Causation in National and International Climate Change Litigation

Meike Krakau

Causation in National and International Climate Change Litigation

Springer

Meike Krakau
Faculty of Law
Ludwig Maximilian University of Munich
Munich, Germany

ISBN 978-3-031-74692-5 ISBN 978-3-031-74693-2 (eBook)
https://doi.org/10.1007/978-3-031-74693-2

Diss., Ludwig-Maximilians-Universität München, 2024

This Springer imprint is published by the registered company Springer Nature Switzerland AG
The registered company address is: Gewerbestrasse 11, 6330 Cham, Switzerland

To my parents.

Acknowledgements

The present book is the result of my research as a doctoral candidate and research assistant at the Chair of Public International Law and Public Law at the Ludwig-Maximilians-Universität in Munich. It was there that I defended my thesis in July 2024.

This journey would not have been possible without the tremendous support of many different people.

First and foremost, I am incredibly grateful to my supervisor, Professor Dr Christian Walter, for giving me the opportunity to embark on this wonderful and enriching journey in the first place and for his unwavering support over these many years. I would also like to thank Professor Dr Ann-Katrin Kaufhold for acting as my second examiner and providing me with her generous report, and Professor Dr Jens Kersten for serving as my oral examiner and challenging me on issues of sovereignty and solidarity in the new WHO Pandemic Treaty.

I also want to express my deepest thanks to the German Federal Environmental Foundation (Deutsche Bundesstiftung Umwelt) for their financial support, as well as for enabling me to meet many brilliant minds from all different fields and areas of environmental research. Knowing that so many talented young researchers are working on all kinds of innovative solutions to the numerous environmental challenges we face today still fills me with awe.

To all my colleagues at the Chair of Public International Law and Public Law at the LMU Munich—a big and heartfelt thank you. Especially to Kathrin, whom I am now proud to call not only a former colleague but also a good friend, for sharing the ups and downs of the PhD process with me. I will certainly miss our breaks, when we watched endless sports tournaments and discussed the appropriate way to drink our coffee—to this day: coffee with rose lemonade is not it.

Next, I would like to thank the University of Oslo, Norway, and the entire PluriCourts team for welcoming me with open arms during my three-month research stay. The long lunches, discussions and seminars gave me so much food for thought and great motivation when new energy was desperately needed. I would especially like to thank Johannes for the many heated conversations over a coffee or two in which we delved deep into the philosophy of causal theories—and mostly disagreed.

Last but not least, I would like to express my sincere gratitude to my wonderful family and friends who have been an integral part of this journey.

I am incredibly grateful to my amazing parents, Kristin and Bernd, for their moral, motivational and unconditional support, not only throughout my PhD process, but throughout my entire life. Their unwavering support has been the backbone of this project. I am also immensely grateful to my grandmother Siegrid, who has instilled curiosity and a thirst for knowledge in me since I was a young girl. Special thanks also go to my partner Frederik, who has been a great source of strength and encouragement, especially towards the end of this huge project.

Finally, I am beyond grateful to all my wonderful friends who have accompanied me on this incredible journey. They have always stood by me with advice, criticism and much-needed laughter at times when the weight of completing this project felt overwhelming. While it is almost impossible to name everyone, I would like to extend special thanks to Frederika, Lukas and Philipp for pointing out the little hiccups when I could no longer see the forest for the trees, to Isabel, Caroline, Steffie and Tamina for always knowing when a glass of wine and a heartfelt conversation were deeply needed, and to Cansu and Britta for the greatest emotional support one could ask for during our many canteen lunches.

Autumn 2024

Meike Krakau

Contents

List of Abbreviations

AFOLU	Agriculture, forestry and other land use
ALI	American Law Institute
API	American Petroleum Institute
APP	Ability to pay principle
BPP	Beneficiary pays principle
CBDR	Common but differentiated responsibilities
CH_4	Methane
CO_2	Carbon dioxide
CPP	Contribution to problem principle
DES	Diethylstilbestrol
ECJ	European Court of Justice
ECtHR	European Court of Human Rights
EIA	Environmental impact assessment
EPA	United States Environmental Protection Agency
EU	European Union
EU ETS	EU Emission Trading System
GDP	Gross domestic product
GHG	Greenhouse gas
GLAN	Global Legal Action Network
GLOF	Glacial lake outburst flood
Gt	Gigatons
$GtCO_{2eq}$	Gigatons of CO_2 equivalent
H_2O	Water vapour
HNO_2	Nitrous acid
HNO_3	Nitric acid
IACHR	Inter-American Commission on Human Rights
IACtHR	Inter-American Court of Human Rights
ICC	International Criminal Court
ICJ	International Court of Justice
ICSID	International Centre for Settlement of Investment Disputes

ICTR	United Nations International Criminal Tribunal for Rwanda
ICTY	United Nations International Criminal Tribunal for the former Yugoslavia
ILA	International Law Association
ILC	International Law Commission
INUS	Insufficient but necessary part of an unnecessary but sufficient condition
IPCC	Intergovernmental Panel on Climate Change
ITLOS	International Tribunal on the Law of the Sea
KETS	South Korea's Emissions Trading Scheme
LGTBQ+	Lesbian, gay, transgender, bisexual, queer and others
LULUCF	Land use, land-use change and forestry
N_2O	Nitrous oxide
NAS	National Academy of Sciences
NDC	National determined contribution
NESS	Necessary element of a sufficient set
NGO	Non-governmental organization
NO	Nitrogen monoxide
NO_2	Nitrogen dioxide
O_2	Ozone
OECD	Organization for Economic Co-operation and Development
OHCHR	Office of the United Nations High Commissioner for Human Rights
PETL	Principles of European Tort Law
Pg	Petagram
Ppm	Parts per million
PPP	Polluter pays principle
SIDS	Small island developing state
SO_2	Sulphur dioxide
SO_3	Sulphur trioxide
Tg	Teragram
VDEW	Association of German Electricity Companies
WMO	World Meteorological Organization
WTO	World Trade Organization

Chapter 1
Introduction

The causal relation between one's action and a specific event has preoccupied legal scholars for a long time. At the intersection of philosophy, natural science and jurisprudence, scholars and practitioners are faced with the question of the right way to handle causal relata. And while much has been written about causal relationships and the resulting problems, new metaphysical approaches have been developed and new ideas introduced, plaintiffs and courts are once again faced with the challenge of establishing attributable chains of causation in the context of climate claims.[1] Not only are the already well-known obstacles of building causal chains pertinent but due to the emission of greenhouse gases since the industrial era, the extremely complex scientific processes of the climate system and the global nature of climate change, the intricacy of establishing coherent causal chains enhances further.[2] That climate change litigation is particularly susceptible to a difficult determination of causation is illustrated by the statement of the High Commissioner for Human Rights, in which it was argued that

> it is virtually impossible to disentangle the complex causal relationship linking historical greenhouse gas emissions of a particular country with a specific climate change-related effect, let alone with the range of direct and indirect implications for human rights.[3]

In the same vein, the District Judge in the case *Comer et al. v. Murphy Oil et al.* held that

---

[1] See for a detailed elaboration on the substance and history of metaphysics van Inwagen et al. (2023). See further Sect. 3.1.1 and Chap. 4. The references, legal cases (with the exception of the analysis in Sect. 3.4), and scientific developments cited in this book reflect the state of knowledge and sources available up to September 2023. Internet-based sources were reviewed and updated where necessary in October 2024.

[2] The IPCC records an increase in GHG emissions in the atmosphere since the year 1750. IPCC (2021), 4, A.1.1.

[3] Office of the United Nations High Commissioner for Human Rights (2009), para 70.

M. Krakau, *Causation in National and International Climate Change Litigation*,
https://doi.org/10.1007/978-3-031-74693-2_1

> (t)he assertion that the defendants' emissions combined over a period of decades or centuries with other natural and man-made gases to cause or strengthen a hurricane and damage personal property is precisely the type of remote, improbable, and extraordinary occurrence that is excluded from liability.[4]

Other decisions in climate change litigation further demonstrate the inherent challenges that courts and plaintiffs encounter when attempting to establish stringent causal chains in climate change litigation. These include, in particular, the failure of traditional counterfactual tests, uncertainty surrounding the scientific foundation of the causal chain at issue, and normative implications that suggest the incompatibility of scientific findings with their use in law.[5] Thus, courts frequently reject or dismiss climate change claims for failing to provide a comprehensive causal chain.[6] Arguments such as the influence of the natural climate variability, the complexity of the chain, intervening causes and a large number of different contributions by large and small emitters are commonly used by defendants to counter climate change claims on the premise of a lack of causation.[7] A number of scholars have also argued that the law's approach to establishing causation generally does not lend well to overall climate change litigation.[8] The point of contention, nonetheless, does not reside in the general negation of causation in the law. Rather, it builds upon the discrepancy between how causation is perceived in the legal system and how it operates in natural cause-and-effect relations. It, thus, concerns the dissociation between scientific knowledge, the ethical and moral perception of justice, and the legal realm.

This thesis does not aim at a detailed analysis of a specific, domestic approach to the establishment of climatic causation but rather, based on the global character of climate change, elaborates on a holistic account that focuses on a more general approach to the obstacles posed by climate change.[9] Despite the different jurisdictions and areas of law in which climate claims are brought, the fundamental and central problems surrounding the establishment of causal relations remain the same. As *Aust* accurately puts it:

---

[4] US Court of Appeals for the 5th Circuit, 28 May 2010 – 07-60756, *Ned Comer et al. v. Murphy Oil USA, Inc., et al.*, Memorandum opinion and order, 35.

[5] See for a detailed elaboration on counterfactual tests Sect. 4.2.

[6] In stating that *"[…] there is no realistic possibility of tracing any particular alleged effect of global warming to any particular emissions by any specific person, entity, group at any particular point in time"* US District Court for the Northern District of California, 30 September 2009 – 4:08-cv-01138-SBA, *Native Village of Kivalina v. ExxonMobil Corp.*, 20, paras 17–19. Similar *Essen Regional Court, 15 December 2016 – 2 O 285/15, Luciano Lliuya v. RWE AG*, paras 41–47.

[7] See e.g. in the case *Neubauer et al. v. Germany*, the arguments brought forward by Germany, Germany Federal Constitutional Court, 24 March 2021 – 1 BvR 2656/18 – 1 BvR 78/20 – 1 BvR 96/20 – 1 BvR 288/20, *Neubauer et al. v. Germany*, para 89.

[8] Counterfactual causation is generally perceived as being the 'common' approach of the law to causation. See for further explanations on counterfactual causation Sect. 3.2. Arguing that standard approaches, such as the but-for test, do not work in climate-related tort cases, Duffy (2009); Steingart (2021); Nitsch (2021), p. 446.

[9] In this book, climatic causation is understood as any type of causation that contains at least one reference to climate change or its impacts within its causal chain per se, see further Sect. 3.3.2.1.

> Given the widely held view that issues of causation have less to do with the individual legal field or system than with the idea of law itself, it thus appears possible to transfer some insights into our field which allow us to lend some doctrinal coherence to the issue of causation [...].[10]

Even the varying methods of courts to establish and elaborate on causation do not contradict the transference of causal relata. Rather, it can be seen as an opportunity to establish a universally applicable approach by resorting to particularly climate-friendly dogmas. Such an approach is supported by the increasing willingness of courts to draw on the results and methods of other jurisdictions in climate issues.[11] Monocentric concepts would stand in the way of such a development, especially in view of climate change as a universal problem which requires solutions based on a global effort. Nevertheless, it is important to note that, despite many similarities, particularly in the legal spheres of common law and civil law countries, differences between legal systems and even different areas of law do persist.[12] This is particularly the case with regard to the adaptation of traditional tests to reflect notions of fairness, justice and further normative perceptions of causation in law. Conversely, in light of the problems posed by climate change, it will be shown that all of the different normative approaches, nevertheless, carry specific core elements at heart. Commonalities and similar approaches, however, can be seen, in particular, with regard to the establishment of factual causation and the application of these respective tests.

The primary objective of this thesis ultimately is to offer a comprehensive and practical strategy for establishing causation in climate claims, and thus to counter arguments opposing the establishment of stringent causal chains in climate change litigation. It further aims to emasculate the divergence between scientific and legal epistemology.[13] Although it is shown that full coherence between a scientific and a legal perception of climatic causation is not feasible based on the normative component that is introduced to the causal inquiry in the law, the thesis provides means to bring scientific and legal causal assessments closer together. In doing so, it lends legitimacy to causal elaborations in the law and demonstrates how scientific evidence and findings can be implemented in court cases with more ease.

[10] Aust (2011), p. 214. In citing Hart and Honoré (1985), p. 9; Becker (2006), p. 288; Rigaux (2005), pp. 82–92.

[11] For example in the case of *Neubauer, et al. v. Germany* the Court referred to the judgment of the Supreme Court of the Netherlands in the case *Urgenda Foundation v. The State of The Netherlands* or to the case *Friends of the Irish Environment v. The Government of Ireland* before the Supreme Court of Ireland, Germany Federal Constitutional Court, 24 March 2021 – 1 BvR 2656/18 – 1 BvR 78/20 – 1 BvR 96/20 – 1 BvR 288/20, *Neubauer et al. v. Germany*, inter alia paras 157, 161, 200, 203, 253, Supreme Court of the Netherlands, 20 December 2019 – 19/00135, *Urgenda Foundation v. The State of The Netherlands*, Supreme Court of Ireland, 31 July 2020 – 205/19, *Friends of the Irish Environment v. The Government of Ireland*.

[12] See in regard to the different areas of law Lahav (2022), p. 114. See further Sect. 6.2.2.

[13] See for the initial differences in scientific and legal epistemology Sect. 3.3.3.

In order to achieve coherence and, thus, to oppose the divergence between causation as understood in law and in science, this thesis makes extensive use of a transdisciplinary account of legal research. It hereby draws upon various doctrines and theories from different areas of law as well as on causal conceptions used in computer science, metaphysics, the overall philosophy of science, as well as formal logic. The viability of such an interdisciplinary approach is assessed in terms of both legal theory and dogmatics and ultimately weighed against practical considerations. To provide a fundamental and comprehensive basis for the considerations made in this work, the thesis relies heavily on an in-depth analysis of the application of causal approaches throughout a diverse range of different climate change lawsuits.[14] The analytical content is, thus, presented within a functional comparative framework which focuses on a micro-comparison.

One of the main challenges in the field of causation studies is the correct use of terminology. While academics in the field of causation research are well aware and sensitized to the overall issue, the arbitrary use of different definitions in a multitude of legal works and court decisions makes it difficult to analyse the usage of causal considerations in depth. Special attention, therefore, had to be paid to terminological peculiarities, connotational differences and the special setting of the wording.[15]

The overall thesis is structured into six chapters. Chapter 2 provides the basis for the following considerations by first outlining climate change from a scientific perspective. The main emphasis hereby resides within the explanation of the climate system, its natural as well as anthropogenic change and the effects accompanied by such. Shifting the focus to the legal sphere, Chap. 2 also provides preliminary remarks on the litigation-specific dimension, with the central question of the proper classification and definition of climate change litigation at the heart of this section. Finally, the chapter concludes with a brief overview of the background, objectives and current trends in climate change litigation.

Chapter 3 is dedicated to causation in the law. In questioning the function and the purpose of causation, it further offers an account of the approaches and doctrines used to establish cause-effect relations both on a domestic, as well as on a regional and international level. After clarifying how causation is used in the law, it is then compared with the scientific determination of causation, placing particular emphasis on climate and attribution science and the divergence in legal and scientific

[14] See in this regard Sect. 3.4.

[15] The terms '*causation*' and '*causality*' are used in this work interchangeably. Also not distinguishing between causation and causality Garner (2009), pp. 249–250. Defining causation as *"(o)ne of the central problem areas of metaphysics. Causation is the relation between two events that holds when, given that one occurs, it produces, or brings forth, or determines, or necessitates the second; equally we say that once the first has happened the second must happen or that the second follows on from the first."* Law (2022), term: causation. Causation is furthermore to be distinguished from mere 'correlation'. Correlation describes the association between two events. Conversely, correlation lacks the causal link, i.e. the cause-and-effect relationship. Correlation is therefore merely a mutual relationship between two components that works in both directions, i.e. not only from cause to effect, but also vice versa. See for the term '*climatic causation*' as it is understood in this work Sect. 3.3.2.1.

epistemology. Finally, the chapter concludes by presenting the findings of the empirical, systematic and substantive analysis, which provide a strong indication for the use of climatic causation, its doctrines and normative accounts in current climate change litigation. The analysis also suggests possible ways of resolving the causation dilemma by building on more recent approaches discussed in the respective decisions.

In strongly relying on the results of the respective analysis, Chap. 4 focuses on the first step of causal determination in the law, namely factual causation. Within this chapter, different approaches to factual causation are introduced, both metaphysically grown concepts and doctrines that have just recently been emerging and are mainly developed in a broader case law dynamic. In this context, reference is commonly drawn to transdisciplinary approaches, originating from natural science and mathematics. The overarching focus of Chap. 4 persists in reconciling perceptions of causation with actual causation and scientific findings. The ultimate aim is to show how the application and adaptation of specific causal doctrines can resolve the dilemma of the divergence between actual causation and causation in law.

Chapter 5 then targets the second step of the causal inquiry in the law by focusing on the normative dimension of cause-effect relations. In elaborating on the normative principles that find entrance into the assessment and doctrines of normative causation, it depicts how factual causal chains are to be adapted in light of normative causation. The main emphasis hereby resides on the concept of climate justice, which finds considerable use and implementation in the tests of foreseeability and materiality. Of further importance are the general principles of international environmental law. This chapter aims to provide a comprehensive elaboration of the specific normative doctrines in terms of their applicability to climate scenarios and, ultimately, their use in climate change litigation.

The final chapter, Chap. 6, builds heavily on the previous findings to demonstrate the feasibility of establishing causation in climate change litigation within different groups of cases. By distinguishing between different jurisdictions, actors and areas of law, it demonstrates how approaches to climatic causation alter within different scenarios. Ultimately, this chapter lays the groundwork for parties in climate change litigation to overcome the hurdle of establishing causation and clarifies the requirements for its ultimate consideration.

Climate Change Cases

Native Village of Kivalina v. ExxonMobil Corp. – US District Court for the Northern District of California, 30 September 2009 – 4:08-cv-01138-SBA

Ned Comer et al. v. Murphy Oil USA, Inc., et al. – US Court of Appeals for the 5th Circuit, 28 May 2010 – 07-60756

Neubauer et al. v. Germany – Germany Federal Constitutional Court, 24 March 2021 – 1 BvR 2656/18 – 1 BvR 78/20 – 1 BvR 96/20 – 1 BvR 288/20

Luciano Lliuya v. RWE AG – Essen Regional Court, 15 December 2016 – 2 O 285/15

Urgenda Foundation v. The State of The Netherlands – Supreme Court of the Netherlands, 20 December 2019 – 19/00135

References

Aust H (2011) Complicity and the law of state responsibility. Cambridge University Press, Cambridge

Becker T (2006) Terrorism and the state – rethinking the rules of state responsibility. Oxford University Press, Oxford

Duffy M (2009) Climate change causation: harmonizing tort law and scientific probability. Temp J Sci Tech Environ Law 28(2):185–242

Garner BA (ed) (2009) Black's law dictionary. West Publishing, Saint Paul

Hart HLA, Honoré T (1985) Causation in the law. Oxford University Press, New York

IPCC (2021) Climate change 2021: the physical science basis – Working Group I Contribution to the Sixth Assessment Report of the Intergovernmental Panel on Climate Change – Summary for Policymakers. Geneva

Lahav AD (2022) Chancy causation in tort law. J Tort Law 15(1):109–135

Law J (2022) Oxford dictionary of law. Oxford University Press, Oxford

Nitsch S (2021) Liability for climate change damages under the German Environmental Liability Act. In: Kahl W, Weller M-P (eds) Climate change litigation: a handbook. C.H. Beck, Munich, pp 430–447

Office of the United Nations High Commissioner for Human Rights (2009) Report on the relationship between climate change and human rights, A/HRC/10/61, 15 January 2009

Rigaux F (2005) International responsibility and the principle of causality. In: Ragazzi M (ed) International responsibility today – essays in memory of Oscar Schachter. Martinus Nijhoff, Leiden, pp 81–91

Steingart G (2021) #176 – Ferdinand von Schirach: Warum Europa neue Grundrechte braucht (2 April 2021). In: Steingarts Morning Briefing – Der Podcast

van Inwagen P, Sullivan M, Bernstein S (2023) Metaphysics. Available via The Stanford Encyclopedia of Philosophy. https://plato.stanford.edu/archives/sum2023/entries/metaphysics. Accessed 24 Oct 2024

Chapter 2
Setting the Stage for Climate Change Litigation

2.1 The Scientific Framework of Climate Change

This section on the scientific framework of climate change forms the basis for all the following considerations on climate change litigation, factual causal chains and normative adaptations. Its purpose is to provide a general account of the fundamental nature of the Earth's climate system, climate change and climate science. The first section, therefore, discusses the concept of 'climate', how the climate system works and the causes of climate change (Sect. 2.1.1). The second step then turns towards the impacts of climate change, both directly as well as indirectly (Sect. 2.1.2). Given that the elaboration of potential causes and impacts of climate change is strongly based on scientific evidence, calculations, and future forecasts, reference will be taken throughout this book to the likelihood scale introduced by the Intergovernmental Panel on Climate Change (IPCC). Accordingly, the IPCC classifies the occurrence of events and their likelihood into seven different probabilistic categories, reaching from very low, which is expressed throughout their reports as '*exceptionally unlikely*' (0–1%) to '*virtually certain*' (99–100%).[1] In addition to the likelihood scale, the IPCC makes further use of the level of confidence that is implied in one's statement or observation. The confidence scale hereby refers to the scope of evidence that is accessible and the respective weight that the statement thus carries. It ranges from '*very low*' confidence through '*low*', '*medium*' and '*high*' confidence to '*very high*' confidence.[2]

[1] If the probability of an outcome is between 99–100%, the outcome is '*virtually certain*'. If the probability only consists of 0–1%, the outcome is '*exceptionally unlikely*'. In between one differentiates in '*very likely*' (90–100%), '*likely*' (66–100%), '*about as likely as not*' (33–66%), '*unlikely*' (0–33%) and '*very unlikely*' (0–10%), see IPCC (2010), p. 3, Table 1.

[2] Ibid.?3.

M. Krakau, *Causation in National and International Climate Change Litigation*,
https://doi.org/10.1007/978-3-031-74693-2_2

2.1.1 *Understanding Climate Change*

2.1.1.1 The Earth's Natural Climate System

2.1.1.1.1 Climate and the Climate System

The Earth's climate system consists of highly complex natural processes that are interdependent and strongly influenced by each other. The result of such a scientific process is what is now referred to as climate, a state of the atmosphere that is strongly related to temporal parameters, which ultimately leads to the climate being the measurement of the "*mean and variability of relevant quantities over a period of time*".[3] While the respective period under consideration can vary from a few months to thousands of years, the World Meteorological Organization (WMO) calculates climate on a 30 years basis.[4] Weather, on the other hand, refers to the temporary state of the atmosphere and is, therefore, calculated over a much shorter period of time than climate.[5] Both conditions hereby take reference from the condition of the atmosphere, which is a layer of different gases that surrounds the Earth up to an altitude of approximately 1000 km.[6] Due to the temporal differentiation, an unusually warm summer provides only limited information about the climate per se; it would rather fall into the category of an (extreme) weather phenomenon. Based on the definition of climate, climate change indicates a change "*in the mean and/or the variability of its properties and that persists for an extended period.*"[7] It is due to these merging processes and their associated complexity that the climate and climate change are so hard to determine and predict.

2.1.1.1.2 The Earth's Average Temperature

The Earth's average near-surface temperature measures about 15 °C and is crucial for life on Earth.[8] It is the result of several different, mutually dependent factors.

---

[3] IPCC (2018), p. 544.

[4] See World Meteorological Organization (2024).

[5] Njau (2011), p. 3; IPCC (2018), p. 543; Schönwiese (2020), p. 18.

[6] Ibid. The Earth's climate system, however, does not only consist out of the atmosphere but of the synergy and interaction of five different subsystems, namely the atmosphere, the hydrosphere, the cryosphere, the lithosphere and the biosphere. See IPCC (2018), p. 544.

[7] Ibid. It should be noted that occasionally the definition refers exclusively to changes due to human influence and does not include natural changes in the climate. The definition of climate change in Art. 1 FCCC, accordingly defines climate change as "*a change of climate which is attributed directly or indirectly to human activity that alters the composition of the global atmosphere and which is in addition to natural climate variability observed over comparable time periods.*"

[8] Mutter (2020), p. 7.

Solar radiation, in particular, plays a major role in maintaining the Earth's average temperature, as do the Earth's albedo and the greenhouse effect.[9]

The Sun produces radiation, more specifically electromagnetic waves. These electromagnetic waves consist of long-wave infrared radiation and short-wave ultraviolet radiation. When radiation hits matter, different interactions can occur. Radiation can be absorbed, reflected or transmitted. Some matter, especially aerosols and gas molecules, absorb the incoming short-wave radiation and convert some of it into longer wavelength radiation. This process generates heat and warms the surrounding atmosphere.[10] When radiation from the Sun hits the Earth directly, it is either reflected by the Earth's surface (known as the surface albedo) or absorbed and re-emitted as longwave radiation, again producing heat.[11] Whether a surface, or matter in general, absorbs or reflects incoming radiation depends strongly on the materials and surface conditions, with snow, clouds and sand having the highest albedo (about 40–80% of incoming radiation) and water and forests having the lowest (about 5–15%).[12] In total, almost 30% of the incoming radiation is reflected back into space. Of the remaining 70% of incoming radiation, 50% is absorbed by the Earth's surface and about 20% by the atmosphere. The short-wave radiation absorbed by the Earth's surface and re-emitted as long-wave radiation is then partly absorbed by specific greenhouse gases and radiated back to the Earth as so-called contra-radiation.[13] The resulting radiation is about twice as strong as the Sun's, causing further warming.[14] This process is called the greenhouse effect and is essential for life on Earth.[15] Compared to the energy and heat produced in this process, the energy coming from the Earth's core contributes only an insignificant amount to the average temperature of the Earth.[16]

2.1.1.2 Natural Causes of Climate Change

2.1.1.2.1 Climate Epochs

Throughout thousands of years, Earth's climate has not been consistent but underwent many changes, divided into different climate epochs with alternating glacial and interglacial eras. The current epoch represents an interglacial climate period called the '*Holocene*', although it is increasingly argued that the rise in

---

[9]Ibid. 10–11. See for the anthropogenic greenhouse effect later on in this chapter Sect. 2.1.1.3.1.

[10]Buhofer (2017), p. 16.

[11]Ibid.?17.

[12]See e.g. Mutter (2020), p. 23, Figure 1.13.

[13]Buhofer (2017), p. 18.

[14]This radiation is also commonly known as '*contra-radiation*'.

[15]See further on the anthropogenic greenhouse effect Sect. 2.1.1.3.1.

[16]Mutter (2020), pp. 10–11.

surface temperature has led to a transition to a new climate epoch, the '*Anthropocene*'.[17] The last interglacial period with temperatures comparable to the present was the '*Eemian interglacial period*' 120,000 years ago.[18] Those alternations are proven to be caused by the so-called '*Milankovitch cycle*'. The Milankovitch cycle describes the variation of Earth's orbital movement around the Sun, especially its eccentricity, obliquity and equinoxes.[19] Those cycles can also be used to calculate the beginning of the next glacial era. Although glacial eras generally and historically last much longer than inter-glacial periods, namely about 90,000 years, according to the current state of research, the next cold period is not expected for about 50,000 years.[20] This variation is based on the minimum eccentricity of the Earth's orbit.[21]

2.1.1.2.2 Natural Climate Variations

The Earth's climate has been changing since the beginning of time. Despite the Milankovitch cycle causing long-term climate variations, the Earth's climate can and has been naturally affected by short-term climate fluctuations as well. Those variations have not been caused by individual, independent events but rather by the interplay of several phenomena commonly referred to as '*climate forces*'. These '*forces*' can be divided into internal terrestrial causes and external extra-terrestrial drivers, as well as into positive forces that cause the temperature to rise and negative forces that have a cooling effect on the atmosphere.[22] Terrestrial factors include, amongst others, volcanism, forest and bushfires, continental drifts and plate tectonics, orogeny, the circulation in the atmosphere, its synergy with the ocean, the ice and snow coverage, and the vegetation.[23] Extra-terrestrial forces, on the other hand, comprise the influence of the Moon, tidal powers, the rotation of the Milky Way and irregularities in solar radiation due to sunspots and solar flares.[24] To evaluate and determine the influence of certain events and processes on the climate, the IPCC

[17] The term '*Anthropocene*' was first developed by *Crutzen and Stoermer*, see Crutzen and Stoermer (2000). In favour of this new climate epoch i.a. Meyer and Newman (2020), pp. 43–45; Zalasiewicz (2008).

[18] Mutter (2020), p. 64.

[19] See Rahmstorf and Schellnhuber (2019), pp. 21–23, Wilby (2020), p. 284; Milankovic (1941).

[20] In contrast, the length of warmer periods is typically around 10,000 years. See Rahmstorf and Schellnhuber (2019), pp. 21–22.

[21] Ibid.?22.

[22] Schönwiese (2020), pp. 329–330; Brooke (2014), pp. 548–549.

[23] Atmospheric pressure and pressure patterns, such as the North Atlantic Oscillation (NAO) and the Atlantic Multidecadal Oscillation (AMO), have a major influence on the Earth's climate. The most important is the influence of the Southern Oscillation, which leads to higher sea surface temperatures, also known as the El Niño phenomenon, or its opposite, the cooler La Niña phenomenon (ENSO).

[24] Schönwiese (2020), p. 330.

developed a scale to classify the change in the radiative flux, called the '*radiative forcing*', which is expressed in Wm^{-2}.[25] Negative results indicate a decrease in temperature in the troposphere (the lowest layer of the atmosphere), while positive figures result in a temperature increase. Exemplary, the eruption of Mount Tambaro, a volcano in Indonesia, in 1816 aggregated a radiative forcing of about $-25\ Wm^{-2}$ and led to a global temperature decrease of 1 °C to 2.5 °C that lasted about one to two years.[26] Because of the interconnectedness of the climate system, changes in this respect can either be balanced by other components or have a feedback effect that causes increasing perturbations in other parts of the climate system.

2.1.1.3 Anthropogenic Climate Change

The Earth's climate is naturally variable and has always been subject to change. In recent years, nonetheless, the Earth's climate has changed much more rapidly than in other climatic periods. This has been majorly attributed to human influence. The most widely known and discussed cause of anthropogenic climate change is the change in the composition of the atmosphere caused by the release of greenhouse gases or climate-relevant trace gases, mainly from the use of fossil fuels and industrial processes (Sect. 2.1.1.3.1). In addition, there are other human activities that also affect the Earth's climate (Sect. 2.1.1.3.2).

2.1.1.3.1 The Greenhouse Effect

As previously discussed, the greenhouse effect is crucial for life on Earth.[27] It was first discovered in its broad outlines by *Joseph Fourier* in 1824, *Eunice Foote* in 1856 and *John Tyndall* in 1861, followed by *Svante Arrhenius,* who was the first to establish the connection between greenhouse gases and human influence.[28] Greenhouse gases cause the short-wave radiation (with a low radiative forcing) from the Sun to pass through them to the surface of the Earth. At the surface, the short-wave radiation is either reflected back into space or absorbed, converting the short-wave radiation into long-wave radiation. Greenhouse gases obstruct the long-wave radiation absorbed by the Earth from leaving the atmosphere. The radiation is rather re-absorbed by the gases and radiated back to the Earth (counter-radiation), leading again to an increase in temperature.[29] The more these gases are concentrated in the

[25] IPCC (2021a), pp. 90, 941–967.

[26] Wirakusumah and Rachmat (2017), pp. 7–8. Other sources suggest a temperature drop between 0.5 °C and 1.3 °C below the twentieth century average. See in this regard Pfister and White (2018), p. 552.

[27] See in this regard Sect. 2.1.1.1.2.

[28] Fourier (1824); Foote (1856), pp. 382–383; Tyndall (2014); Arrhenius (1896).

[29] Renneboog (2018), pp. 265–269.

atmosphere, the less radiation and energy is able to leave the Earth, and the more the surface temperature increases. The main gases contributing to this process are water vapour (H_2O), carbon dioxide (CO_2), nitrous oxide (N_2O), methane (CH_4) and ozone (O_2).[30] While the radiative forcing of all greenhouse gases combined between 1750 and 2011 amounted to a radiative forcing of 2.83 Wm^{-2}, the total amount of anthropogenic influence only added up to 2.3 Wm^{-2}.[31] This distinction in radiative forcing is caused by the overall cooling factor of anthropogenic aerosols, which have a negative radiative forcing factor.[32] In contrast to greenhouse gases, aerosols do not absorb the long-wave radiation but reflect the incoming short-wave radiation of the Sun back to space without causing the atmosphere to heat up. In terms of the warming factor of greenhouse gases and with respect to the overall concentration in the atmosphere, CO_2 is the most important and influential gas with a radiative forcing of 1.82 ± 0.19 Wm^{-2} in 2011.[33]

Even though all greenhouse gases are of natural origin, their concentration has risen dramatically in recent decades. From a concentration of around 280 ppm in the pre-industrial era (around 1750), the amount of CO_2 in the atmosphere has increased by around 48% to an average concentration of 415.01 ppm at the end of June 2021.[34] The main factor contributing to an increase in the greenhouse gas concentration in the atmosphere is the usage of fossil fuels, which is strongly linked to incremental economic growth and the increase in the world's population.[35] Economic growth automatically leads to more prosperity of the population, and thus also to an increased energy demand which automatically results in increased emissions. Although there are large regional differences in per capita GHG emissions, population growth due to humans as the primary source of emissions automatically leads to an increase in the GHG concentration in the atmosphere.[36]

Emissions are measured in gigatons (Gt) and are expressed in terms of the amount of CO_2 that would be required to have the same effect on the temperature of the atmosphere as the gas in question, resulting in a unit of $GtCO_{2eq}$. In 2019 about 59.1 $GtCO_{2eq}$ (±5.9) of GHG emissions have been emitted globally.[37] CO_2 still constitutes the main source of GHG emissions with 76% of the overall anthropogenic emissions in 2010.[38] With about 32 $GtCO_2$/year in 2010 of CO_2 emissions and

[30] IPCC (2018), pp. 550–551.

[31] The radiative forcing then increased by a further 0.43 Wm^{-2} between the Fifth and the Sixth Assessment Reports. IPCC (2013), p. 696, Table 8.6.; IPCC (2021a), p. 11, A.4.1.

[32] IPCC (2013), p. 696, Table 8.6.

[33] Other greenhouse gases have the following radiative forcing: CH_4: 0.48 ± 0.05; N_2O: 0.17 ± 0.03; see IPCC (2014a), p. 678, Table 8.2.

[34] Data drawn from the Global Monitoring Laboratory – Earth System Research Laboratories (2023); IPCC (2013), p. 676; IPCC (2021b), p. 69.

[35] Schönwiese (2020), pp. 347–348; IPCC (2014a), p. 46.

[36] Buhofer (2017), pp. 89–93.

[37] United Nations Environmental Programme (2020), p. 4.

[38] IPCC (2014a), p. 46.

an increasing amount in the following years (about 38 $GtCO_2$/year in 2019), the usage of fossil fuels produces with *high confidence* about 78% of the overall CO_2 emissions.[39] When CO_2 emissions are broken down by economic sector, the energy sector leads with around 14 $GtCO_2$/year, followed by the transport sector with around 8.2 $GtCO_2$/year in 2019.[40] Looking at the total of all greenhouse gas emissions, the energy sector is again the largest, accounting for about 35% of all GHG emissions in 2010. Other GHG emissions are generated by economic sectors such as industry, with about 21% of emissions; buildings, with about 6.4%; transport, with about 14% of GHG emissions; and agriculture, forestry and other land use (AFOLU), with about 24% of total GHG emissions in 2010.[41]

2.1.1.3.2 Non-Emissive Sources of Climate Change

While the greenhouse effect and human influence on this process are the most common and probably the most discussed impacts on the climate, other human behaviours also have a major impact on and contribute to overall climate change.

One of the most significant anthropogenic influences is the change in land usage. Deforestation for agricultural or mining purposes transforms a former storage of carbon dioxide into a source of greenhouse gases, resulting in about 3.8 $GtCO_{2eq}$/ year of GHG emissions between 2001 and 2010.[42] The impact of deforestation on large forest areas is particularly visible in a new study that compares the eastern Amazonian with the western areas and concludes that the eastern Amazonian has now evolved from a carbon sink to a carbon source.[43] This is mainly caused by deforestation, degradation, expansive tree mortality and an increasing amount of forest fires.[44] Furthermore, forest clearing also has significant effects on biodiversity and soil fertility. Particularly in tropical forests with a fundamentally high precipitation rate, clearing the existing forest leads to leaching of the soil that is thus unprotected and hence leads to a considerable loss of nutrients. At the same time, this prevents the regeneration of vegetation. High temperatures and little precipitation, especially in the mid-latitudes, prevent the forest from recovering in the long term as well as is the case in the Mediterranean region, for instance.[45]

---

[39] In 2019 the total CO_2 emissions amounted in 38 $GtCO_2$ (Crippa (2020), p. 14) IPCC (2014a), p. 46.

[40] Data drawn from International Energy Agency (2021).

[41] IPCC (2014a), p. 47, Figure 1.7.

[42] Wilby (2020), pp. 285–286; IPCC (2014b), p. 829.

[43] A carbon sink is "*(a) reservoir (natural or human, in soil, ocean, and plants) where a greenhouse gas, an aerosol or a precursor of a greenhouse gas is stored. Note that FCCC Article 1.8 refers to a sink as any process, activity or mechanism which removes a greenhouse gas, an aerosol or a precursor of a greenhouse gas from the atmosphere.*" IPCC (2018), p. 558.

[44] Gatti et al. (2021), pp. 392–393; Denning (2021), pp. 345–346.

[45] Schönwiese (2020), pp. 340–341.

At the same time, however, forests represent one of the major opportunities for considerable CO_2 reduction. Through afforestation, sustainable forest management and further mitigation measures in forests and other natural ecosystems, studies have shown that 7.3 mean $GtCO_{2eq}$/year could be removed from the atmosphere between 2020 and 2050.[46] But the positive influence of forests on the climate is not limited to their function as carbon sinks; they also act as ventilation systems, cooling the air around them and reducing the impact, force and ferocity of extreme weather events such as storms, hurricanes and cyclones.[47]

Furthermore, urbanization plays a major role in regard to anthropogenic climate change. The increased construction of urban areas contributes to an increase in surface temperatures through its lower reflection rate and its function as a heat storage. This phenomenon is mainly caused by the usage of materials with a higher heat capacity, such as concrete and asphalt.[48] As a consequence of the diminished vegetation and the mostly tared and hence sealed grounds, the evapotranspiration and its cooling factor is lower in urban areas than in rural regions.[49] Additionally, factors like a higher and denser construction, urban-produced air pollution and higher waste generation rates contribute to an increase in temperature.[50]

2.1.2 *Impacts of Climate Change and Global Warming*

Due to the complexity of the climate system, the impacts of climate change are likewise diverse and multi-layered, touching upon almost all areas of life. Because of this complexity and the pending scientific research, it is impossible to provide a definitive assessment of the impacts of climate change. Hence, only the most far-reaching impacts are discussed below.

2.1.2.1 Melting of Glaciers, Ice Sheets and Polar Sea Ice

One of the greatest impacts of rising surface temperatures and, consequently, climate change is the melting of glaciers, as well as ice sheets and polar sea ice.[51] Especially

---

[46] IPCC (2022), p. 750.

[47] Seymour and Busch (2016), p. 33.

[48] Rohli and Vega (2018), p. 307.

[49] Ibid. 307–308.

[50] Schönwiese (2020), pp. 342–345; Rohli and Vega (2018), pp. 307–308.

[51] Glaciers are "*a perennial mass of ice, and possibly firn and snow, originating on the land surface by the recrystallization of snow and showing evidence of past or present flow*" IPCC (2018), p. 550. Ice sheets are defined as a "*mass of land ice of continental size that is sufficiently thick to cover most of the underlying bed, so that its shape is mainly determined by its dynamics (the flow of the ice as it deforms internally and/or slides at its base)*", ibid. 551. Today, only two ice sheets remain on Earth,

glaciers are currently losing mass on a global scale.[52] Although a decrease in glacial land-ice masses has been observed since about 1850, it is likely that anthropogenic climate change has played a role in the increased glacier loss since the end of the twentieth century.[53] This development can be observed on almost every glacier in the world and also includes the Vadret da Morteratsch, a glacier in the Swiss Alps that has been losing ice and volume since the end of the Little Ice Age. However, from the scope of its decline alone, it becomes evident that the recession of the glacier is accelerating due to anthropogenic climate change.[54] Based on scientific models, it can be assumed that glacier loss will continue in the future, even if the Earth's surface temperature does not increase any further.[55] In order to counteract such a development, Pontresina, the municipality in which the Vadret da Morteratsch is located, commissioned a study to identify the best possible methodology for artificially preserving the glacier.[56] Although it is possible to preserve glaciers artificially to a certain extent, it is almost impossible to regain the mass lost through previous melting. Some glaciers, particularly those in the Tropics and the Andes, are already considered to be at serious risk of 'dying', with some of them having already disappeared entirely. This development is also taking place faster than previously expected. While scientists predicted in 2001 that the Chacaltaya glacier in Bolivia would disappear in about 15 years, it has been melting much faster and was ultimately declared lost in 2009.[57]

The decline of the Arctic sea ice can be observed quite distressingly, as well. Compared to 1980, the Arctic ice cover has already decreased by about half its size.[58] The melting of large parts of the ice surface also changes the energy balance in this region. In contrast to snow and ice, the now exposed dark ocean has a lower albedo, meaning it absorbs significantly more radiation and thus leads to stronger warming. This phenomenon is called the Arctic or polar amplification and results in a temperature increase over twice as high as in the rest of the world.[59] According to the IPCC, it is *very likely*, that human influence contributed to this process.[60] In comparison to Arctic sea ice, the sea ice in the East Antarctic increased slightly since

the Greenland Ice Sheet and the Antarctic Ice Sheet, ibid. Sea ice is "*ice found at the sea surface that has originated from the freezing of seawater*", ibid.?557.

52 IPCC (2014a), p. 42.

53 IPCC (2021a), pp. 76–77.

54 Zekollari et al. (2014), pp. 1158–1159.

55 Concerning the Vadret da Morteratsch, ibid. 1160–1161.

56 Oerlemans et al. (2017).

57 Ramírez et al. (2001), p. 193.

58 Rahmstorf and Schellnhuber (2019), p. 57.

59 Even stating that "*the Arctic has been warming nearly four times faster than the globe.*" Rohli and Vega (2018), p. 309.

60 IPCC (2014a), p. 48.

1979. However, there is still *low confidence* in the understanding of the causes of this phenomenon due to insufficient scientific research and contradicting evidence.[61]

The melting of glaciers and ice sheets, combined with the thermal expansion of the ocean due to its warming and the decrease in its density, has thus accounted with *high confidence* for 75% of the total sea-level rise since 1970.[62] It is also *very likely* that the total sea level rise between 1993 and 2010 was about 3.2 mm/year, an increase of about 1.5 mm/year compared to the rise between 1901 and 2010.[63]

Another, more indirect, effect of the melting of glaciers and continental ice sheets is the impact on their function as a source of freshwater. As they continue to melt, this important source of freshwater will be increasingly lost, with serious implications for cities and regions that rely on this freshwater source, ultimately leading to significant water scarcity.[64] The fact that water scarcity due to glacial retreat is already a real problem is demonstrated by the impact of the disappearance of the Chacaltaya glacier on the water supply of La Paz, Bolivia.[65] However, water scarcity does not only result from the melting of glaciers as sources of fresh water; higher temperatures also lead to the lowering of groundwater levels, which again can lead to the contamination of groundwater sources due to the intrusion of water with a higher salinity and ultimately the drying up of surface water sources.

2.1.2.2 Melting Permafrost and the Release of Methane

Climate change and warmer surface temperatures not only cause glaciers and ice masses to melt but also cause permafrost to thaw. According to the IPCC, the thawing of the permafrost is occurring with *high confidence,* but the consequences for the resulting CO_2 concentration in the atmosphere remain unpredictable to this day.[66] Calculations have shown that the CO_2 and CH_4 emissions in the twenty-first century (240 $GtCO_2$) due to the thawing of the permafrost may lead up to 240 PgC of CO_2 and up to 5300 Tg of CH_4 (=5.3 Gt CH_4).[67] Yet, based on current climatic models, the main emissions of carbon caused by the melting of the permafrost are expected to occur after the year 2100.[68] Although the concentration of methane in the atmosphere is low compared to that of carbon dioxide, CH_4 is about 33 times more potent as a greenhouse gas than CO_2, contributing about 25% to anthropogenic

61 Ibid.

62 Ibid.?42.

63 Ibid.

64 Ibid.?51.

65 Soruco et al. (2015).

66 IPCC (2021a), inter alia 16, 24, 76, 677.

67 Ibid.?739.

68 It is estimated that around 60% of all emissions from melting permafrost will occur after 2100, Schaefer et al. (2014), p. 7; IPCC (2018), p. 104.

warming.[69] Due to the huge amounts of CO_2 and CH_4 stored in the frozen soil (about 1700 Gt), the melting of the permafrost is often referred to as one possible '*tipping point*' for Earth's climate.[70]

As well as releasing large amounts of methane and carbon dioxide, thawing permafrost poses other major risks. One of these potential risk factors involves massive rockslides which occur given that the permafrost that has previously stabilized certain rock formations, is destabilized by its melting.[71] Furthermore, there is a general threat to infrastructure and especially to cities that are anchored in permafrost soils, mainly in the northern hemisphere. As the ground melts and softens, buildings, roads and other infrastructure are sinking and becoming unusable. At the same time, the thawing is causing lakes that were previously above the permafrost, to seep away, resulting in the loss of habitat and water sources.[72]

2.1.2.3 Extreme Weather Events

Another impact of anthropogenic climate change, and arguably one of the impacts which accrues the most uncertainty, concerns the occurrence of extreme weather events. According to the IPCC, extreme weather events are "*event(s) that (are) rare at particular place and time of year*".[73] If the extreme event persists over a longer period of time, it might also be called a climate extreme.[74] Extreme weather or climate events include, for example, droughts, floods, heat waves and storms, depending on the timely occurrence of the phenomenon in question. The affectedness and the classification of weather as an extreme weather event varies from country to country and from climate zone to climate zone. Tropical countries that annually experience monsoon rainfalls, for example, would not classify heavy rainfalls or even floods as extreme weather events in comparison to countries located in drier climatic regions. Although it could be argued that the frequency of extreme weather events is increasing, attributing these events to climate change has so far posed major problems due to a lack of historical records and comparative data.[75,76]

Despite the scientific uncertainty that still surrounds some events, extreme weather events that can already be broadly linked to human influence include

[69] Renneboog (2018), p. 344; IPCC (2018), p. 104; Schaefer et al. (2014), p. 2.

[70] Schaefer et al. (2014). A tipping point is "*(a) level of change in system properties beyond which a system reorganizes, often abruptly, and does not return to the initial state even if the drivers of the change are abated. For the climate system, it refers to a critical threshold when global or regional climate changes from one stable state to another stable state.*" IPCC (2018), p. 559.

[71] See for a intensive study on the permafrost and its changes at the Matterhorn, Switzerland Weber et al. (2019), p. 1203.

[72] See Rahmstorf and Schellnhuber (2019), p. 58.

[73] IPCC (2018), p. 549.

[74] Ibid.

[75] See e.g. for the situation in Germany Umweltbundesamt (2019), p. 22.

[76] IPCC (2014a), p. 53.

high-temperature variability, with an increase in warmer temperatures and a decrease in colder ones, as well as regional increases in heavy rainfall.[77] Considering the changes in temperature in Germany over a period of more than 60 years, an increase in the number of extremely hot days can be observed. The number of days above 30 ° C increased from about 3 days per year to an average of 10 days per year in 2018. With regard to a possible decrease in cold days, no consistent and scientifically proven statements can be made so far as it regards the temperature variability in Germany.[78] On a global scale, it is *likely* that the occurrence of heat waves increased in large parts of the world, and it is *very likely* that human influence contributed to this development.[79] A major study of the 2003 heatwave in Europe concluded that although the heatwave might have occurred without human influence on the climate, the risk of exceeding a certain temperature threshold was likely to be doubled by human interference.[80] Furthermore, current research states that the number of record-breaking rainfall events in general increased by about 12% from 1981 to 2010.[81] While attributing this trend to anthropogenic climate change on a global scale is only possible with *medium confidence*, it is *likely* that the amount of precipitation in North America and Europe has increased.[82]

2.1.2.4 Indirect Impacts of Climate Change

2.1.2.4.1 Impacts on Oceans, Nature and Biodiversity

The Earth's climate is strongly influenced by ocean currents such as the North Atlantic Oscillation (NAO) and the Southern Oscillation (SO), as well as by other ocean conditions such as the El Niño phenomenon or the opposite phenomenon, la Niña.[83] These periodic ocean conditions also have a major impact on the weather. The ocean and the atmosphere are in constant interaction. Warmer atmospheric surface temperatures contribute to the warming of the ocean's surface layers. And although the warming process takes much longer than that of the atmosphere because of the ocean's thermal inertia, warmer ocean surface temperatures increase the intensity of storms such as cyclones.[84]

---

[77] Ibid.

[78] Umweltbundesamt (2019), pp. 22–23. The time period refers to data collected between 1951 and 2018.

[79] IPCC (2014a), p. 53.

[80] Scott et al. (2004), p. 610.

[81] Lehmann et al. (2015), pp. 512–513.

[82] IPCC (2014a), p. 53.

[83] The El Niño-Southern Oscillation (ENSO) "*was initially used to describe a warm-water current that periodically flows along the coast of Ecuador and Peru, disrupting the local fishery. It has since become identified with warming of the tropical Pacific Ocean east of the dateline.*" IPCC (2018), p. 548.

[84] Mutter (2020), p. 144.

Oceans are not only influencing Earth's climate through their currents but function as a major reservoir of carbon dioxide itself.[85] Although the oceanic CO_2 intake increased throughout the years and, therefore, resulted in a positive effect on Earth's climate, the aggrandized amount of carbon dioxide in the ocean led to its growing acidification.[86] As saturation has not yet occurred, this is a pending process. Ultimately, the destruction and salinization of the oceans and marine ecosystems are reducing their function as carbon sinks.[87] The effect of climate change on the ocean's thermohaline circulation is still very controversial, in contrast to its function as a carbon sink. If the warmer and denser water does not sink to the lower layers of the ocean as quickly as it used to before the anthropogenic influence on the climate system, the ocean's thermohaline circulation could shift slightly, possibly leading to a change in the trajectory of the Gulf Stream, which would mark another tipping point in the impending anthropogenic climate change.[88]

Climate change also affects different species. While some species, such as ice bears, seals and walruses, are already losing habitat as sea ice retreats, only a few species have been distinct due to climate change yet (*high confidence*).[89] However, significant changes are occurring as species adapt to changing climate patterns. In particular, it has already been observed that migration patterns and geographical activities have shifted (*high confidence*).[90] A new study based on data from 1993 to 2017, focusing on migration within the Arctic, shows changes in the migration of golden eagles and caribou.[91] The study finds that golden eagles are migrating later to their summer habitats. The study further reveals evidence of adaptations that have already taken place in the caribou population.[92] While southern woodland caribou stick to their usual birth timing and patterns, barren ground and northern woodland caribou, which usually live in colder climates, tend to give birth earlier in the year. This occurrence has partly been attributed to a changing climate in the respective climatic spheres.[93] In addition to the increased migration of species, vegetation is also migrating. The migration, however, happens at a much slower rate than in the animal realm and with a higher risk of extinction before the migration process can be completed.[94]

---

[85] Ibid. pp. 72–73.

[86] Abate (2015), p. 6.

[87] IPCC (2014a), p. 62.

[88] Roy-Barman and Jeandel (2016), p. 355.

[89] Rahmstorf and Schellnhuber (2019), p. 57; IPCC (2014a), p. 51.

[90] IPCC (2014a), p. 51.

[91] Davidson et al. (2020).

[92] Ibid.?712.

[93] Ibid.?713.

[94] Schönwiese (2020), pp. 370–371; Moore (2011).

2.1.2.4.2 Social Impacts

In addition to the primary impacts on biodiversity and nature, the social impacts of climate change are increasingly materializing as well. Indigenous peoples are particularly affected, losing their habitat to melting ice sheets, desertification and bush and forest fires.[95] In addition, coastal erosion due to melting ice sheets and thawing permafrost, as well as rising sea levels, are forcing people to leave their homes. Already affected are, for instance, the small town of Shishmaref in western Alaska and the island nation of Kiribati in the North and South Pacific.[96] Due to its low altitude (much of the country is less than 2 m above sea level), the Republic of Kiribati, with a population of around 110,000, is at risk of becoming uninhabitable by 2050 and completely submerged by 2070.[97] Other '*small island developing states*' (SIDS) face the same risk of sea-level rise and more frequent extreme weather events such as tropical storms and cyclones.[98]

In addition to the loss of living environment, climate change is also expected to have direct effects on human health. Particularly elderly and infants will be affected by the spread of diseases and an increase in the mortality rate.[99] The IPCC, however, still classifies health issues as secondary impacts and makes statements on the increase in diseases and mortality rates due to global warming with only *medium confidence*.[100] This relates especially to the lack of scientific data based on the fact that the full impact of climate change on human health is likely to become apparent only in the near future. Nonetheless, the increased spread of mosquitoes and other disease vectors due to milder temperatures in Germany, for instance, also indicates a potential increase in the diseases they transmit.[101]

Climate change also affects and impedes the food security in large parts of the world. Food scarcity on the other hand is closely linked to an increase in the risk of social conflicts, which can, in turn, lead to violent and armed conflicts. Climate

---

[95] See e.g. International Work Group for Indigenous Affairs (2008), p. 5. These include indigenous peoples living in the Arctic, northern Finland, Norway and Sweden, the Amazon rainforest and the Kalahari Desert in Africa.

[96] See e.g. Gregg (2010). The relocation of the village of Shishmaref failed due to a lack of financial support.

[97] See e.g. Donner and Webber (2014), p. 333. See in regard the lawsuit of a Kiribati citizen against New Zealand in the case before the UN Human Rights Committee, 24 October 2019 – SC 7/2015, *Ioane Teitiota v. The Chief Executive of Ministry of Business, Innovation and Employment.*

[98] IPCC (2019). Following the United Nations, "*Small Island Developing States (SIDS) are a distinct group of 39 States and 18 Associate Members of United Nations regional commissions that face unique social, economic and environmental vulnerabilities.*" See Office of the High Representative for the Least Developed Countries Landlocked Developing Countries and Small Island Developing States (2023).

[99] Umweltbundesamt (2019), pp. 32–35; Rahmstorf and Schellnhuber (2019), pp. 76–77. European Court of Human Rights, pending – 53600/20, *KlimaSeniorinnen v. Switzerland.*

[100] IPCC (2014a), p. 51.

[101] In regard to the spread of the Asian Tiger Mosquitos see e.g. Umweltbundesamt (2019), pp. 38–39.

change, thus, indirectly influences and exacerbates the usual drivers of social conflicts, such as water and food scarcity, poverty and a higher unemployment rate (*medium confidence*).[102] However, there is still a lack of sufficient empirical evidence and data to draw any meaningful conclusions and predictions about the relationship between climate change and social conflicts.[103]

2.1.2.4.3 Economic Impacts

The economic impact of climate change is usually measured in terms of the gross domestic product (GDP). Accordingly, the impact of an increase in surface temperatures by 1 °C is calculated to cost about 1.2% of the GDP per year, with every 1 °C increase adding another 1.2%.[104] Based on data provided by the World Bank and relying on the GDP of the United States in 2021, a 1 °C temperature increase would constitute a damage amounting to about US $246,353.516 million.[105]

One of the economic sectors that has already been severely affected by climate change is the tourism industry. Countries and regions that rely on natural snow conditions and winter tourism as their main source of income are currently having to adapt to milder climate conditions, which thus also makes it commonly necessary to either shift their business strategy to other tourism spectrums or to make use of artificial methods to obtain their traditional way of income. For regions that focus on summer tourism, the effects strongly vary depending on their geographical location. For tourist regions with a historically milder and colder climate, the tourist season could extend due to longer and hotter summers and thus enhances the profitability of this economic sector (e.g. in central and northern Europe). At the same time, regions that already suffer from very hot and dry summers, such as Spain and Cyprus, could lose large parts of their tourist season due to unbearably hot climates and related impacts such as the increased risk of forest and bush fires as well as water scarcity.[106] Another effect resides in the loss of tourist attractions as a result of climate change. This has already been demonstrated for the Morteratsch glacier in Switzerland but also includes coastal formations, beaches, coral reefs and biodiversity in general.[107]

Yet the tourism sector is not the only one to be affected by climate change. Another sector already affected by climate change is, for example, the agriculture and land use sector, with an increasing need to adapt agricultural production to

---

[102] IPCC (2014a), p. 16.

[103] Buhaug et al. (2009), p. 75.

[104] This statement is based on calculations for the United States of America, see IPCC (2018), p. 243; Hsiang et al. (2017).

[105] World Bank Group (2023).

[106] See Schönwiese (2020), p. 373; IPCC (2018), pp. 242–243.

[107] Oerlemans et al. (2017); IPCC (2018), p. 243.

changes in climate, which may well involve high investment costs due to the increased use of fertilisers and the need to adapt cultivation methods.[108]

2.1.3 Conclusion

The climate has been changing for thousands of years. However, based on current scientific knowledge, it is impossible to deny the anthropogenic influence of the massive changes in climate that can be felt and experienced today. Over the years, climate science has evolved considerably to the point where it is now possible to? attribute climate change not only to the emission of greenhouse gases but also to identify other climate-forcing factors and drivers. Scientific consensus continues to prevail on most of the impacts of climate change. Although some of the more remote impacts of climate change, such as extreme weather events and some social impacts, remain subject to considerable uncertainty as to their attribution to human behaviour, the argument of lack of scientific consensus and verifiability does not apply to most impacts. Climate change is, therefore, a truly man-made problem.

2.2 Climate Change Litigation: An Overview

The judicial enforcement of climate regulations and laws, as well as the implementation of stricter regulations, is becoming increasingly relevant in the course of advancing climate change, leading to a growing number of lawsuits being brought before courts, tribunals and other administrative bodies.[109] The purpose of this section is to give an overview of the global scope of climate change litigation. The first step in doing so consists of a discussion on the mere definition of climate change litigation. The definition ultimately forms the basis of all further elaborations in deciding which lawsuits should be classified as climate claims (Sect. 2.2.1). Based on those results, this section then enrolls in identifying the status and the characteristics of climate change litigation by assessing which parties are involved (Sect. 2.2.2.1.1), the jurisdiction and area of law in which those claims are being raised (Sect. 2.2.2.1.2), as well as the respective objectives that are being pursued (Sect. 2.2.2.1.3). Lastly, the section outlines the generations of climate lawsuits (Sect. 2.2.2.2) and identifies current trends of climate change litigation (Sect. 2.2.2.3).

---

[108] See e.g. Schönwiese (2020), p. 370.

[109] See the database of the Sabin Center for Climate Change Law (2024).

2.2.1 *Defining Climate Change Litigation*

Climate change litigation is a term that has been at the forefront of media coverage for some time. The concept has also been widely used by lawyers and academics to refer to lawsuits in which climate change is at issue. However, there has been little debate about which claims actually fall into the category of climate change litigation and how climate change litigation should ultimately be defined.[110] This, in turn, is essential to the latter empirical, systematic and substantive analysis of climate change cases and to the broader understanding of causation in climate change litigation.[111]

On the basis of a systematic literature review conducted to ascertain which approaches are currently being advocated in different jurisdictions, two main areas of divergence have been identified. For one, there are differences in how the authors refer to climate change per se, while there are also variations in the institutions before which the cases are brought. Other minor distinctions exist, notably regarding the inclusion of claims and lawsuits aimed at challenging existing climate and emissions reduction targets (also known as '*anti-climate litigation*').[112]

The climate change reference represents the core constituent within the definition of climate change litigation. Concepts thereby vary from very narrow perceptions that use climate change as an issue of fact or law to very broad understandings that focus more on the motivation of the litigants or even the impact of the lawsuit.[113] One of the first, and to this day arguably most commonly held views was introduced by *David Markell* and *J.B. Ruhl* in their article *An empirical assessment of climate change in the Courts: A new Jurisprudence or business as usual?*[114] In their approach, climate change litigation is defined

[110] A clear stance on their definitional approaches is taken e.g. by Setzer and Vanhala (2019); Alogna et al. (2021), p. 15. A clear position was also taken by *Abel* in stating that "*(t)his paper, on the other hand, focuses on a narrow understanding of the term and looks at procedures in which climate protection is the main argument for obliging states or state sub-units to do more to protect the climate.*" (translation by author), Abel (2023), pp. 13–14. Also *Gerrard* (Gerrard (2020), p. 33). However, *Pleming* (Pleming and Keating (2020)) is addressing the definitional problem only indirectly and *Torre-Schaub* (Torre-Schaub (2020)) are not giving definition at all.

[111] See for the analysis Sect. 3.4.

[112] See Sect. 2.2.2.1.3.

[113] See for the discussion e.g. Vanhala and Hilson (2013), pp. 144–145. See for advocates of a narrow understanding of climate change litigation, Burger and Metzger (2020), p. 6; Grantham Research Institute (2021), pp. 8–9; Dwyer (2021), p. 130; Hilson (2010), p. 3. The impact is used as a point of reference by Bouwer (2018), p. 504. By aiming at the motivation of the claimants Peel and Osofsky (2015), pp. 6–9. In an even wider sense, Carlarne (2021), p. 112. Some authors base their work and its classification as climate change litigation on the use of terms in the complaint or judgment, such as 'climate' or 'litigation'. See, for example, in the context of a comparative analysis of existing literature on climate change litigation, Setzer and Vanhala (2019), p. 2. Also adopted out of comparability reasons but criticized, Peel and Osofsky (2020), p. 24. Another approach distinguishes lawsuits on the basis of different narratives Bogojevic (2014), pp. 545–546.

[114] Markell and Ruhl (2012), p. 27. With reference to this definition also Lin (2015), p. 579.

> as any piece of federal, state, tribal or local administrative or judicial litigation in which the party filings or tribunal decisions directly and expressly raise an issue of fact or law regarding the substance or policy of climate change causes and impacts.[115]

This definition established by *Markell* and *Ruhl* has been used frequently by other authors in their scientific work on climate change litigation and constitutes one of the stricter conceptions of climate change litigation.[116] It convinces by its definitional clarity, which ensures its usability for empirical analysis and leaves little room for ambiguity. It, nevertheless, significantly restricts the scope of covered claims, even in regard to cases which have a fundamental impact on the climate system, in which the issue of climate change, however, is not expressively but only implicitly raised.[117]

The second part of the definition then relates to the relevant institutions before which lawsuits are being brought. *Markell* and *Ruhl*, hereby include all cases that are being brought before "*federal, state, tribal or local administrative or judicial*" institutions.[118] However, this wording indirectly excludes regional and international judicial bodies. It is also contested whether disputes before non-judicial bodies or general petitions and complaints can be classified as climate change litigation. While *Markell* and *Ruhl* exclude such cases from being qualified as climate change litigation, the Sabin Center for Climate Change Law applies a broader definition and includes rulemaking petitions, requests for reconsideration of regulations, notices of intent to sue and subpoenas, as well.[119]

The definition of climate change litigation for this book depends heavily on its usability and relevance to the following analysis of climate change decisions.[120] It is therefore important that the definition is both easy to use on an empirical basis, and that it provides a comprehensive account and reflection of overall climate change litigation.

With regard to the climate change reference, restricting the definition only to cases that raise climate change as an issue of fact or law would considerably fall too short and exclude a considerable number of cases that have not only a fundamental impact on the climate system, but are influential for the entire climate change debate. Given that climate change litigation is a very strategic area of litigation, it would be amiss not to include the motivation of the litigants in the definitional approach. However, including the motivation is only compatible with the empirical aim of this work and the following analysis if the motivation of the parties involved is clearly

[115] Markell and Ruhl (2012), p. 27.

[116] See e.g. Dwyer (2021); Hilson (2010), p. 3.

[117] Markell and Ruhl (2012), pp. 26–27.

[118] Ibid. 26. *Dwyer* also limits his assessment to domestic adjudicative bodies, Dwyer (2021), p. 130.

[119] Markell and Ruhl (2012), p. 27. Concerning the methodology of the Sabin Center for Climate Change Law see Sabin Center for Climate Change Law (2024).

[120] See a concretization of the term 'climatic causation' Sect. 3.3.2.1. In regard to the analysis Sect. 3.4.

evident from the complaint itself. It is imperative to avoid any subjective assessments and interpretations without a sound basis. Hence, only the motivation that carries climate change as a central topic to the claim is suitable for empirical as well as overall legal work and should, thus, be included in this definitional approach.[121] It is hereby of irrelevance whether the motivation is based on mitigating the consequences of climate change, requiring further adaptation or questioning enforced climate legislation; so-called '*anti-climate litigation*' cases necessarily need to be qualified as climate change litigation as well. Both the wording of the term climate change litigation, as well as the importance of 'anti climate' in light of their regulatory impact, do not allow for a contrary interpretation.

Concerning the institutional component of the definition, it is quite reasonable not only to focus on judicial bodies but also to accept cases before administrative and quasi-judicial institutions.[122] The inclusion of non-adjudicative cases significantly expands the scope of climate change litigation, but still maintains a clear framework that further guarantees its empirical usability. At the same time, it ensures that innovative approaches, which are rather pursued by quasi-judicial bodies and might have an effect on the climate or on the climate change policy, also become part of the overall analysis, especially on a substantial and systematic level. In addition, this also guarantees the increased inclusion of anti-climate change litigation, as these are often located in dispute settlement proceedings. Due to the innovative power and the willingness of regional and international courts to embrace climate change as a legal matter, the widening of the case category beyond the national borders and the inclusion of the respective lawsuits in the definition of climate change litigation are further indispensable. The definition thus does justice to the character of climate change as a universal and global challenge.

Based on the previous remarks, climate change litigation is, therefore, understood as *including all cases before national, regional and international judicial, quasi-judicial or administrative bodies in which a party directly raises an issue of law or fact or is demonstrably motivated by the substance of the climate, climate change or climate science.*

---

[121] This is reflected by the two outer circles, see Peel and Osofsky (2015), p. 8 Figure 1.1.

[122] Quasi-judicial bodies are institutions with a "*mandate to monitor compliance with a body of norms, settle disputes regarding those norms, or make determinations on the basis of investigations of one form or another, yet none empowered to make final, binding decisions on questions of international law*", Tignino (2016), p. 242. They comprise, inter alia, the Economic, Social and Cultural Rights Committee, World Trade Organization Dispute Settlement or the Aarhus Compliance Committee.

2.2.2 *Categorizing Climate Change Litigation*

Climate change litigation is building on a long tradition of national and international environmental adjudication and legal debate.[123] With the growing discourse and public awareness of the impacts and dangers of anthropogenic climate change, the number of climate change lawsuits is steadily increasing. While only 884 lawsuits were filed by 2007, the number has now risen to over 2000 cases worldwide by June 2023.[124] In terms of the global allocation, most lawsuits to date have been initiated in the United States with over 1500 cases, followed by Australia with about 128 cases and the United Kingdom with 90 proceedings.[125] Although climate change litigation in the Global South, especially in Asia and South America, is on the rise, the Global North still remains the main driver of climate claims.

2.2.2.1 Characteristics of Climate Change Lawsuits

2.2.2.1.1 Parties to the Proceeding

Climate lawsuits are brought by a variety of different plaintiffs, including individuals, corporations, non-governmental organizations (NGOs) and governments. According to an analysis of the complaints filed, individuals and NGOs constitute the largest group of plaintiffs, with the number of lawsuits still on the rise.[126] Especially in international proceedings, individual claimants are frequently accompanied by non-governmental organizations, such as the Global Legal Action Network (GLAN), Greenpeace or Oxfam.[127] Corporations constitute the second largest

---

[123] Carlarne (2021), pp. 112–113. One of the first, and arguably one of the most important, cases in international environmental law that led to the development of the no-harm principle: Arbitrational Tribunal, 16 April 1938, 11 March 1941 – 3 R.I.A.A. 1905, *United States v. Canada (Trail Smelter Case)*. Furthermore, Arbitrational Tribunal, 16 November 1957 – 12 R.I.A.A. 281; 24 I.L.R. 101, *France v. Spain (Lac Lanoux)*, International Court of Justice, 25 September 1997 – I. C. J. Reports 1997, p. 7, *Gabčíkovo-Nagymaros Project (Hungary v. Slovakia)*.

[124] Data drawn from the database of the Sabin Center for Climate Change Law (Sabin Center for Climate Change Law (2024).

[125] Data drawn from the database of the Sabin Center for Climate Change Law (ibid.). The definition used by the database appears to be somewhat narrower than the one used in this paper, although it is not possible to make a clear statement as the definitional approach used is not explicitly mentioned. Therefore, the figures may vary slightly, in particular due to the inclusion of cases based on the motivation of the litigants.

[126] Grantham Research Institute (2021), p. 12.

[127] Cases supported by those NGOs include e.g., New Zealand Supreme Court, 19 December 2008 – NZSC 112, *Greenpeace New Zealand Inc. v. Genesis Power Ltd*, Administrative Court of Berlin, 31 October 2019 – VG 10 K 412.18, *Family Farmers and Greenpeace Germany v. Germany*, Commission on Human Rights (Philippines), 9 December 2019 – CHR-NI-2016-0001, *Greenpeace Southeast Asia and Others*, District Court in Administrative Matters, 21 September 2020 – Amparo No. 372/2020, *Greenpeace Mexico v. Ministry of Energy and Others*. Administrative Court of Paris,

group of plaintiffs, with lawsuits often categorized as anti-climate litigation, targeting environmental impact assessments and administrative permits. The third major group of plaintiffs then consists out of governments and state actors.[128] However, the group of plaintiffs is increasingly diversifying, with claims being brought by political parties, minorities and indigenous groups, as well.[129]

On the defendant side, the majority of lawsuits are filed against governments, followed by lawsuits against multinational corporations and notably against so-called '*carbon majors*'.[130] Only few climate change cases have been brought against individuals to this date. Those that have been brought are mostly criminal cases criminal cases involving climate protesters demonstrating against the construction of a new airport runway, oil pipelines or coal mining.[131] Inter-state climate change disputes, albeit much discussed in the legal discourse, have just scarcely found any equivalent in practice.[132]

2.2.2.1.2 Jurisdiction, Area of Law and Subject Matter

In terms of jurisdiction, most cases are still brought before national courts. Few climate cases have been filed at the international level, mainly before international and regional human rights bodies. Yet, this number is steadily increasing.[133]

Initially, climate change litigation was brought on administrative law grounds. In particular, early litigation in the United States involved challenges to agency permits

---

3 February 2021 – N° 1901967, 1904968, 1904972, 1904976/4-1 *Notre Affaire à Tous and Others v. France*, Spain Supreme Court, 07. January 2021 – 002/0000162/2021, *Greenpeace v. Spain II.*

[128] Grantham Research Institute (2021), p. 12. See in this regard Sect. 2.2.2.1.3.

[129] See e.g. Brazil Federal Supreme Court, 1 July 2022 – ADPF 708, *PSB et al. v. Brazil*, Guyana Supreme Court, pending – n/a, *Thomas & De Freitas v. Guyana.*

[130] The term 'carbon majors' is used to describe companies that account for the largest share of industrial greenhouse gas emissions internationally. The concept is based on *Richard Heede's* 2014 report, in which he attributes 63% of global industrial CO_2 emissions to just 90 oil, gas, coal and cement producers the so called carbon majors. See in this regard Heede (2014). In an updated report from 2017, 71% of industrial CO_2 emissions could be attributed to 100 gas, oil and coal producers, including Shell, BHP and ExxonMobil among others (Griffin (2017)) Grantham Research Institute (2021), p. 12.

[131] Queensland District Court, 28.08.2020 – QDC 205, *EH v. Queensland Police Service; GS v. Queensland Police Service*, West London Magistrates' Court, 24.02.2016 – *Crown Prosecution Service v Basto et al.* Other lawsuits are e.g. Federal District Court for the Eastern District of Virginia, note of voluntary dismissal: 30 April 2015 – 1:15-cv-00486, *Wegman v. Mashey*, Arizona Supreme Court, 29 August 2018 – CV-18-0194-SA, *Energy & Environment Legal Institute v. Arizona Board of Regents*. For an international action, see International Criminal Court, pending – n/a, *The Planet v. Bolsonaro.*

[132] See in this regard e.g. Voigt (2008) and Barton (2002). Based on the announcement of Vanuatu' Foreign Minister to pursue legal actions against sovereign states, see Wewerinke-Singh and Salili (2020). One step in that direction was just recently made by Resolution 77/276 on the request for an advisory opinion of the International Court of Justice on the obligations of States in respect of climate change, 2023.

[133] Data drawn from the Sabin Center for Climate Change Law (2024).

and regulations and disputes over the results of environmental impact assessments.[134] Today, climate litigation is being brought in almost every area of law with the subject matter varying from actions that promote new regulations or enforce existing ones at the national and international level to claims for personal injury resulting from climate-related events. Arguments, therefore, arise from international obligations, constitutional and administrative law, human rights, environmental law, tort law and public trust law.[135]

In terms of the cause of action, two types of cases can be distinguished. The first category includes cases in which the plaintiff seeks regulation or mitigation of greenhouse gas emissions in order to meet national and international emission reduction targets and climate objectives. These cases belong to the category of '*source attribution*'.[136] The second and much more complex category in terms of constructing causal chains includes cases in which the plaintiff invokes the effects of climate change and seeks monetary compensation for the damage it has caused.[137] Those cases are called '*impact attribution*' cases.[138] In terms of subject matter, there are basically four different categories to consider: adaptation cases, mitigation cases, risk management cases and claims for loss and damage.

Some criminal proceedings can also be qualified as climate change litigation. However, these are quantitatively only of minor importance. These cases mainly concern pro-climate activism involving a misdemeanour or criminal offence committed by protesters during a demonstration, as well as cases involving violations of climate criminal law, especially by corporations.[139] Nonetheless, as environmental and climate criminal law continues to develop and become more concrete at the national and international level, it is likely that more and more criminal cases will end up in court in the future.[140] This development is also being enhanced by discussions on the inclusion of ecocide as a fifth crime in the Rome Statute, which could also lead to the strengthening of the prosecution of climate change cases at the

---

[134]Markell and Ruhl (2012), pp. 38–39. See in this regard especially Sect. 2.2.2.2.

[135]Grantham Research Institute (2021), pp. 26–27, Figure 2.1.

[136]Germany Federal Constitutional Court, 24 March 2021 – 1 BvR 2656/18 – 1 BvR 78/20 – 1 BvR 96/20 – 1 BvR 288/20, *Neubauer et al. v. Germany*, Hague District Court, 26 May 2021 – C/09/571932/HA ZA 19-379, *Milieudefensie et al. v. Royal Dutch Shell plc.*

[137]Burger and Metzger (2020), p. 44.

[138]This includes among others: US Court of Appeals for the 5th Circuit, 28 May 2010 – 07-60756, *Ned Comer et al. v. Murphy Oil USA, Inc., et al*, Higher Regional Court Hamm, pending – 5 U 15/17, *Luciano Lliuya v. RWE AG.*

[139]See also in the previous Sect. 2.2.2.1.1. Further e.g. Southwark Crown Court, 23 April 2021 – n/a, *Simon Bramwell et al. v. the Crown (The Shell Six case)*, West London Magistrates' Court 24 February 2016 – n/a, *Robert Anthony Basto et al. v. the Crown*, Queensland District Court, 28 August 2020 – QDC 205, *EH v. Queensland Police Service; GS v. Queensland Police Service.*

[140]Regarding developments at EU level, see Saliger (2020), pp. 9–11, paras 22–23a. For a comprehensive account on 'green criminology' see Kramer (2020). See further Levenson (2020). For an international account, see Minha (2020).

international level.[141] Even without relying on a fifth crime in the Rome Statute, the NGO AllRise, together with other environmental organisations, lawyers and scientists, has called for the former Brazilian head of state Jair Bolsonaro to be indicted by the International Criminal Court for crimes against humanity for his inaction and for promoting the deforestation of the Amazon rainforest.[142]

2.2.2.1.3 Objectives and Motivation

Based on the motivation of the plaintiffs, climate claims can be divided into strategic and routine cases. Strategic climate change lawsuits are characterized by the fact that the plaintiffs do not exceptionally want to achieve a positive outcome of the case but also and predominantly pursue the goal of bringing about a more far-reaching political, societal and social change.[143] In some respects, the actual outcome of the case is merely of secondary matter. Rather, the aim is to elicit public interest, achieve media presence and establish a broader public discourse by filing the lawsuit. Thus, it is essentially a matter of political participation through the use of judicial elements.[144] Developed initially in the Anglo-American legal sphere, with a focus on constitutional and human rights, the concept was particularly well received in the Global South due to the strong interconnectedness of law with political activism.[145] Albeit lawyers from Western European countries adopted the idea of strategic litigation only with scepticism and restraint at first, strategic litigation is now used in almost all jurisdictions and with regard to a wide range of legal matters.[146] These include the assertion of women's rights in the United States and the rebellion against military dictatorships in Latin America in the 1970s, as well as the pursuit of socio-economic and indigenous rights in African courts.[147] Today, strategic litigation is associated, in particular, with climate change litigation. The scope of application is not only limited to lawsuits against states but increasingly also includes corporations.[148]

Routine cases, on the other hand, are not necessarily characterized by a decrease in public and climate-related relevance, but the parties predominantly pursue private

---

141 Sands et al. (2021).

142 International Criminal Court, pending – n/a, *The Planet v. Bolsonaro.*

143 Grantham Research Institute (2021), p. 5.

144 See Fuchs (2019).

145 Concerning judicial activism in Latin America Rodríguez-Garavito (2011). With regard to the 'activist tribunals' in India, South Africa, and Colombia Maldonado (2013), pp. 21–22.

146 Probably one of the first lawsuits in this regard Supreme Court of the United States, 17 May 1954 – 347 U.S. 483, *Brown v. Board of Education of Topeka*, For an overview of the different practical accounts, see different authors in Graser and Helmrich (2019), pp. 53–144.

147 Helmrich (2019).

148 Geneva Association (2021), 21, US Court of Appeals for the 5th Circuit, 28 May 2010 – 07-60756, *Ned Comer et al. v. Murphy Oil USA, Inc., et al*, Hague District Court, 26 May 2021 – C/09/571932/HA ZA 19-379, *Milieudefensie et al. v. Royal Dutch Shell plc.*

interests.[149] The decisive factor for a distinction is thus not the actual effect but rather the will and motivation of the plaintiffs with regard to the reason for bringing the action. However, it is often difficult to classify a climate claim as strategic or non-strategic, as very few claims can be clearly placed in a specific litigation category.

Considering anti-climate litigation lawsuits, the most frequent cases are lawsuits that are either directed against a negative administrative decision, for example, with regard to the operation of coal-fired power plants or demand the issuance of a positive decision.[150] This has become particularly relevant in relation to oil pipelines, the extraction of coal and other minerals, as well as in regard to other power plants. Further complaints are directed against the strengthening of legal regulations and increasingly strict climate protection regulations.[151] Especially at the regional and international level, investment protection law plays a fundamental role in the filing of lawsuits. Investors base their claims, which are predominantly brought within the framework of dispute settlement mechanisms, on provisions of investment and trade agreements, which states might violate due to the launch of strict environmental and climate protection regulations.[152] In other lawsuits, nature and climate activists collide in regard to the construction of renewable energies, such as wind farms or solar parks, that could potentially threaten the habitat, reproduction or flight paths of endangered animal species.[153] Meanwhile, others are based on the ideological rejection and defamation of anthropogenic climate change per se.[154] However, such lawsuits are still relatively limited in number compared to other areas of anti-climate action. As to lawsuits that seek to have a positive impact on the climate, anti-climate lawsuits are still far behind on a global scale in general. Still, with states pursuantly implementing stricter climate provisions, more and more anti-climate lawsuits, especially on the basis of investment protection law, can be expected.[155] At the same time, as countries continue to build wind and solar farms to meet their climate targets under the Paris Agreement, more legal challenges to administrative approvals and the construction itself can be expected.

---

[149] Grantham Research Institute (2021), pp. 12–13; Geneva Association (2021), pp. 18–19.

[150] See Markell and Ruhl (2012), p. 67.

[151] See Alogna et al. (2021), p. 19. In regard to its coal phase out International Centre for Settlement of Investment Disputes, pending – ARB/21/4, *RWE v. Kingdom of the Netherlands.*

[152] Savaresi (2020), p. 367.

[153] Massachusetts District Court, pending – 1:21-CV-11390, *Nantucket Residents Against Turbines et al. v. United States Bureau of Ocean Energy Management et al.*

[154] Hilson (2010), pp. 5–6, Queen's Bench Division, Administrative Court, 10 October 2007 – [2007] EWHC 288 (Admin), [2008] 1 All ER 367, *Stuart Dimmock v. Secretary of State for Education and Skills.*

[155] Markell and Ruhl (2012), pp. 66–67, Figure 3. Recent cases include International Centre for Settlement of Investment Disputes, withdrawn – ARB/21/22, *Uniper v. Netherlands*, International Centre for Settlement of Investment Disputes, 21 November 2022 – UNCT/15/2, *Lone Pine Resources Inc. v. Canada.*

2.2.2.2 Generations of Climate Change Litigation

The development of climate change litigation can be divided into different generations based on its time frame and scope. To date, three generations can be distinguished in particular.[156] As previously addressed, the first climate change lawsuits were filed in the United States, soon followed by lawsuits in Australia. With only a small number of cases and little publicity, these lawsuits, filed up to the year 2007, represent the first generation of climate change litigation. The main objective of such lawsuits remained on specific project-related challenges to approvals and demands for the integration of climate considerations into political, administrative and legislative processes. Lawsuits, in this sense, were mainly directed against governments and state authorities.

The second generation of climate change litigation, which took place between 2007 and 2015, is notable not only for the diversification of the litigants, but also for the geographical expansion of the litigation. Plaintiffs increasingly focused on transnational corporations to hold them responsible for climate change. This development was fuelled by the '*Carbon Majors – Report*' by *Richard Heede*, which was published in 2014.[157] Lawsuits began to be filed in other parts of the world, as well, particularly in Europe. With the entry into force of the Kyoto Protocol in 2005, its increasing ratification and the resulting growing public discourse on climate change, the number of climate lawsuits increased steadily.

The third generation of climate litigation demonstrates the increasing creativity of plaintiffs. Not only has the range of plaintiffs and defendants expanded since 2015 especially triggered by the adoption of the Paris Agreement, but lawsuits are increasingly being filed in other parts of the world, particularly in the Global South.[158] Moreover, the trend from 2015 onwards, in contrast to the second generation, testifies to the increasing success of such claims in national and international courts. The increasing number of cases and their progress is also largely due to the growing consensus on anthropogenic climate change, the findings of climate science, and the reports of the IPCC.[159] At the same time, plaintiffs are increasingly using other areas of law, arguments, and claims to drive the debate on the climate-related implementation of regulatory provisions in national legislation.

---

[156] See concerning the generations of climate change litigation Peel and Osofsky (2020), p. 30; Geneva Association (2021), pp. 13–17; Carlarne (2021), pp. 114–116. A different approach is taken by *Bouwer* in dividing the generations of climate change litigation into a tort wave, a public trust wave and a carbon major wave. See in this regard Bouwer (2018), p. 489.

[157] See again Heede (2014).

[158] See e.g. Supreme Court of Pakistan, 15 April 2021 – C.P.1290-L/2019, *D. G. Khan Cement Company v. Government of Punjab*, Guyana Supreme Court, pending – n/a, *Thomas & De Freitas v. Guyana*.

[159] IPCC (2023).

2.2.2.3 Current Trends and Developments

As the number of climate lawsuits increases, plaintiffs are also becoming more creative, both in terms of potential defendants as well as in terms of the areas of law and the causes of action.

On the defendant side, a clear trend towards climate change litigation against corporations is increasingly materializing.[160] While lawsuits against transnational corporations have been filed since the inception of climate change litigation and have been increasingly successful in the third generation of climate change litigation, there is now an emerging diversification in terms of the parties to the litigation and the area of law. The focus of such lawsuits no longer exclusively rests on large worldwide operating corporations and carbon majors but is also spreading to smaller companies and greenhouse gas-intensive projects.[161] Furthermore, the scope is now broadening to include economic sectors that were initially not directly associated with climate change and greenhouse gas emissions, such as banks, financial institutions and funds.[162] In terms of the parties themselves, there is a clear trend towards a diversification of litigants. While indigenous groups were among the first to take the legal route to protect their habitats and the climate as a whole, other minorities and vulnerable groups are increasingly turning to the courts as well.[163] These include, in particular, women, children, and young people, as well as senior citizens and elderly people.[164] The heterogeneity of claimants goes hand in hand with the increasing focus on human rights-based claims. In addition, and as noted above, parties from the Global South are also gradually discovering the possibility of enforcing and promoting climate protection in and through the courts.[165]

---

[160] Grantham Research Institute (2023), p. 21.

[161] See e.g. District Court of Łódz, 22 September 2020 – n/a, *ClientEarth v. Polska Grupa Energetyczna.*

[162] See e.g. Federal Court of Australia, 17 January 2019 (settlement agreement – 02 November 2020) – NSD1333/2018, *McVeigh v. Retail Employees Superannuation Trust.* Brussels Court of First Instance, withdrawn – 21/38/C, *ClientEarth v. Belgian National Bank.* See in this regard also Grantham Research Institute (2021), pp. 7, 28 Figure 2.2.

[163] Concerning one of the first lawsuits pursued by Indigenous, see US District Court for the Northern District of California, 30 September 2009 – 4:08-cv-01138-SBA, *Native Village of Kivalina v. ExxonMobil Corp.*

[164] See in regard to women, Lahore High Court, pending – No. 8960 of 2019, *Maria Khan et al. v. Federation of Pakistan et al,* Swiss Federal Supreme Court, 20 May 2020 – 1C_37/2019, *Association of Swiss Senior Women for Climate Protection v. Federal Department of the Environment Transport, Energy and Communications (DETEC) and Others ("Verein KlimaSeniorinnen Schweiz v. Bundesrat").* With reference to children and young people e.g., United Nations Committee on the Rights of the Child, ongoing – *Sacchi et al. v. Argentina et al.*, Superior Court of Lima, pending – n/a, *Álvarez et al. v. Peru.* In regard to elderly, see e.g. Swiss Federal Supreme Court, 20 May 2020 – 1C_37/2019, *Association of Swiss Senior Women for Climate Protection v. Federal Department of the Environment Transport, Energy and Communications (DETEC) and Others ("Verein KlimaSeniorinnen Schweiz v. Bundesrat"),* European Court of Human Rights, pending – 53600/20, *KlimaSeniorinnen v. Switzerland.*

[165] Grantham Research Institute (2021), p. 5.

In addition to the diversification of the parties involved in litigation, there has also been a broadening of the areas of law in which claims are being brought. Plaintiffs are increasingly turning to corporate and commercial law, relying on protective and fiduciary duties of companies to support their claims.[166] At the same time, and in the wake of growing social pressure and increasing consumer demand for sustainably produced and climate-neutral products, a new category of litigation is evolving in the form of '*greenwashing*' or even more so '*climatewashing*' cases.[167] Plaintiffs specifically target advertising and marketing campaigns by companies that make statements or promises about the sustainability, climate friendliness and environmental awareness of the company or a particular product but which are misleading or not reflected in practice.[168] The aim of such campaigns is to imply that the company is as environmentally and climate-friendly as possible. These include especially the framing of products as carbon neutral.[169] Other cases of greenwashing involve false, misleading or undisclosed information to shareholders on the assessment of environmental and climate-related risks to the company's business model and future economic development.[170]

Especially since the high-profile case of *Milieudefensie et al. v. Royal Dutch Shell plc,* corporate human rights obligations have come to the fore for plaintiffs.[171] In its judgment in this respective case, the Court stated that, although the applicants cannot rely on Art. 2 ECHR, Art. 8 ECHR and human rights directly, "*[…] the court will factor in the human rights and the values they embody in its interpretation of the unwritten standard of care.*"[172] This jurisprudence is consistent with the substance of the UN Guiding Principles on Business and Human Rights.[173]According to these principles, companies have a responsibility to respect human rights and to take them into account in their deliberations. It remains to be seen, however, whether human rights obligations can be imposed on companies in relation to climate change outside of the above precedent. In an earlier case, the Commission on Human Rights (Philippines) argued that while companies may be liable for climate change damages, they do not have any obligations under the international human rights frame-

---

[166]See in this regard also Carlarne (2021), p. 117; Grantham Research Institute (2021), pp. 29–30.

[167]Grantham Research Institute (2021), p. 29; Grantham Research Institute (2023), pp. 39–41.

[168]See e.g. Federal Court of Australia, 17 January 2019 (settlement agreement – 02 November 2020) – NSD1333/2018, *McVeigh v. Retail Employees Superannuation Trust,* National Contact Point for the OECD Guidelines, 16. June 2020 – n/a, *Complaint against BP in respect of violations of the OECD Guidelines.*

[169]Grantham Research Institute (2023), p. 40.

[170]Federal Court of Australia, withdrawn – VID879/2017, *Abrahams v. Commonwealth Bank of Australia,* United States District Court Northern District of California, Oakland Division, pending – 4:19-cv-06971, *Sierra Club v. U.S. Securities & Exchange Commission.*

[171]Hague District Court, 26 May 2021 – C/09/571932/HA ZA 19-379, *Milieudefensie et al. v. Royal Dutch Shell plc.*

[172]Ibid. Judgement in its translated version (eng.), para 4.4.9.

[173]UN Guiding Principles on Business and Human Rights (2011), pp. 13–16.

work in this regard.[174] Nevertheless, given the large body of literature and discourse on both general human rights and climate-related corporate obligations, it seems only a matter of time before plaintiffs and even courts push this development further.[175]

It is not only in the corporate arena that plaintiffs are increasingly turning to human rights. There is also a growing trend towards a rights turn in other areas of law.[176] In doing so, the plaintiffs rely both on national rights enshrined in their respective constitutions and on regional and international human rights.[177] This is commonly called a '*greening*' of human rights.[178] The plaintiffs argue that, in the absence of precautionary measures by the state or due to other state behaviour (possibly also corporate conduct), they perceive a violation of the state's obligation to protect and, thus, a violation of their human rights.[179] Of particular relevance are the rights to life, health, water and food, as these are directly linked to climate change and the resulting climate variability. In addition, the right to culture and cultural life, which has been particularly raised by indigenous groups, is of considerable importance.[180] However, due to the universality and complexity of climate change, possible approaches are not limited to the above-mentioned rights; on the contrary, all human rights can, in principle, be directly or indirectly affected. In this respect, the Federal Constitutional Court of Germany stated in its landmark decision concerning an increased emission reduction burden on future generations that "*(p)-ractically all forms of freedom are potentially affected because virtually all aspects of human life involve the emission of greenhouse gases [...]*".[181] Yet, the potential of human rights-based litigation is not limited to the outcome of the court case itself. Such lawsuits have great potential to attract public attention outside the courtroom and to further advance the debate on anthropogenic climate change.

In addition to the greening of some human rights guarantees, the direct assertion of the right to a clean and healthy environment is also becoming increasingly common, provided that such a right is enshrined in the respective constitution or

---

[174]Commission on Human Rights (Philippines), 9 December 2019 – CHR-NI-2016-0001, *Greenpeace Southeast Asia and Others.*

[175]Arnold (2016), Brabandere (2010), Ganguly et al. (2018), and Roos (2013).

[176]Peel and Osofsky (2018); Alogna et al. (2021), p. 19; Grantham Research Institute (2021), pp. 6, 32–34.

[177]See e.g. US Court of Appeals for the 9th Circuit, pending – 18-36082, *Juliana v. United States*, Supreme Court of the Netherlands, 20 December 2019 – 19/00135, *Urgenda Foundation v. The State of The Netherlands.*

[178]See e.g. Pirjatanniemi (2016).

[179]See in regard to the positive obligations Sects. 3.2.3 and 3.3.2.4.

[180]See exemplary Inter-American Court of Human Rights, 6 February 2020 – C No. 400, *Indigenous Communities of the Lhaka Honhat (Our Land) Association v. Argentina*, UN Human Rights Committee, 24 October 2019 – SC 7/2015, *Ioane Teitiota v. The Chief Executive of Ministry of Business, Innovation and Employment.*

[181]Germany Federal Constitutional Court, 24 March 2021 – 1 BvR 2656/18 – 1 BvR 78/20 – 1 BvR 96/20 – 1 BvR 288/20, *Neubauer et al. v. Germany*, paras. 37, 117.

human rights treaty and is ultimately also enforceable.[182] In jurisdictions where such a right does not yet exist in law or in the constitution, litigants are progressively endeavouring to derive it from existing legal norms.[183] This development is part of an evolving '*climate constitutionalism*'.[184] Along with this development, and even beyond it, claimants are also increasingly asserting a right to a stable climate.[185]

Another recent trend is the increased focus by plaintiffs on the judicial enforcement of natural rights.[186] At least since the publication of the renowned article '*Should Trees Have Standing*' by *Christopher Stone*, legal scholars have been discussing the legal standing and personhood of natural entities such as lakes, rivers, and mountains and beyond that of nature itself.[187] This development is based, in particular, on the efforts of indigenous peoples and states in the Global South, which have traditionally lived very close to nature. While *Stone*, in the new edition of his book, ventures the thought experiment of extending this model to grant rights also to the climate, this has not yet found a counterpart in legislation and jurisprudence.[188]

Where will climate litigation head next? Will there still only ever exist three generations of climate litigation, or is the climate litigation movement already on the verge of a fourth wave? This much is clear: the climate litigation train has picked up speed and is unlikely to be stopped in the near future.

Climate Change?Cases

A Request for an Advisory Opinion from the Inter-American Court of Human Rights Concerning the Interpretation of Article 1(1), 4(1) and 5(1) of the American Convention on Human Rights – Inter-American Court on Human Rights, 15 November 2017 – OC-23/17

---

[182] The right to an healthy environment is enshrined in the constitutions of e.g. Nigeria (Section 20) and Portugal (Art. 66). See in this regard also Inter-American Court of Human Rights, 15 November 2017 – OC-23/17, *A Request for an Advisory Opinion from the Inter-American Court of Human Rights Concerning the Interpretation of Article 1(1), 4(1) and 5(1) of the American Convention on Human*. Concerning the growing lawsuits in this field Burger and Metzger (2020), pp. 13–20.

[183] See exemplary US Court of Appeals for the 9th Circuit, pending – 18-36082, *Juliana v. United States*, Federal District Court of Curitiba, pending – N° 5048951-39.2020.4.04.7000, *Institute of Amazonian Studies v. Brazil*, Germany Federal Constitutional Court, 24 March 2021 – 1 BvR 2656/18 – 1 BvR 78/20 – 1 BvR 96/20 – 1 BvR 288/20, *Neubauer et al. v. Germany*.

[184] Grantham Research Institute (2021), pp. 33–34, Box 2.6. On a more critical note McHarg (2011), pp. 483–484.

[185] See in the case of Federal District Court of Curitiba, pending – N° 5048951-39.2020.4.04.7000, *Institute of Amazonian Studies v. Brazil*. On the same note Jegede (2020), pp. 196–206.

[186] See among others Burger and Metzger (2020), p. 17.

[187] Stone (1972). Concerning legal rights of rivers, e.g. the rights of the Whanganui river in New Zealand granted by the Te Awa Tupua Act. Concerning mountains, Art. 10, 71–74 of the Ecuadorian Constitution. Regarding the legal situation in Bolivia, see e.g. Ley de Derechos de la Madre Tierra and Ley Marco de la Madre Tierra y Desarrollo Integral para Vivir Bien. Also Calzadilla and Kotzé (2018).

[188] Stone (2010), pp. 33–77.

Abrahams v. Commonwealth Bank of Australia – Federal Court of Australia, withdrawn – VID879/2017

Álvarez et al. v. Peru – Superior Court of Lima, pending – n/a

Association of Swiss Senior Women for Climate Protection v. Federal Department of the Environment Transport, Energy and Communications (DETEC) and Others ("Verein KlimaSeniorinnen Schweiz v. Bundesrat") – Swiss Federal Supreme Court, 20 May 2020 – 1C_37/2019

Crown Prosecution Service v Basto et al. – West London Magistrates' Court, 24 February 2016 – n/a

ClientEarth v. Belgian National Bank – Court of First Instance, withdrawn – 21/38/C

ClientEarth v. Polska Grupa Energetyczna – District Court of Łódz, 22 September 2020 – n/a

Complaint against BP in respect of violations of the OECD Guidelines – National Contact Point for the OECD Guidelines, 16 June 2020 – n/a

D. G. Khan Cement Company v. Government of Punjab – Supreme Court of Pakistan, 15 April 2021 – C.P.1290-L/2019

EH v. Queensland Police Service; GS v. Queensland Police Service – Queensland District Court, 28 August 2020 – QDC?205

Energy & Environment Legal Institute v. Arizona Board of Regents – Arizona Supreme Court, 29 August 2018 – CV-18-0194-SA

Family Farmers and Greenpeace Germany v. Germany – Administrative Court of Berlin, 31 October 2019 – VG 10 K 412.18

Gabčíkovo-Nagymaros Project (Hungary v. Slovakia) – International Court of Justice, 25 September 1997 – I. C. J. Reports 1997, p. 7

Greenpeace Mexico v. Ministry of Energy and Others – District Court in Administrative Matters, 21 September 2020 – Amparo No. 372/2020

Greenpeace New Zealand Inc. v. Genesis Power Ltd. – New Zealand Supreme Court, 19 December 2008 – NZSC?112

Greenpeace Southeast Asia and Others – Commission on Human Rights (Philippines), 9 December 2019 – CHR-NI-2016-0001

Greenpeace v. Spain II – Spain Supreme Court, 7 January 2021 – 002/0000162/2021

Indigenous Communities of the Lhaka Honhat (Our Land) Association v. Argentina – Inter-American Court of Human Rights, 6 February 2020 – C No. 400

Institute of Amazonian Studies v. Brazil – Federal District Court of Curitiba, pending – N° 5048951-39.2020.4.04.7000

Ioane Teitiota v. The Chief Executive of Ministry of Business, Innovation and Employment – UN Human Rights Committee, 24 October 2019 – SC 7/2015

Juliana v. United States – US Court of Appeals for the 9th Circuit, pending – 18-36082

KlimaSeniorinnen v. Switzerland – European Court of Human Rights, pending – 53600/20

Lone Pine Resources Inc. v. Canada – International Centre for Settlement of Investment Disputes, 21 November 2022 – UNCT/15/2

Luciano Lliuya v. RWE AG – Higher Regional Court Hamm, pending – 5 U 15/17

Maria Khan et al. v. Federation of Pakistan et al. – Lahore High Court, pending – No. 8960 of?2019

McVeigh v. Retail Employees Superannuation Trust – Federal Court of Australia, 17 January 2019 (settlement agreement – 2 November 2020) – NSD1333/2018

Milieudefensie et al. v. Royal Dutch Shell plc. – Hague District Court, 26 May 2021 – C/09/571932/HA ZA 19-379

Native Village of Kivalina v. ExxonMobil Corp. – US District Court for the Northern District of California, 30 September 2009 – 4:08-cv-01138-SBA

Nantucket Residents Against Turbines et al. v. United States Bureau of Ocean Energy Management et al. – Massachusetts District Court, pending – 1:21-CV-11390

Ned Comer et al. v. Murphy Oil USA, Inc., et al. – US Court of Appeals for the 5th Circuit, 28 May 2010 – 07-60756

Neubauer et al. v. Germany – Germany Federal Constitutional Court, 24 March 2021 – 1 BvR 2656/18 – 1 BvR 78/20 – 1 BvR 96/20 – 1 BvR 288/20

Notre Affaire à Tous and Others v. France – Administrative Court of Paris, 3 February 2021 – N° 1901967, 1904968, 1904972, 1904976/4-1

PSB et al. v. Brazil – Brazil Federal Supreme Court, 1 July 2022 – ADPF?708

Robert Anthony Basto et al. v. the Crown – West London Magistrates' Court, 24 February 2016 – n/a

RWE v. Kingdom of the Netherlands – International Centre for Settlement of Investment Disputes, pending – ARB/21/4

Sacchi et al. v. Argentina et al. – United Nations Committee on the Rights of the Child, ongoing – CRC/C/88/D/107/2019

Sierra Club v. U.S. Securities & Exchange Commission – United States District Court Northern District of California, Oakland Division, pending – 4:19-cv-06971

The Planet v. Bolsonaro – International Criminal Court, pending – n/a

Thomas & De Freitas v. Guyana – Guyana Supreme Court, pending – n/a

Uniper v. Netherlands – International Centre for Settlement of Investment Disputes, withdrawn – ARB/21/22

Urgenda Foundation v. The State of The Netherlands – Supreme Court of the Netherlands, 20 December 2019 – 19/00135

Simon Bramwell et al. v. the Crown (The Shell Six case) – Southwark Crown Court, 23 April 2021 – n/a

Cases

Brown v. Board of Education of Topeka – Supreme Court of the United States, 17 May 1954 – 347 U.S. 483

France v. Spain (Lac Lanoux) – Arbitrational Tribunal, 16 November 1957 – 12 R.I.A.A. 281; 24 I.L.R. 101

Stuart Dimmock v. Secretary of State for Education and Skills – Queen's Bench Division, Administrative Court, 10 October 2007 – [2007] EWHC 288 (Admin), [2008] 1 All ER?367

United States v. Canada (Trail Smelter Case) – Arbitrational Tribunal, 16 April 1938, 11 March 1941 – 3 R.I.A.A. 1905

Wegman v. Mashey – Federal District Court for the Eastern District of Virginia, note of voluntary dismissal, 30 April 2015 – 1:15-cv-00486

References

Abate RS (ed) (2015) Climate change impacts on ocean and coastal law: U.S. and international perspectives. Oxford University Press, Oxford

Abel P (2023) Klimaklagen gegen Staaten: Ein systematischer Überblick. Nachhaltigkeitsr 3:13–20

Alogna I, Bakker C, Gauci J-P (2021) Climate change litigation: global perspectives – an introduction. In: Alogna I, Bakker C, Gauci J-P (eds) Climate change litigation: global perspectives. Brill, Leiden, pp 1–30

Arnold DG (2016) Corporations and human rights obligations. Bus Hum Rights J 1(2):255–275

Arrhenius S (1896) On the influence of carbonic acid in the air upon the temperature of the ground. Philos Mag J Sci 41(251):237–276

Barton P (2002) State responsibility and climate change: could Canada be liable to small island states? Dalhous J Leg Stud 11:65–87

Bogojevic S (2014) EU climate change litigation: all quiet on the Luxembourgian front? In: Calster GV, Vandenberghe W, Reins L (eds) Research handbook on climate mitigation law. Edward Elgar, Cheltenham, pp 543–559

Bouwer K (2018) The unsexy future of climate change litigation. J Environ Law 30(3):483–506

Brabandere ED (2010) Human rights obligations and transnational corporations: the limits of direct corporate responsibility. Hum Rights Int Leg Discourse 4(1):66–88

Brooke JL (2014) Climate change and the course of global history. Cambridge University Press, Cambridge

Buhaug H, Gleditsch NP, Theisen OM (2009) Implications of climate change for armed conflict. In: Mearns R, Norton A (eds) Social dimensions of climate change: equity and vulnerability in a warming world. World Bank Publications, Washington, pp 75–101

Buhofer S (2017) Der Klimawandel und die internationale Klimapolitik in Zahlen. Oekom, Munich

Burger M, Metzger D (2020) United Nations Environment Programme, Global Climate Litigation Report 2020 Status Review. Nairobi

Calzadilla PV, Kotzé LJ (2018) Living in harmony with nature? A critical appraisal of the rights of mother earth in Bolivia. Trans Environ Law 7(3):397–424

Carlarne CP (2021) The essential role of climate litigation and the courts in averting climate crisis. In: Mayer B, Zahar A (eds) Debating climate law. Cambridge University Press, Cambridge, pp 111–127

Crippa M, Guizzardi D, Muntean M, Schaaf E, Solazzo E, Monforti-Ferrario F, Olivier J, Vignati E (2020) Fossil CO_2 emissions of all world countries – 2020 Report, EUR 30358 EN. Publications Office of the European Union, Luxembourg

Crutzen PJ, Stoermer EF (2000) The "Anthropocene". IGBP Glob Chang Newsl 41:17–18

Davidson SC, Bohrer G, Gurarie E, LaPoint S, Mahoney PJ, Boelman NT, Eitel JUH, Prugh LR, Vierling LA, Jennewein J, Grier E, Couriot O, Kelly AP, Meddens AJH, Oliver RY, Kays R, Wikelski M et al (2020) Ecological insights from three decades of animal movement tracking across a changing Arctic. Science 370:712–715

Denning S (2021) Southeast Amazonia is no longer a carbon sink. Nature 595:354–355

Donner SD, Webber S (2014) Obstacles to climate change adaptation decisions: a case study of sea-level rise and coastal protection measures in Kiribati. Sustain Sci 9(3):331–345

Dwyer G (2021) Climate litigation: a red herring among climate mitigation tools. In: Mayer B, Zahar A (eds) Debating climate law. Cambridge University Press, Cambridge, pp 128–144

Foote E (1856) Circumstances affecting the heat of the sun's rays'. Am J Sci Arts 22:382–383

Fourier J (1824) Remarques Générales sur Les Températures Du Globe Terrestre et des Espaces Planetaires. Annal Chim Phys 27:136–167

Fuchs G (2019) Was ist strategische Prozessführung? In: Graser A, Helmrich C (eds) Strategic litigation. Nomos, Baden-Baden, pp 43–52

Ganguly G, Setzer J, Heyvaert V (2018) If at first you don't succeed: suing corporations for climate change. Oxf J Leg Stud 38(4):841–868

Gatti LV, Basso LS, Miller JB, Gloor M, Domingues LG, Cassol HLG, Tejada G, Aragão LEOC, Nobre C, Peters W, Marani L, Arai E, Sanches AH, Corrêa SM, Anderson L, von Randow C, Correia CSC, Crispim SP, Neves RAL (2021) Amazonia as a carbon source linked to deforestation and climate change. Nature 595(7867):388–393

Geneva Association (2021) Climate change litigation insights into the evolving global landscape. Zurich

Gerrard MB (2020) Climate change litigation in the United States: high volume of cases, mostly about statutes. In: Alogna I, Bakker C, Gauci J-P (eds) Climate change litigation: global perspectives. Cambridge University Press, Cambridge, pp 33–46

Global Monitoring Laboratory – Earth System Research Laboratories (2023) Trends in atmospheric carbon dioxide. Available via Earth System Research Laboratories. https://gml.noaa.gov/ccgg/trends/gl_trend.html. Accessed 24 Oct 2024

Grantham Research Institute on Climate Change and the Environment and Centre for Climate Change Economics and Policy, London School of Economics and Political Science (2021) Global trends in climate change litigation: 2021 snapshot. London

Grantham Research Institute on Climate Change and the Environment and Centre for Climate Change Economics and Policy, London School of Economics and Political Science (2023) Global trends in climate change litigation: 2023 snapshot. London

Graser A, Helmrich C (2019) Strategic litigation – Begriff und Praxis. Nomos, Baden-Baden

Gregg R M (2010) Relocating the Native Village of Shishmaref, Alaska due to coastal erosion [Case study on a project of the Shishmaref Erosion and Relocation Coalition]. Version 2.0. Product of EcoAdapt's State of Adaptation Program

Griffin P (2017) The Carbon Majors Database CDP Carbon Majors Report 2017. London

Heede R (2014) Tracing anthropogenic carbon dioxide and methane emissions to fossil fuel and cement producers, 1854-2010. Clim Chang 112:229–241

Helmrich C (2019) Strategic litigation rund um die Welt. In: Graser A, Helmrich C (eds) Strategic litigation. Nomos, Baden-Baden, pp 115–140

Hilson C (2010) Climate change litigation in the UK: an explanatory approach (or bringing grievance back in). In: Fraccia F, Occhiena M (eds) Climate change: La Riposta del Diritto. Editoriale Scientifica, Napoli, pp 421–436

Hsiang S, Kopp R, Jina A, Rising J, Delgado M, Mohan S, Rasmussen DJ, Muir-Wood R, Wilson P, Oppenheimer M, Larsen K, Houser T (2017) Estimating economic damage from climate change in the United States. Science 356(6345):1362–1369

International Energy Agency (2021) Global CO_2 emissions by sector, 2019. https://www.iea.org/data-and-statistics/charts/global-co2-emissions-by-sector-2019. Accessed 24 Oct 2024

International Work Group for Indigenous Affairs (2008) Report of the conference on indigenous peoples and climate change. Copenhagen

IPCC (2010) Guidance note for lead authors of the IPCC Fifth Assessment Report on consistent treatment of uncertainties. Geneva

IPCC (2013) Climate Change 2013: the physical science basis. Contribution of Working Group I to the Fifth Assessment Report of the Intergovernmental Panel on Climate Change. Cambridge

IPCC (2014a) Climate Change 2014: synthesis report. Contribution of Working Groups I, II and III to the Fifth Assessment Report of the Intergovernmental Panel on Climate Change. Geneva
IPCC (2014b) Climate Change 2014: mitigation of climate change. Contribution of Working Group III to the Fifth Assessment Report of the Intergovernmental Panel on Climate Change. Cambridge
IPCC (2018) Global warming of 1.5°C. An IPCC Special Report on the impacts of global warming of 1.5°C above pre-industrial levels and related global greenhouse gas emission pathways, in the context of strengthening the global response to the threat of climate change, sustainable development, and efforts to eradicate poverty. Cambridge
IPCC (2019) Sea level rise and implications for low-lying islands, coasts and communities. In: IPCC Special Report on the Ocean and Cryosphere in a Changing Climate. Geneva
IPCC (2021a) Climate Change 2021: the physical science basis. Contribution of Working Group I to the Sixth Assessment Report of the Intergovernmental Panel on Climate Change. Geneva
IPCC (2021b) Climate Change 2021: the physical science basis – Contribution of Working Group I to the Sixth Assessment Report of the Intergovernmental Panel on Climate Change – summary for policymakers. Geneva
IPCC (2022) Climate Change 2022: mitigation of climate change Working Group III Contribution to the Sixth Assessment Report of the Intergovernmental Panel on Climate Change. Geneva
IPCC (2023) Climate Change 2023: synthesis report – Contribution of Working Groups I, II and III to the Sixth Assessment Report of the Intergovernmental Panel on Climate Change – summary for policymakers. Geneva
Jegede AO (2020) Arguing the right to a safe climate under the UN human rights system. Int Hum Rights Law Rev 9(2):184–212
Kramer RC (2020) Carbon criminals, climate crimes. Rutgers University Press, New Brunswick
Lehmann J, Coumou D, Frieler K (2015) Increased record-breaking precipitation events under global warming. Clim Chang 132(4):501–515
Levenson LL (2020) Climate change and the criminal justice system. Environ Law Rev 51(2): 333–381
Lin J (2015) Climate change litigation in Asia and the Pacific. In: Calster GV, Vandenberghe W, Reins L (eds) Research handbook on climate change mitigation law. Edward Elgar, Cheltenham, pp 578–599
Maldonado DB (ed) (2013) Constitutionalism of the Global South – the activist tribunals of India, South Africa, and Colombia. Cambridge University Press, Cambridge
Markell D, Ruhl JB (2012) An empirical assessment of climate change in the courts: a new jurisprudence or business as usual? Florida Law Rev 64(1):15–86
McHarg A (2011) Climate change constitutionalism: lessons from the United Kingdom. Clim Law 2(1):469–484
Meyer K, Newman P (2020) Planetary accounting – quantifying how to live within planetary limits at different scales of human activity. Springer, Singapore
Milankovic M (1941) Kanon der Erdbestrahlung und seine Anwendung auf das Eiszeitenproblem. Royal Serbian Academy, Belgrade
Minha D (2020) The possibility of prosecuting corporations for climate crimes before the International Criminal Court: all roads lead to the Rome Statute? Mich J Int Law 41(3):491–539
Moore TT (2011) Climate change and animal migration. Environ Law 41(2):393–405
Mutter JC (2020) Climate change science – a primer for sustainable development. Columbia University Press, New York
Njau EC (2011) Modern science of climate changes. Nova Science Publishing Inc., New York
Oerlemans J, Haag M, Keller F (2017) Slowing down the retreat of the Morteratsch Glacier, Switzerland, by artificially produced summer snow: a feasibility study. Clim Chang 145(1-2): 189–203
Office of the High Representative for the Least Developed Countries Landlocked Developing Countries and Small Island Developing States (2023) About small island developing states.

Available via United Nations. https://www.un.org/ohrlls/content/about-small-island-developing-states. Accessed 24 Oct 2024
Peel J, Osofsky HM (2015) Climate change litigation: regulatory pathways to cleaner energy. Cambridge University Press, Cambridge
Peel J, Osofsky HM (2018) A rights turn in climate change litigation? Trans Environ Law 7(1): 37–67
Peel J, Osofsky HM (2020) Climate change litigation. Annu Rev Law Soc Sci 16(1):21–38
Pfister C, White S (2018) A year without a summer 1816. In: White S, Pfister C, Mauelshagen F (eds) The Palgrave handbook of climate history. Springer, London, pp 551–561
Pirjatanniemi E (2016) Greening human rights law – a focus on the European Convention on Human Rights. In: Bos G, Düwell M (eds) Human rights and sustainability. Routledge, London, pp 11–24
Pleming N, Keating R (2020) Climate change litigation in the United Kingdom: planning, energy and protest. In: Alogna I, Bakker C, Gauci J-P (eds) Climate change litigation: global perspectives. Cambridge University Press, Cambridge, pp 79–102
Rahmstorf S, Schellnhuber HJ (2019) Der Kimawandel. C. H. Beck, Munich
Ramírez E, Francou B, Ribstein P, Descloitres M, Guérin R, Mendoza J, Gallaire R, Pouyaud B, Jordan E (2001) Small glaciers disappearing in the tropical Andes: a case-study in Bolivia: Glaciar Chacaltaya (16°S). J Glaciol 47(157):187–194
Renneboog R (ed) (2018) Principles of climatology. Salem Press, Ipswich
Rodríguez-Garavito C (2011) Beyond the courtroom: the impact of judicial activism on socioeconomic rights in Latin America. Tex Law Rev 89(7):1669–1698
Rohli RV, Vega AJ (2018) Climatology. Jones and Bartlett Publishers, Burlington
Roos SR (2013) Climate change and human rights: what follows for corporate human rights responsibility? In: Ruppel OC, Roschmann C, Ruppel-Schlichting K (eds) Climate change: international law and global governance. Nomos, Baden-Baden, pp 299–322
Roy-Barman M, Jeandel C (2016) Marine geochemistry: ocean circulation, carbon cycle and climate change. Oxford University Press, Oxford
Sabin Center for Climate Change Law (2024) Climate change litigation databases. http://climatecasechart.com/. Accessed 24 Oct 2024
Saliger F (2020) Umweltstrafrecht. Vahlen, Munich
Sands P, Sow D F, Mackintosh K, Rogers R, Cabanes V, Fajardo P, Hasan S R, Jalloh C, Lledo R, Slade T N, Voigt C, Whiting A, Mehta J (2021) Stop ecocide foundation independent expert panel for the legal definition of ecocide: commentary and core text
Savaresi A (2020) Inter-state climate change litigation: 'neither a Chimera nor a Panacea'. In: Alogna I, Bakker C, Gauci J P (eds) Climate change litigation: global perspectives. Martinus Nijhoff Publishers, Leiden, pp 366–392
Schaefer K, Lantuit H, Romanovsky VE, Schuur EAG, Witt R (2014) The impact of the permafrost carbon feedback on global climate. Environ Res Lett 9(8):085003
Schönwiese C-D (2020) Klimatologie – Grundlagen, Entwicklungen und Perspektiven. Utb, Stuttgart
Scott PA, Stone DA, Allen MR (2004) Human contribution to the European Heatwave 2003. Nature 432(7017):610–614
Setzer J, Vanhala LC (2019) Climate change litigation: a review of research on courts and litigants in climate governance. Wiley Interdiscip Rev Clim 10(3):1–19
Seymour F, Busch J (2016) Why forests? Why now?: The science, economics and politics of tropical forests and climate change. Center for Global Development, Washington
Soruco A, Vincent C, Rabatel A, Francou B, Thibert E, Sicart JE, Condom T (2015) Contribution of Glacier Runoff to water resources of La Paz City, Bolivia (16° S). Ann Glaciol 56(70):147–154
Stone CD (1972) Should trees have standing? – towards legal rights for natural objects. South Calif Law Rev 45:450–501
Stone CD (2010) Should trees have standing? – Law, morality, and the environment. Oxford University Press, New York

Tignino M (2016) Quasi-judicial bodies. In: Brölmann C, Radi Y (eds) Research handbook on the theory and practice of international lawmaking. Edward Elgar, Cheltenham, pp 242–261

Torre-Schaub M (2020) Climate change litigation in France: new perspectives and trends. In: Alogna I, Bakker C, Gauci J-P (eds) Climate change litigation: global perspectives. Cambridge University Press, Cambridge, pp 124–142

Tyndall J (2014) Heat considered as a mode of motion: being a course of twelve lectures delivered at the Royal Institution of Great Britain in the Season of 1862. Cambridge University Press, Cambridge

Umweltbundesamt (2019) Monitoringbericht 2019 zur Deutschen Anpassungsstrategie an den Klimawandel (DAS), Bericht der Interministeriellen Arbeitsgruppe Anpassungsstrategie der Bundesregierung. Dessau-Roßlau

United Nations Environmental Programme (2020) Emissions Gap Report 2020. Nairobi

Vanhala L, Hilson C (2013) Climate change litigation: symposium introduction. Law Policy 35(3): 141–149

Voigt C (2008) State responsibility for climate change damages. Nord J Int Law 77(1-2):1–22

Weber S, Beutel J, Da Forno R, Geiger A, Gruber S, Gsell T, Hasler A, Keller M, Lim R, Limpach P, Meyer M, Talzi I, Thiele L, Tschudin C, Vieli A, Vonder Mühll D, Yücel M (2019) A decade of detailed observations (2008-2018) in Steep Bedrock Permafrost at the Matterhorn Hörnligrat (Zermatt, CH). Earth Syst Sci Data 11(3):1203–1237

Wewerinke-Singh M, Salili DH (2020) Between negotiations and litigation: Vanuatu's perspective on loss and damage from climate change. Clim Policy 20(6):681–692

Wilby RL (2020) Climate change. In: Wang Y (ed) The handbook of natural resources, atmosphere and climate. CRC Press, Boca Raton, pp 283–292

Wirakusumah AD, Rachmat H (2017) Impact of the 1815 Tambora eruption to global climate change. IOP Conv Ser Earth Environ Sci 71:012007

World Bank Group (2023) GDP (constant 2015 US$) – United States. Available via World Bank. https://data.worldbank.org/indicator/NY.GDP.MKTP.KD?end=2021&locations=US&start=1960&view=chart. Accessed 24 Oct 2024

World Meteorological Organization (2024) Climate. https://wmo.int/topics/climate. Accessed 24 Oct 24

Zalasiewicz J, Williams M, Smith A, Barry T, Coe A, Bown PR, Brenchley P, Cantrill D, Gale A, Gibbard P, Gregory FJ, Hounslow MW, Kerr AC, Pearson P, Knox R, Powell J, Waters C, Marshall J, Oates M, Rawson P, Stone P (2008) Are we now living in the Anthropocene? GSA Today 18(2):4–8

Zekollari H, Fürst JJ, Huybrechts P (2014) Modelling the evolution of Vadret da Morteratsch, Switzerland, since the Little Ice Age and into the future. J Glaciol 60(224):1155–1168

Chapter 3
Causation in Climate Change Litigation

3.1 Causation as a Precondition of Law

Causation forms a fundamental pillar of law in any legal system. The rationale for its elementary position derives essentially from the function and purpose of causation itself (Sect. 3.1.1), which is also supported by a comprehensive and supra-legal understanding of causation as a two-tiered conception (Sect. 3.1.2). The need to establish causation in law can, thus, arise from a wide variety of different sources, each of which places different demands on the determination of causation per se (Sect. 3.1.3). The following sections provide a general and essential framework for the determination of causation in the law. They form the basis for the subsequent elaborations on causation in climate change litigation and provide the basis for the considerations applied in this regard.

3.1.1 The Purpose of Causation in Law

From time immemorial, causation has preoccupied scholars, scientists and thinkers in a multitude of different disciplines. And while the substance of the causal inquiry hereby stayed the same, namely the finding of a link between a cause and its effect, the way in which the finding of causation was approached varied significantly. Concurrently differs the purpose of the causal inquiry throughout different disciplines. Whereas the field of natural science is mainly concerned with proving the mere existence of causation, philosophers are more concerned with explaining the nature of causes and elaborating on the requirements for the finding of actual causal relata.[1] One of the first philosophers that deeply engaged with the question of

[1] Actual causation in this work strongly relies on modal logic and refers to causation *"as it is"* cf. Law (2022), term: actual. Often used synonymously, actual causation is used in this work

M. Krakau, *Causation in National and International Climate Change Litigation*,
https://doi.org/10.1007/978-3-031-74693-2_3

causation was *Aristotle*.[2] He distinguished between four different kinds of causes: '*causa formalis*', '*causa finalis*', '*causa materialis*' and '*causa efficiens*'.[3] The last of these different causes, the '*causa efficiens*', closely relates to our present understanding of causation. It was also his work, or rather the editing of his works, to which the concept of metaphysics can likely be attributed.[4] One of the most influential philosophical thinkers of our time and the founder of modern causal philosophy, however, was *Hume*, whose work shapes the philosophical understanding of causation and the discourse about it to this day.[5]

Some authors have been quick to argue for the obsolescence of causation in law. Causation is considered by some to be an archaic concept and to be a "*relic of bygone age, surviving, like the monarchy, only because it is erroneously supposed to do no harm.*"[6] It is, thus, perceived as being in fundamental decline.[7] Associated with the supposed decay of significance is the increasing reference to probabilities, especially in the natural sciences.[8] Nonetheless, this argument is flawed because it assumes that causation and probability are mutually exclusive. However, the following explanations show that probabilities and causation can be reconciled and that doing so can even justify an understanding of causation based on probabilities.[9] The reproach that causation in law is merely a means to an end is also myopic and, therefore, misguided given that its purpose in law goes far beyond this. Factual causal inquiries connect the highly socially and morally influenced legal world that is dependent on cultural, ethical and religious norms, with the actual, natural world. It constitutes a bridging function and forms the factual base for nearly every legal transaction and interconnection. Causation, accordingly, serves justice by comprising a means for establishing the truth while concurrently functioning as a channel to find the relevant legal behaviour.[10] As *Becker* aptly describes, "*causal principles are intrinsic to the very idea of law.*"[11] Causation in its factual form, therefore, is a means to grant legitimacy to not only legal reasoning but to legal statutes as well. In

differently from the term 'factual causation', since factual causation in this work is strongly oriented towards legal findings of fact and their doctrinal implementation, and therefore differs in part from actual causation. See further Garner (2009), p. 41.

[2]See especially Aristotle (n.d.b).

[3]Ibid. B 3, 192b-200b.

[4]Aristotle (n.d.a). See for a detailed elaboration in the history of the term 'metaphysics' van Inwagen et al. (2023). For a summary of the causation understanding of Aristotle see Falcon (2023).

[5]See Hume (1978). See for further elaborations on the History of Causation Kleinberg (2012), pp. 11–42.

[6]Russell (1912–1913), p. 1.

[7]Rigaux (2005), p. 83. Accepting that causation is a more philosophical grown construct but opposing its complete negligibility Wright (1971), p. 35.

[8]Rigaux (2005), p. 83.

[9]See in this regard especially Sect. 4.4.

[10]Chong (2020), p. 502. *Chong* hereby refers to Verheyen (2015), p. 163.

[11]Becker (2006), p. 288.

doing so, however, the law must harness scientific findings to prove the existence of factual causation.

Apart from the factual-centred purpose of causation, causation in the law, and especially in regard to the here so-called normative causation, functions as an instrument to establish moral responsibility, as well.[12] Under the influence of socio-legal concepts such as corrective and distributive justice, normative causation, and, even more so, causal responsibility builds the foundation of overall legal responsibility and blameworthiness. *Moore,* in this regard, argues that causal responsibility, which is understood by *Moore* as a combination of factual and normative considerations, is intertwined with moral responsibility, which emphasizes that a "'*cause' in law must mean what it means in morality*".[13] He, nevertheless, concludes that although causation in law should be understood in the same way as in morality, the right way to identify and understand a cause is in its "*natural relation*", meaning the natural relation between cause and effect.[14]

Causation, thus, functions as the naturalistic factual, as well as ontological base of other legal concepts such as moral and legal responsibility, culpability and blameworthiness. It is the foundation of every judicial decision and its anchor to the 'real' and 'natural' as well as societal world. As has been shown, the purpose of causation in the law is consequently multifarious. Its legal understanding, thereby, is strongly reliant on legal theory and philosophical considerations. In law, scientific and philosophical deliberations of causation are, therefore, brought together within legal structures.

3.1.2 The Two-Tiered Approach to Causation in Law

The foregoing has shown that causation is of great importance for the understanding of the law. How causation is ultimately approached and how causal chains are formed diverges slightly in different jurisdictions, and even more so in a national to international comparison. However, those differences mostly regard the broader outlines of the specific causal inquiry rather than its core substance and the heart of the construct. Nevertheless, while the establishment of causation is done more stringently in national terms and, disregarding jurisdiction-immanent peculiarities, more uniformly, regional and international courts do not seem to follow a consistent line even within their own jurisprudence.[15] This renders both the analysis and the evaluation of an appropriate understanding of causation for climate issues thoroughly difficult, which is why it is even more so of importance to refer to the core

---

[12] See in this regard Moore (2009). Also Orakhelashvili (2022), p. 5. See for a detailed analysis on the substance of normative causation Chap. 5.

[13] Moore (2009), p. 4.

[14] Ibid. 5.

[15] See Sect. 3.2.

content and the foundation of causation rather than getting lost in the minutiae. Ultimately, it is exactly this core structure and this foundation which allows for generally valid perceptions of the establishment of causation in the law.

Causation in law can, in principle, be approached from both a factual-objective and normative-subjective perspective. Yet contrary to some beliefs, causation in the law is two-fold, meaning it consists of both factual and normative causal components.[16] Factual or scientific causation hereby forms the basis of overall causal considerations. Factual causation is concerned with finding the actual, natural cause of an event in building upon the mere cause-effect relationship between the action or omission and the outcome in the given situation. It is, thus, closely connected with the scientific understanding of causation and the only 'true' causal component of the causation inquiry in the law. Although factuality and the best possible representation of actual causation is the ultimate aim of factual causation in law, discussions about the 'right' way and the 'right' legal doctrine to prescribe and permute factual causation still prevail.[17] The choice of the correct approach to factual causation is in fact a decision in which normative and subjective-practical considerations are taken into account. However, such a normative choice does not per se contradict the factuality of the chosen doctrine itself.[18]

Normative causation, on the other hand, introduces socio-legal considerations into the general assessment of a legally relevant cause-effect relationship.[19] It is this second step that ultimately ascribes legal responsibility to the party in question. The foundation, therefore, however, is the existence of causation in its factual terms.[20] The requirement of a normative evaluation of factual causation sets the causal inquiry in law apart from other disciplines. Especially technical fields do not know or even apply such considerations. The purpose for the application of normative notions to factual causation is to render the general causal inquiry applicable for its usage in the law. A purely factual assessment carries the danger of producing causal results that are sociologically and morally contrary to the principles of fairness and justice and contradict the bases and foundation of the law per se. This is even more so the case under the application of traditional legal approaches and doctrines of

[16] A prime example of the omission of factual considerations in assessing causation in law is the 'common sense' test of causation proposed by *Hart* and *Honoré* (Hart and Honoré 1985), which is occasionally used in Australian courts. However, it has been heavily criticized in legal and philosophical scholarship and has not received much attention outside the Australian jurisdiction. See for climate cases referring to the 'common-sense' test Sect. 3.4.3.3.1.2.2. Against such an approach Stapleton (2010), pp. 469–471; Orakhelashvili (2022), p. 10. In favour of applying a common sense test Becker (2006), pp. 289–306. Arguing for a partial departure from factual approaches in the context of so-called 'chancy causation' Lahav (2022).

[17] See for a definition of actual causation again Law (2022), term: actual.

[18] Also raising the concern that deciding which factual causes are legally relevant involves inherent normative judgements, but ultimately arguing that such decision-making does not affect the factuality of the respective approach Fumerton and Kress (2001), p. 86.

[19] See for a detailed analysis of normative causation in climate change litigation Chap. 5.

[20] This is the reason why legal causation does not replace the factual inquiry as described in Orakhelashvili (2022), p. 9, but amends it.

factual causation, such as the theory of counterfactuality.[21] Consequently, the social usability of factual causation is evaluated under normative terms. In many cases, this leads to a limitation of the factual inquiry, negating causation in law, although factual and scientific causation exists and causation is present in the 'actual' world. That the law, in general, on an international, regional as well as on a domestic level, knows of and applies a two-tiered understanding of causation in the law is without question.[22] Such an approach is also supported in legal theory and more general legal scholarship.[23]

It is common ground that causation in law consists of two components. The national and international understanding of the concept coincides here.[24] However, the way in which both components are intertwined varies significantly. As will be shown in the following sections, domestic legal systems, in particular, have moved towards a clear separation and disclosure of factual and normative causation. Most of the domestic legal systems hereby use a two-step approach. The first step consists of the elaboration of factual causation under the usage of mainly counterfactual theories such as the conditio-sine-qua-non formula and the but-for test.[25] In a second step, normative considerations are applied, and the results are adapted in accordance with socio-legal understandings.[26] Yet, international and regional courts, in particular, tend to combine both concepts and, therefore, blur the lines between mere factual causation and legally adaptive results.[27]

From a result-oriented perspective, whether both notions are merged or strictly separated might be considered irrelevant. Both, a strict differentiation, as well as the merged appliance should ultimately result in the same outcoming. However, the clarity, structure and comprehensibility of the result-finding process and the outcome itself that derives from the causal inquiry clearly speak for the strict distinction between both concepts. Scientific analysis and inter-jurisdictional comparability also benefit from a two-step approach. Furthermore, a clear separation of factual and normative components leads to considerably more legal certainty for the parties in a court case. It guarantees that the parties of the proceeding can assess and partly foresee the outcome of the causal inquiry as an essential element of the legal proceeding, which at the same time reduces the risk of litigation in general. Without a clear separation of both concepts, it is moreover unclear which requirements are placed upon both components of causation in law. It, therefore, depends largely on

---

[21] See in this regard Sect. 4.2.

[22] See in this regard Sect. 3.2.

[23] See in this regard Plakokefalos (2015), p. 475; Moore (2024); Fumerton and Kress (2001), pp. 84–87.

[24] See again Sect. 3.2.

[25] See for the use of both concepts in domestic law Sect. 3.2.1. For a detailed elaboration of both concepts in climate change litigation see Sect. 4.2.

[26] For a detailed elaboration of normative causation in climate change litigation see Chap. 5.

[27] See for a detailed analysis of the approaches used by regional and international courts Sects. 3.2.2 and 3.2.3.

the judges and the courts how causation in the specific case is to be assessed and modifies the inquiry from a partially factual to a highly evaluative and fluctuating doctrine that is at risk of being interpreted differently not only throughout different jurisdictions but even more so in the same jurisdictional realm. Without a clear distinction, the court's requirements for the causal inquiry resemble a legal lottery rather than a legally arguable and grounded element.[28] Such inconsistency also has an impact on other aspects of judicial decision-making. Especially in tort law, liability cases in light of specific cost allocation depend to a large extent on the establishment and the classification of causation.[29] Mono-causation is rare, and the law is mainly characterized by multi-causal events and different numeric amounts of causal contributions. With the existence of multiple causers, liability and cost allocation are often referenced accordingly.

In favour of a clear distinction between the factual causal inquiry and the following normative considerations also speaks the state practice in numerous domestic jurisdictions. Nowadays, most common law, as well as civil law countries, follow a separate two-step causal approach.[30] However, in some jurisdictions, such an approach has only been common for a limited amount of time. Particularly the causal understanding in the tort law of the United States has evolved over time. As the First and Second Restatements of Tort of the American Law Institute (ALI) have shown, the predominant causal understanding was characterized by the substantial factor test.[31] This, nonetheless, intertwines factual causation with normative notions leading to major uncertainty in regard to its scope and application in general. The legal uncertainty entailed in the doctrine then led to its abandonment in the Third Restatement of Tort, although the terminology and the test itself can still be found occasionally in recent court decisions.[32] With distancing itself from the substantial factor test, the American Law Institute followed the overall trend of a clear separation between factual causation and normative considerations, concurrent with other domestic jurisdictions.

---

[28] On the dangers of mixing factual and normative elements, in particular the criticism of the 'substantial factor' test and the confusion surrounding its application, see in citing the decision of the Court of Appeals of Texas, Fith District, Dallas, 26 August 2010 – 05-08-01390-CV, *Georgia-Pacific Corp. v. Bostic*, 596, Sebok (2017), pp. 3–4. This also applies for the 'common-sense' test.

[29] Liability is not to be confused with causation, rather it asks whether the person is actually responsible for the damage or the outcome of an action, with causation often being a prerequisite for liability as such. Following Black's Law Dictionary, liability is perceived as *"(t)he quality or state of being legally obligated or accountable"* Garner (2009), p. 997. The scope of liability is ultimately concerned with the extent of the obligation to compensate. Total liability in law is an overarching concept that also includes causal considerations, but with many more prerequisites for its assessment. Causation as such does not involve any prediction of the existence of liability.

[30] See e.g. Sect. 3.2.1.

[31] See American Law Institute (1934, 1965).

[32] See in this regard the American Law Institute (1934, 1965). Significant is, in particular, the reform done by the ALI in regard to the Third Restatement (see American Law Institute 2010) in dividing between factual causation and the scope of liability rather than using the terms normative causation or substantial factor. See for a broader discussion Sebok (2017).

The broad majority of legal scholarship as well can be considered in favour of a distinction between both concepts, although the scope of the approaches applied differs to a large extent.[33] In contrast to domestic jurisdictions, regional and international courts greatly lack consistency when it comes to the distinction between actual cause and legal adaptation.[34] Courts, in this regard, often do not disclose expressively which account is used or whether they distinguish between both concepts at all. Nevertheless, the previous explanations have shown that in light of practical as well as metaphysical considerations, the usage of a clearly separated, two-step approach to causation in the law is favourable.

3.1.3 Sources of Causal Inquiries

Despite its profound purpose and its fundamental function in law, not every legal elaboration presupposes an existing and stringent chain of causation. Rather, an explicit or implicit source is required for the establishment and determination of causation, which can operate at both the substantive as well as the procedural level. These sources of causal inquiry form the cornerstone of the reason why causation enters the legal assessment at all, and may differ, especially in terms of their degree of salience, but also within their assessment, especially at the normative level.[35] In an attempt to group and further classify the ways in which causation appears in law, four main sources of causal inquiry can be distinguished. These categories not only form the basis for the subsequent analysis of different approaches to causation in climate change litigation, but also serve to provide a general understanding of causation and its use in law.

The first and thus probably the most obvious source of causal inquiry in law arises from the specific national and international norms itself. The requirement of causation is hereby specifically enshrined in the wording and the terminology of the norm, making the existence of causation a precondition for the claim to be substantiated.[36]

---

[33] See in this regard Moore (2009), p. 83; Wright and Puppe (2016), p. 464; West (2013), p. 3. Favouring a two tiered approach even in international law Bederman (1990), p. 349. Advocating that the differentiation be kept to a minimum, while not denying the existence of the two components, Orakhelashvili (2022), pp. 9–10. Opposing a clear separation between factual and normative causation, Hoffmann (2011), p. 9; Steward (2012), p. 19.

[34] In favour of a two-step approach in international law, Bederman (1990), p. 349. See further Sects. 3.2.2 and 3.2.3.

[35] See for the elaboration of causation in climate change litigation on a normative level Chap. 5.

[36] See in this regard concerning national law especially tort law provisions Art. 45 Bulgarian Obligations and Contracts Act in its English translation (*"Every person must redress the damage he has guiltily caused to another person. In all cases of tort guilt is presumed until proven otherwise"*), §1 Danish Liability and Damages Act (*"Any person who is liable for injury to another person must pay compensation for lost earnings, medical and rehabilitation expenses and any other loss caused by the injury as well as remuneration for pain and suffering"*), Section 3 Art. 1 lit. a UK Compensation Act (*"(1) This section applies where – lit. a. a person ('the responsible person') has*

Causal inquiries of this group mainly stem from liability- and damage-related provisions and are mostly grounded in the law of torts.

However, causation requirements can not only be imposed in a direct manner, i.e. by expressively requiring a cause-effect relationship in the wording. Rather, causal inquiries can also be indirectly inherent in the respective provision without naming the requirement expressively.[37] Words such as 'through', 'due to' or 'because of' can hereby function as indicators for the requirement of causal relata. Yet, even without such indicating words, causation can be inherent in the norm itself. Such preconditions result from logical considerations and can further be inferred from relevant case law or overall legal views, which are often summarized in legal commentaries to the respective provision. These cases belong to the second group of sources of causal inquiries.

The third group entails causation as a requirement of formal and procedural law. In this category, the establishment of a causal link is required for the accessibility of the claim or the overall jurisdiction of the court. Causation can further form part of a precondition for the standing of the plaintiff or constitute a requirement for the (extraterritorial) jurisdiction of the court or the application of a specific treaty.[38]

The last, and thus probably the most difficult category of causation to determine, are considerations which are inherent in legal decision-making. In this context, judges subjectively use causation as an evaluative criterion which ultimately contributes to the decision but does not constitute a prerequisite for the respective claim or offence. Rather, causation is addressed as one of several different criteria in light of the margin of appreciation of the court. In doing so, it contributes to the normative assessment, even though the argument, i.e. the existence of a causal link, may be based on a purely factual approach.

negligently or in breach of statutory duty caused or permitted another person ('the victim') to be exposed to asbestos"). In international law especially Art. 139 II UNCLOS, stating that "*(...) damage caused by the failure of a State Party or international organization to carry out its responsibilites (...) shall entail liability. (...)*" and Art. 31 I DARS stating that *"(t)he responsible State is under an obligation to make full reparation for the injury caused by the internationally wrongful act."*.

[37] See exemplary § 823 BGB. Moore (2009), p. 5. *Moore* also points to that factum in reference to criminal law provisions.

[38] Under Art. III United States Constitution, plaintiffs have to demonstrate an injury-in-fact, causation and redressability. Standing was e.g. in question in the case, United States Court of Appeals for the Ninth Circuit, 17 January 2020 – 6:15-cv-01517-AA, *Juliana v. United States.* It is further at debate in the pending case before the ECtHR, European Court of Human Right, pending – 53600/20, *KlimaSeniorinnen v. Switzerland.* Extraterritoriality is especially in question in regard to the application of regional human rights frameworks, inter alia the Inter-American Charta of Human Rights, see e.g. Inter-American Court of Human Rights, 15 November 2017 – OC-23/17, *A Request for an Advisory Opinion from the Inter-American Court of Human Rights Concerning the Interpretation of Article 1(1), 4(1) and 5(1) of the American Convention on Human Rights.*

3.2 Causation in Legal Practice

Providing a comprehensive analysis of causal approaches across different jurisdictions is an arduous task. Therefore, instead of focusing on a particular region, this section endeavours to offer a broad comprehension of how various jurisdictions, on a national (Sect. 3.2.1) as well as on a regional and international level (Sects. 3.2.2 and 3.2.3), typically handle the establishment of causation.

3.2.1 Causation in Domestic Law

The terminology under which the concepts of causation are applied in different jurisdictions varies greatly.[39] Nevertheless, courts in both civil and common law countries generally adopt a bifurcated approach, consisting of factual causation and its normative adaptation.[40] The predominant understanding of factual causation, especially within tort and criminal law, is shaped by a counterfactual approach, with the but-for test applied in common law countries and the condition-sine-qua-non formula mainly preferred in civil law jurisdictions.[41] In their substance, however, both tests coincide. The same is true for the inherent logical and natural inconsistencies that exist in the current tests, which is why different jurisdictions have come up with unique exceptions to address the posed conceptual incongruities.[42]

In the process of determining normative causation, a number of factors are taken into account. These considerations include the foreseeability of the harm, as well as the question of whether the action is covered by the purpose and protective scope of the norm.[43] Further factors refer to the materiality of the contribution, the proximity between the action taken and the outcome, and the handling of intervening causes.[44] As normative causation depends on a wide range of ethical, moral and social understandings, different jurisdictions apply normative considerations in different ways. This is particularly the case where cultural and religious traditions are concerned. Factual causation, on the other hand, is a constant conjuncture

---

[39] See especially concerning the divergence in light of normative causation Sect. 5.1.

[40] See e.g. Chapter 3 of the Principles of European Tort Law, dividing into conditio-sine-qua-non qualifications (Section 1) and the scope of liability (Section 2), and the American Law Institute (2010) in regard to the case law of the United States. For further elaboration on the necessity of applying a two-step approach see Sect. 3.1.2.

[41] For a detailed elaboration on factual causation see Sect. 4.2.

[42] See for some of the exceptions Sects. 4.2.3, 4.5.1 and 4.5.2.

[43] For a detailed elaboration on normative causation see Chap. 5. See on foreseeability Sect. 5.3, and on the protective scope of the norm Sect. 5.8.

[44] See in regard to materiality Sect. 5.4, in regard to the theory of proximate cause Sect. 5.7 and in regard to intervening causes Sect. 5.5.

throughout jurisdictions and allows, based on its interconnectedness with scientific epistemology, for a more consistent approach to its doctrinal and conceptual frame. Although highly desirable, national courts have not always been clear in distinguishing between factual and normative understandings of causation. In some cases, normative criteria have even been presented as alternatives to factual approaches to causation in the light of their failure.[45] However, this has not gained acceptance in the overall legal sphere.[46]

Causation in the law is often mistakenly associated with tort law claims alone. This is based on the fact that the requirement of causation is often either directly or indirectly anchored in the corresponding liability-based statutes and in tort law in general. They, thus, qualify as cases of the first and second groups of causal inquiries, which are commonly the most dominant ones.[47] Nonetheless, causation is also of great relevance in other areas of law. In regard to fundamental, constitutional and human rights, the infringement in question has to be causally linked to the specific conduct of the actor. In criminal law, causation is required to link the action or omission to the offence and correspondingly to the right infringement, as well. In administrative law, again, it is often relevant to establish a stringent causal chain between an administrative decision and its effects. Causation, therefore, becomes relevant in every area of law, often, however, in a more indirect manner than it is the case under liability-based accounts.[48]

The substantiation of a claim often requires the establishment of two independent chains of causation, particularly in relation to a claim for compensation and cost allocation. The differentiation becomes especially apparent in German tort law, in which it is distinguished between a causal link between someone's action or omission and the right infringement, as well as a causal link between the right infringement and the actual damage.[49] In other jurisdictions, this distinction, in the end, does not become as obvious as in German tort law as it is well acknowledged to fuse both causal chains into one. The distinction persists in a separation of the causal chain, which, although it has its own raison d'être, ultimately has no significant implications for the assessment of factual causation in this book.

[45] E.g. in the British Wagon Mound case, in which the Court considered foreseeability as an alternative to traditional, factual approaches Privy Council, 25 May 1966 – [1966] UKPC 10, [1967] AC 617; [1967] 2 All ER 709, *Overseas Tankship (UK) Ltd v The Miller Steamship Co (Wagon Mound No. 2)*.

[46] E.g. Orakhelashvili (2022), p. 42.

[47] See in this regard Sect. 3.1.3.

[48] Some exceptions, where a causal requirement is not necessary to substantiate the claim, can be found, for example, in the light of positive human and fundamental rights obligations. See in this regard more specifically Sect. 3.2.3.1 and Sect. 3.3.2.4.

[49] In German law this is referred to as 'haftungsbegründende Kausalität' and 'haftungsausfüllende Kausalität'.

3.2.2 *Causation in Regional and International Law*

While national courts and tribunals have largely adopted a two-tiered understanding of causation, including a largely uniform approach to factual causation, regional and international courts are more ambiguous and have yet to coalesce around a common understanding of causation. This is all the more the case as international courts and tribunals, in particular, are neither consistent in their terminology nor in their use of causation doctrines. Causation analysis at the regional and international levels is also a largely under-researched area of law, which further complicates the assessment.[50] Nevertheless, by drawing on some examples from regional and international courts, with a particular focus on regional human rights frameworks, this section attempts to give an idea of how courts at the regional and international level deal with causation in general. At the same time, the analysis is not intended to be exhaustive, but merely to provide an indication of how causation is dealt with at the broader jurisdictional level.

3.2.2.1 International Law and the International Court of Justice

Within the realm of international law, causation is particularly relevant either as a direct or indirect legal requirement or as an evaluative factor in decision-making.[51] Typically, the legal inquiry involves exploring two causal links. The first link connects the act or omission that is being challenged to the violation of the norm at hand. The second link further connects the violation of the norm to the resulting damage.[52] While the first causal relatum is characterised by dogmatic inconsistency within the international jurisprudence, decisions are more coherent with regard to the causal link between the respective violation and the damage and usually require "*a sufficiently direct and certain causal nexus between the wrongful act […] and the injury suffered by the Applicant […].*"[53]

A particular characteristic of international law is the existence of general principles. Those principles are set out in Art. 38 I c) of the ICJ Statute, although those listed do not claim to be exhaustive. While the extent, scope and effect are still highly

---

[50] Improvements in this regard have been made by two just recent publications. See Gascoigne (2023) and Orakhelashvili (2022).

[51] See here esp. Art. 31, 34, 36 DARS and Art. 139 UNCLOS. Also Plakokefalos (2015); Chong (2020), p. 502. *Chong* introduces a third way by referring to causation in due diligence obligations. This, however, goes hand in hand with group two of presumed causation. See for the division of different sources of causation in the law Sect. 3.1.3.

[52] This separation is closely connected to the causation approach used in German tort law, see in this regard Sect. 3.2.1.

[53] International Court of Justice, 26 February 2007 – I.C.J. Reports 2007, p. 43, *Bosnia and Herzegovina v. Serbia and Montenegro*, para 462. Reiterated in International Court of Justice, 9 February 2022 – n/a, *Armed Activities on the territory of the Congo (Democratic Republic of the Congo v. Uganda)*, para 93.

controversial, causation is well-recognised as a general principle of international law.[54] As *Becker* aptly points out, "*causal principles are intrinsic to the very idea of law*".[55] However, there are still some authors who reject the recognition of causation as a general principle of international law, referring to the large amount of various domestic approaches used in different jurisdictions.[56] Conversely, this argument does not convince, especially since the recognition of causation as a general principle does not presuppose a uniform definition on a national level. Rather, Art. 38 I lit. c) ICJ Statute recognises the importance of the principle notwithstanding its specific conceptualization. And although causation as a principle of international law does not specify any particular way or approach of establishing causation, a basic structure, nevertheless, can be derived consisting of factual-objective and normative-subjective components. This basic component ultimately transpires from the basic two-fold structure that is widely acknowledged by national legal systems.[57] Yet, the extent to which the factual and normative relata are to be determined and the concept that has to be used for the respective assessment is not enshrined as a general principle of international law according to Art. 38 I lit. c) ICJ Statute, but takes place on a case-by-case basis and is at the discretion of the respective court.

The International Court of Justice (ICJ), unsurprisingly, does not follow a specific causation approach either but applies causation requirements on a per-case basis as well. Nevertheless, it can be observed that the Court is not averse to the idea of counterfactual causation but rather employs it in specific situations.[58] One of the cases in which the Court dealt most extensively with causation and ultimately considered causation on the basis of a counterfactual substantiation is the *Bosnian Genocide* case. In this case, the Court stated that:

> (t)he question is whether there is a sufficiently direct and certain causal nexus [...]. [...] (S)uch a nexus could be considered established only if the Court were able to conclude from the case as a whole and with a sufficient degree of certainty that the genocide at Srebrenica would in fact have been averted if the Respondent had acted in compliance with its legal obligation.[59]

---

[54] Kotuby and Sobota (2017), p. 143; Plakokefalos (2015), p. 474; Becker (2006), p. 288.

[55] Becker (2006), p. 288.

[56] See e.g. Orakhelashvili (2022), p. 72.

[57] Kotuby and Sobota (2017), pp. 145–146.

[58] International Court of Justice, 2 February 2018 – I.C.J. Reports 2018, p. 15, *Certain Activities Carried Out by Nicaragua in the Border Area (Costa Rica v. Nicaragua)*, Compensation, 26, paras 32–34. In this regard as well Plakokefalos (2015), p. 477. Finding implicit factual causation also in the Corfu Channel Case (International Court of Justice, 25 March 1948; 9 April 1949; 15 December 1949 – I. C. J. Reports 1948 p. 15; 1949 p. 4, 244, *Corfu Channel Case (United Kingdom v. People's Republic of Albania)*.) See Orakhelashvili (2022), p. 135. An counterfactual assessment was also proposed by the applicants in the case International Court of Justice, 9 February 2022 – n/a, *Armed Activities on the territory of the Congo (Democratic Republic of the Congo v. Uganda)*, para 86.

[59] International Court of Justice, 26 February 2007 – I.C.J. Reports 2007, p. 43, *Bosnia and Herzegovina v. Serbia and Montenegro*, para 462.

In considering whether the omission was a causal factor in the genocide in Srebrenica, the Court conducted a hypothetical assessment of whether the outcome would have been avoided had the respondent complied with its duty. The ICJ thus indirectly applied the but-for test.[60] However, it is erroneous to draw conclusions about a particular trend in causal dogmatics from the *Bosnian Genocide* case, as the Court has approached causation in a very different way in other cases.[61] The ICJ even indirectly rejected a counterfactual approach in the case of *Democratic Republic of the Congo v. Uganda* when it affirmed causation despite the existence of concurrent causes and multiple actors. The fact that the Court deliberately does not apply a uniform causation approach is also shown by the statements of Uganda that "*the causal nexus must be assessed differently depending on the internationally wrongful act at issue*".[62] This statement was later confirmed by the the ICJ in the case at hand.[63] Furthermore, such an approach does not preclude the ICJ from resorting to normative causal doctrines without first having factually examined the causal approach. In addition to the resulting confusion between factual and normative causation, such an unconceptualised approach also creates considerable legal uncertainty for the parties.[64] This is due, in particular, to the fact that the ICJ nevertheless makes strong references to normative concepts and criteria. Concurrent with other courts and legal bodies, the ICJ considered notions such as the remoteness of the outcome or damage, its foreseeability or its proximity in general.[65]

3.2.2.2 Causation and State Responsibility

Central to the question of how to deal with causation in international law is the law of state responsibility, largely based on the International Law Commission's Draft Articles on the International Responsibility of States (ILC DARS). It is also precisely this area of law in which causation is closely linked to the socio-normative concept of attribution, even more so than in light of other fields of international law.[66]

---

[60] See for a detailed elaboration on the but-for test Sect. 4.2.

[61] Stating that international law does not require counterfactual causation, Nedeski and Nollkaemper (2022). Referencing Stoyanova (2018) and Lanovoy (2022).

[62] International Court of Justice, 9 February 2022 – n/a, *Armed Activities on the territory of the Congo (Democratic Republic of the Congo v. Uganda)*, para 88.

[63] See ibid. 93.

[64] See for further elaborations on the dangers of a mixture of factual and normative causation Sect. 3.1.2.

[65] E.g. in International Court of Justice, 25 March 1948; 9 April 1949; 15 December 1949 – I. C. J. Reports 1948 p. 15; 1949 p. 4, 244, *Corfu Channel Case (United Kingdom v. People's Republic of Albania)*.

[66] This became especially relevant in inter alia International Court of Justice, 2 February 2018 – I.C.J. Reports 2018, p. 15, *Certain Activities Carried Out by Nicaragua in the Border Area (Costa Rica v. Nicaragua)*, International Court of Justice, 24 May 1980 – I.C.J. Reports 1980, p. 3, *United States Diplomatic and Consular Staff in Tehran (United States of America v. Iran)*.

Decisive for the strong interrelation is the terminology of Art. 2 DARS, which requires the attribution of the act or omission to the respective state as an element of the internationally wrongful act. And while the term 'attribution' in general is a highly vague concept, in contrast to other areas of international law (see, e.g. Art. 9 Rome Statute), the wording and the reference to attribution do not per se imply the necessity of a causal relationship; while, at the same time not precluding it.[67] The ILC elaborated hereby concerning Art. 2 DARS that "*[…] the attribution of conduct to the State is necessarily a normative operation. What is crucial is that a given event is sufficiently connected to conduct (whether an act or omission) which is attributable to the State under one or other of the rules set out in chapter II.*"[68] Still, the ILC stays silent in regard to the requirements posed by its terminology of a 'sufficient connection'.[69] It becomes apparent, however, that the Commission nevertheless presupposes some form of factual connection, whether it is causation as such or a weaker standard of connection, such as contribution or involvement.[70]

In its emphasis on the 'normative operation' of attribution, on the other hand, the ILC runs concurrent especially to the private law sector of national legal systems in which attribution is often treated independently and without any regard to factual causal relationships. This is again emphasized by the ILC stating that "*(t)he attribution of conduct to the State as a subject of international law is based on criteria determined by international law and not on the mere recognition of a link of factual causation.*"[71] It could be assumed at first that the ILC hereby strongly diverges from attribution as it is understood and used in overall natural science. In its latest report, the IPCC defines attribution as "*the process of evaluating the relative contributions of multiple causal factors to a change or event with an assessment of confidence.*"[72] With respect to the definition of the IPCC, attribution is regarded as an additional factor to be applied, presupposed that the factual assessment of causation is yet concluded. Attribution in natural sciences, at least following the perception of the IPCC, is not considered to be a factual causal conception but more so an evaluative and, thus, a normative-subjective component in ascribing overall relations. It, consequently, strongly coincides with attribution as it is used and perceived by the ILC, which also does not consider it to be a comprehensive indication of overall

[67] 'Attribution' in general does not presuppose the existence of a causation. It is rather used to describe a relation in a more vague way, which ultimately can result in causation but does not have to do so. The term attribution, thus, does not indicate or provide any information on the existence of a causal relationship per se. See also for a description of the term attribution in the normative context Sect. 5.1. See further Orakhelashvili (2022), p. 55.

[68] International Law Commission (2001), Art. 2 p. 35 para 6.

[69] Orakhelashvili hereby argues that "*[…] causation is the only reliable guide that any decision-maker could possibly use to demonstrate that 'sufficient connection'.*" Orakhelashvili (2022), p. 59.

[70] The term 'contribution' does not imply a causal statement per se. Contribution also has nothing to do with a particular relationship between two events, but merely states that someone has contributed to a particular outcome.

[71] International Law Commission (2001), pp. 38–39.

[72] IPCC (2021b), p. 2219.

causation but more so as a conception to assign responsibility and blameworthiness in light of a subjective-normative account. Yet, scientific and legal approaches diverge in their manner of finding and applying attribution, with the law commonly making use of criteria such as the foreseeability of the outcome, the proximity of the link or the materiality and substantiality of the action in question.[73] Attribution in the legal context and also in its perception which is accounted for by the ILC, hence, implies an actual causal component, however, not as factual but more so as a normative element. Attribution thereby functions as a limiting factor for too far-reaching factual causation and, at the same time, determines the question of responsibility in light of an existing factual connection.[74]

Apart from the strong reliance on attribution, which is perceived by Art. 2 DARS, and the concurrent account of a normative understanding of causation, a factual causal link in the law of state responsibility may, nevertheless, also be required res materiae. This is the case in the light of Chapter IV DARS for any act of support by another state. In order to avoid the unlimited responsibility of states concerning Art. 16 et seq. DARS, the ILC requires a more comprehensive, factual and, therefore, stronger account of the interrelation between the state's aid and the international wrongful conduct.[75] The ILC, in that regard, stated that *"(t)hus, the articles in this chapter require that the former State should be aware of the circumstances of the internationally wrongful act in question, and establish a specific causal link between that act and the conduct of the assisting, directing or coercing State."*[76] This enhanced understanding of causation does not imply a commitment by the ILC to a particular doctrine of causation. By referring to a 'specific causal link', it, nevertheless, emphasizes the requirement of a factual causal relatum rather than applying a looser approach as it is done by Art. 2 DARS. The ILC further goes on to elaborate:

> In accordance with article 16, the assisting State is responsible for its own act in deliberately assisting another State to breach an international obligation by which they are both bound. It is not responsible, as such, for the act of the assisted State. In some cases this may be a distinction without a difference: where the assistance is a necessary element in the wrongful act in absence of which it could not have occurred, the injury suffered can be concurrently attributed to the assisting and the acting State. In other cases, however, the difference may be very material: the assistance may have been only an incidental factor in the commission of the primary act, and may have contributed only to a minor degree, if at all, to the injury suffered.[77]

Although the ILC's statement recognises, and in part even refers to, a counterfactual perception of causation in relation to Art. 16 DARS, it explicitly rejects its exclusive understanding and again refers only to a lowered standard of factual causation.[78]

[73] See in regard to the criteria applied by the law in light of normative causation Chap. 5.

[74] See in regard to attribution as a limiting factor in international law Becker (2006), pp. 306–328.

[75] See for a detailed elaboration on causation in Art. 16 DARS, Aust (2011), pp. 210–219.

[76] International Law Commission (2001), p. 65 para 8.

[77] Ibid. 67 para 10. Criticizing the ILC for such inconsistency and understanding of causation, Orakhelashvili (2022), p. 88.

[78] See also Aust (2011), pp. 212–213.

However, the commentary goes on to emphasise that counterfactual causation may be required as a general precondition for the link between the actual act and the infringement in question, as a contributory act may be perceived as an actual act in the light of a counterfactual relation.[79]

The most explicit reference to causation, nonetheless, can be found in Art. 31 DARS, which concerns the payment of reparations for the damage caused by the internationally wrongful act. Art. 31 (1) DARS concludes that "*(t)he responsible State is under an obligation to make full reparation for the injury caused by the internationally wrongful act.*"[80] The second paragraph then, in its definition of 'injury', elaborates that "*(i)njury includes any damage, whether material or moral, caused by the internationally wrongful act of a State*."[81] In the light of Art. 31 (II) DARS, the ILC accepts and clearly emphasises a bifurcated and two-step approach to the nexus between the wrongful act and the inquiry in question.[82] Recognising that there are a number of different ways in which a cause may, in fact, be described, the ILC ultimately establishes as a core element of the causal assessment in Art. 31 (II) DARS the existence of a necessary but not sufficient condition.[83] Although the ILC hereby makes use of causal language that is also often utilized in regard to traditional counterfactual approaches to causation, the statement, nevertheless, does not tie Art. 31 DARS to a specific counterfactual inquiry. It merely emphasizes the requirement of a factual causal chain. In a second step, however, the ILC then refers to normative elements, among those are the 'directness', 'foreseeability', 'remoteness' or 'proximity', all of which are "*associated with the exclusion of injury*".[84] Considering these elements as notions of restriction is consistent with the common understanding of normative causation. Further consistency is provided by noting that different international obligations may require different normative assessments, which is why the ILC refrains from defining a specific causal doctrine.[85]

Similar to the description of 'attribution' in Art. 2 DARS, the term 'contribution' in Art. 39 DARS leaves a great deal of uncertainty as to the nature of the relationship and the requirements necessary for its fulfilment. Art. 39 DARS limits the amount of reparation that the injured state can receive in accordance with its own contribution to the overall damage. Whether 'contribution' should be read and interpreted as a doctrine of causation or whether it should be deprived of any causal relation is still

[79] International Law Commission (2001), p. 67.

[80] Art. 31 (I) DARS.

[81] Art. 31 (II) DARS.

[82] International Law Commission (2001), Art. 31, 92–93 para 10. See in that regard also Plakokefalos (2015), p. 490. *Plakokefalos* is proposing a causation test based on regularity followed by a policy-driven inquiry. Against such a specific understanding Orakhelashvili (2022), p. 110.

[83] See again International Law Commission (2001), Art. 31, 92–93 para 19.

[84] Ibid. Art. 31, 92–93 para 10. Most likely opposing the foreseeability criterion as drafted by the ILC, Orakhelashvili (2022), p. 69. See for a detailed elaboration on normative causation Chap. 5.

[85] International Law Commission (2001), Art. 31, 93 para 10.

largely disputed. While some authors even see contribution as part of factual causation, others reject this interpretation with reference to its normative content.[86] The ILC commentary also fails to provide a viable approach as it does not specify the concrete requirements to be met by the contribution in Art. 39 DARS.

Ultimately, it can be concluded that although causation plays a fundamental role in the law of state responsibility, the ILC has failed to clarify the requirements for such causal links. Furthermore, it can be emphasised that the law of state responsibility consists of a variety of different accounts for assigning responsibility and linking the act in question to the result. While it has been shown that strict approaches to causation in the light of counterfactual tests persist in international law, reduced perceptions of causation are also an important part of the legal inquiry. The law is also significantly shaped by evaluative and normative assessments, which in turn strongly influence the nature of causal relations in the law of state responsibility.

3.2.2.3 International Criminal Law, the International Criminal Court and International Criminal Tribunals

In parallel with national criminal law, causation as an element underlying the offence and a factor justifying the relevant conviction also plays an important role at the international level. The assessment of the factual truth and the further interrelation with natural and actual causation acquire relevance in the area of criminal law, even more so than in other areas of law.[87] Causation is, therefore, also present in the international criminal legal realm and specifically in the Rome Statute, in which it finds its way into the assessment explicitly based on the decision of the Assembly of States Parties according to Art. 9 Rome Statute as a constitutive element of the crime. However, causation in international criminal law does, in contrast to national legal systems, not constitute a separate element of the offence; rather, causation must be examined in light of the referenced outcome.[88] In coherence with other international courts, the International Criminal Court (ICC) and international criminal tribunals, among those especially the United Nationas International Criminal Tribunal for the former Yugoslavia (ICTY) and the International Criminal Tribunal for Rwanda (ICTR), do not show any stringency in their requirements posed on the establishment of causal links, either. However, the underlying usage of a two-stage causal approach is recognised both directly and, for the most part, implicitly.[89] In contrast to other international courts, including the ICJ in particular, the ICC, nevertheless, shows an

---

[86] In favour of reading causation into Art. 39 DARS and the term 'contribution', Stern (2010), p. 570. Similar also Orakhelashvili (2022), pp. 104–105. Against the interpretation as doctrine of at least concurrent causation, Crawford (2013), p. 500.

[87] See for the purpose of causation Sect. 4.1.1.

[88] Werle and Jeßberger (2016), p. 221 para 482, fn 54.

[89] Clark (2022), pp. 746–747, para 23.

increasing reference to causation tests based on a strong necessity criterion and, thus, on a naturalistic understanding of causation.[90] Despite the lack of explicit reference to a concrete causation approach beyond its strong necessity requirement, counterfactual approaches such as the but-for test and the conditio-sine-qua-non formula have been proposed and applied multiple times and may moreover increasingly prevail.[91] There are, nonetheless, some cases in which a causal relation was considered a necessary criterion for the offence but a reference to causal counterfactuality was ultimately omitted.[92]

Despite the consensus on a rather strict understanding of causation, a specific constellation based on Art. 28 Rome Statute calls into question the general concept of causation and is, therefore, the subject of much debate, not only in academic circles but also in practice and in the courts. This exception concerns Art. 28 Rome Statute, which refers to the responsibility of commanders and other superiors. Here the Court is often confronted with indirect contributions of persons in leading positions, superior responsibility and the scenarios of instigation and aiding and abetting, which raise the difficult question of the assignment of subsequent, indirect and oblique acts and omissions.[93] The main discussion is based on the question of how the phrase 'as a result of*'* in Art. 28 Rome Statute should be interpreted and whether the terminology indicates the requirement of a causal chain or not. In this respect, it is also not possible to identify a clear line of causation concepts, either on the basis of case law or jurisprudential discussion.[94] Different positions have emerged, all, however, based on the judgment or dissenting and separate opinions in the case of *Bemba Gombo*.[95] The views range from a complete rejection of the necessity of any causal link to the recognition of a causal link in cases of the obligation to prevent and ultimately to the necessity of causation in all respects.[96] Interestingly, in cases of instigation and aiding and abetting outside of military commanders and other superiors, i.e. outside of Art. 28 Rome Statute, the necessity of a causal link is undoubtedly required (according to Art. 25 (III) b), c) Rome

[90] See in regard to Art. 28 Rome Statute and referencing the *Delalic* case (International Criminal Tribunal for the former Yugoslavia, 16 November 1998 – IT-96-21-T, *Prosecutor v. Zejnil Delalic et al.* para 396.), Orakhelashvili (2022), p. 166; Werle and Jeßberger (2016), p. 221 para 482.

[91] Kiss (2015), p. 634. Calling it empirical causation and treating it as an either/or decision, Cupido (2021), pp. 6–22; Clark (2022), pp. 746–747 para 24.

[92] E.g. in regard to Art. 25 (III) lit. b), c) Rome Statute and in regard to a joint criminal enterprise, O'Keefe (2015), p. 190 para 5.71, 173 para 5.22.

[93] For a detailed discussion of these cases, see Cupido (2021).

[94] Kiss (2015), pp. 635–638.

[95] International Criminal Court, 21 March 2016 – ICC-01/05-01/08, *Prosecutor v. Jean-Piere Bemba Gombo*.

[96] For a detailed discussion of the various positions and arguments put forward, and ultimately advocating the exclusion of the general causation requirement in Art. 28 Rome Statute, while acknowledging that each approach is plausible, see Jackson (2022), paras 40–51. Not requiring a causal link Olásolo (2009), p. 99. In favour of the recognition of causality as a requirement of Art. 28 of the Rome Statute Triffterer (2004), pp. 203–205; Ambos (2002), pp. 860–861.

Statute, Art. 7 (1) ICTY Statute, Art. 6 (1) ICTR Statute). Conversely, according to the prevailing opinion and jurisprudence of the Court and the Tribunals, counterfactual causation is not a respective precondition. A substantial contribution to the crime suffices for the affirmation of causation.[97] The ICC thus demonstrates that, although its main conception of causation is based on a rather strict understanding of causation which often refers to counterfactual theories, the Court is nevertheless willing to abandon such a strict understanding in cases where it is normatively incentivised to find causation despite the inconclusiveness of counterfactual tests.

In contrast to the ICC, the International Tribunals, in particular, the ICTY and ICTR, have already taken a more explicit stance in addressing the question of causation in relation of superiority and subordination. This is based, among other things, on the terminological difference between the Statutes of the ICTY (Art. 7 (3) ICTY Statute), ICTR (Art. 6 (3) ICTR Statute) and the Rome Statute. The jurisprudence of the ICTY and ICTR has clearly emphasized a common understanding which rejects the need for counterfactual causation in subordinate and superior relations and thus builds upon a lowered perception of causation in light of the contributions of those in superior positions.[98] In the case against *Tihomir Blaškić*, the ICTY stated that "*(a)lthough it must be proved that the instigation was a clear contributing factor to the commission of the crime, it need not be a conditio sine qua non. Instigation can take many different forms; it can be express or implied, and entail both acts and omissions.*"[99] This statement thus denies the necessity of counterfactual causation between the instigation and the crime and merely presupposes a contribution to the offence as sufficient for the required connection. Rather than assessing whether a causal link existed or not, *Clark*, therefore, suggests asking for "*(w)ho is [justly] responsible for that result?*"[100] In referring to 'responsibility' rather than to causation, *Clark* furthermore advocates for a normatively-based and morally-infused conception of the required relatum between the act and the offence.[101] Yet, the application of a criterion of responsibility also introduces a high degree of uncertainty into the criminal proceedings since the discussion is no longer based on factual elements and can, therefore, be verified, but the Court has an excessively large discretionary scope. Another peculiarity of this scenario is the relevance of its backwards-looking chain of causation, which was confirmed by the Tribunal in the case of *Tihomir Blaškić*.[102] On the basis of an omission-related

[97] See Olásolo and Rojo (2015), p. 564; O'Keefe (2015), p. 185 para 5.59, 188 para 5.65.

[98] E.g. in International Criminal Tribunal for the former Yugoslavia 3 July 2008 – IT-03-68-A, *Prosecutor v. Naser Orić*, partly dissenting opinion Judge Liu para 32.

[99] International Criminal Tribunal for the former Yugoslavia, 3 March 2000 – IT-95-14-T, *Prosecutor v. Tihomir Blaškić*, para 270.

[100] Clark (2022), p. 747 para 24.

[101] Ibid. para 24.

[102] International Criminal Tribunal for the former Yugoslavia, 3 March 2000 – IT-95-14-T, *Prosecutor v. Tihomir Blaškić*, para 85.

responsibility, an instigation and aiding and abetting relation also implies cases where the superior fails to punish a crime committed.[103]

Concurrent to the ICTY and ICTR cases, and neglecting the question of whether causation is required at all in Art. 28 Rome Statute, the ICC in *Bemba Gombo* also rejected the application of a causation doctrine based on but-for causation and in relation to omissions in Art. 28 Rome Statute. The Court instead applied the increase in risk doctrine.[104] That such an approach to Art. 28 Rome Statute is not uncontroversial, however, is shown by the numerous separate opinions that have subsequently addressed the question of the correct causation doctrine.[105] Of particular note is the separate opinion of *Judge Steiner,* in which she explicitly developed a normative model for the determination of causation on the basis of probabilities.[106] Also worth noting is the approach taken by *Judge Ozaki*, who introduced foreseeability as an equivalent causal approach.[107] She thereby widened the foreseeability criterion from a mere normative factor to a causal, factual approaching criterion. Nevertheless, this approach, unlike Steiner's, has not been revisited and should be rejected on the grounds of metaphysical divergence and instringency alone. Ultimately, the question of whether Art. 28 Rome Statute presupposes a causal link or not must remain open.

3.2.2.4 European Law and the Court of Justice of the European Union

Turning to the law on a regional level and looking at the jurisprudence of the Courts of the European Union (European Court of Justice (ECJ) and the General Court), here as well does causation come into play in numerous ways. Particularly in European liability law (enshrined in Art. 340 TFEU), the determination of causation is of increased relevance. It is reasonable to assume that the European system tends to reflect the Member States' understanding of causation. Ultimately, however, the European Court of Justice is autonomous in its treatment of causation, which requires the existence of a sufficiently direct causal chain.[108] In this context, and at least with regard to Art. 340 TFEU, many authors refer to the causal approach of adequate causation, which originated in German law.[109] In building solely on

[103] Jackson (2022), p. 1299 para 39.

[104] International Criminal Court, 21 March 2016 – ICC-01/05-01/08, *Prosecutor v. Jean-Piere Bemba Gombo*, Pre-Trial Chamber II, 15 June 2009, para 425.

[105] See ibid.

[106] Ibid. Separate Opinion of Judge Sylvia Steiner, 01/05-01/08-3343-Anx I, paras 18–24. Acknowledging the causation approach by Steiner ibid. joint DissOp. of Judge Monageng and Judge Hofmański, para 339.

[107] Ibid. Separate Opinion of Judge Ozaki, – 3343-Anx II, para 23. Rejecting foreseeability as an approach to causation ibid. Separate Opinion of Judge Sylvia Steiner, -3343-Anx I, para 22.

[108] Inter alia Bagińska and Majkowska-Szulc (2018), p. 132.

[109] See e.g. Gellermann (2018), para 28; Terhechte (2017), para 40; Kottmann (2022), para 117; Frantzen (2017), p. 272.

adequate and, consequently, a normatively influenced conception of causation, this understanding of causation implicitly excludes a counterfactual and, hence, a factual perception of causation.[110] It, therefore, stands opposite to the application of a two-step causal approach consisting of factual and normative requirements. Nevertheless, some authors argue that a two-tier understanding of causation becomes apparent in the jurisprudence of the Court despite divergent rulings and a lack of conceptual unambiguity, even in regard to the European liability regime.[111] This is derived, in particular, from the terminology concerning the requirement of a '*certain and immediate causal connection*'.[112] The factual component is considered to result from the reference to a '*certain*' causal connection, while the '*immediacy*' represents the second step and, thus, the normative criterium of the causal dogmatic. This view is supported by the fact that the Court nevertheless is aware of and applies a counterfactual understanding of causation in specific decisions, even within the framework of the European (external) liability regime. Increasing support in the literature further enhances the importance of a counterfactual conception building upon the conditio-sine-qua-non formula, in particular.[113] In the case *van den Berg v. Council and Commission*, for example, the Second Chamber of the Court stated that

> [...] an act of the Community institutions is the cause of damage only where such damage can be attributed directly and exclusively to such act. The requisite causal link does not exist where the damage would also have occurred in the absence of the relevant act of the Community institutions.[114]

Still, no exclusivity of a counterfactual approach to causation can be inferred from the statement of the Court, which is shown by numerous other decisions in which the Court simply affirmed or denied causation without referring to any specific causal doctrine or even without elaborating on that matter in any regard.[115] A clear causal approach cannot, therefore, be deduced from the case law of the ECJ.[116]

There is no doubt, however, that in addition to the question of the necessity of counterfactual causation and, rather, factual causation, a great number of normative aspects find their way into the decision of the Court of Justice of the European Union, as well.[117] This is mainly owed to the lack of definition of the requirement of '*immediacy*'. As a result, the Court often applies criteria concurrent to the theory of

---

[110] Frantzen (2017), p. 272.

[111] In this regard especially Weitenberg (2014), pp. 317–320, 792–793.

[112] Ibid. 320–326.

[113] European Court of Justice, 28 October 2004 – C-164/01 P *van den Berg v. Council and Commission*. See in this regard also Kottmann (2022), para 117; Weitenberg (2014), inter alia 421–423.

[114] European Court of Justice, 28 October 2004 – C-164/01 P *van den Berg v. Council and Commission*, para 57.

[115] Weitenberg (2014), p. 364.

[116] With regard to Art. 340 TFEU see Ruffert (2022), para 27; Gellermann (2018), para 28.

[117] See in this regard again Weitenberg (2014), pp. 578–597.

adequacy.[118] Nonetheless, in addition to the requirement of an adequate cause, other normative factors have become relevant as well. Ultimately, there is no exhaustive list of normative factors that are exclusively applied by the Court but rather a wide variety of different considerations that find their way into the legal assessment. These include, inter alia, the foreseeability of the outcome, whether the outcome is a typical or atypical result of the alleged act or omission, or whether there are other intervening causes to be taken into account.[119]

Causation naturally also finds relevance in European law outside its liability regime. The European Charter of Fundamental Rights, for example, poses causation requirements directly and indirectly in several of its provisions.[120] Among those are exemplary Art. 41 CFR, which requires a causal link between the procedural errors and the decision taken, and Art. 21 CFR, which addresses the link between the unequal treatment in question and the disadvantage alleged.[121]

3.2.3 *Causation in the Regional and International Human Rights Framework*

Causation forms a cornerstone of liability for violations in both regional and international human rights frameworks as well. However, questions of causation in the universal human rights framework have been widely overlooked by legal scholars to date, even though causal relata are a significant factor in the jurisprudence of human rights courts. Nevertheless, it should be emphasised that human rights courts generally do not pursue a clear, determinable causal approach but rather proceed on the basis of in casu judgments and only occasionally express themselves clearly on the establishment of causation.[122] In principle, causation can be relevant in the human rights framework at two different junctures. On the one hand, as already mentioned, there must be a causal link between the action or omission of a state and the violation of the convention; the violation of the convention, on the other hand, is further linked to the resulting damage of a material or immaterial nature. This closely resembles the approach inherent in the German liability and tort law system and is reinforced by the legal distinction between violation, compensation and cost allocation.

---

[118] See in this regard Sect. 5.6.

[119] For example, foreseeability was at issue in Federal Court of Australia, 15 March 2022 – [2022] FCAFC 35, *Minister for the Environment v. Sharma* inter alia paras 253, 307, 414–442, District Court of Central Jakarta, 11 January 2021 – 445/Pdt.G/2019/PN.Jkt.Pst, *Ministry of Environment and Forestry v. PT Rambang Agro Jaya*, United Kingdom Court of Appeal (Civil Division), 17 February 2022 – [2022] EWCA Civ 187, *R (Finch on behalf of the Weald Action Group & Others) v. Surrey County Council (& Others)*.

[120] See e.g. Art. 21, 41 CFR.

[121] See e.g. Jarass (2021), Art. 41 para 5; Chen (2011), p. 64.

[122] See, in particular, on the causal link established by the ECtHR Stoyanova (2018), p. 317.

3.2.3.1 Negative Versus Positive Obligations

A major difference between regional and international courts and the human rights framework, in general, persists in the significant importance of positive obligations in light of human rights. Positive obligations require the respective state not only to avoid any action that leads to a right infringement (negative obligation) but to safeguard the right itself from any, even external forces that might lead to a violation of the right in question. How far such a duty to protect reaches is up to the discretion of the courts, as well as implementing such duties in the respective provisions itself. However, considering the new challenges with which courts are frequently confronted, among those, the heightened relevance of supply chains in light of pending globalization, climate change, and a further intensifying refugee crisis, positive obligations are becoming increasingly relevant.

With positive obligations moving at the forefront of legal claims, their impact also extends to the respective determination of causation. Not only are positive obligations granting the claimants far-reaching rights to manoeuvre, positive obligations also considerably simplify the establishment of causation, provided one even assumes that causation is ultimately required by positive obligations at all. Whereas negative obligations require a causal chain between one's conduct and the right infringement, causation in light of positive obligations only requires the determination that a protected right has been violated and the state had a feasible obligation to protect the respective right. Whether the state itself infringed on the right due to its own conduct or the violation occurred by another actor does not become of relevance in the positive realm. Positive obligations are, therefore, blind to metaphysical and dogmatic problems inherent in concurrent causes. Whereas the occurrence of a large number of cumulative causes or even alternative, sufficient conditions might lead to the rejection of causation in regard to negative obligations and under the application of traditional counterfactual tests of factual causation, such challenges do not arise in regard to positive obligations. How far the obligation to protect the respective right reaches and respectively the scope of the obligation, however, is determined on a case-by-case basis. Completely unusual, unforeseeable and hardly avoidable intervening actions can, thus, be excluded from the positive obligations and a duty to protect. This, nonetheless, resides at the discretion of the courts. Ultimately, establishing causation in light of positive obligations, due diligence, and an existing duty of care poses much fewer hurdles and is, therefore, considerably easier to achieve than it is the case with negative obligations.[123]

[123] See e.g. Quirico (2018), pp. 191–193; Campbell-Duruflé and Atapattu (2018), pp. 332–333.

3.2.3.2 The European Convention on Human Rights and the European Court of Human Rights

Causation also plays an important role in the European Convention on Human Rights. In the context of the admissibility of the claim, the first causal link that has to be established concerns the standing of the plaintiff, as set out in Art. 35 ECHR. Although it is to be assumed that the criteria for the causal link required by the assessment of standing are rather low and commonly do not pose a great hurdle to the admissibility of the claim, the Court still presupposes a link between the plaintiff and the alleged violation. What requirements are ultimately set out for the establishment of causation in light of the standing of the plaintiff currently is in question in the precedent case *KlimaSeniorinnen v. Switzerland*.[124] The decision in the respective case will grant an opportunity to the Court to shed light on the preconditions in question.

However, unlike other courts (e.g. the Inter-American Court of Human Rights (IACtHR) in the context of extraterritoriality), the European Court of Human Rights (ECtHR) does not require a causal link for the recognition of its jurisdiction, neither in relation to the common ratione loci nor in regard to the extraterritorial application of the Convention.[125] Rather, the Court conducts a highly normative assessment for the establishment of its extraterritorial jurisdiction based on different case-law-grown criteria.[126] At the substantive level, causation is contained in the individual norms themselves. This applies, in particular, to the link between the action of the state in question and the resulting right infringement and, therefore, highly coincides with general causation requirements.[127]

Considering the case law of the ECtHR, it becomes apparent that the Court follows the general trend of international courts and does not clearly commit itself to a specific causal doctrine or to a certain way of establishing causation in general.[128] Despite this instringency and methodological ambiguity in the way causation is implemented, a denial of causation, however, would also lead to a negation of the violation of the European Convention of Human Rights before the ECtHR.[129] Nevertheless, the jurisprudence of the European Court of Human Rights reveals that the Court frequently employs counterfactual causation theories, which are

---

[124] European Court of Human Rights, pending – 53600/20, *KlimaSeniorinnen v. Switzerland*.

[125] The ratione loci is set in Art. 1 ECHR by referring to the 'jurisdiction' of the parties to the Convention.

[126] The most influential cases concerning the territorial application of the ECHR are among others European Court of Human Rights, 12 December 2001 – 52207/99, *Banković and others v. Belgium and others*, European Court of Human Rights, 7 July 2011 – 55721/07, *Al-Skeini and others v. The United Kingdom*.

[127] For an in-depth discussion of Art. 3 ECHR, see Orakhelashvili (2022), pp. 171–173.

[128] Ugrekhelidze (2007), p. 479.

[129] Conforti (2004), p. 134.

likewise acknowledged in domestic tort and criminal law.[130] In doing so, the Court employs both the but-for test and the conditio-sine-qua-non formula without, however, confining itself to utilizing only one of these approaches.[131] The application of counterfactual causation has been a subject of heated debate, with opposing views on its level of strictness. While some decisions have been critical of the causal approach, citing insufficiency or misleading outcomes, others have advocated for a lowering of the causation threshold.[132] The latter receives further support by increasing calls in the legal scholarship for a generally lowered standard of causation.[133] Nevertheless, the overall need for a factual causal component as such is widely recognised in the literature.[134] *Orakhelashvili* states in this regard, *"[...] finding a violation is always a matter of fact and hence causation has to be identified as a factual link between governemnt's conduct and the applicant's or victim's condition*".[135] And while this statement can be unreservedly endorsed in relation to negative obligations, the case law of the ECtHR does not reflect factuality in relation to positive obligations. Although the connection between a positive obligation and a violation of rights can also constitute a factual determination of causation, and a factual perception would also be desirable here, it is precisely in cases of positive obligations that the Court increasingly makes normative considerations and either directly or indirectly does not mention or does not apply a factual concept of causation.[136] In principle, the Court tends to adopt a weaker approach to causation in the context of positive obligations than in the case of a traditional infringement of

---

[130] Ugrekhelidze (2007), p. 478. With regard to the strict rejection of counterfactual theories in the case law of the ECtHR Stoyanova (2018), p. 316. See, for example, a case in which the Court recognised a causal link on the basis of a strong criterion of necessity European Court of Human Rights, 31 May 2018 – 46454/11, *Abu Zubayday v. Lithuania*, para 656.

[131] See for the application of the conditio-sine-qua-non test European Court of Human Rights, 24 October 2002 – 37703/97, *Mastromatteo v. Italy*, para 74.

[132] In *Mastromatteo v. Italy*, the Court held that, although there was a counterfactual causal link between the release from prison and the murder of A. Mastromatteo, such a conditio-sine-qua-non causal link was not sufficient to establish the State's overall responsibility under Art. 2 ECHR (see European Court of Human Rights, 24 October 2002 – 37703/97, *Mastromatteo v. Italy*, para 74). It further emphasized a normative assessment including the 'ought to have known' standard, involving the question of reasonable foreseeability. In *Opuz v Turkey*, on the other hand, the Court affirmed overall causation even though counterfactual causation could not be established (European Court of Human Rights, 9 June 2009 – 33401/02, *Opuz v. Turkey*.).

[133] See in this regard e.g. Cordes-Holland (2008), p. 435 who is advocating for a transfer of the approach established in Massachusetts v. EPA. In stating that one should "*move beyond causation based attribution*", Bellinkx et al. (2022), p. 73; Lavrysen (2018), pp. 708–709. Opting for a contributing to risk approach Campbell-Duruflé and Atapattu (2018), pp. 332–333.

[134] See inter alia Orakhelashvili (2022), p. 175.

[135] Ibid. 184.

[136] Stoyanova (2018), p. 311. See further for a strict understanding of causation in light of counterfactuality *E. and Others v. the United Kingdom*. The Court rejected the but-for test in the light of positive obligations under Art. 3 ECtHR (European Court of Human Rights, 26 November 2002 – 33218/96, *E. and others v. The United Kingdom*, para 99.

rights and negative obligations.[137] This, however, not only follows from the case law of the Court but is inherent in the nature of positive obligations in general, which does not require such a stringent causal chain as it is presupposed by negative obligations.[138] With regard to Art. 3 ECHR and the positive obligations enshrined therein, the Court stated:

> The test under Article 3 however does not require it to be shown that "but for" the failing or omission of the public authority ill-treatment would not have happened. A failure to take reasonably available measures which could have had a real prospect of altering the outcome or mitigating the harm is sufficient to engage the responsibility of the State.[139]

The Court, therefore, rejects the necessity of applying a doctrine of counterfactual causation in light of the positive obligations in Art. 3 ECHR and affirms the sufficiency of the simple existence of a 'real prospect' of change. The 'real prospect' test, however, does not preclude a factual analysis of the link between the reasonable measures and the change in the outcome. It solely entails the refrainment from a strict counterfactual understanding of causation and indicates a lowered conception of causation while leaving open the question of how the respective link should further be established. Decisive for the assessment, thus, are the criteria which are applied by the Court to analyse this hypothetical link.

The Court, nonetheless, also makes extensive use of normative criteria. The most important of these are the remoteness, proximity and foreseeability of the outcome, which have been applied in numerous decisions of the ECtHR.[140] Especially in regard to positive obligations and the 'real and immediate risk' standard, the Court often uses the 'ought to have known' test, which is one way of applying a conception of foreseeability to the legal assessment.[141] The 'ought to have known standard' is highly subjective and depends greatly on the ability and capacity of the party in question. The Court thereby takes into account the nature and manner of the violation as well as the substance of the legal interest affected while still deciding

---

[137] This is due, inter alia, to the general facilitation of the establishment of links in relation to positive obligations, see e.g. Sects. 3.2.3 and 3.3.2.4.

[138] See in this regard again Sects. 3.2.3 and 3.3.2.4.

[139] European Court of Human Rights, 26 November 2022 – 33218/96, *E. and others v. The United Kingdom,* para 99.

[140] Concerning the remoteness criteria and in stating that *"(t)he Commission therefore finds that the effects of the contested measures are of a too indirect and remote nature as to affect the applicant's rights under Article 9 (Art. 9) of the Convention."* European Court of Human Rights, 29 April 2003 – 56673/00, *Iglesias Gil and A.U.I. v. Spain,* § 70. Concerning a proximate link, see European Court of Human Rights, 10 October 2000 – 22947/93, 22948/93, *Akkoç v. Turkey*, partly dissenting opinion of judge Gölcüklü in its english translation, 25–26, Stoyanova (2018), pp. 338–339; Conforti (2004), p. 314. Regarding the foreseeability criteria European Court of Human Rights, 24 October 2002 – 37703/97, *Mastromatteo v. Italy*, paras 74–79. Also Conforti (2003), pp. 7–8.

[141] See e.g. in European Court of Human Rights, 24 October 2002 – 37703/97, *Mastromatteo v. Italy,* European Court of Human Rights, 28 October 1998 – 87/1997/871/1038, *Osman v. The United Kingdom*, paras 116, 121, 128, Stoyanova (2020), pp. 612–615.

on a case-by-case basis.[142] Although the Court thus recognises and applies both factual and normative causal standards, only occasionally can a clear two-step causal approach be derived from the case law of the ECtHR.[143]

In addition to the causal link between the state's conduct and the violation of a Convention right, causation is also relevant considering compensation for the occurred right infringement and overall damage. This requirement is outlined in Art. 41 ECHR. In contrast to other norm-related causal links, greater consensus prevails about the causal standard that is applied by the Court. Inherent in the terminology of a 'clear causal link' between the Convention violation and the damage suffered is the precondition of a stricter causal standard in factual terms.[144] Here it seems that the Court does have a tendency towards the application of counterfactual theories, at least in regard to negative obligations, even if, as is so often the case in decisions, these are not clearly articulated.[145]

3.2.3.3 The American Convention on Human Rights and the Inter-American Court of Human Rights

The Inter-American Court of Human Rights (IACtHR), like the ECtHR, also requires a cause-effect relationship between the state's actions or omissions and a violation of the Convention. However, this is not the only case in which plaintiffs need to establish causal relata. Parallel to Art. 41 ECHR, the American Convention on Human Rights also contains a provision on compensation and reparation for violations of the Convention in Art. 63-1 ACHR. The phrase 'the consequences' implies the need for a causal link. Yet, the IACtHR has not committed itself to an unambiguous doctrine of causation in this respect but requires a direct, certain, pure and transitive chain of causation.[146] Whether the 'certainty' or the 'directness' entailed in this wording hints towards the acceptance of an inquiry of factuality as it is proposed in regard to the European liability regime, cannot be deduced from the current jurisprudence of the Court. What is certain, however, is that the IACtHR uses a highly normative approach based on policy considerations which lacks uniformity as well as stringency and not only builds upon actual evidence but also falls back to mere presumptions in regard to the existence of causation.[147] This is due, in particular, to the requirement of pure- and transitiveness.

[142] Ugrekhelidze (2007), pp. 471, 478.

[143] Such was e.g. applied in European Court of Human Rights, 24 October 2002 – 37703/97, *Mastromatteo v. Italy*, 74.

[144] See Kellner and Durant (2012); Meyer-Ladewig and Brunozzi (2017), para 13; Wenzel (2015), para 16.

[145] See on liability aspects in the case law of the ECtHR, Kellner and Durant (2012), pp. 457–460.

[146] Hennebel and Tigroudja (2022), pp. 1314–1315.

[147] Again ibid. 1314.

In a 2017 published Advisory Opinion regarding the interplay between human rights and the environment, the Court paved the way for its jurisdiction even in light of an extraterritorial application of the Convention.[148] According to previous judgments of the Court, what was necessary for the exercise of jurisdiction over acts outside the territory of the state concerned, was either authority or effective control over the person in question.[149] Nonetheless, proving effective control in cases of environmental damage is nearly impossible. Therefore, the Court lowered its requirements and elaborated that

> (f)or the purposes of the American Convention, when transboundary damage occurs that effects treaty-based rights, it is understood that the persons whose rights have been violated are under the jurisdiction of the State of origin, if there is a causal link between the act that originated in its territory and the infringement of the human rights of persons outside its territory.[150]

The Court did not comment on the precise requirements for the existence of a causal link. Given, nonetheless, the fact that the Court once adopted a rather restrictive understanding of the extraterritorial application of the law and that jurisdictional questions are increasingly subject to an objective discussion of the facts, it can at least be assumed that a factual causal assessment rather than a mere normatively-indulged determination is required.[151] This presumption is further supported by the explanation of the Court that *"(a) determination must be made, based on the factual and legal circumstances of each specific case [...]."*[152]

Beyond the extraterritoriality in the case of transboundary damage and the reparations under Art. 63-I ACHR, the Inter-American human rights system is strongly influenced by socio-political considerations, which also transpires to the requirements the Court poses on the violation of rights.[153] A discussion of factual causation tends to be conducted implicitly, if, however, at all. It is, therefore, difficult to assess whether the IACtHR even applies a two-step approach to causation,

---

[148] Inter-American Court of Human Rights, 15 November 2017 – OC-23/17, *A Request for an Advisory Opinion from the Inter-American Court of Human Rights Concerning the Interpretation of Article 1(1), 4(1) and 5(1) of the American Convention on Human Rights.*

[149] Ibid. paras 81–82. Campbell-Duruflé and Atapattu (2018), pp. 333–334. See also Hennebel and Tigroudja (2022), pp. 46–52.

[150] Inter-American Court of Human Rights, 15 November 2017 – OC-23/17, *A Request for an Advisory Opinion from the Inter-American Court of Human Rights Concerning the Interpretation of Article 1(1), 4(1) and 5(1) of the American Convention on Human Rights,* 101.

[151] Hennebel and Tigroudja (2022), pp. 48–49. In referring to Inter-American Court of Human Rights, 15 November 2017 – OC-23/17, *A Request for an Advisory Opinion from the Inter-American Court of Human Rights Concerning the Interpretation of Article 1(1), 4(1) and 5(1) of the American Convention on Human Rights*, para 81.

[152] Inter-American Court of Human Rights, 15 November 2017 – OC-23/17, *A Request for an Advisory Opinion from the Inter-American Court of Human Rights Concerning the Interpretation of Article 1(1), 4(1) and 5(1) of the American Convention on Human Rights,* para 93.

[153] Socio-political considerations have e.g. led to the recognition of the right to a healthy environment in the case Inter-American Court of Human Rights, 6 February 2020 – C No. 400, *Indigenous Communities of the Lhaka Honhat (Our Land) Association v. Argentina.*

let alone which particular doctrine the Court follows. It can be concluded that the Court does not consider causation to be a rigid and unyielding concept. Rather, it is viewed as a dynamic and versatile tool that can be adapted to fit various situations and circumstances. This suggests that the Court may take a nuanced and flexible approach when evaluating causation in legal cases.

3.2.4 Conclusion

The concept of causation holds great significance in the realms of both national and international law. This principle forms the foundation for any legal proceeding and has the power to convert an objective act or omission into a legal wrong. However, especially regional and international law lacks a universal understanding of causation. In contrast to domestic law, nonetheless, normative criteria and political considerations are given more importance. Factual causation is only explicitly considered in the context of liability regimes, while normative considerations and the adaptation of overall perceptions are generally discussed in every international and regional jurisdiction. Yet again, it is in the context of liability regimes that the two-stage approach to causation is increasingly evident and adopted.[154] As far as the particular causal approach is concerned, no stringency persists, either. In light of factual approaches, however, counterfactual doctrines predominate over other existing metaphysical concepts, such as theories of regularity or more economic-based theories of factual causation.[155] Depending on the regime, the but-for-test or the conditio-sine-qua-non formula takes precedence.[156]

Nevertheless, this result has to be approached with caution as an extensive amount of decisions consider factual causation without explicitly referencing a particular doctrinal approach. Even more so, decisions refrain from mentioning factual causation at all. It is, therefore, not uncommon to encounter inconsistencies, ambiguity, and vagueness, which can impede a clear understanding of the concepts at play. Among the terminology employed in such discussions, the phrase 'direct chain of causation' is frequently utilized as a means of clarifying and distinguishing the relationships between various causal factors. Concerning the requirement of normative causation, the decisions show a wide variety of normative criteria used. Criteria such as the foreseeability of the outcome, its remoteness or the absence of intervening causes are decisive. These are also partly integrated into other overarching principles, such as the adequate or proximate cause test.

The reason why regional and international courts, in particular, are largely unconceptual in their approach to causation, in contrast to national courts, seems

[154] In favour of a strict distinction and application of a two-stage causal approach in international law, see Bederman (1990), p. 349.

[155] See on those approaches of factual causation later on in Chap. 4.

[156] Supporting the but-for test in international law Orakhelashvili (2022), pp. 62, 113, 208, 216.

to be caused by the great interaction and influence of different legal systems and legal concepts. In an effort to avoid the reproach to specific national approaches and, thus, to evade the allegation of being biased, international courts and tribunals tend to be nonconceptual. In addition, regional and international courts have a much more recent case law history in comparison with the widely matured national legal systems, which gives them less time to develop a comprehensive understanding of cause-effect relations and enhances the vagueness and ambiguity of the concepts used. A further reason is grounded in the base of the legal considerations and, therefore, also in the base of the causal determination themselves. Whereas in most national, especially civil law, legal systems, the norms are rich in detail, and their scope and substance are largely determined by a mature literature, international treaties and statutes, in particular, are characterised by their vagueness and vastness. This is certainly a consequence of the considerably more difficult consensus-building process but, again, does not support the stringency of the jurisprudence based on it.

3.3 Causation and Climate Change

In law, causation not only functions as a link between an act or omission and a resulting legal position but also as a way of attributing legal responsibility and moral blameworthiness. It is, hence, highly distinct from general scientific epistemology, which can lead to significant discrepancies in the translation of scientific scenarios into the legal sphere. The following section discusses causation in the context of climate change. In particular, it draws attention to the particular obstacles to establishing causation in law in light of the pending climate crisis. At the same time, it provides insights into the divergence between causal understandings in natural sciences and those used in law and attempts to find common ground in their elaboration.

3.3.1 Scientific Causation and Climate Change

3.3.1.1 Model of a Climatic Chain of Causation

One of the main problems when it comes to establishing causation in climate change litigation results from the extensive causal chain that needs to be formed within the climate change process.[157] In line with the scientific understanding of climate

[157] In natural sciences, dependencies are often represented not as causal chains but as Bayesian networks. In contrast to causal chains, random variables and probabilities can be integrated into a Bayesian network. The network structure of interdependencies has also been referred to in the climate case Land Court of Queensland, 25 November 2022 – [2022] QLC 21, *Waratah Coal Pty*

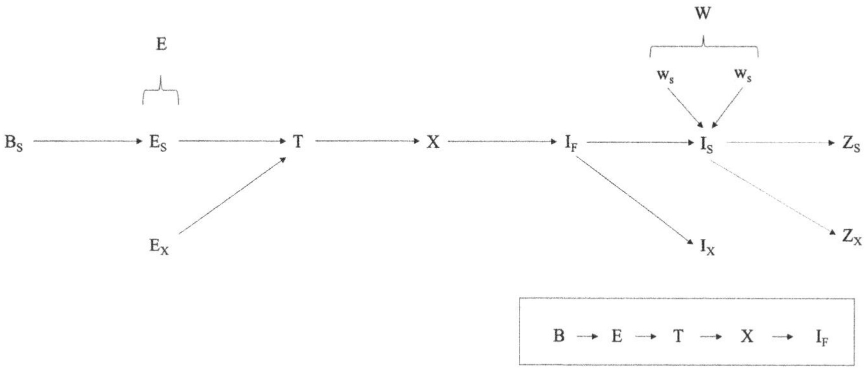

Fig. 3.1 Model of a climatic causal chain

change, the decomposition of a comprehensive causal chain requires the differentiation of numerous individual causal links, such as between emissions (E) and a temperature increase (T), the temperature increase (T) and the resulting warming of the uppermost ocean layers (X) for example, and in turn the resulting effects (I) in a general (I_F) and specific conception (I_S). To illustrate this complex causal chain and in order to simplify its applicability and the visualization of those causal relata, a generalized model has been developed. This model fundamentally founds itself on common acronyms used in climate science (E, T, I_F, I_S) and has been further adapted and extended (B_S, Z, W) to meet the needs of causal chains in climate change litigation.[158] The acronyms used in this model, therefore, have only the purpose and scope described below, and are free of other meanings and connotations, especially those used in science.

Figure 3.1 depicts a typical, standardised form of an emission-related climatic causal chain: $B_{S,}$ as the first link in the model, constitutes a specific action or omission that does not in itself consist of the emission of greenhouse gases. This encompasses, for example, the authorization of administrative permits. Actions or omissions which are considered to be categorized as the initiation of the chain and concurrently present a B_S condition can also be referred to as '*anthropogenic drivers*'. E then denotes the total amount of anthropogenic greenhouse gases in the atmosphere, while E_s quantifies the amount emitted by a single, i.e. specific emitter. Other emissions underlie E_X. T then refers to the increase in the global mean surface temperature, and X to general other impacts resulting out of such an increase as, for example, an increase in ocean surface temperature. The causal relation to X not only persists in one link in the chain but can be extended by further links between T and

Ltd v. Youth Verdict Ltd & Ors (No 6), paras 1338–1339. It is important to recognise that network structures can represent causal relationships better than pure chains. For the sake of simplicity, however, causal relata are referred to here as causal chains. For more details on causal networks, see Williamson (2009), pp. 8–10.

[158] See also similar Minnerop and Otto (2020), pp. 73–77.

I_F, depending on the case and the required scientific accuracy. It is in the subject matter of climate change that a rigid causal chain would not be compatible with reality and thus also not with the general requirements within legal proceedings. I_F thereupon represents general impacts, which can lead to a specific climate-related effect depicted as I_S while also resulting in further specific impacts (I_X). I_S, in turn, can lead to further overall impacts Z_X, with Zs representing a further specific impact. W combines the sum of all causes that have led to I_S beside and in addition to I_F, with w_s representing individual and specific contributions. W_s hereby especially refers to natural climate variability and other man-made factors. However, W and w_s as intervening factors are not only possible at the level of a specific outcome I_S but at basically every stage of the causal chain. A factor that has not found its way into the model but becomes of relevance in regard to a metaphysical substantiation of causation is the factor of time t.[159] (t) often represents an additional account to yet existing and occurring conditions, placing them into a temporal sphere. The present model, in general, focuses on emissions-based litigation as one of the major groups of climate claims. Nevertheless, climate change litigation can also be pursued in the context of other, not emission-related and influenced intrusions into the natural climate system. In light of such emission-independent chains, the foregoing model has to be adapted accordingly, which mainly consists in the omission of emission-related links E and E_S. In such scenarios, B_S directly leads to T or X as those links embody the changes in the climate system.

In addition to the predominant specific causal chain, the subjacent figure illustrates the chain in its generalized form, which simultaneously refers to general causation. General causation hereby asks whether a general behaviour, e.g. the emission of GHG, causes a general increase in global mean surface temperatures and would generally be able to cause an outcome such as sea level rise or generally extreme weather events. Specific causation, on the other hand, refers to the question of whether a specific amount of GHG-emission, e.g. the emission of a specific actor, caused the specific climate change-induced event. Consequently, specific causation is highly more complex to establish than general causation.

The length of the causal chain in climate-related lawsuits, furthermore, greatly depends on the kind of climate change impact the plaintiff is referring to. Thus, a distinction must be made between so-called slow onset events and sudden onset events.[160] Slow onset events are, in contrast to its wording, not a specific, narrowly

[159] See for the relevance of time e.g. Sect. 4.2.3.4.3.3.

[160] Slow onset events include sea level rise, rising temperatures, ocean acidification, glacial retreat and related impacts, salinisation, land and forest degradation, biodiversity loss and desertification, as stated in paragraph 25 of the Cancun Agreements. Similar also van der Geest and van den Berg (2021). Unlike slow-onset events, sudden-onset events do not belong to a clear and identifiable group of events. The demarcation must therefore be made in the negative, with sudden onset events referring to events that occur suddenly and unexpectedly, often reaching the status of extreme weather events. See in this regard also the terminology of the Sendai Framework on sudden onset disasters which are defined in Resolution A/71/644, at 13 as *"triggered by a hazardous event that emerges quickly or unexpectedly"*.

limited event but a development that progresses over a long period. Typical slow onset events include the rise in sea level and, above all, the melting of glaciers and polar sea ice. Sudden onset events, on the other hand, are occasions with an immediate and often unforeseen effect. Such sudden onset events are generally caused by their counterpart, videlicet slow onset events, which generally precede them within the causal chain. Causal chains concerning slow onset events are, therefore, gradually shorter than sudden onset events. Extreme weather events such as storms, floods or heat waves are typically classified as such. While there is already a sound scientific basis for linking slow onset events to anthropogenic climate change and greenhouse gas emissions, there is still a fundamental lack of scientific knowledge about sudden onset events.[161] In addition, sudden onset events are generally influenced to a greater extent by factors that are not immediately climate-related, which in turn raises problems of cumulative causation and intervening causes. The impacts of a flood and the damage caused by it thereby significantly hinge on the flood protection measures taken beforehand, potential changes in the course of the river and other natural or man-made interventions. All these factors have to be considered within the causal dogmas in law and especially in regard to the traditional understanding of counterfactual causation.[162]

To illustrate how both the specific and the general model work as well as to explain its function and the influence of the kind of climate change impact the plaintiff is commonly referring to, the following fictitious case is introduced: Due to a devastating flood, the house owned by the plaintiff (A) became uninhabitable. A, thus, seeks compensation for the damage, i.e. the expenses for repairing the house and restoring its habitability. A considers corporation B, which has been operating a coal mine for years, as responsible for the flood and the damage that occurred. To substantiate A's claim against B, regardless of the statutory provisions and the respective jurisdiction, A must provide the following factual causal chain.

The extraction and sale of coal, under the neglect of GHG emissions resulting from the extraction per se, does not directly harm the climate (B_S). However, coal generally is used to generate energy, which is done by burning the mineral. This combustion by the customers of B produces GHG emissions (E_S) that increase the density of anthropogenic greenhouse gas emissions (E) in the atmosphere, which in turn leads to an increase in the global average temperature (T).[163] The increased average temperature leads to an increased degree of evaporation (X), which in turn

[161] IPCC (2021a), p. 5. See for more detail Sect. 2.1.

[162] See for more detail Sect. 4.2.

[163] The question of whether companies are responsible for emissions caused by the end user as a result of the use of their product has been a highly contentious issue in recent climate change cases. However, courts are increasingly inclined to accept corporate responsibility for so-called scope 3 emissions. This debate is irrelevant to the factual elaboration of causation and the establishment of the relevant causal chain, as long as a factual, rigorous chain can be established. Since 'responsibility' is a morally induced and therefore normative concept of law, possible deviations from the factual causal relation are to be discussed with regard to the elaboration of normative causation. See in this regard Chap. 5.

can lead to an increased occurrence of heavy rainfall with an elevated amount of precipitation (I_F). The enhanced rainfall causes the rivers in the specific region of A's house to swell and deplete the absorption capacity of the soil, which eventually leads to a flood (I_S) that renders A's house uninhabitable (Z_S). Nevertheless, the assertion of A's claim requires not only the presence of such a stringent causal chain but further attention also must be paid to the question of other possible causes and contributions. Thus, the totality (W) of other conditions or even single conditions alone (w_s), such as the straightening of the river, the sealing of large areas of soil or even natural weather and climate variability, may have contributed to the flood, if not caused it alone.

3.3.1.2 Attribution Science

Attribution science is a subfield of climate science that focuses on the attribution of climate change and its consequences to human activities. Having emerged around the turn of the millennium, it remains a fairly young field of research.[164] However, despite it being a rather newly developed area of climate science, four different attribution strands have emerged, namely climate change attribution, impact attribution, source attribution and ultimately, event attribution. Each of these strands has its own unique focus and provides valuable insights into the intricate and multifaceted nature of climate change. Climate change attribution hereby concerns the effect of greenhouse gases on the overall climate system, impact attribution relates to changes in the climate system and their effect on ecosystems and humans in general, whereas source attribution deals with relative contributions by specific actors and their effect on the climate system.[165] Event attribution ultimately asks how changes in the climate system affect the occurrence of extreme weather events. The general procedure in all areas is to detect a possible change and then attribute that change to a forcing factor. Nonetheless, the methods and techniques used to achieve this vary widely. These include, in particular, the use of physical knowledge, observational data, statistical analysis and the application of specific climate models. Reliable and scientifically sound results generally make use of more than one of these techniques.[166] And while the methodologies within the different branches of climate attribution science differ to some extent, they all aim at establishing scientific relations by making use of counterfactual models. Counterfactuality results from a

[164] One of the first climate attribution study is a 2004 paper on the 2003 European heat wave and its anthropogenic influences, see Scott et al. (2004).

[165] See for an account of the different field of attribution science Baldrich (2021); Mikhailova et al. (2022), p. 2.

[166] Burger et al. in this regard aptly conclude "*The most robust attribution approaches combine good observations. Physical understanding, rigorous statistical analysis, and detailed models to generate findings, along with clear communication and transparency with respect to research parameters, assumptions made, confidence in findings, and potential areas of uncertainty or bias.*" Burger et al. (2020), p. 75.

model-based and statistical comparison of the scenario and the outcome in question with and without the corresponding attributable driver.[167] The respective results are usually communicated with references to two divergent kinds of uncertainty. Dual uncertainty arises, on the one hand, from the expression of probability of whether the attributed link actually exists and, on the other hand, from the level of confidence with which such a statement can be made.[168] This methodology is also used by the IPCC.[169]

Yet, climate science still faces fundamental problems inherent in its attributional realm. Despite the increasing standardisation of climate models and the growing volume of publications, leading to greater transparency and verifiability of the results presented, there are still some uncertainties in the assessment and evaluation of specific climate forcings as well as in general climate variability. Those uncertainties particularly influence the assessment of observational data.[170] Moreover, the main difficulty, especially concerning observational evidence, still constitutes the lack of appropriate data sets and their selection. The latter, in particular, carries the risk of hand-sight bias due to the selection of particular data that suits the desired result best.[171] In climate science, this relates, in particular, to the scope and nature of the emissions being assessed. For example, whether the assessment is based on land-based or consumption-based emissions can have a significant impact on the scientific outcome.[172] The same applies to the type of emissions considered. Although CO_2 emissions pose the largest amount of greenhouse gases in the atmosphere, the inclusion of other greenhouse gases as well, such as methane, can considerably alter the respective results. The same is true in considering the negative radiative forcing of aerosols.[173] However, hand-sight bias are not a problem exclusively

---

[167] This methodology is similar to that used in traditional normative causation tests. However, the presentation of the results is very different, which makes it difficult to apply the scientific findings to normative causation.

[168] See for more detail Minnerop and Otto (2020), pp. 70–71.

[169] See in this regard Sect. 2.1.1.

[170] This results especially out of the mere *"complexity of the physical systems modeled."* Burger et al. (2020), p. 72.

[171] Referring to the statement of the World Weather Attribution initiative and stating that data should go back at least to the 1950s, see Cho (2021).

[172] A consumption-based approach attributes the emissions of a specific good and its production to the end user. The consumer thus bears the full responsibility for the product and its emissions. Industrialised countries, with their large number of consumers and high purchasing power, are particularly emission-intensive. A land-based or territorial approach, on the other hand, addresses and quantifies emissions based on the territory where they are actually emitted, which can lead to a divergence of the qualification as emission-intensive based on the reliance on the respective approach.

[173] See in more detail Burger et al. (2020), p. 76. The inclusion of consumer-related emissions (more commonly known as scope 3 emissions) has also been an issue in a number of different climate claims.

inherent in the field of attribution science alone but lies in the general scientific process and methodology. Countering those obstacles respectively requires a transparent disclosure of the selection criteria used and the capacity of the user to evaluate the information provided accordingly.

The complexity of the climate system poses further obstacles to attribution science. Particularly problematic is the accounting of natural and climatic variability, the weighting of climate forcings, and the inclusion of the effect of aerosols into the climatic model.[174] Unlike greenhouse gas emissions, aerosols do not distribute uniformly in the atmosphere but vary in concentration from region to region, resulting in different negative radiative forcing factors. Whether a specific area showed a high density of aerosols at a specific point in time or not is often difficult to assess in a retrospective.[175] In addition, to assess a specific event and its scientific causes, the influence of so-called exogenous variables, i.e. factors outside the climate system, must also be taken into account to obtain accurate results.[176] These include the vulnerability of a population to specific events or other population risk factors.[177] However, these are much more difficult to measure, especially as they are linked to a fine-scaled location and are further dependent on societal factors such as the political situation and cultural habits as well. The spatial sphere, in general, poses major difficulties to the field of event attribution studies. In contrast to general climate change attribution, event attribution studies tend to have a smaller data set due to their temporal and spatial limitations, which are also more influenced by regional characteristics and exogenous variables. In addition, there still remains a large number of events for which reliable models in the context of event attribution do not yet exist.[178] But it is not only the area of specific event attribution that regularly encounters specific, field-immanent obstacles. Also studies in the area of source attribution are regularly confronted and deal with uncertainties due to their strong dependence on documentary evidence, for it is precisely the documentary evidence that may well be influenced by normative, political and socio-economic factors. This can lead to distorted results, which, when utilised, result in an increased uncertainty variable.

As noted above, attribution science is still a relatively new area of climate science. However, this should not be taken as a reason to deny the legitimacy of the results obtained. With the aspiration of general climate science and the increasing public, as well as political attention to the impacts of climate change, which in turn enhances the funding of scientific research, gaps in data sets are being filled more and more each year. Attribution science is further increasingly capable of linking climate

[174] See here again ibid. 73–74.

[175] See for more detail on the effect of aerosols Sect. 2.1.1.

[176] Burger et al. (2020), p. 74; Lloyd and Shepherd (2021), p. 6.

[177] The vulnerability of a population is particularly evident in the climate claims of indigenous peoples and other minorities.

[178] Further highlighting that, see Minnerop and Otto (2020).

change drivers, sources and impacts in a reliable and resilient manner.[179] Increased publications, transparency and extensive peer review also significantly add to the acceptance and, thus, the weight and legitimacy of the results in this field of research.

3.3.2 Law-Inherent Obstacles to Finding Climatic Causation

3.3.2.1 Delimiting Climatic Causation

Causal relationships within climate change litigation do not immediately imply the existence of climate change as a component of the causal chain per se. Based on a rather broad understanding of climate change litigation, the qualification of the lawsuit as such may also result from other causal-independent reasons.[180] This is, of course, in no way reproachable, but is intrinsic to the great diversity of climate change-related claims. For the purpose and function of this thesis, however, some limitations have to be made. The starting point for the specific discussion of causation within climate change litigation are the particular demands that climate change places on the establishment of causation. This, however, presupposes that climate change or its underlying effects are also an essential part of the causal chain. The specific form and manner in which this takes place can be very diverse. Whether the reference relates to climate change itself, a cause of climate change or an impact and effect of climate change is immaterial, as long as the causal chain contains a climate-relevant link at some point.

The lack of a climate-related link in the causal chain and the accompanying problems are particularly apparent in criminal proceedings. At the forefront of this are cases against demonstrators in the context of climate protests. These lawsuits can in principle be classified as climate change litigation. However, the causal chain is often completely independent of climate change, as the relationship is based solely on the behavior of the demonstrators and the obstruction of traffic, coercion or damage to property caused by them.[181] In the case of *R v. Brown* for example, the necessary causal chain that the Court had to establish was between Mr Brown's action of trespassing and gluing himself on top of an aircraft at the London City Airport and the offence of public nuisance.[182] The causal chain was thus free of any reference to climate change, as only the context in which the offence occurred and

---

[179] For a selection of climate attribution studies see e.g. Mergili et al. (2020); Scott et al. (2004); Vautard et al. (2020).

[180] See for the definition of climate change litigation Sect. 2.2.1.

[181] See e.g. Court of Appeal (Criminal Division), England and Wales, 14 January 2022 – [2022] EWCA Crim 6, *R. v Brown (Extinction Rebellion protest, London City Airport)*, Maidstone Crown Court, n/a – T20080116, 8, *The Kingsnorth Six Trial.*

[182] Crown Court at Southwark, 28 July 2021 – n/a, *R v. Brown (Extinction Rebellion protest, London City Airport)*, Court of Appeal (Criminal Division), England and Wales, 14 January 2022 – [2022] EWCA Crim 6, *R. v Brown (Extinction Rebellion protest, London City Airport).*

the motivation of the demonstrator led to the case being defined as a climate change dispute. The same applies to permitting procedures for mines or other environmental or climate-related infrastructure such as wind farms. Here, too, special attention must be paid to distinguishing between climatic causation and causation independent of climate change.

In the following thesis, the discussion of causal relations in climate change litigation will focus exclusively on causal chains that entail a climate change relevant link. As has been previously discussed, the obstacles that the establishment of causation in climate change litigation face are exclusively bound to climate change being part of the causal chain itself. Causal chains that are independent of climate change are, therefore, neither part of the following analysis, nor are they generally considered in the following remarks on the establishment of factual and normative causation. Causal chains that entail a climate change reference are thus also occasionally referred to as climatic causation.

3.3.2.2 Minimal Contributions and the 'Drop-in-the-Ocean Argument'

Anthropogenic climate change is the result of many different actions and omissions by various actors, all of which have contributed to the rise in the Earth's temperature but none of which has caused climate change alone. Climate change is rooted in a combination of a conglomerate of different factors and is, therefore, a multi-causer problem. However, the collective involvement of a large group of different actors minimises the size of the individual contributions, making them appear relatively small when considered individually. This even holds true when one adds up the entire carbon emission of a single country, as the percentage of that country's contribution to the overall climate change problem may still be less than 1%.[183] The situation becomes even more complex when the contributions of private actors are also taken into account.[184] The matter has particularly gained attention concerning the effectiveness of mitigation measures, where it has found its way into the climate debate, both in the literature and in climate litigation itself. Especially in the latter is the negligible size of particular contributions frequently employed as a rebuttal to climate-related assertions in climate change lawsuits.[185] This respective argument has ultimately manifested itself in the growing debate as

[183]Countries with less than 1% share of global CO_2 emissions in 2021 are e.g. Norway (0.11%), Azerbaijan (0.10%), New Zealand (0.09%), Bolivia (0.06%), Ghana (0.06%). Data drawn from Ritchie et al. (2024).

[184]Although studies have shown that about 90 corporations account for nearly 63% of overall CO_2eq between 1751 and 2010, see Heede (2014a, b).

[185]Court of Appeal of Alberta, 24 February 2020 – 2020 ABCA 74, *In the Matter of the Greenhouse Gas Pollution Pricing Act*, paras 851–852, Land Court of Queensland, 25 November 2022 – [2022] QLC 21, *Waratah Coal Pty Ltd v. Youth Verdict Ltd & Ors (No 6)*, para 1316.

the *'drop-in-the-ocean'* argument. According to this argument, an individual's contribution is so small, only a 'drop', that it is of irrelevance in the aggregate of all anthropogenic emissions 'in the ocean'. Due to the allegedly negligible size of the contribution in the context of overall climate change, some argued that it would not be fair, nor justified, to be held responsible, even partially, for it.[186]

Another factor to consider in regard to the drop-in-the-ocean argument is the notion of causation inherent in it. This pertains more to the normative side of causation in the law than to its factual account.[187] In fact, even minimal contributions can be factually causal for the outcome of an event. The factual relation is independent of the size and the scope of a contribution. The difficulty, nevertheless, lies in two places. The first obstacle pertains to the normative component that was already previously referred to. The second obstacle, moreover, relates to the factual component of causation, which requires the transfer and the conversion of the factual into a factual but legally applicable causation doctrine.[188] As the particular contribution cannot be held entirely accountable for the onset of climate change and its repercussions and does not cause climate change on its own, the law considers this scenario to fall into the category of concurrent and cumulative causation. This relates to the fact that the resultant impact is the culmination of numerous factors and contributions acting in conjunction. Attaining a comprehensive factual causal doctrine in the law that corresponds to cumulative causation and minimal contributions still poses a complex task.[189]

Nevertheless, it is the second step of the normative causation test, that faces considerable challenges in light of minimal contributions. The main point of contention is that these contributions lack the necessary moral blameworthiness and unlawfulness element that would typically prevent causation from being established in a legal context.[190] Applying criteria of fairness, reasonableness and justice, this is certainly true for the most trivial of actions. Consider, for example, the act of buying a banana. While it may appear to be a straightforward transaction, the purchase of bananas is associated with heightened levels of emissions in the atmosphere, which stem from the involved processes of intensive cultivation, pesticide application, air and sea transportation, storage, and trade. When examining the concept of normative causation in light of minimal contributions, it is further necessary to consider the mere matter of attribution. Namely, who ought to be deemed responsible for the emissions? Is it the consumer, the producer, or the transporter? Should normative causation further encompass everyday actions such as the purchase of a banana or solely pertain to significant emissions?

---

[186] Land Court of Queensland, 25 November 2022 – [2022] QLC 21, *Waratah Coal Pty Ltd v. Youth Verdict Ltd & Ors (No 6)*, para 1316, Court of Appeal of Alberta, 24 February 2020 – 2020 ABCA 74, *In the Matter of the Greenhouse Gas Pollution Pricing Act*, paras 851–852.

[187] See for the normative side of causation in the law Sect. 5.4.

[188] This is also where the distinction between multi- and mono-causal approaches manifests itself.

[189] See also for a multi-causal approach Chap. 4.

[190] See for the normative side of causation in regard to the materiality of a contribution Sect. 5.4.

Finally, the above has shown that considerations of scope and scale are relevant both in relation to the factual doctrines of causation but even more so in relation to the normative component of causation. However, recent case law has shown that courts frequently tend to reject the application of the drop-in-the-ocean argument, especially concerning claims raised against states.[191] How, ultimately, the substance and materiality influence the normative account of causation in the law will be discussed at a later point in this book.[192]

3.3.2.3 The Temporal Sphere of Causing Climate Change: Historical and Future Emissions

The tremendous impact of climate change and its current effects have not occurred out of the blue. Climate change is a slow and gradual process that has been taking place for several decades now, initiated with the substantial rise in anthropogenic greenhouse gas emissions during the industrial era. Climate change is, therefore, embossed by a temporal sphere, which also transpires to the causal conception that is applied in climate claims. The temporal component of climate change becomes of relevance in climatic causation within three different accounts. Within the factual, it concerns the length of the causal chain; within the normative, the question of fair and equitable treatment; and within the procedural, the question of provability.

Causation, in the factual, naturalistic sense, is independent of time and lacks a temporal component. It is immaterial to the determination of factual causation when exactly something happened.[193] However, it is not the time itself that constitutes difficulties when considering factual causation, it is more so the effects that the passing of a longer period of time has on the causal chain itself. Humankind has always emitted greenhouse gases but it really started to do so excessively at the beginning of the industrial era, leading to a growing imbalance in the climate system. Finding causation between a climate-damaging behaviour that has been conducted a long time ago or over a long period of time resumes into an extensive causal chain with a lot of different, singular steps and a multitude of different possible intervening factors that have to be considered when approaching causation in its original factual state. Nevertheless, time has no bearing on whether or not there is an actual causal

[191] See for rejection e.g. Germany Federal Constitutional Court, 24 March 2021 – 1 BvR 2656/18 – 1 BvR 78/20 – 1 BvR 96/20 – 1 BvR 288/20, *Neubauer et al. v. Germany*, para 202, Land and Environment Court New South Wales, 18 October 2021 – [2021] NSWLEC 110, *Mullaley Gas and Pipeline Accord Inc v. Santos NSW (Eastern) Pty Ltd*, para 66, Prague Municipal Court, 15 June 2022 – 14A 101/2021, *Klimatická žaloba ČR v. Czech Republic*, para 326, Peel (2011), pp. 16–17; Schirmer (2021), p. 1104.

[192] See Sect. 5.4.

[193] However, the temporal sphere may become relevant in the context of factual causation in law if it is intended to create a means of bringing legal doctrines of factual causation closer to actual causation. See e.g. the strategy of factual concretization that also entails a timely component, see Sect. 4.2.3.

link. What matters is how the climatic causal chain can be reconstructed and made comprehensible.

Closely related to the extensive causal chain is the difficulty of proving the factual causal relata. Given the extensive duration that such a chain may cover, proving whether there is a causal link between the alleged behaviour and the resulting outcome can become a highly challenging endeavour. Determining emissions from 100 years ago is a daunting task due to the complex natural processes involved in climate. The intricate interplay of factors such as the thermal inertia and emission sinks makes it extremely challenging to trace the causal chain accurately and respectively to provide sufficient proof.

The third issue that relates to the temporal sphere of causing climate change is its normative component. More so known under the term 'historical emissions', scholars have discussed quite extensively how to treat climate-influencing behaviour that was conducted a long time ago. The discussion about historic emissions most dominantly refers to the liability of developed states, which have benefited greatly from the emission of greenhouse gases in contrast to most of the developing states. Criteria such as corrective and distributive justice come into play here.[194] The same applies to future obligations. Just recently has the German Federal Constitutional Court ruled in *Neubauer v. Germany* that it is unfair to shift the bulk of the burden of reducing emissions to a future scenario, and thus to burden future generations, in order to meet the 1.5 °C target posed by the Paris Agreement.[195] Such considerations find their application in the area of normative causation.[196] Particularly in the case of historical emissions, the question arises as to whether it is fair and just to establish causation in law when the actual causer was unaware of the impact of his action.[197]

3.3.2.4 Negative Versus Positive Obligations

The distinction between negative and positive obligations is particularly important in the national and international human rights framework and regarding overall fundamental and constitutional rights. It has a particular impact on the construction of the causal chain in the context of climate change.[198] The distinction between negative and positive obligations is hereby closely related to the previously mentioned issue of minimal contributions, the drop-in-the-ocean argument and the associated problem of cumulative causation that dominates causal chains within climate claims. While concurrent causes of climate change must be included and taken into account in the assessment of the causal chain in the case of negative obligations and can

---

[194] See for more elaborations on the accounts of climate justice Sect. 5.2.3.

[195] Germany Federal Constitutional Court, 24 March 2021 – 1 BvR 2656/18 – 1 BvR 78/20 – 1 BvR 96/20 – 1 BvR 288/20, *Neubauer et al. v. Germany*.

[196] See in this regard again Chap. 5.

[197] See for the requirement of foreseeability Sect. 5.3.

[198] See for the general distinction Sect. 3.2.3.1.

easily lead to the negation of a strict causal chain if only because of the considerable difficulties of proof, cumulative factors, in particular, are of little importance in the case of positive obligations. Within the negative dimension of climate change-related human rights claims, the standard case consists of a human rights violation caused by the state's contribution to climate change or a specific climate change-based event (such as extreme weather events). However, the fact that the specific contribution is causal for the specific violation, in light of many other contributions to climate change, poses increased problems, at least in the context of its provability. The existence of an obligation to protect, nevertheless, obliges the state to take all relevant measures to protect the specific right despite the possible contributions of others.[199] If the distinction between negative and positive obligations is broken down to the causal chain, it becomes clear that the chain is significantly shorter for positive obligations than for negative obligations. In the case of positive obligations, the causal chain to be established consists only of proving that climate change or its consequences, such as extreme weather events, have led to a human rights violation.[200] Based on the numerical model of an exemplary climatic causal chain, this would constitute a causal relatum between T and I_S (T-I_S). For negative obligations, however, it is furthermore necessary to establish a causal link between the state's actions and climate change as such (B_S-T-I_S). Yet, it is precisely the link between B_S and T that poses significant problems in the context of cumulative causation and multiple contributions to climate claims. In contrast to the discussion of causation under negative obligations, problems of cumulative causation are, therefore, highly irrelevant under positive obligations. On a normative causal level, there is hardly any difference between the two dimensions.

The fact that it is much easier to establish causation, and thus a breach of positive obligations, in the context of climate claims than in relation to negative obligations was also evident in the *Urgenda* decision, where the Court relied heavily on the positive dimension of the relevant rights.[201] Further climate claims show a similar strategy, with plaintiffs relying more and more on positive rather than on negative obligations, which further enhances the greening of the provisions pleaded for.[202]

[199] A positive obligation may include, for example, the monitoring of flood risks and the control of highly polluting industries, see Braig and Panov (2020). Hereby citing the case European Court of Human Rights, 28 February 2012 – 17423/05, 20534/05, 20678/05, 23263/05, 24283/05, 35673/05, *Kolyadenko et al. v. Russia*. Also in regard to the jurisprudence of the ECtHR, see Kahl (2022), p. 166.

[200] See also Braig and Panov (2020), pp. 287–290; Kahl (2022), p. 166.

[201] The Hague District Court, 24 June 2015 – C/09/456689/HA ZA 13-1396, *Urgenda Foundation v. The State of the Netherlands*, The Hague Court of Appeal, 9 October 2018 – 200.178.245/01, *Urgenda Foundation v. The State of the Netherlands*, Supreme Court of the Netherlands, 20 December 2019 – 19/00135, *Urgenda Foundation v. The State of The Netherlands*.

[202] See e.g. United Nations Human Rights Committee, 22 September 2022 – CCPR/C/135/D/3624/2019, *Daniel Billy et al. v. Australia (Torres Strait Islanders Petition)*.

3.3.3 *Connecting Law and Science in Climatic Causation*

Attribution science plays a fundamental role in establishing and ultimately proving causation in law. Scientific results are to be used not only at the level of factual causation but also in establishing normative causation. The latter concerns, in particular, the question of the materiality of the contribution in question, as well as the proximity required in some legal systems.[203] Scientific results can also provide information on intervening factors.[204] The main benefit, however, lies in the use of scientific results in the context of factual causation. Since factual causation in law also aims at the best possible representation of the actual, natural truth, the use of scientific results is obvious. This is done in the context of source attribution, in particular, through the inclusion of documentary evidence in the relevant legal proceedings.[205] Yet, the integration of scientific studies is complicated by several factors. On the one hand, this is due to the mere nature of the causal chain to be proven (Sect. 3.3.3.1); on the other hand, however, the scientific and legal, or at least causal, determination and reproduction of results also differ to a large extent (Sect. 3.3.3.2). Another challenge lies in the demands that legal matters place on scientific studies (Sect. 3.3.3.3). This relates to the temporal and spatial limitation of the scenarios to be considered but also to the possible additional exogenous factors that may have contributed to the outcome in question.

3.3.3.1 The Nature of Climatic Causal Chains

A special peculiarity of causal attribution in climate-related litigation is the complexity of the causal chain, which has to be factually established in accordance with and based on strong scientific findings. Natural processes are not linear. Rather, they are conditioned and influenced by numerous different climate-inherent and exogenous factors which, even with the current state of science, can hardly be fully and comprehensively fathomed and determined. While some of those 'external' factors only influence the outcome in question, some might even be able to have caused the outcome alone. Such additional factors are classified in law as alternative causes and constitute a long-standing and well-known problem in legal epistemology. Due to the complexity of climatic causal chains and scientific processes in general, such challenges to the legal inquiry are also relatively common in establishing climatic causation.

One of the main factors that was considered to pose an alternative cause was the natural variability of the Earth's climate itself. That the climate has changed over the millennia, even in the absence of an anthropogenic forcing, is undisputed.[206] In law,

[203] See for the issue of materiality Sect. 5.4. For the proximity cause doctrine Sect. 5.7.

[204] See for intervening causes Sect. 5.5.

[205] Mikhailova et al. (2022), pp. 12–13.

[206] For further explanation of the Milanovich Cycle and the different climate zones, see Sect. 2.1.1.

this fact was especially used under the so-called '*force majeur*' provision in the first generation of climate litigation to argue that humans per se have not been the cause of today's climate change.[207] However, this should not be confused with climate and weather variability in the context of extreme weather and climate events. Particularly in the field of event attribution, the measurement and quantification of such variability still plays an important role. Whereas climate and weather variability in the context of extreme weather events only applies to short periods of time and considers that weather extremes could occur without the influence of anthropogenic climate change, the force majeure argument aims to dismiss anthropogenic climate change as a whole. Based on today's scientific knowledge, negating the anthropogenic influence on the general climate system and its change from a scientific point of view is no longer tenable. With the development of climate change litigation, new approaches to such litigation and greater reliance on scientific evidence, the force majeure argument has lost much of its relevance in the law, as well.[208] However, as already briefly addressed, the Earth's climate variability still comes into play concerning more specific climate change effects and impacts. It has also previously been shown that natural and climate variability still is of great importance in models and studies of attribution science and further increases the uncertainty level inherent in the respective studies. In light of alternative causation in law, it is questioned whether, for instance, an extreme weather event or a sudden onset event was caused by climate change or whether the occurrence was entirely independent of anthropogenic drivers. Although climate science is not usually able to establish with complete certainty that human-induced climate change is occurring, it can often be shown that human influence has at least increased the likelihood of the effect materialising. How to translate such a finding into legal reasoning is not an easy task. This is even more so the case since decisions have to be made on a case-by-case basis using different scientific methodologies and data.

3.3.3.2 Scientific and Legal Fact-Finding

Climatic causation in the law is fundamentally based on the results of climate science. This especially holds true for factual causation as the first step of the causal inquiry. However, the obstacles posed by and inherent in scientific fact-finding are, by implementing those results into the legal assessment, automatically transferred to the causal inquiry in the law, as well.[209] Among the major hurdles are, for example, the lack of comparative data (notably regarding extreme weather phenomena and sudden onset events) and comprehensive methodologies.[210] At the same time,

---

[207] See in more detail on the elaboration of force majeure and climate change in public international law Dellinger (2017).

[208] Ibid.

[209] See for obstacles of attribution science Sect. 3.3.1.2.

[210] See again Minnerop and Otto (2020), p. 70.

recourse to the results of climate science also implies that the manner in which those results are obtained and displayed in science has to be processed in law accordingly. This, in particular, involves dealing with probability, confidence levels, the possibility of deviations in scientific findings and general scientific uncertainty. Those well-known factors in science do not run concurrent with legal epistemology and, therefore, increase the difficulty of transferring those results into the legal realm. The Commission on Human Rights of the Philippines, in their report on climate change, stated in that regard:

> There is a distinction between the science of event attribution and the establishment of legal causation. Event attribution is not a direct reconstruction of how each carbon contribution of an individual caused damage through climate change. Instead, it seeks to establish: (a) whether the likelihood or strength of a natural event has changed in the observational record, and (b) whether this change is consistent with the anthropogenic influence as found in one or more climate models.[211]

The Commission furthermore recommended courts to take notice of further developments in the field of climate science without addressing the question of how to tackle and ultimately bridge these methodological differences. They moreover refer to the '*fraction of attributable risk*' and highlight that this concept is often wrongly applied in law without again stating how to overcome these obstacles.[212] Nevertheless, several initiatives have started to provide additional educational resources and programs to judges to better understand the scientific background of climate change, as well as to sensibilize for the obstacles inherent in that particular matter.[213]

3.3.3.3 Judicial Demands Versus Scientific Studies

In addition to the differences in methodology and the overall manner of finding results, there are also differences between the scientific and the legal community in terms of the requirements imposed on the respective studies to ultimately make use of the findings inherent in them. This especially arises in the context of the spatial sphere of scientific results. In climate change litigation, the region and locality of the attributable event are of great importance.[214] However, the attribution of an event also requires the precise temporal and local specification of the scientific result.

[211] Commission on Human Rights of the Philippines, 6 May 2022 – CHR-NI-2016-0001, *In re Greenpeace Southeast Asia and Others*, 147. It can be assumed that the Commission did not intend to use the term 'legal' causation in the same way as in the second step of the causal inquiry, but wanted to emphasise the difference between scientific causation and causation in the law.

[212] Ibid.

[213] See e.g. just recently the cooperation between ClientEarth and the government of China, ClientEarth (2018).

[214] See in this regard especially the case of *Juliana v. United States*: United States Court of Appeals for the Ninth Circuit, 17 January 2020 – 6:15-cv-01517-AA, *Juliana v. United States*. A further explanation and assessment of the arguments put forward by the plaintiff can be found in Lloyd and Shepherd (2021).

Missing data or the inclusion of local-specific exogenous variables can lead to scientific difficulties. This is particularly the case when scientific models only allow calculation over a larger local sphere than would be necessary for their usage in the respective lawsuit. Climate change lawsuits often require a down-scaled scientific analysis, which, nonetheless, is only scarcely covered by general scientific studies. *Cho*, for this purpose, gives the example of heavy precipitation, which is usually analysed with reference to so-called grid boxes.[215] These grid boxes are often very broad, usually covering an area of 100 by 100 miles, which allows conclusions to be drawn about the rainfall for such wider region. In this grid box, however, precipitation frequencies and amounts might vary considerably, relating to specific geographical and geological factors. A specific area, therefore, might be exposed to a considerably higher precipitation rate, while others might experience less frequent and lighter rainfall. It is, thus, highly difficult to deduce any valid statements from such a general perception for a specific, smaller spatial realm. The same applies to a temporal delineation. Especially in the context of the utilization of source attribution studies, does a confinement in terms of time become of relevance. Although scientific studies are often restricted to a specific timeframe, judicial demands in terms of the time period and scientific studies often do not coincide.

Further divergence in demands and offerings does not specifically relate to the content of the relevant scientific studies but more so relate to the presentation of the results. Climate and, even more so, attribution science constitutes a complex scientific field, which for most legal practitioners, judges, and parties to the proceeding, embodies a black box in large parts. Studies of attribution science are frequently published only for a scientific community without, however, breaking down or summarizing the results for a more general readership. It is often difficult for litigants and judges to understand and evaluate the methods, models and scientific results that have been used, which on the one hand, hinders the overall awareness about specific results and studies and, on the other hand, impedes the general usage of scientific results in court even further.[216]

3.3.3.4 Finding Common Grounds

It is undoubtedly the case that climate action depends on scientific knowledge. And while some hurdles to the application of attribution studies in law do exist, most of them are surmountable. Starting with the difficulties in using scientific findings due to their challenging accessibility for legal practitioners. Significant progress has already been made in this regard through the development of so-called attribution science databases. In collecting and preparing attribution studies for climate change

[215] See Cho (2021).

[216] See also Stuart-Smith et al. (2021), pp. 13–17.

litigation, databases can provide efficient tools for litigators and courts to scientifically underlay their claims and legal questions. A comprehensive selection, for example, is provided by the Climate Attribution Database by the Sabin Center for Climate Change Law.[217] Such databases thus enhance the usability of scientific studies and greatly facilitate the implementation of scientific resources in courts. Databases, nonetheless, are not able to counter the general lack of mainly observational and spatial-specific data. Such obstacles concurrent with not yet developed models and methodology, especially in the area of event attribution, are, however, inherent problems of science, and solutions, therefore, must result and be developed by the scientific community. Still, the law can contribute to a better and facilitated implementation of yet existing results. This can be achieved, in particular, through a scientific-oriented epistemological approach, which again is better equipped to deal with exogenous factors and, respectively, alternative causation.[218] The same is true for the utilization of uncertainty, probability and confidence levels. The challenge for the law will be to learn to adapt and handle exactly such scientific accounts. Ultimately, all these factors depend on a better cooperation between the scientific and legal communities. The law must clearly communicate its demands for more effective litigation, while science must clarify the limits of the possibilities of its attribution studies. Only in this way will it be possible to adjudicate climate claims not only more effectively but also on a more factual basis.[219]

3.4 The Status Quo of Causation in Climate Change Litigation: An Empirical, Systematic and Substantive Analysis

Causation has been identified in legal scholarship to be one of the main issues and hurdles when it comes to the prospects of success of a climate change-related lawsuit. Whether this assumption is covered by actual court cases is in question in the following analysis. The overall aim of the analysis is to better understand how courts are processing, adapting and evaluating causation in light of the growing demands and hurdles posed by complex climatic processes. How and to what extent are courts encountering problems in establishing causation in the context of such claims? Are such issues specifically occurring in certain jurisdictions or fields and areas of law? And might some separate understandings of climatic causation have already emerged in climate change lawsuits?

---

[217] Sabin Center for Climate Change Law, Climate Change Litigation Databases, available at http://climatecasechart.com/ (24 Oct 2024).

[218] See in particular for a probability-based approach Sect. 4.4.

[219] See for further proposals and recommendations Stuart-Smith et al. (2021), pp. 14–15.

3.4.1 *The Methodological Interface*

3.4.1.1 Overall Parameters

The analysis itself is based on the database provided by the Sabin Center for Climate Change Law in cooperation with the Grantham Research Institute, which was then developed even further in coherence with the definition established and used in this book.[220] Encountered inconsistencies and errors in the respective database have been rectified to the best knowledge.[221] Owing to varying interpretations of climate change litigation of the Sabin Center and this book, the admission of cases might vary to some degree. However, such minor deviations are not decisive for the purpose of this analysis. Beyond the existing data and categorization provided by the database, new criteria have been introduced in the assessment as well, particularly to enrich and support the analysis and the treatment of cause-effect relationships in those judgments.[222] Absent judgments and gaps in the dataset have been filled by a diligent scouring of the pertinent legal databases of the corresponding regions and jurisdictions. In 28 cases, judgments ultimately could not be located.[223]

Court decisions and lawsuits were considered until 31 December 2022, resulting in overall 668 climate change cases stemming from 47 countries as well as further international and regional jurisdictional bodies.[224] Of the overall amount of cases,

[220] Data drawn from Sabin Center for Climate Change Law, Climate Change Litigation Databases, available at http://climatecasechart.com/ (24 Oct 2024). During the preparation of this analysis, the Grantham Research Institute still maintained its own database (Grantham Research Institute on Climate Change and the Environment, Climate Litigation Database, available at https://climate-laws.org/ (22 June 2022). This has now been merged into the Climate Change Litigation Database of the Sabin Center for Climate Change Law. For the definition of climate change litigation for the purposes of this book, see Sect. 2.2.1.

[221] Some judgments have been linked to the wrong cases, see e.g. in the case Land and Environment Court of New South Wales, 27 November 2006 – [2006] NSWLEC 720, *Gray v. Minister for Planning*. Other judgments were sometimes missing or had not been updated in the databases referred to. Some judgments were listed twice in the respective databases, see e.g. Federal Court of Australia, 25 August 2017 – [2017] FCAFC 134, *Australian Conservation Foundation Incorporated v. Minister for the Environment and Energy*.

[222] This applies in particular to the categorisation of pro- and anti-climate lawsuits, the geographical distribution in terms of socio-economic reference to the Global South and Global North, and a more detailed analysis in terms of field and areas of law.

[223] e.g. Lviv Administrative Court, 17 June 2010 – n/a, *Environment-People-Law v. Cabinet of Ministers of Ukraine and National Agency of Environmental Investments*, High Court of Gansu Province (Gansu State Grid), 28 December 2018 – Decision No. 679, *The Friends of Nature Institute v. Gansu State Grid (自然之友环境研究所诉国家电网甘肃公司案, 甘肃省高级人民法院 (2018) 甘民终679 号民事裁定书)*, Supreme Court of Spain, n/a – n/a, *Spain v. Apostolos Mangouras & Others (“Prestige” case)*.

[224] These include cases before the East African Court of Justice, the ICJ, the ICC within the Inter-American System of Human Rights, the Court of the European Union, the WTO and the International Centre for Settlement of Investment Disputes.

about 528 have already been decided, whereas 138 are still pending before courts and judicial bodies.[225] Two claims have been withdrawn.[226]

The analysis focused exclusively on the decisions rendered in the highest instance the lawsuit reached until the respective date.[227] The highest instance hereby often did not run concurrent to the last available instance of the entire judicial procedure. Excluded, however, are decisions that are solely based on procedural grounds, such as, e.g. the grant for leave of appeal or the decision of transfer to another court.[228] In lawsuits in which the decision from the higher court is still pending, the judgment of the lower court was referred to. The same was done with cases in which the appeal was allowed but not yet conducted by the parties, and the deadline of the appeal period has not yet been reached.

As a result of the diverse range of assessments and corresponding languages, it was necessary to produce translations for judgments that were published in languages other than English, Spanish, or German. Whenever feasible, official translations that were provided by the court have been used. However, in situations where no official translations were available, own translations have been created to ensure accuracy and clarity. In exceptional cases, translations provided by alternative sources—including those by NGOs and the plaintiffs themselves—were taken into consideration as well. At times, language barriers posed a challenge in carrying out an analysis. In some cases, the unavailability of dependable translations rendered it impossible to proceed with the assessment.[229]

A wide range of decisions from different jurisdictions and countries have been considered and analysed. However, climate change cases from the United States have been omitted due to the unique circumstances and different reasons surrounding these cases. The emergence of climate change litigation can be traced back to its origin in the United States, where it was largely shaped by the country's legal system.[230] However, it is important to note that the sheer volume of cases brought before American courts would pose some analytical challenges and could potentially

[225] A case is considered 'decided' if a verdict has been reached at least in the first instance. This also applies if the case is dismissed. However, purely procedural decisions are not considered as 'decided' (e.g. decisions to transfer a case to another court). The classification is made on a case-by-case basis.

[226] Federal Court of Canada, withdrawn – T-1836-16, *SkeenaWild Conservation Trust v. Government of Canada*, General Court of the European Union, withdrawn – C-121/21, *Czech Republic v. Poland (Mine de Turów)*.

[227] In cases where the highest instance made several decisions (e.g. costs and merits), all decisions were taken into account.

[228] See High Court of New Zealand, 21 October 2021 – [2021] NZCA 552, *Smith v. Fonterra Co-Operative Group Limited*.

[229] E.g. in the case Osaka High Court, 26 April 2022 – 平成30(行ウ)184; 令和3年(行コ)第46号 (second judgment), *Citizen's Committee on the Kobe Coal-Fired Power Plant v. Japan*.

[230] See for a further historical outline Sect. 2.2.2.

lead to biased results if included in a broader global analysis.[231] First of all, including such cases would distort the results of the analysis due to the long history and the immense development of American-based climate change lawsuits. Given that the focus of the analysis rests on causation and the respective dogmas applied in recent days, cases brought before courts early on in the climate change movement would not contribute to the current debate but would warp the conclusion drawn from it and hinder a comprehensive analysis in general. This is especially the case since climate science has evolved tremendously over time, and with it, the judicial reasoning, which is based on those scientific findings. Due to the strong connection between natural sciences and causal perception in the law, approaches to causation have also considerably shifted and evolved over time. This does not imply that cases brought before courts in the United States have been left out entirely in this book. Throughout the book, reference will be made on various points to judgments and decisions pursued in the United States. However, they haven't been taken into account in the dataset of the following analysis itself.

3.4.1.2 Contextual Analysis and Subject of Research

The overall analysis of the climate change decisions consisted mainly out of two parts. The first step, hereby, involved an empirical approach by analysing and dissecting the decisions based on different causation-related keywords.[232] This was done in full awareness of the extensive weaknesses of relying exclusively on a terminological-based approach, which is why the frame of reference, linguistic peculiarities and the substance of the decisions have been taken into account as well.[233] Special emphasis was placed on the context of the linguistic utility per se, given that causation-related terminology is also often used in a non-causal way. Concurrently and in line with the causal limitation undertaken earlier in this chapter, only decisions that entail a reference to climate change within their causal chain and thus fall into the category of climatic causation, were considered.[234]

---

[231] Obviously, the omission of the American cases has some impact on both the overall findings and the specific results of the analysis. It is difficult to foresee the impact beyond the geographical distribution of claims. However, a shift in the results is likely, particularly with regard to the rejection of specific causation. Due to the relatively large number of earlier cases, a significantly higher rejection rate of climatic causation seems likely. Furthermore, this could also have an impact on the grouping of causal arguments, in particular an increase in the use of the drop-in-the-ocean argument.

[232] This included among others eng: 'causation/causation', 'cause', 'causal', 'link'; spa: 'causalidad', 'causal', 'relación'; fra: 'causalité'; por: 'causalidade', 'causa', 'causal', 'nexo'; nl: 'causaliteit', 'causaal', 'causaal verband'; ind. 'Kausalitas', 'sebab-akibat', 'hubungan kausalitas'; deu: 'Kausalität', 'kausal', 'verursachen'.

[233] Using exclusively terminological methods Setzer and Vanhala (2019).

[234] See for the delimitation to climatic causation Sect. 3.3.2.1.

In line with the overall methodology of the analysis, even in cases in which a lower court decision entailed a causal analysis, decisive in the end was the decision of the highest instance to date. As a result, despite the fact that previous courts have been involved in the assessment of causation, very few cases have been classified as not involving such respective considerations.[235] Based on this methodology, judgments have been categorized on whether they entail a causal analysis or not. Decisive, however, was only how the judges and courts themselves engaged with issues of causal relata. Mere repetitions and reiterations of the statements of parties, witnesses, experts or intervening parties have not been considered and categorized as causal perceptions per se. Nevertheless, in individual cases, exceptions were allowed for judgments in which the higher court referred to and possibly also evaluated causal assessments of the lower court. This was especially the case in lawsuits in which the applicable causal test or the treatment of causal relata was in question or subject to appeal.

The second phase then consisted out of a systematic and substantive analysis of the manner and the scope in which courts approached and handled climatic causation in the respective climate change decisions. Particular attention was paid to the distinction between general and specific causation and to the substance of the analysis.[236] In doing so, four different types of causal assessments were identified in the decisions analysed.

The first type of causal reasoning consists of judgments in which the court places a significant emphasis on the fundamental nature of causation itself. This involves the examination by the court of whether a specific statute, formal standard, or cause of action mandates the establishment of a clear and definitive cause-effect relationship.[237] The second group entails decisions and judgments dealing with the question of the right causal understanding. The court hereby elaborates on the doctrinal approach that should be applied in the current case and for the establishment of causation in general. This type of causal assessment has been commonly used when courts encounter difficulties in establishing causation on the basis of conventional concepts such as counterfactual causation. It has also been at issue in cases in which the plaintiffs have fallen back on just recently emerged and largely case law grown concepts of causation or have been trying to implement models from other areas of law into climate considerations. The third type of cases are based on evaluating the necessary requirements set out by the chosen causal approach. This involves identifying the specific conditions and prerequisites that are demanded in order to successfully apply the causal concept. It further concerns possible distinctions between the application in regard to positive doings and omissions. Such

---

[235]Multicompetent Chamber of the Provincial Court of Justice of Sucumbíos, 29 July 2021 – 21201202000170, *Herrera Carrion et al. v. Ministry of the Environment et al. (Caso Mecheros)*.

[236]For a differentiation between general and specific climatic causation see here Sects. 3.4.3.3.2 and 3.4.3.3.3.

[237]This category strongly concurs with the first and second group of causal inquiries existent in the law, see Sect. 3.1.3.

assessments have especially been pertinent in lawsuits in which either party pursues the application of a newer model of causation in which the requirements concerning the composition of the relevant link could not be ascertained on a long-standing judicial tradition and case law. The fourth and probably the most obvious notion of causal consideration rests in the assessment of the court whether there was a causal link or causation in general or not. This assessment can be carried out through the standard judicial review process, even if it was not explicitly brought up by the parties involved.

3.4.2 Overall Findings

In the course of the analysis, over 668 climate change cases have been examined. The overwhelming majority of these cases, around 75.9%, are concerned with mitigating climate change in general and its specific effects and are, therefore, classified as mitigation cases.[238] The second largest group is made up of actions seeking adaptation measures to climate change. Requiring the defendant to either provide financial support or take measures to protect vulnerable groups from the negative effects of climate change, 18.9% of cases involve or are entirely based on such claims.[239] Loss and damage cases (around 2.9%) and disaster risk management cases (around 2.3%) round off the overall climate change litigation picture. As climate and weather extremes occur more frequently, it is likely that demands for reparation and compensation for climate-related damages will gradually increase over time.[240] In terms of geographical allocation, Australia and the United Kingdom have been heavily involved in climate change litigation and have issued the most climate change judgments, to date.[241]

[238] In the course of the analysis, results are truncated to one decimal place and rounded up or down accordingly.

[239] See as a reference for a successful adaptation case United Nations Human Rights Committee, 22 September 2022 – CCPR/C/135/D/3624/2019, *Daniel Billy et al. v. Australia (Torres Strait Islanders Petition).*

[240] 1% of cases could not be classified at all. These include in particular criminal cases and cases concerning contractual obligations, see e.g. Court of Appeal (Criminal Division), England and Wales, 14 January 2022 – [2022] EWCA Crim 6, *R. v Brown (Extinction Rebellion protest, London City Airport).* Court of Justice of the State of São Paulo, 7 October 2021 – 1072768-63.2021.8.26.0100, *Carbonext Tecnologia em Soluções Ambientais Ltda. v. Amazon Imóveis (Voluntary Carbon Market).*

[241] In total, Australia recorded 127 cases, the United Kingdom 88, the statement is relative to the absence of cases from the United States of America; For further geographical analysis, but also for an analysis of climate change litigation beyond its geographical distribution, see Sect. 2.2.2. Further analysis was also provided by e.g. Grantham Research Institute (2021).

3.4.3 *Causation in Climate Change Decisions and Judgments*

The second phase of the substantial analysis of climate change decisions focused, in particular, on three crucial aspects of causal approaches. Firstly, particular attention was paid to the number of judgments, decisions and orders which actually contained causal considerations (Sect. 3.4.3.1). Secondly, the geographical distribution and the area of law in which causal considerations did and did not play a role in the respective judgments were considered (Sect. 3.4.3.2). Finally, and certainly most relevant for the drawing of systematic and substantial conclusions from this analysis, the structure of the arguments used by the courts to describe and consider causal relationships was assessed (Sect. 3.4.3.3). This included an evaluation of the considerations of causal reasoning provided by the courts on the basis of the four notions of causation introduced earlier. Further attention was paid to the numerical distribution and the framework in which courts applied the relevant assessments, as well as to the distinction between general and specific causation. Final emphasis was then placed on the handling of cumulative causation, which also included an assessment of the reasoning in light of minimal contributions and the drop-in-the-ocean argument.

3.4.3.1 The Marginal Existence of Causal Considerations

Legal scholars have often identified causation as one of the key hurdles and difficulties in climate litigation.[242] Interestingly, after conducting the analysis, it was discovered that a significantly small number of court cases actually delved into the matter of causation. In fact, out of the entire pool of cases that were scrutinized, only 48 were found to have concrete evidence of such considerations being taken into account. This amounts to approximately 7.2% of all climate change litigation.[243] A similar result was obtained by including only cases that have already been decided by the respective courts and judicial bodies. With a slight increase, the proportion of cases rose to around 9.1%. The fact that the percentage of lawsuits, in contrast to the general perception, is rather low, depends on the interplay of a large number of different factors.

One of the most obvious explanations relies on the assumption that, contrary to the current and prevailing legal opinion, causation does not pose a significant obstacle to climate change claims overall. However, this conclusion is not only at

---

[242] See Burger and Metzger (2020), p. 44, Office of the United Nations High Commissioner for Human Rights (2009), para 70. Also discussed in US Court of Appeals for the 5th Circuit, 28 May 2010 – 07-60756, *Ned Comer et al. v. Murphy Oil USA, Inc., et al.*, Memorandum opinion and order, 35, US District Court for the Northern District of California, 30 September 2009 – 4:08-cv-01138-SBA, *Native Village of Kivalina v. ExxonMobil Corp.*, paras 17–19.

[243] For further information of the respective cases see Annex II.

odds with the above explanations but also, to a large extent, with the following results of this analysis.[244]

It is pertinent that not all legal disputes before courts call for causal considerations as such. In some cases, considering causation may be superfluous. This is particularly the case in disputes in which causation is either not at issue or the parties do not disagree about its establishment, dogmatic structure or occurrence. In such cases, the courts are not obliged, nor do they need to address the causal relationships surrounding such cases. It is sufficient that they simply assume the existence of such causal relations. Moreover, the substance of the claim, its admissibility or the subject matter of the action may not require causation at all. On the face of it, some areas of law, especially public law, may appear to be subject to lower, or perhaps no, causation requirements. However, such an assessment does not correspond to the truth, as the analysis ultimately shows.[245] The area of law, nevertheless, still gains relevance and influences the outcome of the analysis in another way. The difference between several areas of law corresponds closely to the overall distribution of climate claims. The area that is most explicitly and by far the most familiar with causation is the realm of tort and liability law. Although liability claims can arise in the public sector as well, the bulk of liability cases is located in the area of private law. The weakness of the analysis in this respect is based on the availability of the respective judgments and the publicity of those lawsuits in general. Lawsuits in the private sector, and even more so the judgments handed down in it, are hardly the focus of public attention and, therefore, have largely not found their way into the databases. Even in cases in which the lawsuits have attracted public attention, the specific decision itself is mostly not accessible to the public. The same is valid for criminal lawsuits in which the qualification of the claim as a climate change lawsuit is already problematic.[246] Exceptions are precedents, which were deliberately brought to public attention by the plaintiffs themselves and thus also found their way into the databases.[247]

Notwithstanding the foregoing elaborations, the actual cause of action and the intention of the plaintiff may also determine the need for an in-depth causation analysis. For example, in the *Urgenda* decision, the Court of Appeal stated that *"[...] (the proceeding in question) concern a claim for imposing an order and not a claim for damages, so that causation only plays a limited role."*[248] While this may

[244] See in this regard especially Sect. 3.4.3.3.

[245] See in this regard especially Sect. 3.4.3.3.

[246] One exception is the legal action taken in the context of the climate protests, see e.g. Maidstone Crown Court, n/a – T20080116, 8, *The Kingsnorth Six Trial.* One case in which the judgment was actually made available was the decision in Court of Appeal (Criminal Division), England and Wales, 14 January 2022 – [2022] EWCA Crim 6, *R. v Brown (Extinction Rebellion protest, London City Airport).*

[247] E.g. Essen Regional Court, 15 December 2016 – 2 O 285/15, *Luciano Lliuya v. RWE AG*, Higher Regional Court Hamm, pending – 5 U 15/17, *Luciano Lliuya v. RWE AG.*

[248] The Hague Court of Appeal, 9 October 2018 – 200.178.245/01, *Urgenda Foundation v. The State of the Netherlands*, para 64.

be true for the case in question, the analysis once again has shown that it is not possible to attribute general validity to this statement.[249]

Another, albeit highly hypothetical, reason rests in the difficulty of establishing causation per se. The analysis carried out has shown that courts and judges only deal with the existence of causation in very few cases in an explicit and dogmatically coherent way. The considerable complexity, the strong link with climate science and the lack of expertise in assessing highly complex atmospheric processes frequently lead to an inconsistent and incoherent approach, ultimately even to the complete omission of any causal consideration. This aspect is supported by the numerous references to IPCC findings in a wide range of different judgements.[250] Without discussing or even addressing the legal causal link, reference is made to the IPCC's findings on scientific relata to illustrate the existence of a factual link.

3.4.3.2 The Factual and Formalistic Analysis

In the following, the decisions in which courts engage with causation are examined in terms of their factual and formalistic, i.e. external, characteristics. The analysis focuses on the extent to which certain jurisdictions, areas of law or causes of action demonstrate a more developed assessment of cause-effect relationships than others.

3.4.3.2.1 The Geographical Allocation

As briefly mentioned previously, Australia provides by far the largest amount of climate change decisions in which judges considered climatic causation. With almost 25% of all cases, Australia accounts for exactly 1/4 of the relevant litigation. This result is consistent with the total number of Australian cases classified as climate change litigation and reflects well the proportion within the total number of cases assessed. The reason for the high number of cases before Australian courts lies in the long history of Australian environmental and climate change jurisprudence, reinforced by the existence and concurrently the decisions of specific environmental tribunals.[251] In addition, the Australian economy is heavily dependent on the extraction of fossil fuels, including coal, which is generally considered to be very emission-intensive, especially when one also takes into account scope 3 emissions. With resources playing such a large role in Australia's economy and society, it is not

---

[249] See in this regard especially Sect. 3.4.3.3.

[250] See among others Germany Federal Constitutional Court, 24 March 2021 – 1 BvR 2656/18 – 1 BvR 78/20 – 1 BvR 96/20 – 1 BvR 288/20, *Neubauer et al. v. Germany*, inter alia para 210, Prague Municipal Court, 15 June 2022 – 14A 101/2021, *Klimatická žaloba ČR v. Czech Republic*, inter alia para 199.

[251] See e.g. the Land and Environment Court of New South Wales available at www.lec.justice.nsw.gov.au (17 May 2022), or the Environment Court of New Zealand available at https://environmentcourt.govt.nz/ (17 May 2022).

surprising that most of the cases reviewed in this context are cases challenging mining approvals or coal mines in general, as well as cases challenging the conduct of environmental impact assessments in relation to the approval process.[252] Although the United Kingdom ranks right behind Australia in terms of the total number of cases brought before courts, in terms of the causal considerations entailed in the final reasonings, decisions from the United Kingdom play only a minor role. They account for 6.3% of the total number of cases. The same is true of decisions from New Zealand and Germany. However, twice as many cases are provided by international judicial and quasi-judicial bodies (11.8%), with Indonesia ranking right behind with around 10.4%. Other decisions originate from jurisdictions such as the Netherlands, France, the Philippines, Norway, Mexico, the Czech Republic, Brazil and the European Union.

While the overall geographical distribution of the number of decisions entailing assessments of causation is not surprising, the result is even more telling when the total number of climate decisions in one jurisdiction is compared to the number of decisions with causal considerations.

The chart in Fig. 3.2 shows the relation between the total number of climate decisions and the number of decisions in which the court considered climatic causation. The graph hereby depicts the percentage of overall climate claims that contain causal assessments in individual jurisdictions. It turns out that the highest percentage of decisions with causal considerations are not found in jurisdictions with the most climate claims per se. While in Australia, only about 9.4% of climate decisions entail causal assessments, the number is even lower in the United Kingdom, with only about 3.4% of the cases. On the other side, however, in Colombia (about 33.3%), Indonesia (41.7%), and the Philippines (about 66.7%), climate decisions do encounter causal considerations to a great extent. The countries most likely to address causality in their climate decisions, with the exception of Brazil, are those in the Global South. Given that climate decisions from the Global North still outnumber those from the Global South, and that climate litigation in the Global South is rapidly catching up and gaining momentum, it will be interesting to see how this outcome evolves in the coming years.[253]

The reasons for the still persisting large number of cases from the Global North in relation to cases from the Global South are versatile. With the climate litigation movement starting in the United States, spreading to Australia and the United Kingdom before slowly expanding to other European countries, plaintiffs of the Global South started relatively late to bring climate change lawsuits before their

[252]E.g. New South Wales Land and Environment Court, 8. February 2019 – [2019] NSWLEC 7, *Gloucester Resources Limited v. Minister for Planning*, Land and Environment Court of New South Wales, 27 November 2006 – [2006] NSWLEC 720, *Gray v. Minister for Planning*, Federal Court of Australia, 25 August 2017 – [2017] FCAFC 134, *Australian Conservation Foundation Incorporated v. Minister for the Environment and Energy*.

[253]In terms of judgments involving causal considerations, about 62.5% were handed down in the Global North, about 22.9% in the Global South and about 14.6% in regional and international judicial and quasi-judicial bodies.

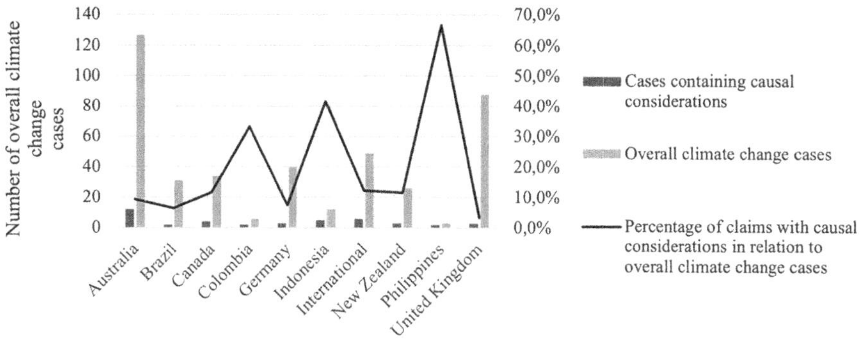

Fig. 3.2 Model of the number of climate cases relative to the entailed causal reasoning (Reference to the data included can be found in the Appendix. Jurisdictions in which no or only one causal climate change decision could be found have been excluded from the graph. This applies in particular to Czech Republic, France, the European Union, Mexico, the Netherlands and Norway.)

respective courts.[254] Although climate change will affect countries in the Global South unproportionable high, most of the climate change cases of the Global South are still pending.[255] Therefore, climate change litigation can still be seen as a phenomenon of the Global North, which also has an impact on the assessment of causation. However, due to the broad and increasing number of lawsuits pending before courts of the Global South, one can expect a shift in the distribution of cases in the North–South divide in the near future. A further reason for the low number of cases from the Global South and, respectively, also the lower number of decisions containing causal considerations persist out of structural reasons. Although scholars from the Global North are increasingly aware and receptive to legal scholarship originating in the Global South, the law of countries of the Global South, which is often fundamentally more progressive in light of environmental matters than it is in countries of the Global North, is still often overlooked and disregarded by the legal realm of Global North jurisdictions. Concurrently, the relevant databases have just recently begun to increasingly focus on countries and jurisdictions of the Global South. It is consequently very likely that quite a large number of lawsuits and climate decisions from jurisdictions of the Global South have not been included in the databases yet.

Jurisdiction-wise, common law countries slightly dominate the causal debate on climatic causation with about 45.8% of the cases, while civil law countries account

[254] Exceptions in this regard are e.g. Federal Court of Nigeria, 30 November 2005 – FHC/B/CS/53/05, *Gbemre v. Shell Petroleum Development Company of Nigeria Ltd. and Others*, Superior Court of Justice, Brazil, 2 December 2009 – 650.728 – SC (2003/0221786-0), *Public Prosecutor's Office v. H Carlos Schneider S/A Comércio e Industria & Others*.

[255] Most SIDS reside in the Global South. See Vanuatu's global campaign, which led to Resolution 77/276 on the request for an advisory opinion of the International Court of Justice on the obligations of States in respect of climate change, Vanuatu ICJ Initiative (2023).

for about 35.4% of judgments containing causal considerations.[256] 14.6% refer to regional and international judicial and quasi-judicial bodies, while about 4.1% are issued in jurisdictions that cannot be fully assigned to a particular legal tradition.[257] The reason for this slight disparity still lies in the different levels of overall climate change litigation per se, with common law countries still being at the forefront of bringing climate change issues to court. On the other hand, the common law as a legal system per se may be more flexible, open and adaptable to newer causal concepts than the civil law realm.[258] The way in which the law can be shaped by judicial reasoning in common law countries allows courts to respond more quickly and comprehensively to new challenges and developments. This observation will be elaborated on later in the analysis, but it shows that judges and courts in common law countries may be more open to discussing and transferring concepts from other areas of law and to develop newer approaches to the causal dilemma than courts of civil law countries.[259]

3.4.3.2.2 The Field and Area of Law, Response and Direction of Action

In a second step, the analysis is narrowed down from the geographical distribution of claims to a categorisation within the area of law and the direction of action. Initially, and especially based on the extensive literature on liability for climate change-induced damage and tortious acts, it was expected that tort law cases correlating with public nuisance and negligence would be the dominant area of law in which causal considerations would come into play.[260] However, the analysis shows a different picture. Only about 20.8% of the cases containing causal considerations are private law cases. This result is inevitably influenced by the fact that a large number of potential climate litigation cases in private law are not captured by the databases. The availability of private law decisions is strongly limited, given that courts do not publish their judgments in full or the parties conduct the litigation outside the public eye. Thus, unless the dispute is one in which a carbon major or other multinational is being sued, private law cases can easily fall below the radar of climate change litigation. The lacking availability most certainly does not constitute the only reason for the low amount of private law cases and does not explain why causal considerations have not been applied in the included and recorded lawsuits, as well. A further reason persists in the fact that although climate liability law has often

[256] Although Quebec also applies civil law to some extent, Canada is classified as a common law jurisdiction.

[257] This includes in particular the Philippines, which applies both common law and civil law concepts.

[258] See in this regard also Sect. 6.1.

[259] See in this regard Sect. 3.4.3.3.

[260] See for a selection of literature on climate liability law Pöttker (2014), van Dijk (2011), Haritz (2011), Kloepfer and Neugärtner (2021), Wagner and Arntz (2021), Kosolapova (2011), and Nitsch (2021).

been addressed in the scholarly debate and constitutes an interesting line of thought, claiming damages for climate change impacts on the basis of delinquent and tortious conduct has not been at the forefront in practice and in climate change litigation in general.

Nevertheless, with respect to the remaining private law cases, which include causal assessments, tort law is the dominant area of law.[261] Plaintiffs are mainly seeking monetary compensation for the risk of damage to their legal property or cultural heritage caused by climate-damaging actions or omissions. The same applies to cases in which the damage has already occurred.[262] It is the Indonesian judiciary that has been at the forefront of considering causation in private climate lawsuits, most of which involve claims for financial compensation for the deforestation of large areas of land which was cleared to make way for palm plantations.[263] It is interesting to note that most of these cases do not constitute legal disputes between two private parties but that rather the Indonesian state itself takes action against private entrepreneurs. By international standards, this is an important feature of Indonesian cases. Similar constellations hardly occur in other jurisdictions.

Dominating, however, are with 79.2% of the overall climate change lawsuits cases of public law, especially ones based in the area of administrative law (37.7%). The majority of such lawsuits are, hereby, either directed against already existing operating permits of potentially climate-damaging or at least climate-influencing projects, such as lawsuits against the operating permits of coal mines in Australia or against inadequate, deficient or non-existent environmental impact assessments by the responsible authority.[264] It is certainly true that the number of lawsuits in this sector has increased significantly, mainly due to the disproportionate number of Australian lawsuits that address precisely these kinds of issues.[265] Nevertheless,

---

[261] Cases include Essen Regional Court, 15 December 2016 – 2 O 285/15, *Luciano Lliuya v. RWE AG*, High Court of New Zealand, 21 October 2021 – [2021] NZCA 552, *Smith v. Fonterra Co-Operative Group Limited*.

[262] Cases include Essen Regional Court, 15 December 2016 – 2 O 285/15, *Luciano Lliuya v. RWE AG.*, Banjarmasin Court of Appeal, 21 February 2018 – 48/PDT/2018/PT.BJM, *Ministry of Environment and Forestry v. PT Palmina Utama*, District Court of Central Jakarta, 11 January 2021 – 445/Pdt.G/2019/PN.Jkt.Pst, *Ministry of Environment and Forestry v. PT Rambang Agro Jaya*, Palembang Court of Appeal of Indonesia, 12 February 2016 – 51/PDT/2016/PT.PLG, *Ministry of Environment and Forestry v. PT Bumi Mekar Hijau*, Supreme Court of Indonesia, 18 April 2017 – 1 PK/Pdt/2017, *Minister of Environment v. PT Kalista Alam*.

[263] Supreme Court of Indonesia, 18 April 2017 – 1 PK/Pdt/2017, *Minister of Environment v. PT Kalista Alam*, Palembang Court of Appeal of Indonesia, 12 February 2016 – 51/PDT/2016/PT. PLG, *Ministry of Environment and Forestry v. PT Bumi Mekar Hijau*, Banjarmasin Court of Appeal, 21 February 2018 – 48/PDT/2018/PT.BJM, *Ministry of Environment and Forestry v. PT Palmina Utama*, District Court of Central Jakarta, 11 January 2021 – 445/Pdt.G/2019/PN.Jkt.Pst, *Ministry of Environment and Forestry v. PT Rambang Agro Jaya*.

[264] It is precisely within these cases that the existence of climatic causation can be denied in the subsequent causal analysis, despite the elaboration of the court concerning 'normal' causation. See for a distinction between 'normal' causation and climatic causation Sect. 3.3.2.1.

[265] Cases include Federal Court of Australia, 15 June 2006 – [2006] FCA 736, *Wildlife Preservation Society of Queensland Proserpine/Whitsundry Branch Inc. v. Minister for the Environment &*

numerous lawsuits from other jurisdictions can also be attributed to the area of administrative law.[266] Causal considerations relate, in particular, to the cause-effect relationship between administrative decisions on greenhouse gas concentrations in the atmosphere, the management of scope 3 emissions, and the operation of specific businesses and potential environmental and climate impacts.

Contrary to initial expectations, causation has also been at issue in many cases based on constitutional law, fundamental rights and human rights. With a share of 37.7%, this type of litigation is as well represented as administrative lawsuits. In contrast to the cases based on administrative law, the subject matter of rights-based lawsuits differs significantly. The main issues hereby revolve around inadequate constitutional provisions on climate change or inadequate government reduction targets, which could lead to a violation of the constitutional, fundamental and basic human rights of the plaintiffs, most of whom are minority groups such as indigenous peoples, children and youth. Other decisions include the greening of rights or the establishment of a fundamental new human right, such as the right to a healthy environment.[267] Although it was primarily unexpected that decisions based on constitutional provisions involved so many causal considerations, the fact that more and more plaintiffs are invoking their fundamental and constitutional rights is in line with the current prevailing trend, also known as the third wave of climate change litigation.[268]

One area of law that is completely absent from the class of cases in which causal considerations could be proven is the area of criminal law. Although such cases do exist in the climate change context, particularly in relation to protestors convicted for their behaviour in relation to climate change demonstrations, in none of these cases did the judge include a causal assessment. This is somewhat surprising since in criminal law, in general, causation plays a fundamental and constituting role and functions as a prerequisite for most offences. What is of relevance in these cases, however, is that the causal link between a particular behaviour and climate change, as well as its effects, is usually not of great importance. In such cases, it is not the climatic link that is decisive but the causal link between the defendant's behaviour or omission and the damage that has occurred. The reference to climate change which

---

Heritage, Land and Environment Court of New South Wales, 27 November 2006 – [2006] NSWLEC 720, *Gray v. Minister for Planning*, Queensland Land Court, 27 March 2012 – [2012] QLC 13, *Xstrata Coal Queensland Pty. Ltd. and Others v. Friends of the Earth – Brisbane and Others*, 18 October 2021 – [2021] NSWLEC 110, *Mullaley Gas and Pipeline Accord Inc v. Santos NSW (Eastern) Pty Ltd.*

[266] See e.g. United Kingdom Court of Appeal (Civil Division), 17 February 2022 – [2022] EWCA Civ 187, *R (Finch on behalf of the Weald Action Group & Others) v. Surrey County Council (& Others)*, High Court of New Zealand, 16 August 2010 – NZHC CIV 2009 412 000980 *Maniototo Environmental Society Inc. v. Central Otago District Council.*

[267] Inter-American Court on Human Rights, 15 November 2017 – OC-23/17, *A Request for an Advisory Opinion from the Inter-American Court of Human Rights Concerning the Interpretation of Article 1(1), 4(1) and 5(1) of the American Convention on Human Rights.*

[268] See Sect. 2.2.2.

ultimately qualifies the lawsuit as climate change litigation, usually lies in the circumstances surrounding the offence, i.e. the offence being committed during a climate change demonstration or as an act of protest, rather than in the matter of the offence itself.[269] Given that the problems of climatic causation are, therefore, unlikely to arise in criminal climate change cases, the only way to assess causation in such cases would be through the usual causal discrepancies and difficulties. As this is not the case in the criminal law cases currently qualified as climate change litigation, and as these are still few in number, this area of law is completely missing from the group of cases in which the court assessed climatic causation. Similar to lawsuits in the private realm and as briefly mentioned above, there is the problem of publicity and access to reasonings of the courts. It is more than likely that quite a few criminal law cases fell under the climate change litigation radar.

Apart from the area of law, some jurisdictions also impose causal standards to the admissibility assessment of the legal case sought. In such cases, climatic causation can furthermore be problematized as a criterion for the existence of legal standing, as well as in reference to the extraterritorial application of treaties.[270] In none of the assessed cases have causal considerations been at issue in regard to the question of standing.[271] Although, in some cases, plaintiffs elaborate on the adequate causal standard in regard to the standing requirements, courts have not taken over such considerations or engaged in its discussion until this point in time.[272]

---

[269] A prime example for this consideration is the growing body of criminal law cases surrounding protests of the activist group 'Last Generation', which are known for their enhancing climate protests. Some of the members of the organization have been convicted in light of protests by which they clued themselves on to busy streets, rappelled down motorway bridges or poured tomato sauce on works of art in museums (see e.g. District Court Freiburg im Breisgau, 22 November 2022 – 28 Cs 450 Js 23773/22.). In the context of these lawsuits, the courts did not have to address the link between anthropogenic actions and climate change, but rather the link between the actions of the protesters ('cluing', 'abseiling', 'throwing') and the damage or risk that occurred. In the case of abseiling, for example, this refers to the risk to traffic, and even more so to road users, created by the protesters through their actions.

[270] For legal standing, see for example Supreme Court of the United States, 2 April 2007 – 05-1120, *Massachusetts v. EPA*, dissenting opinion Judge Roberts, 9 (this case was not part of the analysis). Standing is further at issue in the pending case European Court of Human Rights, pending – 53600/20, *KlimaSeniorinnen v. Switzerland.* See for the extraterritoriality e.g. Inter-American Court of Human Rights, 15 November 2017 – OC-23/17, *A Request for an Advisory Opinion from the Inter-American Court of Human Rights Concerning the Interpretation of Article 1(1), 4(1) and 5(1) of the American Convention on Human Rights*, paras 101, 104, United Nations Committee on the Rights of the Child, 8 October 2021 – CRC/C/88/D/107/2019, *Sacchi et al. v. Argentina et al.*, paras 9.5, 9.7.

[271] This fact might be elevated by upcoming decisions, for example, in the case European Court of Human Rights, pending – 53600/20, *KlimaSeniorinnen v. Switzerland.*

[272] See for such causal considerations by plaintiffs Administrative Court of Berlin, 31 October 2019 – VG 10 K 412.18, *Family Farmers and Greenpeace Germany v. Germany*, statement of claim (25 October 2018), 80–82. The situation is different in US cases. Here, courts are slightly more likely to discuss causation standards in relation to standing requirements, see e.g. Supreme Court of the United States, 2 April 2007 – 05-1120, *Massachusetts v. EPA*.

In light of the distribution of pro- and anti-climate change litigation, the results are not surprising, with pro-climate change cases outnumbering anti-climate change cases by far.[273] This ratio is reflected in the total number of cases examined, as well. Complaints mainly concern the rejection of private sector projects on climate and environmental grounds, as well as climate-related measures taken by public authorities, which can ultimately lead to restrictions on rights and financial losses.[274] The same applies to the distribution of cases between mitigation and adaptation. With no cases falling into the categories of disaster risk management and only seven into loss and damage, 43 cases relate to mitigation.[275] Only four cases in which the court assessed causation refer to or claim adaptation measures.

3.4.3.3 The Systematic and Substantive Structure of Causal Argumentation

3.4.3.3.1 The Four Notions of Causal Argument

As described above, the substantive analysis is based on four different notions of causal considerations. The first notion covers the question of whether causation or a causal link needs to be established at all in the case at hand. The second notion includes cases in which the court assesses the correct doctrinal approach to causation, while the third notion correlates in this respect that courts and judges within this type of cases discuss the necessary conditions and the requirements imposed by the

[273] Anti-climate change litigation case are for example New South Wales Land and Environment Court, 8 February 2019 – [2019] NSWLEC 7, *Gloucester Resources Limited v. Minister for Planning*, Court of Appeal of Alberta, 24 February 2020 – 2020 ABCA 74, *In the Matter of the Greenhouse Gas Pollution Pricing Act*, International Centre for Settlement of Investment Disputes, 9 September 2021 – ARB/16/41, *Eco Oro Minerals Corp. v. Republic of Colombia*, High Court of New Zealand, 16 August 2010 – NZHC CIV 2009 412 000980 *Maniototo Environmental Society Inc. v. Central Otago District Council*.

[274] In regard to projects of the private sector see e.g. New South Wales Land and Environment Court, 8 February 2019 – [2019] NSWLEC 7, *Gloucester Resources Limited v. Minister for Planning*. In regard to measures taken by public authorities see e.g. International Centre for Settlement of Investment Disputes, 9 September 2021 – ARB/16/41, *Eco Oro Minerals Corp. v. Republic of Colombia*.

[275] Cases include International Centre for Settlement of Investment Disputes, 9 September 2021 – ARB/16/41, *Eco Oro Minerals Corp. v. Republic of Colombia*, Supreme Court of Indonesia, 22 May 2014 – 151/K/TUN/2014, *Yayasan Wahana Lingkungan Hidup Indonesia v. Governor of Bali and others*, District Court of Central Jakarta, 11 January 2021 – 445/Pdt.G/2019/PN.Jkt.Pst, *Ministry of Environment and Forestry v. PT Rambang Agro Jaya*, Banjarmasin Court of Appeal, 21 February 2018 – 48/PDT/2018/PT.BJM, *Ministry of Environment and Forestry v. PT Palmina Utama*, Administrative Court of Paris, 3 February 2021 – N° 1901967, 1904968, 1904972, 1904976/4-1 *Notre Affaire à Tous and Others v. France*, Prague Municipal Court, 15 June 2022 – 14A 101/2021, *Klimatická žaloba ČR v. Czech Republic*, European Court of Human Rights, 11 October 2022 – 31612/09, *Pavlov et al. v. Russia*.

specific causal approach. The fourth and last notion describes cases in which the court simply discusses whether a causal link exists or not.

While the first three categories deal with more specific and detailed parts of causal reasoning, the fourth category functions as a residual class, which is also reflected in the distribution and classification of the cases in the different term groups. Of course, not all decisions can be made unambiguously. Some decisions fall into two or more different categories. However, the dominant group of causal reasoning relates to its affirmation or negation and, therefore, consists of the fourth group of causation. With 58.7% of all decisions implementing such considerations, the fourth group is by far the strongest. This is not surprising since an assessment of the existence of a causal link is, on the one hand, the basis of the following claims or breaches of duty and, on the other hand, the logical consequence of considerations applied in the three other groups of causal assessments.

3.4.3.3.1.1 Group 1: The Necessity of Causation

Although one might think that most courts and jurisdictions have already established clear requirements in their statutes or in their case law and have considered whether these require a causal link or not, the analysis has shown that the question of whether a causal link is required or not still occupies the courts.[276] In around 14.3% of the cases, the court considered whether its statute or administrative assessment required a causal link. Group 1 is particularly relevant in relation to two different sources of causal inquiry.[277] On the one hand, courts may ask whether a particular norm indirectly implies the need to consider causation by interpreting the terminology of the text. This relates, in particular, to the second source of causal inquiries. On the other hand, courts may extend their pre-existing norms so that they can be applied in cases that have not been predominantly concerned with climate change and its impacts. As public awareness of the impacts, effects and dangers of climate change gradually increases, so too does the knowledge of the factors that contribute to it. This is true even for areas of law that, at first glance, may not seem to be closely related to climate change, such as finance, antitrust or competition law. With such fields suddenly confronted with the 'new' subject of climate change, existing statutes, formal standards and conditions of assessment need to be adapted, as

[276] Decisions involving causal considerations that fall into group one include, but are not limited to Inter-American Court on Human Rights, 15 November 2017 – OC-23/17, *A Request for an Advisory Opinion from the Inter-American Court of Human Rights Concerning the Interpretation of Article 1(1), 4(1) and 5(1) of the American Convention on Human Rights*, Federal Court of Australia, 25 August 2017 – [2017] FCAFC 134, *Australian Conservation Foundation Incorporated v. Minister for the Environment and Energy*, High Court of New Zealand, 16 August 2010 – NZHC CIV 2009 412 000980 *Maniototo Environmental Society Inc. v. Central Otago District Council*, Environment Court, 28 October 2009 – [2009] NZEnvC 293, *Maniototo Environmental Society Inc. v. Central Otago District Council*, Prague Municipal Court, 15 June 2022 – 14A 101/2021, *Klimatická žaloba ČR v. Czech Republic*.

[277] See for the different sources of causal inquiry Sect. 3.1.3.

well. Such considerations can furthermore extent to the procedural sphere, which then concerns the third source of causal inquiries. A fitting example of such a procedural adaption and, even more so, a clarification and expansion of current practice was provided by the Inter-American Court on Human Rights in their Advisory Opinion. Here the Court elaborated on the requirements of an extraterritorial application of treaty rights in light of the obligation to prevent transboundary harm. The Court hereby stated that

> (i)t is important to stress that this obligation does not depend on the lawful or unlawful nature of the conduct that generates the damage, because States must provide prompt, adequate and effective redress to the persons and States that are victims of transboundary harm resulting from activities carried out in their territory or under their jurisdiction, even if the action which caused this damage is not prohibited by international law. That said, there must always be a causal link between the damage caused and the act or omission of the State of origin in relation to activities in its territory or under its jurisdiction or control.[278]

Other courts, moreover, clarified whether the wording of a statute entailed a strict causal link or not. This was done, for example, by the Prague Municipal Court in the case *Klimatická žaloba ČR v. Czech Republic,* in which the Court stated that

> (t)he Municipal Court observes that the first and fifth conditions for interference are intertwined, as both require that the interference be direct. The wording of Section 82 of the Code of Administrative Justice, in the part "the interference was directly directed against him or her or as a result of which he or she were directly affected", was interpreted by the Municipal Court as requiring a causal link between the interference and the infringement of the applicants' rights.[279]

In essence, it is important to note that only a few cases ultimately fall into group 1. Based on largely established legal traditions, further claims within this causation category can only be expected to a limited extent. If any, they are likely to be found in areas of law that traditionally had little to do with climate change. Given the heavy reliance on case law, such actions are most likely to arise in common-law countries.

3.4.3.3.1.2 Group 2: The Applicable Doctrine of Causation

The second notion of causal consideration contains the question of the applicable causal dogma.[280] About 15.9% of the decisions and judgments assessed include such considerations. A wide variety of tests have been applied and considered by courts in light of finding the most fitting approach to climatic causation. Looking at the results

---

[278] Inter-American Court of Human Rights, 15 November 2017 – OC-23/17, *A Request for an Advisory Opinion from the Inter-American Court of Human Rights Concerning the Interpretation of Article 1(1), 4(1) and 5(1) of the American Convention on Human Right*, para 103, also para 101.

[279] Prague Municipal Court, 15 June 2022 – 14A 101/2021, *Klimatická žaloba ČR v. Czech Republic*, para 324.

[280] Decisions involving causal considerations belonging to group two are Federal Court Canada, 16 November 2020 – 2020 FC 1059, *Lho'imggin et al. v. Her Majesty the Queen*, Ontario Superior Court of Justice, 12 November 2020 – 2020 ONSC 6918, *Mathur et al. v. Her Majesty the Queen in Right of Ontario*.

of the substantial analysis, it becomes obvious that courts and judges are primarily concerned with the issue of factual causal approaches. The question of which normative approach should be used gets hardly ever discussed. This presumably relates to a large extent to the breadth and scope of interpretation and discretion that prevails with regard to the normative causal component. Normative criteria are fluid and transitive. They allow the inclusion of a large number of different criteria, which makes it easier to adapt them to new challenges than is possible within the factual framework. In cases in which courts and judges address normative causation, they are usually concerned with the question of whether the applied criteria are present rather than with the assessment of the right applicable criteria as such. Besides the right causal approaches, however, the overall distinction between factual and normative causation has only been scarcely addressed. In *Ministry of Environment and Forestry v. PT Rambang Agro Jaya*, the Court held that *"[...] proving causation is usually carried out based on testing of two forms of causation, namely in the form of cause in fact and in the form of proximate cause. [...](P)roximate cause is often also called legal cause or the scope of liability"*[281] The lack of decisions addressing this distinction beyond the present case is undoubtedly due in most cases to the existing legal tradition, which in a large number of jurisdictions already presupposes the two-stage approach to causation.[282]

3.4.3.3.1.2.1 Counterfactual Causation

Noticeable is that most judges and courts still fall back on counterfactual tests in climate change cases.[283] This is true for both, decisions stemming from civil law countries and judgements made by courts in common law jurisdictions. The success rate of cases in which a causal link was to be established on the basis of counterfactual tests, especially in regard to specific causal relata, on the other hand, was surprisingly low. In the majority of the cases, the assessment led to the rejection of a specific causal link. And although the Court in *Ministry of Environment and Forestry v. PT Rambang Agro Jaya* ultimately affirmed the existence of specific causation and generally made use of counterfactual theories, it did not apply them in the respective case. The reason for refraining from the counterfactual assessment in the present decision related to the fact that what was at issue was an absolute liability regime, which does not require counterfactual causation based on a hypothetical

[281] District Court of Central Jakarta, 11 January 2021 – 445/Pdt.G/2019/PN.Jkt.Pst, *Ministry of Environment and Forestry v. PT Rambang Agro Jaya*, 208 – translation by author.

[282] See in this regard in more detail Sect. 3.1.2.

[283] See in this regard in more detail Sect. 4.2. Cases in which a counterfactual understanding was applied e.g. Essen Regional Court, 15 December 2016 – 2 O 285/15, *Luciano Lliuya v. RWE AG*, Land and Resources Tribunal Queensland, 15 February 2007 – [2007] QLRT 33, *Re Xstrata Coal Queensland Pty. Ltd. & Ors*, International Centre for Settlement of Investment Disputes, 4 September 2020 – ARB/15/50, *Eskosol S.p.A. in liquidazione v. Italian Republic*, Queensland Land Court, 27 March 2012 – [2012] QLC 13, *Xstrata Coal Queensland Pty. Ltd. and Others v. Friends of the Earth – Brisbane and Others*, 559.

assessment in the context of the Indonesian legal system.[284] This is an alarming result, given that most jurisdictions still use counterfactual tests as their standard test of causation. The picture, however, is quite different in regard to the assessment of general causation. Here courts and judges have been more eager to find counterfactual causation.[285]

With this result at hand, the tide might slowly turn in favour of other causal dogmas. Such a development is supported by quite a few recent decisions in which judges rejected the application of counterfactual concepts. In *Minister for the Environment v. Sharma*, Judge Beach, in coherence with Chief Justice Allsop, expressly rejected the application of the but-for test as inapt for the current case.[286] Judge Wylie argued similarly in *Smith v. Fonterra Co-Operative Group Limited.*[287] Both cases stand out due to the surprisingly clear stance of the judges against the application of counterfactual tests and their approval of other causal tests, which they qualify as more apt for climate change lawsuits.

In addition to these two key decisions, counterfactual causation may no longer be considered generally useful in climate change litigation. Judge Beach stated that *"(i)t seems to me that the common law is going to have to evolve to deal with scenarios such as the present […]."*[288] Such considerations are also in coherence with the judgement in *Family Farmers and Greenpeace Germany v. Germany,* in which the Court elaborated on the necessity of lowering the standard of causation in climate change scenarios.[289] Up to date, however, no clear causal dogma has prevailed. Rather, plaintiffs are constantly proposing newer approaches in their claims, forcing courts and judges to elaborate on possible solutions to causation issues, the transference of other causal approaches to climate change scenarios, and even to think about totally new causal conceptions.

This, nonetheless, is a one-sided development. The analysis has shown that exclusively courts from common law jurisdictions engage with the deployment of new concepts to causation. Courts from civil law countries still mainly fall back on counterfactual theories, which leads to a higher rejection rate of specific causation under their respective application. Although there are single cases in which the court referred to a possible deviation or a reduction of the causal standard, considerations in this regard are still very vague and inconclusive, with no court ultimately having

---

[284] District Court of Central Jakarta, 11 January 2021 – 445/Pdt.G/2019/PN.Jkt.Pst, *Ministry of Environment and Forestry v. PT Rambang Agro Jaya.*

[285] See e.g. in the case Prague Municipal Court, 15 June 2022 – 14A 101/2021, *Klimatická žaloba ČR v. Czech Republic.*

[286] Federal Court of Australia, 15 March 2022 – [2022] FCAFC 35, *Minister for the Environment v. Sharma* judgment by Judge Beach para 438, judgment by Chief Judge Allsop paras 304–333.

[287] High Court of New Zealand, 21 October 2021 – [2021] NZCA 552, *Smith v. Fonterra Co-Operative Group Limited*, para 84.

[288] Federal Court of Australia, 15 March 2022 – [2022] FCAFC 35, *Minister for the Environment v. Sharma* judgement by Judge Beach para 440.

[289] Administrative Court of Berlin, 31 October 2019 – VG 10 K 412.18, *Family Farmers and Greenpeace Germany v. Germany*, 22.

referred to a possible dogmatic structure supporting such development.[290] The most important reason for the divergence between legal systems is the structure and functioning of case law, legal reasoning and decision-making per se in common law countries. In common law countries, the reliance on case law provides the means to establish new legal concepts quicker.[291] The transfer of existing concepts is essentially at the discretion of the individual judges. Civil law jurisdictions, however, are more likely characterised by their rigidity and difficulty to change. Yet, other factors may also be at play, including the long history of climate change litigation, particularly in Australia and the UK and the high profile of environmental jurisprudence in those respective countries. The latter is particularly valid for Australia, where fossil fuels and coal mining, in particular, are crucial to the economy and extreme weather events and their consequences have been observed and endured by the population for years.

3.4.3.3.1.2.2 Common Sense Test

The fact that plaintiffs and courts are becoming increasingly creative in transferring traditional causal standards and concepts to cases of climate change litigation can already be seen in the early climate change case *Gray v. Minister for Planning and Ors*. In this case, the plaintiffs challenged the Environmental Impact Assessment (EIA) carried out prior to and in relation to the granting of a permit for a coal mine. They requested that the burning of fossil fuels, and, in particular, coal, by third parties, resulting in scope 3 emissions, should be considered and implemented in the assessment as well. The plaintiffs argued that due to a broad understanding of the term 'environment' and a wide approach to causation, scope 3 emissions need to be implemented in the assessment. The question arising in this regard, however, was which kind of link would need to exist between the mine, the greenhouse gas emissions resulting from burning the extracted coal by third parties and climate change in general. The applicants hereby relied on the 'common sense test' developed in *Marche v. Stramare* and based upon elaborations of *Hart* and *Honore* in their work *Causation in the Law*.[292] In *Marche v. Stramare*, the Court clarified that an act or omission should be regarded as a cause even where the act or omission in question is concurrent and consistent with common sense.[293] The common sense test thus represents a departure from the traditional but-for test in cumulative and intervening cause cases. Originally developed for negligence cases, claimants argued for its transfer to judicial review cases where the correctness of an

[290] An example for employed considerations e.g. is again the case *Family Farmers and Greenpeace Germany v. Germany*, see ibid.

[291] This is also the reason for a diverging assessment in Sect. 6.1.

[292] Land and Environment Court of New South Wales, 27 November 2006 – [2006] NSWLEC 720, *Gray v. Minister for Planning*, para 83.

[293] High Court of Australia, 24. April 1991 – (1991) 171 CLR 506, *Marche v. Stramare*, Judge Dean paras 6–8, Judge Mason paras 17–22.

environmental assessment was at issue. Nevertheless, the Court in *Gray v. Minister for Planning and Ors* encountered difficulties in applying the concept of causation to the climate change case at hand. Judge Pain stated in that regard that

> (i)t is problematic to apply a rule of causation relying on commonsense, developed to enable legal liability, to be determined in private law matters, where whether actual injury or loss sustained by a plaintiff is sufficiently connected with the breach of a duty of care of the defendant is in issue, to judicial review proceedings concerning the meaning of "environmental assessment" under the EP&A Act.[294]

As a result, the Court in *Gray v. Minister for Planning and Ors* rejected the application of the common sense test.

The common sense test was further in question in the case *Waratah Coal pty Ltd v. Youth Verdict Ltd & Ors.* in which the defendants claimed that *"(t)he common law approach to causation is the common-sense test"*.[295] However, as both the climate cases and the precedent case were brought before Australian courts, it appears that the common sense test is, in fact, a jurisdiction-specific modification of the but-for test, rather than the general 'common law approach to causation'. Outside the Australian legal system, the test has not found any application in climate change litigation before courts.

Although the Court in *Gray v. Minister for Planning and Ors* ultimately rejected the establishment of causation based on common sense, the judges still had to solve the issue of what dogma had to be applied for the causal standard. Hereby, the Court had to assess two other causal standards. First, the Court referred to a standard developed by Judge Bignold in *Bell v. Minister for Urban Affairs and Planning and Prot Waratah Coal Service Ltd* in which a 'real and sufficient link' was required for causation to be established.[296] The Director-General, on the other hand, referred to a stricter concept of causation in demanding that the effects of the mine needed to be significant, proximate and not unlikely to occur. In the end, however, the Court accepted both standards as fulfilled, which led to the establishment of causation in the present case.[297] The case depicts well which obstacles exist in the establishment of causation and, on the other hand, how the transfer of causal standards from other areas of law can actually take place.

---

[294]Land and Environment Court of New South Wales, 27 November 2006 – [2006] NSWLEC 720, *Gray v. Minister for Planning*, para 83.

[295]Land Court of Queensland, 25 November 2022 – [2022] QLC 21, *Waratah Coal Pty Ltd v. Youth Verdict Ltd & Ors (No 6)*, para 1314. Emphasising that a common sense approach is hard to find in both the US and UK legal systems, see Stapleton (2010), p. 468, Fn. 8.

[296]Land and Environment Court of New South Wales – 95 LGERA 86, *Bell v. Minister for Urban Affairs and Planning and Prot Waratah Coal Service Ltd*, para 101.

[297]Land and Environment Court of New South Wales, 27 November 2006 – [2006] NSWLEC 720, *Gray v. Minister for Planning*, paras 97–100.

3.4.3.3.1.2.3 Increase in Risk Test

The 'increase in risk test', first developed in the British case *Fairchild v. Glenhaven Funeral Services Ltd.*, became particularly pertinent in two climate cases; in the Australian case *Sharma and others v. Minister for the Environment* and the judgment of the High Court of New Zealand in the lawsuit *Smith v. Fonterra Co-Operative Group Limited.*[298] In the latter, the plaintiffs argued that the situation and the rationale of climate change and the context of the *Fairchild* decision run concurrently, from which it follows that the increase in risk test should be applied in the beforementioned case as well. The Court ultimately rejected such an analogy without elaborating further on the reasons.[299] In parallel to the decision of the High Court of New Zealand, the Federal Court of Australia also dealt with the question of the applicability of the *Fairchild* criteria. Interestingly, the remarks of Chief Justice Allsop and Justice Beach differed. Chief Justice Allsop stated that *"(u)ntil the High Court says otherwise, causing an increase in the risk of harm occurring does not amount of itself to causing or materially contribution the harm."*[300] And further, *"[...] it is clear that it is not for an intermediate appellate court to say that for proof of causal connection in the causing of harm from global warming increasing the risk of such is a sufficient causal connection to establish liability."*[301] However, Judge Beach, on the other hand, suggested and affirmed the possibility of an analogous applicability of the test. He further pointed out that the increase in risk test, as developed in the British *Fairchild* case, has not yet gained recognition in Australia as a legitimate test for establishing causal chains. In the end, he left the decision on the transfer of the causal concept open, stating on the one hand that the problem in question was one of duty rather than causation and, on the other hand, referring to even more far-reaching causal approaches.[302]

Ultimately, there has been no successful application of the increase in risk tests in climate change lawsuits to date.[303] However, the statements of Justice Beach and Chief Justice Allsop indicate that an application of the increase in risk test may be

[298] House of Lords, 20 June 2002 – UKHL 22, *Fairchild v. Glenhaven Funeral Services Ltd.* See in this regard also Sect. 4.5.2.2.1, Federal Court of Australia, 15 March 2022 – [2022] FCAFC 35, *Minister for the Environment v. Sharma*, High Court of New Zealand, 21 October 2021 – [2021] NZCA 552, *Smith v. Fonterra Co-Operative Group Limited.*

[299] High Court of New Zealand, 21 October 2021 – [2021] NZCA 552, *Smith v. Fonterra Co-Operative Group Limited*, 107–112.

[300] Federal Court of Australia, 15 March 2022 – [2022] FCAFC 35, *Minister for the Environment v. Sharma* judgment by Chief Justice Allsop, para 320.

[301] Ibid. judgment by Chief Justice Allsop, para 323.

[302] Ibid. Judge Beach, paras 433–442.

[303] Further references to increasing risk as an approach to causation can be found, for example, in Land Court of Queensland, 25 November 2022 – [2022] QLC 21, *Waratah Coal Pty Ltd v. Youth Verdict Ltd & Ors (No 6)*, para 1325. Here the Court stated that *"[...] the plaintiff must show the risk 'came home' [...]."*, see ibid. Other references to the increase in risk test were made in High Court of New Zealand, 21 October 2021 – [2021] NZCA 552, *Smith v. Fonterra Co-Operative Group Limited.*

conceivable, provided, in the case of Australia, that the Supreme Court allows the transfer of the criteria. Whether these statements also apply to other jurisdictions, even outside the common law legal realm, is highly doubtful.

3.4.3.3.1.2.4 Further Causal Conceptions

The analysis has shown that approaches introduced to prove and establish causation go far beyond the well-established connotations of causal considerations. As previously mentioned, Judge Beach, in the decision *Sharma and others v. Minister for the Environment*, referred to a very theoretical and metaphysical approach to causation derived from legal philosophy.[304] He advocated for the application of a causal standard based on the theoretical concepts of *Wright,* which build upon a necessary element of a sufficient set of conditions.[305] In the light of the necessary causal adjustment, Judge Beach stated:

> No doubt it might be said that the "but for" test concerning factual causation is inapposite in the present context and that the NESS (necessary element of a sufficient set) test by Professor Richard Wright and others is more suitable, particularly when dealing with a posited causal condition that is neither necessary nor sufficient.[306]

By then further referring to *Stapleton's* remarks on the right understanding of causation in the law, Judge Beach clearly signals that he is in favour of a radical reduction of the factual standard of causation.[307] Although Judge Beach's comments are merely a suggestion of future causal considerations rather detached from the case, it nevertheless shows that theoretical and philosophical conceptions are increasingly permeating through into the jurisprudence per se.

Another causal approach that has been addressed is the 'material contribution test' in differentiated forms. In Canada, for example, initially developed for cases of negligence within tort law, the plaintiffs in the case *Lho'imggin et al. v. Her Majesty the Queen* sought to transfer the approach to Charter claims.[308] The plaintiffs argued that the circumstances in which the material contribution test was developed in the case *Clements v. Clements* were similar to the climate change scenario and, therefore, suggested a transfer of the test.[309] Argumentatively, the plaintiffs further submitted that the mere fact that the action and the claim constitute a novel form

---

[304] Federal Court of Australia, 15 March 2022 – [2022] FCAFC 35, *Minister for the Environment v. Sharma* para 438.

[305] See in this regard Sect. 4.3.

[306] Federal Court of Australia, 15 March 2022 – [2022] FCAFC 35, *Minister for the Environment v. Sharma* para 438.

[307] Ibid. para 439 in referring to Stapleton (2010).

[308] Federal Court Canada, 16 November 2020 – 2020 FC 1059, *Lho'imggin et al. v. Her Majesty the Queen*. See on this further Sect. 4.5.2.

[309] Supreme Court of Canada, 29 June 2012 – [2012] 2 R.C.S, *Clements v. Clements*.

of causal establishment should not be inconsistent with its likelihood of success.[310] The Court accepted the line of thought provided by the plaintiffs but further stated that *"(t)here must be some basis in fact to argue that there could be a material contribution claim for Charter breaches, and that does not exist in this case."*[311] Ultimately, the Court rejected the application of the material contribution test in the case *Lho'imggin et al. v. Her Majesty the Queen.* However, provided that a factual basis could be established, the application of the test to Canadian climate litigation may well be conceivable.

In the Australian case *Sharma and others v. Minister for the Environment,* the Court also addressed the question of causation based on material contributions.[312] While the plaintiffs relied on the standard of the increase in risk test established in *Fairchild,* the defendants claimed the application of the material contribution test based on the *Bonnington Castings* decision.[313] Consequently, Chief Judge Allsop discussed a possible application of the *Bonnington Castings* criteria but, in the end, refrained from taking a clear stance on how to deal with such an approach in the current case.[314] Judge Beach, on the other hand, clearly rejected the application of the material contribution test. He argued that the situation surrounding the decision in *Bonnington Castings* could not be analogously applied to the situation in the *Sharma* case, as the question of the impact of scope 3 emissions on temperature increase and climate change was only a question of an increase in risk but not a direct consequence or a direct contribution to the occurrence of the damage itself.[315] The same conclusion was reached by the third judge, Judge Wheelahan, who stated that *"(t)he "tiny" contribution to which the primary judge referred would at most amount to a contribution to an increased risk of harm but not a risk of contribution to the harm itself, still less a material contribution that would attract the principles in Bonnington Castings."*[316]

In other climate decisions, courts have often tended to refer only briefly and rather vaguely to the applicable standard of causation. In *Costa Rica v. Nicaragua,* the ICJ argued for the existence of 'a direct and certain causal link', in *Mullaley Gas and Pipeline Accord Inc v. Santos NSW (Eastern) Pty Ltd,* the Court referred to a 'real and sufficient link', and in *Smith v. Fonterra Co-Operative Group Limited,* the Court

[310] Federal Court Canada, 16 November 2020 – 2020 FC 1059, *Lho'imggin et al. v. Her Majesty the Queen,* para 99.

[311] Ibid.

[312] Federal Court of Australia, 15 March 2022 – [2022] FCAFC 35, *Minister for the Environment v. Sharma.*

[313] House of Lords, 25 March 1995 – [1956] AC 613, *Bonnington Castings Ltd. Wardlaw.* See on this in Sect. 4.5.2.2.1.

[314] Federal Court of Australia, 15 March 2022 – [2022] FCAFC 35, *Minister for the Environment v. Sharma* paras 876–882.

[315] Ibid. para 436.

[316] Ibid. judgment by Judge Wheelahan para 882.

ultimately rejected the application of the market share liability doctrine.[317] All those different approaches to factual causation show that the discussion about the right causal dogma in general, but even more so in regard to climatic causation, has not yet come to an end. With traditional approaches still prevailing and newer approaches being rejected by the courts, it is clear that there is still much potential for development.

3.4.3.3.1.3 Group 3: Prerequisites of Factual Causation

Concurrent with the first notion of causal arguments, cases of group 3 are rare and only constitute about 11.1% of the overall cases which consider climatic causation in their reasoning.[318] Cases of group 3 often imply the question of what requirements need to be present and assessed to establish causation. In addition to the requirements of causation per se, what acts and omissions should be taken into account may also be of relevance. In *Public Prosecutor's Office v. H Carlos Schneider S/A Comércio e Industria & Others*, the Court elaborated on the relevance of the immediacy of the respective acts. Ultimately, the Court concluded that not only direct actions are significant but that persons who contribute only indirectly to an event may also be held causally responsible for the damage that has occurred. The Court hereby stated that

> (f)or the purpose of determining the causal link in environmental damage, the following are equalized: whoever does it, whoever does not do it when they should do it, whoever lets them do it, whoever does not mind them doing it, whoever finances their doing it, and whoever benefits when others do it.[319]

The issue which requirements are needed for the establishment of factual causation and the search for the right causation doctrine are often closely connected.[320] Thus, the call for a lowering of the standard of causation in *Family Farmers and Greenpeace Germany v. Germany* entails both, a requirement for causation per se,

---

[317] International Court of Justice, 2 February 2018 – I.C.J. Reports 2018, p. 15, *Certain Activities Carried Out by Nicaragua in the Border Area (Costa Rica v. Nicaragua)*, para 72, 18 October 2021 – [2021] NSWLEC 110, *Mullaley Gas and Pipeline Accord Inc v. Santos NSW (Eastern) Pty Ltd*, para 14, High Court of New Zealand, 21 October 2021 – [2021] NZCA 552, *Smith v. Fonterra Co-Operative Group Limited*, paras 107–111. See for further reference to the market-share doctrine Sect. 4.5.1.

[318] Decisions which entail causal considerations falling in group three are inter alia Administrative Court of Berlin, 31 October 2019 – VG 10 K 412.18, *Family Farmers and Greenpeace Germany v. Germany*, 22, Superior Court of Justice, Brazil, 2 December 2009 – 650.728 – SC (2003/0221786-0), *Public Prosecutor's Office v. H Carlos Schneider S/A Comércio e Industria & Others*, District Court of Central Jakarta, 11 January 2021 – 445/Pdt.G/2019/PN.Jkt.Pst, *Ministry of Environment and Forestry v. PT Rambang Agro Jaya*.

[319] Superior Court of Justice, Brazil, 2 December 2009 – 650.728 – SC (2003/0221786-0), *Public Prosecutor's Office v. H Carlos Schneider S/A Comércio e Industria & Others*, 11 – translated by author.

[320] As it is e.g. in Federal Court Canada, 16 November 2020 – 2020 FC 1059, *Lho'imggin et al. v. Her Majesty the Queen*, paras 96–102.

i.e. a lowering of the stringency and rigour of the causal link, and a call for a weaker causal dogma.[321] However, as the Court in the respective case did not in any way refer to a specific applicable causal doctrine or propose the application of a dogma that complies with a lowered causal perception other than the concepts traditionally applied, the classification of this respective case leans rather towards group three, than group two. Nevertheless, it should not be precluded that cases fall in two or more causal groups based on the very same causal argument. This does not speak against the groupings as such but is intrinsic to the very idea of using causal arguments. Cases of group 3 are, moreover, frequently followed by the question of whether causation actually exists or not and, thus, also fall into the realm of group 4.

3.4.3.3.1.4 Group 4: The Existence of Causation

The fourth notion of causal argumentation is by far the most common. In more than 58.7% of the cases, the existence of causation is at the centre of decisions that involve a causal debate per se.[322] This is also reflected in the high proportion of decisions that deal exclusively with this issue and do not fall into another category (about 39.7%). In cases in which the court addressed causation not exclusively in light of category four, judges most commonly referred to the question whether causation is necessitated at all (group 1) before applying the chosen approach to the facts of the case. However, whether causation was ultimately accepted depended largely on the type of causal chain that was required and the proof that had been brought forward by the claimants.

3.4.3.3.2 General Causation

A key issue in analysing the reasoning used by judges in assessing causation is the distinction between general and specific causation. In the vast majority of cases, general causation had to be assessed either in regard to the relation between overall greenhouse gas emissions and a general effect on rights or concerning the relation between a general behaviour or omission and the composition of the atmosphere.[323]

---

[321] Administrative Court of Berlin, 31 October 2019 – VG 10 K 412.18, *Family Farmers and Greenpeace Germany v. Germany*, 22.

[322] Decisions which entail causal considerations falling in group four are among others Supreme Court of Indonesia, 22 May 2014 – 151/K/TUN/2014, *Yayasan Wahana Lingkungan Hidup Indonesia v. Governor of Bali and others*, Essen Regional Court, 15 December 2016 – 2 O 285/15, *Luciano Lliuya v. RWE AG*, International Centre for Settlement of Investment Disputes, 9 September 2021 – ARB/16/41, *Eco Oro Minerals Corp. v. Republic of Colombia*, Supreme Court of Indonesia, 18 April 2017 – 1 PK/Pdt/2017, *Minister of Environment v. PT Kalista Alam*, 15th Civil Federal Court, Brazil, 3 February 2021 – 1010603-35.2019.4.01.3800, *Federal Environmental Agency (IBAMA) v. Siderúrgica São Luiz Ltd. and Martins.*

[323] See e.g. Federal Court of Australia, 15 March 2022 – [2022] FCAFC 35, *Minister for the Environment v. Sharma*, Federal Court Canada, 16 November 2020 – 2020 FC 1059, *Lho'imggin*

While some courts did not address general causation at all, the overwhelming majority found the existence of general causation, particularly with respect to the impact of greenhouse gas emissions on anthropogenic climate change, to be affirmative. The Supreme Court of the Netherlands in the case *Urgenda Foundation v. State of the Netherlands,* stated that *"(t)here is a direct, linear connection between the greenhouse gas emissions caused by humans, which are partly caused by the burning of fossil fuels, and the warming of the planet."*[324] Only in one individual case did the judicial body reject the existence of a general causal link. In the case *In re Xstrata Coal Queensland Pty. Ltd. & Others,* the Tribunal did not accept the IPCC's Fourth Assessment Report as conclusive enough to comprehensively explain and elaborate on a general causal relationship.[325] However, as the Tribunal's decision was issued in 2007 and is, therefore, relatively old in the eyes of the climate change litigation movement, the Tribunal's reasoning becomes less meaningful for climate change litigation today. This is especially true given the growing acceptance of the IPCC's scientific findings and a broader societal understanding of the nature of climate change in general. It is further supported by the widespread acknowledgement of general causation within different fields and areas of law. In both private and public law, courts overwhelmingly affirm the existence of general causation. The same result can be seen when looking at the different areas of law. In administrative law, as well as in fundamental rights or tort law, courts consider general causation to be given.

What the Tribunal in *In re Xstrata Coal Queensland Pty. Ltd & Others* still rejected can now be seen as commonly given and even as a trend in climate change cases. Nearly all decisions that involved general causal statements have fallen back on reports provided by the IPCC, despite possible scientific uncertainties and probabilities. Even in cases which do not entail causal considerations as such, courts referred to the IPCC concerning the scientific background of climate change.

3.4.3.3.3 Specific Causation

In contrast to the general causal link, the establishment of specific causation has proven to be considerably more difficult. The number of cases in which judges affirm the existence of a specific causal chain is significantly lower than for general causation, with only 25% of the total number of cases in which courts assessed causation at all. The ratio slightly changes to 38.7% if only the cases in which the

---

et al. v. Her Majesty the Queen, Supreme Court of Norway, 20 April 2020 – 20-051052SIV-HRET, *Greenpeace Norway v. Government of Norway*.

[324] Supreme Court of the Netherlands, 20 December 2019 – 19/00135, *Urgenda Foundation v. The State of The Netherlands*, para 2.1.

[325] Land and Resources Tribunal Queensland, 15 February 2007 – [2007] QLRT 33, *Re Xstrata Coal Queensland Pty. Ltd. & Ors*, para 17, IPCC (2007).

courts actually addressed the problem of specific causation are considered.[326] The analysis further shows that even in cases in which courts affirmed general causation, specific causation was often denied. In this respect, the Administrative Court in the case *Notre Affaire à Tous and Others v. France* also stated that *"(c)onsequently, even supposing that the commitments given by all the States Parties were insufficient, the applicant associations do not establish that this inadequacy was the direct cause of the ecological damage relied on."*[327] In another decision the Court stated that *"(i)ndeed even if this mine's GHG emissions were eliminated completely, QCC failed to show that that would have the slightest effect on global warming and climate change."*[328]

In comparing the results of the analysis in light of the different fields of law, it becomes clear that the outcome is not conditioned by them. In both private and public law, there is an equal ratio of affirming and denying specific causal relationships. Surprisingly, there are hardly any differences even when comparing the individual legal areas. While it was initially assumed that causation would be more likely to be affirmed in human rights and fundamental rights litigation, the results of the analysis do not support this assumption. Rather, it appears that even within tort law, specific climatic causation has been able to be affirmed.[329] This result is again subject to the objection of the paucity of data. Nevertheless, the result can at least be interpreted as an indication that the establishment of specific causation and its chances of success are, in principle, neither dependent on the field nor on the area of law. With regard to the responses, it is difficult to make a well-founded statement. This is due to the low number of lawsuits being brought in regard to adaptation measures, loss and damage or disaster risk management.

Differences in the handling of specific causal relata, however, also exist considering the geographical allocation of the proceeding, especially in light of a Global North – Global South divide. Climate change litigation from the Global South has clearly proved to be much more adaptable to specific causal problems than reasoning in jurisdictions from the Global North. The Indonesian decisions, in particular, stand out due to both, the extensive discussion of specific causation and the high degree of susceptibility to the affirmation of specific causal relationships.[330] This result can

---

[326] This is also reflected in the ratio of positive to negative causal decisions.

[327] Administrative Court of Paris, 3 February 2021 – N° 1901967, 1904968, 1904972, 1904976/4-1 *Notre Affaire à Tous and Others v. France*, para 32 in its unofficial translation.

[328] Land and Resources Tribunal Queensland, 15 February 2007 – [2007] QLRT 33, *Re Xstrata Coal Queensland Pty. Ltd. & Ors*, 21.

[329] See e.g. Supreme Court of Indonesia, 18 April 2017 – 1 PK/Pdt/2017, *Minister of Environment v. PT Kalista Alam*, Banjarmasin Court of Appeal, 21 February 2018 – 48/PDT/2018/PT.BJM, *Ministry of Environment and Forestry v. PT Palmina Utama*, 15th Civil Federal Court, Brazil, 3 February 2021 – 1010603-35.2019.4.01.3800, *Federal Environmental Agency (IBAMA) v. Siderúrgica São Luiz Ltd. and Martins*.

[330] District Court of Central Jakarta, 11 January 2021 – 445/Pdt.G/2019/PN.Jkt.Pst, *Ministry of Environment and Forestry v. PT Rambang Agro Jaya*, Banjarmasin Court of Appeal, 21 February 2018 – 48/PDT/2018/PT.BJM, *Ministry of Environment and Forestry v. PT Palmina Utama*,

certainly be interpreted as a strong indication of the progressiveness of these jurisdictions in assessing climatic causation.[331] On an international, as well as European level both the affirmation and negation of specific causation are represented in equal shares.

In contrast to the argumentation of judicial bodies in the context of general causation, the IPCC's findings could not be relied upon in the context of specific causation. Still, the divergence between general and specific causation shows the immense difference that the incorporation of well-founded scientific findings can make in legal proceedings. The length of the reasoning of the courts is indicative of this. While the court's statements on general causation with reference to the IPCC's findings are significantly shorter, and the effort to substantiate them also appears to be significantly less, the extensive statements on specific causation show that the judges have significantly more difficulty in establishing a causal connection without referencing the IPCC's findings.

Looking at the distribution of climate lawsuits over time gives cause for optimism. Even if it is not yet possible to make a clear prediction about the treatment and eventual confirmation of specific causation in future climate cases, the general trends point in the direction of an increasing confirmation of specific causal chains. In particular, the second generation of climate change litigation shows a clear trend shift. Nevertheless, the fact that the growing willingness of judicial bodies to accept specific causal relata does not give rise to unqualified hope for a simplified determination of climatic causation is shown by the large number of causation-denying decisions that have been handed down in the third wave of climate litigation to date.[332]

3.4.3.3.4 Cumulative Causation, Minimal Contributions and the Drop-in-the-Ocean Argument

A further focus of the substantial analysis was to dissect the way in which courts and judges deal with the problem of multiple causal contributions. The existence of multiple different contributions to the change of the climate was hereby often addressed as the drop-in-the-ocean argument. In a more factual and theoretical

---

Supreme Court of Indonesia, 22 May 2014 – 151/K/TUN/2014, *Yayasan Wahana Lingkungan Hidup Indonesia v. Governor of Bali and others.*

[331] Only few countries of the Global South have been subject to climate change litigation. The few cases stem from Brazil, The Philippines, Indonesia and Colombia.

[332] In this regard e.g. United Kingdom Court of Appeal (Civil Division), 17 February 2022 – [2022] EWCA Civ 187, *R (Finch on behalf of the Weald Action Group & Others) v. Surrey County Council (& Others)*, High Court of New Zealand, 15 July 2022 – [2022] NZHC 1693, *Smith v. Attorney-General*, Federal Court of Australia, 27 May 2021 – [2021] FCA 560, *Sharma and others v. Minister for the Environment*, European Court of Human Rights, 11 October 2022 – 31612/09, *Pavlov et al. v. Russia.*

way, however, it reflects the issue of cumulative causation.[333] The analysis has shown that courts in several jurisdictions have frequently addressed the issue of the proper treatment of multiple contributions, albeit often in a non-dogmatic manner and not infrequently neglecting the causal issue involved. Concurrently, in the minority of cases, the courts actually used causal terminology to describe the problem. For example, in *Gray v. Minister for Planning*, the judges stated: *"The fact there are many contributors globally does not mean the contribution from a single large source such as the Anvil Hill Project in the context of NSW should be ignored in the environmental assessment process."*[334] In *Sacchi et al. v. Argentina et al.*, the Committee further elaborated that *"[...] the Committee finds that the collective nature of the causation of climate change does not absolve the State party of its individual responsibility [...]."*[335] As is depicted by the latter decision in *Sacchi v. Argentina*, courts also often referred to responsibility rather than actual causation when it came to the assessment of multiple (minor) contributions. This terminological inconsistency does not, however, get in the way of the causal component entailed in such an analysis.

In contrast to other factors, the analysis has shown that there is considerable agreement on the procedure for dealing with such arguments, particularly in the case of multiple polluters and emitters, even in different jurisdictions. The broad consensus on the collective nature of emissions and, intrinsically, the affirmation of claims despite the existence of cumulative causation is also reflected in the decision in the case *Gloucester Resources Limited v. Minister for Planning*, in which the Court took a very broad view on that issue.[336] The Court respectively analysed in detail the practice and methodology of other courts, including, for example, the US Supreme Court in *Massachusetts v Environmental Protection Agency* and The Hague District Court in *Urgenda Foundation v. The State of the Netherlands*.[337] In the latter case, the Court's approach to the drop-in-the-ocean argument and the link between responsibility and causation is again evident. In this regard, the District Court stated the following:

> After all, it has been established that any anthropogenic greenhouse gas emission, no matter how minor, contributes to an increase of CO2 levels in the atmosphere and therefore to

[333] See for a more detailed analysis of the issue Sect. 3.3.2.1.

[334] Land and Environment Court of New South Wales, 27 November 2006 – [2006] NSWLEC 720, *Gray v. Minister for Planning*, para 98.

[335] United Nations Committee on the Rights of the Child, 8 October 2021 – CRC/C/88/D/107/2019, *Sacchi et al. v. Argentina et al*, para 9.10.

[336] New South Wales Land and Environment Court, 8. February 2019 – [2019] NSWLEC 7, *Gloucester Resources Limited v. Minister for Planning*.

[337] Ibid. See Supreme Court of the United States, 2 April 2007 – 05-1120, *Massachusetts v. EPA*, paras 523–525, New South Wales Land and Environment Court, 8. February 2019 – [2019] NSWLEC 7, *Gloucester Resources Limited v. Minister for Planning*, paras 514–524.

> hazardous climate change. Emission reduction therefore concerns both a joint and individual responsibility [...]. Therefore, the court arrives at the opinion that the single circumstance that the Dutch emissions only constitute a minor contribution to global emissions does not alter the State's obligation to exercise care towards third parties [...].[338]

And further:

> From the above considerations, particularly in 4.79 [which is cited above], it follows that a sufficient causal link can be assumed to exist between the Dutch greenhouse gas emissions, global climate change and the effects (now and in the future) on the Dutch living climate.[339]

Despite the undoubted reference to cumulative causation, i.e. to the (causal) contribution of other parties to the effect in question (here climate change), courts have mainly refrained from developing a clear dogmatic structure. In referring to decisions rooted in civil law jurisdictions, which, therefore, ought to refer to the conditio-sine-qua-non formula as the traditional standard of causation, the strict application of the counterfactual approach in the cases at issue would usually lead to the negation of causation.[340] However, since the courts ultimately refrain from doing so and assume partial responsibility on the part of the actors, this leads either to the affirmation of the causal connection (as, for example, in the decision in the case *Urgenda Foundation v. The State of the Netherlands* at first instance) or a presumption of it.[341] Due to the lack of recurrence to strict dogmatic approaches, however, the courts fall back on policy-driven methods of argumentation in a thoroughly imprecise and vague manner. In doing so, courts also increasingly resort to well-known concepts from international environmental law for further reasons of legitimacy in terms of their argumentation. In *Sacchi et al. v. Argentina et al.*, the Court founded the partial responsibility of the states despite the collectivity of climate change on the principle of common but differentiated responsibilities, which is anchored among others in the Paris Agreement.[342] The Court also used the same principle in the case *Family Farmers and Greenpeace Germany v. Germany*.[343] The Supreme Court of the Netherlands, in the case *Urgenda Foundation v. The State of the Netherlands,* also referred to the principle of common but differentiated responsibilities but grounded it on the preamble of the United Nations Framework Con-

[338] The Hague District Court, 24 June 2015 – C/09/456689/HA ZA 13-1396, *Urgenda Foundation v. The State of the Netherlands*, para 4.79.

[339] Ibid. para 4.90.

[340] See for further explanation of this issue Sect. 4.2.

[341] Supreme Court of the Netherlands, 20 December 2019 – 19/00135, *Urgenda Foundation v. The State of The Netherlands*.

[342] See Art. 2 II Paris Agreement, United Nations Committee on the Rights of the Child, 8 October 2021 – CRC/C/88/D/107/2019, *Sacchi et al. v. Argentina et al*, 9.10.

[343] Administrative Court of Berlin, 31 October 2019 – VG 10 K 412.18, *Family Farmers and Greenpeace Germany v. Germany*, 22.

vention on Climate Change (FCCC) in conjunction with the no-harm principle, which again stems from the preamble of the FCCC.[344]

Thus, the analysis has shown that a broad consensus now seems to have emerged on how to deal with cumulative causation within public law and international claims. Plaintiffs are, therefore, also increasingly referring to the argumentations of precedent decisions from other jurisdictions. For example, the Climate Action Network Europe stated in their intervention in the *Duarte Agostinho and Others v. Portugal and 32 Other States et al.* case:

> They [the courts in Urgenda Foundation v. The State of the Netherlands and Neubauer] also both clarified that not only was cumulative causation present but that – despite global climate change being a global phenomenon – states must do their fair share and cannot shift responsibility to other states, which also allow emissions to continue.[345]

While most of the cases in which such considerations have become relevant to date have been cases located in the public sphere, i.e. where the defendant is usually a public institution or a state, the fundamental debate is not limited to this field and area of law. The above considerations applied by courts could also play a role in private law cases but have not yet been successfully addressed so far, as it is shown by the German case *Luciano Lliuya v. RWE AG* and the case *In the Matter of the Greenhouse Gas Pollution Pricing Act.*[346] Rather, in both decisions, the courts denied the existence of a causal relatum due to the existence of cumulative causation. Although the drop-in-the-ocean argument is nowadays also broadly rejected by legal scholars all around the world, the judges still relied upon the argument in their reasoning.[347] Why decisions in private law cases are generally more restrictive than decisions in public law cases remains questionable. However, one possible reason for such a divergence between private law cases and public law cases might persist in the stronger linkage of private law cases to dogmatic structures, increased causation requirements and reduced discretionary powers of courts.

3.4.4 Results of the Analysis

One of the main questions preceding the analysis was whether the results would show a disparity between different legal systems and jurisdictions in their causal

---

[344] Supreme Court of the Netherlands, 20 December 2019 – 19/00135, *Urgenda Foundation v. The State of The Netherlands*, para 5.7.2.

[345] Climate Action Network Europe (2021) See European Court of Human Rights, pending – 39371/20, *Duarte Agostinho and Others v. Portugal and 32 Other States.*

[346] Essen Regional Court, 15 December 2016 – 2 O 285/15, *Luciano Lliuya v. RWE AG*, Court of Appeal of Alberta, 24 February 2020 – 2020 ABCA 74, *In the Matter of the Greenhouse Gas Pollution Pricing Act.*

[347] Scholars rejecting the drop-in-the-ocean argument inter alia Schirmer (2021), p. 1104. In more detail Peel (2011), pp. 17–18.

understanding and their handling of climatic causation overall. The analysis also aimed to explore the variability in causal approaches with a special emphasis on newer conceptions of causation in light of the obstacles posed to causation by climate change. Additionally, the analysis sought to determine whether a particular jurisdiction, area of law or type of case would specifically prove effective for the establishment of, in particular, specific causal chains.

Overall, the analysis found that courts only marginally deal with causal considerations in climate change cases per se. However, in the rare instances when they do, the handling of causation varies considerably between general and specific causal chains. While the establishment of general causation with recourse to the results of the IPCC frequently succeeds in a dogmatically clean and structured manner and thus demonstrates the coherent development between science and jurisprudence, the establishment of specific causation still poses considerable obstacles for plaintiffs and courts. Jurisdictions that follow civil law traditions especially encounter challenges due to their adherence to traditional, counterfactual causal approaches. In contrast, the analysis has shown that common law legal systems are more receptive to innovative causal approaches and the transfer of concepts from other areas of law. Despite this, the establishment of specific causation in climate-related cases remains a challenging issue, even in common law jurisdictions. Currently, there is no established method to effectively tackle the establishment of specific causal chains.

Contrary to the prevailing view that private law, and, in particular, tort actions, would predominate the causal debate, the analysis has shown that the area of administrative law provides for the largest number of lawsuits in which courts and judges engage with the establishment of causation. Influencing factors are, nonetheless, not only the area of law but also the geographical distribution of the proceedings being brought. Geographically, lawsuits from the Global North still clearly predominate not only general climate change litigation but also its causal discourse. However, with a large number of climate litigation from the Global South already pending before courts and increasing public awareness and interest, this is likely to change in the near future.

In considering the causal approaches used to assess causal chains in climate change litigation, the substantial analysis has shown that courts have not resorted to a homogeneous understanding of climatic causation yet. The analysis has clarified that establishing causation still is one of the major difficulties in the climate debate. Especially the usage of counterfactual approaches fails in light of their restrictive and mono-causal nature.[348] Even by comparing climate cases that have been brought before courts in the same jurisdiction, it was not possible to deduce a comprehensive causal dogma which is able to face the obstacles posed by climate change.[349]

[348] See also Sect. 4.2.

[349] E.g. comparing cases from Australia with the permission of a coal mine at issue, see Land and Environment Court of New South Wales, 27 November 2006 – [2006] NSWLEC 720, *Gray v. Minister for Planning*, Queensland Land Court, 27 March 2012 – [2012] QLC 13, *Xstrata Coal Queensland Pty. Ltd. and Others v. Friends of the Earth – Brisbane and Others*, Federal Court

Although deviations from counterfactual perceptions of causation have been proposed by plaintiffs and have even been partly discussed by courts, no effective approach has found its way into climate jurisprudence to date. Nevertheless, the analysis has brought to light that courts are still becoming more inclined to acknowledge causation even when multiple minimal contributions and cumulative causation exist. This is often done without strict adherence to dogmatic principles but rather through relying on international treaties like the Paris Agreement and the FCCC, as well as further environmental principles such as the principle of common but differentiated responsibilities. This factor particularly applies to court rulings pertaining to public and international law claims. The analysis has further indicated that courts in common law countries are much more innovative and willing to consider and evaluate newer causation approaches than civil law courts. There is a strong likelihood that the common law courts will take the lead in tackling the complex issues stemming from climate change through the development of a comprehensive causal approach.

3.5 Summary of Findings

The foregoing discussion has shown that there are still great differences and uncertainties in both the terminology and the way in which causation is established. What most jurisdictions have in common, however, is the acceptance of a two-tiered factual and normative approach to causation. In this regard, this thesis advocates for a clear separation of the two concepts not only given general theoretical considerations but also building on fundamental needs of climatic causation. The strong link between climate science and jurisprudence in climate litigation implies the need for a comprehensive consideration of factuality. Such perception can, nonetheless, only be accommodated under the strict separation of factual and normative approaches; mixing both understandings of causal inquiry would lead to the falsification and relativization of scientific data and, ultimately, causation itself. Climatic causation, therefore, argues strongly for the separation between factual and normative causation, in addition to the already perceived general considerations of logic, practicability and applicability.

It further has been shown that establishing causation in climate cases can pose major hurdles, particularly in the face of the considerable length and complexity of the causal chain, as well as given the complex underlying climate system. Those difficulties arise uniformly in all jurisdictions and, more specifically, in all areas of law. Yet, it has been shown that most obstacles can be countered based on an enhanced inclusion of scientific data, and a better collaboration between the scientific community and the law in general. By better communicating the demands and

of Australia, 25 August 2017 – [2017] FCAFC 134, *Australian Conservation Foundation Incorporated v. Minister for the Environment and Energy.*

necessities of climate change litigation and concurrently disclosing the limits of attribution science, a significant amount of current legal obstacles could be countered.

Climate change is a global problem that transcends national boundaries and affects the entire world. Despite the efforts of individual countries to protect the environment and the climate system itself, significant progress can only be made through a concerted global effort. Global climate change, therefore, requires global solutions. This does not mean that there is a single solution to the obstacles faced to date by climate change litigation. However, in overcoming the hurdles, courts should, and obviously can, look beyond their own horizons to find solutions and ways of dealing with causation obstacles in the context of climate change.

Climate Change Cases

A Request for an Advisory Opinion from the Inter-American Court of Human Rights Concerning the Interpretation of Article 1(1), 4(1) and 5(1) of the American Convention on Human Rights – Inter-American Court on Human Rights, 15 November 2017 – OC-23/17

Australian Conservation Foundation Incorporated v. Minister for the Environment and Energy – Federal Court of Australia, 25 August 2017 – [2017] FCAFC 134

Carbonext Tecnologia em Soluções Ambientais Ltda. v. Amazon Imóveis (Voluntary Carbon Market) – Court of Justice of the State of São Paulo, 7 October 2021 – 1072768-63.2021.8.26.0100

Certain Activities Carried Out by Nicaragua in the Border Area (Costa Rica v. Nicaragua) – International Court of Justice, 2 February 2018 – I.C.J. Reports 2018, p. 15

Citizen's Committee on the Kobe Coal-Fired Power Plant v. Japan – Osaka High Court, 26 April 2022 – 平成30(行ウ)184; 令和3年(行コ)第46号 (second judgment)

Czech Republic v. Poland (Mine de Turów) – General Court of the European Union, withdrawn – C-121/21

Daniel Billy et al. v. Australia (Torres Strait Islanders Petition) – United Nations Human Rights Committee, 22 September 2022 – CCPR/C/135/D/3624/2019

Duarte Agostinho and Others v. Portugal and 32 Other States – European Court of Human Rights, pending – 39371/20

Eco Oro Minerals Corp. v. Republic of Colombia – International Centre for Settlement of Investment Disputes, 9 September 2021 – ARB/16/41

Environment-People-Law v. Cabinet of Ministers of Ukraine and National Agency of Environmental Investments – Lviv Administrative Court, 17 June 2010 – n/a

Eskosol S.p.A. in liquidazione v. Italian Republic – International Centre for Settlement of Investment Disputes, 4 September 2020 – ARB/15/50

Family Farmers and Greenpeace Germany v. Germany – Administrative Court of Berlin, 31 October 2019 – VG 10 K 412.18

Federal Environmental Agency (IBAMA) v. Siderúrgica São Luiz Ltd. and Martins – 15th Civil Federal Court, Brazil, 3 February 2021 – 1010603-35.2019.4.01.3800
Gbemre v. Shell Petroleum Development Company of Nigeria Ltd. and Others – Federal Court of Nigeria, 30 November 2005 – FHC/B/CS/53/05
Gloucester Resources Limited v. Minister for Planning – New South Wales Land and Environment Court, 8 February 2019 – [2019] NSWLEC 7
Gray v. Minister for Planning – Land and Environment Court of New South Wales, 27 November 2006 – [2006] NSWLEC 720
Greenpeace Norway v. Government of Norway – Supreme Court of Norway, 20 April 2020 – 20-051052SIV-HRET
Herrera Carrion et al. v. Ministry of the Environment et al. (Caso Mecheros) – Multicompetent Chamber of the Provincial Court of Justice of Sucumbíos, 29 July 2021 – 21201202000170
Indigenous Communities of the Lhaka Honhat (Our Land) Association v. Argentina – Inter-American Court of Human Rights, 6 February 2020 – C No. 400
In the Matter of the Greenhouse Gas Pollution Pricing Act – Court of Appeal of Alberta, 24 February 2020 – 2020 ABCA 74
In re Greenpeace Southeast Asia and Others – Commission on Human Rights of the Philippines, 6 May 2022 – CHR-NI-2016-0001
KlimaSeniorinnen v. Switzerland – European Court of Human Rights, pending – 53600/20
Klimatická žaloba ČR v. Czech Republic – Prague Municipal Court, 15 June 2022 – 14A 101/2021
Lho'imggin et al. v. Her Majesty the Queen – Federal Court Canada, 16 November 2020 – 2020 FC 1059
Luciano Lliuya v. RWE AG – Essen Regional Court, 15 December 2016 – 2 O 285/15
Luciano Lliuya v. RWE AG – Higher Regional Court Hamm, pending – 5 U 15/17
Maniototo Environmental Society Inc. v. Central Otago District Council – Environment Court, 28 October 2009 – [2009] NZEnvC 293
Maniototo Environmental Society Inc. v. Central Otago District Council – High Court of New Zealand, 16 August 2010 – NZHC CIV 2009 412 000980
Massachusetts v. EPA – Supreme Court of the United States, 2 April 2007 – 05 1120
Mathur et al. v. Her Majesty the Queen in Right of Ontario – Ontario Superior Court of Justice, 12 November 2020 – 2020 ONSC 6918
Minister for the Environment v. Sharma – Federal Court of Australia, 15 March 2022 – [2022] FCAFC 35
Ministry of Environment and Forestry v. PT Bumi Mekar Hijau – Palembang Court of Appeal of Indonesia, 12 February 2016 – 51/PDT/2016/PT.PLG
Minister of Environment v. PT Kalista Alam – Supreme Court of Indonesia, 18 April 2017 – 1 PK/Pdt/2017
Ministry of Environment and Forestry v. PT Palmina Utama – Banjarmasin Court of Appeal, 21 February 2018 – 48/PDT/2018/PT.BJM
Ministry of Environment and Forestry v. PT Rambang Agro Jaya – District Court of Central Jakarta, 11 January 2021 – 445/Pdt.G/2019/PN.Jkt.Pst

Mullaley Gas and Pipeline Accord Inc v. Santos NSW (Eastern) Pty Ltd, 18 October 2021 – [2021] NSWLEC 110

Native Village of Kivalina v. ExxonMobil Corp. – US District Court for the Northern District of California, 30 September 2009 – 4:08-cv-01138-SBA

Ned Comer et al. v. Murphy Oil USA, Inc., et al. – US Court of Appeals for the 5th Circuit, 28 May 2010 – 07-60756

Neubauer et al. v. Germany – Germany Federal Constitutional Court, 24 March 2021 – 1 BvR 2656/18 – 1 BvR 78/20 – 1 BvR 96/20 – 1 BvR 288/20

Notre Affaire à Tous and Others v. France – Administrative Court of Paris, 3 February 2021 – N° 1901967, 1904968, 1904972, 1904976/4-1

Opuz v. Turkey – European Court of Human Rights, 9 June 2009 – 33401/02

Pavlov et al. v. Russia – European Court of Human Rights, 11 October 2022 – 31612/09

Public Prosecutor's Office v. H Carlos Schneider S/A Comércio e Industria & Others – Superior Court of Justice, Brazil, 2 December 2009 – 650.728 - SC (2003/0221786-0)

Re Xstrata Coal Queensland Pty. Ltd. & Ors – Land and Resources Tribunal Queensland, 15 February 2007 – [2007] QLRT 33

R (Finch on behalf of the Weald Action Group & Others) v. Surrey County Council (& Others) – United Kingdom Court of Appeal (Civil Division), 17 February 2022 – [2022] EWCA Civ 187

R v. Brown (Extinction Rebellion protest, London City Airport) – Crown Court at Southwark, 28 July 2021 – n/a

R. v Brown (Extinction Rebellion protest, London City Airport) – Court of Appeal (Criminal Division), England and Wales, 14 January 2022 – [2022] EWCA Crim 6

Sacchi et al. v. Argentina et al. – United Nations Committee on the Rights of the Child, 8 October 2021 – CRC/C/88/D/107/2019

Sharma and others v. Minister for the Environment – Federal Court of Australia, 27 May 2021 – [2021] FCA 560

SkeenaWild Conservation Trust v. Government of Canada – Federal Court of Canada, withdrawn – T-1836-16

Smith v. Attorney-General – High Court of New Zealand, 15 July 2022 – [2022] NZHC 1693

Smith v. Fonterra Co-Operative Group Limited – High Court of New Zealand, 21 October 2021 – [2021] NZCA 552

Spain v. Apostolos Mangouras & Others ("Prestige" case) – Supreme Court of Spain, n/a

The Friends of Nature Institute v. Gansu State Grid (自然之友环境研究所诉国家电网甘肃公司案, 甘肃省高级人民法院 (2018) 甘民终679 号民事裁定书) – High Court of Gansu Province (Gansu State Grid), 28 December 2018 – Decision No. 679

The Kingsnorth Six Trial – Maidstone Crown Court, n/a – T20080116, 8

Urgenda Foundation v. The State of the Netherlands – The Hague District Court, 24 June 2015 – C/09/456689/HA ZA 13-1396

Urgenda Foundation v. The State of the Netherlands – The Hague Court of Appeal, 9 October 2018 – 200.178.245/01
Urgenda Foundation v. The State of The Netherlands – Supreme Court of the Netherlands, 20 December 2019 – 19/00135
Waratah Coal Pty Ltd v. Youth Verdict Ltd & Ors (No 6) – Land Court of Queensland, 25 November 2022 – [2022] QLC 21
Wildlife Preservation Society of Queensland Proserpine/Whitsundry Branch Inc. v. Minister for the Environment & Heritage – Federal Court of Australia, 15 June 2006 – [2006] FCA 736
Xstrata Coal Queensland Pty. Ltd. and Others v. Friends of the Earth – Brisbane and Others – Queensland Land Court, 27 March 2012 – [2012] QLC 13
Yayasan Wahana Lingkungan Hidup Indonesia v. Governor of Bali and others – Supreme Court of Indonesia, 22 May 2014 – 151/K/TUN/2014

Cases

District Court Freiburg im Breisgau, 22 November 2022 – 28 Cs 450 Js 23773/22
Abu Zubayday v. Lithuania – European Court of Human Rights, 31 May 2018 – 46454/11
Akkoç v. Turkey – European Court of Human Rights, 10 October 2000 – 22947/93, 22948/93
Al-Skeini and others v. The United Kingdom – European Court of Human Rights, 7 July 2011 – 55721/07
Armed Activities on the territory of the Congo (Democratic Republic of the Congo v. Uganda) – International Court of Justice, 9 February 2022 – I.C.J. Reports 2022 p. 13 (judgment on the reparations)
Banković and others v. Belgium and others – European Court of Human Rights, 12 December 2001 – 52207/99
Bell v. Minister for Urban Affairs and Planning and Prot Waratah Coal Service Ltd – Land and Environment Court of New South Wales – 95 LGERA 86
Bonnington Castings Ltd. Wardlaw – House of Lords, 25 March 1995 – [1956] AC 613
Bosnia and Herzegovina v. Serbia and Montenegro – International Court of Justice, 26 February 2007 – I.C.J. Reports 2007, p. 43
Clements v. Clements – Supreme Court of Canada, 29 June 2012 – [2012] 2 R.C.S
Corfu Channel Case (United Kingdom v. People's Republic of Albania) – International Court of Justice, 25 March 1948; 9 April 1949; 15 December 1949 – I. C. J. Reports 1948 p. 15; 1949 p. 4, 244
E. and others v. The United Kingdom – European Court of Human Rights, 26 November 2002 – 33218/96
Fairchild v. Glenhaven Funeral Services Ltd. – House of Lords, 20 June 2002 – UKHL 22

Georgia-Pacific Corp. v. Bostic – Court of Appeals of Texas, Fith District, Dallas, 26 August 2010 – 05-08-01390-CV
Iglesias Gil and A.U.I. v. Spain – European Court of Human Rights, 29 April 2003 – 56673/00
Kolyadenko et al. v. Russia – European Court of Human Rights, 28 February 2012 – 17423/05, 20534/05, 20678/05, 23263/05, 24283/05, 35673/05
Mastromatteo v. Italy – European Court of Human Rights, 24 October 2002 – 37703/97
Marche v. Stramare – High Court of Australia, 24. April 1991 – (1991) 171 CLR 506
Osman v. The United Kingdom – European Court of Human Rights, 28 October 1998 – 87/1997/871/1038
Overseas Tankship (UK) Ltd v The Miller Steamship Co (Wagon Mound No. 2) – Privy Council, 25 May 1966 – [1966] UKPC 10, [1967] AC 617; [1967] 2 All ER 709
Prosecutor v. Jean-Piere Bemba Gombo – International Criminal Court, 21 March 2016 – ICC-01/05-01/08
Prosecutor v. Naser Orić – International Criminal Tribunal for the former Yugoslavia, 3 July 2008 – IT-03-68-A
Prosecutor v. Tihomir Blaškić – International Criminal Tribunal for the former Yugoslavia, 3 March 2000 – IT-95-14-T
Prosecutor v. Zejnil Delalic et al. – International Criminal Tribunal for the former Yugoslavia, 16 November 1998 – IT-96-21-T
United States Diplomatic and Consular Staff in Tehran (United States of America v. Iran) – International Court of Justice, 24 May 1980 – I.C.J. Reports 1980, p. 3.
van den Berg v. Council and Commission – European Court of Justice, 28 October 2004 – C-164/01 P

References

Ambos K (2002) Superior responsibility. In: Cassese A, Gaeta P, Jones JRWD (eds) The Rome Statute of the International Criminal Court – a commentary. Oxford University Press, Oxford, pp 823–872
American Law Institute (1934) Restatements of the Law, Torts. St. Paul, Minnesota
American Law Institute (1965) Restatements of the Law, Second, Torts. St. Paul, Minnesota
American Law Institute (2010) Restatements of the Law Third, Torts: liability for physical and emotional harm. St. Paul, Minnesota
Aristotle (n.d.a) Metaphysica. In: Jaeger W (ed) Oxford classical texts (1957). Oxford University Press, Oxford
Aristotle (n.d.b) Physica. In: Ross WD (ed) Oxford classical texts (1950). Oxford University Press, Oxford
Aust H (2011) Complicity and the law of state responsibility. Cambridge University Press, Cambridge
Bagińska E, Majkowska-Szulc S (2018) Causation as a requirement for the Member State Liability under Art. 7 TEU in Conjunction with Art. 2 TEU. Europarecht 2018 Beiheft 1:125–143

Baldrich R (2021) The role of climate science in litigation against carbon majors. Available via ISIpedia. https://www.isipedia.org/story/the-role-of-climate-science-in-litigation-against-carbon-majors/. Accessed 24 Oct 2024
Becker T (2006) Terrorism and the state – rethinking the rules of state responsibility. Oxford University Press, Oxford
Bederman DJ (1990) Contributory fault and state responsibility. Va J Int Law 30(2):335–370
Bellinkx V, Casalin D, Türkelli GE, Scholtz W, Vandenhole W (2022) Addressing climate change through International Human Rights Law: from (extra) territoriality to common concern of human rights. Trans Environ Law 11(1):69–93
Braig KF, Panov S (2020) The doctrine of positive obligations as a starting point for climate litigation in Strasbourg: The European Court of Human Rights as a Hilfssheriff in combating climate change? J Environ Law Litig 35:261–298
Burger M, Metzger D (2020) United Nations Environment Programme, Global Climate Litigation Report 2020 Status Review. Nairobi
Burger M, Wentz J, Horton R (2020) The law and science of climate change attribution. Colum J Environ Law 45(1):60–240
Campbell-Duruflé C, Atapattu SA (2018) The Inter-American Court's Environment and Human Rights Advisory Opinion: implications for international climate law. Clim Law 8:321–337
Chen C-H (2011) Die speziellen Diskriminierungsverbote der Charta der Grundrechte der Europäischen Union – Eine Strukturanalyse unter besonderer Berücksichtigung des Verbotes der Altersdiskriminierung. Nomos, Baden-Baden
Cho R (2021) Attribution science: linking climate change to extreme weather. Available via Columbia Climate School. https://news.climate.columbia.edu/2021/10/04/attribution-science-linking-climate-change-to-extreme-weather/. Accessed 24 Oct 2024
Chong A (2020) State responsibility for climate change damage and the evolving regime of human rights. German Yearb Int Law 63:481–509
Clark RS (2022) Art. 9 – elements of crimes. In: Ambos K (ed) Rome Statute of the Internatinonal Criminal Court – article-by-article commentary, 4th edn. C.H. Beck, pp 727–756
ClientEarth (2018) China launches unprecedented judge training for environment cases. Available via ClientEarth. https://www.clientearth.org/latest/latest-updates/news/china-launches-unprecedented-judge-training-for-environment-cases/. Accessed 24 Oct 2024
Climate Action Network Europe (2021) Amicus Brief in the Case Duarte Agostinho and Others v. Portugal and 32 Other States, 6 May 2021
Conforti B (2003) Reflections on state responsibility for the breach of positive obligations: the case-law of the European Court of Human Rights. Italian D Int Law 13:3–10
Conforti B (2004) Exploring the Strasbourg case-law: reflections on state responsibility for the breach of positive obligations. In: Fitzmaurice M, Sarooshi D (eds) Issues of state responsibility before international judicial institutions. Bloomsbury Publishing, Portland, pp 3–10
Cordes-Holland O (2008) The sinking of the strait: the implications of climate change for Torres Strait Islanders' human rights protected by the ICCPR. Melb J Int Law 9(2):405–438
Crawford J (2013) State responsibility – the general part. Cambridge University Press, Cambridge
Cupido M (2021) Causation in international crimes cases: (Re) concenptualizing the causal linkage. Crim Law Forum 32:1–50
Dellinger M (2017) Rethinking force majeure in public international law. Pace Law Rev 37(2): 445–506
Falcon A (2023) Aristotle on causality. Available via Stanford Encyclopedia of Philosophy. https://plato.stanford.edu/entries/aristotle-causality/. Accessed 24 Oct 2024
Frantzen KI (2017) Staatshaftung für das Vertrauen auf unionsrechtswidrige Gesetze. Peter Lang, Berlin
Fumerton R, Kress K (2001) Causation and the law: preemption, lawful sufficiency, and causal sufficiency. Law Contemp Probl 64(4):83–105
Garner BA (ed) (2009) Black's law dictionary. West Publishing, Saint Paul, Minnesota

Gascoigne C (2023) Causation in the law of the World Trade Organization – an econometric approach. Cambridge University Press, Cambridge
Gellermann M (2018) Art. 340 AEUV. In: Streinz (ed) EUV/AEUV, 3rd edn. C. H. Beck, Munich, pp 2585–2601
Grantham Research Institute on Climate Change and the Environment (2022) Climate Litigation Database. https://climate-laws.org/. Accessed 22 June 2022
Grantham Research Institute on Climate Change and the Environment and Centre for Climate Change Economics and Policy, London School of Economics and Political Science (2021) Global Trends in Climate Change Litigation: 2021 Snapshot. London
Haritz M (2011) Liability with and liability from the precautionary principle in climate change cases. In: Faure M, Peeters M (eds) Climate change liability. Edward Elgar Publishing, Cheltenham, pp 15–35
Hart HLA, Honoré T (1985) Causation in the law. Oxford University Press, New York
Heede R (2014a) Carbon majors: accounting for carbon and methane emissions 1854-2010 methods & results report. Lambert Academic Publishing, London
Heede R (2014b) Tracing anthropogenic carbon dioxide and methane emissions to fossil fuel and cement producers, 1854-2010. Clim Chang 112:229–241
Hennebel L, Tigroudja H (2022) The American Convention on Human Rights – a commentary. Oxford University Press, Oxford
Hoffmann RHL (2011) Causation. In: Goldberg R (ed) Perspectives on causation. Hart Publishing, Oxford, pp 3–10
Hume D (1978) A treatise of human nature. Oxford University Press, Oxford
International Law Commission (2001) Draft Articles on Responsibility of States for Internationally Wrongful Acts, with Commentaries, A/CN.4/SER.A/2001/Add.1 (Part 2). Yearb ILC 2(2): 30–143
IPCC (2007) Climate Change 2007: Synthesis Report – Contribution of Working Groups I, II and III to the Fourth Assessment Report of the Intergovernmental Panel on Climate Change. Geneva
IPCC (2021a) Climate Change 2021: The Physical Science Basis – Contribution of Working Group I to the Sixth Assessment Report of the intergovernmental Panel on Climate Change – Summary for Policymakers. Geneva
IPCC (2021b) Climate Change 2021: The Physical Science Basis. Contribution of Working Group I to the Sixth Assessment Report of the Intergovernmental Panel on Climate Change. Geneva
Jackson RAM (2022) Art. 28 – Responsibility of Commanders and other Superiors. In: Ambos K (ed) Rome Statute of the Internatinonal Criminal Court – article-by-article commentary. Oxford University Press, Oxford, pp 1280–1322
Jarass HD (2021) Charta der Grundrechte der Europäischen Union: GRCh. C. H. Beck, Munich
Kahl V (2022) A human right to climate protection – necessary protection or human rights profileration. Neth Q Hum Rights 40(2):158–179
Kellner M, Durant IC (2012) Causation. In: Fenyves A, Karner E, Koziol H, Steiner E (eds) Tort law in the jurisprudence of the European Court of Human Rights. De Gruyter, Berlin, pp 449–500
Kiss A (2015) Command responsibility under Article 28 of the Rome Statute. In: Stahn C (ed) The law and practice of the International Criminal Court. Oxford University Press, The Hague, pp 608–648
Kleinberg S (2012) Causality, probability, and time. Cambridge University Press, Cambridge
Kloepfer M, Neugärtner RD (2021) Liability for climate damages, sustainability and environmental justice. In: Kahl W, Weller M-P (eds) Climate change litigation: a handbook. C. H. Beck, Munich, pp 23–45
Kosolapova E (2011) Liability for climate change-related damage in domestic courts: claims for compensation in the USA. In: Faure M, Peeters M (eds) Climate change liability. Edward Elgar Publishing, Cheltenham, pp 189–205
Kottmann M (2022) Art. 340 AEUV. In: Hilf M, Nettesheim M (eds) Das Recht der Europäischen Union: EUV/AEUV, 77th edn. C. H. Beck, Munich

Kotuby CT, Sobota LA (2017) General principles of law and international due process: principles and norms applicable in transnational disputes. Oxford University Press, Oxford
Lahav AD (2022) Chancy causation in tort law. J Tort Law 15(1):109–135
Lanovoy V (2022) Causation in the law of state responsibility. Br Yearb Int Law 90:1–84
Lavrysen L (2018) Causation and positive obligations under the European Convention on Human Rights: a reply to Vladislava Stoyanova. Hum Rights Law Rev 18(4):705–718
Law J (2022) Oxford dictionary of law. Oxford University Press, Oxford
Lloyd E, Shepherd TG (2021) Climate change attribution and legal contexts: evidence and the role of storylines. Clim Chang 167(3–4):28–41
Mergili M, Pudasaini SP, Emmer A, Fischer J-T, Cochachin A, Frey H (2020) Reconstruction of the 1941 GLOF Process Chain at Lake Palcacocha (Cordillera Blanca, Peru). Hydrol Earth Syst Sci 24(1):93–114
Meyer-Ladewig J, Brunozzi K (2017) Art. 41 EMRK. In: Meyer-Ladewig J, Nettesheim M, von Raumer S (eds) EMRK Europäische Menschenrechtskonvention, 4th edn. Nomos, Baden-Baden
Mikhailova EA, Lin L, Hao Z, Zurqani HA, Post CJ, Schlautman MA, Post GC, Shepard GB (2022) Delaware's climate action plan: omission of source attribution from land conversion emissions. Laws 11(3):41–56
Minnerop P, Otto F (2020) Climate change and causation. joining law and climate science on the basis of formal logic. Buffalo Environ Law J 27:49–86
Moore M (2009) Causation and responsibility: an essay in law, morals, and metaphysics. Oxford University Press, New York
Moore M (2024) Causation in the law. Available via Stanford Encyclopedia of Philosophy. https://plato.stanford.edu/entries/causation-law/. Accessed 24 Oct 2024
Nedeski N, Nollkaemper A (2022) A guide to tackling the collective causation problem in international climate change litigation. Available via EJIL:Talk! https://www.ejiltalk.org/a-guide-to-tackling-the-collective-causation-problem-in-international-climate-change-litigation/?utm_source=mailpoet&utm_medium=email&utm_campaign=ejil-talk-newsletter-post-title_2 . Accessed 24 Oct 2024
Nitsch S (2021) Liability for climate change damages under the German Environmental Liability Act. In: Kahl W, Weller M-P (eds) Climate change litigation: a handbook. C. H. Beck, Munich, pp 430–447
O'Keefe R (2015) International criminal law. Oxford University Press, Oxford
Office of the United Nations High Commissioner for Human Rights (2009) Report on the Relationship Between Climate Change and Human Rights, A/HRC/10/61, 15 January 2009
Olásolo H (2009) The criminal responsibility of senior political and military leaders as principals to international crimes. Oxford University Press, Oxford
Olásolo H, Rojo EC (2015) Forms of accessorial liability under Article 25 (3) (b) and (c). In: Stahn C (ed) The law and practice of the International Criminal Court. Oxford University Press, Oxford, pp 557–591
Orakhelashvili A (2022) Causation in international law. Edward Elgar Publishing, Cheltenham
Peel J (2011) Issues in climate change litigation thematic focus: climate change governance: policy and litigation in a multi-level system. Carbon Clim Law Rev 5(1):15–24
Plakokefalos I (2015) Causation in the law of state responsibility and the problem of overdetermination: in search of clarity. Eur J Int Law 26(2):471–492
Pöttker E (2014) Klimahaftungsrecht. Mohr Siebeck, Tübingen
Quirico O (2018) Climate change and state responsibility for human rights violations: causation and imputation. Neth Int Law Rev 65(2):185–215
Rigaux F (2005) International responsibility and the principle of causality. In: Ragazzi M (ed) International responsibility today – essays in memory of Oscar Schachter. Martinus Nijhoff Publishers, Leiden, pp 81–91
Ritchie H, Rosado P, Roser M (2024) Share of global CO_2 emissions. Available via Our World in Data. https://ourworldindata.org/grapher/annual-share-of-co2-emissions. Accessed 24 Oct 2024

Ruffert M (2022) Art. 340 AEUV. In: Calliess C, Ruffert M (eds) EUV/AEUV: das Verfassungsrecht der Europäischen Union mit Europäischer Grundrechtecharta: Kommentar, 6th edn. C. H. Beck, Munich, pp 2576–2599
Russell B (1912–1913) On the notion of cause. Proc Aristot Soc 1912-1913 New Ser 13:1–26
Sabin Center for Climate Change Law (2024) Climate Change Litigation Databases. http://climatecasechart.com/. Accessed 24 Oct 2024
Schirmer J-E (2021) Klimahaftung und Kausalität – und es geht doch! Juristenz 76(22):1099–1106
Scott PA, Stone DA, Allen MR (2004) Human contribution to the European Heatwave 2003. Nature 432(7017):610–614
Sebok AJ (2017) Actual causation in the second and third restatements: or, the expulsion of the substantial factor test. In: Zervogianni E, Infantino M (eds) Causation in European tort law. Cambridge University Press, Cambridge, pp 60–84
Setzer J, Vanhala LC (2019) Climate change litigation: a review of research on courts and litigants in climate governance. Wiley Interdiscip Rev Clim 10(3):1–19
Stapleton J (2010) Factual causation. Fed Law Rev 38(3):467–484
Stern B (2010) The obligation to make reparation. In: Crawford J, Pellet A, Olleson S (eds) The law of international responsibility. Oxford University Press, Oxford, pp 563–571
Steward JG (2012) Overdetermined atrocities. Pub Law Leg Theory Pap Ser – N Y Univ School Law 10(5):1189–1218
Stoyanova V (2018) Causation between state omission and harm within the framework of positive obligations under the European Convention on Human Rights. Hum Rights Law Rev 18(2): 309–346
Stoyanova V (2020) Fault, knowledge and risk within the framework of positive obligations under the European Convention on Human Rights. Leiden J Int Law 33(3):601–620
Stuart-Smith R, Saad A, Otto F, Lisi G, Lauta K, Minnerop P, Wetzer T (2021) Attribution science and litigation: facilitating effective legal arguments and strategies to manage climate change damages. Summary Report for FILE Foundation, Oxford
Terhechte JP (2017) Art. 340 AEUV. In: Pechsteich M, Nowak C, Häde U (eds) Frankfurter Kommentar zu EUV, GRC und AEUV, 1st edn. Tübingen, Mohr Siebeck, pp 1428–1464
Triffterer O (2004) Causality, a separate element of the doctrine of superior responsibility as expressed in Article 28 Rome Statute? Leiden J Int Law 15(1):179
Ugrekhelidze M (2007) Causation: reflection in the mirror of the European Convention on Human Rights (A Sketch). In: Caflisch L, Callewaert J, Liddell R, Mahoney P, Villiger M (eds) Liber Amicorum Luzius Wildhaber: Human Rights – Strasbourg Views, Droits de l'Homme – Regards de Strasbourg. N. P. Engel Publisher, Kehl, pp 469–481
van der Geest K, van den Berg R (2021) Slow-onset events: a review of the evidence from the IPCC Special Reports on Land, Oceans and Cryosphere. Curr Opin Environ Sust 50:109–120
van Dijk C (2011) Civil liability for global warming in the Netherlands. In: Faure M, Peeters M (eds) Climate change liability. Edward Elgar Publishing, Cheltenham, pp 206–226
van Inwagen P, Sullivan M, Bernstein S (2023) Metaphysics. Available via The Stanford Encyclodpedia of Philosophy. https://plato.stanford.edu/archives/sum2023/entries/metaphysics. Accessed 24 Oct 2024
Vanuatu ICJ Initiative (2023) ICJ Resolution. Available via Vanuatu ICJ Initiative. https://www.vanuatuicj.com/. Accessed 24 Oct 2024
Vautard R, van Aalst M, Boucher O, Drouin A, Haustein K, Kreienkamp F, van Oldenborgh GJ, Otto FEL, Ribes AE, Robin Y, Schneider M, Soubeyroux J-M, Stott P, Seneviratne SI, Vogel MM, Wehner M (2020) Human contribution to the record-breaking June and July 2019 heatwaves in Western Europe. Environ Res Lett 15(9):094077
Verheyen R (2015) Loss and damage due to climate change: attribution and causation – where climate science and law meet. Int J Glob Warm 8(2):158–169
Wagner G, Arntz A (2021) Liability for climate damages under the German law of torts. In: Kahl W, Weller M-P (eds) Climate change litigation: a handbook. C. H. Beck, Munich, pp 407–429

Weitenberg M (2014) Der Begriff der Kausalität in der haftungsrechlichen Rechtsprechung der Unionsgerichte Nomos, Baden-Baden

Wenzel N (2015) Art. 41 EMRK. In: Karpenstein U, Mayer FC (eds) Konvention zum Schutz der Menschenrechte und Grundfreiheiten – Kommentar, 2nd edn. C. H. Beck, Munich, pp 640–659

Werle G, Jeßberger F (2016) Völkerstrafrecht. Mohr Siebeck, Tübingen

West E (2013) The utility of the NESS test of factual causation in Scots law. Aberd Stud Law Rev 4(1):39–62

Williamson J (2009) Probabilistic theories. In: Beebee H, Hitchcock C, Menzies P (eds) The Oxford handbook of causation. Oxford University Press, Oxford, pp 185–212

Wright G H v (1971) Explanation and understanding. Routledge, London

Wright RW, Puppe I (2016) Causation: linguistic, philosophical, legal and economic. Chic-Kent Law Rev 91(2):461–502

Chapter 4
Factual Causation

4.1 Factual Causation in Climate Change Litigation

Factual causation represents the first of the two requirements for establishing causation in law within a bifurcated understanding. However, the establishment of factual causation, especially in the context of conventional causation doctrines, poses several problems when applied to climatic situations. Most of these obstacles are inherent in the causal doctrines themselves. After a brief introduction to the field of factual analysis, the causal doctrines used by courts in this context are examined in detail. These include the doctrines of counterfactual causation (Sect. 4.2), regularity-based theories (Sect. 4.3) and probability-based concepts (Sect. 4.4). They all build on the common ground of a strong metaphysical foundation and have long been established in legal theory. The main emphasis of each section thus lies in reconciling these doctrines with the obstacles posed by climate change. Moving away from philosophical and metaphysical understandings of causation, the second part of the chapter then analyses newer, more dynamic conceptions of causation in law. These theories have their origins mainly in the jurisprudence of the courts and are, therefore, backward concepts of causation (Sect. 4.5). The most prominent and thus also the most promising approaches in light of climate change are the emission share causation doctrine (Sect. 4.5.1) and a contribution-based approach (Sect. 4.5.2).

The ultimate aim of this chapter is to present possible solutions for dealing with climatic causation. The focus herein does not rest on establishing an overarching, universal doctrine, but rather on identifying the strengths and weaknesses of individual approaches and suggesting options for adaptation through deliberative analysis.

M. Krakau, *Causation in National and International Climate Change Litigation*,
https://doi.org/10.1007/978-3-031-74693-2_4

4.1.1 Introducing Factual Causation

Factual causation refers to the actual cause-effect relation between an action or an omission on the one hand, and the outcome in question on the other. It hereby is considered a basic prerequisite for the establishment of causal relations in virtually every jurisdiction.[1] By asking what the real objective cause for the outcome was, factual causation aims at indicating the factual truth. The main obstacle in establishing factual causation in the law, however, is not posed by the determination of an 'actual' causal connection as such but rather by the transfer of logical considerations into an applicable, practical causal doctrine without producing biased and ultimately incorrect results. This is what most jurisdictions attempt to do by applying counterfactual tests.[2]

However, the translation of actual causality into applicable legal doctrines is always accompanied by a certain loss of actuality. Even if one tries to avoid this through a variety of doctrines and metaphysical approaches, and thus to create a logical, intuitively correct and actual causation depicting doctrine, it has not yet been possible to create a fully comprehensive representation of actual causation in law. Therefore, the goal of a factual doctrine can only be the closest possible representation of actual causation. In this context, the normative-subjective choice of a specific doctrine of factual causality in law does not contradict its overarching factuality, since the normative component refers only to the choice of doctrine and not to the determination of the result per se.[3]

The terminology used to describe factual causal relations varies greatly from one legal system to another. Instead of factual causation, the terms natural, scientific, or pre-legal causation are used, as well.[4] Although terminological differences persist, the distinction between them is largely negligible as they widely refer to the same substance and scope. Nevertheless, in order to avoid confusion and to highlight the differences between the scientific determination of causation and causation in the law, the terms 'scientific' and 'natural' causation are used exclusively when the determination of causation refers to its scientific realm.[5] The term 'pre-legal' causation is likewise eschewed, as this can give the impression that factual causation also implements normative notions causation. For the sake of conceptual consistency, the terminology used is, therefore, limited to the concept of factual causation. In light of a bifurcated understanding of causation in the law, factual causation must further be strictly separated from the notions of the scope of liability, responsibility, and attribution, as these conceptions are usually shaped by normative and evaluative

[1] See in this regard Sect. 3.1.2.

[2] See in more detail Sect. 4.2.

[3] Similarly Fumerton and Kress (2001), p. 86.

[4] In this regard e.g. Pöttker (2014). Some even make use of the term 'nonnormative causation' see Fumerton and Kress (2001).

[5] See in more detail Sect. 3.3.

notions rather than by an objective account of the actual truth.[6] Although it has been argued that socio-political considerations should be incorporated into the overall causation assessment, such approaches are highly contradictory to the purpose and objective of the factual inquiry and should, thus, be discounted.[7]

4.1.2 Omissions as Causes

That active doings can be qualified as causes is undeniable. However, one of the longest-running debates revolves around the question of whether omissions can also be recognized as factually causal for the occurrence of an outcome. On the premise that if a particular person had actively done something, the damage would not have occurred, and in recourse to common parlance, one might consider an omission to be qualified as a cause.[8] Such reasoning relies heavily on an understanding of causation as counterfactual dependence. Counterfactuality itself does not distinguish between omissions or active doings but is rather 'blind' to the substance of the condition.[9] As a result, it is irrelevant whether a counterfactual link has to be established between an omission or a positive action and the outcome.

However, it is widely recognised that mere counterfactual dependence is not equivalent to actual causation as such, which is the premise of those who argue for the exclusion of omissions from causal relations in the law.[10] Nevertheless, there are other valid reasons for not recognising an omission as a cause, especially if one moves away from a mere counterfactual understanding of causation. One of the major arguments in this regard builds upon the naturalistic understanding that omissions are missing an active force. Omissions do not alter the status quo and further do not interfere with the 'normal' cause of events, which leads them to not "*display(ing) 'causal energy'*".[11] This argument goes hand in hand with the more philosophically-grown consideration that the existence of 'nothing' can also set nothing into motion, not even a causal chain.[12] All those arguments ultimately come down to the question of what a cause truly is made of and whether omissions

---

[6]For earlier perceptions Stapleton (2010), pp. 467–468.

[7]See in this regard Sect. 3.1.2.

[8]This is also acknowledged by Wright (2007), p. 288; Beebee (2004), p. 291.

[9]Moore (2009a), p. 399.

[10]Beebee (2004), p. 293; Moore (2009a), p. 399.

[11]In considering that the alteration of a status quo is "*the only morally and legally sound, ontologically sustainable distinction between an action and omission [...].*" Orakhelashvili (2022), p. 38. Events are hereby understood as "*a change or happening*", see Law (2022), term: event. Events are further "*(g)enerally regarded as either a change, usually of short duration, in the qualities or relations such as spatial relations of a thing or as the possession of a property or relation by something at or for a time.*", see Proudfoot and Lacey (2009), p. 129. For the difficult definition and substance of the term 'event' see also Casati and Varzi (2023).

[12]See exemplary Moore (2003), pp. 1222–1223; Moore (2009a), p. 399; Beebee (2004), p. 293.

can be framed in the general perception of causes being events. The prevailing opinion suggests that the latter is not the case.[13] The main arguments of this view persist in the lack of physical interaction and intentional choice, which is considered by this view as a necessary precondition for the qualification as causes.[14] *Moore* argues in this regard that omissions are the sole absence of any type of act.[15] 'Negative acts', consequently, do not exist. Other authors refrain from that general view and argue that every omission entails a positive act consisting of the willingness and the consent not to act.[16] Opposing opinions point out that an omission can, contrary to that presumption, also occur without the will of the person concerned.[17] Some authors, therefore, do not focus on the omission as including a positive will-based act but rather argue that each omission is accompanied by such.[18] Yet others take on a completely different account in emphasising that causation does not describe the relation between different events but between either different facts or propositions.[19] Since an omission does not constitute an event but a fact or a proposition and is, hence, not reliant on positive actions, one can establish causation in the law even in light of omissions.

The difficulty of dealing with omissions within the factual causal inquiry also relates to its application in practice. It particularly becomes apparent when one tries to strictly apply an omission to one of the traditional counterfactual tests. The test requires an analysis of whether the outcome would also have occurred in the absence of the action. However, as the factor in question is an omission and, thus, non-existent, it is hypothetically impossible to 'think away' an already non-existent act. The traditional factual causation test in law, therefore, does not suit an omission-related causal inquiry.

Despite all these ontology-based arguments against the recognition of omissions as causes, a different picture has emerged in practice. In adapting traditional tests of factual causation to conceptualize omissions even in the light of counterfactuality, most jurisdictions nowadays recognize omissions as a cause in the law.[20] By using a method of hypothetical or mental substitution, the decisive counterfactual relation is

---

[13] See e.g. Lewis (1987), p. 190.

[14] Moore (2003), p. 1223; Pundik (2006), p. 1.

[15] Acts are hereby understood as "*(t)he process of doing or performing; an occurrence that results from a person's will being exerted on the external world.*" Garner (2009), p. 27.

[16] For this work acts are to be understood as synonymous with the term 'action', although some see the difference between the two as being that 'acts' are used more technically and 'actions' are used primarily in relation to responsibility, see Proudfoot and Lacey (2009), p. 5; Moore (2009a), pp. 436–437.

[17] Bentham (1789), p. 72.

[18] Hart and Honoré (1985), p. 448.

[19] Facts are understood to be "*(a)n event or state of affairs known to have happened or existed*" Law (2022), term: fact. It is "*(u)sually, that which corresponds to a statement or makes it true*" Proudfoot and Lacey (2009), p. 137; Mellor (1995). Opposing, see Moore (2009a), p. 445; Lewis (1987).

[20] See, for example, the criminal liability for failure to render assistance e.g. in § 323c German Penal Code, but also in international law International Law Commission (2001), Art. 2 para 4.

shifted to the hypothetical assumption of what the outcome would be had a particular event actually taken place. This practice is also, in the view of some authors, a matter of basic socio-legal accounts. *Orakhelashvili* identifies in this regard a particularly liberal perspective in the common law understanding of human autonomy. He argues that quite similar to the understanding of international law runs the liberal conception that "*people do not owe affirmative assistance to each other with a view to avoiding harm that would otherwise materialise but are merely obliged by the law not to proactively harm each other.*"[21] Decisive for the materialization of omission-based causation in most jurisdictions and coherent with a liberal understanding in light of humans' autonomy, nevertheless, is the existence of a duty to act that was ultimately not fulfilled.[22] The duty to act, however, poses a prerequisite of general liability and does not constitute a requirement of counterfactual tests and factual causation as such. It is merely a socio-legal construct that emphasises the recognition of omissions as incentives for the affirmation as causes in practice. Apart from the state practice, other authors propose the inclusion of omissions as causes as well, bringing to use approaches based either on mere dependency or on concepts that rely on physical progress.[23] Yet, such considerations are not covered by current court practice and are moreover opposed by a large number of legal scholars.[24]

Overall, there is a clear case for identifying omissions as causes under the conception that omissions can as well have the same effect as active doings. Whether a non-swimmer is actively thrown into the water or is not rescued (although it would be possible to do so) ultimately does not constitute a significant difference in its effect. Furthermore, it may often not be possible to distinguish between an omission and an action, or a particular scenario may consist of both an omission and an active doing.[25] However, the distinction between omissions and positive actions can become relevant in law. This is particularly the case in criminal law, where it can ultimately lead to different assessments of, for example, the sentencing.[26] This distinction, though, only refers to the effect that omissions as causes ultimately have; it is irrelevant to the question of whether omissions can ultimately be qualified as causes. It is also commonly argued that from a normative-legal perspective, omissions and actions are equivalent.[27] In continuing with a normative account on the matter, reasons of fairness and justice further mandate the infliction of moral, as well as of legal blameworthiness on non-actions. And although normative reasons

[21] Orakhelashvili (2022), p. 38.

[22] Magnus (2007), p. 101.

[23] Lagnado and Gerstenberg (2017), p. 566.

[24] Amongst them Magnus (2007), p. 96; Pundik (2006), pp. 7–29; Lewis (1987), p. 189; Paul (2009), p. 169; David et al. (2005), pp. 222–223.

[25] E.g. Magnus (2007), p. 98; Infantino and Zervogianni (2017), p. 593. In cases in which both, an omission and an active doing are apparent, the German criminal theory would then focus on the main emphasis of the scenario (*Schwerpunkttheorie*).

[26] See e.g. in German criminal law the differentiation between § 13 I and § 13 II German Penal Code.

[27] Orakhelashvili (2022), p. 94.

cannot be the sole reason for deciding how to deal with a factual dilemma, and traditional 'the same as always' state practice as well is not an indicator of the righteous way, it is inevitable for the purpose and the aim of this work to acknowledge omissions as causes. It is here that metaphysical and philosophical accounts diverge from legal theory and ultimately legal practice.

4.1.3 Evaluative Criteria of Factual Causal Doctrines

The following sections deal with the treatment of various causation doctrines, both in their traditional and in their more recently developed conceptions. In doing so, the approaches are examined for their aptness to be used in climate change litigation on the basis of three differing criteria. Those criteria include, in particular, the metaphysical soundness of the causal conceptions, their accuracy in representing factual causation, and their practical relevance and actual feasibility within a deliberate legal trajectory as well as their overall suitability to be translated into practice. Through this process, the following section aspires to provide a thorough examination that aids in directing forthcoming legal measures in the context of climate change.

When evaluating different causal doctrines for their use in climate change litigation, the first criterion to consider is their metaphysical validity. This involves assessing the theoretical and metaphysical grounding of traditional approaches, as well as doctrines building regularities and probabilities.[28] While a comprehensive analysis of all accounts and variations within the metaphysical frameworks of those respective approaches is not feasible, the focus of the evaluation mainly rests within the generally valid components of each causal approach. Case law-grown approaches, on the other hand, cannot be analysed in the same manner as traditional concepts due to their way of originating. Rather the aim in regard to those more recent theories of causation resides in the evaluation as to how those approaches could be reconciled with existing metaphysical accounts to be granted further legitimacy and legal acceptance.

Closely connected to the first aspect of the metaphysical soundness of the approaches is the criterion that seeks to evaluate how the respective account captures actual factual causation. As already discussed previously, it is a two-step account that is crucial for the assessment of causation in the law.[29] The objective of factual causation as the first step within this bifurcated understanding hereby resides in the anchoring of the causal assessment with reality and thereby legitimizing the causal chain for its use in the law. Therefore, the second evaluation criterion consists in the extent to which the relevant causal doctrines can approximate factual causation in the

[28] See in this regard Sects. 4.2, 4.3, and 4.4.

[29] See in this regard Sect. 3.1.2.

law to actual causation. The actual causal reality, hereby, is subject to a scientific causal understanding of cause-effect relations.[30]

In addition to the theoretical considerations, the third and final criterion concerns the practical relevance of the approaches. This criterion acts as a bridging factor between the more abstract considerations of theory and philosophy of the correct causal understanding and the realisation and application of these theories in legal practice. Crucial factors are the general applicability of the doctrines by courts and litigants, and their suitability in a climate change-induced scenario. The latter aspect, in particular, is given considerable weight in assessing the viability of the respective accounts. This depends largely on the extent to which the approaches can deal with the causal difficulties inherent in climate change litigation, such as the large number of different small and large contributions, the scientific uncertainties and the complexity of the climate system in general.[31] Within this factor, recourse is taken to the results of the analysis as indicative factors by dissecting and evaluating the implementation and application of causal approaches in climate cases that already have been decided by courts.[32] In the case of causal doctrines and accounts that have not yet found their way into legal practice, or have done so only to a limited extent, the focus is placed on a simulated application of the respective approach to an exemplary climate case in order to assess its usefulness and suitability. Recourse is often, but not exclusively, drawn to the judgment and case of *Luciano Lliuya v. RWE AG.*[33]

These three criteria thus form the main construct of the causal analysis of different factual approaches and their applicability in climate change litigation. In the final evaluation of the feasibility and the overall soundness of the respective approaches, all three criteria carry the same weight. Thus, the argument that an approach makes it ‘easier’ for courts and litigants to establish causation may serve as an indication of the general applicability of the approach, but without a sound metaphysical basis and without meeting the general requirement of factual causation that the legal analysis be anchored in scientific causal relations, the approach is of little use. Having clarified the evaluation criteria, and as explained at the outset, it is generally understood that the emphasis is not on an all-or-nothing approach. Instead, the strengths and weaknesses of each approach are identified on the basis of the criteria introduced, in order to allow for an individual and jurisdiction-specific identification of the account that best fits the specific conditions and legal framework.[34]

---

[30] See for a scientific understanding of causation Sect. 3.3.1.

[31] See for more detailed elaborations on the obstacles of causation in regard to climate change litigation Sect. 3.3.2.

[32] See for the comprehensive analysis Sect. 3.4.

[33] See Essen Regional Court, 15 December 2016 – 2 O 285/15 -*Luciano Lliuya v. RWE AG.*

[34] See in this regard Chap. 6.

4.2 Counterfactual Causation

4.2.1 The Metaphysical Interface of Counterfactual Theories of Causation

Within legal practice and jurisprudence, factual causation is generally established by applying counterfactual tests, also known as a concept of strong necessity. Although first but most confusingly and rather unintentionally introduced by *Hume*, it was *Lewis* who developed a functional and comprehensive account of counterfactual causal relations.[35] *Lewis* emphasized that

> (w)e think of a cause as something that makes a difference, and the difference it makes must be a difference from what would have happened without it. Had it been absent, its effects – some of them, at least, and usually all – would have been absent as well.[36]

Lewis's understanding of causation is strongly based on the interrelation of two factors. It constitutes a highly bilateral and bi-depended conception of cause-effect relations. Building upon the understanding developed by *Lewis*, two tests of counterfactual causation, in particular, have gained acceptance in national, regional and international law.[37] The but-for test, mainly used in common law jurisdictions, asks whether, but for the existence of an act, the outcome would have occurred.[38] The conditio-sine-qua-non doctrine, which is predominantly used in civil law jurisdictions, is based on the same premises as the but-for test but differs slightly in the level of proof required within the test.[39] Substance-wise, however, both conceptions depict the same understanding of causation in that they both ground their assessment on a hypothetical, ex-post reflection of the relevant scenario without the particular act in question. If the outcome would still occur, although the relevant action was dismissed, the condition would not be qualified as necessary for the specific outcome, thus leading to a rejection of factual causation. As the standardized phrase of counterfactuality does not comprehensively takes account of the need of qualifying

---

[35]Hume (1975) revised text and notes by P.H.Nidditch, Lewis (1973).

[36]Lewis (1973), p. 161.

[37]Counterfactual tests have e.g. stood in question in European Court of Justice, 11 March 1987 – C-265/85, *Van Den Bergh En Jurgens v. Commission*, para 1155, European Court of Justice, 7 April 1992 – C-358/90, *Compagnia Italiana Alcool v. Commission*, 2457. Concerning the establishment of causation by European Courts see Weitenberg (2014), p. 421.

[38]Countries such as the United States of America and Great Britain would normally use the term 'but-for' to describe counterfactual causation.

[39]The standard of proof required for the respective causal chain varies greatly from jurisdiction to jurisdiction. Most use a probability or certainty-based account, ranging from a 'more-probable-than-not' approach commonly used in, e.g. England and Denmark, to near certainty or the conviction of the court used in Germany. Infantino and Zervogianni (2017), pp. 611–612. For a critical account on the 'more-probable-than-not' standard see Strandberg (2019). In highlighting the different accounts inherent within different areas of law within the same jurisdiction, see Sorabji (2019). Concerning the standard of proof presupposed in German tort law and especially its alteration Althammer and Tolani (2019).

omissions as causes, courts have made use of a modified version of traditional counterfactual tests. According to such adapted dogmas, an omission is perceived as causal if the outcome would not occur, if the necessary action was fulfilled.

Conceptual-wise, counterfactual theories depend largely on the necessity of the condition for the outcome of the specific event, however, they do not require full sufficiency. Proportional sufficiency is fully satisfactory in this respect.[40] Nevertheless, counterfactual theories are mono-causal conceptions, meaning they aim at finding only one relevant cause for the outcome in question. Respectively such theories encounter multiple problems when an outcome is not only caused by one sufficient condition, but several sufficient and/or necessary acts or omissions contribute to the occurrence of the very same. The main complaint raised against the use of counterfactual conceptions of causation involves the criticism that these tests yield unjust results due to their inability to deal with cases of overdetermination and multiple tortfeasors. Despite this criticism, the use of counterfactual tests still dominates legal practice and also transpires to climate cases. Focusing, in particular, on the moral value of counterfactual theories, *Orakhelashvili* emphasized that

> (t)he key relevance of a but for cause is that it expresses distinctly the idea of blameworthiness based on contribution to actus reus of a crime or more generally to material content of a legal wrong. It is the most natural criterion rationalising the link of a harmful outcome to conscious action of persons and entities who act independently and autonomously.[41]

And further:

> The but for test is not just a random tool in the box; instead, it explains the actual change and alteration of status quo. Also, and frequently voiced criticism notwithstanding, the but for test also puts emphasis on the agent's blameworthiness, and is the most manifest indication of moral choices made by an agent.[42]

In concluding that counterfactual causation forms the natural component of legal culpability and thus legal blameworthiness, *Orakhelashvili* spans the arc from the doctrine and its substance per se to its ultimate use and significance in the law. In implementing counterfactuality, the doctrines also function as an anchor for the legal assessment in the natural, actual world. It is, therefore, of paramount importance in almost any legal assessment.

4.2.2 The Viability of Counterfactual Tests in Climate Change Litigation

As has previously been shown, the but-for test and the conditio-sine-qua-non formula form the basis of factual causal analysis in the vast majority of jurisdictions

---

[40] See for the obstacles posed by the conception of necessity and sufficiency Sect. 4.2.2.

[41] Orakhelashvili (2022), p. 22.

[42] Ibid. 23.

around the world. The use of both tests, hereby, is not limited to a particular field or area of law but is widely accepted across different legal disciplines. The tests are also precedingly applied in light of climate change claims and require a demonstration that, but for a particular act or omission, a particular outcome would not have occurred. Accordingly, the conduct must be qualified as a necessary and partly sufficient condition for the occurrence of the outcome. The difficulty of establishing such a comprehensive causal chain depends largely on its length, the responsibility for the outcome and its nature.

The length of the causal chain, in turn, strongly depends on whether general or specific causation is in question.[43] Whereas general causation in climate litigation aims at the establishment of a causal link between a generalized conduct, for example, the overall emission of greenhouse gases, and a general impact, specific causation targets a specific conduct, e.g. the emission of greenhouse gases of an individual emitter and a concrete outcome. Specific causal chains are, therefore, considerably longer and more dendritic than it is the case with general causal chains and, in turn, pose great obstacles to the establishment of causation in climate lawsuits. The fact that courts are generally confronted with fewer problems when establishing general causal relations is shown by the decision of the Supreme Court of the Netherlands in the case *Urgenda Foundation v. State of the Netherlands*, in which the High Court did not border to deal with the causal relation between anthropogenic greenhouse gas emissions from the burning of fossil fuels and global warming but instead affirmed general causation as a scientifically proven fact.[44] The same can be observed in similar cases, which exclusively concern the general influence of greenhouse gas emissions on climate change.[45] In supporting this argument, the results of the analysis also indicate that courts are generally more open to affirming general causation than it is the case with specific causation.[46]

On the other hand, cases that involve determining the precise causal chain for a particular outcome can be extremely challenging and difficult to navigate in climate matters. Cases of specific causation are inherently characterized by significantly longer causal chains. While a causal link between emissions E_S and climate change as an effect I_F can still be established rather unproblematically, fundamental problems arise when a counterfactual causal chain is necessary to be constructed between a not emission-imminent behaviour B_S and a specific damage or violation of a legal good I_S. A link shorter but no less problematic is the case *Luciano Lliuya v. RWE AG*, which is currently pending before the Higher Regional Court of Hamm.[47] In this

[43] See in more detail Sect. 3.3.1.1.

[44] Supreme Court of the Netherlands, 20 December 2019 – 19/00135, *Urgenda Foundation v. The State of The Netherlands*, para 2.1.

[45] Ibid., Germany Federal Constitutional Court, 24 March 2021 – 1 BvR 2656/18 – 1 BvR 78/20 – 1 BvR 96/20 – 1 BvR 288/20, *Neubauer et al. v. Germany*.

[46] In 90% of the cases general causation has been affirmed. See for the results in more detail Sects. 3.4.3.3.2 and 3.4.3.3.3.

[47] Higher Regional Court Hamm, pending – 5 U 15/17, *Luciano Lliuya v. RWE AG*.

case, Luciano Lliuya, a Peruvian farmer and mountaineering guide, is claiming the assumption of costs for the construction of flood protection measures by the RWE AG. The plaintiff argues that the proportionate emissions of the RWE AG (E_S) amounting to 0.47% of the worldwide anthropogenic greenhouse gas emissions (E) have led to a proportionate increase in the global surface temperature T and thus to an enhanced melting of the glaciers of the Cordillera Blanca and retreat, in particular, of the Palcaraju glacier (X_S). As a result, the water volume of the Palcacocha lagoon had risen (I_F), and the risk of a so-called glacial lake outburst flood (GLOF) in the area in which the plaintiff lives and whose house is located had increased (I_S). The Essen Regional Court then dismissed the action in the first instance as inadmissible and partly unfounded. In particular, the Court ruled that a causal chain could not be formed based on the conditio-sine-qua-non formula, as the alleged flood hazard would continue to exist even without the greenhouse gas emissions of the RWE AG. Above all, the Court focused on the problem of the cumulative effect of emissions.[48]

The District Court for the Northern District of California also denied the existence of a causal chain based on counterfactual tests in the case of the *City of Oakland v. BP p.l.c.*[49] Here, the cities of Oakland and San Francisco claimed that five corporations should bear the costs of the city's climate adaptation measures. In particular, they urged the assumption of the costs necessary for the construction of protective measures against an increasing sea level rise, which would, in return, damage the city's infrastructure. In its order, however, the Court argued that "*global warming would have continued in the absence of all California-related activities of defendants. Plaintiffs have therefore failed to adequately link each defendants' alleged California activities to plaintiffs' harm.*"[50] In the absence of causation, the Court dismissed the motion due to a lack of standing.

In addition to positive acts, such as the emission of greenhouse gases, omissions also play a major role in climate change lawsuits. The difficulty of distinguishing between an omission and an active doing is particularly evident in scenarios of non-compliance with emission reduction targets. In the case of *Urgenda Foundation v. The State of The Netherlands* and the case *Neubauer et al. v. Germany*, the plaintiffs urged that current reduction targets fail to meet the temperature threshold set by the Paris Agreement.[51] Both cases raise the question regarding the specific nature of the action being referenced. On the one hand, setting emission reduction targets that are too low might qualify as a positive action, while on the other hand, not setting sufficient targets can be seen as an omission. To solve this dilemma,

---

[48] Essen Regional Court, 15 December 2016 – 2 O 285/15, *Luciano Lliuya v. RWE AG*, para 42. See also later in Sect. 4.2.2.1.

[49] United States District Court for the Northern District of California, pending – 3:17-cv-06011, *City of Oakland v. BP p.l.c.*

[50] Ibid. order (27 July 2018) (Doc. 287), 5.

[51] Supreme Court of the Netherlands, 20 December 2019 – 19/00135, *Urgenda Foundation v. The State of The Netherlands*, Germany Federal Constitutional Court, 24 March 2021 – 1 BvR 2656/18 – 1 BvR 78/20 – 1 BvR 96/20 – 1 BvR 288/20, *Neubauer et al. v. Germany*.

different jurisdictions draw on different methods and principles.[52] However, as seen in the previous section, and from a universal and more abstract perspective, the distinction is negligible.[53] Since in the predominant literature as well as in the case law of courts, omissions are widely regarded as causes, even within a (slightly modified) counterfactual test, the qualification as a positive act or omission is only of limited significance and of dogmatic and philosophical nature but does not pose a significant obstacle to climate change litigation claims.[54]

Although there have been attempts to employ counterfactual tests in climate change cases, a number of obstacles to their successful implementation remain. It is not only the courts that consider counterfactual causation in climate scenarios a major hurdle, some scholars argue that the conditio-sine-qua-non formula and the but-for test are entirely unsuitable for climate scenarios, as well.[55] The main problem, particularly with respect to emissions-based claims, emanates from the large number of emitters, which raises the issue of concurrent causes and scientific verifiability. However, this can also become of relevance in emission-independent lawsuits since numerous factors influence the natural climate system and its change. With the problem of concurrent causes being the generic category in light of multiple tortfeasors, it can further be distinguished between the types of cumulative (Sect. 4.2.2.1) and alternative causation (Sect. 4.2.2.2). Furthermore, problems in the temporal and local sphere of emissions need to be addressed (Sect. 4.2.2.4).

4.2.2.1 Cumulative Causation and Causal Over-Determination

Cumulative causation is present when an act or an omission does not suffice to cause the outcome alone but is accompanied by other conditions, with each of those conditions lacking the sufficiency to cause the outcome without the others. Cumulative causation thereby falls in the category of concurrent causes, which is often used in common law countries to describe causation in the case of multiple actors. Others, especially in the metaphysical, philosophical discourse, turn to the term

[52] In Germany, for example, the so-called '*Schwerpunkttheorie*' applies to distinguish between offences by omission and offences by an active doing in criminal law. The classification depends solely on where the main emphasis of the offence lies.

[53] See in this regard Sect. 4.1.2.

[54] A limiting difference is the necessity of the existence of a duty to act for legal reproachability in the case of omissions. This requirement lies outside the realm of causation and causal determinations per se.

[55] In this regard Dijk (2011), p. 219; Frank (2013), p. 30; Kaminskaitė-Salters (2011), p. 183; Duffy (2009), p. 221; Minnerop and Otto (2020), p. 50. Concerning cases with multiple emitters Voigt (2016), p. 484. In regard to the inadequacy of the but-for test in general, see Stapleton (2010), pp. 474, 476. In favour of the application of counterfactual tests, see Schirmer (2021) and Zeidler (2022).

causal overdetermination.[56] Depending on the conceptual qualification of conditions as necessary, two different scenarios emerge within the class of cumulative causation cases.

In the first scenario, the specific emissions E_S are necessary for the outcome but do not represent a sufficient condition alone. Only with the inclusion of several other conditions (E_{XS}) does this set exceed the threshold of sufficiency.[57] The counterfactual tests strictly applied would, however, still lead to the affirmation of the causal relation of E_S since, without its contribution, the necessary threshold would not be passed. Thus the outcome would not occur without the contribution of E_S. The prerequisite for such a scenario, nonetheless, is that each specific condition (E_{XS}) is a necessary one. In this regard, establishing counterfactual causal relations by courts or plaintiffs is not a heavy task. Rather, the nature and, above all, the extent of liability is proving difficult. Whether each defendant is liable to the full extent (joint and several liability) or only to a certain amount (several liability) varies from jurisdiction to jurisdiction. This question only concerns the extent of liability and not causation per se. Therefore, this question shall be neglected at this point. Nonetheless, even this scenario is not completely without problems. While the construction of the causal chain may be perfectly obvious in theory and when the laws of formal logic are applied, the question arises as to its applicability in reality. Due to various different contributions and the variability of the climate system itself, it is often difficult to determine an exact necessity threshold. And even if such a threshold could be scientifically determined, there are still obstacles in regard to the handling of scientific evidence and uncertainties.[58]

Within the second scenario, E_S is merely part of a multitude of conditions E_X subsumed under set E. E is, in its entirety, necessary and sufficient for the outcome in question. Within E, however, the individual E_X are neither sufficient nor necessary.[59] The lack of necessity, in particular, results from the fact that the set of conditions in its entirety has already exceeded the threshold for the occurrence of the outcome in such a way that the outcome would still occur even if individual conditions were omitted. In overstepping the threshold (which was met in scenario one), it could even be said that scenario two is a further evolution of scenario one. Assuming that it would be possible to calculate a sufficiency threshold, all conditions up to this threshold would be considered necessary and thus counterfactually causal (scenario one). If the conditions exceed this threshold by a certain amount, the conditions would retrospectively no longer be considered necessary, which in turn would qualify them as no longer causal. This follows from the fact that even if the

[56] In this regard e.g. *Moore* in describing causal overdetermination as cases in which two or more conditions are independently sufficient to produce a certain outcome, see Moore (2009a), p. 354.

[57] See for further explanation Pöttker (2014), p. 52. *Moore* also calls those types of cases "*ordinary garden-variety concurrent causation cases*" see Moore (2009a), p. 411.

[58] See in this regard especially Sect. 3.3.

[59] *Moore* calls such types of cases "*mixed concurrent overdetermination cases*", Moore (2009a), pp. 411–412.

conditions were removed, the later ones would now take the place of the omitted ones, so the result would remain the same. Applied to climate scenarios and greenhouse gas emissions, this means that even if a threshold for the occurrence of damage could be scientifically calculated (e.g. a temperature threshold, density of CO_2 emissions in the air, etc.) and the specific emissions in question were emitted before the threshold was reached, the necessity of some of the contributions could still be eliminated by the addition of further emissions. Yet, not every transgression of this threshold leads to the rejection of counterfactual causation. What is decisive is that the sum of the excess is considered to be greater than or equal to the specific condition. This consideration may appear to be merely theoretical at first, in the determination of causation, nevertheless, it is crucial.

Assuming that E_S is equal to the sum of ten and E_1, E_2, E_3 and E_4 are also ten, the threshold Y at which the sum E of all $E_{S\text{-}4}$ can be regarded as a causal condition for the outcome is 50. In scenario one, this constellation persists. All emissions, E_S, E_1, E_2, E_3 and E_4, are necessary conditions for exceeding the threshold. The sum E of $E_{S\text{-}4}$ is, therefore, necessary and sufficient, which in turn leads to $E_{S\text{-}4}$ also being counterfactual causal. Assuming that E_5 is now added to E and equates to a sum of five. Y is now exceeded. However, E_S is still a necessary condition and thus counterfactually causal since when E_S is removed, the sum of $E_{1\text{-}5}$ (45) does not exceed the necessary threshold of 50. Thus scenario one is still relevant for E_S. Conversely, this does not apply to E_5 since E_5 is already not to be regarded as a necessary condition for the outcome under this scenario. In another step, however, E_6 is added with a sum of five. With the addition of E_6, all $E_{S\text{-}6}$ are automatically no longer counterfactually considered necessary conditions and thus no longer causal. This ultimately clarifies the difference between scenarios one and two. The threshold itself is particularly relevant, as is the scope of E_S and all additional factors. Within climate change litigation, it is, therefore, scenario two that courts are most frequently confronted with. Although there are, of course, other types of cases that fall within the scope of climate change litigation, the standard case involves the emission of greenhouse gases and a claim either to reduce them or to pay for the damage they cause. Under the strict application of counterfactual tests to emission-based climate change lawsuits, factual causation would frequently have to be rejected.

In 1987, the Federal Court of Justice of Germany was confronted with the question of the effects of emissions, more specifically of sulphur dioxide (SO_2) and nitrogen oxides (including nitrogen monoxide (NO) and nitrogen dioxide (NO_2)), on the environment and biodiversity.[60] The so-called *Forest-Dieback* case (*Waldsterbensfall*) dealt with the question of whether the owner of a forest, which had suffered considerable damage due to air pollution and acid rain, could claim compensation from public authorities. Even though this case did not deal with CO_2 emissions but with SO_2 emissions, the case has often been referred to and has been proclaimed comparable to current climate change lawsuits when it comes to the

[60] Federal Court of Justice, 10 December 1987 – III ZR 220/86, *Forest Dieback.*

cumulative effect of emissions. The Federal Court of Justice emphasized in that regard that

> [...] a large number of large and small emitters [...] are involved in the generation of air pollutants [...]. Their emission contributions are indistinguishably mixed (summed emissions), so that it is practically impossible to individually attribute the damage incurred by the individual forest owner to one or more specific emitters.[61]

Based on this statement, the Federal Court of Justice ultimately negated the existence of a stringent causal chain. However, the fundamental difference, and consequently the reason for the limited transferability of the judgement, is that SO_2 emissions change, transform and mix in the air due to the influence of other gases, making it much more difficult to track them and their effects. To form acid rain, which is precipitation with a lower ph-level than normal rainwater and is, therefore, harmful to nature and biodiversity, SO_2 must react with oxygen in the air to form SO_3.[62] When SO_3 reacts with water, it forms sulphuric acid, which in turn, lowers the pH of the precipitate. Nitrous oxides react with water and oxygen to form nitrous acid (HNO_2/HNO_3), which has the same effect. This is not a concern when emissions of CO_2 are in question; CO_2 emissions cause the climate-changing effect directly, without the need to react with other substances in the air to produce the harmful effect. The causal chain between the substance itself and its effect is, thus, much shorter, making it difficult to apply the judgement to current climate lawsuits. Another problem is the distribution of SO_2 molecules in the atmosphere, as not all SO_2 emissions react with water, but only a small individual amount contributes to the formation of acid rain. This makes individualisation of SO_2 emissions necessary but difficult due to natural thermal variations and wind currents. Nonetheless, attribution science and climate science, in general, have evolved, making it easier to trace emissions today. Furthermore, CO_2 emissions are not subject to such distributive peculiarities since CO_2 emissions tend to be evenly dispersed in the atmosphere. These fundamental differences impede the transference of the reasoning in *Forest Dieback* to climate change lawsuits.

In the same context, the Court in the case *Native City of Kivalina v. Exxon Mobil et al.* ruled, and even the plaintiffs acknowledged, that

> there is no realistic possibility of tracing any particular alleged effect of global warming to any particular emissions by any specific person, entity, group at any particular point in time. [...] (T)he genesis of global warming is attributable to numerous entities which individually and cumulatively over the span of centuries created the effects they now are experiencing.[63]

Courts have recognized the issue of cumulative emissions in light of counterfactual causation numerous times, and while they rejected claims based on causation before, recent cases, in particular, show that courts are becoming more willing to affirm

[61] Ibid. para 13 (translated by the author).

[62] Water usually has a pH of 7 and is neutral, whereas rainwater is calculated to have a pH of around 5.7. Acid rain is said to occur when the pH falls below 5.

[63] US District Court for the Northern District of California, 30 September 2009 – 4:08-cv-01138-SBA, *Native Village of Kivalina v. ExxonMobil Corp.*, 20.

causation despite possible conceptual inconsistencies. The Committee on the Rights of the Child stated in its decision in the case *Sacchi et al. v. Argentina et al.* that "*the Committee finds that the collective nature of the causation of climate change does not absolve the State party of its individual responsibility [...].*"[64] In the same context but concerning the necessary climate protection measures to stop climate change, the Federal Constitutional Court of Germany stated in the case *Neubauer, et al. v. Germany* that "*(i)t is true that Germany would not be capable of preventing climate change on its own. Its isolated activity is clearly not the only causal factor determining the progression of climate change and the effectiveness of climate action.*"[65] In doing so, the Court indirectly addressed the drop-in-the-ocean principle often invoked as a defence in pro-climate change lawsuits, according to which each state's contribution is only a small, insignificant part of a large sum of causes.[66] And while such an argument could also be fine-grained to individual emissions, courts, however, seem to be more and more reluctant to accept such a defence.[67]

The elaboration of both cases has shown that the cumulative occurrence of different emissions is no longer used as an argument for rejecting causation. However, this is done without any dogmatic or conceptual substantiation since a strict, purely objective application of the counterfactual test would most likely have led to a rejection of causation in these cases as well.[68] The above shows that there is a need to depart from strict counterfactual analysis, as without such deviation, no emission would be considered causal, which, in a further step, would lead to the failure of any climate claim. However, the main objection to the handling of cumulative causes in counterfactual causation does not reside in its general rejection of factual causation but in the deviation of causation in the law with actual, natural causation and reality. A rejection of causation due to the application of counterfactual tests would further be contrary to the factual truth. Even the smallest contributions can be qualified as causes within the framework of 'actual' and 'natural' processes. Whether such minimal contributions should ultimately also be perceived as causal in the law is a question that has to be answered in the second step of the causal analysis but does not need to be implemented in the factual assessment.[69] A deviation from the traditional dogma of causation is necessary to correspond to actual and even scientific causation in order to ultimately fulfil the purpose of its factual account. Without a reflection of

[64] United Nations Committee on the Rights of the Child, 8 October 2021 – CRC/C/88/D/107/2019, *Sacchi et al. v. Argentina et al.*, para 9.10.

[65] Germany Federal Constitutional Court, 24 March 2021 – 1 BvR 2656/18 – 1 BvR 78/20 – 1 BvR 96/20 – 1 BvR 288/20, *Neubauer et al. v. Germany*, para 201 (engl. translation).

[66] See for materiality as criteria of normative causation Sect. 5.4. See for more detail also Sect. 3.4.3.3.4.

[67] See e.g. Administrative Court of Berlin, 31 October 2019 – VG 10 K 412.18, *Family Farmers and Greenpeace Germany v. Germany*, 22, New South Wales Land and Environment Court, 8. February 2019 – [2019] NSWLEC 7, *Gloucester Resources Limited v. Minister for Planning*, 515–524.

[68] See for the validity of this statement also the results obtained in the analysis in Sect. 3.4.3.3.4.

[69] See in this regard Sect. 5.4.

reality, factual causation loses its function of anchoring legal evaluation in the real world and thus ceases to serve as a basis for overall legal evaluation. A departure from counterfactual tests in cases of cumulative causation has further been recognized outside the realm of climate change litigation for quite some time, although different jurisdictions handle the dilemma differently.[70] In legal scholarship, a denial of causation in cases of cumulative causation is regarded to be an unacceptable and inequitable result, as well.[71] Especially when one considers the difference between both scenarios of cumulative causation, it does not coincide with logical sense and intuition why the first scenario would result in the establishment of causation, while in the second scenario, only because of the excision of the threshold, causation would be rejected.[72] An adaption of counterfactual causation, therefore, has to be achieved in the light of climate change litigation and climatic causal chains.[73]

4.2.2.2 Alternative Causation

Cases of alternative causation concern two or more independent but sufficient sets of conditions, which in themselves could have caused the outcome alone.[74] Such alternating causes can also be described as symmetrically overdetermined concurrent causation, duplicative causation or additional competitive causation.[75] The description as symmetrical thereby relies on the fact that all conditions are equally sufficient ones. From a theoretical point of view, such a problem may arise when not only the specific emission E_S but also E_1 and E_2 constitute a sufficient set of conditions alone. In addition to emissions as causes, climate lawsuits may also concern other emission-independent factors w_x that can cause the outcome in themselves. In the event of a flood, the straightening of the river, the faulty construction of dams, the lack of necessary flood protection measures or many other factors could also constitute a single-handed sufficient condition or a sufficient set of conditions parallel to the emissions of greenhouse gases.

Based on their temporal sphere, two scenarios of alternative causation can be distinguished. The first scenario, and arguably the default case was already described

[70] Infantino and Zervogianni (2017), p. 652.

[71] For example, *Moore*, who states the denial of causation in such cases as metaphysically, morally, and legally unacceptable, see Moore (2009a), p. 410.

[72] Of the same tenor, see Moore (2009), p. 418.

[73] E.g. Verheyen (2005), p. 253. Concerning the case law of courts of the European Union, see Weitenberg (2014), pp. 433–434.

[74] The concept of alternative causation is not used uniformly but can vary slightly, see e.g. Verheyen (2005), p. 254. *Verheyen* only qualifies conditions as alternative, when all conditions have been sufficient, but only one condition truly lead to the outcome and it cannot be ascertained which condition finally did.

[75] For the terminology of overdetermined concurrent causation, see Moore (2009a), pp. 411, 414–417. For the term duplicative causation, see Puppe and Wright (2017), p. 35. For the term additional competitive causation, see Verheyen (2005), p. 254.

above and constitutes two or more sufficient conditions occurring at the same time t. The second scenario is characterised by the temporal differentiation of the sufficient conditions, with both or all conditions occurring not at the same time but one after the other. One sufficient condition, therefore, pre-empts other sufficient conditions. So-called cases of pre-emptive overdetermination raise a lot of problems given that neither of both (or more) conditions would be considered counterfactually causal. Assuming a flood I_{S1} fully destroyed the house of the plaintiff at a specific point in time $t_1(I_{S1\text{-}t1})$.[76] Some days later, at t_2, another flood I_{S2} occurs, with the same destructive strength ($I_{S2\text{-}t2}$). Without the occurrence of $I_{S1\text{-}t1}$, $I_{S2\text{-}t2}$ would have destroyed the house of the plaintiff in the same way as $I_{S1\text{-}t1}$ did. However, given that $I_{S1\text{-}t1}$ already destroyed the house, $I_{S2\text{-}t2}$ does not leave any impact on the house of the plaintiff. Still, based on common sense and logic, at least $I_{S1\text{-}t1}$, the pre-empting sufficient condition, would be considered as a cause of the destruction of the house, whereas $I_{S2\text{-}t2}$ would not. Nonetheless, in applying counterfactual tests, neither of both conditions would be a cause since without the first condition, $I_{S1\text{-}t1}$, the house would still be destroyed by $I_{S2\text{-}t2}$ and vice versa. Consequently, while both conditions are sufficient conditions for the destruction of the house, none of them would be necessary, resulting in the negation of counterfactual causation as a whole.

From a more practical-oriented perspective, pre-emptive causation in climate change litigation is especially conceivable in light of sudden onset and extreme weather events. Since extreme weather events often are followed by other extreme events, alternating conditions do occur in climate change cases as well. Amongst those are mainly droughts, wildfires, and heat waves, as well as floods, frost and storms. Similar alternative, pre-emptive situations occur concerning heavy precipitation. Heavy rainfall in correlation with other factors, such as preceding droughts or sealed floors, frequently not only leads to a swelling of rivers but also to an increased risk of landslides due to the precipitation-induced destabilization of large earth masses.[77] Pre-emptively occurring sufficient conditions in light of climate change are, therefore, quite conceivable.

More difficult, however, are cases in which emission-related conditions are in question. One of the scenarios in which emission-related pre-emptive overdetermination can occur in climate change cases is in cases of regulatory government failure in terms of emission reduction and climate protection. The same applies to sufficient emission-bundles of different actors which diverge timewise. Assuming that the emissions of industrialised country A lead to a certain outcome, for example, a specific extreme weather event in a sufficient manner, but that the emissions of country B following in time would also have led to such an

[76] This terminology is used by e.g. *Moore*, see Moore (2009a), pp. 412, 419–425. Of the same tenor, see Puppe and Wright (2017), p. 35. Others also use the term of '*hypothetical causation*', '*superseding*' or '*overriding causation*' or of a '*reserve cause*'. See in this regard Oetker (2019), para 207; Pöttker (2014), pp. 56, 200.

[77] In early February 2022, heavy rains flooded parts of the city of Quito, Ecuador, followed by a landslide that killed more than a dozen people. Just two weeks later, flash floods and landslides in the Brazilian city of Petropolis also claimed more than 100 lives.

outcome. Within the strict application of counterfactual tests, causation would have to be rejected. Highly problematic, however, is the slow and decelerated effect of emissions, making it difficult to assess the exact moment in which the sufficiency threshold is exceeded, or the outcome has occurred. Equally questionable is the temporal frame between the pre-empting and subsequent conditions raising the issue of whether a time limit needs to be set and to what extent future events should also be included in the consideration. If no limits were to be set in terms of time, further emissions of greenhouse gases could render causation inapplicable in the future due to previous causal conditions, which would lead to inequitable results and make responsibility solely dependent on the time of action. This problem, in addition to the question of the correct grouping of emissions, represents a major hurdle for cases of alternating, pre-emptive causation under the counterfactual approach. Most jurisdictions, thus, deviate from the strict application of counterfactual tests in instances of alternative causation and consider only the first, both or all conditions as causal.[78]

4.2.2.3 The Outlier of Asymmetrical Overdetermined Concurrent Causes

Following the terminology of symmetrically overdetermined concurrent causation as introduced by *Moore*, which reflects on cases that fall in scenario one of the present understanding of alternative causation, the counterpart is posed by asymmetrical scenarios.[79] In difference to symmetrical overdetermined concurrent causes, asymmetrical cases consist of one or more sufficient conditions accompanied by not sufficient ones. Provided that there is only one sufficient condition in addition to further insufficient ones, only the sufficient condition would be qualified as a counterfactual causal condition. Nevertheless, under a strict classification, asymmetrical causation cases that contain only one sufficient condition do neither qualify as an alternative nor as a cumulative case. Alternative causation is characterized precisely by the fact that two or more sufficient conditions are present. Simply put, alternative causation requires an 'either-or' situation. Either one condition brings about the outcome or the other. While this can certainly occur in asymmetrical cases when two or more sufficient conditions fall together with insufficient ones, this is not the case when only one sufficient condition is accompanied by an insufficient one. In the latter scenario, only the sufficient condition is regarded as a cause which would ultimately not pose an obstacle to the establishment of counterfactual causation per se. However, in cases in which the insufficient condition is of heightened relevance and concurrently greatly contributes to the outcome in question, some might consider it intuitively false to deny the insufficient condition the status as a cause.[80]

[78] This is how it is handled, for example, in Italy, Sweden, Germany, Denmark and England, see Infantino and Zervogianni (2017), p. 633.

[79] Moore (2009a), pp. 411, 417–418.

[80] In that regard also Lewis (1987). Opposing, see Moore (2009a), p. 418.

The difference between asymmetrical scenarios and scenarios of cumulative causation or cases of symmetrical overdetermined causation, nonetheless, persists in the facts that asymmetrical cases, provided there is only one sufficient condition, do not lead to the rejection of causation regarding all conditions. Both in cumulative causation and the other scenarios of alternative causation, no single condition would be considered causal. In the scenario of asymmetrical overdetermination, however, a necessary and sufficient condition exists which can lead to a confirmation of causation even under the strict application of counterfactual tests. Naturally, there can be exceptions in which the affirmation of causation for the second condition is to be perceived as logical and 'just' in a normative, deterministic way. Particularly in the case of conditions that contribute to the outcome in a disruptive way and which, despite their lack of necessity and sufficiency, are regarded as an elementary component of the outcome from an ex-post perspective, the question arises as to whether they should not also be regarded as causal in a counterfactual way. Asymmetrical constellations of conditions are in practice and even more so in climate change litigation, not inconceivable. Assuming that worldwide emissions qualify as a sufficient and necessary set of conditions for the occurrence of a flood, with the straightening of the river and missing flood-protection measures still contributing to the outcome. Both of the latter conditions cannot be classified as a cause on the basis of counterfactual tests since, without the reconstruction of the river or even with the necessary flood protection measures, the flood would still have occurred. Further asymmetrical cases might occur in regard to administrative permits and environmental impact assessments that are ultimately followed by further climate damaging behaviour. Asymmetrical cases, therefore, are highly relevant for climate change cases, although they don't fall in the category of alternative causation.

4.2.2.4 The Spatial and Temporal Sphere of Causal Relata

In contrast to issues of cumulative and alternative causation, which are default obstacles to counterfactual causal analysis, issues of spatial and temporal spheres are inherent to the particularities of climate change lawsuits. Anthropogenic climate change is characterised by the fact that the result of one's action or omission does not materialise at the same origin and at the same time as its cause.[81] These problems are referred to as issues of spatial damage and delayed harm.

4.2.2.4.1 The Spatial Sphere of Counterfactuality

Climate change litigation is often concerned with the fact that the effects of one's actions do not occur in the same local sphere as their origin but affect processes in

[81] See in this regard Sects. 3.3.2 and 3.3.3.

completely different parts of the world.[82] This is not surprising, as climate change is indeed a global phenomenon. However, the issue of the long distance between someone's action and the outcome poses significant problems for plaintiffs. In particular, it is difficult to trace the damage or outcome back to emitters who operate far from the site of the event. From a procedural point of view, questions also arise as to the jurisdiction and the court in which the claim must be brought. Finally, further hurdles for the plaintiff and the court are posed by the much more difficult nature of proof.[83] Although the long distance between someone's action and the outcome in question is often perceived as a causal dilemma, traditional counterfactual tests are blind to the spatial scale of the causal chain. The factual causal chain remains the same regardless of where the outcome ultimately occurs. It is a procedural requirement rather than a factor that is taken into account in factual causation. The application of the but-for test and the conditio-sine-qua-non formula do not rely on a local component. The spatial sphere, conversely, can become of relevance in the second step of the causal inquiry in law when normative considerations are introduced in the analysis.[84]

4.2.2.4.2 The Temporal Sphere of Counterfactuality

The Earth's climate system itself is the reason for the temporal hurdles that climate lawsuits face in light of 'delayed' and 'latent' harm.[85] The dilemma builds upon the fact that the impacts of climate-damaging behaviour do not become apparent immediately after the harmful conduct but instead materialize with considerable delay. The delay mainly derives from the inertia of the climate system, with oceans and carbon sinks significantly contributing to the temporal lag.[86] However, climate cases are not the only type of litigation in which the problem of latent harm arises. In particular, in earlier toxic tort cases, which involved health hazards resulting from exposure to either harmful drugs or toxic substances in general, courts have been confronted with the problem of the long temporal distance between cause and effect.[87] In these cases, the time between the damage becoming apparent and the

---

[82] See e.g. the impact of German-based RWE AG's emissions on the risk of a glacial lake outburst flood in Huaraz, Peru, Essen Regional Court, 15 December 2016 – 2 O 285/15, *Luciano Lliuya v. RWE AG*. Also the impact of inadequate climate change mitigation in Germany on complainants from Nepal and Bangladesh, Germany Federal Constitutional Court, 24 March 2021 – 1 BvR 2656/18 – 1 BvR 78/20 – 1 BvR 96/20 – 1 BvR 288/20, *Neubauer et al. v. Germany*.

[83] See again Higher Regional Court Hamm, pending – 5 U 15/17, *Luciano Lliuya v. RWE AG*. In this case, the preliminary investigation was delayed due to a lack of cooperation from the Peruvian authorities. On the general difficulty of dealing with long-distance damage in court, see Chatzinerantzis and Appel (2019), pp. 885–886.

[84] See in this regard especially the requirement of foreseeability in Sect. 5.3.

[85] See in this regard Sect. 2.1.

[86] See e.g. IPCC (2021), pp. 79–80, Box TS.5. See in this regard further Sect. 2.1.

[87] See i.a. Biber (2009), pp. 976–977.

cause was well over 30 years. After the damage had occurred, this long period of time made it much more difficult to trace back the causal chain to its factual cause.

But the temporal sphere is not only relevant in a retrospective. In climate change litigation, issues of delayed harm also arise in the context of claims challenging the potential occurrence of future harm. Such cases primarily concern the adjustment of climate protection targets and the reduction of greenhouse gas emissions. To prevent future harm by actions of today, plaintiffs more and more resort to claims brought forward in place for future generations, which will be even more affected by today's actions as already living generations.[88] Such cases are, therefore, forward-looking, requiring the courts to establish chains of causation even though a particular loss may not yet have materialised. The only way of doing so is by resorting to a risk-based assessment. It is not possible to establish a counterfactual causal link between a condition and a future outcome that has not yet occurred. It is, consequently, only possible to consider the risk of a loss arising but not to predict the precise time at which that risk will materialise. Nevertheless, the problem of delayed damage hasn't gone unnoticed and unaddressed by the courts.

On the contrary, several courts have already recognised the problem, although only a few have dealt with it explicitly. For example, the District Court of The Hague stated in its judgment in the case of *Milieudefensie et al. v. Royal Dutch Shell plc.* that "*the climate system has a delayed response to the greenhouse gas emissions: the warming effect of greenhouse gases which are emitted today will only become apparent in thirty to forty years' time.*"[89] Delayed impacts imply that causal chains must extend over several years, with the risk that various other intervening causes may influence the outcome. Although the problem of delayed damage poses severe difficulties in climate change litigation, it does not affect the application of counterfactual tests given that neither the conditio-sine-qua-non formula nor the but-for test require a temporal frame for the occurrence of the outcome. Counterfactual tests are, thus, also independent of time.

Although issues of delayed harm and distant consequences pose difficult obstacles for plaintiffs in climate change litigation, counterfactual tests generally do not require a particular time or place of occurrence. They are spatially and temporally neutral and, therefore, do not impede the construction of factual causation. Still, this problem may arise regarding the requirements of normative causation or within the procedural requirements of proof.[90] In the context of forward-looking climate demands, the temporal component may also become relevant due to the expected

---

[88] Most expressively see Supreme Court of Colombia, 8 April 2018 – 11001-22-03-000-2018-00319-01, *Future Generations v. Ministry of the Environment and Others.*

[89] Hague District Court, 26 May 2021 – C/09/571932 / HA ZA 19-379, *Milieudefensie et al. v. Royal Dutch Shell plc.*, para 2.3.2.

[90] In the case of *Luciano Lluyia v. RWE AG*, the Court was confronted with a number of problems. In particular, the lack of cooperation from the Peruvian authorities with regard to the preparation of expert reports has significantly delayed the evidentiary proceedings. (Essen Regional Court, 15 December 2016 – 2 O 285/15, *Luciano Lliuya v. RWE AG.*).

output. In general, however, for the establishment of counterfactual causation in its conventional form, the temporal and local sphere is irrelevant.

4.2.2.5 Conclusion

Counterfactual tests, in general, have been confronted with significant criticism due to their alleged unjustness of the results and their incompatibility with actual causal relata. The weakness of the conditio-sine-qua-non formula and the but-for test, however, becomes particularly apparent in cases of climate change litigation in light of causal overdetermination and concurrent causes. The complexity of the climate system itself leads to a convergence of cumulative and alternative causes, which further complicates the assessment of causation. In particular, claims that target greenhouse gas emissions are prone to complex causal chains, with cumulative and alternative, especially pre-emptive, causal situations coinciding. Such scenarios are at odds with the monocentricity of counterfactuals. Nonetheless, it is not only concerning greenhouse gas emissions that counterfactual tests fail in their conventional application. Due to the universal nature of climate change, the complexity of the climate system, and the many factors that can influence and alter the outcome, the issue of establishing factual causation based on counterfactual analysis arises in almost every climate change lawsuits. To put it in the apt wording of *Spier*, "*we face a legal nightmare.*"[91]

Still, unlike cumulative and alternative causation cases, counterfactual tests do not present an obstacle to the often raised issues of delayed harm and the local sphere of damage because counterfactual tests, as conventionally applied and according to the prevailing view, do not involve either a local or a temporal component.[92]

4.2.3 *The Strategy of Factual Concretization*

The previous section has shown that counterfactual tests quite often pose major hurdles or lead to the overall rejection of causation in cases of climate change litigation. It is, therefore, questionable whether an adaptation of the conditio-sine-qua-non formula and the but-for test can lead to an improvement in counterfactual causation, especially in its convergence with actual causation and factual truth. The aim of this section is not to abandon counterfactual tests altogether but instead to interpret or extend the concepts that already exist and have been applied in such a way that they are increasingly applicable to the challenges posed by counterfactuals and climate change.

---

[91] Spier (2007), p. 74.

[92] In opposition and including a temporal sphere, Teichmann (2021), para 26.

One way to solve the problem of counterfactuals in light of concurrent causes, in general, is to add more information to the setting of the outcome of one's action until this specified outcome would not occur without the action in question.[93] Concretizations may include the temporal and local sphere, as well as the overall impact, strength, and pattern of the outcome.[94] By applying this 'strategy of concretization', one eliminates as many conditions from the group of conditions that either one necessary and sufficient condition remains in the end, or only those conditions are left that are not sufficient but necessary.[95] *Moore* refers to this approach as the "*fine-grained individuation of effects strategy*".[96]

What is decisive for the application of such methodologies in law is the standard of the counterfactual tests themselves for the concretization of damages. It may not be necessary to change the existing tests at all but only to subordinate them to a more concrete application. The relevant doctrine would then turn to consider whether the damage would cease to exist in its concrete form.[97] While the concretization of the result has largely been a product of conceptual and theoretical scope and has been discussed predominantly in legal philosophy, the theory of factual concretization has been occasionally adopted and advocated in the literature and practical scholarship, as well.[98] The latter is particularly concerned with a temporal concretization, which in turn would solve problems of pre-emptive causation in particular. This temporal component would presuppose the counterfactual at a certain point in time while at the same time excluding later occurring alternative causes. In addition to a concretization in terms of time, a specification in other respects seems conceivable as well. How specific the outcome would need to be, and whether such concretization would solve counterfactual problems in the context of climate change litigation, indicates the need for further elaboration of the strategy of factual concretization.[99]

4.2.3.1 Concretizing Climatic Causation

Applying the strategy of factual concretization in its comprehensive, unlimited manner to climate change litigation would result in a refinement of I_S not only as a

[93] In favour of this approach, see Böhm (2021), pp. 120–121. In parts also Toepel (2013). Similar also Becht and Miller (1961), pp. 15–17. Discussing this approach Moore (1987), pp. 510–511. Against such an approach in international law, see Orakhelashvili (2022), p. 151.

[94] Puppe and Wright (2017), p. 36.

[95] This strategy is also known as '*targeted but-for test*' (see e.g. Wright 2001).

[96] Moore (2009a), pp. 409–417.

[97] See e.g. Böhm (2021), p. 121; Schmitz and Wulf (2019), para 292. Indications of this also in Verheyen (2005), pp. 256–257; Rengier (2021), p. 78. Relying on a concretization in terms of time, see Teichmann (2021), para 26.

[98] See e.g. Teichmann (2021).

[99] In the literature and in legal scholarship in general, this question is extremely neglected and hardly addressed at all. An exception is provided by *Teichmann* who focuses only on the specification of the temporal sphere (ibid. para 26).

specific climate change impact but as an impact at a very specific time t and location l, to a particular extent and with specific consequences Z_S. Those consequences Z_S could then again be redefined and specified, as well. If such a substantiation does not yet lead to the establishment of the required counterfactual causal chain, causation could eventually be achieved by specifying further links in the causal chain. As this model abstractly shows, the degree of the specification can vary up to a great extent, whereby cases of alternative causation frequently pose a smaller obstacle than cumulative causation cases. The reason for this deviation rests in the fact that cases of cumulative causation in climate change lawsuits usually occur earlier in the causal chain than alternative causation issues. Cumulative causation cases are furthermore defined by fundamentally smaller contributions, which in turn require an increased concretization for their differentiation.

4.2.3.1.1 Concretizing Cases of Cumulative Causation

Within cases of cumulative causation, the individualization of the outcome is greatly of relevance for scenarios in which the overall conditions exceed the threshold of sufficiency in a manner in which the individual conditions would not qualify as necessary for the outcome anymore (scenario two). Due to the fact that all individual conditions already classify as necessary for the outcome and are, therefore, to be considered causal, a further fine-graining of the causal chain is not relevant for cumulative cases falling under scenario one. The strategy of factual concretization, consequently, focuses exclusively on cases of the second scenario with the aim of adding more information to the setting in such a manner that the sufficiency threshold of the outcome is no longer overstepped and the remaining conditions, in turn, qualify as necessary. The concretization thus aims to convert a cumulative scenario two into a scenario one and thereby to achieve factual causation.

The default case of cumulative causation resorts to the occurrence of one single sufficient condition. It is hereby highly different to cases of alternative causation, which usually entail two or more sufficient conditions. This distinction also affects the concretization of cumulative cases. While the establishment of counterfactual causation within alternative cases can basically be restricted to the distinction between the two or more sufficient sets themselves, and thus a temporal differentiation, for example, offers a relatively simple option for factual concretization, a distinction within cumulative causation has to take place at least one step earlier in the causal chain. At the same time, climate-related cumulative conditions, in particular, are often characterised by relatively similar contributions, which makes the differentiation even more difficult. With regard to the factors within a concretization that can lead to the creation of counterfactual causation, the mono-sufficiency of the condition implies that a concretization with regard to the spatial sphere of the outcome, in particular, is only seldom conceivable. However, the causal analysis might change by a specification of the outcome in light of the time of its occurrence, its scope, and its manner, respective to the concretizing factors applied.

Whether the concretization of an outcome is considered to be problematic largely depends on the number of cumulative factors that are involved in the causal assessment. Cases that only refer to a low number of cumulative causes might be solved without further effort by employing a concretization concerning the manner of the outcome. More problematic, then again, are scenarios of emission-related cumulative causation, which are considered standard cases within climate change litigation. Difficulties, in particular, arise from the fact that all greenhouse gas emissions, at least within their individual substance group, have the same effect on the climate and behave in the same way. Greenhouse gas emissions are stringent in their terms and direction of action and, therefore, difficult to diversify. A method of concretization, nonetheless, which is applicable even though the manner in which greenhouse gas emissions come into effect is coherent, is a concretization based on the scope and the time of the outcome. With fewer emissions contributing to the outcome, the outcome in its concrete form would most likely not be as substantial as with the contribution of the emissions in question. At the same time, the outcome in question in its whole degree might only occur later in time, as with the contribution of the emissions in question. As a result, a concretization concerning both time and scope, provided their scientific provability, would lead to the affirmation of counterfactual causation in emission-based climate claims.

Ultimately, one could think about focusing on the conditions themselves in narrowing down the set of conditions to only ones that result out of a certain behaviour or for a certain purpose. In an emission-related setting, this could involve focusing only on traffic-related emissions, emissions resulting out of land usage or heavy industries. A further concretization could relate to a restriction on emissions produced only within a specific time frame. And while the decision about which set of conditions to focus on is a highly normative one, it does not lead to the normativisation of the factual causal inquiry in general, given that ultimately the establishment of causation and the respective determination itself remains factual in nature.[100] However, such concretization does not cohere with the specification of the outcome but with a concretization further up the causal chain and can ultimately lead to a concretization of the potential cause itself. It is further highly misleading, as it results in circular reasoning. Establishing individual, specific causation of a condition cannot result in concretizing and individualizing precisely this condition itself. To grant legitimacy to the concretization of the causal chain in cumulative cases of climate change litigation, it is thus imperative to relate to the outcome exclusively.

---

[100]The charge of normativisation of factual causation can in principle be levelled at any causal doctrine, given that the decision for or against the use of such a doctrine, as well as its design, is in principle of a subjective-normative nature. However, factuality does not depend on the question of why such a doctrine is used, but only on the application of the doctrine itself, which must be fundamentally factual.

4.2.3.1.2 Concretizing Cases of Alternative Causation

In contrast to cases of cumulative causation, and as already emphasized above, cases of alternative causation are frequently easier to be dealt with in terms of a concretization of the outcome. Basically, three different scenarios can be distinguished. The first scenario consists of causes that follow each other in time. In the second scenario, the causes do not differ in time, i.e. they occur at exactly the same time, but differ in scope and magnitude. The third and final scenario, does not allow for differentiation either in terms of time or scope.

The first and most feasible scenario relates to conditions that succeed each other in terms of time. Those cases of pre-emptive overdetermination only require a concretization in light of the temporal occurrence of the outcome. Even if both sufficient sets of conditions would occur in the same manner, substantiating the 'when' of their occurrence would lead to the establishment of counterfactual causation. Assuming flood I_{F1} destroys a house on a specific day t_1. Without the first flood $I_{F1\text{-}t1}$, a second flood $I_{F2\text{-}t2}$ would have destroyed the house as well, however, only one day later at t_2. With the strict application of counterfactual tests, neither the first nor the second flood would be causal for the destruction of the house. Yet, in requiring causation for the destruction of the house at t_1 and, thus, concretizing the outcome in terms of its temporal sphere, only $I_{F1\text{-}t1}$ is considered causal, given that without flood $I_{F1\text{-}t1}$, the destruction of the house on day t_1 would not have occurred. The temporal concretization also leads to results that correspond to overall principles of logic and depict factual, actual causal truths. Even if day t_2 were to be used in the above scenario, flood $I_{F2\text{-}t2}$ would not qualify as causal because a house that has already been destroyed cannot be destroyed again. Therefore, coinciding with actual causation, only the first flood $I_{F1\text{-}t1}$ would be considered counterfactual causal under a temporal concretization. This further coincides with the problem of hypothetical causal processes, which are also of considerable relevance in the application of the law. In legal practice, the imperative of practicability requires the drawing of a temporal line beyond which reserve causes or so-called hypothetical causal processes no longer find their way into judicial considerations. If a potential cause, nevertheless, arises after such a point in time, the hypothetical cause remains out of consideration. Without such a limitation, a causal decision would clearly depend on chance, rather than on factual events.

More explanatory effort is required when the sufficient conditions do not deviate in a timely manner, meaning two or more independent sufficient conditions or sets of sufficient conditions occur at the same time (scenario two). Such cases cannot be resolved by a timely concretization but require a concretization concerning the substance of the outcome, targeting the *manner* of its occurrence rather than its temporal sphere. Assuming the plaintiff is claiming the uninhabitability of a house due to the occurrence of two sufficient, simultaneously occurring conditions. The first sufficient condition is constituted by a flood, and the second one by a rockfall. Due to the flood, the cellar and ground floor of the house was filled with water which slowly drenched all the walls. To some degree, water damage can be rectified through the disclosure and drying out of the walls and material affected.

Nevertheless, this is only possible to a certain degree. Assuming that at the time this threshold of unremovable water damage was reached, a rockfall hit the house, destroying it completely and leaving no wall standing. With both conditions leading to the uninhabitability of the house at the same moment, counterfactual causation concerning both conditions would have to be negated due to a lack of necessity. However, in focusing on the 'how', meaning the manner of the outcome, one would be able to establish counterfactual causation despite the presence of a second condition. In focusing on the whole demolition of the house in question and asking for the cause of the whole demolition of the house, the rockfall would result in the mere cause of the outcome. Even though the house was uninhabitable due to the water damage, the corpus of the house was still intact. This result also corresponds to actual, factual causation, as was already the case in the context of pre-emptive causation. Nonetheless, it requires considerably more justification than in the case of alternative pre-emptive causes. It further leads to the significant dangers of causal excesses depending on the manner of the occurrence of the outcome in question.

The third and most likely also the most problematic case within alternative causation concerns cases in which both or all conditions occur at the same time and in the same way. Assuming the house is hit by a second rockfall B which reaches the house at the same time as the first rockfall A. Neither in terms of time nor in terms of manner or direction of action can a differentiation be made. The concretization requirement would, therefore, have to be applied earlier within the causal chain. Consideration could, consequently, be given to the prior link in the causal chain and refer to the initiation of action. Assuming that rockfall A is triggered by an earthquake and B by general weathering. Thus, rockfall A would be considered counterfactual causal for the earthquake-induced destruction of the house, and rockfall B for the weathering-induced destruction. Whether a specification further up the causal chain is in coherence with logical and overall legal considerations will be substance to a later discussion.[101] From a mere effective point of view, considering causal links as concretizing factors, however, leads to the establishment of counterfactual causation. Even more difficult are cases in which even the most appropriate description of the event does not lead to a differentiation between the conditions. Rockfalls A and B are set off by the same event, at the same time and place and evolve in the same way. Under the assumption that such scenarios exist in real life and even more so in climate change lawsuits, even a concretization would not lead to the establishment of counterfactual causation.[102] Whether such scenarios ultimately exist in practice, then again, is doubtful. Sufficient sets of coherent greenhouse gas emissions are, in light of climate change litigation, probably the closest to such a theoretical scenario in practice.

[101] See in this regard Sect. 4.2.3.4.1.

[102] See especially in regard to the last scenario Hart and Honoré (1985), p. 124.

4.2.3.1.3 Conclusion

The above discussion has shown that the strategy of concretization, when applied to counterfactual causal chains, can lead to the affirmation of factual causation. The most prominent ambit lies in cases of pre-emptive overdetermination, where the addition of a temporal sphere to the outcome usually leads to the establishment of a continuous causal chain. In other cases of alternative causation, adding more information to the outcome can also solve the problem of counterfactual definiteness. In particular, the question of the nature of the outcome becomes relevant. However, the spatial concretization of the outcome is only of minor relevance. Although a concretization in this respect may lead to concrete factual results, in most cases, a reference to the temporal sphere or to the manner of occurrence is sufficient for the establishment of a stringent causal chain based on counterfactuality. Even in the context of cumulative causation, the temporal sphere may become significant. More relevant, nevertheless, is the scope of the outcome, which is particularly important for emissions-based climate lawsuits. In sum, it has been shown that the strategy of concretization can lead to the establishment of factual causation and, moreover, bring counterfactual causation doctrines closer to actual causal truth. It thus makes their application in law more legitimate and tenable.

4.2.3.2 Translating Causal Concretization into Climate Practice

Having concluded that the strategy of factual concretization can enhance the establishment of counterfactual causation, the question remains if such a methodology is covered by current court practice. Some authors argue that this is indeed the case in some jurisdictions.[103] However, up to this date, in none of the analysed climate change lawsuits have the courts fallen back on this methodology. In spite of this, the applicability of the strategy to climate change lawsuits can be aptly illustrated by the case *Luciano Lliuya v. RWE AG*.[104] In the first instance, the Court applied a strict counterfactual test and ultimately dismissed the claim for lack of causation. The case represents a default case of emission-based and thus cumulative causation, in which, however, if natural climate variations are taken into account, alternative causation cannot be completely ruled out but plays only an ancillary role either way. Furthermore, the outcome of the causal chain does not refer to damage that has already occurred but only to an increase in the risk of damage, which further affects the concretization. In limiting the outcome based on its temporal sphere, one must come to the conclusion that the risk to the plaintiff's property would still exist. The timely specification would, therefore, not render the alleged emissions of the RWE AG

[103] Wright and Puppe (2016), p. 479. Quite a few authors that apply the approach do so without discussing its account, among those Böhm (2021), pp. 120–121; Teichmann (2021), para 26.

[104] Essen Regional Court, 15 December 2016 – 2 O 285/15, *Luciano Lliuya v. RWE AG*, Higher Regional Court Hamm, pending – 5 U 15/17, *Luciano Lliuya v. RWE AG*.

counterfactual causal. Nonetheless, would the Court have considered the temporal concretization in conjunction with the scope of the respective risk, counterfactual causation most likely would have been established. Without RWE AG's emissions, the general risk would still persist, but the scope of the risk would have been reduced without RWE's emission or would have materialized in the same scope, but not at that exact point in time. A specification in terms of time and scope would, thus, lead to an affirmation of counterfactual causation in the case *Luciano Lliuya v. RWE AG*.

A similar approach was taken by the plaintiff in the present case, although he commenced significantly earlier in the causal chain and referred to the difference in the overall surface temperature rather than the difference in the outcome. However, this methodology was largely due to the framing of the statement, which was intended as a counter-argument to the defendants' assessment of the *Forest Dieback* case.[105] In the statement, the plaintiff noted:

> A causal linkage can therefore be affirmed for all CO2 emissions, because according to the conditio sine qua non formula, none could be 'theoretically eliminated' without decreasing the temperature by a corresponding amount— regardless of where exactly the emissions are released and how great the distance between the emission source and climate impacts.[106]

As most climate change litigation claims build upon the effects of emissions, the argumentation and the results are highly transferable to other climate change lawsuits. Although the Court of the first instance did not support and admit the respective considerations, the Court in the second instance seems more open given that it transferred the proceeding to the evidentiary phase of the lawsuit.

4.2.3.3 Shortcomings of the Strategy of Concretization

While the concretization of the outcome can lead to the establishment of counterfactual causation in cases in which factual causation would otherwise have to be denied, whether and how a concretization should take place is still a matter of debate. Clearly, applying the strategy of concretization leads to fairer results which in turn are closer to the actual truth. It further leads to the affirmation of more conditions as causes in scenarios in which jurisdictions otherwise had to deviate completely from counterfactual tests to comply with the laws of logic. This in itself is a strong argument for its usefulness and applicability. However, apart from its actual practicability, it remains questionable to what extent such an approach is justifiable from a legal and metaphysical perspective.

---

[105] Federal Court of Justice, 10 December 1987 – III ZR 220/86, *Forest Dieback*.

[106] Essen Regional Court, 15 December 2016 – 2 O 285/15, *Luciano Lliuya v. RWE AG*, written submission of the plaintiff (11 July 2016), 14. On Appeal, the plaintiffs traced the causal chain even more precisely, see Higher Regional Court Hamm, pending – 5 U 15/17, *Luciano Lliuya v. RWE AG*, Appeal by the plaintiff, unauthorised translation, provided by Germanwatch e.V. Interestingly, in their original statement of claim, the plaintiffs still referred to the doctrine of conditio-sine-qua-non in its unconcreted version, see Essen Regional Court, 15 December 2016 – 2 O 285/15, *Luciano Lliuya v. RWE AG*, statement of claim (23 November 2015), 32 para 4.2; 34 para 4.2.5.

Uncertainty already prevails in regard to the definitional coverage of counterfactual tests. Especially within the framework of the conditio-sine-qua-non test, concepts differ within the requirement of the conditions. While some commentaries and, thus, legal scholars apply the conditio-sine-qua-non formula in its form as an appropriated counterfactual test and thus require the reference to a *concrete* outcome, this aspect is widely absent in other definitional approaches.[107] Up to this day, it is still unclear in which situations courts and judges apply the conditio-sine-qua-non formula in its concretized version and in which situation they refer to the conventional form of the test. Even within individual jurisdictions, the standard of application of the tests varies.[108] It, therefore, seems that whether the outcome is put into a microscopic perspective, or viewed from a distanced, more generalized point of view depends on the convenience of the respective account. Correspondingly, the strategy of concretization is still subject to great arbitrariness. Furthermore, uncertainty prevails concerning the application of this strategy to common law jurisdictions and, thus, to the but-for test.

In addition to the definitional uncertainty, teleological aspects and the principle of formal logic also become of relevance in the determination of the strategy. A significant issue pertains to the extent of the strategy of concretization. In a scientific-philosophical perception, every event, no matter how small it might be, can have an impact on the outcome in question. As a result, the relevant question persists whether such an understanding of causal relata can and should also be applied in light of the strategy of concretization. Ultimately, every outcome can be fine-grained in a way that relates to the desired act. However, influencing one's outcome in a way is not to be equated with actually causing it. Otherwise, every insignificant, irrelevant condition could be regarded as causal under the right concretization, even if it was only an accidental occurrence and would diverge from actual causation.[109] Such an ascertain runs counter to the mere base of counterfactuality. Especially since it would include factors in the causal chain that would not be regarded as influential, at least causal, from the perspective of formal logic. While it hence might be true that in a philosophical way and even in a scientific regard, every action, no matter how small it is, is influencing and, therefore, somehow contributing to an event, such a broad and far-reaching approach would indeed contravene the legal applicability of causal tests in general and would not remain within the scope of the determination of causation in the law.[110]

In opposition to the inclusion of any criteria of concretization, it is argued that legal reasoning has no interest in any additional concretizing fact, even not in spatial

---

[107] In applying counterfactual tests in their concrete form, see Böhm (2021), pp. 120–121; Toepel (2013). In refraining from such an approach e.g. Oetker (2019), para 103; Flume (2022), para 280; Brand (2022), p. 219; Orakhelashvili (2022), p. 151.

[108] This, for example, is the case in Germany.

[109] In this regard also Puppe and Wright (2017), pp. 36–37; Toepel (2013), p. 119.

[110] See concerning materiality in a normative sense Sect. 5.4.

and temporal terms.[111] Fine-graining factors are only considered to identify the event in question but do not contribute to its legal evaluation.[112] Some authors even argue that most information and details added to an outcome are, in principle, irrelevant to the legal assessment.[113] In some instances, however, the legally relevant properties precisely include the temporal or the local sphere of an event or even contain further information. *Toepl* hereby points to the example of manslaughter.[114] Since it is a fact that every human being must ultimately die of natural causes, the bringing about of death due to other (manmade) conditions is decisive in terms of time. Without the reference to time, no manslaughter could be considered a counterfactual condition since the death of the person is unavoidable. Decisive is, thus, not the death itself, but the death by manslaughter at a specific time t. It is exactly in situations and scenarios like this that law as such cannot be denied an interest in the differentiation of various conditions. Nonetheless, it is precisely in the interest of law to establish conditions that constitute a scientifically verifiable and provable chain of causation. The objection of boundlessness, nevertheless, also prevails here, which is why a limitation, in general, is needed.[115]

A further challenge with using individualized counterfactual tests is the need to establish specific causal chains in a scientifically verifiable manner. The more intricate the causal chain, the harder it is to prove causation scientifically. Although climate and attribution science are constantly advancing, it remains unclear whether climate science is able to establish a precise causal chain and whether the findings can ultimately be admissible in court.[116]

4.2.3.4 Introducing Criteria of Concretization

The explanations provided earlier have highlighted several challenges associated with the concretization strategy. One of the main criticisms of this methodology is its vastness and illimitability. Thus, based on the validity of the arguments, a fundamental delimitation has to be carried out.

4.2.3.4.1 Chain-Related Individualization

The first restriction builds upon the causal chain itself. As the previous section has already indicated, a causal chain relating to a specific condition can be established by

---

[111] In this regard for example Puppe and Wright (2017), p. 38.

[112] Ibid. In opposition and with regard to the temporal component, see Toepel (2013), p. 120.

[113] Puppe and Wright (2017), p. 37. Similar also Moore (2009a), p. 413.

[114] Toepel (2013), p. 120.

[115] *Moore* refers concerning the vastness to the "*extraordinary promiscuity introduced into the counterfactual theory*", see Moore (2009a), p. 412. See for criteria on the limitation Sect. 4.2.3.4.3.

[116] See also Sect. 3.3.1.

focusing on different links in the causal chain (T; I_F; X) and, ergo, not exclusively on the outcome I_S. However, the difficulty and the dangers of such a methodology have already been explained previously. Especially the individualization of the primary condition itself (B_S; E_S) leads to circular reasoning.[117] It further harbours the dangers of illimitably and opposes the ratio of finding and establishing causation in the first place. Thus, the potential of fine-graining the event has to be restricted to the outcome alone. Nevertheless, in considering longer causal chains, which ultimately contain several links within the cause-effect relatum, the question persists whether these individual links may also be subjected to a specification or whether this still only applies to the outcome alone. Due to logical considerations, one might assume that the former must apply here; after all, each link within the causal chain is already a causal relation in its own right. If every individual link is considered separately, as its own self-contained causal relata, every outcome in itself would be a factor to concretize. The fact that these individual causal links are part of a longer causal chain can, therefore, not be held against such a concretization. Otherwise, it would merely depend on chance whether a concretization may take place or not.

Even more decisive is the interconnectedness of the causal links themselves. Causal chains are a fundamental simplification of science to better depict relata and make relations understandable. In reality, however, all actions and omissions are interconnected and interwoven. This is especially true for climate change, which is influenced by a multitude of different factors. Thus, each causal relation is in itself only one link in another causal chain. This causal chain, in turn, is only another link in an even longer chain of conditions. To better reflect reality and the influence of other conditions, be they causal or not, natural sciences more and more refer to causal nets than to causal chains. Although it is impossible to depict a comprehensive 'net' of causal linkages either, this methodology, nevertheless, overtrumps the application of chains in relation to the actual world. It would thus further limit the law's depiction of factual reality and simply be outside logical considerations to limit the concretization to the artificially constructed end of the causal chain since it is precisely not the end as such but only a further condition in an even longer causal chain.[118] And although such methodology widens the application and the possibility of concretizing the outcome further, it nevertheless does not result either in circular reasoning or contradicts formal logic, as long as the condition in question is not individualized itself.

4.2.3.4.2 The Necessity for Legally Relevant Information

The second limitation that has to be applied for the adaptation of counterfactual causation rests within the nature of the specification and concretization itself. With the inclusion of a multitude of different factors, respectively the manner, time, and

[117] Also Toepel (2013), p. 119.

[118] Opposing that view, ibid. 121, Wright and Puppe (2016), p. 479.

location of the occurrence, a causal chain can almost always be concretized in such a way that, in the end, only one strongly necessary condition remains. And although such width is useful from an economic perspective, it considerably hinders the applicability and the ratio of counterfactual causation in the law, especially when the added information does not carry any legal implication or relate to the underlying legal assessment.[119] This not only contradicts the sense and purpose of the entire reason why such methodology is implemented in the first place but ultimately undermines the purpose of any restrictions per se. Therefore, a restriction to information and concretization features is required, which on the one hand, have legal relevance and, on the other hand, represent a fundamental property of the outcome.[120]

Naturally, it can be argued that the focus on such legal constructs contradicts factuality and the strong reliance and argumentative focus on reflecting the actual truth as such. By applying a legal conception, normative aspects undoubtedly find their way into the discussion of factual causation. However, this pretext is contradicted by the fact that counterfactual tests are not a mere reproduction and translation of facts into law but rather an attempt to make the factual accessible to the law in an approachable manner, through which legal considerations implicitly find their way into the discussion. This is tantamount to the introduction of legal information within the framework of the strategy of factual concretization. The claim of factuality must, nevertheless, remain as the main objective of every legally accessible causal consideration. This is taken into account by the fact that the strategy of concretization brings the result of the counterfactual tests closer to actual causation, despite ingesting counterfactual doctrines with further evaluative and legal perceptions of factual causation. At the same time, considering only legally relevant information hinders the ingress of accidental causes and opposes the problem of illimitable breath.

The issue that remains is the process of determining pertinent information. One potential solution is to evaluate each matter on a case-by-case basis, scrutinizing each causal inquiry separately.[121] Nevertheless, this method may generate inconsistent and conflicting interpretations, producing a considerable degree of legal ambiguity. Instead of relying on a vague approach, it is, therefore, more effective to establish specific and clear individualizing criteria beforehand. This guarantees that all important factors are determined before the causal inquiry is carried out, which avoids any extraneous influences on the final outcomes.

[119] Moore (2009a), pp. 413–414; Toepel (2013), pp. 120–121; Wright and Puppe (2016), p. 475. With most added details being irrelevant to the description. Also Wright (2001), p. 1114. Further raising the issue of the inclusion of "*irrelevant details*" and on a rather critical note, Fumerton and Kress (2001), pp. 96–97.

[120] Moore (2009a), pp. 413–414, also Toepel (2013), pp. 120–121.

[121] In favour see Toepel (2013), p. 120.

4.2.3.4.3 Factors of Legal Individualization

The third and thus probably also the most important restriction is directed at the core question of the topic and refers to the actual factors that can be used for concretization. In particular, four different factors come into question. The manner and reason of the outcome, its spatial sphere, its temporal sphere and finally its scope.

4.2.3.4.3.1 The Manner and Reason of the Outcome

Whereas in the previous examples (flood and avalanche), the question of how the damage was caused met with great success, it is precisely this factor that allows for an infinite number of concretizations. Apart from overly theoretical models, a distinction is, at least in practice, always possible within the manner of the outcome, even if one has to fine-grain the outcome to the core. However, the manner of the outcome also carries a lot of ambiguity and uncertainty. Often, the way in which an outcome came into existence does not constitute a fundamental difference to the reason why it occurred. As it will later be shown, the reason for the occurrence cannot pose legally relevant information and, therefore, function as a distinctive factor in light of the concretization of the outcome. And even in cases in which the manner of the outcome can ultimately be distinguished from the mere reason, considering the way in which a particular outcome came into being constitutes a highly subjective decision of the relevant factors. Moreover, decisive is whether the manner can pose a piece of legally relevant information. It certainly does in quite a few cases, especially when the provision in question imposes specific responsibility not only on the occurrence of the outcome per se but on the manner in which the outcome was achieved. This specific responsibility does not apply to all legal scenarios, however, it does cover a broad amount of legal cases. Nevertheless, and although a concretization in regard to the manner has proven both efficient and legally relevant, factorization in this regard has to be approached with the necessary care, as it can easily lead to an overbreadth of the approach. Decisive is that the manner based on which the outcome is specified, is already inherent in the legal provision, both explicitly and indirectly. What, conversely, is not legally required and, therefore, does not entail legal information is the concretization in whatever manner the required result serves best. Such would elementarily contradict the ratio behind the requirement of a legally relevant factor. Concretizations in regard to the manner, consequently, have to be approached with due care, although without excluding such factors from the realm of concretization entirely.

A concretization concerning the reason ('why') for an outcome must, nonetheless, be handled with even more caution. In principle, the reason why something was done or not can play a role in the legal assessment. Especially in criminal law, a specific reason for someone's doing or omission can have an aggravating or mitigating effect on the punishment.[122] In differentiation to the terminology and the understanding of 'reason' in a mere factual sense, the 'reason' turned to in the law itself usually relates to the 'why' of the active doing, rather than the outcome of such. It ties in with the beginning of the causal chain. Concurrently, a reason in a causal sense that relates to the outcome can only partly be equated with the more subjective understanding of reason as the intention of the actor or omitter. And while the intention of someone's doing therefore might carry legal relevance and represent a legally relevant information, it most frequently does not comply with the second requirement of being a fundamental property of the outcome. It can rather constitute a fundamental property of the cause itself. The reason in a causal factual sense must thus be approached and handled free of subjective and intentional choice that ties in with ones doing or omission and more so relate to the reason of the factual outcome occurring.

Whereas it has been clarified that the reason for someone's doing or omission does ultimately not constitute a factor that is suitable for concretizing the outcome, a possible point of departure might nevertheless rest in the reason for the outcome itself. The reason for the outcome reflects the cause in its own singular causal chain, allowing a fine-graining of the reason ultimately leading to the concretization of the initial condition. This problem becomes, above all, apparent in single-link causal chains, in which the reason correlates directly to the specification of the condition, which is why an concretization in this regard needs to be rejected. As it was previously mentioned, fine-graining the initial condition leads to circular reasoning and uncontrollable miscellany in the approach. The question of whether the 'why' can potentially constitute a legally relevant factor, therefore, does not have to be decided.

4.2.3.4.3.2 The Spatial Sphere of the Outcome

While the reason for the outcome occurring unambiguously cannot constitute reliable criteria for a concretization, the question of including a spatial component in consideration of counterfactual tests is more difficult.[123] In legal practice and in reliance on jurisdictions that occasionally make use of a similar approach, it is especially the temporal sphere that often finds implementation. However, it is uncertain whether the spatial sphere also holds any legal significance und ultimately is even fit as a concretizing factor. Whether a particular outcome occurs in one place or another has most frequently no legal implication as such. In other words, the event

[122] Thus, in German criminal law, the addition of factors such as greed ('*Habgier*'), murderousness ('*Mordlust*') or malice ('*Heimtücke*') aforethought leads to the qualification of the act as murder, and not as manslaughter, see §§ 211, 212 of the German Penal Code.

[123] With regard to the temporal component, this is clearly affirmed by *Toepel* (Toepel 2013). Also acknowledged by Wright (2007), p. 292 Fn. 14. *Wright* still argues against that approach due to incorrect results, see Wright (2001), p. 1114. Wright and Puppe (2016), pp. 477–481. Reluctant with regard to the local component Toepel (2013), pp. 121–122. In opposition, see Wright and Puppe (2016), p. 476.

and the outcome remain the same no matter where they occur. The location of the occurrence frequently only serves to single out and identify the specific condition but not to legally or even causally assess the output.[124] Whether a glacier in the Peruvian Andes or the Swiss Alps is melting as a result of the specific behaviour is of no significance for the legal causal assessment as such. In contrast to the temporal component, this arises from the fact that the causal chain alone acts independently of local factors. Here, the local component, the scope, as well as the manner and the reason of the causal outcome converge.

Only in individual cases can the place of the outcome hold any legal significance. One such example is the use of regional and international treaties, particularly human rights treaties. These are usually bound in their application to the jurisdiction of the contracting parties, which can further imply that the place of occurrence has to lie within the territory of the respective actor.[125] Even if there are exceptions to this limitation, which allow for extraterritorial applicability, the question of applicability and, thus, also of the place of the event or the place of the violation can play a central role in the legal consideration.[126] The same applies to statutes that regulate the legal order in a specific, delimitable area or that are legally bound to a specific local sphere, such as traffic rules.[127] While traffic rules are mainly only applicable on public grounds, speeding would commonly not be enforceable in the private realm. The sphere in which the action and ultimately also the outcome happened (public grounds versus private grounds), therefore, matters and imposes a piece of legally relevant information. A delimiting factor that must nevertheless also be taken into account with regard to the local scope is the question of the effect on the outcome. The requirement that the legal information must also be a fundamental property of the outcome sets limits to the inclusion of the local component. This is not an obstacle in areas where the outcome must also lie within the locally delimitable

---

[124] Even on a more rigid note, see Wright and Puppe (2016), p. 476.

[125] See Art. 1 ECHR, Art. 1 IACHR, Art. 2 Arab CHR. Exceptions have been developed in regard to nearly every regional and international treaty. See for the jurisprudence of the ECtHR on the widening of the spatial sphere of the ECHR, see European Court of Human Rights, 7 July 2011 55721/07, *Al-Skeini and others v. The United Kingdom*, European Court of Human Rights, 18 December 1996 – 15318/89, *Loizidou v. Turkey*.

[126] The ECHR entails in its requirement of jurisdiction in Art. 1 ECHR also its applicability 'ratione loci'. This implies jurisdiction ratione loci on the State's own territory (provided that the contracting state also has effective control over this territory), but may in exceptional cases extend to extraterritorial scenarios. However, jurisdiction ratione loci is primarily territorial in nature. See Johann (2022), pp. 58–68 paras 18–35, Meyer-Ladewig and Nettesheim (2017), pp. 60–63 paras 26–34. See for the jurisdiction ratione loci of the American Convention on Human Rights which mainly focuses on the 'authority and control' over a territory rather than on the territory of the contracting parties itself Antkowiak and Gonza (2017), p. 17. In highlighting the restrictiveness of the extraterritorial dimension of the American Convention, see Hennebel and Tigroudja (2022), pp. 46–49. See for the extraterritoriality in regard to environmental harm also Inter-American Court of Human Rights, 15 November 2017 – OC-23/17, *A Request for an Advisory Opinion from the Inter-American Court of Human Rights Concerning the Interpretation of Article 1(1), 4(1) and 5(1) of the American Convention on Human Rights.*

[127] Examples here refer to, for example, a nature reserve, but also to a local, community level.

zone of special rights (cf. e.g. traffic rules). In other respects, however, it may cause hurdles to the concretization by spatial components.

In addition to the question of its legal relevance, the usefulness of a spatial concretization is also in question. While spatial concretization is conceivable for some scenarios in climate change litigation (particularly in relation to the above-mentioned areas of law), and with particular emphasis on emission-based lawsuits, a spatial concretization might fall short. Given the global impact of climate change and the uniformity of greenhouse gas effects, emission-based lawsuits often do not vary in terms of the local component of the outcome. In the case of *Luciano Lliuya*, requiring the emissions of the RWE AG to be a necessary factor for the risk of the GLOF in Huaraz would most likely not lead to a different evaluation of the counterfactual causal chain. Conclusively, spatial concretization only offers a solution to counterfactual obstacles in a few cases. In cases of pre-emptive causation, they naturally can hardly provide a way of resolving the causal dilemma.

Whether a differentiation based on the spatial sphere of the norm is suitable for application in court, thus, remains questionable. However, in considering whether the additional information they pose on the outcome is a piece of legally relevant information about the offence or the applied norm and constitutes a fundamental property of the outcome, courts can circumvent this criticism and provide for legal compliance.

4.2.3.4.3.3 The Temporal Sphere of the Outcome

Another factor of concretization refers to the inclusion of a temporal sphere. Hereby, every action is considered causal if the outcome at a certain time t would cease to exist without the relevant action or omission. For a condition to be causal, the condition would have to be a necessary condition for the outcome at a specific point in time. This becomes important, especially for cases of alternative causation. It is further relevant in pre-emptive cases in which the inclusion of the temporal component can eliminate subsequent conditions and thus create a stringent causal chain. As the case of *Luciano Lliuya* has shown, the temporal component can also lead to the establishment of a stringent causal chain in cases of cumulative causation.[128]

Apart from the efficiency of a temporal sphere as a resounding argument for its inclusion in the causal chain, the temporal component further gains relevance as a legally relevant factor. This can certainly be affirmed if the relevant norm provides for a time indication. However, the time also holds legal significance even though it is not explicitly mentioned in the provision itself. The law has a fundamental interest in a temporal limitation, even if this is not explicitly anchored in the respective norms. This results, in particular, from the objective to exclude further alternative causes in a causal assessment, may it be the natural death in the case of homicide or the first offence in the context of several alternative causes. A temporal component is

[128] See in this regard Sect. 4.2.3.1.1.

thus frequently present in the law. In difference to the spatial sphere, temporal components constitute information on a substantial and material level of the relevant legal consideration in question. Whereas the spatial sphere often becomes of importance in regard to the applicability of the law and the place of jurisdiction and is hence relevant on a procedural rather than on a material level, the time of the behaviour in question and the respective outcome is inherent in every legal consideration, often more implicitly than explicitly. This already dictates the necessity of excluding hypothetical and reserve causes. The temporal sphere further, and again in contrast to other factors of concretization, constitutes a fundamental property of the outcome. It, therefore, provides for a metaphysically sound, reliable and even more so applicable form of general concretization in the realm of counterfactual tests. Its relevance even extends to the consideration that time, as a concretizing factor, must always be taken into account whenever a specification of the causal chain and the outcome is in question.

4.2.3.4.3.4 The Scope of the Outcome

Beyond the temporal sphere, it is especially the scope of the outcome that becomes of importance in climate change lawsuits. Such does not only apply to the damage itself but also to the respective risk of damage. Would the risk of damage be of that specific scope without the condition in question? In reference to the case of *Luciano Lliuya*, such considerations would fundamentally change the assessment of the causal chain. Without the action by the defendant, the scope of the risk for the property of the plaintiff would be lower and thus counterfactually causal by applying a scope-concretized strategy. A concretization regarding the scope would, beyond this specific case, lead to the establishment of factual causation in a large number of emission based climate cases, advocating for its economic importance. Even in a more general sense, a scope-related concretization would lead to the establishment of a counterfactual causal chain in cases of particularly cumulative, but also alternative and possibly even pre-emptive causation.

The main difficulty, however, that consists in the application of a scope-related concretization still is based on the issue of whether the scope of the outcome also constitutes a legally relevant information. This is inevitably the case for statutes that aim at allocating cost and damages, as well as for provisions that behold a sufficiency threshold for their own application and enforcement. To return to the traffic example that was introduced in regard to the spatial sphere, if someone is driving at an excessive speed, they could be in breach of traffic regulations. However, the penalty varies depending on the speed and the deviation from the speed limit. Some countries, including Germany, even provide for a certain tolerance margin within which the increased speed is not yet punishable.[129] Another example where the scope carries legal significance is in the classification of incidents into the correct

[129]In Germany, this generally amounts to 3 km/h in urban areas and a certain percentage in other traffic areas, also depending on the method that was used to measure the speed.

alternatives of the statutory definition of the offense. For example, in Art. 3 ECHR, the individual alternatives within the prohibition of torture can be distinguished on the basis of the severity of the violation of the right.[130] The scope of the event and concurrently the outcome therefore carries legal relevance.

Beyond its explicit implementation in the respective statutes, the scope can also essentially be of implicit legal significance. It hereby strongly corresponds with the temporal sphere, which can provide in their interplay for a sufficient fine-grained outcome. In contrast to the temporal sphere, however, the scope of the outcome might not always be of legal significance. Some legal scenarios are free of considerations of scope and the ultimate extent of the outcome. What matters is rather whether or not there has been an infringement of the respective right or provision or not. In such circumstances, the scope of the infringement is frequently not legally relevant. It concurrently does not form a fundamental property of the outcome. Whether a provision is legally relevant to the scope of the outcome must thus also be considered in the light of the particular situation and the overall rationale of the norm. Similar as to the spatial sphere of the outcome, the possibility of concretizing the result on the basis of the scope must be assessed on an individual basis. Since the legal relevance of the scope and its qualification as a property of the outcome varies from one instance to another, it is ultimately an individual decision on a case-by-case basis whether or not the scope can be used for concretization. Given that most legal judgments also make use of and take into account the scope of the result, it is safe to say that, at least with regard to the first requirement of legal relevance, the scope of the outcome becomes more important than its spatial sphere. The crux of the qualification, nevertheless, resides in the prerequisite that the scope is also a fundamental property of the outcome.

4.2.4 Conclusion

Counterfactual tests (unlike other theories) are monocentric at heart, meaning that they are aimed at finding exactly one single cause for a particular outcome. This monocentrism is often at the root of the metaphysical obstacles that counterfactual theories face, especially in the face of cumulative and alternative causes. In addition to the metaphysical difficulties that counterfactuals generally encounter, a major concern is their account of actual and scientific causation. At the scientific level, outcomes are almost never caused by a single cause, but are determined by a large number of different acts and omissions that collectively increase the probability of the particular outcome. Actual causation is thus generally opposed to a monocentric understanding of factual causation in law.

[130] This theory is called '*Stufentheorie*'. Others distinguish the different alternatives based on the purpose of the use of force (also known as '*Zwecktheorie*').

From a practical and utilitarian point of view, counterfactual theories can build on a fairly long legal tradition of their application in law. Several legal systems use counterfactual theories to assess factual causation, making them the most common way of establishing cause-effect relations. To overcome the metaphysical obstacles, courts have often developed exceptions and new rules to the traditional counterfactual approach to ensure its soundness and general applicability. The metaphysical obstacles further affect, and even contradict, the practical application of the approach in the context of climate change litigation. The complexity of the climate system not only makes it objectively impossible to identify a single cause of a climate-induced outcome, but would consequently always lead to a rejection of specific causation in climate scenarios. This has been demonstrated by a large number of court cases to date, in which a strict application of counterfactual tests has predominantly led to the rejection of causation. While there is nothing inherently wrong with such a result, actual and scientific causation dictates a generally broader understanding of cause-effect relationships. In particular, the cumulative effect of contributions (especially in the case of greenhouse gas emissions) from a variety of large and small emitters emphasises a multi-causal understanding in law.

One approach to bring the results of counterfactual theories closer to their factual truth is the theory of factual concretization, by which cases of causal overdetermination can be generally avoided. Some also see this strategy as already inherent in the definition of counterfactual tests, at least in the conditio-sine-qua-non formula. However, to avoid the approach being overused and to make it conform with the grounds of legal considerations, the concretization must be restricted to apply only to legally relevant information. The added information, furthermore, has to represent a fundamental property of the outcome.

The above considerations have shown that especially three factors are able to provide enough legal relevance to constitute restricting factors as required by the strategy of factual concretization. Among these are the spatial sphere of the outcome, as well as its scope. Both constitute legitimate and legally valid factors that can be applied to specialize and concretize the outcome with respect to the strategy of concretization. Yet, both factors are dependent on the provisions enabled and are not of legal importance in every legal scenario in question. Particularly the spatial sphere easily loses its legal significance in cases in which the local sphere only resorts to a procedural requirement that is not inherent in the substantial considerations which are inflicted upon the situation. Whether the spatial sphere, therefore, also carries material weight has to be elaborated on a case-by-case basis. Different to the spatial sphere and the extent of the outcome, nonetheless, are considerations in terms of time. As the previous elaborations have shown, the temporal sphere is inherent in almost every legal assessment and thus frequently constitutes legally relevant information. A concretization can, in light of the strategy of concretization, thus always be based on a temporal component.

However, the strategy of concretization also harbours difficulties. Besides theoretical arguments speaking against the implementation of such a strategy, it is notably the practical realm that still poses challenges to the application of the strategy of concretization. Based on the concretization in a very delicate and comprehensive manner, especially in regard to the time and scope, the legal assessment is strongly dependent on particular scientific results. Although every factual causal doctrine faces the question of scientific provability, it is even more difficult when the scientific findings have to relate to an even more specific outcome. Yet, attribution science has shown that they are able to provide for such distinct analyses in specific cases, even though the risk of high uncertainty and low confidence levels still persists.[131] The more detailed the concretization becomes, the more difficult it is to access the necessary data and, thus, to find scientific causation.[132] The strategy of factual concretization in sum, therefore, constitutes a promising approach to solve at least parts of the factually resorted causation problem in climate-related matters.

4.3 Regularity Theories of General Causation

4.3.1 Metaphysical Substantiation of Theories of Regularity

Regularity theories form a counterpart to the traditional theories of causation that still dominate legal practice. In contrast to the but-for test and the conditio-sine-qua-non formula, they ultimately do not ground their causation assessment in mono-causal counterfactuals but in the regular occurrence of certain sequences of events (Sect. 4.3.1.1). However, theories of regularity are confronted with several general objections which address the way of epiphenomenon as well as the usage of regularities per se. The latter mainly concerns the occurrence of imperfect regularities. Moreover, the multi-causal nature of regularity-based theories leads to scenarios in which the qualification of more than one condition as causal might be perceived as unsatisfactory, as might be especially the case in situations of pre-emptive causation (Sect. 4.3.1.2). From a practical point of view, significant concerns can be expressed regarding the way of forming a sufficient set of conditions (Sect. 4.3.1.3), which also implies how to handle scientific uncertainties and omissions in light of theories of regularity.[133] Ultimately it will be discussed whether a combination of different metaphysical approaches, such as counterfactual theories and regularity-based theories, could constitute a solution posed by climatic causation (Sect. 4.3.1.4).

4.3.1.1 The General Principles of Theories of Regularity

Theories of regularity provide, at least in philosophy and legal theory, a nowadays increasingly advocated counterpart to counterfactual approaches that still

131 Stuart-Smith et al. (2021).

132 See in this regard Sect. 3.3.

133 Moore (2009a), pp. 488–489; Kelmann (1987).

predominate in legal scholarship and practice.[134] Founding causation on experiences of regularity traces back to *Hume*, who first introduced a concept of constant conjunction without the involvement of a necessity criterion.[135] The approach was later redefined by *Mill*, who broadened the concept extensively and introduced the regularity requirement to a law of nature.[136] *Mill* hereby considered all positive and negative factors that are conjunctly sufficient for the outcome as causes.

Regardless of the different connotational approaches, regularity theories are generalist theories of causation, meaning that fundamentally applicable law is concluded based on a recurring event.[137] In this process, singular statements, statements of specific causation, are translated into generally applicable laws. According to the Humean theories of regularity, a causal relationship between events *a* and *b* is established when exactly three conditions are met: (I) Events *a* and *b* follow each other closely both in spatial relation and in time (spatiotemporal proximity). (II) Event *a* precedes event *b*, and (III) events of type b always follow events of type a.[138]

The most significant difference to counterfactual tests is the requirement placed on the specific condition itself. Despite founding the conception of causation on inferentiality, regulatory theories only partially refrain from the necessity criterion. However, whereas counterfactual tests require a strongly necessary condition for the specific event and, therefore, presuppose the necessity of the condition for the outcome itself, regularity theories deviate from this strict perception in only requiring necessity for a specific set of conditions, independent of its effect for the outcome itself. Regularity theories, hence, apply a weaker perception of necessity. The focus of regulatory theories, moreover, rests on the requirement of sufficiency. As a result, for an action to be qualified as a cause, the act is required to be part of a sufficient set of conditions, irrespective of its necessity for the respective outcome. The sufficient set itself, again, does not need to be a necessary one. Yet, the action has to be necessary for the sufficiency of the specific set, while at the same time, it is not required to be sufficient for the set itself. Broken down, a specific action is causal for a specific outcome if the action is necessary for a sufficient set of conditions. In cases where only one sufficient set of conditions exists, regularity theories do not deviate from counterfactual assessments in their perception of necessity and sufficiency since the specific conditions would also be regarded as causal under counterfactual aspects.[139]

[134] Wright and Puppe (2016), pp. 469–470; Birnbacher and Hommen (2012), pp. 60–61. As an advocate of *Mackies'* INUS approach, see Toepel (2013), p. 111. Against such an approach, see Moore (2009a), pp. 471–495.

[135] Hume (1975), revised text and notes by Nidditch. Also, see Psillos (2009).

[136] Mill (2011).

[137] See for a detailed assessment of theories of general causation, Moore (2009a), pp. 471–495.

[138] Hume (1978).

[139] Concerning the NESS-test, Baldwin (2003), p. 6.

Theories of regularity and counterfactuality, however, do not only deviate in their requirements laid upon the dependency of the condition and the outcome, they, furthermore, differ in their basic understanding of causation itself. Whereas counterfactuals in law aim to identify precisely one single cause for a given effect and are, therefore, mono-causal concepts of causation, regularity-based theories allow for more than one condition to be qualified as a causative one, which in turn opens up the prospect of shared causation.[140] The plurality of causes is based both on the viability of different sets of sufficient conditions and on the different conditions allowed within each set. In rejecting singular causes, multi-causal concepts are closer to actual, natural causation than counterfactuals. The perception of multi-causation is also consistent with the understanding of causation promoted in other disciplines, most notably social, computer, and other fields of natural science.[141]

Nowadays, two concepts of regularity based on *Hume's* metaphysical approach have been promoted in particular. The INUS test ('Insufficient but Necessary part of an Unnecessary but Sufficient condition') and the NESS approach ('Necessary Element of a Sufficient Set').[142]

The development of the INUS test is considered to be one of the most significant developments in causal theory in modern times. It can be traced back to *Hart* and *Honoré*, who first described the new causal conception in their monograph *Causation in the Law.*[143] Today, *Mackie* is often wrongfully credited as the originator of the theory. He was, nonetheless, the first to refer to the theory by its acronym INUS. In his monograph, *The Cement of the Universe, Mackie* referred to the approach of *Hart* and *Honoré* as the INUS theory based on a '*causally relevant factor*' without, however, explicitly acknowledging them as the originators of the theory.[144] Nevertheless, the INUS approach significantly enhances *Hume's* understanding of causation. In particular, it extends the still mono-causal Humean conception of regularity-based causes to the now dominant notion of regularity-based multi-causation, which in turn leads the approach to its practical relevance. However, *Mackie* also introduced a limitation to the application of the approach. He suggested that the theory should only apply to laws of nature, which further implies that the conditions themselves are based on such laws.

[140] The multi-causal perception was not inherent in the original Humean understanding but is now a fundamental factor in the prevailing conceptions of regularity-based theories.

[141] This does not mean that these fields also apply theories of regularity. They most often refer to probabilistic accounts of causation, but they coincide in their perceptions of the legitimacy of multiple causes.

[142] The INUS test is also known as the '*nomic sufficiency theory of causation*', see Moore (2009a), pp. 89, 174–175. See for the NESS test, Wright (1985), pp. 1788–1803. Although it is argued that this approach was also already taken by *Hart* and *Honoré* in their work 'Causation in the Law' see Hart and Honoré (1959). See in this regard Stapleton (2009), p. 756.

[143] Hart and Honoré (1959), pp. 106–107. In this regard e.g. Puppe and Wright (2017), p. 26.

[144] Mackie (1974), p. 62. Already indicated in Mackie (1965).

The second, and the more prominent approach to regularity-based causation today, is the NESS test introduced by *Wright* in 1985.[145] Based on the INUS test, the NESS approach expands on the original concept developed by *Hart*, *Honoré*, and later by *Mackie*. In the same way as the INUS test, it builds on the understanding of weak necessity and strong sufficiency. Although there is only a slight difference between the NESS and the INUS test in their fundamental approach to causation, and some authors even state that the NESS test represents merely a simplification of the INUS approach, *Wright* insists on its fundamental differences and better applicability to legal causal assessments.[146] Nowadays, the NESS test is regarded as a further conceptual evolution and dogmatic consolidation of the INUS test, which is why *Wright's* approach dominates legal and philosophical discourse today.

One of the main differences contrasting the initial INUS test is its applicability to singular causal scenarios. While *Mackie* only advocates his approach in scenarios of general causation between events and applies counterfactual theories in cases of singular causal relations instead, *Wright* expands his regularity-based theory to scenarios of singular causation, as well.[147] Besides this expansion, he further develops the concept of strong sufficiency beyond its abstract principles.[148] One of the main scenarios that illustrate the difference between both approaches is a sequence of events in which the condition is neither sufficient nor necessary. *Hart* and *Honoré* consider such a condition, following counterfactual theories, as not causal.[149] *Wright*, nevertheless, concludes differently, given that the condition, in conjunction with other conditions, may still be a necessary part of a sufficient set, leading to the affirmation of regularity-based causation.[150]

Unlike counterfactual concepts of causation in the law, regularity theories have only occasionally found their way into jurisprudence. However, without explicitly referring to the NESS or the INUS test, references to similar causal perceptions of the law can be found—at least implicitly—in some decisions.[151] Furthermore, although case law in this area lags far behind the use of counterfactual tests, expositions of

---

[145] Wright (1985), pp. 1788–1803.

[146] See for the argument of the NESS-test being a simplification of the INUS-approach, Pearl (2009), p. 314. See on Wrights account Wright (2011), Wright (1988), p. 1023. See also Fumerton and Kress (2001), p. 90.

[147] Mackie (1974), pp. 59–60; Toepel (2013), p. 114. See for differentiation between *Mackies* INUS test and *Mills* and *Hume's* perception of regularity, Holger and Guenther (2021). See for the difference this distinction enables in climate change scenarios Sect. 4.3.2.

[148] See Puppe (2013), p. 74; Wright (2007); Wright (1985); Wright and Puppe (2016); Wright (2011).

[149] Hart and Honoré (1985).

[150] The difference is most directed at the treatment of cases of overdetermination, which are also excluded by *Mackies* INUS approach but are entailed in *Wrights* understanding. See e.g. Mackie (1965), p. 33. See also in comparison to the approach chosen by *Mackie*, Wright (1988), pp. 1023–1028.

[151] Plakokefalos (2015) in citing the case, 30 June 1930 – 2 R.I.A.A. 1035, *Responsabilité de l'Allemagne en raison des actes commis postérieurement au 31 juillet 1914 et avant que le Portugal ne participât a la guerre (Portugal v. Allemagne) (Naulilaa)*, 1070.

regularity-based theories can be encountered not only in purely theoretical and metaphysical works but also increasingly in commentaries as well as practice- and application-oriented works. The American Law Institute, for example, in its comprehensive revised Restatement of the Law Third, speaks of multiple sufficient causes:

> In some cases, tortious conduct by one actor is insufficient, even with other background causes, to cause the plaintiff's harm. [...] Moreover, the fact that the other person's conduct is sufficient to cause the harm does not prevent the actor's conduct from being a factual cause of harm according to this Section, if the actor's conduct is necessary to at least one causal set.[152]

However, the ALI leaves open the question of how to deal with a situation in which one or more sufficient conditions or sets of sufficient conditions are present in addition to the insufficient condition in question by stating that

> (s)ometimes, one actor's contribution may be sufficient to bring about the harm while another actor's contribution is only sufficient when combined with some portion of the first actor's contribution. Whether the second actor's contribution can be so combined into a sufficient causal set is a matter on which this Restatement takes no position and leaves to future development in the courts.[153]

The statement made by the ALI addresses the question of the correct set-setting of conditions, which is one of the main metaphysical and ultimately application-oriented concerns in the application of regularity-based theories.[154]

Given that the NESS account constitutes a further refinement of the INUS approach and is, therefore, predominantly used in more recent literature, the NESS approach will also be primarily referenced in the following. Nevertheless, this does not preclude the general validity and transferability of regularity-specific conceptions to the INUS approach.

4.3.1.2 Imperfect Regularities, Spurious Regularities and Epiphenomenal Causes

The mode of epistemology and the fundamental inference of causation of theories of regularity can sometimes be in conflict with the natural and realistic perception of causal sequences. Regularity-based theories infer general principles from repetitive results. However, even if a causal relation based on regularities is metaphysically established, such regularity does not ensure that the outcome of the next scenario will be the same as in the previous one.[155] There might be a higher probability of the outcome occurring, but it is not possible to deduce a particular outcome

[152] American Law Institute (2010), § 27 Comment f.

[153] Ibid. § 27 Comment f.

[154] See for a broad discussion on this issue Sect. 4.3.1.3.

[155] Mayor criticism brought forward by Haas (2002), pp. 175–176. Also acknowledging the problem, but deferring it to epistemology and natural science, Puppe (2013), pp. 86–87.

unambiguously and with complete empirical certainty from such a coherent sequence. Known as the issue of imperfect regularities, the occurrence of a multitude of stringent events does not allow the assumption of an all-encompassing regularity or law, especially when the sequence of events or the regularity does not occur in a homogenous field. Regularity-based theories, therefore, fundamentally confuse non-actual events with reality because regularities are alien to nature. And, although the perception of multi-causation corresponds better to reality than mono-causal concepts, in its fundamental core, theories of regularity diverge significantly from the natural and actual world.

Strongly connected with the aforementioned issue of imperfect regularities is the concern that the regularity-based approach increases the number of events that can be considered causal conditions in a way that would not only lead to an overbreadth of the approach (see below) but includes events that are only correlated and happen accidentally. However, these conditions are usually not considered causal in a logical and intuitive sense, which is why they are treated as issues of '*spurious regularities*' and '*epiphenomenal causes*'.[156] Considering the case that deforestation of the rainforest in a minimally sufficient way would regularly lead to both the extinction of native species and the release of significant amounts of CO_2, as well as a measurable increase in atmospheric temperatures. According to theories of regularity, and because of the correlation with deforestation, the extinction of native species would also be causally linked with the increase in temperature. The regularity approach would thus result in the establishment of a causal link between both events, ultimately leading to a spurious and, hence, false regularity. *Mackie* himself introduced another epiphenomenal example. In his example, he addresses the situation between Manchester factory hooters sounding at five o'clock and workers regularly leaving their factories in London just moments later (*Manchester-Factory-Hooters*).[157] *Mackie* himself concludes in the above example that although the sounding of the hooter at five o'clock and the workers leaving the factory with the sounding of the horn would not intuitively be regarded as a causal relation, these correlations would have to be considered as a causal factor when applying a regularity approach. He, therefore, explains that

> the sounding of the Manchester factory hooters, plus the absence of whatever conditions would make them sound when it wasn't five o'clock, plus the presence of whatever conditions are, along with its being five o'clock, jointly sufficient for the Londoners to stop work a moment later—including, say, automatic devices for setting off the London hooters at five o'clock, is a conjunction of features which is unconditionally followed by the

---

[156] See for a more detailed explanation of the problem and possible solutions Baumgartner (2008). In regard to the issue of perfect correlations Birnbacher and Hommen (2012), pp. 101–102. *Moore* also calls such epiphenomenal events, Moore (2009a), pp. 481–482. However, these conditions are usually not considered causal in a logical and real sense.

[157] Mackie (1974), pp. 83–87. Countering this example, see Wright (2011), p. 297. Also addressing this example in more detail, Moore (2009a), pp. 481–483.

> Londoners stopping work. In this conjunction the sounding of the Manchester hooters is an essential element, for it alone, in this conjunction, ensures that it should be five o'clock.[158]

Based on this difficulty, it is argued that it is nearly impossible to establish a causal law that semantically justifies this difference and excludes sole correlations and events that occur accidentally or circumstantially.[159] Although based on *Mackie's* view, one might argue that results achieved by regularity theories are flawed (especially concerning the application of the INUS approach), *Wright* argues that the NESS test offers correct results even in the aforementioned scenario since *"(n)either horn's sounding, nor even its existence, is part of the instantiation of the antecedent of any causal generalisation for which the consequent is the state of its being five o'clock"*.[160] Thus, the sounding of the hooters is not considered a causal condition for workers leaving the factory according to the NESS approach. The NESS test following *Wright*, therefore, better complies with one's intuition and relates more accurately to natural and factual causation. In addition to *Wright*, other scholars, on the forefront of them *Baumgartner*, argue that accidental and spurious regularities do not obstruct regularity theories.[161] However, they hereby often refer to slightly modified versions of theories of regularity.[162]

4.3.1.3 The Set-Setting Dilemma

The greatest uncertainty in regularity theories of causation remains in the formation of individual sufficient sets of conditions. In general, the formation of sets is based on individual decisions and, thus, on specifications about the grouping of the respective sets. This method, however, is at cross purposes with the core of regularity theories and fundamentally contradicts their qualification as a generalistic theory of factual causation in law by introducing singular causal statements into a generalistic assessment.[163] Yet, apart from the individualization of generalistic theories, the right way of grouping and set-setting relevant conditions in light of the INUS and NESS tests still is at issue. Generally, set-setting allows the user of the causal approach in law to influence the result by deciding on the specific grouping of the sets, not only leading to an individualisation but also to a subjectification of a fundamentally objective and factual dogma which again contradicts the core essence

---

[158] Mackie (1974), p. 83.

[159] Mayor criticism expressed by Pearl (2009), p. 314.

[160] Wright (2011), p. 297.

[161] Baumgartner (2008), pp. 342–346.

[162] *Baumgartner* hereby introduces the '*minimal theory*' that ultimately should lead to intuitively correct results, see Baumgartner (2013), pp. 90–91.

[163] Criticizing, see Moore (2009a), pp. 491–492. Also Toepel (2013), pp. 128–129.

of a two-step causal approach to causation.[164] Especially in cases of alternative and pre-emptive causation, the approach taken is crucial, can it ultimately depend on whether a condition is to be recognised as causal or not. In his NESS approach, *Wright* resorts to the greatest possible flexibility in forming the relevant sets.[165] In doing so, he also advocates for the splitting of fixed and established units to obtain minimally sufficient sets. This is possible in his view because it does not change the relevant properties of a condition or the outcome, respectively but only its quantity.[166]

Regarding the so-called duplicative causation cases, and similar to what is called here a cumulative cause, *Wright*, most fittingly for climate matters, gives the example of a case concerning multiple polluters.[167] He elaborates the following:

> [...] (A)ssume that five units of pollution were necessary and sufficient for the injury and that each of seven defendants discharged one unit of pollution. Each defendant can truthfully say that its one unit was neither necessary nor independently sufficient of the injury. But each defendant's one unit was necessary of the sufficiency of **a** set of actual antecedent conditions that included only four of the other units, and the sufficiency of this particular set of actual antecedent conditions was not affected by the existence of two additional duplicative units.[168]

In principle, every unit would be able to be grouped into a sufficient set of conditions, leaving two of the units out of the equation. However, grouped differently, they could also be qualified as necessary for a sufficient set which would render them causal in the respective setting, then again, excluding two other units.

As the example given by *Wright* shows, the dilemma of multiple, cumulative contributions and the right set-setting becomes particularly relevant in cases of multiple-source pollution. Such cases, in turn, coincide closely with scenarios and considerations applied in regard to emissions-based climate change claims.[169] Given the occurrence of many cumulative conditions, causation in these cases would have to be denied under conventional (not-appropriated) counterfactual accounts. Yet, given that the requirement of regularity-based theories, and, in particular, the NESS account, is that the specific emissions E_S are a necessary condition for any sufficient set of conditions, E_S is deemed to be causal. It is irrelevant whether E_S would form a

[164] This issue is also raised by *West* (West 2013). Concerning *Wright*, see Wright (2007), p. 297. Also stating that it would *"(set) the stage for the arbitrary and selective apportioning of blame."*, see Orakhelashvili (2022), p. 32.

[165] Wright (1985), pp. 1793–1794.

[166] Ibid.

[167] *Wright* defines duplicative causation cases as "*cases in which a factor other than the specified act would have been sufficient to produce the injury in the absence of the specified act, but its effects [...] combined with or duplicated those of the specified act to jointly produce the injury.*" *Wright* gives the following example: "*C and D independently start separate fires, each of which would have been sufficient to destroy P's house. The fires converge and together burn down the house. Each fire was a duplicative cause of the destruction of the house.*" Ibid. 1775–1776.

[168] Ibid. 1793.

[169] West (2013), p. 48.

necessary part of only a few of these sufficient sets of conditions. As long as E_S can be included as a necessary part of any sufficient set, E_S is to be considered a cause of the outcome in light of regularity theories.

While the result seems intuitively correct for cases of cumulative causation, difficulties arise for cases of alternative and pre-emptive causation. As seen above, and in contrast to the application of counterfactual tests, under the strict application of regularity theories, both alternative and pre-emptive conditions would or can be considered causal based on the fact that it is possible to have multiple sufficient sets of conditions. Allowing for the existence of different sufficient sets, especially with respect to concurrent cases of alternative causation, addresses one of the criticisms often levelled at counterfactual theories of causation. However, unlike conventional counterfactual theories, which in their strict application lead to the negation of the existence of any cause and are criticised for not giving any result, regularity theories face the opposite criticism of generating too many causes. This is notably true in staggered cases of alternative causation, where both or all of the preceding and succeeding necessary conditions of sufficient sets would have to be regarded as causal. Such a result, however, contradicts the nature of causal inquiry and legal cases in general and is contrary to factual reality.[170] It further moves away from actual, naturalistic causal relata. Cases of alternative or pre-emptive causation are characterised by the fact that despite several sufficient conditions or sets of conditions, in reality, only one condition causes the specific outcome. Whether the causal scenario revolves around alternative, pre-emptive, or similar cases of causation is not decisive.

Proponents of theories of regularity have sought to demonstrate that the traditional approach of INUS and NESS is also applicable to such overdetermination cases. In applying a further condition to his initial theory, *Wright* argues that for a condition to be a cause in the sense of the NESS approach, the outcome does not have to be already brought about by another set.[171] Therefore, only the pre-emptive set of conditions is regarded as causal for the outcome. Nevertheless, some scholars claim that such a result contradicts the strict application of regularity theories.[172] *Wright* counters those objections by introducing the term 'causal sufficiency'.[173] However, quite a few scholars are of the view that such would result in circular reasoning.[174] Apart from cases of pre-emptive causation and their qualification as causes in the NESS approach, it remains to be considered that there are only limited scenarios of alternative causation in which the categorisation of two conditions as a cause seems to be valid. This is the case with simultaneous sufficient conditions or

[170] In this regard also, Moore (2009a), p. 491.

[171] Wright (1985), p. 1795.

[172] See Fumerton and Kress (2001), pp. 100–101; West (2013), p. 51; Stapleton (2008), p. 477.

[173] Wright (2011), p. 289. Similarly, see Fumerton and Kress (2001), pp. 101–102.

[174] Moore (2009a), p. 492; Stapleton (2009), p. 765. Arguing that instead of causal sufficiency, legal sufficiency is required, see West (2013), p. 50. Also acknowledging the potential of seeing causal sufficiency as a "*vicious form of circularity*", Fumerton and Kress (2001), p. 102.

sets of conditions, where it is not possible to determine whether set A or set B caused the effect in question.

In dealing with cumulative and alternative causation, one of the main concerns of theories of regularity arises from the fact that the causal condition in each respect would constitute an enormous number of causes, leading to an alleged over-breadth of this approach.[175] The same concern was also addressed regarding the counterfactual-grown strategy of concretization, nonetheless, regularity-based theories are further enhanced by allowing conditions to be grouped in a variety of different ways without imposing strict requirements and constraints on the manner in which they are set.[176] In further contrast to the strategy of concretization, the regularity-based set setting allows for individualised grouping to such an extent that it is almost inconceivable that a particular contribution could not be arranged in such a way as to constitute a necessary element of a sufficient set of conditions. In accepting the qualification of a more comprehensive range of conditions as causes, regularity theories are even broader than counterfactual theories. The breadth of the regularity-based approach, however, is criticised, in particular, with regard to its practical application in law, its function as a factual causation dogma and even its raison d'être per se. The latter is particularly questioned on the assumption that the acceptance of almost any condition as cause renders the discussion of factual causation superfluous. However, as discussed above, the utility and purpose of causation in law lies not merely in the determination and sorting out of conditions and even less in the delimiting function of factual causation.[177] Rather, the benefit lies in the legitimating function that factual causation achieves. To counter the argument that the breadth of regularity-based theories would hinder their legal applicability, it is precisely the function of legal, not factual, causation to constitute a limiting factor on the results achieved by factual causation and thus to ensure its legal applicability. It is, moreover, not the role of factual causal assessments to limit the amount of causes to a legally applicable amount. Therefore, the breadth of causal approaches cannot serve as an argument against their application, provided that it does not render the examination of factual causation redundant.

The breadth of the approach further goes hand in hand with the fact that mono-causal events do not occur in reality. Instead, as already mentioned, actual causal relations are characterized by multi-causal components. Nevertheless, and despite this argument in favour of broader approaches to causation, the criticism raised against theories of regularity still persist that even irrelevant and accidental conditions and conditions that would not be considered to be a cause from an intuitive,

---

[175] Kelmann (1987), pp. 603–604. Also concerning the practicability of the NESS-test, see West (2013), pp. 52–62. *Moore* calls it the *"promiscuity problem"*, see Moore (2009a), pp. 477–478. Also raising this issue, see Fumerton and Kress (2001), p. 99.

[176] See for the requirements and restrictions by the theory of factual concretization Sect. 4.2.3.

[177] See in this regard Sect. 3.1.1.

factual point of view are considered to be a cause of the outcome in the right set-setting and with the right grouping of conditions.[178]

Closely related to the breadth provided by the possibility of individual set-setting is the risk of an unintuitive splitting of already existing adhesive units. This is particularly relevant for cases of asymmetric causation, in which one unit (E_1) constitutes a sufficient condition. However, additional conditions ($E_{2\text{-x}}$) exist that, taken individually, are not sufficient for the event's outcome. Even a combination of these individual conditions, e.g. E_2, E_3 and E_4, to a coherent set would not overstep the sufficiency threshold. In a synopsis with unit E_1, nonetheless, each unit ($E_{2\text{-x}}$) would also not be necessary for a sufficient set of conditions since the sufficiency limit has already been far exceeded by E_1. A qualification of $E_{2\text{-x}}$ as causes would only succeed based on splitting the unit E_1 into subunits $E_{1.x}$, which then, combined with the conditions $E_{2\text{-x}}$, lead to the qualification of those units as necessary for a sufficient set of conditions.[179] However, this fragmentation, often articulated as artificial, has been criticised in the literature.[180] It also raises the question of whether E_1, despite being split into different subunits, can still be a cause on its own. At least the latter must be affirmed in any case since E_1 would undoubtedly be a cause of the result even without its division. To deny this would only lead to a further distortion of the conditional relations.

The right way of set-setting, furthermore, poses practical issues. Particularly in cases of multiple contributions of different magnitude and time, which in law most frequently relates to instances of pollution or the conjunction and intermixture of various chemical substances (toxic tort), breaking down the causal chain to every single contribution poses significant challenges. This reflects not only on the law itself but also overshadows the scientific determination of results, which in turn leads to an increased level of uncertainty. Theories of regularity are much more dependent on the exact determination of conditions and units than counterfactual theories, especially when it comes to the correct set-setting or possible splitting of certain pre-existing and compound units. For this reason, some scholars argue that theories of regularity, and, in particular, the NESS test, are not useful and appropriate for dealing with scientific uncertainty.[181] However, while acknowledging the difficulties of proving the existence of factual causation in general, this argument must be countered on two grounds. First, it is not apparent why regularity theories pose more extensive problems in dealing with scientific uncertainty than other theories of causation. Proving factual causation in the face of scientific uncertainty is a significant difficulty for all theories of causation in the law.[182] Furthermore, whether it is scientifically proven that a particular causal link exists is not a legal issue but a

---

[178] Although he advocates such an approach, even *Moore* sees this as a central concern, see Moore (2009a), p. 490.

[179] Wright (1985), p. 1793.

[180] Problematizing but accepting such fragmentation West (2013), pp. 48–49.

[181] See, e.g. Ibid. 50–51, Hogg (2011), pp. 48–49.

[182] Acknowledging that, ibid. at 48.

purely scientific one on which the legal argument should not depend. Therefore, theories based on regularities should not be opposed by such arguments.

A more specific challenge to the set-setting and the right way of grouping units within theories of regularity is posed by negative events and omissions.[183] However, unlike adherents of other theories, generalists allow almost exclusively the inclusion of omissions in causal chains.[184] This admissibility reflects the lower requirements posed on causal relata by theories of regularity, which do not account for whether the sequence of regular events occurs between positive or negative actions. The difficulty lies in the actual handling of omissions, both in terms of the appropriate set setting as well as beyond. Strongly responding to the widespread problem of set-setting and indeterminate causation, *Fisher* argues that the regularity theories fail to produce just results concerning multiple, independently sufficient omissions. The inequitable outcome hereby stems from the fact that the relevant scenarios and sets of conditions can easily be adjusted in ways that lead to the desired result.[185] This is mainly due to the unlimited number of omissions which can be grouped arbitrarily for the 'right' result. In contrast to counterfactual tests that fail to produce any causal relata in such cases, he argues that regularity theories (both the INUS and the NESS test and although differing in their applicability) deliver too many possible causal options.[186] It thus once again responds to the criticism of the breadth of a regularity-based approach but also has to meet the counter-arguments of the limiting function of normative causation.

4.3.1.4 Combining Counterfactuals and Regularities

Some authors, including *Mackie,* in reliance on his INUS approach and *Toepel,* most likely building on the NESS test, argue for using both regularity approaches and counterfactual methods.[187] They distinguish the application of the concept based on the establishment of singular or general causal relations. Thus, it is argued that the application of counterfactual tests, the conditio-sine-qua-non formula in particular, lead to intuitively correct results in the case of singular causal relations. However, in the presence of general causal relations, regularity theories and especially (following *Mackie*), the INUS test is applicable. Both tests are connected by general causal statements as the basis on which singular causal relations are ultimately founded.[188]

---

[183] For a more general account of the debate on the qualification of omissions as causes, see Sect. 4.1.2.

[184] Moore (2009a), p. 480; Birnbacher and Hommen (2012), pp. 101–102.

[185] Concerning the NESS-test, see Fisher (1992), pp. 1358–1359.

[186] Ibid. 1360.

[187] Mackie (1974), pp. 59–60. Also affirmative of such an approach, see Toepel (2013), pp. 130–132. *Fumerton* and *Kress* also raise the question of a combined appliance of both tests, however, reject such an approach right away as not being able to resolve dilemma of causal overdetermination, see Fumerton and Kress (2001), p. 98.

[188] Toepel (2013), p. 131.

Toepel considers his approach particularly vindicated in cases of scientific uncertainty. In situations, mainly in the field of medicine, in which a specific counterfactual cannot be established due to a lack of scientific knowledge, general causal considerations within the framework of the INUS test act as a backbone for the causal chain that, as argued, can nevertheless be established.[189] Assuming a degree of comparability between medical and climate cases, at least in regard to the scientific uncertainties entailed in both situations, one could consider *Toepel's* approach as a possible solution also in the realm of climatic scenarios.

However, this position is unconvincing on a number of grounds. First, both theories are based on fundamentally different understandings of the nature of causes at the metaphysical level. The rationale of causes in terms of counterfactuals contradicts the basic understanding of causes in terms of regularities. Furthermore, it is not convincing why, especially in the case of scientific uncertainties and the failure of specific, counterfactual causation, regularity-based theories represent a fall-back function within the framework of general causation. Regularity-based theories face the same difficulties as counterfactual theories in dealing with scientific uncertainty.[190] In principle, it can be assumed that general causation offers less potential for assailment in the counterfactual than in the determination of special causation. Moreover, mixing the two theories does not resolve the specific problems of counterfactual tests with respect to specific cases of causal overdetermination.[191] To solve counterfactual problems of overdetermination, *Toepel* uses the fine-graining method.[192] Yet, it is not comprehensible why it is necessary to mix two different theories of causation and not to focus only on counterfactual theories, notably if one, like *Toepel*, ultimately adopts a fine-grained approach. *Toepel* is led in part by his use of the INUS approach, which simply does not account for special causation. While *Wright's* NESS test affirms its applicability to singular causal statements, it is *Mackie* who promotes the use of counterfactuality. Finally, and especially with regard to the applicability and functionality of a unified approach, the conflation of the two approaches is overall not convincing. The aim should, therefore, be to establish a unified, metaphysically-founded approach.

4.3.2 Reconciling Theories of Regularity with Climatic Causation

The multi-causal concept and the associated handling of regularity-based theories with cumulative causation, in particular, could also argue for greater efficiency and conceptualisation in substantiating climatic causation. Emissions-based climate

[189] Ibid. 131–132.

[190] See in this regard Sect. 4.2.

[191] See in this regard Sect. 4.2.2.

[192] See in this regard Sect. 4.2.3.

claims are characterised by many cumulative contributions, without any single contribution exceeding the threshold of sufficiency and necessity alone. As a result, grouping emissions into specific sets of conditions that are sufficient in themselves could also be advantageous from an economic and application-oriented perspective. A sectoral breakdown (among others, industry, transport, and land use), already familiar in climate and related sciences, could particularly be suitable for a reference of set-setting itself. The utility and usability of regularity-based theories for climatic causation are moreover highlighted by the early reference of legal scholars to the applicability of the respective approach to pollution cases and hereby advocating a concept of weak necessity—strong sufficiency.[193] Similarly, in emission-based scenarios, too, the issue arises as to what extent emission clusters, consisting, for example, of the emissions of a particular actor or even within a sectoral reference, can be artificially divided for the purpose of establishing causation. The divisibility per se, nonetheless, is not an obstacle in emissions-based litigation, given the vast possibilities for fine-graining emission clusters and even emissions themselves down to the molecular level. In addition, the enormous potential to divide clusters of emissions reduces the risk of unintuitive, artificial splitting of relevant conditions. Within the constraints of the greatest possible effectiveness of a regularity-based approach, and with reference to *Wright's* understanding in the context of the NESS account, every emission, independent of its general or its specific account, would be causal for climate change in general and most likely also to a large extent for climate change-related damage. In contrast, *Mackie's* INUS approach can only partially produce such a result. While regularity-based causation between emissions and climate change, as well as between emissions and general climate change-related effects, can be ascertained, the INUS test cannot be used for singular causal statements, which relates to statements about the causal link between the emissions of a specific emitter and a specific consequence. According to *Mackie*, this would require the use of counterfactual theories.

Less relevant in the context of climate change litigation than cumulative and emissions-based claims are cases of alternative causation. Dealing with two or more sets of sufficient conditions, however, also poses some challenges within regularity-based theories. But unlike counterfactual theories, difficulties arising with alternating causes do not consist in the attainment of too few or no causal outcomes at all but rather result in too many conditions being qualified as such, which in turn is inconsistent with the actual, factual situation. In principle, regularity-based theories allow for the existence of several sufficient sets, which can be reflected, for example, in several sufficient emission clusters, or can also have repercussions on general climate variability or other human influences. The multi-causation of the regularity-based approaches can refute the often-used argument of other contributions to the specific outcome since it is not just a single condition that can be considered causal but one that can occur alongside other causal conditions. Furthermore, the reference to the contributions of others or even to the—now very outdated—'force majeur'

193 West (2013), p. 10.

argument cannot be raised within the framework of regularity-based theories.[194] In this respect, regularity-based theories are quite advantageous for climate lawsuits, at least in their economic dimension and in their practical application. Yet, difficulties arise from the temporal sequence of sufficient conditions within the framework of pre-emptive causation. Nevertheless, unintuitive and even incorrect results can be avoided by referring to a temporal condition, which requires that no other cause has already preceded the cause in question.[195]

Applying the NESS concept to the case of *Luciano Lliuya v. RWE AG* also shows that regularity-based theories can help establishing causation in climate litigation.[196] Leaving aside the metaphysically-bound question of the applicability of regularity theories to individual cases, the specific emissions of the RWE AG E_S must prove to be a necessary condition of a set of conditions that qualifies as sufficient for the occurrence of the outcome I_S, viz the increase in the risk of a glacial lake outburst flood. As there is no specific requirement as to how the different conditions must be cumulated, and the condition E_S only needs to be a necessary condition of any set of conditions, the establishment of causation is relatively straightforward. In the case of *Luciano Lliuya v. RWE AG,* however, the main problem lies in the area of concurrent causes and cumulative causation. One must construct a set of conditions that includes all relevant conditions up to the point where the set's sufficiency threshold is reached but without the set exceeding the sufficiency threshold in such a way as to reduce the necessity of E_S. This could lead to the omission of other emissions E_X, as their addition to the set would not satisfy the necessity element. In addition, the impact of negative events and omissions is also highly relevant in this case. Those omissions concern, in particular, the failure to construct sufficient flood protection measures and to ensure the diversion of water to relieve the pressure building up on the natural moraine. Other factors, such as the absence of extreme natural climate variations, which could have significantly increased the risk of a glacier outburst flood, or other human influences, can furthermore provide for conditions that are of influence for the set-setting, in particular, but also the general outcome in question. Yet, it must be acknowledged that, at least in its practical application, a precise determination of each set of conditions to be established borders on the impossible. This does not only refer to the current climate case but is valid for all cases where regularity-based theories are involved. A practical application of regularity-based causal theories can hence only take place on the premise that there is no need for a detailed and precise definition of a set, especially when individual contributions are of such a similar nature and mode of action in their fine-grained perception that the specific set-setting is no longer of importance. In summary, then, even if the relevant set of conditions in the present case cannot be determined comprehensively, and even if significantly more negative events play a role, the specific emissions of RWE AG can be regarded as factually causal within the framework of regularity theories,

[194] See for 'force majeure' as an intervening cause Sect. 5.5.

[195] At least this is how *Wright* would perceive the problem of pre-emptive causation.

[196] Essen Regional Court, 15 December 2016 – 2 O 285/15, *Luciano Lliuya v. RWE AG.*

even if this case is highly simplified for technical reasons. This finding is supported by scientific evidence that indicates at least a high probability ('*virtually certain*') that the retreat of the Palcaraju glacier is not due solely to natural causes.[197]

The beforementioned examples have shown that despite the multi-causal conception of regularity-based theories, as well as their closer perception to actual causation, courts and actors, in general, are still reluctant to fall back on the INUS or NESS theory. The debate on regularity-based approaches remains mainly at a philosophical and legal-theoretical level, although the merits of applying the conception in different jurisdictions and legal systems are increasingly being argued for.[198] Nevertheless, the analysis has shown that, to date, no climate change case has been found in which either the plaintiffs, the defendants or the court have made active or even successful use of the INUS or NESS concept. An exception to this fundamental observation, however, was made by Judge Beach in the case of *Minister for the Environment v. Sharma*, in which a possible duty of care on the part of the Minister for the Environment concerning the effects of climate change on children was at issue.[199] Questions have also arisen as to whether a strict chain of causation is required and, if so, what type of causation test should be applied in this context. In this regard, Judge Beach stated that

> (n)o doubt it might be said that the "but-for" test concerning factual causation is inapposite in the present context and that the NESS (necessary element of a sufficient set) test advocated by Professor Richard Wright and others is more suitable, particularly when dealing with a posited causal condition that is neither necessary nor sufficient.[200]

Despite those remarks, Judge Beach refrains from actually applying the NESS approach in the relevant case stating that the decisive factor for the decision in the case of *Minister for the Environment v. Sharma* is not how causation is to be established but whether the duty owed was reasonably foreseeable. He, therefore, leaves the question of the applicable causal doctrine open. However, he later expresses his view that newer approaches to factual causation must be assessed and adopted in light of the new concept of climate change lawsuits.[201]

As a result, and despite Judge Beach's suggestion of a change in the application of causal dogmas, the NESS and INUS tests have so far had little practical significance. The reasons for this are complex. One of the main factors is that courts, especially in civil law countries, still largely adhere to a counterfactual

---

[197] Stuart-Smith et al. (2021).

[198] E.g. Minnerop and Otto (2020), pp. 67, 73–77. Some jurisdictions, particularly common law countries, occasionally recognise a weak necessity standard as sufficient to establish causation, see in this regard especially the domestic approaches described concerning contributory causation (Sect. 4.5.2.2.1).

[199] Federal Court of Australia, 27 May 2021 – [2021] FCA 560, *Sharma and others v. Minister for the Environment*, Federal Court of Australia, 15 March 2022 – [2022] FCAFC 35, *Minister for the Environment v. Sharma.*

[200] Federal Court of Australia, 15 March 2022 – [2022] FCAFC 35, *Minister for the Environment v. Sharma* para 438.

[201] Ibid. para 440.

understanding of causation. Furthermore, the complexity of its metaphysical construct and methodology certainly plays a decisive role in the lack of implementation in practice. For an actual practical application, and thus an increase in recognition of regularity approaches, it is necessary to translate them into a general legal understanding that enables their functional legal application.

4.3.3 Conclusion

As multicentric theories, theories of regularity form a counterpart to the monocentrically bound counterfactual conceptions of causation in law. By dispensing with the notion that a particular result can only be caused by a particular cause, theories of regularity are mostly able to deal with concurrent causes in a metaphysically sound way. Concurrent to counterfactual theories, however, there are also multi-causal scenarios in which the general perception and metaphysical realisation of the theory would lead to results that differ from an actual and also scientific understanding of cause-effect relationships. Especially in the case of preventive causation, it is necessary to slightly adapt the general theories, for example by adding a temporal component. The necessary deviations in the light of regularity theories are, nevertheless, much more limited than in the case of counterfactual theories. Furthermore, theories of regularity are often closer to the actual, factual nature of causality and to a scientific understanding of causality that allows multiple conditions to be qualified as causes.

The foregoing discussion has also shown that theories of regularity, in addition to their popularity in the metaphysical discussion among legal philosophers, have their raison d'être in practical application as well. One of the undoubted advantages of such an approach to causation in law is its ability to deal with cases of overdetermination and concurrent causation, which makes it particularly suitable for emission-based climate lawsuits and climate change litigation in general. Due to the complexity of the climate system, climate scenarios are shaped by many different conditions, which in turn affect the outcome in many different ways.

However, regularity theories are also subject to valid criticism, not only from a metaphysical point of view, but also from an application-oriented perspective. The main concern hereby relates to the criticism of an artificial and unnatural splitting of units of conditions and their respective grouping. Yet, as discussed above, the former is unlikely to occur in the context of emission-based climate claims. While it cannot be ruled out that such a problem will ever emerge, it is at least mitigated by the subject matter of climate change scenarios. Furthermore, concerning the grouping and, in particular, the rendering of the relevant sets, the requirement imposed on actors and courts cannot consist of a precise depiction of the whole constituents that are included in the set. Such high preconditions would render any application of the approach impossible. The demand can only relate to a coherent and conclusive disclosure of the set of conditions so that it can be inferred from this that the set itself is sufficient and the condition in question qualifies as necessary. The further criticism that regularity-based approaches lead to overly broad results due to their multi-causal conception can also be refuted on the basis of the inherent consistency with actual factual causal relations.

4.4 Probabilistic Theories of Causation

4.4.1 Metaphysical Substantiation of Probabilistic Theories of Causation

4.4.1.1 The General Principles of Probabilistic Causation

Probabilistic theories to causation stand in opposition to the deterministic approaches established and founded by *Hume*.[202] In contrast to regularity-based and counterfactual theories, probabilistic causation does not rely on qualifying conditions or sets of conditions as necessary and sufficient for a specific outcome.[203] It eschews the elaboration based on these two factors altogether. Instead, to establish causation on the basis of probabilities, it is sufficient to show that the condition increases the probability of the outcome occurring, i.e. that the likelihood of a given outcome occurring without the condition is lower than with the condition. To move from mere scientific probabilities to causation in general, however, it is necessary to interpret probabilistic results objectively rather than from an epistemic perspective. First developed and proposed by *Reichenbach*, the determination of causation on the basis of probability is now a common way of expressing causal relations, especially in medicine, natural and social sciences.[204] Although still relatively rare, an increasing number of scholars and legal theorists are advocating the application of such theories in law, as well.[205] In doing so, they draw heavily on scientific findings in their determination of causation.

The greatest merit of probabilistic theories over counterfactual and regularity-based, i.e. deterministic, understandings of causation lies in their compatibility with reality, actual causation and scientific truth.[206] As probabilistic theories do not rely on counterfactuals and hypothetical assumptions to establish causation but on well-founded and scientifically sound probabilistic statements, they convince through

[202] With one of his most influential works being, see Hume (1978).

[203] See for a detailed assessment as to why probabilistic theories refrain from defining causes as either necessary and/or sufficient, see Eells (1988), pp. 189–190.

[204] Reichenbach (1956).

[205] Among the first, see *Suppes* (e.g. in Suppes 1970), *Cartwright* (e.g. in Cartwright 1979), *Skyrms* (e.g. in Skyrms 1980), *Eells* (e.g. in Eells 1991) and *Peñalver* (e.g. in Peñalver 1998, pp. 582–587). More recently also Schauer and Spellman (2020). "*Sound(ing) a death-knell for the approach except for the fact that the alternatives' vital signs are equally weak*", Davis (1988), p. 157. Against a probabilistic understanding of causation, see Moore (2009a), p. 4.

[206] See e.g. Peñalver (1998), p. 583 in citing Dupré (1993), pp. 185–186, 214.

their provability and thus their close relation to the actual world and reality. Probabilistic theories truly carry factuality at their heart. Therefore, proponents of this view are particularly opposed to the assumption of universal truth and provability implied by counterfactual theories, which, in their opinion, cannot be reconciled with the laws of nature.[207] Rather, the natural course of events is based on alternating probabilities, where 'virtual certainty' (i.e. a probability of 99–100%) is only theoretically conceivable but does not correspond to a scientific determination of results and even less so to reality. Furthermore, and concurrent to theories of regularity, probabilistic approaches to causation function as a possible alternative to the 'all-or-nothing' principle established by counterfactualism, which greatly affects judicial decision-making in practice.[208] They constitute concepts of multi-causation rather than the mono-causal conception advocated by counterfactual theories, which again brings them closer to an actual, natural understanding of factual causation. However, in comparison with regularity-based theories, probabilistic causation convinces by its facilitated, intuitively correct applicability, the avoidance of biased results, as is the case, for example, with imperfect, asymmetric, and spurious regularities, and its solid metaphysical basis.[209] Moreover, it is argued that a probabilistic approach prevents the great vastness that arises from counterfactual and even more so from regularity-based approaches.[210]

As one of the more recent approaches to causation, at least in its application to causation in the law, the metaphysical substantiation of probabilistic theories still constitutes a model in flux. The most authoritative for today's understanding of probabilistic causation, nonetheless, is the model developed by *Suppes*. To qualify an action or omission as a cause, *Suppes* presupposes that the cause is positively relevant to the effect from a probabilistic point of view and no screening factors exist.[211] In doing so, he relies on the positive deviation of probability in a conditional sense.[212] A screening factor, moreover, refers to events that are positively relevant but ultimately do not cause the effect in question. These factors, however, increase the probability of the effect in the same way as the respective cause and are, therefore, able to 'screen off' the cause from its specific outcome. According to *Suppes*, specific emissions E_S are a cause when E_S increases the probability of I_S and no screening factors W exist, resulting in:[213]

[207] See in this regard Soar (1996), p. 143.

[208] Ibid. Advocating its usage in cases of toxic tort, see Schauer and Spellman (2020), pp. 12–15.

[209] See in this regard Sect. 4.3.1.2, as well as Hitchchock (2021).

[210] See e.g. Davis (1988), pp. 135–136.

[211] The methodology is merely presented here in a highly condensed form. For a more detailed discussion, see Suppes (1970); Reichenbach (1956).

[212] Davis (1988), pp. 133–137.

[213] This theory again builds upon ibid. 135 and is called '*the basic conditional probability theory*'.

$$((P(I_s|E_s) > P(I_s) \text{ and there is no factor W such as } P(I_s|E_sW) = P(I_s|W))$$

Conversely, *Giere* deviates from probabilities in a conditional sense and refers to counterfactuals. He, furthermore, does not deal with possible screening conditions, which raises the question of his handling of additional, interfering conditions.[214] Further modifications concern the requirement of a continuous causal chain, as well as the inclusion of further background conditions.[215] However, the most advocated modification persists, similar to deterministic theories of causation, in temporal limitations, which most frequently relate to the precondition that the cause has to precede the effect (temporal precedence).[216] In particular, temporal precedence seems to have gained acceptance in the literature as a means of avoiding backward causation resulting in the requirement of a positively relevant condition at time t:[217]

$$((P(I_s|E_s) > P(I_s) \text{ and there is no factor W such as } P(I_s|E_sW) = P(I_s|W) \text{ at t})$$

Criticism was raised regarding the temporal precedence, arguing that such limitation would also lead to unsatisfactory results due to the fact that conditions that are cumulative in time can find further exclusion.[218] Yet, such an argument does not militate against the inclusion of a temporal component but rather speaks in favour of restructuring the approach so that such cases of temporal simultaneity can also be covered in a comprehensive manner. Ultimately, the reasons for including a temporal precedence in the probabilistic assessment of causation outweigh those against it. Again, the further development of the approach for its application in law can draw on experience from other disciplines and thus provide a coherent approach.

4.4.1.2 The Dichotomy Between Logic, Intuition and Theory

Despite its advantages over regularity-based and counterfactual theories of causation, building causation on probabilities also faces some obstacles. One of the main

---

214 Giere (1980). Also in favour of probabilistic counterfactuals, see Lewis (1987), pp. 178–179. Supporting *Lewis* approach in broad parts, see Menzies (1996). See for more detail on *Giere's* Theory Davis (1988), pp. 137–140.

215 See for the requirement of a continuous causal chain Menzies (1989). For the inclusion of background conditions, see e.g. Otte (1981). *Otte* presupposes the existence of specific background information.

216 While *Hume* did not envisage a temporal limit in the sense that the cause precedes the effect, *Suppes* (e.g. in Suppes 1970, p. 12) advocates such an approach. For a deviation between the temporal precedence in general and singular causal statements see Davis (1988), pp. 149–154. Against including a temporal sphere, see Giere (1980). Also accepting '*backward causation*', see Cartwright (1979). Sceptical due to the exclusion of '*simultaneous causation*', see Davis (1988), pp. 153–154.

217 This formula again builds upon Davis (1988), p. 135.

218 Ibid. 157.

difficulties with probability-based theories concerns the relationship between cause, effect and probability per se, which reveals that even a factual, probabilistic account of causation is not free of contradictions. In particular, there are causes that, contrary to the core of probabilistic theories, do not increase the probability of the outcome but rather decrease it or have no effect on the probability of the outcome at all ('*non-probability raising causation*').[219] On the other hand, some events or facts significantly increase the probability of the outcome but cannot be qualified as causes in their actual, factual causal understanding since it would contradict ones intuitive and logical understanding of causation per se ('*probability-raising non-causation*').[220] How to deal with such events continues to be one of the most controversial issues in the current probabilistic literature.[221]

4.4.1.2.1 Non-Probability Raising Causation

Non-probability raising causation is concerned with actions or omissions that, from a logical and even factual point of view, could be considered as causes but which do not in themselves increase the probability of the outcome. Rather they do not change the probability at all or even lead to a reduction of it. More generally speaking, the problem revolves around the fact that there are actions or events which, from the perspective of a neutral observer and based on logical considerations, are undoubtedly evaluated as causes but which, from a scientific point of view, reduce the probability of an outcome. The best-known example for such cases goes back to *Hesslow*. *Hesslow* herein describes the relationship between contraceptive pills, thrombosis, and pregnancy.[222] While both contraceptive pills, as well as pregnancies raise the probability of thrombosis, contraceptive pills, however, reduce the risk of becoming pregnant. Since the pregnancy itself carries a much higher risk of thrombosis than contraceptive pills and contraceptive pills reduce the probability of becoming pregnant much more considerably than they itself pose the risk of thrombosis, contraceptive pills result in a probability reduction of the risk of thrombosis, even though they may themselves be a cause of thrombosis. The method of dealing with and solving this problem is still controversial today. Some philosophers solve this dilemma by referring to a stringent causal chain.[223] According to this, only the increase in probability within each link in the causal chain is to be considered, but

---

[219] Hesslow (1976), p. 291. See for a further description of the problem Davis (1988), pp. 140–141. In opposition, see Otte (1981); Soar (1996); Rosen (1978). See in this regard the following Sect. 4.4.1.2.1.

[220] See in this regard Sect. 4.4.1.2.2.

[221] Rejecting the probabilistic approach inter alia due to those issues and calling it the "*noncausal concept of probabilistic causation*", see Wright (1988), p. 1043.

[222] See for an explanation in detail Hesslow (1976), p. 290. In opposition, see Soar (1996), pp. 138–141.

[223] See e.g. Menzies (1989), p. 656. In opposition, see Glynn (2011), pp. 349–353. *Glynn* is stating that such a causal chain (so-called '*sequence*') does not always exist.

not the probability between the initial cause and the final effect. Yet, such a methodology does not resolve the fact that even within a causal chain, individual links can have negative probabilities in their causal relations. *Rosen* presents a further approach to the dilemma in that, similar to the counterfactual theory of factual concretization, it focuses on the more precise specification of the cause, thereby including the circumstance in which the causal relation is embedded. Thus, with increasing concretization and specification, a probability-reducing cause can be moulded into probability-increasing cause.[224] Concurrent to the strategy of factual concretization, this approach also runs the risk of normativising a factual causal approach. However, this is even more significant than with deterministic approaches since the reference to probabilities is dedicated to the greatest possible realism and the depiction of actual causation. *Otte* advocates a similar approach but with a different formulation in that he requires the probability increase to be related to a specific reference class.[225] In the same context, it is also argued that a specific causal relation must always exist within a specific and concrete causal field. Outside this causal field, the causal relation in question might not be of existence.[226]

4.4.1.2.2 Probability Raising Non-Causation

Cases of probability raising non-causation, on the other hand, represent facts and actions that per se increase the probability of the outcome but ultimately do not actually contribute to the outcome in any actual way, i.e. are not to be considered as causes in any intuitive, factual understanding. One of the main examples, which has been illustrated by a number of scholars with some variations, depicts the situation in which two people throw stones towards a window with the aim of breaking it (stone A and stone B).[227] However, only stone A hits the window, destroying it. The other stone, stone B, misses. Based on logical considerations and actual factual circumstances, only the throwing of stone A would be considered as the cause of the breaking of the window.[228] Stone B, on the other hand, would not be considered a cause at all. Nevertheless, the throwing of stone B has increased the probability of the window breaking. According to probabilistic theories, stone B would also have to be regarded as a cause. Yet, this contradicts logical considerations. To solve this problem, different approaches have been put forward by different scholars, and no consensus has yet been reached. Consistent with cases of non-probabilistic causation, one solution advocated is the reference to a strict and continuous causal

[224] See Rosen (1978), p. 608.

[225] Otte (1981).

[226] See Suppes (1970). More critical and proposing other accounts, see Soar (1996), pp. 139–141.

[227] For example by Glynn (2011), pp. 33–34.

[228] Whether or not common sense can be used as a legitimate tool of analysis and argument should be left aside at this point.

chain.[229] Since throwing stone B did not cause the window to break, it is argued that there is no causal chain between throwing stone B and the window breaking. According to this approach, throwing stone B would not qualify as a cause in a probabilistic sense because of the instringency and the gap in the causal chain. However, such an argument runs the risk of circularity since the determination of a causal chain depends on the probability in question. Moreover, this approach would first require a normative-subjective judgement of what constitutes the causal chain. Determining the relevant causal chain without the reference to probabilities, nonetheless, contradicts probabilistic approaches, which assume that the relevant causal chain can only be constructed at all through the probabilities.

Another approach builds on a preposition that has already been generally made with regard to probabilistic theories and considers the introduction of different factors as a specification of the theory. At the forefront of such individualisation is the temporal concretization that can lead to unambiguous and unbiased results. Supposing throw B would be conducted to a time t_2, whereas throw A was conducted at t_0 with the window breaking at t_1 and t_1 being a time before t_2. Then a specification of the outcome concerning the time of the window breaking would lead to the omission of throw B as a cause since throw B would not raise the probability of the window breaking at t_1. Throw B would simply be a neutral factor without any positive or negative influence on the probability. As argued earlier, the introduction of a temporal component is effective in producing unbiased results and provides a comprehensive way of dealing with cases of pre-emptive causation. However, it is also important to recognise the limitations of the temporal factor, particularly in the presence of simultaneous alternating conditions. Nevertheless, the lack of universality of a temporal component does not detract from its fundamental usefulness, which is why at least a concretization in this respect, in coherence with the strategy of factual concretization and regularity-based approaches, is to be considered positive for the factual causation assessment.

The obstacles of non-probabilistic causation and probabilistic non-causation illustrate one of the major weaknesses of the probabilistic causal approach. Although several scholars have already pointed out possible solutions to this problem, no uniform way of dealing with this group of cases has yet been established. For an application in law, it will be crucial that this explicit problem is addressed and a comprehensive solution is found, consistent with measures of feasibility and applicability. A step in the right direction may be the introduction of a temporal component. However, this is not a comprehensive solution to the dilemma of the dichotomy between probabilistic theories and logical, intuitive causes.

[229] Menzies (1989), p. 656. Opposing such an approach due to its obstacles in dealing with omissions, see Glynn (2011), pp. 36–37.

4.4.1.3 Singular Probabilistic Causal Statements

Causal theories are frequently confronted with the obstacle of their application to singular causal statements. The same also applies to theories of probabilistic causation.[230] Quite a number of scholars share the view that while probabilistic assessments work well for general causation, they fail when it comes to singular and specific causal relations.[231] This short-coming is mainly ascribed to the nature of the probabilities on which causal reasoning is based and is consistent with the criticisms raised within regularity-based theories.[232] It is argued that, although there are different kinds of probability (namely empirical, subjective and logical probability), only empirical probability can and should be used in causal reasoning due to its objectivity.[233] Yet, because empirical assessments are based on the frequent occurrence of events, it is not possible to draw singular and specific causal conclusions from them. An example often cited in this context is the link between smoking and cancer. While smoking generally increases the likelihood of developing cancer, such an increase does not imply that smoking was the actual cause of cancer in a particular case.[234] The issue, therefore, strongly correlates with the problem of cases of probability raising non-causes.

In addition to the specific objection in regard to the way of epistemology, it is further argued that probabilistic causation, in general, does not fit specific causal links due to the nature of singular causal statements which is conceived as "*transitive, asymmetric, and irreflexive*".[235] *Menzies*, furthermore, also argues against the application of probabilistic causation to singular causal claims. In particular, he refers to the pre-emption problem as an argument for not extending the conception to such instances.[236] The starting point of any criticism in regard to singular causal statements is that probability-based theories are based on empirical data as well as empirical causation. One can certainly agree with this choice. However, the resulting conclusions and the associated rejection of the application of probabilistic approaches, in theory, appears to be too short-sighted since the determination of the applicability on specific causal relations tends to be a question of natural science

[230] Some authors use the term '*token-level causation*' instead of singular causal statement see e.g. Eells (1991), pp. 278–392.

[231] In favour of this statement, see Giere (1980); Cartwright (1979); Davis (1988); Parascandola (1997), p. 200. Also raising the concern in regard to singular causal statements, see Pöttker (2014), p. 419. Opposing such a statement and applying probabilistic theories to general causal statements as well as to singular or specific causal statements, see Suppes (1970), pp. 79–80. Also in regard to his notion of probabilistic causation, see Lewis (1987), pp. 178–179. Providing an overview to this issue Davis (1988), pp. 145–149.

[232] See for a more detailed analysis and explanation of that problem Davis (1988), pp. 145–146.

[233] Ibid. 146.

[234] This example is e.g. referred to by *Pöttker* under the rejection of potential solutions, see Pöttker (2014), pp. 419–420.

[235] Davis (1988), p. 146.

[236] Menzies (1996).

per se rather than of metaphysical, theoretical considerations. Particularly in the natural sciences and especially in attribution science, a large area of study lies in the analysis of probabilities regarding the occurrence of single events, ergo singular causal statements.[237] If, in natural sciences, it is possible to draw causal conclusions based on probabilities in cases of singular causal statements, why should legal theory object to applying it to the factual causal component of law? Notably, given that the purpose of factual causation lies within a close relation to the actual, natural truth.

While quite a few authors reject the application of probabilistic causation to singular causal claims, the overall majority still intends to apply a probabilistic approach, either by addressing the concerns raised above or by adapting the traditional theory so that it is also compatible with specific causation.[238] Although the problem is well known, and a number of scholars are working on the phenomenon, there hasn't been a unified understanding of how such an adapted probabilistic singular causal explanation would work or how it would be compatible with probabilistic theories of causation in general.[239] However, as mentioned above, the option that a stronger link to scientific knowledge and scientific fact-finding could pose a possible solution to the problem of singular causal statements still must be considered.

4.4.1.4 Simpson's Paradox

The close relation of probabilistic causation theories in law to the application of such theories in mathematics and social science can also be seen in the problem of Simpson's paradox.[240] Originating from statistical considerations and arguably first discovered by *Simpson* in 1951, it has now entered the discussion in legal theory and law in general.[241] Simpson's paradox refers to the fact that, statistically speaking, the interpretation of a study can turn out differently and lead to differing results depending on whether the results of comparative groups are ultimately combined or not.[242] In terms of causation, this means that the assessment, i.e. whether an action or inaction is to be classified as probability increasing or probability decreasing, varies depending on whether a third action is included or not.

---

[237] See in this regard Sect. 3.3.1.2.

[238] See again against the application of probabilistic accounts to singular causal statements Giere (1980); Cartwright (1979); Davis (1988); Parascandola (1997), p. 200.

[239] See Hitchchock (2021), para 4.5.

[240] The approaches and principles presented here are only a fragment of the problem at hand. Because of its complexity, it is simply impossible to present the full discourse and the full range of views represented in this regard. The problem was explicitly explained by *Cartwright* in Cartwright (1979), p. 419.

[241] Simpson (1951).

[242] See for an easy description of the problem from a statistical point of view, see Pearl and Mackenzie (2018), pp. 200–217. *Pearl* and *Mackenzie* hereby proposes to implement causal considerations into statistical considerations.

Cartwright, who was one of the first to discuss this problem in detail, refers to the relationship between smoking, exercise and the likelihood of smoking-related heart disease.[243] While smoking undoubtedly increases the likelihood of developing heart disease at an earlier age, exercising at the same time—if it is considered 'healthier' than smoking is considered 'unhealthy'—may lead to an overall reduction in the likelihood of developing heart disease.[244] Whether smoking is considered to be a cause of heart disease, therefore, depends heavily on the inclusion of other 'intervening' factors. It is, hence, crucial to identify the factors to be included and, ultimately, the causal cluster to be considered.

A similar problem, albeit in a different context, can also be found within regularity-based theories of causation, with the question of which potential causes should be grouped into sets.[245] Furthermore, and again in probabilistic terms, it is closely related to the question of how to deal with probability-reducing causes per se, since depending on the grouping or omission of causes, a probability reduction can take place.[246] However, the difference between Simpson's paradox and the example given in the context of non-probability increasing causes is that, in the latter, there is a close relationship between the different conditions. It is only because of this close relationship that such an effect occurs. Simpson's paradox, on the other hand, refers to a much broader set of conditions, some of them accidental, all of them, however, completely independent of the cause in question. *Cartwright* solves this problem by what she calls 'causal homogeneity'.[247] Here, all potential cause-effect relationships are to be considered singularly, i.e. without potential correlations. With the omission of any correlations, *Cartwright* considers all causes to be causal in the probabilistic sense, which have a probability-increasing effect in any stand-alone situation, i.e. without the influence of further correlations.[248] Smoking would thus lead to a fundamental increase in the risk of developing heart disease without taking physical exercise into account and would, therefore, be considered causal according to *Cartwright's* approach.

However, the adjustment of the theory proposed by *Cartwright* and, in particular, the 'notion of causal homogeneity' contained therein have been met with considerable criticism. On the one hand, it has been argued that such a view of causation is inconsistent with reality, unintuitive, and thus very difficult to identify.[249] On the other hand, it has been claimed that despite the introduction of causal homogeneity, this notion would nevertheless not be exempt from probability reductions in cases of

[243] Cartwright (1979).

[244] Ibid.

[245] See in this regard Sect. 4.3.1.3.

[246] See in this regard Sect. 4.4.1.2.1.

[247] Cartwright (1979), pp. 423–424.

[248] Ibid. Against the approach of using singular causal statements, see Pöttker (2014), p. 419.

[249] In this regard e.g. Soar (1996), p. 141. In regard to the reproach of unintuitivity Otte (1985), p. 114.

actual causes.[250] *Otte,* in particular, argues that despite the detachment from any correlation in the sense of a homogeneous causal field, certain causes can still have a probability-reducing effect.[251] He criticises, among other things, the assertion that an action or omission can only be regarded as a cause if it acts as a probability-increasing cause in every single and possible homogeneous causal field. This would lead to a too-narrow, unintuitive understanding of causation.[252] *Skyrms,* on the other hand, presents a solution to such a narrow understanding of causation in that he does not require that an action or omission must be probability-increasing in every homogeneous causal field but rather is never probability-reducing and is probability-increasing in at least one scenario (so-called 'pareto-dominance condition').[253]

This debate, which was initially confined to scientific and especially statistical discourse, has now reached the legal determination of causation and poses a fundamental problem for the application of probability-based theories in the law. The proposal to exclude correlating events and to consider only individual causal relations has already been put forward in relation to other probabilistic dilemmas and has a growing number of supporters. Since, however, both natural sciences as well as philosophy, in the broadest sense, still disagree on how to deal with Simpson's paradox, it is highly questionable to what extent law can provide upstream approaches. This is particularly the case since the legal discourse on specific obstacles arising in regard to probabilistic theories in law has been rather scarce. This raises the question of whether a solution should not rather come from the field of probabilistic fact-finding and whether the law, as a mere means of applying the results found, should not rather concur and avoid deviating from scientific approaches and solutions.

4.4.2 Assessing Probabilistic Climatic Causation

4.4.2.1 Climate Change Litigation and Probabilistic Causation

For law, probabilities are not an unknown concept; on the contrary, the law has long made use of probabilities in various areas, even within the determination of causation based on traditional approaches. Traditional, counterfactual-based theories, nonetheless, do not rely on assessments of probability in their causal considerations per se; instead, they focus on degrees of probability within the question of proof and

[250] Otte (1981), p. 110; Otte (1985), p. 115.

[251] Otte (1985), pp. 114–115.

[252] Ibid. 116–117.

[253] Skyrms (1980), p. 108.

the introduction of evidence in court.[254] In contrast to causation based on counterfactuals or even regularities, a purely probability-based concept of causation has hardly found its way into legal practice and is only sparsely advocated in legal theory.[255] However, one way of implementing probabilistic accounts into legal practice was perceived by the nowadays controversial '*doctrine of risk aggravation'*.[256] Originating as a doctrine inherent in German criminal law and first developed by *Roxin,* the concept is based on the understanding that someone is also causally responsible for an outcome in cases in which the person in question has ultimately increased the risk of the occurrence of damage.[257] In referring explicitly to the doctrine of risk aggravation, such a probabilistic concept has occasionally been proposed for application to climate cases in the climate law literature, as well.[258] Nevertheless, a closer look at this straightforward approach and its dogmatic structure reveals its weaknesses and ultimately renders the concept too cumbersome and dogmatically intrinsic for its application to climate claims. The inapplicability of the doctrine of risk enhancement arises from the fact that it is not a factual causal approach but a theory that allows attribution within the normative causal component under reduced requirements. The adoption of the doctrine of risk aggravation as a universal doctrine of climatic causation, as proposed by some scholars, thus dangerously blurs the distinction between factual and normative causation. As a result, its application is neither justified from a dogmatic nor a metaphysical point of view. The doctrine of risk aggravation in its form under German criminal law is, therefore, not a suitable model for a transfer to the general account of causation in climate claims.

However, the rejection of the risk enhancement doctrine does not lead to a fundamental dismissal of any probability-based approaches. Instead, the main criticism is its lack of dogmatic transferability. There remains, nonetheless, no objection

[254] The degree of probability varies widely between jurisdictions, with common law jurisdictions generally setting lower probability hurdles for proving counterfactual causation than civil law jurisdictions. See in relation to tort law von Bar (2000), pp. 469–470, paras 449–450. See in regard to probabilistic liability in environmental law Greinert (2007).

[255] In favour of a (but not universal) probability-based conception in law and arguing that law is certainly more open to probability-based approaches than generally advocated, see Peñalver (1998), Schauer and Spellman (2020), Canale (2020), Braig and Panov (2020). Most of the relevant argumentation does not refer to a probability-based causation approach, but rather to probability considerations within the determination of evidence. Also in regard to normative causation and applying *Suppes* approach to theories of probabilistic causation, see Soar (1996), p. 146. *Soar* presupposes a probabilistic theory of causation as standard test and also hints towards the application of the approach in other common law jurisdictions. Opposing the application of a probabilistic account in regard to climate liability cases, see Pöttker (2014), p. 420; Kahl (2022), p. 167.

[256] Roxin (1962). The doctrine is widely rejected in German criminal law, see e.g. Freund (2020), para 223; Puppe (2017), paras 204–205. Also rather rejecting, see Frisch (2011), pp. 207–208; Eisele (2016), para 90. The main concerns are that it violates the principle of *'in dubio pro reo'*, and that it transforms the qualification of the crime from an objective crime into a crime of endangerment ('*Gefährdungsdelikt*').

[257] See again Roxin (1962).

[258] Voigt (2008), p. 16; Verheyen (2005), pp. 292–293.

to the basic probabilistic design per se, which allows for a consideration of a probabilistic approach outside of this specific doctrine. An operational advantage of probabilistic theories is that courts are quite familiar with dealing with probabilities in assessing evidence. While the inference from pure probabilistic evidence to a complex causal system is a non-trivial challenge, it does not represent an entirely unfamiliar conceptual approach.[259] From an economic perspective, it is also argued that probabilistic methods, especially in climate issues and based on complex climate data, lead to fairer outcomes in terms of their compliance with corrective justice considerations. They are further said to reduce the overall costs of accidents.[260] Another advantage is the ability to use the results of the probabilistic causation assessment in the further legal proceeding. By providing detailed information on the extent of a person's contribution, based on the probability increase caused, the exact distribution of costs, as well as the determination of compensation and reparations, is significantly more facilitated, as there is no need to determine the extent of the contribution any further. And even at a more metaphysical level, probabilistic theories of causation can help to address the challenges posed by climate change litigation. The easement applies, in particular, to the cumulative nature of emissions, which, because of the firm reliance on scientific accounts, can be more easily causally attributed to an outcome concerning probabilistic conceptions than is the case with other theories of causation.[261]

The fact that probability-based assessments are not unfamiliar to courts and judges, in general, is evidenced by the terminology often used in decisions, particularly in cases related to natural events, which also includes climate change litigation. The reference to probabilities, moreover, becomes apparent concerning the prediction of future impacts within considerations of proportionality. However, the usage of probabilistic language does not militate in favour of the establishment and use of a probabilistic causal approach per se but rather stands for a terminological idiosyncrasy. A fitting example for the usage of probabilistic language is shown by the case *Gloucester Resources Limited v. Minister for Planning*, in which the Court stated that

> (t)he Project's cumulative GHG emissions are therefore likely to contribute to the future changes to the climate system and the impacts of climate change. In this way, the Project is likely to have indirect impacts on the environment, including the climate system, the oceanic and terrestrial environment and people.[262]

The Court's use of probabilistic terminology, such as 'likely' or 'very likely', does not implicitly suggest the use of a probabilistic approach to causation in the law.

---

[259] See for a metaphysical and dogmatic critique on the use of evidence to establish causation, Wright (1988), pp. 1043–1044.

[260] Referring from toxic tort to climate claims, Peñalver (1998), pp. 588–591.

[261] Such a conclusion can only be drawn if one allows the application of probabilistic approaches to singular causal statements, as is advocated here.

[262] New South Wales Land and Environment Court, 8 February 2019 – [2019] NSWLEC 7, *Gloucester Resources Limited v. Minister for Planning*, para 525.

Rather, the choice of the words 'likely to contribute' indicates that the Court is lowering the standard set for the relation between effect and outcome rather than applying a probabilistic approach to causation per se. In most cases, the court only refers to probabilistic terminology when making use of scientific evidence. Distinguishing between mere scientific findings and probabilistic causal considerations hereby poses a significant challenge. The core of a probabilistic approach to causation, however, lies in assessing whether the possible cause increases the likelihood of an event. Such considerations, nonetheless, cannot be inferred from the Court's statements. It would require a tremendous argumentative effort to suggest otherwise.

The metaphysical nature of probability-based causation theories and the challenges inherent therein, nevertheless, also affect their application in climate change litigation. Although causation based on probabilities is preponderantly fit to deal with cumulative emissions and thus has significant advantages over other theories of causation, the way in which the approach deals with cases in which theory and logic diverge is also perpetuated in climate change litigation. Even more problematic, however, is the application of probabilistic theories to climatic scenarios if one assumes that such a conception of causation does not apply to singular causal statements because it is precisely the establishment of specific causation that still is significantly in question in climate change litigation. Yet, by following the argumentation above and referring to attribution science as a basis for singular causal statements, the fact that the law has not found a metaphysical answer to create coherence, despite its firm reliance on such scientific findings, should not be held against the application of probabilistic causation.

From a more application-oriented perspective, the probabilistic conception of causation still represents the most distant approach compared to the deterministic theories applied so far. This 'distance' concerns, in particular, the use of causal language and inherent constructs, with probabilistic theories not relying on the qualification of conditions as necessary and sufficient. The absence of recourse to such already familiar constructs may hinder, or at least impede, the willingness of legal practitioners and courts to apply such a new understanding of causation. It may, therefore, be preferable to apply theories of regularity which, although based on a different metaphysical understanding of cause-effect relations, still make use of generally known causal concepts. And although the law has made use of probabilistic statements concerning the law of evidence, the introduction of such a concept into causal reasoning has found no precedent in practice. Furthermore, it has been argued that a probabilistic account of causation is inconsistent with general principles of environmental law, which precludes its application to climate change claims.[263] *Kohler* has argued in this regard that the polluter pays principle, in particular, stands in the way of the application of such a probabilistic account, as it would lead to liability on the basis of mere suspicion.[264] This criticism takes up the

[263] Kohler (2017), para 166.

[264] Ibid.

metaphysical problem according to which conditions can also be regarded as causes based on an increase in probability, even though the result is not realised in precisely these conditions, i.e. these conditions did not contribute to the outcome. It is, thus, closely related to the problem of probability increasing non-causes and thus builds on the same criticism raised in that context.[265]

First, and in response to *Kohler's* objection, the establishment of causation does not imply the existence of liability but is merely a further precondition on the basis of which liability can ultimately be found. In line with the arguments made concerning the metaphysical impediment, the introduction of a temporal component may also lead to fairer results. And although the problem needs to be addressed, *Kohler's* criticism still remains inadequate in that it leads to circular reasoning. The use of probabilistic accounts does not lead to a relation based on suspicion, but the condition that *Kohler* refers to as 'suspicion' is to be regarded as a legitimate cause because it increases the probability. And although *Kohler's* argument is misguided, his criticism remains valid in the respect that the polluter pays principle focuses only on the natural and actual condition. A mere increase in risk or probability, without the actual contribution, is not sufficient for its substantiation. A probabilistic approach in its original form deviates from the polluter pays principle and is, hence, difficult to justify in the context of climate claims. To achieve applicability in the climate context, it is, therefore, necessary to adapt the approach to reflect actual, factual causation.

Concurrent with theories of regularity, the practical applicability of a probabilistic account to causation is to be tested on the basis of the case of *Luciano Lliuya v. RWE AG*.[266] In applying probabilistic approaches, a causal link between RWE's emissions (E_S) and the risk of flooding and the danger to Luciano Lliuya's property (I_S) would be affirmed if RWE's emissions had added to the probability of the risk increase occurring and no other screening factors (W) existed, resulting in:[267]

$$(P(I_s|E_s) > P(I_s) \text{ and there is no factor W such as } P(I_s|E_sW) = P(I_s|W).$$

If the requirement of temporal precedence is additionally applied, then the emissions of RWE would have to precede the risk of flooding and the risk of damage to the house, as well as constituting an increase in probability at time t further developing the relevant relation to:

$$(P(I_s|E_s) > P(I_s) \textit{ at time t} \text{ and there is no factor W such as } P(I_s|E_sW) = P(I_s|W)$$

With the relevant emissions of RWE having occurred before the increased risk of the flood, the timely precedence is undoubtedly given. Beyond the existence of the

[265] See in this regard Sect. 4.4.1.2.2.

[266] Essen Regional Court, 15 December 2016 – 2 O 285/15, *Luciano Lliuya v. RWE AG*.

[267] The following example focuses only on the standard probabilistic approaches. A treatment and consideration of all the nuances and forms of the theories would clearly go too far at this point.

temporal component, however, the determination of causation based on this probabilistic relation is not feasible without the reference and the inclusion of scientific data. Without these, no judgement, not even a preliminary one, can be made on the possible existence of a factual causal link. The case shows the proximity of the approach to the scientific determination of results and thereby reveals its great difficulty. While courts within counterfactual and regularity-related causal theories ultimately also have to fall back on scientific results, initial causal conclusions can, nevertheless, already be derived from logical considerations and the mere application of such theories. Such initial logical causal inferences, however, guarantee in practice a certain—and in that sense faster—handling of court cases, in that obvious causally unsound cases can be sorted out immediately. By applying probabilistic causal theories, the discretionary power and, in particular, the room for manoeuvre of courts is severely restricted. Thus, probabilistic approaches in this aspect pose a significantly more complicated procedure in their legal application.

On the other hand, due to that same reason, the probabilistic causal considerations are closer to actual, scientific reality and the scientific truth per se. Yet, due to the availability of an attribution study on the respective case and concerning *Heede's* overall calculation of contributions by carbon majors, one will have to assume that a probabilistic account of causation would lead to the establishment of a factual causation chain in the case of *Luciano Lliuya v. RWE AG.*[268] The same holds true for other climate claims. Apart from the metaphysical difficulties concerning its practical usability, probability-based theories in climate change litigation would, in many cases, lead to the establishment of a continuous causal chain in climate damage scenarios. From an economic point of view, the approach is, therefore, highly suitable for use in climate claims.[269]

4.4.2.2 Scientific Data, Probabilistic Causal Analysis and Climate Cases

4.4.2.2.1 The Need for Scientific Results

Climate action cannot persist without climate science. The results of climate science, and, in particular, attribution science, are a fundamental part of any climate litigation process.[270] As scientific methods for attributing extreme weather events, in particular, continue to advance, climate litigation is gaining momentum. Building causal dogmas directly on the results of climate science is effective in many ways. On the one hand, linking dogmatic theories of causation and scientific results lends legitimacy to causation in the law. The avoidance of hypothetical causal reasoning (as is the case with counterfactual approaches) results in an unassailable causal relation that is comprehensible and fathomable to all parties. The causal relationship thus

268 Heede (2014a, b).

269 Affirming, Peñalver (1998), p. 587.

270 See in more detail Sect. 3.3.1.2.

greatly reflects reality and actual, factual causation. The fact that courts are not averse to considering and incorporating scientific findings and often gratefully accept the possibility of a scientific basis for their legal assessment is also supported by the practice of implementing results by the IPCC. The general acceptance of the IPCC's findings has already led to the fact that courts no longer explicitly comment on causation concerning general climatic relations regarding the results of the IPCC, let alone expressly applying legal causal doctrines.[271] Numerous different climate lawsuits and their decisions have shown such a conception.[272] In addition to the legitimacy thus established, scientific findings are crucial for the courts' fact and truth-finding mission. By refraining from assessing causal chains on a hypothetical (counterfactual) basis, courts come closer to the actual, natural and universal truth. Under the enhanced implementation of scientific findings, courts will increasingly fulfil their role as fact-finders. On the other hand, and as briefly mentioned above, referring to scientific results in the assessment of causation provides a further basis for allocating the damage and, ultimately, the costs without requiring an additional evaluation of such apportionment. It is primarily the law of tort and cases of delict in which this becomes particularly useful.

4.4.2.2.2 On Terminological Coherency and Methodological Discrepancies

One of the main arguments raised in favour of probabilistic theories of causation relates to their coherency with scientific results and findings. Using probabilities rather than factual truths even outside the realm of proof strongly refers to methodologies and terminology used in natural sciences. Thus, the presentation of results, especially within attribution science, is often based on language referring to increased probability. The terminological coherence is illustrated, for example, by the results of a study on the anthropogenic impact of a heat wave in Western Europe in 2019.[273] In this study the researchers concluded:

> At all locations analyzed, the change in probability of the event is large. In France and the Netherlands, we find changes of at least a factor 10. Without climate change, this event would have been extremely improbable (return period larger than about 1000 years). For the other locations, changes in probabilities were smaller but still very large, at least a factor of 2–3 for the U.K. station, and 3 for the German station.[274]

The implication of this statement suggests that the probability of a heatwave occurring in France and the Netherlands has increased by a factor of ten due to

[271] See in this regard the results of the analysis in Sect. 3.4.

[272] Supreme Court of the Netherlands, 20 December 2019 – 19/00135, *Urgenda Foundation v. The State of The Netherlands*, Germany Federal Constitutional Court, 24 March 2021 – 1 BvR 2656/18 – 1 BvR 78/20 – 1 BvR 96/20 – 1 BvR 288/20, *Neubauer et al. v. Germany*.

[273] Vautard et al. (2020).

[274] Ibid. 7–8.

climate change. Transferred to probabilistic causal statements in law, this would render climate change a cause of the occurrence of the respective heatwave.

Despite this terminological consistency, the level at which this methodology is applied also partly differs between the legal application for establishing causation and the scientific modelling of results. Whereas at the legal level, probability-based approaches use an increase in probability per se to justify causation, probability statements in climate science often refer to the reliability of the results themselves. In other words, they merely represent the validity of the results by including uncertainty factors but do not justify the outcome per se. The reports by the IPCC provide useful examples. In the IPCC's recent report, the Panel concluded in its Summary for Policymaker: "*Human influence has likely increased the chance of compound extreme events since the 1950s, including increases in the frequency of concurrent heatwaves and droughts (high confidence).*"[275] The term 'likely' used by the IPCC hereby refers to a probability of 66–100%.[276] However, this percentage rate does not relate to the increase in the probability of the event's occurrence but to the validity of the mere statement about the probability of the outcome occurring. The comment by the IPCC, therefore, does not contain any valid raison that could be used to infer causation in its probabilistic sense from it. Instead, the term 'likely' hints towards the statement's validity. As a result, when using scientific accounts in the sense of probabilistic causation production, great care must be taken to capture the actual probability-based content correctly.

4.4.2.2.3 The Dependency of Legal Assessments on Scientific Evidence

Within probability-based theories, finding factual causation in the law is closely linked to scientific evidence. In practice, nonetheless, this also entails that the jurisprudential determination of results depends to a considerable extent on the comprehensiveness of scientific findings per se. Although attribution science, despite its relatively recent emergence, has developed fundamental and comprehensive methodologies and is characterised by advanced attribution methods, there still remain events, particularly in the field of extreme event attribution, that are not yet accessible to any scientific attribution methodology.[277] Naturally, these problems also arise with other theories of causation. The big difference, however, is that the scientific conceit of probabilistic theories already takes place at the material and substantive level of the causation-finding in law and not, as with deterministic theories, at the evidentiary and, thus, procedural level. The scientific considerations are decisive for substantiating the claim, which increases the dependence of

[275] IPCC (2023), 5, A.2.1.

[276] See further for an explanation of the likelihood-scale used by the IPCC Sect. 2.1.1.

[277] See for the relation between attribution science and law Burger et al. (2020). See furthermore Sect. 3.3.1.2.

probabilistic causation on scientific evidence and even more so on the further development of attribution science per se.

However, the heavy reliance of probability-based theories on scientific results carries other risks as well. Scientific results, even outside the specific field of attribution science, are inherently subject to the danger of incorrect or biased results due to, among other things, different parameter choices, limited data sets, or errors in the scientific model itself.[278] In the context of attribution science, the risk is even slightly higher due to the progressiveness and novelty of the field of climate science, which implies that methods and procedures have not been subjected to the same level of scrutiny and testing as in other areas of science. Furthermore, there are certain climatic or climatic-related events for which climate science is not yet able to make well-founded scientific statements.[279] In such cases increased reliance on scientific evidence, as is the case with probabilistic theories of causation in law, further complicates the legal determination of causation.

The inability to obtain scientific results could also affect the determination of causation in the law in such a way that ultimately renders the establishment of it impossible. The same applies to the risk of false scientific findings. However, the law can certainly counteract this specific risk by setting standards for the inclusion of scientific data on the substantive and material determination of causation. A particularly appropriate way of doing this is to adopt standards that are already applied at the level of proof. The requirements to be met by the evidence to be introduced in court proceedings is a very jurisdiction-specific concept. If one takes the '*Daubert standard*', which is predominantly used in the US legal system, as a reference, the criteria for the valid inclusion of scientific studies refer in particular to the verification and general scientific recognition of the methodology used. Further requirements are the accessibility of the results to and the possibility of verification by the public (including through an appropriate peer review process), as well as a comprehensive assessment of the uncertainties and possible variables.[280] Such criteria need to be defined and assessed on a case-by-case basis but can be facilitated by legitimated findings based on a broad scientific consensus.

The best example for the possibility and feasibility of establishing a scientific consensus is the work of the Intergovernmental Panel on Climate Change. The reports and results of the IPCC show that it is possible to arrive at scientific

---

[278] See in particular Sect. 3.3.3.

[279] This fact is also acknowledged and problematized by Minnerop and Otto (2020), p. 70. This is particularly true for extreme and sudden events. In this regard, and particularly in relation to toxic tort cases and probabilities of risk increase, see Pöttker (2014), p. 319. For further elaborations see Sect. 3.3.

[280] The Daubert standard that is used today was first developed in United States Supreme Court, 28 June 1993 – 509 U.S. 579, *Daubert v. Merrell Dow Pharmaceuticals*. It was further refined in United States Supreme Court, 15 December 1997 – 522 U.S. 136, *General Electric Co. v. Joiner*, United States Supreme Court, 23 March 1999 – 526 U.S. 137, *Kumho Tire Co. v. Carmichael*. The Canadian Supreme Court also referred to the Daubert standard as valid way of evaluating evidence in Supreme Court Canada, 10 December 2000 – 2 S.C.R. 600, *R. v. J.-L.J.*

statements on climate change in a consensus-based manner. Particularly concerning general causal statements, the IPCC is an essential instrument for litigants and courts. Yet, the IPCC does not make any statements regarding individual and specific causal relations, which is why recourse to the IPCC is only possible to assess general causation in the law. That the IPCC at one point in time indulges in specific causal statements seems highly unlikely, does it ultimately not relate to the task and competence of the institution itself. Nevertheless, at least concerning general causation, the use of IPCC findings regarding probability-based causation can provide for some relief to the obstacles presented above. Beyond that, the establishment and, ultimately, the use of specific standards is essential for the determination of factual, probability-based causation, whereby a reference to the criteria for the introduction of proof can ensure legal certainty and coherence at the substantive level.

However, the strong dependency of probabilistic theories of causation on scientific studies carries further challenges for its application in court. Probabilistic doctrines demand the strong reliance of judges on the validity of the results presented to them by science, even more so than with other theories of causation. It is often not explicitly clear, or difficult for the layman to see, whether the results presented are valid and in accordance with the principles of good science or whether they have been distorted by possible hindsight-bias and other criteria. This is further complicated by the fact that many judges do not necessarily have any further training in climate-specific litigation, let alone in attribution and climate science. Strict criteria (such as those outlined above) and reliance on studies by reputable institutions such as the IPCC also provide further assistance in this regard.

4.4.3 Conclusion

As this section has shown, a probabilistic approach to causation in climate change litigation can certainly lead to a factual determination of causation in the law. In legal practice, however, and particularly in climate and environmental law, such approaches have been used only to a limited extent when referring to causation. Nevertheless, probability-based statements are not entirely alien to jurisprudence. In the law of evidence, in particular, the weighing of probabilities forms a basis for the inclusion and legitimacy of scientific studies and findings. Occasionally but with increasing frequency, legal scholars also advocate the application of a probabilistic conception of causation. This is particularly common in areas and fields of law that rely heavily on scientific evidence, which is, for example, the case in toxic tort and climate litigation cases.

The strongest argument for the use of probabilistic causation in law is undoubtedly its close connection to the natural sciences and the resulting proximity to actual, factual causation. Probabilistic climatic causation is consistently based on climate and attribution studies and, therefore, does not allow, or run the risk of allowing, a subjectification of the factual causal assessment. The causal assessment is, hence genuinely factual and lends a high degree of reliability and legitimacy to causation in the law as a whole. Furthermore, scientific and legal terminology correlate in their application of probabilistic theories, which further enhances the universal application of the approach in climate change litigation.

However, the terminological consistency is also a significant threat to the use of scientific studies in legal assessments. Great care must be taken in the precise formulation, methodology, and use of scientific probabilities to avoid erroneous and biased conclusions. The firm reliance on valid scientific results is another obstacle to the application of the theory but can be countered by a coherent and comprehensive standard on the requirements of good science and the validity of scientific studies in general. From an epistemological point of view, the suitability of the approach for law can also be seen in the light of the metaphysical obstacles mentioned above. Moreover, probabilistic theories are an evolving concept of causation that has not yet reached the metaphysical and theoretical maturity of counterfactual or even regularity-based theories. It has become clear, mainly when applied to current cases, that this approach is rather cumbersome in practice. The heavy reliance on scientific evidence, even at a substantial level (and not at the level of proof), does not allow for simple causal statements by the courts but requires reliance on costly and complex scientific studies. In addition, probabilistic causation is subject to the same difficulties as scientific fact-finding, be it the risk of biased results due to missing data, the incorrect weighting of exogenous factors, or the pervasive uncertainty of the climate system's own influence.

Probabilistic theories in law are ultimately a concept that is well equipped for its application in climate change litigation and its respective implementation of scientific results. Especially as attribution science and the dogmatic behind probabilistic causal theories continues to develop in mathematical sciences and other scientific fields, probabilistic causal theories will soon constitute a viable metaphysical alternative to traditional causal approaches in law. For such development, however, it is essential that coherent and even more so comprehensive standards for the incorporation of scientific studies on a substantial level have been considered, and the dangers of relying so heavily on scientific findings have been evaluated accordingly. It remains questionable, nevertheless, whether such a development will take place in time and with recourse to the rapidly developing global climate crisis.

4.5 Climatic-Specific Causation as an Emergent and Dynamic Construct

In the face of growing global challenges to legal systems and the law in general, and in order to adapt to new legal realities and overcome the hurdles posed by traditional conceptions of causation, courts and legal practitioners have developed and advocated newer understandings of causal relations. Based on considerations of efficiency and feasibility, these newer doctrines are not grounded in metaphysical and epistemological conceptions of causal relations, nor are they concerned with the nature of law and general legal theory. They largely abandon the deterministic and probabilistic notions that have been commonly advocated and, thus, represent a policy-driven, result-oriented and pragmatic-based conception of causation that returns to philosophical, theoretical and dogmatic thinking only as a corollary.

By starting from the ultimate goal of establishing causation in scenarios where actual, natural causation exists, those newer theories of factual causation form legal accounts based on the achievable result without linking them to legal philosophy and theory. They could, therefore, be perceived as 'backwards-looking' doctrines of causation. Usually, such theories have been developed by courts and have found their way into general jurisprudence, especially in common law jurisdictions. Ultimately, all of these theories carry at their core their effectiveness and the goal of making factual causation in law consistent with natural causation. In the context of climate change litigation, two causal concepts are particularly noteworthy: the emission share causation doctrine developed from the framework of the market share liability doctrine (Sect. 4.5.1) and a contribution-based approach (Sect. 4.5.2).

4.5.1 *Emission Share Causation Doctrine*

In the 1980s, courts in the United States developed a comprehensive case law on the effects of specific drugs on pregnancies and babies in general.[281] In light of this legal development, courts also established a new liability doctrine, the so-called '*market share liability doctrine*'. Based on this specific liability regime that will be further discussed and elaborated on later, the discussion is increasingly turning to its transfer to other comparable situations and subject matters. One of these potential transfer areas concerns environmental and, more specifically, climate law by replacing the market share with an overall and global emissions share. Whether such an emission share doctrine could prove beneficial for the establishment of causation, thus also transforming from a comprehensive liability approach to a mere causation doctrine, is elaborated on in the following.

4.5.1.1 The Tenets of the Market Share Liability Doctrine

The market share liability doctrine as a product liability doctrine was developed by a US Court in the case *Sindell v. Abbott Laboratories* and further enhanced in *Collins v. Eli Lilly Co.*[282] The doctrine is one of several attempts in negligence cases to

[281] See e.g. Supreme Court of California, 20 March 1980 – 607 P.2d 924, *Sindell v. Abbott Laboratories*, Supreme Court of Wisconsin, 4 January 1984 – 82-1844, *Collins v. Eli Lilly & Co.*

[282] See Supreme Court of California, 20 March 1980 – 607 P.2d 924, *Sindell v. Abbott Laboratories*, Supreme Court of Wisconsin, 4 January 1984 – 82-1844, *Collins v. Eli Lilly & Co.* Further

obtain relief despite difficulties in establishing liability. It, therefore, builds upon considerations of equity and justice. The case of *Sindell v. Abbot Laboratories* was mainly concerned with the question of the attribution of negligent actions in the production of Diethylstilbestrol (DES), which was prescribed to pregnant women in particular.[283] Children of these women, who had already been exposed to this drug in utero, showed a conspicuous susceptibility to a specific type of cancer at an early age. Scientifically, it was eventually feasible to causally attribute the use of this drug to the particular cancer, but the plaintiffs failed before the courts due to the difficulties in attributing the disease to a specific producer given that it could no longer be proven which drug from which manufacturer was taken by their mothers.

As a result, the Court developed the market share liability doctrine and imposed liability on each producer of the specific drug based on its market share at the relevant time. By further shifting the burden of proof, it was ultimately up to the producers to prove that they had acted lawfully. The basis of the market share liability doctrine is thus a proportionality-based liability linked back to the market position of the respective producer and reflecting the risk the producer set throughout its participation in the market in general.[284] As the doctrine developed, four particular conditions became immanent. First, the producer of the product had to cover a substantial part of the market. Second, the product had to be fungible. Thirdly, the producers had to be active on the market at the time of the event, and, finally, the failure to identify the specific cause must not be the fault of the injured party or the plaintiff himself.[285]

A comparable concept can now be found in at least one other jurisdiction besides the United States of America. In Austria, despite the lack of a comprehensive body of case law, liability founded on the market shares of the producers is commonly advocated, at least in the academic and scholarly sphere.[286] An equivalent of the concept can also be found in Art. 3:103 of the Principles of European Tort Law.[287]

enhanced in New York Court of Appeals, 4 April 1989 – 539 N.E.2d 1069, *Hymowith v. Eli Lilly & Co*, Washington Supreme Court, 4 October 1984 – 49359-6, *Martin v. Abbot Laboratories.* Rejecting the application of the market share liability doctrine Supreme Court of Illinois, 3 July 1990 – 137 Ill. 2d 222 (Ill. 1990); 560 N.E.2d 324, *Smith v. Eli Lilly & Co.* Also applied outside of DES litigation in United States Court of Appeals, 26 July 2013 – 10–4135–cv (L), 10–4329–cv (XAP), *In Re: Methy Tertiary Butyl Ether (MTBE) Products Liability Litigation.*

[283] See again Supreme Court of California, 20 March 1980 – 607 P.2d 924, *Sindell v. Abbott Laboratories.*

[284] *Lahav* sees in the market-share liability doctrine an example of "*chancy causation*", see Lahav (2022), pp. 130–131.

[285] See here in regard to the prerequisits prescribed by the Court Supreme Court of California, 20 March 1980 – 607 P.2d 924, *Sindell v. Abbott Laboratories.*

[286] Steininger (2017), pp. 288–289. A codification of the principle was also discussed in the context of an amendment to the Austrian Tort Law initiated in 2005, but did not find a counterpart in actual law.

[287] Art. 3:103 (1) PETL states that "*(i)n case of multiple activities, where each of them alone would have been sufficient to cause the damage, but it remains uncertain which one in fact caused it, each activity is regarded as a cause to the extent corresponding to the likelihood that it may have caused*

However, the majority of other jurisdictions still apply different approaches to similar issues.

4.5.1.2 The Convergence of the Market Share Liability Doctrine to Climatic Causation

4.5.1.2.1 From Market-Share to Emission-Share

The core value of the market share liability doctrine rests in the establishment of liability despite consistent scientific uncertainties as to the distribution and existence of specific causation, attribution and provability. The doctrine, therefore, addresses and answers to obstacles, which are also prominent in climate change cases and climatic scenarios in general. Due to those apparent similarities and the need to further develop traditional causal approaches in light of the challenges posed by climate change, one could consider the transferability of the market share-based doctrine to emission shares and a reduction of the concept to a mere causal perception.

4.5.1.2.2 DES and Climate Change

To explore the possibility of extending the doctrine used in product liability cases to cases involving emission-based liability, it is crucial to first determine if such a transfer is viable in terms of its substance and underlying notions. This entails evaluating the practicality of implementing the doctrine within the context of emissions and climate change in general. The comparability of both scenarios clearly indicates that it is worth considering transferring this approach to emission-based cases. The legal difficulties in DES cases built upon the attribution of the effects of the drug to a specific manufacturer, which resulted mainly from the long-time period between the ingestion of the medication and the occurrence of the negative impacts. Climate change cases are also characterised by long-lasting impact relationships, mainly due to the thermal inertia of the ocean, carbon sinks, and numerous other reasons, which further carry the same problem of difficult individual attribution as in the respective DES cases.[288] Besides the similar temporal component, both scenarios coincide in their requirement of proportionality between the damage or outcome and the risk posed.[289] A further convergence consists of the fundamental problem of establishing causation. Based on the temporal disperse and missing differentiability

---

the victim's damage.", see European Group on Tort Law, PETL, Art. 3:103 (1), Šaltinytė (2017), pp. 290–291.

[288] See, in particular, the chapter on the scientific framework of climate change Sect. 2.1.

[289] Regarding the proportionality as a prerequisite for market share liability doctrines, since otherwise it would contradict the principle of efficiency Grimm (2007), pp. 218–221.

between the medication produced by the manufacturers, establishing a comprehensive causal chain with respect to DES cases borders on the impossible. The same applies to climate change cases. Although the connection between greenhouse gas emissions and climate change in general grounds on verifiable scientific findings, causation in climate change litigation certainly fails to a great extent in cases in which specific causation is in question, i.e. the attribution of a specific event to an individual emitter.[290]

Considering responsibility for environmental damage based on one's share of the overall pollution is not an entirely new concept but was proposed by *Friedland* as early as 1985.[291] In doing so, *Friedland* introduced a pollution share liability doctrine in cases of damage resulting from air pollution, which would further be carried by a strong social consensus and public policies.[292] However, in proposing such a far-reaching approach, she also recognised that a restriction is required in light of the nature of harmful air pollution, the possibility of chemical combination, the reaction of relevant substances in the air, and the geographically specific effects of pure air pollution.[293] Those difficulties strongly refer to air pollution in general. Due to their immutability in the air, greenhouse gas emissions are largely unaffected, or only slightly influenced, by such impediments. Providing comprehensive scientific data on the specific impacts of greenhouse gases on the climate system is highly more feasible than it is in regard to specific air pollution cases.[294]

When considering a shift towards policies that prioritize emission shares, it is crucial to acknowledge that the standards established in the DES cases may not be entirely feasible to execute. While CO_2-emissions may well be considered fungible and, therefore, fulfil the requirement set out by the courts, the question of the temporal component, in particular, poses difficulties.[295] This arises, in particular, from the fact that emissions only have a certain dwell time in the atmosphere. The retention time, in general, varies depending on the type of greenhouse gas, nevertheless, emissions that have already been emitted years ago may no longer have contributed to the effect in question. In the same way, greenhouse gases that have only recently been emitted may not yet have found their equivalent in climate change-induced changes from a scientific point of view. Another problem resides in the possible absorption of emissions by greenhouse gas sinks, which would eliminate the effect of the specific emission on climate change.[296] A further issue

[290] See e.g. IPCC (2021).

[291] Friedland (1984).

[292] Ibid. 317. The doctrine still constitutes a doctrine of liability, not to be confused with a doctrine of causation.

[293] Ibid. 315. See concerning the problem of mixed emissions also Federal Court of Justice, 10 December 1987 – III ZR 220/86, *Forest Dieback*.

[294] For a detailed analysis of the applicability of the *Forest Dieback* case to GHG emissions, see Sect. 4.2.2.1.

[295] Grimm (2007), pp. 219–220. In regard to the problems regarding the temporal sphere also Pöttker (2014), pp. 364–365.

[296] See for the scientific background Sect. 2.1.1.

closely related to the temporal sphere arises in light of the long duration of the effects of the emissions. Although the effects of the emissions may still be present, the original emitter may no longer persist in its legal form. This danger also arises in cases under the market share liability doctrine. However, due to the multitude of large and small emitters on a corporate level and the highly economical fluctuation accompanied by this, the probability of a contributor not abiding until the respective claim is raised, does pose a significantly higher risk than with emissions-based lawsuits. It is further often not possible to determine the exact point in time of the tortious act. Relevant is rather a time period which contrasts the introduction of a harmful product to the market as an exactly determinable point in time. The difference in time frames further contradicts the comparability to a market share doctrine.[297]

Influential in climate scenarios are further climate-damaging omissions, which object to a specific quantification in terms of their impact and, therefore, emission-share, although they generate considerable impacts on the climate system and its change. The inclusion of factors other than emission-generating behaviour is also proving to be rather complicated. And although it has been suggested that omissions as contributing shares should be considered in the calculation of the plaintiff's compensation, there must be considerable doubt as to its feasibility and, above all, as to the amount and calculability of the respective reduction.[298] Alongside this line of thought, an emission-based approach also does not allow for liability of otherwise climate-damaging and precisely non-emission-based behaviour. While some actions can still be quantified and calculated in emission-related terms, such as deforestation or the extraction of fossil fuels, specific actions are denied such translation. The sealing of soils, the increasing expansion of cities and gentrification are just a few examples.[299] Supposed an emission share doctrine would be applied, its scope of application would only resort to emission-based climate change impacts and would leave out other forms of contributions. The doctrine hence could not claim universality.

The last and probably most significant factor of comparability concerns the conceptual scope of the doctrine and its metaphysical grounding.[300] DES cases are salient due to several sufficient conditions, which thus forms a case of alternative causation. Emission-based cases, on the other hand, predominantly involve a multitude of small and, therefore, non-sufficient conditions, which places these cases in the area of cumulative causation. The lack of sufficiency concerning individual contributions results in the inability to comprehensively infer the setting of the risk. After all, the contribution was not yet sufficient to cause the outcome alone. It is, however, exactly the fundamental risk-setting on which the market-share doctrine founds its blame. Each shareholder beholds full blameworthiness because

---

[297] Rostron (2004), pp. 208–210.

[298] Grimm (2007), pp. 224–232.

[299] See for scientific explanations Sect. 2.1.1.3.2.

[300] Pöttker (2014), pp. 361–362.

his contribution could have produced the outcome alone. Based on this fundamental and conceptual consideration, transferring the market-share doctrine as a doctrine of alternative causation to a cumulatively grown emission-share doctrine falters. DES cases are further characterised by their identifiable and delimitable number of manufacturers, who can be named concisely. Climate change cases, on the other hand, are defined by a large number of different actors contributing to varying degrees and over a much longer period of time. Given the lack of comparability and, in particular, the impossibility of identifying all potential polluters, the New Zealand Court of Appeal in the case *Smith v. Fonterra* concurrently refused to apply the market share liability doctrine adopted in *Sindell* to a climate change case.[301] Consequently, a potential emissions share doctrine, if it were to be successfully applied, cannot be based on the existing case law of *Sindell v. Abbott Laboratories* but requires a new concept separate and independent from the existing case law. An analogous application of the doctrine is consequently foreclosed.

4.5.1.2.3 Delineating a 'Market' for Emissions

One of the main components of the market-share liability doctrine persists in the idea that the action and participation in the market by tortious means already carries blameworthiness. This perception of the concept, however, prerequisites the existence of a delimitable realm of action and, therefore, concerns the spatial sphere which is set by the doctrine. In doing so, the 'market' itself does not merely constitute a criterion for the application of the doctrine but is entailed in the ratio of the approach itself. Whereas in the respective DES cases, the market was clearly delimitable as the distribution of the particular drug in the United States, market delimitations in light of emissions are considerably widened, if not ultimately impossible, given the global nature of climate change.[302] This ultimately results in questions of the spatial scope of the market and the further feasibility of an emission share doctrine.

A blueprint for arguably a limited but nevertheless comprehensive and workable emission-market is provided by the EU Emission Trading System (ETS).[303] Given the existing market structure, the ETS not only provides for a delimitable market itself but also for a procedural framework that allows for the application and eventual feasibility of attributing emissions in a precise manner according to the EU-wide contribution to the global atmospheric emission density.[304] The ETS itself was

[301] High Court of New Zealand, 21 October 2021 – [2021] NZCA 552, *Smith v. Fonterra Co-Operative Group Limited*, Judgment of the Court of Appeal para 111.

[302] See for a detailed analysis of the different market sectors and their issues Pöttker (2014), pp. 358–365.

[303] Other similar schemes have been established e.g. in Canada, South Korea (KETS), New Zealand, Switzerland and the US.

[304] Peeters (2011), pp. 100–101. Opposing such a solution due to its short existence and its local limiations Pöttker (2014), p. 359.

established to monitor carbon-based emissions and to safeguard compliance with reduction targets of the EU set out under the Kyoto Protocol. In creating a market for CO_2 emissions, prizing them accordingly and reducing the 'emission-cap' starting from 2013 over time, the ETS also sets an incentive for reducing overall corporative emissions. The ETS furthermore allows for the selling of surplus shares, setting another incentive for the reduction of carbon emissions. By initiating and constructing a cap on the overall carbon emission of the included industrial sectors, the EU not only draws the authority of the number of carbon emissions in these respective sectors but also controls the amounts emitted. In doing so, it is not only possible to track exactly how much is emitted but also what share is contributed by whom and in which year. It, therefore, greatly facilitates the attribution and quantification of various emissions-based contributions and sets the framework for the market, which is partially comparable to the market structure of the DES cases. Such can at least be invoked by considering sector-specific carbon emission caps, provided those industries are included in the EU ETS mechanism.[305]

In contrast to the DES cases, one of the major downsides of looking at the EU ETS is that the scheme does not cover all potential sources of threat to the climate system. Since the EU ETS does only refer to the most high-emitting industries (which still account for about 45% of overall EU emissions), it does not cover the entire 'market' but only a fraction of it. Nevertheless, the sectoral emission share can function as an indicator of substantiality or even as an indicator of contribution, but deriving well-founded factuality from the EU ETS is deceived by its fractiousness.[306] Similar objections can be raised against comprehensive, but only national, systems. Unlike in the case of DES, no certainty can be provided that the threat originates from a source that is resilient in its national market. Climate change as a global phenomenon arises from emissions around the world without the ability to reduce or comprehensively delineate the market. An emissions-based market must, therefore, operate on a global, worldwide scale.[307]

Limiting an emission-share approach only to actual 'markets' per se (such as the EU ETS, the KETS or national economic markets) is, nevertheless, too short-sighted. Moving away from the actual economic concept of a market and abstracting the concept back to its basis as a framework in which supply and demand meet and the supply is constrained by internationally agreed temperature limits, one could well make use of the idea of a 'market share' on a global scale. That it is possible to attribute specific emission shares to individual entities was already shown by the calculations by *Heede*, which have been renewed and continued repeatedly.[308] By

[305] The industries covered by the ETS are particularly emission-intensive. These include inter alia metal and energy production and mineral processing.

[306] See for the use of the market share as an indicator of substantiality Sect. 5.4.2.3.

[307] On the difficulty of introducing such an approach, see Pöttker (2014), p. 360. In relation to the share of fossil fuels, and only indirectly in relation to its CO_2 equivalent, but still in a global context Peñalver (1998), p. 592. In this respect presumably also Grimm (2007).

[308] Heede (2014b) and Griffin (2017).

broadening the scope of the relevant market beyond carbon emissions (a restriction still maintained by the EU ETS) and eventually including other greenhouse gas emissions, the concept of 'market share' would eventually evolve into a comprehensive approach, regardless of its applicability. It would further increasingly reflect existing international climate agreements. Given the almost insurmountable task of reaching a global consensus on climate issues, it is highly unlikely that the future will involve emissions caps, reductions and pricing similar to the ETS at the global level.

The economic focus of the market or, respectively, the emission share doctrine further means that emissions from other non-economic sources, such as emissions from individuals and government contributions, are not reflected in the share per se. In addition to the bias already introduced by the ETS restriction to emission-intensive industries, a restriction to purely economic emissions leads to a further distortion of the shares in light of overall climate change. Including non-economic emissions would be a more defensible and realistic approach, but it also contradicts the basic intention of a market share approach.

4.5.1.2.4 Conceptualizing Causation Under an Emission Share Approach

The market share liability doctrine is in itself not an exclusive method for establishing causation, rather, it is founded on the idea of establishing liability in cases in which the lack of causation would hinder such doing. As previously addressed, the main obstacles DES cases faced concerned scientific uncertainties and the impossibility of attributing the effect of the medication to one specific actor. Whereas general causation between the ingestion of the drug in general and the children's higher risk of cancer could be affirmed, it was ultimately the specific causal chain that was lacking. As a solution for the lack of provability of specific causation, the market share liability doctrine first applied a presumption of existing causation and further reversed the burden of proof by placing it on the defendant. The necessity of a market share liability doctrine, therefore, strongly builds upon the determination and establishment of causation, which further enables the consideration of whether the ratio of the market share liability doctrine would allow for a reduction of the concept to a mere causation-based dogma. Its effectiveness, as well as its logical underpinnings, certainly argue in favour of such a reduction. In contrast to these economic considerations, one of the main concerns relates to the nature of the doctrine as an approach to liability. Liability is based on the understanding that one who has breached a duty is responsible for the outcome and must hence face the consequences of their own breach. Applying the original doctrine to climate change cases would, therefore, imply that the emissions occurred in breach of an obligation, further imposing blameworthiness and responsibility.[309] In metaphysical,

[309] In this regard Pöttker (2014), p. 361. In regard to state responsibility and negating a duty to care in this regard Verheyen (2005), p. 294. In proposing a certain amount of permissible CO_2 (permissible level) Grimm (2007), pp. 233–236.

epistemological terms, the market share liability doctrine continues to rely on a counterfactual and thus mono-causal perception of causation (the use of a drug caused specific harm), whereas emission shares rely heavily on multi-causal considerations based on their cumulative occurrence. Cumulative and alternative causation thus converge, which leads to major metaphysical and epistemological difficulties in the transference of the liability doctrine to a mere causation approach.

4.5.1.3 Conclusion

The foregoing discussion has shown that the transfer of the market share liability doctrine as it was developed in *Sindell v. Abbott Laboratories* to an emission-based causation approach seems conceivable from an economic and application-oriented perspective. The challenges that the courts were confronted with in light of the DES cases are comparable to the obstacles posed to legal actions by climate change, namely the lack of proof and scientific uncertainty. Nonetheless, an emission share doctrine faces two major and ultimately fatal points of contention. The first concern relates to the conceptual scope of the market share liability doctrine. While the market share liability doctrine greatly builds upon the establishment of causation in an alternative setting, breaking it down to an emission-related cumulative scenario would result in dogmatic, epistemological and metaphysical inconsistencies and predicaments. The second point of contention addresses the delineation of the right market. Reference has been alluded to the EU ETS, as well as to a possible global model, without, however, providing for a feasible conception of how to approach an emission-related model itself. Based on these two grounds as well as on further concerns, the applicability of the market share liability doctrine to climatic causation must ultimately be denied. While the transference of the market share liability doctrine to climate change litigation ultimately fails, a market share may, nevertheless, be a sector-specific indicator for the substantiality of someone's contribution, as well as for the causal relevance of its contribution in general.

4.5.2 Contribution-Based Approach to Causation

A broad consensus has emerged among legal scholars and, in particular, environmental and climate lawyers in recent times that the requirement of causation in climate claims can only be maintained and satisfied by lowering the high standard of causation posed by current, mainly counterfactual concepts. One approach that has been advocated in this regard is a contribution-based approach.[310] The following

---

[310] Also proposing such an approach Verheyen (2005), pp. 254–256, as well as Voigt (2008), p. 16. An indication was also given in Arbitrational Tribunal, 16 April 1938, 11 March 1941 – 3 R.I.A.A. 1905, *United States v. Canada (Trail Smelter Case)*. Similarly, for American

sections, therefore, first discuss the substance of a contribution-based approach (Sect. 4.5.2.1) and the extent to which such a concept is already being applied in other areas of law and jurisdictions (Sect. 4.5.2.2), before looking specifically at its application within climate change litigation (Sect. 4.5.2.3). On the basis of the results obtained, the conceptual framework of the approach is then to be evaluated and metaphysically reconciled before the principles of the contribution-based approach are further elaborated and developed beyond the previous remarks, especially in terms of their practicability and applicability (Sect. 4.5.2.4).

4.5.2.1 The Substance of a Contribution-Based Perception of Factual Causation

Contrary to counterfactual theories or theories of regularity and more akin to the pollution share liability doctrine, the contribution-based account has its origin in legal practice and is not based on metaphysical approaches or anchored in doctrines of legal theory. Establishing causation on mere contributions was rather born out of the necessity of reducing the high causal hurdles in cases in which scientific uncertainty, the lack of provability, and the failing of traditional approaches hindered the establishment of causation. In considering reasons of justice and fairness, and despite the lack of e.g. counterfactual but-for causation, the account builds upon normative, socio-politically driven considerations. The aim of a contribution-based approach lies in constituting a factual test of causation, independent from any normative influences and considerations. The contribution-based approach is built on the understanding that any contribution to an outcome, and in the climate context any emission-related contribution to climate change is to be considered causal. At a factual level, the size of the contribution is irrelevant. Whether a contribution alone has caused the outcome or whether the contribution takes effect concurrent to a number of other conditions is immaterial within the contribution-based approach. Rather, the extent of the contribution is a question of normative significance, which is why it must be discussed at the secondary level of the determination of causation.[311]

Due to its case law grown development and origin, the approach lacks a metaphysical foundation. If, however, the substance of the approach is transferred to causal-theoretical structures and translated into a dogma of necessary and sufficient conditions, one has to abandon the requirement of a strong necessity criterion, such as is required, for example, within counterfactual theories. A contribution-based approach is qualified precisely by the fact that a condition does not have to be necessary for the outcome per se, let alone the requirement of sufficiency. Rather, the

environmental liability jurisprudence in public and private nuisance cases, see Pöttker (2014), pp. 344–346. Acknowledging the existence of contributory causation without discussing its substance further, Lahav (2022), p. 118.

[311] See in this regard Sect. 5.4.

approach converges to metaphysical structures of weak necessity that are argued for in regularity-based theories. Nonetheless, this does not yet imply the same metaphysical substantiation.

Apart from the above explanations, the contribution-based approach is largely a concept in flux, without already existing, long-established structures and methodologies. However, one of the aims of the subsequent sections is to place the contribution-based approach within a coherent dogmatic structure and, in part, a metaphysical framework.

4.5.2.2 The Contribution-Based Approach in Practice

Lowering the causation threshold is not a new concept for legal thinking and jurisprudence in general. Common law countries, in particular, have been at the forefront of adapting traditional concepts of causation and thus reducing the standard of causation in the law. Within these jurisdictions, the field of clinical and medical law, as well as negligence cases in general, have raised the awareness of the importance of thinking about causation in different ways. In the following sections, some of these exemplary approaches from national and international jurisprudence are elaborated on with the aim of finding a fundamental structure for a reduced and contribution-based perception of causation.

4.5.2.2.1 Domestic Approaches to Reduced Standards of Causation

4.5.2.2.1.1 The Canadian Material Contribution to Risk Test

A reduced approach to causation has already been evolving in Canadian jurisprudence for quite some time. The most significant decision in this regard was made by the Supreme Court of Canada in the case *Resurfice Corp. v. Hanke.*[312] In this case, the Supreme Court refined the previously existing but only vaguely applied '*material contribution to risk*' approach established for cases of unprovable negligence. The case concerned an explosion of vaporised gasoline caused by the plaintiff's inadvertent introduction of water into a gas tank, which in turn led to his injury. One of the key issues in the case was the correct causation doctrine to apply, with the Trial Judge relying on the but-for test but the Court of Appeal rejecting its usage and instead adopting the material contribution to risk test.[313] The Supreme Court then

---

[312] Although the case cannot be regarded as the origin of a contribution-based approach in the Canadian legal system, it is regarded as the most significant case and the most explicit application of it, see Supreme Court of Canada, 8 February 2007 – 1 S.C.R. 333, 2007 SCC 7, *Resurfice Corp. v. Hanke*.

[313] Court of Appeal of Alberta, 7 November 2005 – ABCA 383, *Hanke v. Resurfice Corp*, para 14, Court of Queen's Bench of Alberta, Judicial district of Edmonton, 22 July 2003 – ABQB 616, *Hanke v. Resurfice Corp.*

had to clarify the requirements for using a reduced standard of causation and argued for a restrictive conception of the test. The Court set out two conditions that must be met before the test can be applied at all.[314] First, the existence of two or more tortfeasors must make it impossible for the plaintiff to establish but-for causation. The tortfeasors and their actions, in general, must also be placed outside the plaintiff's responsibility and control. The second requirement demands that the defendant has breached a duty of care which has resulted in damage to the plaintiff.[315] Only when these two conditions are met does the Court decide on the application of the material contribution to risk test. These two requirements were further refined in the Supreme Court's decision in *Clements v. Clements.*[316] Here the Court stated that the material contribution test is only applicable if

> the plaintiff, through no fault of her own, is unable to show that any one of the possible tortfeasors in fact was the necessary or "but for" cause of her injury, because each can point to one another as the possible 'but for' cause of the injury, defeating a finding of causation on a balance of probabilities against anyone.[317]

The Court in *Resurfice* further clarified that the material contribution to risk approach does not function as an exception to the but-for test concerning the establishment of causation but only provides liability even though no causal link or only a general link can be found.[318] As the Court stated in a later case, a "*material contribution [to risk] does not signify a test of causation at all; rather it is a policy driven rule [...].*"[319] The test thus functions as a bridge between the offence and the liability of the defendant in cases in which traditional approaches to causation fail. Yet, the Supreme Court made clear that the material contribution to risk test in its function as a 'gap-filler' should only be applied in exceptional cases. Due to the strictness of the approach, its application and decisions in favour of this conception are rare. Ultimately, the material increase in risk test has never been upheld by the Supreme Court of Canada.

However, despite its strictness, more and more plaintiffs are falling back on the assertion of a contribution-based approach. Having in mind the two prerequisites set out by the Supreme Court in *Resurfice* and especially concerning the presupposed failure of but-for causation due to multiple tortfeasors, the application of the material contribution test to cases of climate and environmental harm is not far-fetched. This

---

[314]Concerning the discussion whether the prerequisites are requirements of the test itself, or requirements for the test to be applied, see Hansen (2011).

[315]Supreme Court of Canada, 8 February 2007 – 1 S.C.R. 333, 2007 SCC 7, *Resurfice Corp. v. Hanke*, para 25, Supreme Court of Canada, 29 June 2012 – [2012] 2 R.C.S, *Clements v. Clements*, paras 27, 34.

[316]Supreme Court of Canada, 29 June 2012 – [2012] 2 R.C.S, *Clements v. Clements*.

[317]Ibid. para 46.

[318]Supreme Court of Canada, 8 February 2007 – 1 S.C.R. 333, 2007 SCC 7, *Resurfice Corp. v. Hanke*.

[319]Supreme Court of Canada, 29 June 2012 – [2012] 2 R.C.S, *Clements v. Clements*. For a review of the *Clements v Clements* decision, see Galway and McKee (2016). For a discussion of the requirements for applying the material contribution to risk approach, see Hansen (2011).

is shown in particular by the recent decision of the Federal Court of Canada in the case *Lho'imggin et al. v. Her Majesty the Queen.*[320] The plaintiffs—Dini Ze'Lho'Imggin and Dini Ze'Smogilhgim, on behalf of all members of two Wet'suwet'en Indigenous houses—alleged a violation of their fundamental and constitutional rights based on insufficient climate change mitigation efforts by Canada. The plaintiffs' claims were based, inter alia, on international climate and environmental treaties as well as a potential breach or rather an exceeding of Canada's Nationally Determined Contribution (NDC) under the Paris Agreement.[321] The case has been in appeal before the Federal Court of Appeal since December 2020. However, the first-instance decision is already of considerable interest in terms of extending the scope of application of the material contribution test. In particular, the question of the applicable causal standard for Section 7 of the Charter was disputed. Section 7 of the Charter states that *"(e)veryone has the right to life, liberty and security of the person and the right not to be deprived thereof except in accordance with the principles of fundamental justice."*[322] A violation of Section 7 ultimately presupposes a causal link between the government's conduct at issue and the impairment of the applicants' rights. The plaintiffs argued that the material contribution standard, which had been established in Canada only for negligence cases, should be applied to the present case, as well. Until then the material contribution test had only been discussed in the context of tort cases. It has never been applied to claims based on the Canadian Charter of Rights and Freedoms.[323] And while the Court ultimately rejects the claim for the application of the material contribution test, its reasoning nevertheless shows that a transfer of the approach, despite its restrictiveness, is not inconceivable. The Court stated that *"(i)t is true that the novelty alone is not a reason to strike a claim but at the same time, it does not mean that novel claims will never be struck."*[324] Yet, even though the Court ultimately denied the Charter claim, it did so based on a lack of facts and evidence and explicitly not because a transference of the material contribution standard outside of negligence cases would not be possible.

Despite the negative outcome for the plaintiffs and the Court's rejection of the material contribution argument in the *Lho'imggin* case, the ruling shows that a transfer of the material contribution standard, despite its restrictive nature, to other areas of law is not precluded and may well be possible with the right argumentation and presentation of the facts. This is particularly the case given that the requirements of the approach established in *Resurfice* fit into the realm of constitutional and fundamental rights, notably in light of positive obligations. Furthermore, the case

[320] Federal Court Canada, 16 November 2020 – 2020 FC 1059, *Lho'imggin et al. v. Her Majesty the Queen.*

[321] See ibid. statement of claim (10 February 2020), paras 42–58.

[322] Section 7 Canadian Charter.

[323] Federal Court Canada, 16 November 2020 – 2020 FC 1059, *Lho'imggin et al. v. Her Majesty the Queen*, para 98.

[324] Ibid. para 99.

shows that the concept does not stand in the way of being transferred to cases that carry climate change at heart. Notwithstanding the attempt to apply the material contribution standard in the above-mentioned climate change case, the contention remains that the test has had limited application in Canadian courts to date. This is due to its—now seemingly fragile—limitation to negligence cases and, in particular, to the high demands placed on its applicability. However, the former appears to be weakening. Nevertheless, the fact that the standard does not involve a new qualification and substantiation of causation per se should not be disregarded. Rather, the material contribution test merely has a bridging function to overcome non-existent counterfactual causation.

4.5.2.2.1.2 The British Account of Contributory Causation

4.5.2.2.1.2.1 The Material Contribution to Risk Test

Concurrent with the Canadian approach, courts in the United Kingdom are also applying a similar contribution-based concept in cases of negligence with a specific emphasis on medical and clinical cases. Based on the traditional but-for test, courts in several cases had to deal with the question of how to handle situations in which a counterfactual conception of causation would fail, although actual causation still existed. One of the precedent cases in which the Court referred to a reduced threshold of causation due to the occurrence of an indivisible injury was the judgement in the case *Fairchild v. Glenhaven Funeral Services Ltd.*[325] In *Fairchild*, the House of Lords had to deal with the question of how to approach the problem that the actual cause of lung cancer (mesothelioma) resulting from the exposure to asbestos could no longer be determined. The plaintiffs had worked for several different employers and had been exposed to asbestos on several occasions. However, even a single exposure to the highly toxic substance is sufficient for the development of lung cancer. Due to the uncertainty and lack of evidence regarding the primary causative agent, counterfactual causation tests failed. Therefore, the House of Lords, in establishing a '*material contribution to risk*' test, ruled that if the plaintiff could prove that a party had contributed to increasing the risk of such a disease, the plaintiff could still recover compensation for the harm he suffered.[326]

The *Fairchild* case is particularly relevant in that several courts have considered the applicability of the concept developed in that case to climate change claims. So far this has only happened outside the British jurisdiction. Of particular relevance to the debate on the application of the contribution to risk test to climate change claims are the Australian decision in *Minister for the Environment v Sharma* and the decision of the High Court of New Zealand in *Smith v Fonterra Co-Operative*

[325] House of Lords, 20 June 2002 – UKHL 22, *Fairchild v. Glenhaven Funeral Services Ltd.*

[326] Ibid.

Group Limited.[327] In the latter, the plaintiff argued that the situation and purpose of the case were consistent with the principles in *Fairchild*. In *Smith v Fonterra*, the plaintiff targeted numerous high-emitting companies, including in particular the Fonterra Co-Operative Group Limited, which operates dairy farms that use coal for energy production. The plaintiff relied on three distinct courses of action. First, he claimed public nuisance, arguing that emissions and related climate change and sea level rise were damaging his family's property through the physical loss of land, the loss of fertility, and correlated the loss of value. He further supported the claim by arguing that public health was being violated by the defendants. As a second cause of action, Mr Smith relied on a negligent breach of a duty of care owed to him by the corporations and violated due to the emission of greenhouse gases and the production of emission-generating products. Finally, the plaintiff alleged a breach of a legally enforceable duty not to damage the climate system.[328]

In its judgment, the High Court first determined the inapplicability of the but-for test before addressing the possibility of transferring the material contribution to the risk test. In the end, however, such a transfer was rejected. The negated analogy was justified in particular by the lack of comparability of lung cancer caused by asbestos and climate change per se. It was particularly relevant that the failure of the but-for test in *Fairchild* was based solely on the lack of provability, although all employers could, in principle, be but-for causers. Concerning climate change, nonetheless, the picture is different. The failure of counterfactual causation in climate lawsuits in large parts cannot be accounted to the lack of provability but consists in the presence of numerous cumulative causal contributions, with no single but-for causer. *Justice Whylie* thus rejected the analogous application of the *Fairchild* criteria in the present case.[329]

The case of *Smith v. Fonterra* clearly demonstrates the problematic nature of applying the *Fairchild* criteria to climatic issues. While the case law in *Fairchild* was developed based on a problem of alternative causation, climate change lawsuits usually concern numerous different contributions by several different actors without being able to identify one or more individual sufficient causers. Climate change litigation, however, usually deals with cases of cumulative causation rather than alternative causative settings. This argument is very similar to the argument raised in regard to the market share liability doctrine, which also failed in part because of the distinction between alternative and cumulative causation. The scenario in *Fairchild* and climate change, in general, is nevertheless comparable when considering the aim and the purpose of the newly developed contribution-based doctrine. Ultimately, the purpose of the test is to hold potential causers accountable not based on their actual

327 Federal Court of Australia, 15 March 2022 – [2022] FCAFC 35, *Minister for the Environment v. Sharma* , High Court of New Zealand, 21 October 2021 – [2021] NZCA 552, *Smith v. Fonterra Co-Operative Group Limited*, para 107.

328 High Court of New Zealand, 21 October 2021 – [2021] NZCA 552, *Smith v. Fonterra Co-Operative Group Limited*, inter alia paras 94–98, 114–126.

329 Ibid. para 88.

contribution or condition that caused the outcome but solely on their contribution to the risk increase. Whether the risk increase, herby concerns the danger of developing lung cancer, or the increase of the risk of climate change or climate change-induced damages, is highly extraneous. Therefore, unlike *Justice Whylie* in *Smith v. Fonterra*, *Justice Beach* in *Minister for the Environment v. Sharma* hinted at the possibility of transferring the *Fairchild* case but ultimately left open the question of whether such a transfer would be feasible.[330]

Nevertheless, the argument of a lack of factual analogy weighs heavily. While applying the *Fairchild* criteria still seems feasible for cases within the realm of alternative climatic causation, comparability within cumulative cases fails. Yet, as most climate litigation is based on cumulative scenarios and few address alternative causes, the value of an analogue application within climate scenarios is severely limited. More useful than the analogous transfer of the principles themselves, however, is the transfer of the reasoning behind the *Fairchild* considerations. The idea that plaintiffs should not be denied their claims solely on the basis of lack of provability regarding the actual causer and thus for lack of causation, even though the contribution itself is fully provable, can certainly be transferred to climate issues. This underlines the importance of evaluating and including mere but provable contributions to causal conceptions.

4.5.2.2.1.2.2 The Material Contribution Test

In addition to the risk-oriented projection of a contributory approach, the British jurisprudence developed a purely material contribution test even earlier. In the case of *Bonnington Castings Ltd v. Wardlaw,*[331] the plaintiff, similar to the *Fairchild* case, contracted a lung disease, in this case, pneumoconiosis. This was due to silica dust inhaled at the workplace, which originated from two sources. The first was a pneumatic hammer, for which the employer complied with the prescribed health and safety regulations, and the second was a grinding machine for which the employer was obliged to provide a dust extraction plant but negligently failed to do so and was subject to a breach of a duty of care. Thus, the plaintiff had to prove that it was precisely the employer's breach concerning the grinding machine that had led to his illness. However, this was not possible retrospectively based on the but-for test. The House of Lords finally decided in their judgment that the dust from both sources had led to the illness but that this did not prevent the affirmation of causation because the negligently caused dust due to the breach of duty of care constituted a material contribution to the damage, i.e. the illness.[332] The contribution was also material as it did not constitute mere de minimis causation.

---

[330] Federal Court of Australia, 15 March 2022 – [2022] FCAFC 35, *Minister for the Environment v. Sharma* para 436.

[331] House of Lords, 25 March 1995 – [1956] AC 613, *Bonnington Castings Ltd. Wardlaw.*

[332] Ibid. para 3. The decision was further developed in House of Lords, 15 November 1972 – 1 WLR 1, *McGhee v. National Coal Board.*

Two facts distinguish the test in *Bonnington Castings* from the causation standard developed in the *Fairchild* decision. Firstly, the conduct complained of differed. Whereas in *Fairchild,* only the contribution to an increase in risk was of relevance, in the *Bonnington* decision, the reproachable conduct was defined more narrowly and was based on a contribution to the actual damage. The second difference lies in the nature of causation. While in *Fairchild,* even a single exposure to asbestos led to the disease at hand and several contributions interacted alternatively, in *Bonnington,* the pneumoconiosis disease was an effect of the cumulative impact of various dust particles.

The *Bonnington* case, and the test developed in it, are also significant for climate issues, as it has already been invoked in some climate cases to establish causation. In the decision *Minister for the Environment v. Sharma*, already briefly mentioned concerning the analogous application of the *Fairchild* criteria, the Court also dealt with the question of the analogous application of the material contribution test established in *Bonnington.*[333] However, this was ultimately denied by *Judge Beach.* The immediacy of the negligent act on the effect in question, and the proximity of the causal chain, played a major role. The Court emphasised that such immediacy was lacking in the present case. While in *Bonnington,* the dust directly led to the disease, in *Fairchild,* the asbestos only led to an increase in the risk of contracting lung cancer but not directly to the outcome itself. Since the emission of greenhouse gases rather increases the risk than directly leading to specific climate-related damage, *Judge Beach* considered the emission of greenhouse gases as being not comparable to the *Bonnington* decision but rather to *Fairchild.* It has been argued that there are further steps in the causal chain between the emission and the damage, such as an increase in temperature, sea level rise, etc., which make the proximity of the contribution even more difficult. The same applies to the risk of damage.[334]

If one follows the reasoning of *Judge Beach* in the *Sharma* decision, the application of the material contribution test qualifies as fundamentally unsuitable for climatic circumstances. After all, climate change is characterised by a considerably long causal chain with many scientific components and intermediate causalities. If this is seen as an obstacle, a general transfer of the contribution-based approach is not possible. However, it could also be argued that immediacy can be inferred even when intermediate steps are necessary, such as the increase in temperature and the rise in sea level, but such intermediate steps are also part of a direct, uninterrupted causal chain. Although numerous other components play a role within climatic scenarios and contribute to the climate-relevant outcome, it is scientifically provable that emissions contribute to and generally enhance climate change. It can thus only be concluded from the reasoning of *Judge Beach* that the application of the immediacy criteria is to be read in the most restrictive way possible and needs to be built on a direct, unilateral causal relation. With the strict and narrow perception that is

[333] Federal Court of Australia, 15 March 2022 – [2022] FCAFC 35, *Minister for the Environment v. Sharma* paras 432–442.

[334] Ibid. esp. para 436.

presented by *Judge Beach*, the immediacy will most likely have to be universally denied within climate change litigation, even under this assumption, as well.[335] This conclusion is rather unfortunate because, at least on the basis of the dogmatic and metaphysical qualification of the contributions as cumulative, the *Bonnington* case is more comparable to an emissions-related climate claim than the alternative contributions in the *Fairchild* case. However, the perception of immediacy pictured in the *Bonnington* case does not run concurrently with the normatively induced requirement of a stringent causal chain that is presupposed by some doctrines of normative causation. If the perceptions of immediacy and proximity are aligned with the reading of these factors in normative causation, there certainly is a chance of transmission and analogy based on an arguably direct, but not unilateral, chain of causation. Furthermore, it is questionable whether such normatively induced factors should be decisive for a factual approach after all. However, as the immediacy concerns only the transferability and analogous application of the concept to climate claims and not the establishment of factual causation per se, no objections are to be raised. Nevertheless, under the perception elaborated on in *Sharma*, an analogous transfer of the material contribution test as developed in the *Bonnington Castings* case to climate claims is not feasible. Ultimately, the considerations show that, in principle, a mere contribution to damage does not necessarily exclude causation but can certainly lead to an existing causal chain.

4.5.2.2.1.3 The American Substantial Factor Test

Theories of causation that allow multiple acts as causes based on a reduced threshold are also not unknown in the American legal system. The so-called *'substantial factor test'* has a long history in American jurisprudence and has become increasingly relevant in environmental law, especially concerning pollution-based claims.[336] In abandoning the strict requirements of counterfactual causation, the substantial factor test allows a contribution of substantial size to suffice for the establishment of causation. The test is defined as *"(t)he principle that causation exists when the defendant's conduct is an important or significant contributor to the plaintiff's injuries."*[337] Yet, unlike the British or Canadian approach, the substantial factor test is not limited to either alternative or cumulative cases but extends to all cases in which multiple contributions are present. Originally, this test was developed not to replace counterfactual tests but to adapt the but-for test in two specific scenarios. On the one hand, the test should lead to the establishment of causation in cases of multiple actors, i.e. in cases of causal overdetermination. On the other hand, it should

[335] The perception of immediacy described in *Bonnington* is not consistent with the normatively induced requirement of a strict chain of causation presupposed by some doctrines of normative causation.

[336] See in this regard especially the Restatements (Second) of Torts para §§ 431, 432, Pöttker (2014), pp. 344–350.

[337] Garner (2009), p. 1566, term: substantial-cause test.

act as a limiting factor within so-called de minimis or trivial but-for causes and thus prevent an extension of causation to such unimportant, mediocre cases.[338]

From a factual point of view, the first condition is particularly relevant. The second criterion serves the normative side of causation, which for the determination of a factual causal approach to contributory causation, is of no relevance. However, due to the vagueness of the terminology and thus the necessity for further elaboration by the courts, the broad interpretation of the substantial factor test leads to legal uncertainty for the parties to the action. It further provides for the establishment of diverging standards contingent on different areas of law and jurisdictions.[339] Based on this criticism, the Restatements (Third) of Torts refrained from applying the substantial factor test and established a causal approach strictly based on the separation of factual causation and the scope of liability (normative causation).[340] Although the Restatements (Third) of Torts distanced itself from the terminology of a substantial factor, it did not refrain from the substance of the approach as such.[341] Contrary to the developments in the new version of the Restatement of Torts, some authors nevertheless argue for the application of the substantial factor test in cases of considerable evidentiary difficulties, as well. This has been discussed again, particularly in the context of asbestos cases.[342]

In its applicability to climate change claims, the substantial factor test is convincing due to its broad dogmatic and structural scope, which allows both cumulative and alternative conditions to be considered as causes. Given the conceptual vagueness of the approach and the lack of strict requirements for its application, it can be anticipated that at least the factual causal element could be affirmed in climate change litigation. However, the reference to a 'substantial' contribution would require consideration at the level of normative causation under a bifurcated approach and is, therefore, irrelevant to the factual determination of causation.[343] Nevertheless, the original test of substantial contribution is based on a conflation of factual and normative causation, which is at odds with the perception of causal assessments in the law that is advocated here. For this reason alone, a generic and unmodified application of the respective test to a contribution-based approach of causation is to be discounted. Ultimately, the American substantial factor test, and the fact that the Restatement (Third) of Torts has at least retained the substance of the concept, show that American jurisprudence is not averse to a reduced conception of causation.

---

[338] See concerning trivial cases comment a to § 431 in Restatements (Second) of Torts.

[339] Due to the overall vagueness of the approach, courts tend to apply a wide variability of different non-coherent criteria, see summarizing Hensley and Robinson (2013).

[340] See especially § 26 of the Restatements (Third) of Torts.

[341] Sanders et al. (2008), p. 419; Sebok (2017), p. 61.

[342] Sanders et al. (2008); Pöttker (2014), pp. 342–344.

[343] See in regard to materiality Sect. 5.4.

4.5.2.2.2 Regional and International Perceptions of Reduced Causal Standards

Contribution-based concepts of causation can also be encountered in the international legal framework. However, the discussion of such notions in relation to regional and international jurisdictions is much more challenging than in the context of national law owing to the lack of consistency, ambiguity and terminological discrepancies in the usage of causal approaches per se. To this end, some illustrative and non-exhaustive concepts from regional tort law and the law of state responsibility are analysed and evaluated, without claiming to be exhaustive in presenting the use of reduced standards of causation.

4.5.2.2.2.1 The Principles of European Tort Law

The Principles of European Tort Law (PETL) constitute a synopsis of the different concepts advocated in tort law throughout different Member States of the European Union. The principles function as an attempt to harmonise European tort law in providing suggestions and guidelines for national legislation. Although not binding for the Member States, it is particularly Principle 3:105 which is relevant to the aspect of a lowered perception of causation, in which it is stated that

> (i)n the case of multiple activities, when it is certain that none of them has caused the entire damage or any determinable part thereof, those that are likely to have [minimally] contributed to the damage are presumed to have caused equal shares thereof.[344]

Although the principle initially resembles a norm for the attribution of liability rather than an actual cause-effect relation, Art. 3:105 PETL constitutes a rule of causal substantiation. This can already be deduced from the norm's systematic place in Chapter 3 of the PETL, which deals explicitly with causation.[345] The argument finds support in the chosen terminology, which speaks for the assumption of a causal norm. However, it is obvious that the focus of the statute certainly does not respond to a contribution-based conception of causation but a causation establishment in the case of uncertain contribution rates. The provision itself refers to cumulative conditions in which one activity alone does not produce the damage, but several different factors are of relevance for bringing the respective claim. Cases of alternative causation are explicitly excluded from this provision, with them being referred to in Art. 3:102 and Art. 3:103 PETL. Art. 3:105 PETL constitutes a norm of partial causation. In applying a reduced standard of causation, any condition that is likely to have contributed to the outcome is considered causal, provided that no condition could have caused the outcome alone or in large parts. The peculiarity of the application of this particular standard lies in its reference to and presupposition of uncertainty about the interplay between different contributions. However, the exact

[344] Principle 3:105 PETL.

[345] In the same regard Spier (2005), pp. 54–56.

scope and requirements of the provision have been the subject of considerable debate. While some prefer to apply the norm similar to the doctrine of market share liability only in cases in which all conditions contribute minimally to the result, the majority also accepts the application of Art. 3:105 PETL, even if the extent of some of these contributions can be assessed and quantified.[346] Nevertheless, Art. 3:105 PETL explicitly does not apply in cases in which the explicit scope of the contributions is unknown, but it is understood that the individual contributions were not formally equal.[347]

Such an understanding of Art. 3:105 PETL renders the norm highly problematic for its application in climate change cases. Climate cases are built upon the conception of different shares of contributions, even though uncertainty about the scope of those contributions may prevail. This is even more so the case when one follows the understanding that Art. 3:105 PETL presupposes that all of those conditions have to contribute minimally, and no contribution can be prescribed a certain share. The reference to contributions is, therefore, merely a loose shell within Art. 3:105 and can only be deduced here as an existing legal concept without further implications or statements about an actual factual concept of contributory causation.

4.5.2.2.2.2 The Law of State Responsibility

Contribution as a legal concept per se, which is furthermore relevant to the attribution of responsibility, is not unknown to the international legal framework and especially the realm of state responsibility.[348] After all, causation-related contribution has to be distinguished from the general usage of the concept. In the international law of state responsibility, two provisions, Art. 39 DARS (contributory fault) and Art. 25 DARS, refer to the causal dimension of contributions and provide insights on the stance of state responsibility to a low conception of causation.
Art 39 DARS reads as follows:

> In the determination of reparation, account shall be taken of the contribution to the injury by willful or negligent action or omission of the injured State or any person or entity concerning whom reparation is sought.[349]

Apart from the terminology, it is difficult to assess whether the 'contribution' in Art. 39 DARS indicates a causation-based provision or is purely liability-based. The latter is the case when one interprets Art. 39 DARS only as a provision that determines the amount of reparations to be paid, which grants Art. 39 DARS a mere function as a norm of cost allocation and quantification. However, even if Art. 39 DARS is read solely as a cost allocation norm, there must still be a connection between the behaviour of the injured state and the damage. Mere non-causal

[346] Ibid.

[347] Ibid. 55 para 7.

[348] Nollkaemper and Jacobs (2015), pp. 25–27.

[349] Art. 39 DARS.

correlations cannot be imputed to the state in such a way as to reduce the damage and thus be detrimental. The very purpose of the norm requires that the conduct must have led to the result and the damage. Thus, a causal element is to be read into the provision and concurrently into the reference to contribution. This does not have to be done within the framework of counterfactuals. Especially since state responsibility and international law as such are rather restrictive in their treatment of the doctrine of counterfactual causation.[350] That the 'contribution' is thus a standardization of factual causation is, however, undeniable with regard to its implementation in Art. 39 DARS.[351]

Although Art. 39 DARS does not entail a normatively-induced threshold concurrent to national jurisdictions such as 'material' or 'substantial', the phrase '*account shall be taken*' indicates the implementation of normative criteria, including a certain materiality threshold.[352] The extent to which the injured State must contribute to its injury in order for a contribution to be considered substantial within the meaning of Art. 39 DARS must be decided on a case-by-case basis.[353] For the factual determination of causation, the scope of the contribution, however, is negligible.

Art. 39 DARS can also prove to be relevant for climate lawsuits, assuming that climate litigation is brought before international courts.[354] With every state emitting greenhouse gas emissions and promoting or at least tolerating climate-damaging behaviour such as deforestation and climate-positive land usage, every state is, in fact, 'contributing' to climate change and climate change-induced damages. However, whether Art. 39 DARS will be invoked in the climate change context depends on the individual case and the scope of its contribution. One of the cases in which a contribution of the injured state was included in the considerations by the ICJ was the *LaGrand case (Germany v. The United States of America),* in which the Court considered the "*manner in which these proceedings were filed and [...] their timing.*"[355] However, due to the small number of climate cases before the ICJ and other international courts in which Art. 39 DARS can be applied, the practical relevance of the norm and its determination by the courts for climate scenarios remains rather low. Should states, though, seek compensation for climate-related damage before the ICJ, as Vanuatu's campaign partly aims to do, Art. 39 DARS will become highly relevant.[356]

---

[350] See for causation in international law Sects. 3.2.2 and 3.2.3.

[351] In favour of reading causation into the term 'contribution' inherent in Art. 39 DARS, Stern (2010), p. 570. Also Orakhelashvili (2022), pp. 104–105.

[352] International Law Commission (2001), p. 110, para 5.

[353] In this regard also Voigt (2016), p. 489; International Law Commission (2001), p. 110, para 5.

[354] Voigt (2016), pp. 486–489.

[355] International Court of Justice, 27 June 2001 – I. C. J. Reports 2001, p. 466 *LaGrand (Germany v. United States of America)*, 487, para 57.

[356] Vanuatu ICJ Initiative , Resolution 77/276 on the request for an advisory opinion of the International Court of Justice on the obligations of States in respect of climate change, 2023.

Art. 25 No. 2 lit. b DARS also entails a contributing aspect, stating that "*in any case, necessity may not be invoked by a State as a ground for precluding wrongfulness if: [...] (b) The State has contributed to the situation of necessity.*"[357] The evaluations here are very similar to Art. 39 DARS. Besides the fact that Art. 25 DARS entails a causal dimension at least partly as well, the provision also lacks an explicit normative restriction regarding the scope of the required contribution. However, due to the terminology, it is obvious that a substantial contribution is not a prerequisite of the provision.[358] Still, in contrast to Art. 39 DARS, in which the contribution is to be assessed on a case-by-case basis, the ILC clearly stated that the contributing factor in Art. 25 DARS must be of a certain materiality. Merely minor or accidental acts or omissions do not invoke lit. b and therefore do not exclude the defence of necessity.[359]

In general, international law does not seem to be averse to the idea of mere contribution-based causation. In addition to the Draft Articles provided by the International Law Commission, the ICJ in its *Bosnian genocide* case showed that counterfactualism is not necessarily authoritative in international law.[360] In the respective case, the ICJ had to address the question of how to deal with multiple conditions that are neither necessary nor sufficient in themselves. Again, the Court accepted that the State acted causally, while recognising that the State could not have acted on its own to stop and prevent the events from occurring.[361]

From the assessment of the concept of a contribution-based standard of causation in the law of state responsibility, it can at least be concluded that the law is not averse to lowering strict notions of causation and moving away from a conventional counterfactual test of specific causation. Moreover, a mere contribution to the outcome of an event may be sufficient to establish causation in special cases. Nevertheless, an explicit contribution-based approach to causation cannot be derived from the law of state responsibility. However, international law at least does not stand in the way of softening strict approaches based on strong necessity criteria.

[357] Art. 25 No. 2 lit. b DARS came into play, for example, in International Court of Justice, 25 September 1997 – I. C. J. Reports 1997, p. 7, *Gabčíkovo-Nagymaros Project (Hungary v. Slovakia)*, esp. para 57.

[358] Kolb (2017), pp. 131–132.

[359] International Law Commission (2001), p. 84, para 20.

[360] International Court of Justice, 26 February 2007 – ICJ Reports 2007 p. 43, *Application of the Convention on the Prevention and Punishment of the Crime of Genocide (Bosnia and Herzegovina v. Serbia and Montenegro)*.

[361] Ibid.

4.5.2.2.3 Lessons Drawn from Domestic and International Approaches to Contributory Causation

4.5.2.2.3.1 Jurisdiction and Area of Law

National and international jurisprudence has shown that reducing the factual causal conception to a mere contribution-based approach and refraining from factors such as necessity and sufficiency can and certainly has been applied in practice. Most of such deviations, however, have been located in common law or international jurisdictions rather than on a universal, worldwide level. Concurrently to the results obtained in regard to a generally reduced threshold of causation, the previous analysis has shown that also in regard to climate claims, civil law countries are more likely to obtain counterfactual tests, which in turn more often leads to the rejection of factual causation.[362] The reason for both findings builds upon the fundamental difference between the two legal systems and highlights the benefits of applying a case-law-based system which is more agile in responding quickly to new challenges than more donnish civil law systems.

In terms of the dominant area of law, reduced standards of causation have been applied predominantly in the private law sphere, with tort cases being at the forefront of the development of a mere contribution-based conception of factual causation. Other areas of law have so far only restrictively developed or even adopted a similar contribution-based approach. However, especially in international and regional law, different understandings of causation, including weakened conceptions of factual causation, have been applied, although not in a dogmatic and conceptually coherent manner. In addition, terminological discrepancies and inconsistencies have further complicated the analysis, which is why private law, and in particular tort law, still dominates the debate on different standards of causation. In the field of tort law, the emphasis on contributory causation ultimately lies in cases of negligence, with a further preponderance in cases of clinical and medical negligence. And even in international and regional law, the reduction of the causation standard is mainly limited to issues of liability and fault rather than being recognised as a universal approach.

4.5.2.2.3.2 Raison D'Être

The dominance of negligence and tort cases is due, in particular, to the demanding requirements of the claims and the burden of proof placed on the plaintiff to obtain compensation for alleged damages. All domestic approaches have in common that under the strict application of counterfactual approaches (more specifically, the but-for test), causation would have to be denied. The rejection of counterfactual causation thereby rests in the inability to prove a continuous causal chain. The establishment of counterfactual causation is thereby usually hindered by scientific

---

[362] See for the analysis Sect. 3.4.

uncertainty about the 'true' causer of the event or the influence of numerous different contributions by different actors. The raison d'être behind the establishment of causation, despite its inability to cohere with counterfactual tests, however, stems from the fact that courts nevertheless considered actual causation as given. In the attempt to comply with the actual, factual causal status, they adapted their considerations respectively. Lowering the threshold of causation is, therefore, a means to better reflect reality, factuality and the actual truth.

4.5.2.2.3.3 Mode of Action

The function of the aforementioned contribution-based conceptions is, in contrast to their raison d'être, quite diverse. The Canadian approach remains to be the most narrow in many respects. It merely constitutes a way of overcoming counterfactually lacking causation by finding liability nonetheless. In bridging the gap of causation, the Canadian material contribution to risk test can rather be considered a liability approach than a concept of causation. The Canadian model is, thus, not in itself a test of causation. Representing the other extreme is the American substantial factor test, which advocates an adaptation of the traditional but–for test and ultimately leads to the establishment of causation per se. Finally, the British tests form the middle ground by allowing the contribution-based test to be applied as an exception to traditional causal approaches in individual cases. They, therefore, constitute a second test of causation rather than an adaptation as the equivalent American concept is perceived. However, the precondition for their application is the primary failure of the but-for test. Arguably, both tests, the material contribution to risk test and the material contribution test, are concepts that do not merely bridge a lack of causation but lead to the establishment of such per se. The same can be said for the approach manifested in the Draft Articles on State Responsibility. While the terminology does, however, not indicate an explicit approach, great consensus persists on the fact that the contribution in Art. 39 DARS constitutes a test of factual causation or at least involves some form of causal concretization.

4.5.2.2.3.4 Preconditions of Contributory Causation

As with the function of the various tests, Canada is the most demanding in terms of the application and scope of the approach. The Court made it clear that the material contribution to risk test can only be applied in exceptional cases, which must also meet a number of different criteria. These include the presence of two or more tortfeasors and an act or condition beyond the control of the plaintiff.[363] Particularly with regard to the first condition, the different approaches are quite consistent. Scientific uncertainty about causation is decisively shaped by the existence of multiple causal contributions. However, the approaches vary in terms of the specific

[363] Supreme Court of Canada, 8 February 2007 – 1 S.C.R. 333, 2007 SCC 7, *Resurfice Corp. v. Hanke*, Supreme Court of Canada, 29 June 2012 – [2012] 2 R.C.S, *Clements v. Clements*.

scenario of causal overdetermination envisaged. While the British material contribution to risk test depicts cases of alternative causation, the material contribution test is particularly applicable to cases of cumulative causation. Although both tests involve multiple tortfeasors, their applicability to climate scenarios has shown that courts use the scope of the condition, i.e. whether they are sufficient or not for the specific outcome, as a decisive criterion in their application, which in turn may hinder their implementation. Beyond the multi-stakeholder component, the approaches also differ in their further preconditions. The British material contribution tests, for example, presuppose the immediacy of the action in question, whereas the same requirement has not been posed for the British material contribution to risk tests in the case law in question.[364] Case law is also very vague on the substantial factor test. It is almost impossible to lay down specific requirements or conditions for its application because of the wide variety of ways and standards in which it has been applied in US case law. While some courts apply a rather strict concept of the substantial factor, most courts still favour a highly flexible and, therefore, inconsistent account.

4.5.2.2.3.5 Obstacles to the Application of a Contribution-Based Approach

The inherent dangers in the application of a contributory approach are illustrated in particular by the American attempt to reduce the high standard of causation. Its vagueness and ambiguity, and the associated legal uncertainty and risk of abuse, formed part of the reasons why the approach was abandoned by the (Third) Restatements of Torts. However, some courts still refuse to follow the ALI's recommendation and continue to rely on the substantial factor test. In addition, although regional and international approaches also tend towards a reduced understanding of causation, the concepts employed in this regard tend to be vague in their formulation, which in turn makes them difficult to apply for both courts and litigants. They also lack statutory framing, as such concepts are usually either developed in case law or based on mere scholarly interpretation. Another obstacle to the application of existing contributory concepts remains their limitation to specific situations of either cumulative or alternative causation. Apart from the American approach, the Canadian and the two British accounts are very narrow in their scope.

4.5.2.2.3.6 Analogy and Transferability to Climatic Scenarios

The raison d'être and function of existing concepts of contributory causation seem to be closely related to climatic conditions. Cases of clinical and medical negligence are highly comparable to climate lawsuits due to their consistent lack of evidence and scientific uncertainties, even though the actual causal link is either a given fact or based on a delimitable group of possible causers. The latter factor, in particular,

[364] See for the requirement of immediacy House of Lords, 20 June 2002 – UKHL 22, *Fairchild v. Glenhaven Funeral Services Ltd.*

refers to another comparable aspect, namely the involvement of a large number of actors. Whether these causal scenarios represent cases of cumulative or alternative causation does not stand in the way of transferring concepts of contributory causation to climate scenarios.

In practice, however, transferring contributory approaches has largely failed so far. Especially the elaborations in the case *Minister for the Environment v. Sharma* and *Smith v. Fonterra Co-Operative Group Limited* show that the respective Courts ruled on a lack of specific comparability of climatic cases to contributory tests. As to the transfer of the contribution-based approaches to other climate litigation lawsuits and, with respect to both negatively evaluated decisions, the application does not seem very likely at this stage in time. This is true, at least in the relevant Oceanic jurisdictions. The Canadian case *Lho'imggin et al. v. Her Majesty the Queen* was also not decided based on the proposed contribution-based approaches, but unlike the Australian cases, the Court left more room for future devolution of a reduced standard of causation. However, the Court's engagement with the contribution-based approach also shows that a transfer or a lower conception of causation, in general, is not ruled out a priori. The climate cases in which a transfer of the yet existing contributory concepts was attempted only constitute a small number of lawsuits at a very early stage of climatic causal law development. However, the reasoning of the courts also shows that an exact transfer is confronted with considerable hurdles. Therefore, instead of transferring already existing approaches, courts might be more open to developing a new climate and contribution-based approach. This not only allows the development of an approach that is tailored to specific climatic conditions but also avoids the problem of dealing with the requirements of existing yet established conceptions. The extent to which this is feasible from a dogmatic and metaphysical perspective is discussed elsewhere.[365]

4.5.2.3 Climate Case Studies

A differentiated account of factual causation in the law can not only be derived from isolated domestic approaches but can be observed in individual climate change cases, as well. In *Massachusetts v. EPA* (Sect. 4.5.2.3.1) and *Native City of Kivalina v. Exxon Mobil et al.* (Sect. 4.5.2.3.2), the Courts grappled with the issue of causation within the standing of the plaintiff. In *Maniototo Environmental Society v. Central Otago District Council* (Sect. 4.5.2.3.3), the Court had to discuss the extent to which causation plays a role as a prerequisite for a statutory definition of climate change, and in *Family Farmers and Greenpeace Germany v. Germany* (Sect. 4.5.2.3.4), the Court dealt with the requirements of causation within the establishment of a link between governmental inaction and the potential effect. How and under what conditions the Courts ultimately discussed a reduced standard of causation is discussed in the following.

[365] See in this regard Sect. 4.5.2.4.

4.5.2.3.1 Massachusetts v. EPA

In *Massachusetts v. EPA*, the plaintiffs—in this case, an association of numerous states and cities in the United States—challenged the Environmental Protection Agency (EPA) and sought monetary damages from the defendant for the harm caused by climate change in the state of Massachusetts.[366] The plaintiffs argued that the Environmental Protection Agency's failure to regulate pollutant emissions, including, in particular, the failure to regulate CO_2 emissions within the automotive industry, had led to an increase in climate change and thus also to increased damage, e.g. through fast-evolving land loss in Massachusetts accompanied by rising sea levels.

Within the case, causation became particularly interesting concerning the question of Massachusetts' standing to sue. Three requirements persist for the establishment of standing: injury, causation and redressability. The last two requirements, in particular, were at issue in the present case. The ruling was preceded by a discussion on the extent to which greenhouse gas emissions cause climate change. Although the Supreme Court ultimately left the question of the scope of the contribution open in the respective decision, it stated concerning causation:

> EPA does not dispute the existence of a causal connection between man-made greenhouse gas emissions and global warming. At a minimum, therefore, EPA's refusal to regulate such emissions contributes to Massachusetts' injuries.[367]

Thus, the Supreme Court accepted the existence of a causal chain based solely on EPA's contribution. Despite the large number of different emitters and the cumulative effect of the contributions, the Court found that concurrent conditions did not constitute an obstacle to the overall establishment of causation. The Court also rejected the drop-in-the-ocean argument concerning the argued insignificance of the emissions caused by the automotive industry.[368] In the same vein, the Court also opposed the challenge to its own jurisdiction under the political question doctrine and argued that a material cause is not required.[369] However, *Chief Justice Roberts* took a different view in his dissenting opinion and denied the standing of Massachusetts based on the contribution of other states and the merely hypothetical considerations applied by the Court. Today, the case of *Massachusetts v. EPA* and particularly its decision by the Court are one of the most significant decisions within the climate change litigation movement due to their pioneering role in many respects. Especially its approach to the determination of standing has found broad resonance in following climate cases. In *Comer v. Murphy Oil USA Inc.,* the 5th Circuit Court of Appeal revisited the reasoning in *Massachusetts v. EPA* and, based

[366] Supreme Court of the United States, 2 April 2007 – 05-1120, *Massachusetts v. EPA*.

[367] Ibid. 20.

[368] Ibid.

[369] Ibid. 20–22.

on it, also came to an affirmation of the existence of a causal chain. The Court further affirmed standing based solely on the contributions by the defendant.[370]

4.5.2.3.2 Native Village of Kivalina v. Exxon Mobil et al.

As one of the first climate litigation lawsuits, the case *Native Village of Kivalina v. Exxon Mobil et al.* initiated the wave of nuisance-related climate lawsuits.[371] The plaintiffs, the Native Village of Kivalina and the City of Kivalina, herein sued various oil and gas corporations to provide monetary compensation for the damage to their city, which resulted from a climate change-induced flood. One of the key obstacles concerning the admissibility of the claim again constituted the establishment of standing. The plaintiffs tried to do so by building on the argument of contribution.[372] In relying on previous judgments targeting the pollution of waterways and rivers under the Clean Water Act, the plaintiffs argued that "*for purposes of establishing standing, they need only allege that Defendants contributed to their injuries*".[373] However, the Court ultimately did not follow the argumentation by the plaintiffs. The Court argued that the principles developed under the Clean Water Act could not be applied to cases of air pollution and the emission of greenhouse gases. The difference between the two scenarios allegedly persisted in the requirement of a threshold imposed on a federal level. Since, in contrast to the Clean Water Act, the plaintiffs had not been able to build upon a federal limit on GHG emissions that had been exceeded by the defendant, the Judge further stated that without such a limit

> [...] no presumption arises that there is a substantial likelihood that any defendant's conduct harmed plaintiffs. Without that presumption, and especially given the extremely attenuated causation scenario alleged in Plaintiffs' Complaint, is it entirely irrelevant whether any defendant contributed to the harm because a discharge, standing alone, is insufficient to establish injury.[374]

Today, however, this case would have been judged differently on the same grounds. Given that a large number of countries have committed themselves to reduce emissions, at least under the Paris Agreement, and have set emission reduction targets and maximum charges for some industrial sectors at the national level, a violation and, thus, an affirmation would have been anticipated, at least if the respective targets had been exceeded. However, e contrario to the reasoning of the

[370] US Court of Appeals for the 5th Circuit, 28 May 2010 – 07-60756, *Ned Comer et al. v. Murphy Oil USA, Inc., et al*, opinion (16 October 2009), 10–11.

[371] US District Court for the Northern District of California, 30 September 2009 – 4:08-cv-01138-SBA, *Native Village of Kivalina v. ExxonMobil Corp.*

[372] Ibid. order (30 September 2009), 16–19.

[373] Ibid. order (30 September 2009), 16. Previous judgments especially referred to United States Court of Appeals, Third Circuit, 20 August 1990 – 89-5831, 89-5851, 89-5861, *P.I.R.G. et al. v. Powell Duffryn Terminals Inc.*

[374] US District Court for the Northern District of California, 30 September 2009 – 4:08-cv-01138-SBA, *Native Village of Kivalina v. ExxonMobil Corp.*, 19.

Court in the current case, and under the presumption of the fulfilled threshold requirements, the decision does not exclude the sufficiency of a mere contribution for the standing of the plaintiff. Presupposed, however, is a regulation at the federal level comparable to the Clean Water Act.

4.5.2.3.3 Maniototo Environmental Society v. Central Otago District Council

In a classic anti-climate change case, the plaintiffs in *Maniototo Environmental Society v. Central Otago District* challenged the resource consents granted in connection with the construction of a new wind farm by Meridian Energy Ltd.[375] The plaintiffs relied on an impact assessment which they claimed to be flawed, arguing that the disadvantages and the negative impacts associated with the construction of a wind farm were not sufficiently considered. To evaluate the positive effects of a wind farm in light of their negative impacts on the environment, biodiversity and the landscape, the Environment Court, in the first instance, carried out a cost-benefit assessment. In the course of the evaluation, the Court also dealt with Section 7 (i) of the Resource Management Act, which states that

> (i)n achieving the purpose of this Act, all persons exercising functions and powers under it, in relation to managing the use, development, and protection of natural and physical resources, shall have particular regard to— [...] (i) the effects of climate change: [...].[376]

Central to the new assessment by the Court formed the question of the right definition of the term ‘climate change’ under the RMA. It was, in particular, at dispute whether the definition required a causal link between the human activity and the alteration of the composition of the atmosphere or whether a mere contribution to the anthropogenic changes was sufficient under Section 7 (i). In this regard, the Court stated:

> We consider if a party reasonably attributes changes to the composition of the global atmosphere to human activity then it falls within the definition of climate change for the purpose of the Act.[377]

The Environment Court followed up by defining climate change as “*a change: (1) that is attributed to human activity that alters the composition of the global atmosphere; and (2) that is in addition to natural variability*.”[378] It further elaborated on its deviation from strict causation requirements as a measure of establishing

---

[375] Environment Court, 28 October 2009 – [2009] NZEnvC 293, *Maniototo Environmental Society Inc. v. Central Otago District Council*.

[376] Section 7 (i) RMA.

[377] Environment Court, 28 October 2009 – [2009] NZEnvC 293, *Maniototo Environmental Society Inc. v. Central Otago District Council*, para 221.

[378] Ibid.

a relation between human activity and the composition of the global atmosphere. In this regard, the Court stated:

> We assume Parliament's intention was for local authorities to avoid scientific discussion about the existence and extent of anthropogenic climate change and get on with the local circumstances of resource consent applications.[379]

Such an understanding of the connection between human activities and changes in the combustion of the atmosphere was also confirmed by the High Court of New Zealand in the second instance.[380] The Court's comments emphasize that the Court is broadly sensitive to the demands that a causation requirement would place on local authorities. As a strict causation requirement, especially in its factual form, would require extensive scientific research and studies, which would not only be time-consuming but also financially constraining, the Court advocated a reduced standard, taking into account the efficiency and effectiveness of local authorities. These remarks are limited exclusively to the definition of climate change in Section 7 (i) RMA and have not been transferred, at least not at present, to other subject areas. However, the Court's consideration of mere attribution and its dismissal of strict causation shows a novelty in climate matters. The fact that, in the end, the effectiveness and efficiency of the procedure are weighted higher than scientific and legal-dogmatic stringency highlights the absolute necessity of alternative solutions for such complex issues and chains of causation. The endorsement of the approach by the High Court of New Zealand strengthens this view and approach once again.

4.5.2.3.4 Family Farmers and Greenpeace Germany v. Germany

In *Family Farmers and Greenpeace Germany v. Germany*, the plaintiffs—three families supported by Greenpeace—challenged the German government's failure to meet its 40% emissions reduction target.[381] The target, adopted by the German Cabinet in December 2014, called for a 40% reduction in greenhouse gas emissions by 2020 compared to the emission level of 1990. However, according to calculations, the government's efforts only led to a reduction of 32%. On this basis, the plaintiffs claimed a violation of their fundamental rights under Article 2 (2), Article 12 (1) and Article 14 of the German Constitution. However, the Administrative Court of Berlin dismissed the case in October 2021 as inadmissible for lack of standing and unfounded in any case.

What is decisive from a causative point of view, however, is not the outcome of the action itself but the Court's reasoning within its judgment. While the plaintiff's complaint was based on the assumption that causation was not required, as the

---

[379] Ibid.

[380] High Court of New Zealand, 16 August 2010 – NZHC CIV 2009 412 000980 *Maniototo Environmental Society Inc. v. Central Otago District Council*, para 157.

[381] Administrative Court of Berlin, 31 October 2019 – VG 10 K 412.18, *Family Farmers and Greenpeace Germany v. Germany*.

possibility of a violation of fundamental rights was considered sufficient for the establishment of standing, the Court argued that the claim required a "*demonstration of causation between the failure of the federal government to take further climate protection measures and an impairment of the plaintiffs' position protected by fundamental rights.*"[382] Whether the plaintiffs have sufficiently demonstrated causation as such, however, was left open by the Court. Rather, the Court stated:

> Individual legal protection concerning climate change is only conceivable if the requirements for causation between the failure to take national climate protection measures and the impact on the protected legal positions of those affected are not overstretched.[383]

Although the Court did not address the standard of causation to be applied, the statement clearly indicates that the Court distanced itself from a strict application of causation or its doctrines. In connection with the principle of common but differentiated responsibilities, the Court felt obliged to depart from traditional approaches to causation based on the complexity of the climate system and the contributions of multiple emitters. In doing so, the Court explicitly signalled a new understanding of climatic causation and set a precedent that can be followed in other court decisions. Subsequent climate cases have already referred to such a reduced standard of causation based on the reasoning in *Family Farmers and Greenpeace Germany v. Germany*.[384]

4.5.2.4 Framing a Reduced Understanding of Causation

4.5.2.4.1 The Substance of a Contribution-Based Approach

The contribution-based approach has already been introduced as a concept of a reduced standard of factual causation. As such, it accepts the qualification of different contributions as causes of a particular outcome and constitutes a multi-causal approach which concurrently distances itself from a mono-causal counterfactual perception of causation. It, thus, renders broader than traditional counterfactual concepts. From an efficiency and outcome-oriented perspective, a reduced standard of causation offers a solution to the causal obstacles posed by climate change and its scientific basis. The simplification of causal attribution has a particular impact on specific and individual causal chains, which are still the most obstructive when using traditional causal approaches. While general causation, most often depicted by the causal relata between greenhouse gas emissions and climate change or general climate-related impacts, can be scientifically established on the basis of the IPCC

[382] Ibid. 21, translation by the author. As well as ibid. statement of claim (25 October 2018), 81.

[383] Ibid. 22, translation by the author. The reasoning of the Court was adopted and reiterated e.g. in Prague Municipal Court, 15 June 2022 – 14A 101/2021, *Klimatická žaloba ČR v. Czech Republic*, para 326.

[384] See e.g. Germany Federal Constitutional Court, 24 March 2021 – 1 BvR 2656/18 – 1 BvR 78/20 – 1 BvR 96/20 – 1 BvR 288/20, *Neubauer et al. v. Germany*, para 203.

findings and, in turn, also does not pose a hurdle for the establishment of causation in the law, specific causation has often been a major issue. By not relying on counterfactualism and accepting multiple different causes, a contribution-based approach to causation avoids traditional causal hurdles, such as the dilemma that occurs in light of alternative and cumulative causes. By lowering the specific standard of causation, it thus manifests a doctrine of attenuated individualisation. It also facilitates the scientific demonstration of causal chains by not posing unintuitive requirements on the scientific assessment. Such a simplification is particularly necessary in view of the considerable scientific complexity of the climate system itself. At the same time, however, this does not detract from the legitimacy of contributory, factual causation, which nevertheless requires scientific proof. However, not only is the burden of the law eased by a reduced standard of causation but in scientific terms, the attribution of a mere contribution to the outcome also alleviates the scientific determination of results, generates a higher degree of probability of the achieved result, and considerably reduces the uncertainty factor. Moreover, in its multi-causal dimension and its distance from counterfactualism, it represents a dogma that is even closer to actual factual causation than other approaches used to date. It recognises that mono-causation is an artificially developed legal construct that has no parallel in the real world. Contributory causation, therefore, provides a further approximation to factual reality.

A reduction of the causation requirements is furthermore not unknown to domestic jurisdictions. Within most of them, however, the lowering of the causation standard functions as an exception rather than as a rule.[385] Since most of the reduced standards of causation have been developed and used in common law jurisdictions, those exceptions are usually case-law grown. While the rationale within the different national approaches is consistently the same, the requirements differ significantly in terms of the demands they place on the use of a reduced causal approach. The approaches are, to a large extent, geared to very specific scenarios of multi-causation and basically include either cumulative or alternative situations. However, such a restrictive approach does not seem to be profitable in the context of understanding climatic causation, especially since climatic causal relations are largely determined by alternative and cumulative causation. A reduction of the causation approach must, therefore, be developed comprehensively. Civil law countries have been reluctant to depart explicitly from traditional approaches by applying different concepts but have developed rather small exceptions, which are still consistent and implicit in the traditional approaches used. Those exceptions, in particular in relation to the reversal of the burden of proof, have had to be manifested in specific legislation. A comprehensive contributory approach cannot be found in any jurisdiction at present. However, the need for such relief is evident, particularly in the case law of the courts. While it is misleading to speak of a specific trend towards the adoption of a contribution-based approach, it is apparent that courts in some jurisdictions are not averse to applying a reduced standard in specific cases of aggravated individual

[385] See on this aspect Sect. 3.4.3.3.

causation. These include, in particular, the United States, England, Australia and New Zealand.[386]

4.5.2.4.2 The Metaphysical Interface of a Lowered Conception of Causation

4.5.2.4.2.1 Implementing Contributions into Traditional Concepts of Causation

The above considerations have shown that courts have already considered, and in some cases implemented, an approach to causation that imposes weaker hurdles and is similar to, or entirely based on, contribution. However, it is clear that such approaches, in contrast to more traditional approaches (counterfactual, regularity and probability-based), have grown out of the need to find a solution to outcomes that were perceived as 'unfair' under traditionally applied accounts. As such, they represent a dynamic view of factual causation and are generally not based on a metaphysical or philosophical understanding of cause-effect relationships or causes in general. The resulting lack of dogmatic and metaphysical embodiment may well be seen as one of the main reasons for their limited use and implementation. At the very least, such a downward approach excludes legal theory and philosophy from the debate and thus hinders the general discourse in jurisprudence. It also leads to a lack of legitimacy and uncertainty in the actual application of the approach, which is why courts and legal practitioners may still prefer to resort to dogmatically grounded counterfactual tests, such as the but-for test or the conditio-sine-qua-non formula. Dogmatic and metaphysical recourse is, therefore, essential for the legitimacy, general acceptance and ultimately the application of any kind of factual causal concepts. A metaphysical foundation also provides a more detailed conceptual framework for the relevant concepts, which in turn ensures the comprehensiveness and uniformity of the approach itself, as well as its application in law. In administering a conceptual framework, it also guarantees and ensures the factuality of the concept by suspending and excluding normative factors that would lead to confusion between factual and normative causation. In view of this constraint and due to the conception being an judicial-grown understanding of causation, a retrospective analysis of doctrinal and metaphysical approaches is undertaken in an attempt to grant legitimacy to the concept of contribution. It turns out that legal practice and theory have converged to a considerable extent independently of each other but both are driven by the impulse to renew traditional causal doctrines.

If a reduced standard of causation is placed in a metaphysically sound framework and makes use of the concepts of necessity and sufficiency inherent in it, it becomes apparent that contribution-based approaches do not constitute a test of strict necessity but rather are in line with tests that advocate a weak conception. According to the contribution-based approach, causal contributions may but do not essentially have to, qualify as a necessary element for the respective outcome. On the basis of its

[386] See in this regard Sect. 3.4.3.3.

multi-causal understanding, a reduced standard of causation would accept the qualification of these conditions as causes even in cases where the conditions as a whole far exceed the threshold of sufficiency and would, therefore, not in themselves be perceived as necessary for the outcome in question. At the same time, and even more so, conditions need not be qualified as individually sufficient for the outcome in question. A lowered standard of causation also accepts the existence of other sufficient conditions, which consequently also qualify as actual causes. In this way, and in correlation with the multi-causal understanding derived from it, contribution-based approaches preclude the use of counterfactual causal theories since these, as already discussed, and even in their modified form, require a strictly necessary condition and thus qualify as theories of strong necessity. Rather, it becomes clear that the qualification as a doctrine of weak necessity makes the contribution-based theory fit better into the systematics, semantics, or at least the rationale of regularity-based theories. In the absence of a comprehensive discussion and widespread application, the contribution-based approach is also hardly subject to strict formal requirements, which also supports the linkage of such an approach and the implementation of contributions in general to a regularity-based understanding of factual causation. Thus, at least from a purely conceptual point of view, and in terms of the requirements of necessity and sufficiency imposed on the respective conditions per se, contribution and regularity-based theories coincide.

The similarity of both conceptions, however, does not result in the conjecture that the metaphysical considerations behind regularity-based theories are unambiguously equivalent to contribution-based theories. In particular, the philosophical considerations of a metaphysically substantiated factual concept cannot simply be transferred to a mere case law-grown approach. Moreover, it is not a question of transforming the contribution-based approach one-to-one into a metaphysical conception. Rather, the aim is to show the proximity of the attenuated understanding to already existing multi-causal, factual conceptions of causation. Furthermore, it is intended to show that, despite its ratio based on the efficiency of the concept, a reflection into philosophical and metaphysical approaches can take place.

4.5.2.4.2.2 The Scope of Application

Given the various ways in which a reduced standard of causation has been implemented at the national and international level, its scope must now be determined within the climate framework. Two factors, in particular, are becoming increasingly relevant. On the one hand, the epistemological core of the concept is concerned with the question of whether the associated approach can only be used for general causal statements or whether it also extends to singular and specific causal relations (Sect. 4.5.2.4.2.2.1). On the other hand, and in strong reliance on the domestic approaches presented above, it has to be discussed whether the contribution-based approach should only be used exceptionally in the light of the failure of the standard causal tests or whether a fundamental application in the context of climate claims seems preferable (Sect. 4.5.2.4.2.2.2).

4.5.2.4.2.2.1 Distinguishing Between General and Singular Causal Statements

The issue of applying a reduced causal standard arises fundamentally from the metaphysical determination of causation. Within some causal conceptualisations, especially within regularity-based theories, recourse to other causal accounts within singular causal statements is occasionally called for.[387] Concurrently, a distinction between general and specific causal chains might also be conceivable for the application of contribution-based causation. In practice, however, and within the application of a reduced causal approach, such a distinction has not gained acceptance. Rather, the domestic approaches of a reduced causal conception have proved even more relevant in cases of specific, individual causation. And for reasons of effectiveness alone, the application of these principles to specific causal chains is particularly necessary in light of climatic causation. Whether an individual contribution to a specific outcome is in question or the causal chain is approached in a more generalized way is of no difference.

The question of whether there should be a distinction between singular and general causal statements ultimately results exclusively from the metaphysical substantiation of the approach. Since contribution-based theories are similar in their general conceptual structure to regularity-based theories, one would have to grapple with the problems inherent in regularity-based theories if one wanted to go further in the metaphysical and epistemological foundations of a contribution-based theory.[388] The differentiation here relates in particular to the distinction between *Mackie's* original regularity-based approach and *Wright's* further developed NESS concept. While *Mackie* does not include singular causal statements in his INUS approach and refers to traditional theories of counterfactual causation, *Wright* argues for an epistemological substantiation of singular causal relations, as well. The main argument against the application of regularity-based theories to singular causal claims is that while general claims can be grounded on the regular occurrence of events, it cannot be argued that this is the case in regard to specific causal chains. This metaphysical problem is thus strongly rooted in the nature and mode of causal epistemology rather than in the conceptual account and the use of necessity and sufficiency dogmas. For a weakened approach to causation in the light of a reference to contributions, the discussion, therefore, only arises under the implication that the developed approach is grounded entirely on an understanding of regularities as the basis for causal relations. The contribution-based approach would thus function as the practical realisation of a purely regularity-based causal dogma, which would undoubtedly secure its philosophical and metaphysical conception. Unless one goes so far as to see the contribution-based approach precisely as a practical implementation of regularity-based theories of causation, the application of the approach to singular causal relations poses no problem. Moreover, from an application perspective, the value of contribution-based theories lies precisely in their use in specific

[387] See in this regard especially Toepel (2013). Furthermore, Sect. 4.3.1.

[388] See in this regard Sect. 4.3.

causal theories, especially in the context of climatic causation. Restricting the application to general causal claims would not make a contribution-based approach any more effective. Lowering the standard of causation would also be a futile exercise. It is, thus crucial to refrain from an explicit distinction between singular and general causal claims.

4.5.2.4.2.2.2 Arguing Between Exception and Rule

The assessment of national approaches to reduced causation standards has shown that courts vary widely in the manner in which they apply reduced causation requirements. However, there is considerable convergence in the scope of their application. The British and Canadian accounts demonstrate that the material contribution tests are only an exception for cases where traditional concepts would fail and do not constitute a universal and legal rule of causation.[389] However, given the fundamental nature of causation in climate change litigation, it quickly becomes apparent that a contribution-based approach would have to be applied in almost every climate change litigation case, making it the rule rather than the exception in climate law. This is particularly the case in jurisdictions that do not use the strategy of factual concretization within counterfactual tests but rather use these accounts in their general and common way.[390] After all, a large proportion of claims on climate change are, sooner or later, based on the emission of greenhouse gases in their causal chains. This, in itself, raises the fundamental issue of cumulative causation.

In principle, natural climate variability and other influencing factors must always be taken into account when constructing the causal chain, which affects the question of alternative causation. While there may be isolated claims that do not raise such issues, it cannot be denied that courts will be faced with precisely such problems in the majority of climate claims and would, therefore, have to apply the contribution-based approach in each of these cases. Otherwise, courts would have to apply traditional counterfactual tests. The exceptional nature of the contribution-based approach would thus be reversed. While the application of the 'normal', counterfactual tests in court would thus, in practice, only occur in special cases, the contribution-based approach would then become the norm rather than the exception of the causal establishment. As a result, at least within the framework of climatic causation and as long as courts do not find other dogmatic solutions for establishing factual causation within more traditional frameworks such as under appropriated counterfactual tests, the contribution-based approach is to be advocated as a general factual causal approach in climate change litigation. It, however, might regain its exceptional status when courts acknowledge deviations from traditional factual concepts in other ways than under contributory causal dogmas.

---

[389] See Sect. 4.5.2.2.1.

[390] See in this regard the obstacles that counterfactual tests face in regard to cumulative and alternative causation Sect. 4.2.2.

4.5.2.4.3 Legislating Contributory Causation

Causation enters into legal reasoning in many different ways, be it through its explicit reference in the relevant norm, as an implicit precondition of a statute, or as a procedural or evaluative requirement.[391] What is common to all forms of transposition, however, is that they usually refrain from specifying in detail how causation is to be established. A reference to a particular causal doctrine or dogma is rarely found in legal texts. Thus, the type of causation used in most jurisdictions is not a legally established and entrenched concept. Rather, the causal dogma used by a jurisdiction is something that has developed through judicial decision-making and case law in general, and is at best explained in the accompanying commentaries. This is even more the case in common law jurisdictions, which are traditionally more statute independent. As most jurisdictions still use counterfactual tests such as the conditio-sine-qua-non formula and the but-for test, and their use is deeply rooted in the respective legal traditions, some references to the explicit formulation of the tests can be found, nevertheless. However, apart from such minor references, the causation standard is not statutorily prescribed. What is usually referred to in legal texts and norms themselves, conversely, are cases where the approach deviates from the standardised accounts. These deviations often relate to presumptions of causation and the reversal of the standard of proof, which are, therefore, regularly enshrined in the relevant legal provisions.[392]

Although a contribution-based approach neither constitutes a presumption of causation, nor a reversal of the burden of proof, it still comprises a deviation from the traditional and 'normal' understanding of the establishment of causal chains, which is why an embedment in statutory legal provisions is desirable. Given the importance of the rule of law and in the interests of legal certainty, the current conceptualisation of a climatic understanding of causation must also be enshrined in the legal text.[393] An embedment also contributes to and enhances the uniform and comprehensive application of the respective standard. It, furthermore, legitimizes the new understanding of causation in light of the dominating traditional approaches and ensures the involvement of legislative bodies, thus avoiding the objection often raised against climate claims that the courts are overstepping their jurisdiction in terms of the separation of powers.[394] It additionally opens up a broader debate on the attribution of damages and burdens caused by climate change to a wider audience, raising the level of awareness of the dangers of climate change.

---

[391] See in more detail the results of the empirical, systematic and substantive analysis in Sect. 3.4, as well as the general sources of causation in the law in Sect. 3.1.3.

[392] Deviations are often implemented in medical law provisions, see, e.g. § 630 h German Basic Law.

[393] Arguing for the necessity of a statutory basis for an ecological concept of causation, see Kohler (2017), paras 164–165. In the end, *Kohler*, argues against such a concept, given that such an approach would focus too much on the victim and does not reflect an individual account of causation.

[394] Such concern is often raised under the term the '*political-question doctrine*'.

Although quite a few major arguments speak for an implementation of the chosen approach into statutory provisions, whether this ultimately occurs is at the discretion of the respective legislator. Moreover, the implementation concerns not only regulation at the national but also at the international level. Given the global nature of climate change, the co-occurrence of causal problems in a wide range of jurisdictions, and the need for fundamental new regulation or adaptation, global regulation at the cross-jurisdictional level is not only desirable, but entirely appropriate. However, it is questionable whether such comprehensive legislation, for example in the context of the Paris Agreement, is feasible and realistic, partly because of the difficult consensus-building process. Should such a legislative project, especially on the national level, actually be carried out, difficulties further arise concerning the place of statutory embedment of the approach. Since climate change litigation occurs in every area and field of law, a provision in environmental and/or climate-specific law might be considered as falling too short. The same criticism needs to be levelled at the incorporation of the dogma into liability-specific standards. Ultimately, however, and given that legislation is highly jurisdiction-specific and can vary to a great extent, it is up to the legislator to decide where and how such a provision should be established.

4.6 Summary of Findings

Factual causation constitutes the first step of the bifurcated approach to causation in the law. It serves as the basis for further socio-legal and normatively influenced causal considerations, intending to anchor causation in the law on the grounds of actual, factual and scientific causal relata. In order to translate factual causation into an applicable and usable causal doctrine in law, two ways of approaching such an understanding of causation have emerged. On the one hand, and arguably the more traditional way, doctrines have been constructed and developed on the basis of metaphysical and legal philosophical conceptions of causal relations. Such theories persist given their strong philosophical grounding, which gives them particular legitimacy and metaphysical maturity. On the other hand, and especially recently, so-called 'backward-looking', dynamic concepts of factual causation have emerged and are increasingly promoted. Such concepts are not initially based on metaphysical considerations but are developed out of the need to adapt dysfunctional traditional approaches.

The most common approach in practice and across jurisdictions relies on a counterfactual understanding of causation and is expressed in the form of the conditio-sine-qua-non formula, used mainly in civil law jurisdictions, and the but-for test, used mainly in the common law realm. Despite its widespread use, there are significant obstacles to its application in climate lawsuits. Those, in particular, result out of the mono-causal conception of the doctrines, the cumulative nature of greenhouse gas emissions and further contributions to climate change as well as alternating causes. However, a solution to this problem could be provided by a factual concretization of counterfactual causal chains, which has already been proposed and employed in some jurisdictions. Nevertheless, in order to ensure the legitimacy of the concretization and to avoid circularity, it is crucial that only legally relevant factors are used in the application of the approach.

A second way of establishing factual causation in law is based on an understanding of regularities and frequent occurrences. With the NESS and the INUS test being the dominant legal doctrines developed on the base of this account, those approaches persist due to their proximity to the actual, factual and scientific truth. As multi-causal concepts, they are better equipped to deal with climatic causal chains than is the case with mono-causal, counterfactual approaches to causation in the law. Although counterfactual approaches have prevailed in practice so far, some reasoning by courts, also in the climate context, indicates a shift towards a regularity-based conception of causation. Nevertheless, metaphysical indifferences still hinder a universal adoption of such a causal understanding.

The third metaphysically grounded account of causation refers to a determination of causation based on an increase in probabilities. The probabilistic approach to causation appeals due to its similarity to scientific fact-finding. It also represents the causal approach closest to actual, factual causation and is, therefore, widely advocated in climate matters and in relation to the science of probabilistic event attribution. However, in contrast to the other two metaphysically based approaches, the probabilistic account remains the concept that faces the greatest obstacles in terms of its legal application. Because of its close connection to climate science, which goes hand in hand with a considerable dependence on the methodology and verifiability of climatic findings, the scientific difficulties, especially with regard to attribution science, also have a major impact on the legal determination of causation. Nonetheless, as climate data becomes more accessible and scientific methods improve, a probabilistic approach to causation will become increasingly feasible and thus appealing to the law.

Besides the metaphysically grounded, more traditional approaches of factual causation, two dynamic accounts have just recently emerged in the context of climate change litigation. The market share liability doctrine in the form of an emission share causation doctrine and a purely contribution-based approach. However, the analysis has indicated that the former is not viable for establishing causation in climate change litigation. A transfer of the case law per se, in which the doctrine was developed, fails due to the indefinability and obscurity of all potential tortfeasors, as well as the existence of different kinds of multi-causal conceptions. Even attempts to adopt the mere rationale of the concept and to establish a construct detached from its jurisprudential original results in major difficulties, in particular in light of the correct market and, more abstractly, with its delimitation in general. The doctrine of market share liability has thus not proved to be fundamentally applicable to the determination of causation in the law. The contribution-based approach, therefore, offers the most promising dynamic conception of factual causation in law. The preceding sections have shown that similar models already exist—particularly in common law jurisdictions and international law—and that the implications of the principles of international environmental law also support and encourage such an approach. Ultimately, however, its legal legitimacy will require not only its dogmatic and legal but also its metaphysical resonance.

The foregoing has shown that, in the context of the pending climate crisis and the causal obstacles inherent in it, there is no 'one-size-fits-all' approach to factual causation. Rather, several different concepts offer a solution to the problem of causation, all, nonetheless, entailing their own problems and difficulties. Regulatory frameworks will determine whether a given approach is implemented. As a result, the approaches adopted may well differ from jurisdiction to jurisdiction, depending on how well a legal system is equipped to deal with the relevant adaptations and implement them in its legal framework. The availability and processing of climate science, however, will be critical to the success of any factual approach to causation in law.

Climate Change Cases

A Request for an Advisory Opinion from the Inter-American Court of Human Rights Concerning the Interpretation of Article 1(1), 4(1) and 5(1) of the American Convention on Human Rights – Inter-American Court on Human Rights, 15 November 2017 – OC-23/17

City of Oakland v. BP p.l.c. – United States District Court For the Northern District of California, pending – 3:17-cv-06011

Family Farmers and Greenpeace Germany v. Germany – Administrative Court of Berlin, 31 October 2019 – VG 10 K 412.18

Future Generations v. Ministry of the Environment and Others – Supreme Court of Colombia, 8 April 2018 – 11001-22-03-000-2018-00319-01

Gabčíkovo-Nagymaros Project (Hungary v. Slovakia) – International Court of Justice, 25 September 1997 – I. C. J. Reports 1997, p. 7

Gloucester Resources Limited v. Minister for Planning – New South Wales Land and Environment Court, 8 February 2019 – [2019] NSWLEC 7

Klimatická žaloba ČR v. Czech Republic – Prague Municipal Court, 15 June 2022 – 14A 101/2021

Lho'imggin et al. v. Her Majesty the Queen – Federal Court Canada, 16 November 2020 – 2020 FC 1059

Luciano Lliuya v. RWE AG – Essen Regional Court, 15 December 2016 – 2 O 285/15

Luciano Lliuya v. RWE AG – Higher Regional Court Hamm, pending – 5 U 15/17

Maniototo Environmental Society Inc. v. Central Otago District Council – High Court of New Zealand, 16 August 2010 – NZHC CIV 2009 412 000980

Massachusetts v. EPA – Supreme Court of the United States, 2 April 2007 – 05-1120

Maniototo Environmental Society Inc. v. Central Otago District Council – Environment Court, 28 October 2009 – [2009] NZEnvC 293

Milieudefensie et al. v. Royal Dutch Shell plc. – Hague District Court, 26 May 2021 – C/09/571932 / HA ZA 19-379

Minister for the Environment v. Sharma – Federal Court of Australia, 15 March 2022 – [2022] FCAFC 35
Native Village of Kivalina v. ExxonMobil Corp. – US District Court for the Northern District of California, 30 September 2009 – 4:08-cv-01138-SBA
Ned Comer et al. v. Murphy Oil USA, Inc., et al. – US Court of Appeals for the 5th Circuit, 28 May 2010 – 07-60756
Neubauer et al. v. Germany – Germany Federal Constitutional Court, 24 March 2021 – 1 BvR 2656/18 – 1 BvR 78/20 – 1 BvR 96/20 – 1 BvR 288/20
Sacchi et al. v. Argentina et al. – United Nations Committee on the Rights of the Child, 8 October 2021 – CRC/C/88/D/107/2019
Sharma and others v. Minister for the Environment – Federal Court of Australia, 27 May 2021 – [2021] FCA 560
Smith v. Fonterra Co-Operative Group Limited – High Court of New Zealand, 21 October 2021 – [2021] NZCA 552
Urgenda Foundation v. The State of The Netherlands – Supreme Court of the Netherlands, 20 December 2019 – 19/00135

Cases

Al-Skeini and others v. The United Kingdom – European Court of Human Rights, 7 July 2011 – 55721/07
Application of the Convention on the Prevention and Punishment of the Crime of Genocide (Bosnia and Herzegovina v. Serbia and Montenegro) – International Court of Justice, 26 February 2007 – ICJ Reports 2007 p. 43
Bonnington Castings Ltd. Wardlaw – House of Lords, 25 March 1995 – [1956] AC 613
Clements v. Clements – Supreme Court of Canada, 29 June 2012 – [2012] 2 R.C.S
Collins v. Eli Lilly & Co. – Supreme Court of Wisconsin, 4 January 1984 – 82-1844
Compagnia Italiana Alcool v. Commission – European Court of Justice, 7 April 1992 – C-358/90
Daubert v. Merrell Dow Pharmaceuticals – United States Supreme Court, 28 June 1993 – 509 U.S. 579
Fairchild v. Glenhaven Funeral Services Ltd. – House of Lords, 20 June 2002 – UKHL 22
Forest Dieback – Federal Court of Justice, 10 December 1987 – III ZR 220/86
General Electric Co. v. Joiner – United States Supreme Court, 15 December 1997 – 522 U.S. 136
Hanke v. Resurfice Corp – Court of Queen's Bench of Alberta; Judicial district of Edmonton, 22 July 2003 – ABQB 616
Hanke v. Resurfice Corp – Court of Appeal of Alberta, 7 November 2005 – ABCA 383
Hymowith v. Eli Lilly & Co. – New York Court of Appeals, 4 April 1989 – 539 N. E.2d 1069

In Re: Methy Tertiary Butyl Ether (MTBE) Products Liability Litigation – United States Court of Appeals, 26 July 2013 – 10–4135–cv (L), 10–4329–cv (XAP)
Kumho Tire Co. v. Carmichael, – United States Supreme Court, 23 March 1999 – 526 U.S. 137
LaGrand (Germany v. United States of America) – International Court of Justice, 27 June 2001 – I. C. J. Reports 2001, p. 466
Loizidou v. Turkey – European Court of Human Rights, 18 December 1996 – 15318/89
Martin v. Abbot Laboratories – Washington Supreme Court, 4 October 1984 – 49359-6
McGhee v. National Coal Board – House of Lords, 15 November 1972 – 1 WLR 1
P.I.R.G. et al. v. Powell Duffryn Terminals Inc. – United States Court of Appeals, Third Circuit, 20 August 1990 – 89-5831, 89-5851, 89-5861
Responsabilité de l'Allemagne en raison des actes commis postérieurement au 31 juillet 1914 et avant que le Portugal ne participât a la guerre (Portugal v. Allemagne) (Naulilaa), 30 June 1930 – 2 R.I.A.A. 1035
Resurfice Corp. v. Hanke – Supreme Court of Canada, 8 February 2007 – 1 S.C.R. 333, 2007 SCC 7
R. v. J.-L.J. – Supreme Court Canada, 10 December 2000 – 2 S.C.R. 600
Sindell v. Abbott Laboratories – Supreme Court of California, 20 March 1980 – 607 P.2d 924
Smith v. Eli Lilly & Co. – Supreme Court of Illinois, 3 July 1990 – 137 Ill. 2d 222 (Ill. 1990); 560 N.E.2d 324
United States v. Canada (Trail Smelter Case) – Arbitrational Tribunal, 16 April 1938, 11 March 1941 – 3 R.I.A.A. 1905
Van Den Bergh En Jurgens v. Commission – European Court of Justice, 11 March 1987 – C-265/85

References

Althammer C, Tolani M (2019) Proof of causation in German tort law. In: Tichý L (ed) Standard of proof in Europe. Mohr Siebeck, Tübingen, pp 109–121
American Law Institute (2010) Restatements of the law third, torts: liability for physical and emotional harm. St. Paul, Minnesota
Antkowiak TM, Gonza A (2017) The American Convention on Human Rights. Oxford University Press, Oxford
Baldwin RA (2003) A structural model interpretation of Wright's NESS Test. Thesis, University of Saskatchewan
Baumgartner M (2008) Regularity theories reassessed. Philos 36:327–354
Baumgartner M (2013) A regularity theoretic approach to actual causation. Erkenntnis 78:85–109
Becht AC, Miller FW (1961) Test of factual causation in negligence and strict liability cases. Washington Universiy, Washington
Beebee H (2004) Causing and nothingness. In: Collins J, Hall N, Paul LA (eds) Causation and counterfactuals. MIT Press, Cambridge, pp 291–308
Bentham J (1789) An introduction to the principles of morals and legislation. London

Biber E (2009) Climate change, causation, and delayed harm. Hofstra Law Rev 37(4):975–983
Birnbacher D, Hommen D (2012) Negative Kausalität. De Gruyter, Berlin
Böhm I (2021) Staatsklimahaftung – Die klimarechtliche Verantwortlichkeit Deutschlands und der EU. Nomos, Baden-Baden
Braig KF, Panov S (2020) The doctrine of positive obligations as a starting point for climate litigation in Strasbourg: The European Court of Human Rights as a Hilfssheriff in Combating Climate Change? J Environ Law Litig 35:261–298
Brand O (2022) § 249 BGB. In: Gsell B, Krüger W, Lorenz S, Remann C (eds) beck-online Grosskommentar
Burger M, Wentz J, Horton R (2020) The law and science of climate change attribution. Colum J Environ Law 45(1):60–240
Canale D (2020) Three concepts of probabilistic causation in the law. J Inst Theor Econ 176(1):18–26
Cartwright N (1979) Causal laws and effective strategies. Nous 13:419–437
Casati R, Varzi A (2023) Events. Available via The Stanford Encyclopedia of Philosophy. https://plato.stanford.edu/archives/fall2023/entries/events/. Accessed 24 Oct 2024
Chatzinerantzis A, Appel M (2019) Haftung für den Klimawandel. Neue Jur Wochenschau 13:881–886
David H, McCague WP, Yaniszewski PF (2005) Proving causation where the but for test is unworkable. Advocates' Q 30(2):216–238
Davis WA (1988) Probabilistic theories of causation. In: Fetzer JH (ed) Probability and causality. Kluwer Academic Publishers, Dordrecht, pp 133–160
Dijk C v (2011) Civil liability for global warming in the Netherlands. In: Faure M, Peeters M (eds) Climate change liability. Edward Elgar Publishing, Cheltenham, p 206-226
Duffy M (2009) Climate change causation: harmonizing tort law and scientific probability. Temp J Sci Tech Environ Law 28(2):185–242
Dupré J (1993) The disorder of things – metaphysical foundations of the disunity of science. Harvard University Press, Cambridge
Eells E (1988) Probabilistic causal interaction and disjunctive causal factors. In: Fetzer JH (ed) Probability and causality. D. Reidel Publishing Company, Dordrecht, pp 189–209
Eells E (1991) Probabilistic causality. Cambridge University Press, Cambridge
Eisele J (2016) § 10. In: Baumann J, Weber U, Mitsch W, Eisele J (eds) Strafrecht Allgemeiner Teil, 12th edn. Gieseking, Bielefeld, pp 190–247
Fisher D (1992) Causation in fact in omission cases. Utah Law Rev 1992(4):1335–1384
Flume JW (2022) § 249 BGB. In: Hau W, Poseck R (eds) Beck Online Kommentar, 63rd edn.
Frank W (2013) Klimahaftung und Kausalität. Z Umweltr:28–32
Freund G (2020) Vorb. § 13. In: Erb V, Schäfer J (eds) Münchner Kommentar zum Strafgesetzbuch – Band 1, 4th edn. C. H. Beck, Munich, pp 438–605
Friedland E (1984) Pollution share liability. Colum J Environ Law 9(2):297–320
Frisch W (2011) Objektive Zurechnung des Erfolgs – Entwicklung, Grundlinien und offene Fragen der Lehre von der Erfolgszurechnung. Jurist Schul:205–211
Fumerton R, Kress K (2001) Causation and the law: preemption, lawful sufficiency, and causal sufficiency. Law Contemp Probl 64(4):83–105
Galway S, McKee G (2016) Causation in Canada Revisited: material contribution to risk and the impact of Clements (litigation guardian of) v. Clements. Def Couns J:487–495
Garner BA (ed) (2009) Black's Law Dictionary. West Publishing, Saint Paul, MN
Giere R (1980) Causal systems and statistical hypotheses. In: Cohen LJ, Hesse M (eds) Applications of inductive logic. Clarendon Press, Oxford, pp 251–270
Glynn L (2011) A probabilistic analysis of causation. Br J Philos Sci 62(2):343–392
Greinert J (2007) Der Beweis der Kausalität bei der Umwelthaftung. Nomos, Marburg
Griffin P (2017) The Carbon Majors Database CDP Carbon Majors Report 2017. London
Grimm DJ (2007) Global warming and market share liability: a proposed model for allocating tort damages among CO_2 producers. Colum J Environ Law 32:209–250

Haas V (2002) Kausalität und Rechtsverletung: Ein Beitrag zu den Grundlagen strafrechtlicher Erfolgshaftung am Beispiel des Abbruchs rettender Kausalverläufe. Duncker & Humblot, Berlin
Hansen R (2011) Fullowka v. Pinkerton's of Canada LTD. and the material-contribution test for factual causation in negligence. Alta Law Rev 48(3):771–782
Hart HLA, Honoré T (1959) Causation in the law. Oxford University Press, Oxford
Hart HLA, Honoré T (1985) Causation in the law. Oxford University Press, New York
Heede R (2014a) Carbon majors: accounting for carbon and methane emissions 1854-2010 methods & results report. Lambert Academic Publishing, London
Heede R (2014b) Tracing anthropogenic carbon dioxide and methane emissions to fossil fuel and cement producers, 1854-2010. Clim Chang 112:229–241
Hennebel L, Tigroudja H (2022) The American Convention on Human Rights – a commentary. Oxford University Press, Oxford
Hensley CW, Robinson DC (2013) Causation: Giving Teeth to the "Substantial Factor" Analysis. Available via Frost Brown Todd. https://frostbrowntodd.com/causation-giving-teeth-to-the-substantial-factor-analysis/. Accessed 24 Oct 2024
Hesslow G (1976) Two notes on the probabilistic approach to causality. Philos Sci 43(2):290–292
Hitchchock C (2021) Probabilistic causation. Available via Stanford Encyclopedia of Philosophy. https://plato.stanford.edu/entries/causation-probabilistic/. Accessed 24 Oct 2024
Hogg M (2011) Developing causal doctrine. In: Goldberg R (ed) Perspective on causation. Hart Publishing, Oxford, pp 41–56
Holger A, Guenther M (2021) Regularity and inferential theories of causation. Available via Stanford Encyclopedia of Philosophy. https://plato.stanford.edu/cgi-bin/encyclopedia/archinfo.cgi?entry=causation-regularity. Accessed 24 Oct 2024
Hume D (1975) Enquiries concerning human understanding and concerning the principles of morals. Oxford University Press, Oxford
Hume D (1978) A treatise of human nature. Oxford University Press, Oxford
Infantino M, Zervogianni E (eds) (2017) Causation in European tort law. Cambridge University Press, Cambridge
International Law Commission (2001) Draft Articles on Responsibility of States for Internationally Wrongful Acts, with Commentaries, A/CN.4/SER.A/2001/Add.1 (Part 2). Yearb ILC 2(2):30–143
IPCC (2021) Climate Change 2021: The Physical Science Basis – Contribution of Working Group I to the Sixth Assessment Report of the Intergovernmental Panel on Climate Change. Geneva
IPCC (2023) Climate Change 2023: Synthesis Report – Contribution of Working Groups I, II and III to the Sixth Assessment Report of the Intergovernmental Panel on Climate Change – Summary for Policymakers. Geneva
Johann C (2022) Art. 1 EMRK. In: Karpenstein U, Mayer FC, Aichele V (eds) Konvention zum Schutz der Menschenrechte und Grundfreiheiten – Kommentar, 3rd edn. C. H. Beck, Munich, pp 46–67
Kahl V (2022) A human right to climate protection – necessary protection or human rights proliferation. Neth Q Hum Rights 40(2):158–179
Kaminskaitė-Salters G (2011) Climate change litigation in the UK: its feasibility and prospects. In: Faure M, Peeters M (eds) Climate change liability. Edward Elgar Publishing, Cheltenham, pp 165–188
Kelmann M (1987) The necessary myth of objective causation judgments in liberal political theory. Chic-Kent Law Rev 63(3):579–637
Kohler J (2017) Einleitung zum Umwelthaftungsrecht. In: Kohler J (ed) J. von Staudingers Kommentar zum Bürgerlichen Gesetzbuch mit Einführungsgesetzen und Nebengesetzen – Buch 2. Sellier & Co, de Gruyter, Berlin, pp 1–363
Kolb R (2017) The international law of state responsibility – an introduction. Edward Elgar Publishing, Cheltenham
Lagnado DA, Gerstenberg T (2017) Causation in legal and moral reasoning. In: Waldmann MR (ed) The Oxford handbook of causal reasoning. Oxford University Press, Oxford, pp 565–602

Lahav AD (2022) Chancy causation in tort law. J Tort Law 15(1):109–135
Law J (2022) Oxford dictionary of law. Oxford University Press, Oxford
Lewis D (1973) Causation. J Philos 70(17):556–567
Lewis D (1987) Philosophical Papers Volume II. Oxford University Press, Oxford
Mackie JL (1965) Causes and conditions. Am Philos Q 2(4):245–264
Mackie JL (1974) The cement of the universe. Oxford University Press, Oxford
Magnus U (2007) Causation by omission. In: Tichý L (ed) Causation in law. E. Rozkotova, Prag, pp 95–104
Mellor DH (1995) The facts of causation. Routledge, London
Menzies P (1989) Probabilistic causation and causal processes: a critique of Lewis. Philos Sci 56(4):642–663
Menzies P (1996) Probabilistic causation and the pre-emption problem. Mind Assoc New Ser 105(417):85–117
Meyer-Ladewig J, Nettesheim M (2017) Artikel 1 Verpflichtung zur Achtung der Menschenrechte. In: Meyer-Ladewig J, Nettesheim M (eds) EMRK Europäische Menschenrechtskonvention Handkommentar, 4th edn. Nomos, Baden-Baden, pp 50–62
Mill JS (2011) A system of logic, ratiocinative and inductive – being a connected view of the principles of evidence, and the methods of scientific investigation. Cambridge University Press, Cambridge
Minnerop P, Otto F (2020) Climate change and causation. joining law and climate science on the basis of formal logic. Buffalo Environ Law J 27:49–86
Moore MS (1987) Thomson's preliminaries about causation and rights. Chic-Kent Law Rev 63(3):497–522
Moore MS (2003) For what must we pay – causation and counterfactual baselines. San Diego Law Rev 40(4):1181–1272
Moore MS (2009) Causation and responsibility. Soc Philos Policy 16(2):1–51
Moore MS (2009a) Causation and responsibility: an essay in law, morals, and metaphysics. Oxford University Press, New York
Nollkaemper A, Jacobs D (2015) Introduction: mapping the normative framework. In: Nollkaemper A, Jacobs D (eds) Distribution of responsibilities in international law. Cambridge University Press, Cambridge, pp 1–35
Oetker H (2019) § 249 BGB. In: Krüger W (ed) Münchener Kommentar BGB – Band 2, 8th edn. C. H. Beck, Munich, pp 340–529
Orakhelashvili A (2022) Causation in international law. Edward Elgar Publishing, Cheltenham
Otte R (1981) A critique of Suppes' theory of probabilistic causality. Synthese 48(2):167–190
Otte R (1985) Probabilisitc causality and Simpson's paradoxon. Philos Sci 52(1):110–125
Parascandola M (1997) Singular probabilistic causation in the law. Rechtstheor Beiheft 19:199–207
Paul LA (2009) Counterfactual theories. In: Beebee H, Hitchcock C, Menzies P (eds) The Oxford handbook of causation. Oxford University Press, Oxford, pp 158–184
Pearl J (2009) Causality – models, reasoning, and inference. Cambridge University Press, Cambridge
Pearl J, Mackenzie D (2018) The book of why. Basic Books, New York
Peeters M (2011) The regulatory approach of the EU in view of liability for climate change damage. In: Faure M, Peeters M (eds) Climate change liability. Edward Elgar Publishing, Cheltenham, pp 90–133
Peñalver EM (1998) Acts of god or toxi torts? Applying tort principles to the problem of climate change. Nat Resour J 38(4):563–601
Plakokefalos I (2015) Causation in the law of state responsibility and the problem of overdetermination: in search of clarity. Eur J Int Law 26(2):471–492
Pöttker E (2014) Klimahaftungsrecht. Mohr Siebeck, Tübingen
Proudfoot M, Lacey AR (2009) The Routledge dictionary of philosophy. Routledge, Abingdon
Psillos S (2009) Regularity theories. In: Beebee H, Hitchcock C, Menzies P (eds) The Oxford handbook of causation. Oxford University Press, Oxford, pp 131–157

Pundik A (2006) Can one deny both causation by omission and causal pluralism? The case of legal causation. SSRN:1–39
Puppe I (2013) The concept of causation in the law. In: Kahmen B, Stepanians M (eds) Critical essays on causation and responsibility. De Gruyter, Berlin, pp 67–109
Puppe I (2017) Vorb. § 13. In: Kindhäuser U, Neumann U, Paeffgen H-U, Saliger F (eds) Strafgesetzbuch, 5th edn. Baden-Baden, Nomos, pp 513–650
Puppe I, Wright RW (2017) Causation in the law: philosophy, doctrine and practice. In: Infantino M, Zervogianni E (eds) Causation in European tort law. Cambridge University Press, Cambridge, pp 17–59
Reichenbach H (1956) The direction of time. Dover Publications Inc., Berkeley
Rengier R (2021) Strafrecht Allgemeiner Teil. C. H. Beck, Munich
Rosen DA (1978) In defense of a probabilistic theory of causality. Philos Sci 45(4):604–613
Rostron A (2004) Beyond market share liability: a theory of proportional share liability for nonfungible products. UCLA Law Rev 25(1):152–215
Roxin C (1962) Pflichtwidrigkeit und Erfolg bei fahrlässigen Delikten. Z gesamte Strafrechtswiss 74(3):411–444
Šaltinytė L (2017) The case studies, Case 5: a cancerous drug – Lithuania. In: Infantino M, Zervogianni E (eds) Causation in European tort law. Cambridge University Press, Cambridge, pp 290–292
Sanders J, Green MD, Powers WC Jr (2008) The insubstantiality of the substantial factor test for causation. Mo Law Rev 73(2):399–432
Schauer F, Spellman B (2020) Probabilistic causation in the law. J Inst Theor Econ 176:4–17
Schirmer J-E (2021) Klimahaftung und Kausalität – und es geht doch! Juristenz 76(22):1099–1106
Schmitz R, Wulf M (2019) AO § 370. In: Erb V, Schäfer J (eds) Münchner Kommentar zum Strafgesetzbuch – Band 7, 3rd edn. C. H. Beck, Munich, pp 239–445
Sebok AJ (2017) Actual causation in the second and third restatements: or, the expulsion of the substantial factor test. In: Infantino M, Zervogianni E (eds) Causation in European tort law. Cambridge University Press, Cambridge, pp 60–84
Simpson EH (1951) The interpretation of interaction in contingency tables. J R Stat Soc Ser B 13: 238–241
Skyrms B (1980) Causal necessity: pragmatic investigation of the necessity of laws. Yale University Press, New Haven
Soar K (1996) A probabilistic theory of legal causation. UCL Jur Rev:132–148
Sorabji J (2019) The English approach to the standard of proof in civil proceedings. In: Tichý L (ed) Standard of proof in Europe. Mohr Siebeck, Tübingen, pp 249–269
Spier J (2005) 3:105. In: European Group on Tort Law (ed) Principles of European tort law: text and commentary. Springer, Vienna, pp 54–56
Spier J (2007) Inconvenient questions – causation and the eradication of poverty and climate change. In: Tichý L (ed) Causation in law. E. Rozkotova, Prag, pp 69–93
Stapleton J (2008) Choosing what we mean by 'causation' in the law. Mo Law Rev 73(2):433–480
Stapleton J (2009) Causation in the law. In: Beebee H, Hitchcock C, Menzies P (eds) The Oxford handbook of causation. Oxford University Press, New York, pp 744–770
Stapleton J (2010) Factual causation. Fed Law Rev 38(3):467–484
Steininger BC (2017) The case studies, Case 5: a concerous drug – Austria. In: Infantino M, Zervogianni E (eds) Causation in European tort law. Cambridge University Press, Cambridge, pp 288–289
Stern B (2010) The obligation to make reparation. In: Crawford J, Pellet A, Olleson S (eds) The law of international responsibility. Oxford University Press, Oxford, pp 563–571
Strandberg M (2019) The more-probable-than-not standard: a critical approach. In: Tichý L (ed) Standard of proof in Europe. Mohr Siebeck, Tübingen, pp 65–92
Stuart-Smith RF, Roe GH, Li S, Allen MR (2021) Increased outburst flood hazard from Lake Palcacocha due to human-induced glacier retreat. Nat Geosci 14(2):85–90
Suppes P (1970) A probabilistic theory of causality. North-Holland Pub. Co, Amsterdam

Teichmann A (2021) Vorb. §§ 249-253. In: Jauernig O (ed) Bürgerliches Gesetzbuch, 18th edn. C. H. Beck, Munich, pp 271–287

Toepel F (2013) Causal overdetermination. In: Kahmen B, Stepanians M (eds) Critical essays on causation and responsibility. De Gruyter, Berlin, pp 111–132

Vanuatu ICJ Initiative (2023) ICJ resolution. Available via Vanuatu ICJ Initiative. https://www.vanuatuicj.com/. Accessed 24 Oct 2024

Vautard R, van Aalst M, Boucher O, Drouin A, Haustein K, Kreienkamp F, van Oldenborgh GJ, Otto FEL, Ribes A, Robin Y, Schneider M, Soubeyroux J-M, Stott P, Seneviratne SI, Vogel MM, Wehner M (2020) Human contribution to the record-breaking June and July 2019 heatwaves in Western Europe. Environ Res Lett 15(9):094077

Verheyen R (2005) Climate change damage and international law – prevention duties and state responsibility. Brill, Leiden

Voigt C (2008) State responsibility for climate change damages. Nord J Int Law 77(1-2):1–22

Voigt C (2016) Climate change and damages. In: Carlarne C, Gray K, Tarasofsky R (eds) The Oxford handbook of international climate change law. Oxford University Press, Oxford, pp 464–494

von Bar C (2000) The Common European Law of Torts – 2 damage and damages, liability for and without personal misconduct, causality and defences. Oxford University Press, Oxford

Weitenberg M (2014) Der Begriff der Kausalität in der haftungsrechlichen Rechtsprechung der Unionsgerichte Nomos, Baden-Baden

West E (2013) The utility of the NESS test of factual causation in Scots law. Aberd Stud Law Rev 4(1):39–62

Wright RW (1985) Causation in tort law. Calif Law Rev 73(6):1741–1826

Wright RW (1988) Causation, responsibility, risk, probability, naked statistics and proof: pruning the bramble bush by clarifying the concepts. Iowa Law Rev 73(5):1001–1078

Wright RW (2001) Once more into the bramble bush: duty, causal contribution, and the extent of legal responsibility. Vanderbilt Law Rev 54(3):1072–1132

Wright RW (2007) Acts and omissions as positive and negative causes. In: Neyers JW, Chamberlain E, Pitel SGA (eds) Emerging issues in tort law. Hart Publishing, Oxford, pp 287–307

Wright RW (2011) The NESS account of natural causation: a response to criticisms. In: Goldberg R (ed) Perspectives on causation. Hart Publishing, Oxford, pp 285–322

Wright RW, Puppe I (2016) Causation: linguistic, philosophical, legal and economic. Chic-Kent Law Rev 91(2):461–502

Zeidler S (2022) Klimahaftungsklagen – Die internationale Haftung für die Folgen des Klimawandels. Duncker & Humblot, Berlin

Chapter 5
Normative Causation

5.1 Normative Causation in the Law

Normative causation forms the second step in the commonly and predominantly used bifurcated approach to causation in the law.[1] It hereby functions as a criterion of delineation either in cases in which the results stemming from the factual assessment would be considered as 'unjust' or 'unfair' or simply morally irrelevant from a normative point of view, or the factual causal assessment would render too broad. By implementing normative aspects into causal considerations, normative causation adjusts the factual results within the framework of a value-based and policy-driven order. It, therefore, can lead to the dismissal of overall causation, in cases in which normative criteria would hold it necessary to do so. Imperial for the assessment of normative causation, however, is the existence of a factual causal chain per se, as normative causation cannot subsist without factual causation having first been affirmed.[2]

Nearly every jurisdiction is acquainted to normative concepts either directly through developed legal tests of causation or indirectly through unwritten but societal-shaped perceptions. The scope and the manner, nonetheless, in which those concepts find entrance into the legal assessment vary considerably.

The main obstacle to comparing the different normative notions which underly the legal assessment of causation consists in the usage of varying terminology for the

---

[1] See for the necessity of distinguishing between factual and normative causation Sect. 3.1.2.

[2] *Orakhelashvili* additionally introduces another understanding of normative causation in international law which relies solely on normative legal criteria without taking factual or natural relata into consideration. He ultimately, refuses such an approach and reaffirms the understanding that is applied here. See Orakhelashvili (2022), pp. 66–67. The extent to which factual causation can be 'bridged' by normative considerations is not subject of this work. This constitutes a deviation from the principle of the two-stage causal approach, for which a legal exception would be necessary within the framework of a presumption of causation. The same applies to a possible reversal of the burden of proof to avoid causal problems.

M. Krakau, *Causation in National and International Climate Change Litigation*,
https://doi.org/10.1007/978-3-031-74693-2_5

second step of the causal inquiry and normative causation per se. In general, no conceptual consistency exists across different jurisdictions. Besides the term 'normative causation' adopted for this work, other terminological approaches such as the term 'legal causation' are also common.[3] The main advantage of using the term 'normative' instead of 'legal' rests in its clear determinability and the omitted risk of confusing and mixing overall 'legal' causation with the specific legal causal assessments that persists in the second step of the assessment of causation in the law.[4] Some authors further resort to terms such as attribution or scope of liability.[5] And although the term 'attribution' is also used in some jurisdictions such as Germany, it is still subject to a degree of inconsistency and vagueness, as it does not implicitly include a causal factor, but can also be used as a mere description of correlative factors.[6] The 'scope of liability' not only massively limits the causal assessments literally to cases of liability and excludes other cases of causal assessments in the law but furthermore widens the second step of the bifurcated approach beyond the scope of causal deliberations. This is especially the case since the scope of liability entails questions such as the allocation and distribution of liability which can fall in line with the concept of joint and shared responsibility.[7] Those liability-based considerations, however, go beyond the mere causal assessment. Due to the lack of otherwise suitable terminologies, it is, therefore, the term 'normative causation' that constitutes the most precise form of describing the content and scope of the herein-entailed analysis.

Besides those terminological indifferences, the scope and evaluative criteria invoked with regard to the examination of normative causation also differ from jurisdiction to jurisdiction. This is due to the close connection with the respective societal and value-based system, which is influenced by cultural and religious currents, as well as the respective policy-driven order. Even in the tort law of countries of the European Union, the disaccord about suitable normative

[3]See for the usage of the term 'legal causation' in different jurisdictions Infantino and Zervogianni (2017), p. 403. The term 'legal causation' is also used in countries such as Greece, Ireland and Portugal. Other authors also use such terminology e.g. Weitenberg (2014), pp. 579–597; Kohler (2017), para 159; Nitsch (2021), pp. 439–445, paras 34–55.

[4]See for such critique e.g. Koziol (2007), p. 60. The ALI refrains from using the term 'normative causation' due to the fact that they used this terminology as an overarching construct entailing factual as well as normative causal statements. See for further explanations, American Law Institute (2010), § 29.

[5]See for the usage of both concepts Koziol (2007), p. 60. The term 'scope of liability' is also used by the Principles of European Tort Law in Art. 3:201. Using the term 'scope of responsibility', see Plakokefalos (2015), p. 478. The term 'scope of liability' is also used in American Law Institute (2010).

[6]In Germany some legal assessments of causation are conducted in criminal law under the concept of '*objektive Zurechnung*' meaning objective attribution.

[7]This is referred to in the German law as '*Gesamtschuld*' or '*Teilschuld*'.

assessments prevails.[8] Yet all found their assessment of normative causation on criteria such as fairness, equity and moral responsibility. Due to the varying criteria applied by different jurisdictions in the EU, the authors of the Principles of European Tort Law (PETL) thus resorted to the implementation of multiple different normative tests in Section 2 of the statute, which concerns the 'scope of liability', stating that

> (w)here an activity is a cause within the meaning of Section 1 of this Chapter, whether and to what extent damage may be attributed to a person depends on factors such as
>
> a) the foreseeability of the damage to a reasonable person at the time of the activity, taking into account in particular the closeness in time and space between the damaging activity and its consequences, or the magnitude of the damage in relation to the normal consequences of such an activity;
> b) the nature and the value of the protected interests (art. 2:102);
> c) the basis of liability (Art. 1:101);
> d) the extent of the ordinary risks of life; and
> e) the protective purpose of the rule that has been violated.[9]

In using the wording 'such as', the authors of the PETL clearly emphasize that the list in Section 2 does not constitute an exhaustive enumeration but may also include other normative aspects and criteria as well.

The restriction of factual causation due to normative requirements does not resort exclusively to claims raised under the law of tort but is inherent in every area of law, be it in criminal, administrative or public law. Given that from a teleological point of view, different areas of law pose different normative requirements based on the rationale and purpose of the application of the law, the usage of normative tests of causation even varies within the same jurisdiction.[10] Which normative concepts and tests ultimately are used largely depends on the reliance and the interconnectedness of the area of law with the societal value-based order and the underlying objective of the legal framework itself. It is, therefore, especially in the realm of criminal law that stricter tests of normative causation find their way into the assessment of overall causation in the law.[11]

---

[8] In regard to the case law of the Court of the European Union see *Weitenberg* who identifies five test of normative causation. Among them foreseeability, the protective purpose of the norm, the manner of the damage, interruption of causal chains and the theory of adequacy. See Weitenberg (2014), pp. 579–597; Kleinschmidt (2009). More generally on normative causal considerations applied by countries of the European Union, see Infantino and Zervogianni (2017).

[9] Art. 3:201 PETL.

[10] See in more detail Sect. 6.2.2.

[11] In German criminal law it is decisive that the result was the so-called '*Werk*' (literally: work) of the defendant, see on the differences in normative causation in civil and criminal climate change litigation Satzger and von Maltitz (2021), p. 5. See again Sect. 6.2.2.

International law as well knows of normative criteria which function as restrictive mechanisms for sprawling factual causation.[12] Even more variety than in the European law context evolves in the attempt to identify a consistent approach by international courts and tribunals. Even within individual international courts, the application of normative concepts of causation varies considerably. One reason for this divergence lies in the confluence of a wide variety of legal systems and legal concepts, which is ultimately reflected in the different normative concepts inherent in them.[13] Without a comprehensive value-based order, international law is simply unable to provide a comprehensive framework for the use of normative criteria in causal assessments.

In light of the foregoing analysis, the following chapter first assesses which general normative criteria are of importance in regard to causal assessments and explicitly elaborates on the facts that apply in climate change lawsuits specifically (Sect. 5.2). Following the assessment of overall normative criteria, special legal tests of normative causation are discussed. Of importance is hereby, in particular, the correlation between the specific tests of normative causation and the overall climate setting. In which way are these criteria of use in their application to certain climate change lawsuits and how might they have to be adapted? The analysis herein focuses on the most common tests of normative causation, such as the foreseeability of the outcome (Sect. 5.3), the proximate cause (Sect. 5.7) and the theory of adequacy (Sect. 5.6). Another focus lies on intervening causes (Sect. 5.5) and the protective purpose and scope of the rule (Sect. 5.8) as normative criteria of the restriction of factual causation. Furthermore, and in regard to climate-damaging behaviour and omissions a specific climate change–induced focus persists on the materiality threshold of the respective contribution (Sect. 5.4). Ultimately, the aim of this chapter is to elaborate and discuss the necessary tests of normative causation in climate change litigation and to identify possible solutions to the inherent obstacles.

5.2 Normative Implications for Causation

The underlying incentive for the assessment of normative causation is the need to produce fair and equitable results in a moral and ethical way so that the law is acceptable for the usage in society. Since factual causation is ideally based on natural and scientific assessments of the cause—effect relationship without implementing moral and ethical values, such principles are needed to be implemented in the causal assessment in a second step. Which considerations, however, are underlying the

---

[12] Stating that the causal link has to be foreseeable, International Court of Justice, 2 February 2018 – I.C.J. Reports 2018, p. 15, *Certain Activities Carried Out by Nicaragua in the Border Area (Costa Rica v. Nicaragua)*, para 32. Foreseeability has also been applied in International Labour Organization Administrative Tribunal, 10 February 2020 – 4239, *L. v. WHO*, 9 para 14. For the remoteness of the causal link see International Law Commission (2001a), p. 93.

[13] See in this regard also Sects. 3.2.2 and 3.2.3.

applied tests and which concepts should be considered when approaching normative causation is discussed in the following. In a first step, general normative concepts are assessed and evaluated (Sect. 5.2.1) These include, in particular, concepts such as responsibility, justice, fairness and equity. Doctrines of normative causation are, furthermore, shaped by general legal principles that are relevant to the substantive assessment of the issue at hand. In the case of climate change, the framing of the specific tests of normative causation is influenced, in particular, by general principles of international environmental law which also find application in light of climate change (Sect. 5.2.2). A third concept that is overall present in climate change litigation and, thus, shapes the normative doctrines and theories applied in the second step of causation in the law is the notion of climate justice (Sect. 5.2.3). What the concept of climate justice ultimately entails and how it is influencing normative causation forms a fundamental part of this assessment, as well.

5.2.1 General Sources of Normativity

Normative causation is based upon the supposition that there are numerous cases in which sole factual causation would lead to unjust results and contradict moral perceptions of today's society. This is especially the case in scenarios in which the outcome was not foreseeable or the contribution only of such minor substance that it would ultimately seem unfair to introduce legal blameworthiness. One will also talk about unfairness in scenarios in which the outcome of an action or omission is so far beyond any experience of life that the outcome could not be predicted in any way. One of the standard cases in this regard, notably in German literature and scholarship, is the so called '*Bluter-case*'.[14]

In 1920 the German Supreme Court of the Reich was confronted with the question of whether a man was responsible for the death of a student.[15] The man had thrown a rock at the student, which resulted in a minor cut. The immediate injury itself was not life-threatening under normal circumstances. The student, however, suffered from Haemophilia, which was the reason why the minor cut ultimately led to the death of the victim.[16] Given that the factual causal relata between the throwing of the stone and the death of the student was given under counterfactual theories in the present case, the Court in the first instance ruled against the accused and convicted him of negligent manslaughter.[17] Nowadays, the case is a prime example for the debate and the difficulties surrounding the relation of factual and normative causation. The fact that the person throwing the stone would be considered causally

[14]Reichsgericht, 31 May 1920 – I 211/20.

[15]Ibid.

[16]Haemophilia is a bleeding disorder in which the blood does not clot properly or clots very slowly. People with haemophilia are often at risk of bleeding to death from minor injuries.

[17]Reichsgericht, 31 May 1920 – I 211/20.

responsible for the death of the student, although the injury was only minor, the consequences of death nearly unforeseeable and the probability of encountering a person suffering from Haemophilia very low, would nowadays be commonly qualified as unjust and not in line with overall moral considerations.[18] The case is hence used as a prime example of the rejection of normative causation, leading to a general negation of causation in law in such cases.[19]

Two important aspects can be deduced from the aforementioned example. On the one hand, it shows how causal requirements and the overall understanding of the influence of normative criteria shifted over time. While the Supreme Court of the Reich only considered factual causation (in the form of the conditio-sine-qua-non formula) to be relevant for the establishment of the causal relata, courts in the present-day are implementing more and more normative requirements and considering those imperative for overall causal considerations in the law.[20] On the other hand, the case shows the great influence normative considerations can have for the outcome of a court case. While the Supreme Court of the Reich persecuted the accused on the bases of negligent manslaughter, these days courts might resort only to negligent battery, which would result in a considerable difference in the degree of punishment.

The *Bluter-case* has shown that normative considerations are imperative for lawsuits in general and can have a considerable impact on the outcome and the evaluation of a case.

On the forefront of normative considerations in the light of normative causation is the principle of justice. In building on a natural perception of law and justice (justitia naturalis), the Oxford Dictionary of Law defines justice in the context of the law as "*(a) moral ideal that the law seeks to uphold in the protection of rights and punishment of wrongs*".[21] Yet what this 'moral ideal' ultimately entails depends on a wide variety of factors, cultural perceptions and philosophical, as well as legal differentiation.[22] In transference to the requirement of causation, it is the principle of justice that orders factual causation to be adapted through the application of normative criteria in the first place. It is, therefore, the mere reason why normative considerations are being applied in causal assessments at all. Different legal systems

[18]The German Supreme Court of the Reich argued in its judgment that the death of a person hit by a stone was generally foreseeable because of the danger involved in throwing a stone. Today, the jurisprudence has shifted. Although the specific outcome of one's actions still does not have to be entirely foreseeable, events that are completely outside any experience of life are not imputable and therefore not legally causal. See in this regard Federal Court Germany, 10 July 1958 – 4 StR 180/58. Federal Court of Germany, 17 March 1992 – 5 StR 34/92.

[19]In German criminal law, the assessment is based on the concept of objective attribution ('*objektive Zurechnung*'). See e.g. Rengier (2021), p. 93 para 72; Kühl (2017), p. 54 para 65.

[20]See on the need for a bifurcated understanding of causation again Sect. 3.1.2.

[21]Law (2022). See also Garner (2009), p. 942.

[22]For a detailed analysis of different conceptions of justice from a philosophical perspective, see Miller (2021).

hereby apply different legal tests and prerequisites so that the result of the overall causal tests suits their perception of justice best.

The perception of justice not only demands for the adaptation of factual causation per se but also shapes the idea of how the causal assessment should be adapted itself. This is achieved by applying underlying normative notions such as the principles of equity, equality and fairness, as well as criteria of blameworthiness, culpability and responsibility. Although much has been written about those principles in different disciplines, even outside the legal realm, defining or restricting those notions to a uniform definition boarders on the impossible and contradicts the overall aim of normative criteria which carry at their core a fluctuate, adaptive and overall shifting manner.[23] Concurrent with the overarching principle of justice, cultural, religious and societal perceptions and traditions are strongly influencing the sentiment of those normative notions, as well. Thus, without the ability to define them specifically, the scope and aim of the different concepts persists in their delineation from one another, without negating their interconnective and inter-influencing nature.

Equality, as the criterion that is still most tangible, relates to the "*correspondence between a group of different objects, persons, processes or circumstances that have the same qualities in at least one respect but not all respects, i.e., regarding one specific feature, with differences in other features.*"[24] In strongly entailing a distributive component it builds upon the perception of an equal benefit-, as well as burden-sharing. Equality hereby, and different to the criteria of equity, does not incorporate individual characteristics and abilities into consideration but solely focuses on not being biased among different persons, situations or objects.

Often applied as a synonym to justice, equity constitutes an individualized notion of the overarching concept in asking what is required specifically. It, therefore, delineates itself in its distributive notion from the principle of equality by not constituting a burden or benefit sharing in an equal manner but dependent on one's individual ability and need. Despite its definitional lack of clarity, the term equity has been used broadly in legal debates and has found its way into a multitude of international legal treaties.[25] Applying the perception of equity has hereby often been perceived and declared as 'fair' and 'just', which highlights its interconnectedness with further normative criteria.

Although the term 'fair' is often used in common parlance, its usage in actual legal debates and legal frameworks is marginal.[26] This could stem from fairness being an overarching concept rather than a detailed embodiment of a particular normative construct. It relates to the reasonableness of the action, behaviour or

---

[23] See for the difficulties in defining 'moral responsibility' and 'blameworthiness' in computer science the lecture of Halpern (2017).

[24] Gosepath (2021). Black's Law Dictionary defines 'equality' as "*(t)he quality or state of being equal.*" Garner (2009), p. 616.

[25] See e.g. Art. 2, 4, 14 Paris Agreement and Art. 3 I FCC.

[26] The reference to the term 'fair' or 'fairness' in general can only be found once in the Paris Agreement, as equity and equality are mentioned on several different occasions throughout the Agreement.

overall situation in question.[27] Whether something is perceived as reasonable, and fair, is, like the concept of justice, a product of different cultural, societal and religious norms and traditions, and thus different in every jurisdiction.

Strongly interconnected with the perception of fairness and frequently influencing its conception and scope are principles such as responsibility, culpability and moral blameworthiness.[28] Whether someone is to be regarded as responsible, at least in a moral manner, is frequently based on an assessment of their capacities followed by a contextualization of their behaviour in correlation with the former results.[29] It moreover implies the duty to act in a specific, often socially engraved manner and hence to comply with so-called 'social forces'. If someone does not comply with the socially, legally or in any other way established norms or 'forces' of conduct, and their behaviour is, therefore, perceived as wrong, one would render the person blameworthy. Responsibility and blameworthiness are often referred to in the law as a person being legally culpable, which frequently becomes of consideration in assessing someone's delinquent and criminal conduct. Culpability, in contrast to responsibility and blameworthiness, is thus a strongly legalistic concept that, while building on both conceptions, concurrently implies a legal rather than a moral or ethical wrong.[30]

5.2.2 International Environmental Law

The legal framework on which climate change litigation is generally grounded has largely evolved from pre-existing environmental principles. This is evident not only in international climate litigation, but also in domestic litigation, where courts often refer to international treaties and the principles of international environmental law

[27] 'Fair', for instance, is defined by Black's Law Dictionary as "*(i)mpartial; just; equitable; disinterested.*" Garner (2009), p. 674.

[28] For the correlation between causation and responsibility see Moore (2009).

[29] The concept of responsibility and the scope of responsibility are often erroneously used as synonyms for causation or liability in court. For an example of the use of responsibility in relation to liability, see Garner (2009), p. 1427. While liability and causation are primarily legal constructs, responsibility is a multifaceted social and moral concept that strongly influences legal perceptions of what is right and what is wrong. Causal responsibility can therefore be inferred from the existence of factual causation. Normative causation, on the other hand, can be reassessed and influenced by existing and continuing moral responsibility. See in more detail on moral responsibility Talbert (2024).

[30] Black's Law Dictionary, for example, defines 'culpability' as "*(b)lameworthiness; the quality of being culpable. Except in cases of absolute liability, criminal culpability requires a showing that the person acted purposely, knowingly, recklessly, or negligently with respect to each material element of the offense.*" Garner (2009), p. 435.

that they embody.[31] Those principles not only function as general pillars of international environmental and consequently also climate law, but also contain strong normative indications which can also transpire to the understanding and assessment of causation in the respective lawsuits. The focus hereby rests on four principles in particular, namely the principle of prevention (Sect. 5.2.2.1), the precautionary principle (Sect. 5.2.2.2), the polluter pays principle (Sect. 5.2.2.3) and the concept of common but differentiated responsibilities (Sect. 5.2.2.4). In their application to the specific theories of normative causation, it is crucial to consider whether the respective environmental principle actually applies to the actor in question. Since the environmental principles are initially binding only for states, actor-related deviations may occur in the specific determination of the normative doctrines of causation in the law.[32]

5.2.2.1 The Principle of Prevention

The principle of prevention forms one of the central tenets of international environmental law. Based on and further emerged from the 'no-harm rule' developed in the *Trail-Smelter case* in 1938 and 1941, its significance in customary law is now undisputed.[33] In the field of friction between state sovereignty and extraterritoriality, the principle of prevention requires the avoidance of transboundary environmental damage through actions on one's national territory. The state is bound to not only omit any transboundary damaging behaviour but also has the due diligence duty to regulate behaviour conducted by private parties. In a further development of the no-harm rule, the principle now also contains a duty to prevent any transboundary damage. In contrast to the no-harm rule the principle of prevention abandons local (spatial) limitations and requires preventive measures for states both outside the neighbouring sphere and on their own territory. Furthermore, the principle expands the relevant circle of parties by distancing itself from a purely state-centred perspective. Rather it developed into an environment-focused dogma, concurrently affecting the requirement of legal standing, as well as the material and substantial extent of

[31] In relying on the Paris Agreement and national implementations of the principle of prevention and precaution, Prague Municipal Court, 15 June 2022 – 14A 101/2021, *Klimatická žaloba ČR v. Czech Republic*, inter alia paras 258–260. In relying on the principles set out by the European climate policy and especially Art. 191 TFEU. The Hague District Court, 24 June 2015 – C/09/456689/HA ZA 13-1396, *Urgenda Foundation v. The State of the Netherlands*, paras 4.60–4.63. See further, General Court (Third Chamber), 2 March 2010 – T-16/04, *Société Arcelor Atlantique et Lorraine v. [EU] Parliament and Council (environment and consumers)*.

[32] See in more detail Sect. 6.2.1.

[33] Arbitrational Tribunal, 16 April 1938, 11 March 1941 – 3 R.I.A.A. 1905, *United States v. Canada (Trail Smelter Case)*, acknowledging the broad consensus about its recognition as a norm of customary law, but questioning the existence of sufficient state practice Peel et al. (2018), p. 207.

other statutory norms themselves.[34] Principle 21 of the Stockholm Declaration of 1972 resonates with the prevention principle in this sense:

> States have, in accordance with the Charter of the United Nations and the principles of international law, the sovereign right to exploit their own resources pursuant to their own environmental policies, and the responsibility to ensure that activities within their jurisdiction or control do not cause damage to the environment of other States or of areas beyond the limits of national jurisdiction.[35]

Twenty years after the Stockholm Declaration first implemented the principle of prevention, it has also found its way into numerous other environmental treaties, amongst them the Rio Declaration on Environment and Development, which even adopted the wording of the Stockholm Declaration.[36]

The broad wording of the principle of prevention leaves much room for interpretation, particularly with regard to the substance of the damage and implicitly of the damaging threshold, as well as the nature of the act. Which preconditions the principle imposes has further only been addressed sporadically both by the scientific community and by courts in their application of the principle. And while the detailed elaboration of the principle is largely irrelevant to its normative implications for causal determinacy, it can be considered whether the nature and purpose of the principle itself has ramifications for the handling of climatic causation. After all, the prevention principle is not exclusively applied to traditional environmental disputes such as cases of water and air pollution but is increasingly being extended to climatic issues as well.[37] The purpose of the principle lies in the prevention of damage before the harmful conduct even occurs. The underlying ratio consists in the fact that mitigating and reversing yet occurred damage, in particular in environmental scenarios, is either not possible or much more expensive than initiating preventive steps before the damage even occurs. However, this preventive mechanism can only develop its full strength if no excessive demands are made on the causal connection. After all, it is precisely the purpose of the principle to take preventive action even in scientifically complex situations. This is particularly the case in the event of preventive measures within the framework of existing duties to protect. Thus, the principle transpires to and shapes in particular the normative account of requiring a certain degree of foreseeability of the possible outcome, especially in light of intervening causes and the complexity of the climate system.[38]

---

[34] Duvic-Paoli and Vinuales (2015), pp. 113–121.

[35] Principle 21, Stockholm Declaration.

[36] Although with minor changes "*[...] to exploit their resources pursuant to their own environmental and developmental policies [...]*" see Principle 2 Rio-Declaration.

[37] E.g. in The Hague District Court, 24 June 2015 – C/09/456689/HA ZA 13-1396, *Urgenda Foundation v. The State of the Netherlands*, paras 4.58, 4.61.

[38] See in regard to the foreseeability Sect. 5.3. Concerning intervening causes, see Sect. 5.5.

5.2.2.2 The Precautionary Principle

The precautionary principle forms one of the guiding principles of international environmental law and has found its way into domestic environmental legislation and numerous regional and international agreements.[39] It is frequently at the heart of environmental and climate disputes and is regularly invoked in court decisions as well. In essence, the principle acts as a preventive mechanism even in the face of an uncertain scientific factual basis. It is, thus, closely linked to the duty of care arising from positive obligations under fundamental and human rights as well as environmental law. As a transformative concept of environmental risk reduction, the precautionary principle also serves as a means of interpreting legal concepts. Under the application of the principle, an actor cannot justify inaction in managing foreseeable risks on the basis of a lack of scientific evidence but must nevertheless take preventive measures. The precautionary principle differs in this respect from the principle of prevention, which still requires a scientifically sound basis for the application of risk prevention measures.

5.2.2.2.1 Disputing the Precautionary Principle

The differentiation of the requirements which are posed on the existence of scientific certainty also has an impact on its legal status. In contrast to the no-harm rule and the principle of prevention, the precautionary principle cannot (yet) be claimed as a norm of customary law.[40] It rather constitutes a very controversial concept. In particular, two different fields of dispute emerge in the legal debate underpinning the principle. On the one hand, the question of the correct terminology for the concept has given rise to considerable debate. While in the European context, and probably also reflecting a more modern understanding of the precautionary concept, the term 'principle' is commonly used, the United States, in particular, have resisted such terminology, suggesting a more 'neutral' formulation that is at the same time weaker and less binding.[41] The controversy over the terminology of the principle,

---

[39] On an international level e.g. Art. 15 Rio-Declaration. On a regional level, e.g. in Art. 191 II TFEU. On a national level e.g. in Art. 20a German Basic Law. For a detailed assessment of the precautionary principle in the European context and its application in court see European Court of Human Rights, 27 January 2009 – 67021/01, *Tatar v. Romania*, para 109.

[40] Although this fact is slightly controversial. In favour for its status of a norm of customary law, de Sadeleer (2016), p. 21; Trindade (2015), pp. 412–413; Marti (2011), p. 69; von Arnauld (2019), p. 409 para 895. This view is also supported by the ICJ, and the WTO, see Peel et al. (2018), pp. 237, 240. Acknowledging a trend towards its acceptance as a norm of customary law, while still not committing to its actual status as customary law, International Tribunal for the law of the Sea, 1 February 2011 – ITLOS Reports 2011, p. 10, *Responsibilities and obligations of States sponsoring persons and entities with respect to activities in the Area (Request for Advisory Opinion submitted to the Seabed Disputes Chamber)*, para 135. Opposing its customary status e.g. Boyle and Redgwell (2021), pp. 181–183.

[41] de Sadeleer (2021), pp. 168–169.

however, is not only rooted in questions of wording but goes deeper into the discussion of the content and nature of the commitment that the concept implies. Given that the term 'principle' has a more binding and definitive character than the term 'approach', some states have been reluctant to adopt and commit themselves to such terminology.[42]

Beyond the debate on the correct terminology and the related question of the binding nature of the conception, the scope and substance of the principle are even more controversial. Disagreement already prevails on the question of how many different definitions of the principle actually exist.[43] Moreover, disagreement remains as to the preconditions for the application of the principle and as to what arises from the application of the principle at all. The weakest interpretation of the precautionary principle thus implies only an authorisation to act in cases of scientific uncertainty, which is neither binding nor obligatory on the state concerned. The strictest interpretation, on the other hand, advocates a shift in the burden of proof in cases in which all the requirements of the precautionary principle are met.[44] Risk takers must prove that they have complied with all the requirements and obligations laid down by law in order to calculate and assess the risk created by their action. They may also have to prove that they took all necessary measures to prevent the risk from materialising. However, this is still clearly a 'minority' view, which has only been called for in isolated cases and has hardly been implemented in practice.[45] The mediating view, on the other hand, calls for a stricter interpretation of the principle, going beyond a mere authorisation to exercise due care and deriving from its application an obligation or duty to act.[46] However, the measures to be taken in order to fulfil and comply with such a duty are also widely disputed and largely depend on the requirements of national law. At the same time, the different ways in which the principle is implemented are crucial to its application. As the concept of precaution has found its way into a multitude of different international agreements,

[42] For the sake of simplicity, the terms 'approach' and 'principle' will be used here interchangeably, despite the pending terminological discussion. See for a more detailed analysis of the dispute Boyle and Redgwell (2021), pp. 172–173; Trindade (2015), pp. 411–412.

[43] On a general note Wiener (2018), p. 177. Counting more than 12 definitions de Sadeleer (2021), p. 181.

[44] The reversal of the burden of proof e.g. was in question in International Court of Justice, 20 April 2010 – I.C.J. Reports 2010 p.14, *Argentina v. Uruguay (Pulp Mills)*. Against such a strict view with reference to international jurisprudence Boyle and Redgwell (2021), pp. 176–177.

[45] Opposing such a strict application and a shift in the burden of proof Boyle and Redgwell (2021), p. 183, International Court of Justice, 20 April 2010 – I.C.J. Reports 2010 p. 14, *Argentina v. Uruguay (Pulp Mills)*, para 164. Stating that a reversal of the burden of proof would be a misinterpretation or an overinterpretation of the precautionary principle Haritz (2011), p. 25. Hinting that there might be some state practice supporting a shift in the burden of proof Peel et al. (2018), p. 234.

[46] Regarding the different scopes of the precautionary principle see Peel et al. (2018), pp. 234–235; Wiener (2018), pp. 178–179. Only differing between a strong version and a weak version of the concept, see Scott (2004), pp. 57–58.

constitutions and statutory provisions in a variety of different areas of law, the requirements and scope of the principle vary accordingly.

5.2.2.2.2 The Substance of the Precautionary Principle as an Interpretative Device for the Assessment of Normative Causation

Although historically a concept of environmental law, the scope of the precautionary principle now extends beyond purely environmental issues to cover all areas of elevated risk and significant scientific uncertainty.[47] One of the major fields outside the realm of environmental law concerns the application of the principle in the health and medical sector. However, with the emergence of climate law and the growing focus on climate change issues on a global scale, the precautionary principle has become a cornerstone of climate change law as well. The principle can, for example, be found in Principle 15 of the Rio Declaration, stating that

> (i)n order to protect the environment, the precautionary approach shall be widely applied by States according to their capabilities. Where there are threats of serious or irreversible damage, lack of full scientific certainty shall not be used as a reason for postponing cost-effective measures to prevent environmental degradation.[48]

The United Nations Framework Convention on Climate Change addresses the precautionary principle as well. Article 3 Abs. 3 of the Framework sets forth that

> (t)he Parties should take precautionary measures to anticipate, prevent or minimize the causes of climate change and mitigate its adverse effects. Where there are threats of serious or irreversible damage, lack of full scientific certainty should not be used as a reason for postponing such measures, taking into account that policies and measures to deal with climate change should be cost-effective so as to ensure global benefits at the lowest possible cost. [...].[49]

The dispute about the right terminology and the different prerequisites entailed within also becomes apparent in the implementation of the principle introduced above. In order to fully understand the reconciliation of the precautionary principle with climatic causation, it is imperative to redirect the attention from the mere discussion of differing interpretations to the principle itself. It is impossible, and even more misleading, to discuss the preconditions for all variations of codified precautionary principles. Instead, emphasis is placed on the universal aspects and basic and major preconditions of the principle.[50]

---

[47] The precautionary principle originated from the German '*Vorsorgeprinzip*', which in turn was established in 1971 as a core principle in the first German environmental program. The principle quickly found its way into environmental jurisprudence beyond Germany's borders, especially in Great Britain, before it was anchored in the Rio Declaration in 1992.

[48] Principle 15 Rio Declaration.

[49] Art. 3 FCCC.

[50] In regard to requirements posed by Art. 3 III FCCC, de Sadeleer (2016), pp. 24–29.

The first universal requirement concerns a certain degree of scientific uncertainty about the effect of the action or omission in question.[51] Obviously, scientific uncertainty always plays a role in legal considerations when it comes to establishing stringent causal chains, especially in the context of positive obligations. It is generally not possible to determine with complete certainty what the future effects of a particular action or omission will be. However, the level of uncertainty increases in the case of climate-related claims. Due to the innovative character of climate science, including the field of attribution science, uncertainties largely result from insufficient scientific experience. Although the lack of comparative data is closing more and more over time, attributing extreme weather events, nevertheless, often fails based on missing reference variables as well as methodological obstacles. The former notably results from the fact that comparable data was collected relatively late, and the density of data varies greatly from region to region.[52]

Another reason for the increased incidence of scientific uncertainty in climate litigation lies in the very nature of these cases. Because of the close connection with scientific findings and the need to take them into account, the law must also come to terms with their methods and procedures. Since scientific data can never be stated with complete probability, and given that the probability of the accuracy of the results is always reduced by other factors, which results in uncertainty components being built into the scientific determination of results, uncertainties, probabilities and confidence levels are implicitly included in the legal consideration.[53] These obstacles are exacerbated when it comes to positive obligations and future impacts. Due to the variability, fluidity and complexity of the climate system, it is difficult to predict specific rather than general impacts with a high degree of certainty. In general, climate science and, consequently also climate claims are dominated by scientific uncertainty. Scientific uncertainty is, thus, also an integral part of the normative assessment of causation, where it is particularly relevant in the application of the principle of foreseeability, which in turn is closely linked to the question of how to deal with intervening causes.[54]

The second universal requirement addresses the existence of irreversible and serious damage. Such a requirement is set out, for example, in Article 3 III FCCC and Article 15 of the Rio Declaration. The qualification as 'serious' is largely determined by the national legal system and presupposes that a previous threshold set by the legislature in a political act has been exceeded. At the international level and authoritative for climate matters, it is the Paris Agreement that considers a temperature increase of 1.5 °C to be significant. For this reason, the limit, especially in international treaties, will have to be measured as far as possible within the framework of the respective agreement, with a strong reference to the findings and

[51] Recent case law does not see this as a prerequisite. Rather, measures should be taken in spite of, rather than because of, the uncertainties, see Marti (2011), pp. 59–60.

[52] See in this regard Sect. 3.3.3.

[53] See for a determination of uncertainty and confidence levels of the IPCC Sect. 2.1.

[54] See for the principle of foreseeability Sect. 5.3. Concerning intervening causes, see Sect. 5.5.

predictions of the IPCC.[55] As domestic legislation is also strongly influenced by the climate and mitigation targets set out in the Paris Agreement, some of the concepts contained therein can also be used as a reference at the national level.

However, the point at which legislators and jurisprudence consider an impact to be 'serious' per se is still subject to highly subjective interpretation with a wide margin of appreciation. The criterion of irreversibility, in turn, requires a very factual assessment that can be made on the basis of sound scientific evidence.[56] Irreversibility refers to the inability to reverse the effects of an action or omission. In the case of climate, irreversibility consists of the lack of self-regulation and mitigation of the climate system itself with respect to the changes that have occurred.[57] Whereas in a healthy and undisturbed state, the climate system was able to regulate itself by absorbing excess greenhouse gases in carbon sinks, the extensive emissions of the Anthropocene have largely disturbed the balance. The effects of climate change, such as the rise in mean surface temperature and the concomitant rise in sea level, cannot be reversed, only mitigated. Even the use of negative emission technologies, including carbon capture technologies, cannot reverse the damage already done to the climate system. Other technologies, which fall into the category of geo- and climate-engineering approaches, also face significant regulatory hurdles due to the unpredictability of their impact on the overall climate system and regional weather conditions.[58] A further escalation stage will most certainly be reached with the passing of so-called 'climatic tipping points'.[59] In any case, at the current state of science and despite numerous proposals from the scientific community, the reversal of anthropogenic climate change and climate damage per se cannot be achieved. As a result, any action that contributes to climate change must be considered as having an irreversible impact on the climate system. This also applies to damage caused by climate change, including, in particular, the irreversible global disappearance of glaciers or the extinction of fauna and flora. The requirement of the existence of irreversible and serious harm ultimately feeds into the assessment of normative

[55] de Sadeleer (2016), pp. 27–28.

[56] Ibid. 27–29.

[57] Marti (2011), p. 57.

[58] One of the few frameworks regulating climate-engineering on an international level is the London Protocol to the Convention on the Prevention of Marine Pollution by Dumping of Wastes and Other Matter. See for the difficult legal implications of negative emission technologies and geo-engineering Blickle (2022), Burns et al. (2021), and Du (2018).

[59] Climatic tipping points are events that not only contribute to further climate change, but also significantly increase the warming of the atmosphere, leading to the fatal situation that climate change cannot be slowed down even at much higher temperature levels. Tipping points are the starting point of a snowball system of constant temperature rise. Some of the tipping points that have been analysed by climate scientists are, for example, the thawing of the Greenlandic or other ice shields, and the release of large amounts of methane due to the thawing of the permafrost. The *IPCC* defines tipping points as "*(a) level of change in system properties beyond which a system reorganizes, often abruptly, and does not return to the initial state even if the drivers of the change are abated*" see IPCC (2018), p. 559.

causation, in particular within the framework of materiality, in which it might be determinant to the precondition that are placed on the substance of the outcome.[60]

A third requirement of the precautionary principle is strongly influenced by the perception of the nature of the principle itself and is, therefore, only occasionally called for in its application. If the principle is understood simply as a concept of cost-benefit analysis with an emphasis on the economic component, then the cost-effectiveness of an ex-ante action, as opposed to an ex-post repair of damage, may well be a further requirement for its application. Although the prevailing view denies the principle of such nature, the inclusion of a cost factor has nevertheless found its way into a wide range of treaties and regulations.[61] The economic perception of the precautionary principle, however, is at odds with its nature as a principle of environmental law, risk reduction and the preservation of biodiversity. Particularly in the face of irreversible damage, remedying the occurred harm cannot restore the former status quo. Such a perception is fatal, especially in the face of accelerating climate change. In any case, the introduction of a cost factor would not stand in the way of applying the precautionary principle to climate claims. Ex-post measures in climate scenarios relate to adaptation to the damage and other risks, which, in the context of a looming climate catastrophe, far outweigh the costs of ex-ante precautions and mitigation measures. The significant cost difference becomes even more apparent when the costs are considered in a timely perspective, including the burden on future generations to maintain a normal standard of living. Beyond the quantitative conception of the economic approach, there has also been an argument for a qualitative cost-benefit assessment.[62] But even from a qualitative point of view, there is hardly a scenario in which preventive measures take a back seat to reactive ones.[63] The cost-effectiveness of preventive measures in light of climate change, thus, boarders on irrelevance in the determination of normative causation.

5.2.2.3 The Polluter Pays Principle

The polluter pays principle (PPP) constitutes yet another key principle of international environmental and climate law. Concurrent with the debate surrounding the precautionary principle, the content, scope and general application of the polluter pays principle is also highly controversial.[64] In terms of its legal status, however, it has to be denied recognition under customary law.[65] As quintessence, the doctrine contains the dogma that "*the polluter should bear the expense of preventing and*

[60] See for a detailed assessment of materiality Sect. 5.4.

[61] The cost-effectiveness of the measures is also acknowledged by IPCC (2014b), p. 1268.

[62] Marti (2011), p. 62.

[63] Concerning the wording used and the prerequisites set by Art. 3 FCCC, de Sadeleer (2016), pp. 28–29.

[64] See concerning the further problems Schwartz (2018), pp. 268–270.

[65] Acknowledging the principle as a norm of regional custom Schwartz (2015), p. 436.

controlling pollution to ensure that the environment is in an acceptable state."[66] Thus, according to the prevailing view, it is merely a cost allocation norm, even though some authors emphasize the importance of the principle beyond its mere economic factor and recommend its reinforcement as a "*philosophy of responsibility and accountability.*"[67] Although it may seem terminologically correct that the polluter pays principle refers to cost allocation only from an ex-post perspective, this is not the case in practice. In conjunction with the precautionary principle, the polluter pays principle can also be applied from an ex-ante perspective.[68]

Concurrent with the other main principles of international environmental law, the polluter pays principle has found its way into a broad number of international treaties and agreements, with Principle 16 of the Rio Declaration being one of the most prominent reflections.[69] Principle 16 states:

> National authorities should endeavour to promote the internalization of environmental costs and the use of economic instruments, taking into account the approach that the polluter should, in principle, bear the cost of pollution, with due regard to the public interest and without distorting international trade and investment.[70]

Besides its international codification, the polluter pays principle is now increasingly being implemented in regional and national legislation, as well.[71] The polluter pays principle itself is an outgrowth of the principle of climate justice and the corrective component it contains, which in turn carries implications for virtually all normative causal doctrines.[72]

5.2.2.4 The Concept of Common but Differentiated Responsibilities

The principle of common but differentiated responsibilities (CBDR) constitutes another key principle of international environmental law. It is inter alia anchored in Principle 7 of the Rio Declaration, which notes:

> States shall cooperate in a spirit of global partnership to conserve, protect and restore the health and integrity of the Earth's ecosystem. In view of the different contributions to global environmental degradation, States have common but differentiated responsibilities. The developed countries acknowledge the responsibility that they bear in the international

[66] Organisation for Economic Co-operation and Development (1975), p. 15.

[67] In favour of a mere cost allocation norm, see Principle 16 of the Rio Declaration. Also Calliess (2022), para 42; Heselhaus (2017), para 75; Kahl (2018), para 97. Highlighting the importance beyond its economical factor, see Schwartz (2018), pp. 270–271. Proposing that it should be understood as a principle of material responsibility Rehbinder (2021), p. 53 para 23.

[68] Mossoux (2010), pp. 285–286; Monien (2014), pp. 350–352.

[69] Principles 21, 22 Stockholm Declaration.

[70] Principle 16 Rio Declaration.

[71] E.g. §§ 13, 14 German Nature Conservation Act.

[72] See Sect. 5.2.3.2.

pursuit of sustainable development in view of the pressures their societies place on the global environment and of the technologies and financial resources they command.[73]

Despite its lack of recognition as a norm of customary law, the principle is now embedded in a large number of international environmental and climate agreements, including Art. 2 (2) of the Paris Agreement, as well as in Art. 3 (1) and the Preamble of the Framework Convention on Climate Change.[74] The principle consists of two main components.[75] First, the reference to 'common' responsibilities imposes an obligation to cooperate and participate in the management of environmental and climate-related issues. Secondly, fairness and equity considerations are introduced into the principle through the reference to the 'differentiated' sphere of such responsibilities. As the first requirement of 'common' obligations sets the frame for all following environmental efforts, it is especially the concept of their 'differentiated' scope that provides the greatest ground for debate. It is also the latter that takes into account a timely component in evaluating past, current and future implications: The historical contributions to the environmental and climate situation of the individual states (hereby also targeting the problem of historical emissions), the current capacities and situation of the countries, as well as the future implications and effects that certain problems and developments bring with them for the different states. The result of such temporal sensitive consideration is an implicit distinction between developing and developed countries, whereby aspects such as financial and technological obligations, as well as other liabilities, are not reciprocally transferred to the individual countries but rather according to their respective capabilities, possibilities and resources. One major outlet of the principle, for example, is the obligation to transfer technology between developed and developing states as well as the support in basic capacity building. However, the scope of the obligations and their content vary widely and are still the subject of much debate underpinning the implementation of the concept of common but differentiated responsibilities.[76]

The concept of common but differentiated responsibilities does not in itself contain a causal assessment but entails strong indications for the normative assessment of causation. This is shown especially by current climate lawsuits, in which courts are increasingly resorting to the principle of common but differentiated responsibilities in close connection with their causal assessments.[77] The principle is hereby used, in particular, to overcome the now outdated drop-in-the-ocean

[73] Principle 7 Rio-Declaration.

[74] Concerning the CBDR and customary law see Honkonen (2016), pp. 147–148.

[75] For a detailed assessment of the components of the principle see Peel et al. (2018), pp. 245–248; Boyle and Redgwell (2021), pp. 148–149.

[76] In regard to the implementation of the CBDR within the climate regime see Honkonen (2016), pp. 144–145. Also in a broader sense Boyle and Redgwell (2021), pp. 147–148.

[77] See e.g. Administrative Court of Berlin, 31 October 2019 – VG 10 K 412.18, *Family Farmers and Greenpeace Germany v. Germany*, 21–22, Committee on the Rights of the Child, 8 October 2021 – CRC/C/88/D/107/2019, *Decision adopted by the Committee on the Rights of the Child under the Optional Protocol to the Convention on the Rights of the Child on a communications procedure in respect of Communication No. 107/2019*, para 9.10.

argument and, thus, forms an integral part in the normative assessment of materiality.[78] Breaking down the socio-political argument into its legal component can furthermore carry strong implications for the evaluation of the foreseeability of certain climate-change induced impacts.[79] The principle of common but differentiated responsibilities, thus, does justice to its role as a prerogative of consideration and moral imperative in climate change cases. In particular, it deprives states of the possibility of founding their arguments on the contributions of others. As the Administrative Court of Berlin has shown in its judgment in the case *Family Farmers and Greenpeace Germany v. Germany*, the requirements for causation, especially on a normative level, must not be overstretched.[80]

5.2.3 *Climate Justice*

5.2.3.1 Climate Justice as a Principle of Law

The general principles of justice, equity and fairness not only find their way directly and in their genuine form into normative causal considerations but also form and shape thematically specific conceptions. The most important concept within climate change litigation in this respect concerns the normative-based principle of 'climate justice'.

Climate justice is a dogma originally stemming from the American evolved principle of 'environmental justice'. The concept of environmental justice, in turn, arose within the environmental movement of the 1980s in the United States of America. During that time, socio-political factors such as inequity, poverty and racism had risen to the front of public awareness and debate through the approval and construction of environmentally harmful and high-pollutive plants and projects predominantly in the vicinity of neighbourhoods of low-income communities and minorities.[81] Such actions have led to the term known today as 'environmental racism'.[82] In the course of the pending and growing debate about anthropogenic climate change and climate change-induced damages, the principle of environmental justice evolved and expanded beyond its original scope and nowadays also entails a

[78] See in this regard Sect. 5.4.

[79] See in this regard Sect. 5.3.

[80] Administrative Court of Berlin, 31 October 2019 – VG 10 K 412.18, *Family Farmers and Greenpeace Germany v. Germany*.

[81] However, some authors, when referring to international climate and environmental cases, emphasise that the history of justice in environmental law is much older than the notion of environmental justice. See in this regard Ebbesson (2009b), pp. 2, 5–6. *Ebbesson* is hereby referring to Arbitrational Tribunal, 16 April 1938, 11 March 1941 – 3 R.I.A.A. 1905, *United States v. Canada (Trail Smelter Case)*.

[82] See e.g. Atapattu et al. (2021), p. 9; Kloepfer and Neugärtner (2021), pp. 28–30, paras 17–21.

climatic-focused component. This evolvement ultimately shaped the term and the principle of 'climate justice'.

In the context of the growing climate debate, the initially socio-political construct experienced an increasing juridification and nowadays constitutes a widely accepted principle that forms the foundation of environmental and climate efforts by multiple countries as well as the United Nations.[83] Such development is shown especially by the growing number of international treaties referring to and implementing such a concept. Among them is the Paris Agreement, which states in its preamble:

> [...] Noting the importance of ensuring the integrity of all ecosystems, including oceans, and the protection of biodiversity, recognized by some cultures as Mother Earth, and noting the importance for some of the concept of "climate justice", when taking action to address climate change [...].[84]

Other international frameworks with reference to the principle of climate justice are, for example, the FCCC and the 2000 UN Millennium Declaration.[85] However, the fact that the implementation of the principle of climate justice was not uncontroversial in its early days is shown by the terminology of the Paris Agreement, in which the application of the principle is limited by the term "*for some*".[86] From today's perspective and against the background of developments in climate law and the general climate discourse, such a limitation no longer seems feasible.[87]

Besides the embodiment of climate justice in specific climate and environmental treaties, the principle is also entailed in general principles of international and national environmental and climate law such as the principle of common but differentiated responsibilities or the polluter pays principle.[88] It, furthermore, shapes sustainable policy considerations and in turn finds reflection in the Sustainable Development Goals.[89] In addition to its strong focus on climate and environmental law concepts, the principle also has a fundamental impact on other areas of law. In this context, the principle acts as a referent and anchor for the 'greening' of provisions that were not originally conceived in terms of climate law, and also provides a basis of legitimacy for the expansion of such concepts. The principle of climate

[83] Germelmann (2021). Criticism, however, stems from the fact that environmental and climate justice, as they are currently and most commonly understood, do not apply to non-human beings and do not take non-human interests into account. In support of such critique and being in favour of '*ecophilosphical pluralism*' and '*ecological justice*', see Kloepfer and Neugärtner (2021), p. 30 para 24.

[84] Preamble Paris Agreement.

[85] Preamble FCCC, para 6. The 2000 UN Millennium Declaration further states that "*(g)lobal challenges must be managed in a way that distributes the costs and burdens fairly in accordance with basic principles of equity and social justice. Those who suffer or who benefit least deserve help from those who benefit most.*" 2000 UN Millennium Declaration, Section I, Principle 6.

[86] See in this regard Carazo (2017), pp. 117–118; Boer (2021), p. 27 para 78.

[87] See again Boer (2021), p. 27 para 78.

[88] See in this regard Sect. 5.2.2.

[89] See Agenda 2030.

justice is, therefore, of increasing relevance, particularly within the human rights framework.[90]

Furthermore, the principle of climate justice unfurls considerable importance as a balancing prerogative in the structuring and organization of practical and regulatory instruments. In the European Union, the debate about the implications and the implementation of climate justice arose especially in the context of the EU Emissions Trading System (EU ETS).[91] Decisive hereby was the manner of distribution regarding the respective certificates. Which factor would determine how many certificates a specific company would receive? Which scale should be applied in the capping of the certificates? Would considerations of climate justice justify a differentiated treatment among different companies? The ETS is only an example of the implications the concept of climate justice can have in its practical implementation. Nowadays, considerations of justice, equity and fairness can be found in nearly every climate-relevant policy framework and convention. Moreover, the principle is becoming increasingly enforceable, not at least thanks to the growing focus on the principle of climate justice in climate change litigation.[92]

5.2.3.2 The Substance of Climate Justice

Although the principle of climate justice is widely recognized, its scope and content still constitute some issue of debate, with the result of climate justice considerations strongly depending on the manner in which the principle is approached. On the one hand, one could consider aspects of climate justice exclusively in relation to the climate and climate change per se and in complete disregard of other issues, such as economic, social and cultural factors ('*isolationism*').[93] However, this does not find much acceptance among scholars, nor is this approach reflected in the aspiration of climate justice efforts in law in general.[94] International law and treaties, in particular, are characterized by the inclusion of numerous factors to shape the idea of justice. Limiting the idea of justice exclusively to such a small frame would additionally run counter to the general impacts of climate change, which extent to multiple different areas beyond the mere natural component. Thus, the approach that takes into account and integrates different levels of considerations generally prevails ('*integrationism*').[95]

---

[90] See for the implications of climate justice on the human rights framework, inter alia Jegede and Adejonwo (2022) and Giacomini (2022).

[91] See for a more detailed analysis of the debate on distributive justice in particular in relation to the national sphere of implementation Kloepfer (2006), pp. 285–297, paras 613–640.

[92] Climate justice especially comes at the forefront in climate change litigation in respect to the debate surrounding future generations.

[93] Caney (2020).

[94] Stephens (2022b, 2022a). See in regard to a per capita budget Torpman (2021).

[95] See for a more detailed analysis of that matter Caney (2020). In favour for an integrational, holistic approach also Caney (2018).

Following the dominant approach of integrationism, the core content of the principle of climate justice lies within the equitable distribution of climate benefits and burdens, carrying at its heart the reduction of greenhouse gases in a socially just manner and the fair allocation of climate change-related damage.[96] The concept of climate justice beholds the premise that those who have contributed least to anthropogenic climate change are the ones most affected by it, which in correlation are those who have benefited least from greenhouse gas emissions as well. Others refrain in their definition from a merely anthropogenic point of view and pursue climate justice in a more universal and ecocentric way. *Msafiri,* for example, defines climate justice as "*short- and long-term rights and abilities of the earth to regenerate and support all life forms, human and non-human, in a sustainable and dignified manner, with a fair distribution of resources and environmental burdens.*"[97] Regardless of how climate justice is ultimately defined, the principle ultimately bridges the gap between the purely ecological problem of global warming and the resulting changes to the ecosystem and the morally implied and resulting societal and social influences and impacts. It concurrently widens the aspect of justice to a global perspective and opens up the concept to a spatiotemporal sphere. Based on this integrating approach, ethical, philosophical, political and sociological points of views find their way into the ecological discussion on the effects and mitigation of climate change, which is also reflected in discussions of political philosophy.[98]

The multidisciplinarity of the concept further enhances the already inherent discrepancies of the understanding of the principle which are based in particular on the fact that the definition of justice, or the perception of justice as such, varies greatly in different cultural circles and legal systems. Another reason for the divergence of the concept can be perceived from its strong moral interconnectedness and its temporal variability. Moral and societal perceptions alter over time. Climate justice is, therefore, a fluctuating concept, dependent on moral views, political opinions and the cultural and societal values of the time. Notwithstanding these conceptual differences, distinct underlying types of justice can be inferred from the concept of climate justice. Overall there are four overarching notions of justice, which are, although initially self-contained, intertwined and strongly interconnected. The first and one of the most important notions of climate justice, which also constitutes one of the pillars of international climate conventions such as the Paris Agreement, is the concept of distributive justice (a)). Another highly influential notion, especially in light of climate change litigation is the concept of corrective justice, which is also pervasive in the public debate on the distribution and cost allocation of climate damages (b)). Often overlooked and overshadowed by the strong and very present notions of distributive and corrective justice is the procedural component of climate justice (c)). More and more attention, on the other hand, is

---

[96] See in this regard also Huang (2017), p. 25.

[97] Msafiri (2013), p. 662.

[98] See e.g. Torpman (2021).

prescribed to the last of the four notions of justice, which subsumes a wide variety of other conceptions under the frame of social justice (d)).

5.2.3.2.1 Distributive Justice

One of the cornerstones of the principle of climate justice is the fair and equitable allocation of benefits as well as the burdens of climate change in its embodiment as a distributive notion of justice.[99] The debate about the way in which certain benefits and burdens are to be distributed within a definable group, however, already existed long before the development of the principle of climate and environmental justice.[100] The same applies to the decisive criteria that have to be taken into account and that ultimately determine the amount one receives. Despite the tight linkage between climate and environmental justice, both concepts slightly differ in their dimension of their distributional component. The distributive dimension of environmental justice is largely, but not exclusively, positive, i.e. concerned with the equitable distribution of environmental goods, and is thus benefit-oriented.[101] Climate justice, on the other hand, increasingly focuses on the negative dimension of the concept of distributive justice. This reflects the fact that climate change per se is predominantly detrimental. The main component of distributive justice within climate justice is thus the equitable distribution of emission burdens and the costs of protection against climate change-induced damage. Due to its negative and, therefore, burden-sharing connotation, distributive justice correlates strongly with the notion of corrective justice. The positive frame of climate distributive justice, on the other hand, consists of the equitable distribution of the remaining budget of greenhouse gas emissions determined by specific climate change targets (e.g. the aim of keeping the warming of the atmosphere under 1.5 °C).[102]

The conceptualisation and application of the principle of distributive justice is extremely complex. Not only do the divergent perceptions of justice already discussed complicate its material-legal application, but the appropriate application

[99] For a critique of the principle of distributive justice in international law and international environmental law, see Cullet (2010), p. 168; Kloepfer and Neugärtner (2021), p. 34 para 35. *Kloepfer* describes distributive justice as implicit in the concept of environmental justice as "*myopic and superficial*". Ibid.

[100] For a detailed analysis of the historical context of distributive justice in relation to the principle of environmental justice, see Ehemann (2020), pp. 54–57. The origin of the idea of distributive justice is often traced back to *Aristotle* in Aristotle (n.d.), Ethica Nicomachea. For a brief compilation of the ideas contained in this work see again Ehemann (2020), pp. 54–57.

[101] The negative dimension of distribution in environmental justice concerns mainly cases of water and air pollution. Environmental goods include mineral resources, groundwater, oil and gas reserves, renewable materials such as wood, etc.

[102] IPCC (2018).

of distributive standards and parameters also remains highly controversial.[103] Distributive justice is a construct that is strongly influenced by divergent interests and is interpreted differently depending on the point of reference. However, the underlying criterion of distributive justice is undoubtedly the principle of equality (both between states and between individuals). Equality, moreover, is a highly normative concept that is strongly influenced by the perceptions of justice and equality of the respective actors and policy-makers.

In addition, there are formal difficulties in determining the relevant comparative component. In principle, there are two dominating approaches to an equitable distribution of the residual greenhouse gas budget. On the one hand, one could take up a per capita view, which would apportion a certain budget to every individual, which would then translate into a certain greenhouse gas budget for the state regarding its number of inhabitants.[104] On the other hand, one could argue for a state-related reference point. Here, every state would be assigned a certain budget, regardless of its population. However, which components and criteria are decisive for the scope of the budget is still an issue for debate. Conceivable would, for example, be the Gross Domestic Product (GDP), the population (this correlates strongly with a per capita view) or the overall development of the countries.[105] Whether the budget, in turn, should be historically sensitive and take into account former greenhouse gas emissions or be neglectful of such is still subject of major discussion. Furthermore, the principle of equality, despite its predominant recognition as a justice-relevant feature, is also called into question. *Shue,* in particular, argues for a subsistence-based distribution principle.[106] This is opposed by the view of formal equality, which justifies distribution without reference to subsistence, which in turn is very difficult to assess. That the equality criterion is by no means rigidly and strictly applied in practice is shown by the form of emission reduction targets in relevant climate agreements. While on the one hand a division into two different groups of states was made in the light of the Kyoto Protocol, the grouping of China and the concessions made to Spain and Australia, for example, testify to a politically motivated partial dissociation from the idea of equality and also equity-based distributive justice.[107]

Equality, however, does not form the only parameter which has or can be considered in finding the right vantage point for distributive justice. Other factors might include the rule of proportionality, equity or adequacy.[108] Distributive justice

---

[103] See for a more detailed analysis of the different concepts Czarnecki (2008), pp. 163–170. More generally, but also in regard to environmental law Ehemann (2020), pp. 54–57.

[104] See for a more detailed analysis Caney (2020). From a climate ethical point of view Birnbacher (2015). In regard to a per capita distribution ibid. 70–71.

[105] The Kyoto-Protocol, for example, distinguishes between Annex 1 countries (mostly developed countries) and non-Annex 1 countries (mostly developing countries). Those criteria are also referenced in regard to the materiality threshold, see in this regard Sect. 5.4.

[106] Shue (2014), pp. 47–66.

[107] See e.g. in the Kyoto-Protocol.

[108] *Kloepfer* hereby refers to the term '*Prinzipienpluralismus*' see Kloepfer (2006), p. 33 para 35.

is, therefore, a motley bouquet of interdependent conceptions and parameters. Due to the numerous different and interconnected principles, a varying understanding of justice, a divergency in regard to the actor and addressee, as well as the necessary distinction between the distribution of benefits and of damages, a standardized conception on how to approach and consider distributive justice in climate scenarios is simply not feasible.[109] Distributive justice, nevertheless, forms a fundamental part of any justice consideration in climate change lawsuits.

5.2.3.2.2 Corrective Justice

5.2.3.2.2.1 Corrective Justice and Present Emissions

Corrective justice represents the second major notion of overall climate justice considerations. The concept presents a means of retributive and reparative justice, which at its core holds the idea that anyone who has been deprived of rights or has suffered harm should be compensated accordingly. The notion of justice is fulfilled by restoring the status quo or, where this is not possible, by providing compensation for the harm suffered.[110] However, corrective justice is not a self-contained regime; rather, it overlaps in many respects with other principles of justice, including in particular the conception of justice in its distributional dimension. How distributive justice can be distinguished from corrective justice, nevertheless, is still highly disputed in both moral and philosophical discourse.[111]

In the law, corrective justice is mainly entailed and enforced in the areas of tort law, contract law, unjust enrichment and most comprehensively in criminal law.[112] A major influence in the pursuit of corrective climate justice today can also be attributed to the growing movement of climate change litigation. Most of these lawsuits have at their core the idea of correcting past wrongs and preventing or stopping new climate damage. Given the widespread agreement on the harmful effects of climate change and its anthropogenic influence, it is generally accepted that present actions should be viewed and analysed in terms of corrective mechanisms. The extent to which corrective justice is to be fulfilled, however, remains at the discretion of policymakers and courts.

---

[109] Affirming such conception ibid. 32–36, paras 31–39.

[110] For an example of what corrective justice might require, see for the Maldives Atapattu and Simonelli (2021). Highlighting the paucity of research on corrective justice in international law Mickelson (2009), pp. 299–300.

[111] See e.g. Benson (1992). *McKinnon's* distinction is based on the parties involved. Corrective justice is always between individuals, i.e. one party to another, whereas distributive justice must be considered in relation to society as a whole. See McKinnon (2009), p. 261.

[112] As opposed to distributive justice. According to *Thornton*, who sees distributive justice as more prominent in public law, Thornton (2021).

5.2.3.2.2.2 Corrective Justice and Historic Emissions

The treatment of historic emissions is highly controversial as it involves a wide range of philosophical, ethical and moral issues, which are then intertwined with economic and legal considerations. However, the debate on how to deal with past emissions in the light of the corrective dimension of climate justice revolves around four main areas of concern. The first relates to the question of whether historical emissions should give rise to any responsibility or obligation on the part of the parties concerned. The second, and arguably the most debated issue, concerns the perception of responsibility and blame. It is primarily a reflection of the cause of the corrective. Closely related to the second question is the third, which focuses on determining who is or should be responsible: the individual, the state, or both. Finally, the fourth relates to the scope and content of responsibility. In particular, it asks what obligations should be imposed on the party in question.

5.2.3.2.2.2.1 Historic Emissions and General Reproachability

The question of whether there should be any responsibility at all for historical emissions forms the basis for further discussions on the application of corrective justice criteria to past climate damage. It is safe to say that most philosophers and legal scholars nowadays are in favour of imposing responsibility, although in various ways, to the respective actors.[113] The main aspect of reproachability, however, does not relate to the emission of greenhouse gases per se, but the exceeding of a country's budget or nature's ability to compensate for these anthropogenic emissions. Few disagree with this view. The main argument that is put forward in that regard refers to the overall use of corrective justice to climate change scenarios. *Sunstein* and *Posner,* for example, resume "*that the climate change problem poorly fits the corrective justice model, because the consequence of tort-like thinking would be to force many people who have not acted wrongfully to provide a remedy to many people who have not been victimized.*"[114] The overall consensus, nonetheless, rests in the assertion that responsibility for historic emissions does persist. Reference can be drawn, for example, from the frequent discussion of reparations for damage caused by and during the colonial era.[115]

---

[113] See inter alia Mason-Case and Dehm (2021), p. 174; Shelton (2009), p. 72; Zellentin (2015); Neumayer (2000).

[114] Sunstein and Posner (2007), p. 21. In the same sense Posner and Weisbach (2010), p. 103. Refuting historical responsibility overall, Zahar (2021).

[115] Although Germany has rejected any legal claims for damages as a result of colonialism, it has recognized the genocide in Namibia and pledged financial support of around €1.1 billion for the reconstruction and development of Namibia in 2021. See tagesschau (2021). Further on this issue Theurer (2023) and Ebbers and Müller (2023). Similarly, the restitution of the so-called Benin bronzes by the German Foreign Minister Annalena Baerbock on 20 December 2022. See more on this topic Campfens (2018).

5.2.3.2.2.2.2 *Conceptions of Historic Reproachability*

The following aspect of corrective justice in the light of historical emissions relates to the specific concepts and approaches that should be used to assess responsibility. In general, three different approaches are advocated in the literature. The first focuses on the emitter per se and imposes responsibility and a duty to pay on the polluter, the so-called polluter pays principle (PPP).[116] Given that the PPP starting from its development in the *Trail Smelter case* in 1938 and 1941 has now become one of the pillars of international environmental law, it has consequently also been advocated in regard to addressing the harm induced by historic emissions.[117] One of the main objections, however, is that the individual polluters of the past can no longer be held accountable.[118] Some, therefore, argue for a succession of obligations, echoing similar debates about the damage caused by colonialism and war. In view of the difficulties associated with the transfer of obligations, succession seems feasible, if at all, only for states and larger entities.[119]

The second and arguably more modern approach to historic responsibility is formed by the beneficiary pays principle (BPP).[120] Proponents of the BPP cite the economic growth that accompanied the emission of large quantities of greenhouse gases during the industrial era. The main argument consists of the notion that those who have benefited the most should have the greatest obligation to mitigate climate change and to pay for the damages caused by climate change. However, most proponents of this approach only take into account benefits that have been achieved through either unlawful or inequitable actions.

[116] In philosophical literature, this principle is sometimes referred to as the 'contribution-to-problem principle' (CPP), see Heyward (2021). Also Kirby (2016). See also in the previous Sect. 5.2.2.3.

[117] See e.g. Zellentin (2015). *Zellentin* bases her thoughts on the slogan "*You broke it, you fix it*". See for the *Trail Smelter case*, Arbitrational Tribunal, 16 April 1938, 11 March 1941 – 3 R.I.A.A. 1905, *United States v. Canada (Trail Smelter Case).*

[118] Calling it the "*wrongdoer identity problem*", Sunstein and Posner (2007), pp. 22–24; Posner and Weisbach (2010), pp. 103–108. See in regard to the overall problem of who can be defined as polluter, Kloepfer and Neugärtner (2021), p. 35 para 38.

[119] The point of reference, at least for states, could be the international views on the succession of states. Others build their argument on the 'institutional continuity' or the continuity of bilateral agreements, see in more depth Butt (2017), p. 64.

[120] See in favour of the BPP, Okowa (2010), pp. 313–314; Barry and Kirby (2017). Introducing the concept of 'transgenerational free-riding' and advocating for the application of the BPP, Gosseries (2004). Advocating for a slightly changed understanding of the BPP, Berkey (2017), p. 138. Advocating for the BPP in its form as an "*unjust enrichment principle*", see Page (2012). Against the BPP e.g. Karnein (2017). *Karnein* argues that the mere benefit cannot impose obligations on the beneficiary. On the same note Huseby (2015). Applying a modified version and calling it the 'Qualified Beneficiary Pays Principle', see Baatz (2013), p. 15.

Opposing the BPP, academics argue that other, mostly low-emitting countries have also benefited from industrialisation and the associated greenhouse gas emissions.[121] They argue that not only have low-emitting countries benefited economically from industrialisation in terms of increased trade, technology transfer and globalisation in general, but that greenhouse gas emissions have also indirectly led to improvements in living standards and general health. Some even use climate arguments, claiming that some countries will benefit from climate change through milder climates that can increase agricultural productivity and soil fertility.[122] A final objection concerns the reference point for categorising past emitters and beneficiaries. Some argue that although industrialised countries have emitted a lot of CO_2, low-emitting countries in the past have also contributed to climate change through increased deforestation and agricultural land use, releasing large amounts of methane.[123] Therefore, countries with low CO_2 emissions should also be classified as emitters. It goes without saying that this is not an exhaustive list of arguments against the BPP. Especially in the philosophical and ethical discourse, there is still a well-founded debate about the applicability of the principle.[124]

The third approach departs from the backward-looking approaches and considers the capacity of countries to adapt and mitigate climate change. The so-called ability to pay principle (APP) refers to the economic, technological and financial potential of countries, meaning that only those countries that are actually able to compensate for the damage caused should be obliged to support affected nations.[125] However, this approach is rarely advocated on its own, but rather combined with one of the other principles of corrective justice.[126] In particular, proponents of the BPP tend to include some notion of APP to avoid the criticism that countries that have emitted a lot and may have benefited at some point in time may have lost that benefit and may not be able to bear the burden today. Including the APP would exempt such countries from liability.

In international law, all three principles have found their way into the framework of climate law. As the main pillar of international environmental law, the PPP is one of the most dominant conceptions. But the APP has also found its way into the law per se within the framework of CBDR. Insofar as the CBDR imposes responsibility according to individual capabilities, the principle is in line with the idea of the APP. In the climate context, the BPP is also important because it is implicitly anchored in the PPP. This is based on the fact that, contrary to some opinions, reducing or

[121] Arguing against a 'distinctive role' of the BPP, see Heyward (2021), p. 126. For a comprehensive account on the major arguments brought forward against the BPP see Kirby (2016), pp. 44–67.

[122] In this regard e.g. Sunstein and Posner (2007), p. 23. See for the most recent assessment of the impacts of climate change on food, fiber and other ecosystem products also including agriculture and farming, IPCC (2022a).

[123] See e.g. Zahar (2021).

[124] See again Kirby (2016), pp. 44–67.

[125] In favour of the APP, Meyer and Roser (2010). Framing it as a principle of fairness, see Shue (2014), pp. 186–189.

[126] Proposing a combination of the APP and PPP, Caney (2010).

contributing to climate change also correlates with corresponding benefits. There is no clear choice between the two principles. Instead, as normative considerations, they are coherently integrated into the notion of climate justice, and thus also into the resulting understanding of normative causation, in line with the international climate framework.

5.2.3.2.2.2.3 The Perception of the Right Duty Bearer

The third area of concern relates to the question of who exactly should be held accountable for past emissions and who should be the ultimate duty bearer. It thus builds largely on the debate on reproachability and the principles of corrective justice introduced earlier and reflects broadly the discourse on the idea of responsibility, whether from an individualistic or a collective point of view.[127] Particularly in the light of recent international climate agreements, most scholars identify states as the most comprehensive duty bearers.[128] Private actors, in turn, mostly relate to private entities such as companies and corporations. To date, individuals themselves have rarely been held directly accountable under the concept of corrective justice.[129] However, it is precisely this that has been criticised with regard to the accountability of states. Even if states were held responsible, the actual burden of the obligation would be borne indirectly by individuals through their taxes and possible tax increases. Given that such a transfer of burdens seems generally unfair, not a few authors use this argument to reject historical responsibility altogether.[130] Another criticism concerns the identity of the plaintiff. Since current generations have had no opportunity to control the behaviour and emissions of past greenhouse gases, how can current individuals be held accountable?[131] On the other hand, some argue that the ultimate, damaging effects of climate change will not be fully felt until sometime in the future, i.e. they will mainly affect future generations. There is thus a divergence between claimant and victim, which again would not fit into the realm of climate justice considerations.[132]

5.2.3.2.2.2.4 The Scope of the Duty

Finally, disagreement persists over the scope and content of such a levy. While some argue for a full absorption of all benefits, others advocate for a percentage

[127] *Godard*, for example, makes a strong distinction between these two moral concepts and shows how each would function if applied comprehensively to considerations of corrective justice. See Godard (2017), pp. 113–115.

[128] In this regard see e.g. Zellentin (2015); Page (2012), pp. 302–303.

[129] See for an example of the invocation of individual responsibility International Criminal Court, pending – n/a, *The Planet v. Bolsonaro*.

[130] See again Posner and Weisbach (2010) and Sunstein and Posner (2007).

[131] Godard (2017), p. 121.

[132] Calling it the '*victim/claimant identity problem*' Sunstein and Posner (2007), pp. 24–25; Posner and Weisbach (2010), pp. 108–109.

distribution based on the damage caused to a low-emitting country by the benefit derived by the high-emitting country.[133] Others focus on the damage that has been done and demand compensation, regardless of the profits countries have made from past emissions.[134] Which approach is ultimately advocated by which scholar depends to a large extent on whether the PPP, BPP or APP is used in the light of corrective justice. Given that the scope and content of the duty do not affect the normative substance of the principle of corrective justice and the moral and ethical considerations underlying it, the debate may fall short on this point. In particular, the amount of damages and compensation does not affect the normative considerations made in the context of the legal notion of causation.

The incorporation of moral and philosophical considerations into legal thinking is widespread. This applies in particular to the question of which norms and rules should be applied, or whether they even meet the needs of corrective justice as a whole.[135] The main and most morally relevant problem is the treatment and assessment of the foreseeability of the parties involved.[136] Can someone be held responsible for a specific act that was not known to be harmful at the time it was committed? And can someone be held liable retrospectively for something that was not punishable at the time it was done? Although such legal considerations are largely informed by philosophical and ethical discourse, they are usually discussed in the context of evaluating the specific normative test. What is apparent in the legal discourse, however, is that the strong divergence between PPP, BPP and APP is increasingly being broken down. Although the PPP is a well-known principle in international environmental law, legal scholars often combine the PPP with the BPP when talking about corrective justice for historical emissions. This is particularly the case when countries are divided into Annex I and Annex II countries, as was done in the Kyoto Protocol.[137]

5.2.3.2.3 Procedural Justice

In addition to the substantive concepts of distributive and corrective justice, climate justice also entails a procedural notion that implements criteria of fairness and equity

---

[133] Advocating for a transfer of all unjustly received goods, Berkey (2017), p. 138.

[134] Calling for reparations modelled on payments made in regard to colonialism but without advocating a full compensation for the occurred harm, see Mason-Case and Dehm (2021), pp. 187–189.

[135] See e.g. Farber (2017). *Farber* argues that the negligence systems fits the needs of corrective justice better than e.g. the system of product liability.

[136] See for the implementation of corrective justice considerations into the test of foreseeability Sect. 5.3.

[137] See e.g. Kyoto Protocol.

in the decision-making processes.[138] One of the main aspects hereby forms the principle of transparency, as well as public participation, inclusivity and the access to information.

Procedural justice is strongly interrelated with other notions of climate justice. Decisions about the just and fair distribution of climate burdens or benefits, for example, have to be pursued within the framework of a procedure that meets the requirements of procedural justice.[139] One of the main and most common implementations of the concept of procedural justice in climate induced claims is to be seen in light of environmental impact assessments (EIA). In addition to being framed in terms of environmental issues, EIAs often and increasingly tend to include potential climate impacts. The importance of EIAs in relation to climate-damaging projects is reflected in the increasing number of climate-related lawsuits that base their claims on the inadequate and unlawful conduct of EIAs.[140] Only the guarantees of procedural justice, i.e. that EIAs are carried out and accessible to the public, ensure that climate change litigation is possible at all.

Another notion of procedural justice relates to the legal sphere, with the provision of general access to courts also being relevant to climate issues. Procedural justice in this sense has been at issue when courts, particularly in earlier climate change litigation, have rejected claims based on the so-called 'political question doctrine'.[141] By stating that the issue raised by the plaintiffs could not be fully debated in court but had to be decided by the legislature in the light of the separation of powers, courts denied their own jurisdiction and thus denied procedural justice. Today, this argument is by and large no longer valid. Courts are increasingly asserting their jurisdiction. Where the concept of procedural justice comes into play, however, is in the question of the representation of younger and, even more so, future generations. Both groups of claimants do not have access to the courts under normal circumstances, either because of their young age or because they do not yet exist. Procedural justice is, therefore, of paramount importance in the context of climate change litigation.

---

[138] For further elaborations on procedural justice as it relates to environmental justice, and related research, see Kloepfer (2006), pp. 47–53. For the notion of procedural justice in international law and in transboundary law cases, see Ebbesson (2009a), pp. 275–276, 284–285.

[139] See e.g. Ebbesson (2009b), pp. 15–16; Ehemann (2020), p. 471.

[140] See e.g. Federal Court, 3 June 2020 – 2020 FC 663, *Ecology Action, et al. v. Minister of Environment and Climate Change*, Court of Justice at Wagani, 10 September 2021 – OS (JR) 35 of 2021, *Saonu and Morobe Provincial Government v. Minster for Environment and Conservation and Climate Change and Others*, Kenya's National Environmental Tribunal, 26 September 2019 – Net 196 of 2016, *Save Lamu et al. v. National Environmental Management Authority and Amu Power Co. Ltd*, Federal Court of Nigeria, 30 November 2005 – FHC/B/CS/53/05, *Gbemre v. Shell Petroleum Development Company of Nigeria Ltd. and Others*, United Kingdom Court of Appeal (Civil Division), 17 February 2022 – [2022] EWCA Civ 187, *R (Finch on behalf of the Weald Action Group & Others) v. Surrey County Council (& Others).*

[141] Scottish Court of Sessions, 7 October 2021 – [2021] CSIH 53, *Greenpeace v. United Kingdom*, United States Court of Appeals for the Ninth Circuit, 17 January 2020 – 6:15-cv-01517-AA, *Juliana v. United States*, 5.

5.2.3.2.4 Social Justice

Social justice as the fourth notion entailed in the overall principle of climate justice mainly is a result of integrationism. It includes and reflects the fact that climate considerations are highly interconnected and dependent on other aspects of life, as well as being influenced by issues such as poverty, race, gender and other factors. In the following, only a few of those factors are to be addressed, among those are the notions of intergenerational (Sect. 5.2.3.2.4.1) and cultural justice (Sect. 5.2.3.2.4.2) Yet social justice itself is a constantly evolving concept, influenced by social discourse and the challenges of the times.

5.2.3.2.4.1 Intergenerational Justice

Intergenerational justice builds upon the aspect that climate change does not only affect past and present but also and even more so future generations. It bridges the gap between different generations and their interests and provides a solution for generational conflicts with regard to climate issues.[142] Today, intergenerational justice is mainly used in relation to future generations. The principle consequently advocates the inclusion of intergenerational aspects in policy making, judicial decisions and further climate change considerations. It is based on the understanding that current actions should always take into account their impact on children, young people and future generations. However, how the interests of future generations should be taken into account in a fair and equitable way is still widely debated. This is particularly the case when it comes to determining the right temperature threshold and the remaining greenhouse gas budget. Intergenerational justice is also relevant to the question of who should bear the burden of damages caused by climate change. It, therefore, also includes a component of corrective justice.[143]

The notion of intergenerational justice was especially at issue in the judgement of the Supreme Court of Germany in the case *Neubauer, et al. v. Germany*.[144] In this case, the Court ruled that the former Climate Protection Act ('*Klimaschutzgesetz*') violated the fundamental rights of young people and, implicitly, of future generations, by failing to set strict and sufficient emission reduction targets.[145] The main burden of reducing emissions would thus be postponed and imposed on future

---

[142] See on the notion of intergenerational justice in relation to environmental justice Kloepfer (2006), pp. 26–27, paras 18–19. On the implications of climate change litigation for intergenerational justice, see Spentzou (2021).

[143] For a more detailed analysis of the different views and positions on the principle of intergenerational equity, see Caney (2020).

[144] Germany Federal Constitutional Court, 24 March 2021 – 1 BvR 2656/18 – 1 BvR 78/20 – 1 BvR 96/20 – 1 BvR 288/20, *Neubauer et al. v. Germany*. For a detailed analysis of intergenerational justice concerning the decision, see Seibert (2021).

[145] German Climate Act.

generations.[146] Beyond that specific case, there is a general trend of younger generations pursuing climate change lawsuits based on the argument and the substance of climate and thus intergenerational justice.[147] As a result, courts can serve as a forum for shaping and forming the principle of intergenerational justice by defining the scope of the aspect and its implementation in both the political and social spheres.

5.2.3.2.4.2 Cultural Justice

Cultural justice also forms an intrinsic principle in quite a few climate change lawsuits. Especially concerning claims raised by indigenous peoples which address the dangers of climate change to their cultural habits and their culture in general, cultural justice considerations are applied.[148] Cultural justice in general implies that different cultures may be affected differently by overall climate change, as well as by climate-damaging behaviours and mitigation efforts. Cultures that rely heavily on the natural environment for their way of life, and that maintain a close connection and interdependence with nature as such, are particularly affected by climate change. This is even more the case when nature itself becomes the cultural root of the people. This is where cultural resilience to climate change comes into play.

5.2.3.2.4.3 Further Notions of Social Justice

Social justice forms a broad framework under which a multitude of different social aspects can be subsumed. Characteristic hereby is the fact that the vulnerability to climate change damages or climate change in general strongly depends on societal aspects and someone's social status. Intergenerationally, these include, for example, the affiliation to different social classes and groups (especially minorities), a certain age (with a special focus on marginalized groups, i.e. children and the elderly), the

[146] The Court hereby refers to the concept of the intertemporal guarantee of freedom ('*intertemporale Freiheitssicherung*'), Germany Federal Constitutional Court, 24 March 2021 – 1 BvR 2656/18 – 1 BvR 78/20 – 1 BvR 96/20 – 1 BvR 288/20, *Neubauer et al. v. Germany*, paras 116–134, 182–265.

[147] See e.g. Lahore High Court, pending – No. 8960 of 2019, *Maria Khan et al. v. Federation of Pakistan et al*, application (14 February 2019), Brazil Federal Supreme Court, 1 July 2022 – ADPF 708, *PSB et al. v. Brazil*, application (11 November 2020), High Court at Kampala, pending – No. 283 of 2012, *Mbabazi and Others v. The Attorney General and National Environmental Management Authority*, statement of claim (20 September 2012). European Court of Human Rights, pending – 39371/20, *Duarte Agostinho and Others v. Portugal and 32 Other States*.

[148] See e.g. Federal Court of Australia, pending – VID322/2021, *Pabai Pabai and Guy Paul Kabai v. Commonwealth of Australia*, application (26 October 2021), 9th Federal Court of Rio Grande do Sul, pending – 5069057-47.2019.4.04.7100, *Arayara Association of Education and Culture and others v. FUNAI, Copelmi Mineração Ltda. and FEPAM (Mina Guaíba Project and affected indigenous communities)*, esp. decision (20 January 2022), United Nations Human Rights Committee, 22 September 2022 – CCPR/C/135/D/3624/2019, *Daniel Billy et al. v. Australia (Torres Strait Islanders Petition)*.

gender (especially women and members of the LGTBQ+ community), and people with a migration background.[149] Beyond that, factors such as poverty, racism and a colonial past can and must be taken into account within questions of social justice and thus also climate justice as well. The issue of social justice is, therefore, primarily concerned with considerations of equity rather than equality, given that equality is one source of social injustice with respect to climate-vulnerable groups.

5.2.4 Implications for Normative Causation in Climate Scenarios

A variety of normative considerations and principles influence the connotation of normative causation in climate scenarios. However, not all normative considerations are equally important when it comes to adapting factual causation in climate change litigation. And although climate justice is at the forefront of the legal debate, not all of its concepts come into play in the assessment of normative causation. In particular, the notion of procedural justice, while also highly relevant to climate lawsuits in general, plays only a minor role in assessing the scope of factual causation. In contrast, aspects of distributive and corrective justice are of paramount importance. In connection with the principle of social justice and the related notion of intergenerational justice, corrective and distributive justice are invoked in particular when dealing with past emissions. These notions of justice need to be taken into account especially with regard to the legal test of foreseeability and the question of the right temporal threshold.[150] Apart from the aspect of intergenerational justice, other dimensions of social justice are only of minor importance when it comes to the assessment of normative causation.

In addition to these general requirements of climate justice, other normative principles are of relevance, as well. Chief among these is the principle of equity.

---

[149] Social justice in relation to the elderly, for example, is at the heart of the case European Court of Human Rights, pending – 53600/20, *KlimaSeniorinnen v. Switzerland*, Swiss Supreme Court, 20 May 2020 – No. A-2992/2017, *Association of Swiss Senior Women for Climate Protection v. Federal Department of the Environment Transport, Energy and Communications (DETEC) and Others*, Swiss Federal Supreme Court, 20 May 2020 – 1C_37/2019, *Association of Swiss Senior Women for Climate Protection v. Federal Department of the Environment Transport, Energy and Communications (DETEC) and Others ("Verein KlimaSeniorinnen Schweiz v. Bundesrat")*. See for women, e.g. Lahore High Court, pending – No. 8960 of 2019, *Maria Khan et al. v. Federation of Pakistan et al.* The argument was also brought forward in a recent hearing request before the IACHR, see Inter-American Commission on Human Rights, pending – n/a, *Hearing on Climate Change Before the Inter-American Commission on Human Rights*.

[150] See in this regard Sect. 5.3.2.

Its importance in the legal debate on climate change is reflected in the notion of 'climate equity' and its increasing use in climate change litigation.[151] In particular, international climate agreements, most notably the Paris Agreement, have fallen back on demanding an equitable distribution of burdens and benefits.[152] The Kyoto Protocol, too, revolves around the idea of equity in dividing member states into Annex I and Annex II countries, and thus in determining different obligations to reduce emissions and protect the climate. Due to its importance in international climate treaties as well as in climate policy in general, the principle of equity also forms one of the pillars of normative considerations with regard to normative causation in climate change litigation.

It is interesting to note, however, that most climate and environmental treaties, especially in recent times, have refrained from using the terms 'equality' or 'fairness'.[153] This may be due to the fact that the scope of the concept of equity is seen as better reflecting the current challenges and commitments in the face of the impending climate crisis than mere equality. However, despite their lack of implementation in international treaties, equality and fairness are present in the legal debate and are often applied when it comes to equal and fair burden-sharing and emissions budgets. They are fundamental components of considerations of justice in general and are therefore crucial to assess when it comes to normative causation. How and in what way normative criteria are incorporated into the assessment of normative causation, however, is not a matter of uniform application. The close links with the rapidly developing field of climate science, the susceptibility of the issue to political, social, religious and moral beliefs, and the necessary economic and legal constraints associated with climate protection lead to divergent perceptions of the normative components.

5.3 The Principle of Foreseeability

5.3.1 Foreseeability as a General Principle of Normative Causation

Foreseeability is one of the most decisive normative criteria in adapting factual causal results. By assessing whether the outcome and the causal sequence of someone's conduct or omission was foreseeable, normative causation provides a

[151] Equity considerations can be found e.g. in New South Wales Land and Environment Court, 8 February 2019 – [2019] NSWLEC 7, *Gloucester Resources Limited v. Minister for Planning*, paras 398–416. As well as in regard to intergenerational equity Land and Environment Court of New South Wales, 27 November 2006 – [2006] NSWLEC 720, *Gray v. Minister for Planning*, paras 118–126.

[152] Preamble, as well as Art. 2, 4, 14 Paris Agreement. Art. 3, 4, 11 FCCC.

[153] The Paris Agreement e.g. only addresses equality in regard to gender equality, see preamble Paris Agreement.

tool for excluding atypical and unrealistic effects from the factual causal chain. The idea that one can only be held responsible for one's actions or omissions in cases in which it was possible to consider and assess the consequences beforehand generally arises out of notions of fairness and is, furthermore, closely linked to considerations of climate justice. Foreseeability is thus enhancing corrective justice while at the same time being limited by its fundamental substance. The latter is based on the restrictive premise that the party in question does not have to bear responsibility for all climate-related damages but only for those that it could have foreseen. Foreseeability thus carries an ambiguous position in light of climate justice considerations. It, on the one hand, represents as a value-based concept a means to implement climate justice into the assessment of causation in the law. On the other hand, foreseeability also limits the circumference of climate justice under the premise of legal applicability. As an outgrowth of overall fairness criteria, foreseeability thus functions as both, a safeguard for the implementation of climate justice considerations in their form as corrective and distributive conceptions, as well as a limiting factor to the otherwise uninhibited influence of normative criteria on the causal assessment in the law.

Foreseeability itself does only scarcely constitute a test of normative causation in its own.[154] In most jurisdictions, it is rather implemented in a broad variety of other normative-based doctrines and tests. The theory of adequacy and the proximate cause doctrine, for instance, prerequisite foreseeability as one among many other decisive factors for the evaluation of the normative legitimacy of affirming normative causation.[155] The scope of its implementation hereby varies quite substantially, as does the comprehensiveness and continuity with which foreseeability is applied within those doctrines. Nevertheless, it constitutes a principle that finds application in different areas of law and is not limited to specific legal realms.[156] The precondition of foreseeability of a specific outcome or causal link in question has also been acquired in European and international law, although causal assessments therein are strongly based on a case-by-case analysis.[157]

---

[154] Although this was proposed in some common law cases, see Privy Council, 18 January 1961 – [1961] UKPC 2, [1961] AC 388; [1961] 1 All ER 404, *Overseas Tankship (UK) Ltd v Morts Dock and Engineering Co Ltd (Wagon Mound (No. 1))*.

[155] See for the theory of adequacy Sect. 5.6 and for the theory of proximate cause Sect. 5.7.

[156] See for an overview of the requirement of foreseeability in the tort law of EU jurisdictions, Infantino and Zervogianni (2017), pp. 604–605. For foreseeability as a criterion of remoteness see Koziol (2007), pp. 61–62.

[157] International Court of Justice, 2 February 2018 – I.C.J. Reports 2018, p. 15, *Certain Activities Carried Out by Nicaragua in the Border Area (Costa Rica v. Nicaragua)*, para 32, His Majesty Oscar II, King of Sweden and Norway as Arbitrator under Convention of 7. November 1899, 14 October 1902 – 9 R.I.A.A. 15, *Germany v. Great Britain and the United States of America (Samoan Claims Case)*. For an overview see Verheyen (2005), pp. 297–301; Voigt (2016), pp. 486–489. Stating foreseeability as one of "*the most important and most applied factor*." Spier (2005), p. 61 para 13. See also von Bar (2000), paras 454–456; Weitenberg (2014), e.g. pp. 804–805. In referring to the '*known or ought to have known standard*' of the ECtHR in regard to positive obligations, see Stoyanova (2020).

Given the current difficulties in defining the extent and scope of foreseeability, especially regarding different tests for normative causation, it is imperative to explore this standard outside of established legal structures. The rationale behind utilizing this approach lies in the fact that the standards and extent of the test differ significantly across various jurisdictions and fields of law. This is particularly applicable to the degree of foreseeability required for a result to be deemed legally causal. The strictest understanding of foreseeability and, therefore, the narrowest scope of the principle is applied in the sphere of criminal law, requiring the party to foresee the outcome as well as the process leading to such to a much greater extent than is the case in private and particularly in contract and tort law.[158] This variability of the test and its fluctuation among different areas of law has also been a point of major concern. Foreseeability as a limiting factor was critiqued due to its "*uncertainty of what must be foreseen, by whom and at what time*".[159] However, its vacillation is also its greatest strength considering its applicability and its adaptability to new challenges. Taking into account new realities such as the climate crisis, but also the increased use of artificial intelligence, and other legal issues raised by new technological, political and natural developments, the concept of foreseeability can be normatively adapted to make it fit to face new obstacles. By the great discretion which is incumbent on courts in the second step of the causal inquiry in the law, foreseeability can be tailored to face the current needs of adapting the respective causal assessment. The foreseeability test, thus, renders highly alluring for normative causation in climate change litigation.

Whether a specific factor was ultimately foreseeable or not, however, is not only presupposed by assessments of normative causation but is even more so applied and considered outside the scope of cause-effect relationships. Foreseeability, for example, is of great importance when it comes to the violation of a duty to care both in common law, as well as in civil law jurisdictions.[160] Besides that, international courts apply foreseeability tests outside the realm of causal tests, as well.[161] Although the scope and the assessment of foreseeability tests do not coincide with foreseeability as a causal requirement, it is nevertheless possible to draw on some parallels, while some concepts may even be entirely transferable to the assessment of normative causation.

[158] Moore (2009), p. 83. Comparing the requirement of foreseeability in Swiss criminal and civil law, Frei (2010). See in this regard also Sect. 6.2.2.

[159] American Law Institute (2010), § 29 Comment j.

[160] See exemplary for English law on the history of foreseeability as a precondition of the duty of care, Scott (2019). See also for the UK Goudkamp and Plunkett (2019).

[161] See e.g. the ECtHR in regard to the principle 'nullum crimen sine lege', van der Wilt (2015); Stoyanova (2018), pp. 314–315.

5.3.2 *Foreseeability and Climate Change*

In climate change litigation, it is the complexity of the climate system, as well as the close connection of climate lawsuits and the causal inquiry itself to scientific knowledge that pose new challenges to the foreseeability criteria. The foreseeability of slow onset events is hereby as complex as the foreseeability of sudden onset events. And while most aspects are in line with general tests and requirements for establishing foreseeability, the main concern relates to the timely threshold of foreseeability in light of climate change and climate change induced damages.[162] At what point in time was it foreseeable to the party in question that its GHG emissions would contribute to a rise in surface temperatures or even to further damage? This is strongly related to the question of how to deal with historical emissions and further non-emitting but climate-damaging behaviour or omissions.

5.3.2.1 The Scope of Foreseeability

The basic framework on which the further assessment of foreseeability in climate change litigation is based builds on four main determinants. The first factor relates to the vantage point of assessing foreseeability and questions whether foreseeability should be addressed from an ex-ante or an ex-post perspective (Sect. 5.3.2.1.1). The second criterion relates to the requirements and the standards that are placed on the vantage point and the respective observer itself (Sect. 5.3.2.1.2), whereas the third factor determines whether foreseeability should also take account of special and individual knowledge (Sect. 5.3.2.1.3). Ultimately, and arguably most important is the degree as to what the party in question should be able to foresee a specific outcome and the causal chain leading to such an event (Sect. 5.3.2.1.4).

5.3.2.1.1 The Right Vantage Point

The point of commencement for the assessment of foreseeability rests within the determination of the right vantage point, which considers the perspective from which foreseeability must be consolidated. Usually two possible vantage points obtain. The first consists in the application of an ex-ante stance, whereby the occurrence of a specific outcome has to be predictable before or at the time the action or the omission in question took place. According to an ex-post perspective, as the second possible point of departure, the relevant vantage point either relates to the foreseeability of the outcome and the causal chain immediately after the respective action or to the time in which the conduct itself was at dispute. Although applying a substantial ex-post

[162] See in this regard especially Sect. 5.3.2.3.

view and approaching the outcome from the perspective at the time of dispute would considerably facilitate the assessment of foreseeability, not only has such a perception been negated in practice, but major arguments militate against it, as well.[163] Given that there is commonly more information available after the occurrence of the outcome than beforehand, one of the main concerns relates to the overbreadth of a retrospective approach. Using experimental and future knowledge as well as temporally successive standards of foreseeability further can lead to so-called 'hindsight bias', as well as to considerable normative errors.[164] This holds even more true in the context of climate change litigation, given that the effects of a particular conduct usually occur much later than the conduct itself ('problem of delayed harm').[165] Due to the fast-evolving area of climate and attribution science and the changing state of the art of scientific epistemology, what is to be considered ex-post foreseeable changes even faster.

In taking special account on the problems of delayed harm, current climate change decisions show a tendency towards an ex-ante perspective in their assessment of foreseeability. Akin is, for example, indicated by the Human Rights Committee in its decision in the case *David Billy and others v. Australia* as well as by the Committee of the Rights of the Child in *Sacchi et al. v. Argentina.*[166] An ex-ante perspective is also supported by the principle of prevention, and even more so by the precautionary principle, as both principles are based on the idea of avoiding damage altogether and the associated notion of timely recognition of consequences rather than retrospective traceability. But also in legal scholarship, and even outside the climate change debate, a more nuanced view based on an ex-ante perspective is finding strong support across different jurisdictions and areas of law.[167]

On a normative basis, general considerations of fairness and the therein entailed notion of responsibility and blameworthiness concurrently oppose a strict ex-post perspective. Moral and legal blameworthiness accrue from the execution of the act or the omission, even though the party in question could have foreseen and anticipated the consequences. Without the foreseeability of the outcome at the time of the occurrence, however, the conduct or omission in question does not carry any

[163] Stating that the acceptance of ex-post foreseeability in German jurisprudence is based on the misinterpretation of a judgment of the German Federal Court of Justice (Federal Court Germany, 23 October 1951 – I ZR 31/51), Wagner and Arntz (2021), pp. 417–418, para 55.

[164] See in this regard Pöttker (2014), p. 131; Brand (2022), para 239.

[165] See in this regard Sects. 2.1 and 3.3.2.3.

[166] United Nations Human Rights Committee, 22 September 2022 – CCPR/C/135/D/3624/2019, *Daniel Billy et al. v. Australia (Torres Strait Islanders Petition)*, para 8.14, United Nations Committee on the Rights of the Child, 8 October 2021 – CRC/C/88/D/107/2019, *Sacchi et al. v. Argentina et al.*, para 9.11.

[167] See for an ex-ante perspective in European law, Weitenberg (2014), pp. 781, 804. In regard to Swiss civil and criminal law see Frei (2010), pp. 70, 197, 211–212. In regard to the German law of torts, see Oetker (2019), para 111. Also Zeidler (2022), p. 112. Indirectly also Verheyen (2005), pp. 299, 314; Voigt (2008), p. 12. In regard to the jurisprudence of the ECtHR considering positive obligations, see Stoyanova (2020), pp. 619–620.

moral blame. Applying an ex-post perspective would, thus, lead to cases in which the outcome was caused by an action or omission for which the defendant was not morally blameworthy, however, he could be held legally responsible due to the existence of ex-post foreseeability. Finding legal responsibility without moral and legal blameworthiness, contradicts the core of the principle of fairness. To avoid such a normative dilemma, one must avoid applying a perspective to the standard of foreseeability that is too far removed from the actual initiation of the causal chain.[168]

Despite the principle of fairness, it is the notion of climate justice that is of substantial relevance for normative assessments in climate change litigation. Given its multiple objectives and direction of actions, considerations of climate justice do not promise to provide as clear an understanding as considerations of fairness. Considering the aspect of foreseeability from an ex-post point of view would allow for a wider understanding of legal and, thus, overall causation in law, which corresponds to a greater number of climate lawsuits. It is in this aspect that the purpose of foreseeability as a limiting factor of factual causation and its perception as the implementation of climate and even more so corrective justice collide. With the enhancement of scientific knowledge on the causes and impacts of climate change, an ex-post assessment consolidates the establishment of causation in the law for an increasing amount of climate lawsuits, especially in light of historic and past emissions. With the enhanced possibility of prosecuting past wrongs, it aims at the core of corrective justice. It, further, corresponds to the polluter pays principle, which, as the structural concept of corrective justice in the law, also demands the reproachability of the damaging behaviour or omission. Although corrective justice is not concerned with providing for as many lawsuits as possible, and only aims at persecuting wrongful behaviour and providing compensation for the victims, it would sill benefit greatly from a widened perception of foreseeability. In applying an ex-post approach, foreseeability would thus build upon fundamental aspects of overall climate justice.

Although such perception of justice might seem fair particularly considering the resulting compensation victims of climate damage would receive, it runs counter to aspects of moral blameworthiness and overall fairness criteria, as already previously addressed. Without ex-ante foreseeability, the moral wrongfulness of the behaviour automatically ceases to exist. Without a legal wrong, however, the point of contention of moral responsibility is also obliterated, which in turn is a prerequisite for corrective justice to take hold. Thus, the corrective dimension of justice also depends fundamentally on ex-ante foreseeability, even if, in the context of achieving the greatest possible effectiveness, one would like to build on an ex-post approach. Corrective justice is thus also realised in an ex-ante perspective, which in turn resolves the dilemma of foreseeability as both a limiting criterion for factual causation and a form of corrective justice. Without those opposing notions of

[168] Also in favour of an ex-ante perspective concerning the foreseeability of climate change, Pöttker (2014), p. 130; Wagner and Arntz (2021), pp. 417–418. Concerning foreseeability considerations within the assessment of interests of the breach of duty, Zeidler (2022), p. 112.

normative causation and in strong reliance on criteria of fairness and moral blameworthiness it is ultimately the ex-ante perspective that needs to be adopted when assessing foreseeability in climate change litigation.

5.3.2.1.2 The Standard of the Right Observer

The assessment of foreseeability in light of normative causation commonly builds upon the consideration whether a third party could have expected and foreseen the outcome. It is a concept that strongly relies on objective and abstract deliberations, rather than considering what the specific party in question actually foresaw or could have foreseen at the time of the respective conduct.[169] Issue of debate, however, still rests in the required standard of care that has to be placed on the objective observer. Especially two divergent standards are known to overall jurisdictions. The narrower perception refers to the perspective of an optimal observer.[170] Decisive hereby is whether the outcome could have been foreseeable to a person that has unlimited expertise and access to experiential knowledge. In applying a more relaxed standard, others require not an optimal but only a reasonable party. Such is mainly known in common law jurisdictions.[171]

Although the difference amongst those two standards of care seems only minuscular at first and some authors even argue that the standards do not diverge substantially and are equal in their scope and content, they do in fact differ considerably, especially in light of climate change.[172] Given that the standard of an optimal observer also implies access to unlimited scientific knowledge, anthropogenic climate change, its effects and further impacts would be considered foreseeable as soon as scientific knowledge was available. Such perception significantly advances the threshold of foreseeability in regard to general climate change to the beginning of the twentieth century.[173] Specific climate-induced damages could then be considered foreseeable shortly after, at latest, however, in the mid of the twentieth century, depending on what demands one places on the scientific findings per se. It would, thus, result in a considerable shift of foreseeability and ultimately would equate the observer's standard of care with the current state of scientific knowledge of the time of the action in question. By contrast, a standard that builds upon a reasonable observer, would ultimately not lead to such a considerable shift of the threshold of

[169] Spier (2005), p. 61 para 13. For courts of the European Union see Weitenberg (2014), p. 781.

[170] This is particularly the case in German tort law (although not entirely unchallenged), see e.g. Brand (2022), p. 239; Oetker (2019), p. 111; Schulze (2021), para 15.

[171] In regard to foreseeability entailed in the duty of care, see Pöttker (2014), pp. 286, 289, 293–294. Reasonable foreseeability was also a major issue in Federal Court of Australia, 15 March 2022 – [2022] FCAFC 35, *Minister for the Environment v. Sharma.*

[172] Stating that there is no difference in regard to the 'reasonable' and 'optimal' standard by comparing German, English and French law, Wurmnest (2003), p. 326.

[173] Section 2.1.

foreseeability. Rather, the assessment would build upon the extent to which these climate findings are perceived and could be perceived by the general public.[174]

While most judges and courts do not expressively elaborate on the respective standard which they apply in their decisions and even less so in light of climate change lawsuits, *Judge While* considered in the case *Smith v. Fonterra Co-Operative Group Limited* damage to be foreseeable "*[…] only where there is a real risk of damage, that is one which would occur to the mind of a reasonable person in the position of the defendant and one which he would not brush aside as far-fetched.*"[175] Concurrently with common law, he applied the standard of reasonability and, ultimately, qualified the damage occurred to Mr. Smith as not foreseeable.[176]

The decision of *Judge While* would hardly hold in jurisdictions that apply the standard of an optimal observer. Given that an optimal observer would be required to know even of most distant findings and occurrences, nearly every outcome would be considered as foreseeable. The risk that such a broad standard of foreseeability implicitly carries, however, strongly relates to the danger of losing its function as a criterion of normative containment as well as its general value in regard to considering normative causation. Only the most far-fetched and uncommon outcomes would be excluded as not legally causal. This would lead to a convergence of the approach with other normative conceptions that explicitly exclude improbable, completely extraneous impacts from the causal chain.

Another point of concern in light of the 'optimal' standard arises based on the subject matter per se. Climate change litigation is dominated by complex, highly scientific processes that can hardly be understood in their full extent by a reasonable, non-scientific audience without them being considerably facilitated and broken down. The scientific difficulty of climate change and its attribution thus widens the gap between the two perceptions of the necessary standard even more. Based on this high complexity, which is still object to significant scientific research, especially in regard to sudden onset and extreme weather events, an optimal observer constitutes a legal construct, which does not find equivalence in reality. By setting such a high, unsurmountable and, ultimately, in reality non-existent standard, it also runs counter to considerations of justice and fairness. Given that this optimality is nearly, if not entirely, unattainable, it further raises the question of the moral blameworthiness of the conduct. Imposing a standard onto one's action or omission, without the possibility of the party living up to that required standard, it is difficult to justify imposing legal blame on the action in question. The notion of fairness and even more so moral blameworthiness thus already requires a lowered standard of foreseeability. The same holds true for the application and implementation of the conception of

[174] See for the respective threshold of foreseeability later in this chapter, especially Sect. 5.3.2.3.

[175] In citing Privy Council, 25 May 1966 – [1966] UKPC 10, [1967] AC 617; [1967] 2 All ER 709, *Overseas Tankship (UK) Ltd v The Miller Steamship Co (Wagon Mound No. 2)*, para 643, see High Court of New Zealand, 21 October 2021 – [2021] NZCA 552, *Smith v. Fonterra Co-Operative Group Limited*, para 80.

[176] High Court of New Zealand, 21 October 2021 – [2021] NZCA 552, *Smith v. Fonterra Co-Operative Group Limited*, 81–82.

corrective justice. Without moral and legal blame, the corrective mechanism of justice does not find application, which is why this normative conception does not stand in the way of a reduced standard of foreseeability. It hereby concurs with the analysis in regard to the vantage point of foreseeability.[177]

Besides the normative arguments that clearly speak for the adoption of a reasonable observer, applying a stricter standard has, nevertheless, also an important advantage over a reduced requirement. This argument strongly builds upon the unambiguousness and delimitability of the construct. While the requirements for an optimal observer are, based on the current state of knowledge, determinable to a large extent, which in turn provides for a certain degree of legal certainty, the standard that is applied to a reasonable observer is commonly left at the discretion of the courts. This allows for greater individualization and adaptation within different jurisdictions but also harbours risks based on the inherent legal uncertainty. Although in comparison to the optimal observer, reasonableness is a rather vague construct, it, nevertheless, is not without any limitations and frame at all. In determining the standard of reasonableness, reference is taken on a comparable group of addressees. If the action or omission of a private actor such as a corporation is at issue, it is the reasonableness of a similar class of addressees that is taken as a reference. In the context of climate change, this has particular implications and consequences for the standard of foreseeability of individuals in comparison to the standard applied to states.[178]

Ultimately, and especially in light of the intricacy of the climate system and the difficulty in understanding anthropogenic climate change and its effects, assessing foreseeability based on an optimal observer is contrived and remote from reality. Thus, on the basis of the highly scientific topic and due to the otherwise pertaining risk of loss of function of the concept of foreseeability in climate change lawsuits, the benchmark of foreseeability in normative causation rests within a reasonable observer.

5.3.2.1.3 The Implementation of Special Knowledge

Foreseeability is commonly a concept of objectivity.[179] Some notions of subjectivity may, however, be considered based on the specific knowledge of the respective party. Such deliberation, for example, was put forward by the claimants in the case *Milieudefensie et al. v. Royal Dutch Shell.*[180] The plaintiffs referred in their

[177] See in this regard Sect. 5.3.2.1.1 of this respective part.

[178] See in this regard Sect. 5.3.2.3.

[179] Spier (2005), p. 61 para 13. For courts of the European Union see Weitenberg (2014), p. 781.

[180] Hague District Court, 26 May 2021 – C/09/571932/HA ZA 19-379, *Milieudefensie et al. v. Royal Dutch Shell plc.*, statement of claim, paras 530–574. Similar was conducted by the claimants in US District Court for the Northern District of California, 30 September 2009 – 4:08-cv-01138-SBA, *Native Village of Kivalina v. ExxonMobil Corp.*

complaint to studies conducted by the American Petrol Institute (API) in the 1950s which have been available and accessible to Royal Dutch Shell due to their membership in the organization and the chairmanship by the Chief Executive Officer of Shell in 1959.[181] They further referred, among others, to Shell's participation in the World Climate Conference in 1979 and, probably most important, to the internal report conducted by Shell in 1986 (1988) about the effect of greenhouse gases to anthropogenic climate change and Shell's contribution to it.[182] In the respective report, Shell specifically named the amount of greenhouse gases they produced and placed them in the overall context of climate change, resulting in a contribution of about 4% of CO_2 to global carbon emissions in 1984.[183] Under the assumption that general anthropogenic climate change was not yet foreseeable for a reasonable observer, it is, in light of the respective report, difficult to argue that based on the concept of objectivity and reasonable foreseeability, the contribution to anthropogenic climate change by Shell was not legally causal.

Similar arguments were put forward by the plaintiff in the case *Luciano Lliuya v. RWE AG.*[184] Here the claimant referred to a declaration issued by RWE in 1995 through the German Association of Energy and Water Industries which affirmed the knowledge of the corporation about its responsibility for climate change.[185] Ultimately, reference to reports and internal papers that prove special knowledge of, especially, corporate defendants is used by nearly every claimant in substantiating their climate change lawsuit. Thus, in legal practice and even more so in climate change litigation, the acquiescence of special knowledge concerning the requirement of objective foreseeability is of major importance notably in regard to the responsibility of states and corporations for climate change and climate change induced damage. It is, moreover, of importance for claims aimed against all bigger entities which possess the ability to draw on and gain access to knowledge that is disclosed from the broader public. In bringing those actors to court it is imperative for claimants to show that major emitters gained consciousness and knowledge of the impact of their climate-damaging behaviour prior to the timely threshold of reasonable foreseeability. Proofing special knowledge enables claimants to shift the foreseeability threshold forward to the detriment of the defendant and hold them responsible for climate damage induced by their historical emissions.

However, deviations from this principle of foreseeability and special knowledge must be allowed in the light of different legal and liability regimes. In *Ministry of Environment and Forestry v. PT Ramban Agro Jaya*, the Court held that under an absolute liability regime, foreseeability must solely be approached from an objective

---

[181] Hague District Court, 26 May 2021 – C/09/571932/HA ZA 19-379, *Milieudefensie et al. v. Royal Dutch Shell plc.*, statement of claim, paras 533, 534.

[182] Ibid. statement of claim, paras 539, 541.

[183] Greenhouse Effect Working Group (1988), p. 57, table 8.

[184] Essen Regional Court, 15 December 2016 – 2 O 285/15, *Luciano Lliuya v. RWE AG*, statement of claim (23 November 2015), p. 37 para 4.3.

[185] Ibid. statement of claim (23 November 2015), 19.

point of view. This is based on the fact that, in the context of absolute liability, the decisive factor does not lie in what the defendant could have subjectively foreseen but in whether the defendant took prudent measures to minimise the risks. Therefore, it was argued by the Court that it is the general knowledge of the public and not the subjective knowledge of the defendant that is to be considered for the determination of foreseeability.[186]

As the case *Ministry of Environment and Forestry v. PT Ramban Agro Jaya* has shown, it is obvious that differences in regard to different jurisdictions do exist. In jurisprudential discourse, however, it is commonly recognized that special, individual knowledge could be taken into consideration within the assessment of objective foreseeability.[187] This does not lead to an overall subjectivation of foreseeability but only presents an exception to the still generally acknowledged objective stance of the concept of foreseeability. The acceptance of specific factual knowledge is also in line with overall justice considerations, given that the moral blameworthiness continues to persist in cases in which the party in question possesses actual knowledge about an outcome even though in general such outcome would otherwise not be foreseeable for a reasonable party. It further enhances corrective justice considerations by allowing an earlier foreseeability threshold based on the parties legal responsibility rather than refuting the ability to correct the blameworthy behaviour based on objections of objectivity. Moreover, it functions as a remedy to prevent the abuse of law, given the party is not able to draw benefit out of their individual, the objective foreseeability exceeding, knowledge.

5.3.2.1.4 The Extent of Foreseeability

The fourth and also the most comprehensive factor in framing the standard of foreseeability relates to its extent and scope. This factor considers whether foreseeability only has to pertain to the outcome or if the criterion also includes the causal chain (Sect. 5.3.2.1.4.1). Additionally, it addresses the degree to which the observer must foresee the consequences in question (Sect. 5.3.2.1.4.2).

5.3.2.1.4.1 The Substance of Foreseeability: Outcome Versus Chain-Specific Foreseeability

Foreseeability requires the party in question to be able to predict the result of ones doing or omission up to some extent.[188] That foreseeability hereby aims at the

[186] District Court of Central Jakarta, 11 January 2021 – 445/Pdt.G/2019/PN.Jkt.Pst, *Ministry of Environment and Forestry v. PT Rambang Agro Jaya*, 210.

[187] See e.g. in German criminal law Rengier (2021), § 13 para 74. Concerning courts of the European Union, Weitenberg (2014), p. 782. Opposing the inclusion of specific knowledge, von Bar (2000), para 454.

[188] The degree of foreseeability in question will be addressed in Sect. 5.3.2.1.4.2.

outcome as the toehold of its legal blameworthiness is evident. Nevertheless, it remains unclear whether foreseeability also extends to the sequence of events that led to the outcome. Is it necessary for the person to be cognizant of the intermediate steps in the causal chain that eventually led to the outcome? And, if so, to what extent should the causal chain be established in a foreseeable manner?

The majority of jurisdictions and in line with general logical considerations arguably draw on the causal chain in one way or another within the requirement of foreseeability.[189] Given that the assessment of factual causation requires a continuous causal chain leading up to the effect, one could argue in the interest of continuity and comprehensiveness for a similar approach taking into account the respective causal chain in the legal causal considerations as well. The criterion of foreseeability ensures that normative causation does not extend to causes that merely occurred accidentally or are completely atypical. Such cases do not constitute the outcome of the legal wrong but, due to their accidentality, carry no legal blame. Responsibility for those outcomes thus does not lie with the individual chain-setter.

However, there are some instances in which the outcome was foreseeable and the causal chain factually causal, although the chain of events that lead to such an outcome, ultimately was atypical, accidental and intricate to such an extent.[190] Imposing responsibility and affirming overall foreseeability would, thus, contradict general considerations of fairness and justice.[191] By widening the foreseeability standard to the causal chain as well, one is able to eliminate normative causation on the basis of lacking foreseeability and further conform with overall justice perceptions. Ultimately, both normative and logical reasons as well as the argument of continuity speak in favour of extending foreseeability to the causal chain as well.

When assessing foreseeability concerning causal chains, it is crucial to analyse the extent of the foreseeability precondition that is posed on each individual link in the causal chain. It is highly improbable that a fictional observer would have been able to foresee every single step involved in the causal chain to its fullest extent. This level of predictability can only be achieved in instances in which the cause immediately is followed by the impact, resulting in a short, one-link causal chain. The shorter the causal chain, the less likely it is for unexpected actions to interfere and disrupt the chain of events or exclude foreseeability from a normative point of view. However, climate processes are characterized precisely by substantially long causal chains, in which several different factors come into play simultaneously. Even outside climate scenarios, predicting specific links in the causal chain is incredibly challenging. On the basis of the scientific complexity underlying climate change and the climate system in general, foreseeing every step in the climatic causal chain, nonetheless, verges on the impossible. For those reasons alone is it imperative to apply a reduced standard of foreseeability to the causal chain itself.

---

[189] See e.g. for German criminal law Rengier (2021), § 13, para 71. In contrast Zeidler (2022), p. 111.

[190] This aspect coincides with the issue of intervening causes, see Sect. 5.5.

[191] See in this regard especially Sect. 5.5 on intervening causes.

A fitting example of the complexity of climatic causal chains in light of their foreseeability is provided by the case *Luciano Lliuya v. RWE AG*, which also aptly depicts the need to lower the foreseeability standard with respect to the causal chain in question.[192] The causal chain hereby is initiated by the GHG emissions produced over several years by the RWE AG (E_S). Those emissions contributed to an increase in the density of GHG emissions in the atmosphere, which again lead to a decrease of long-wave radiation leaving the atmosphere. The Earth's atmospheric temperature than constantly increased based on the hereby caused counter-radiation (T). Due to the nominal increase in the Earth's surface temperature, glaciers in the Andes melted faster which again lead to an increase in the mountaineered waterflow (X_{S1}). The hereby increased waterflow contributed to the Palcacocha lagoon filling up with water and considerably increasing its volume (X_{S2}), which in turn incremented the pressure on the natural moraine (X_{S3}). The pressure on the moraine again contributed to an increase in risk of the natural barrage breaking which in turn enhanced the risk of a glacier lake outburst flood in the region of Huaraz (I_S).[193] And while the causal chain can be broken down even further, it clearly shows the difficulty in requiring foreseeability at all for the specific links in the chain itself.

This is even more evident given that foreseeability is to be viewed from an ex-ante perspective. Even if the first steps in the causal chain, namely the emission of GHG and the contribution to an increase in the Earth's surface temperature was foreseeable to some extent in the time of the damaging behaviour, the further one proceeds in the causal chain, the more difficult it becomes to determine foreseeability. For this reason alone, it is favorable to reduce the necessary standard of foreseeability in regard to the causal chain. Therefore, it can only be expected for the actor to foresee the causal chain in its broad outlines. This includes the major steps in the causal chain, without however foreseeing every link in its very detail.[194] As major steps in the chain of events in the case of *Luciano Lliuya* could, for instance, be considered the increase in temperature and the melting of the glacier.

The reference to a reasonable observer as the decisive standard imposed on the objective foreseeability also supports a lowered perception of the standard. Even if one would impose the standard of an optimal observer, it could not be expected that the causal chain would be foreseeable in its full extent. This is all the more true for a standard of reasonableness. The decisive standard of foreseeability of the causal chain thus relies on a more general perception, with the main links in the causal chain being required to grant some form of foreseeability, without imposing too high of a standard on the incremental steps. Foreseeability thus relates to what the actor could have expected to happen in the causal chain from the ex-ante perspective of a reasonable observer.[195] In relying on general foreseeability rather than on specific

---

[192] Essen Regional Court, 15 December 2016 – 2 O 285/15, *Luciano Lliuya v. RWE AG*, Higher Regional Court Hamm, pending – 5 U 15/17, *Luciano Lliuya v. RWE AG*.

[193] See for more scientific background on the influence of anthropogenic GHG emissions on the respective glaciers and the risk of a GLOF, Stuart-Smith et al. (2021).

[194] For further elaborations on the extent of foreseeability see Sect. 5.3.2.1.4.2.

[195] In this regard also Rengier (2021), § 13 para 71.

foreseeability, the assessment of the foreseeability strongly builds on case-by-case considerations, which in turn is strongly influenced by the special knowledge the actor had at the time of his conduct or omission. In principle, nonetheless, the chain of causation must have been foreseeable, at least in its broad outlines.

5.3.2.1.4.2 The Degree of Foreseeability

It is verging on impossibility to determine all the details of a future loss in advance. This is all the more the case if, as in the case of climatic events, the damage only occurs after a considerable amount of time which can add up to decades before the real and entire damage becomes apparent. Nevertheless, since the legal culpability and moral blameworthiness of the action or omission is based on the specific outcome, the standard of foreseeability is to be considered stricter than concerning the causal chain. Decisive in regard to the outcome especially is in a first step that the actor ought to have known that his action or omission could be damaging at all. If that is not the case from the perspective of a reasonable observer, normative causation has to be negated on the grounds of missing specific foreseeability.

However, predicting that an action or omission might be harmful is not sufficient for the foreseeability requirement. Overall, the actor has to foresee that his action or omission would result in a damage of a certain kind, regardless of its actual geographical location, the exact time of its occurrence or the exact person that has been affected. Rather it is decisive whether it was foreseeable that the kind of damage would be able to occur in a certain geographical area, during a certain time span and would be damaging for a certain group of people. For the case of *Luciano Lliuya v. RWE AG* this translates to the necessity of foreseeing the risk of flooding, in mountain regions (including the Andes) and the possible impairment of people living in such regions of the world.[196] Within overall climate change litigation and apart from this specific case, foreseeable harms and impacts from the emission of GHG include, among others, rising sea levels, weather extremes, such as droughts, irregularities in precipitation patterns, wildfires, and falling water tables.

Still, those foreseeable impacts only relate to the foreseeability standard for actions and omissions conducted today. What was foreseeable is always dependent and required to be viewed from the perspective of the respective time. However, requiring foreseeability beyond the here described extent would be misguided, not feasible in reality, and contradictory to the standard of reasonableness implied on the right observer. Thus, the standard and the degree in regard to the specific outcome is a matter of general kind-related foreseeability.[197] It must be foreseeable for a reasonable observer from an ex-ante perspective that the effect could occur on the

[196] Essen Regional Court, 15 December 2016 – 2 O 285/15, *Luciano Lliuya v. RWE AG*, Higher Regional Court Hamm, pending – 5 U 15/17, *Luciano Lliuya v. RWE AG*.

[197] See also Pöttker (2014), p. 132. With reference to a reduced 'ought to have known' – standard Voigt (2008), pp. 11–12.

basis of the act or omission per se, without having to foresee the exact extent of it.[198]

Foreseeability was also greatly at issue in the case *Sharma v. The Minister for the Environment*. The case concerned the affectedness of children of a certain age and geographical location to the adverse impacts of climate change. The primary judge, *Judge Bromberg*, herein emphasized that the concept of foreseeability would not require the party to foresee the outcome or potential harm for an exact person, here, the respective children as claimants, but only for a class of persons. The Judge further affirmed that only harm of like-kind needed to be foreseeable for the respondent. This was later affirmed by the Chief Judge in the second instance.[199] The primary Judge, and later again affirmed by the Chief Judge in the second instance, also addressed the different standards placed on the requirement of foreseeability in regard to the invoked claim. They argued that the foreseeability assessment concerning a breach of duty—which was in question in the underlying case—had to be of a higher generalization and abstractness than in regard to the breach of a right.[200] Such differentiation is not only of case-specific nature but is valid for all climate cases in which the foreseeability of the outcome is in question. The differentiation is based on various grounds, but mainly on the nature of the infringement itself. The effects of omissions are fundamentally more difficult to determine than in the case of an active doing. An active doing implies an intentional act and, therefore, requires a more detailed consideration of possible effects than is the case with mere omissions. Those considerations are further reflected in the overall differentiation between positive and negative obligations in human rights law, which also require a relaxed standard of overall causation in light of positive obligations.[201]

---

[198] Such perception is also in line with international law. See with reference to the *Corfu Channel* case (International Court of Justice, 25 March 1948; 9 April 1949; 15 December 1949 – I. C. J. Reports 1948 p. 15; 1949 p. 4, 244, *Corfu Channel Case (United Kingdom v. People's Republic of Albania)*), Verheyen (2005), p. 300.

[199] Federal Court of Australia, 15 March 2022 – [2022] FCAFC 35, *Minister for the Environment v. Sharma* paras 131–153. Judge Weelahan rejected the existence of reasonable foreseeability in its entirety. See for the primary judgment Federal Court of Australia, 27 May 2021 – [2021] FCA 560, *Sharma and others v. Minister for the Environment*, paras 184–204.

[200] See Federal Court of Australia, 15 March 2022 – [2022] FCAFC 35, *Minister for the Environment v. Sharma* paras 131–153, Federal Court of Australia, 27 May 2021 – [2021] FCA 560, *Sharma and others v. Minister for the Environment*, paras 184–204. The Courts hereby cited the following cases, High Court of Australia, 1 May 1980 – 146 CLR 40, *Wyong Shire Council v. Shirt*, High Court of Australia, 21 October 2005 – HCA 62, *Vairy v. Wyong Shire Council*.

[201] See for further elaborations on the differentiation between positive and negative obligations, Sects. 3.2.3.1 and 3.3.2.4.

5.3.2.2 Present-Day Foreseeability of Climate Change and Climate Change-Induced Damage

As of today, there is no doubt of the factual causal relation between the emission of greenhouse gases and anthropogenic climate change in general. Due to the multitude of international climate agreements and the comprehensive reports of the IPCC, it is unquestionably foreseeable for an optimal as well as for a reasonable observer that climate change is caused and intensified by the emission of greenhouse gases.[202] More difficult, however, is the relation between other non-emitting actions and climate change per se, with deforestation and increasing urbanization accompanied by the sealing of surfaces being amongst the more obvious non-emitting interferences. And while those actions are generally known to result in an aggravation of anthropogenic climate change, are scientifically proven, and, therefore, can be considered as foreseeable in causing anthropogenic climate change, other more concealed actions might not yet be commonly regarded as having an impact on the world's climate.[203] Despite today's comprehensive knowledge of the causes and consequences of climate change, due to the complexity of the matter, it cannot be ruled out that certain actions that are currently not regarded as damaging to the climate might prove to be harmful in the future. Nevertheless, the general foreseeability of anthropogenic climate change due to the emission of greenhouse gases is to be affirmed, after all.

In parallel with the general foreseeability of climate change, a large part of specific damages and impacts are also covered by reasonable foreseeability up to date.[204] Not only due to the comprehensive scientific research but also based on the broad public and media coverage of the dangers and impacts of climate change as well as the great popularity of climate change lawsuits, foreseeability in its normative dimension does in most cases not limit factual causation from a current perspective. Even more remote impacts of the emission of greenhouse gases, such as the negative impact of climate change on human health or on children rights, are to be qualified as foreseeable from the perspective of a reasonable observer

[202] The *IPCC* concluded with certainty in its first assessment IPCC (1992a), p. 63. Also in affirmation, see Pöttker (2014), p. 131; Zeidler (2022), pp. 111–112. Germany Federal Constitutional Court, 24 March 2021 – 1 BvR 2656/18 – 1 BvR 78/20 – 1 BvR 96/20 – 1 BvR 288/20, *Neubauer et al. v. Germany*, 119.

[203] See e.g. IPCC (2023).

[204] In affirmation Koch et al. (2011), para 15.77; Hunter and Salzman (2007), p. 1769. See also from a scientific perspective, IPCC (2023), pp. 15–19.

nowadays, as well.[205] This result is favoured by the understanding that the degree and scope of foreseeability do not require the outcome to be foreseeable in all its details but that the generic foreseeability of an outcome suffices the imposed standard.

Especially in earlier stages of climate change litigation, defendants ought to bring forward the argument of so-called 'force majeure'.[206] In claiming that the outcome was not causally linked to their conduct but was deduced from a sudden-occurring, non-predictable nature's whim, they tried to negate their own specific causal conduct. However, such an argument is no longer tenable today.[207] Given the broad scientific consensus on the impact of human behaviour on the climate system, anthropogenic climate change and other climate change-induced impacts, the argument against anthropogenic impacts no longer holds water in court. Although nature's own climate variability does exist and also has been subject to major research, the fast and intense climate variations that can be experienced today are not attributable to mere climate variability.[208] Natural climate variations as, for example, influenced by the Milankovitch cycle, are changes that occur over the period of thousands of years. Anthropogenic climate change, however, is characterized by its fast-emerging and major influence which does not allow nature to adapt as fast as it would be required.

5.3.2.3 Historic Emissions and the Timely Threshold of Foreseeability

Highly problematic, in spite of the foregoing considerations, is the question of foreseeability in regard to past emissions. As already comprehensively addressed, climate change and climate change-induced damages resulting from GHG emissions and other acknowledged climate-damaging behaviour are foreseeable in current times. Greenhouse gas emissions, however, have been emitted for a long time even before scientific studies of climate change and its anthropogenic influences were available, let alone covered by scientific consensus and made known to the

---

[205] See the argumentation brought forward in regard to health e.g. in the case Swiss Federal Supreme Court, 20 May 2020 – 1C_37/2019, *Association of Swiss Senior Women for Climate Protection v. Federal Department of the Environment Transport, Energy and Communications (DETEC) and Others ("Verein KlimaSeniorinnen Schweiz v. Bundesrat")*, Swiss Supreme Court, 20 May 2020 – No. A-2992/2017, *Association of Swiss Senior Women for Climate Protection v. Federal Department of the Environment Transport, Energy and Communications (DETEC) and Others*, European Court of Human Rights, pending – 53600/20, *KlimaSeniorinnen v. Switzerland.* In respect to the impacts on children, see United Nations Committee on the Rights of the Child, 8 October 2021 – CRC/C/88/D/107/2019, *Sacchi et al. v. Argentina et al.*

[206] See for international public law, Dellinger (2017). See also in more detail Sect. 5.5 on intervening causes.

[207] In this regard also Chatzinerantzis and Appel (2019), pp. 881, 884; Hänni (2021), p. 18, Regional Court of Kassel, pending – n/a, *Barbara Metz et al. v. Wintershall Dea AG*, statement of claim, 65–66.

[208] See in this regard Sect. 2.1.

broader public. Given the lack of scientific knowledge about the influence of greenhouse gases on the Earth's climate and the respective lack of foreseeability, the moral blameworthiness of emitters for the conduct concurrently ceases to exist as the conception is ultimately bound on the normative reproach of their action. Factual causation is thus limited by a threshold based on reasonable foreseeability. The difficult obstacle in that regard, nonetheless, is the setting of a specific timely threshold. Considerate for the establishment of a threshold ultimately is the point in time at which the climate-damaging influence of the emission of greenhouse gases is considered foreseeable for a reasonable observer. In assessing the respective threshold, two specific scenarios have to be differentiated based on their substance, their scope of factual causation and ultimately, the degree of foreseeability they require. The first scenario refers to the general foreseeability of anthropogenic climate change due to the emission of greenhouse gases and other climate-damaging behaviour (Sect. 5.3.2.3.1). The second scenario in turn addresses specific foreseeability, which relates to the foreseeability of specific climate change induced harm and runs concurrent to the assessment of overall specific causation in the law (Sect. 5.3.2.3.2).

5.3.2.3.1 General Foreseeability of Climate Change

That greenhouse gas emissions contribute to and cumulatively cause anthropogenic climate change is an undisputed fact.[209] However, disagreement still prevails regarding the explicit timely threshold as of when the effect of GHG emissions and anthropogenic climate change was reasonably foreseeable outside the scientific community and in respect to the broader public.

As previously mentioned, the standard of foreseeability strongly depends on the right observer, which, on the one hand, has to be reasonable but, on the other hand, requires a perspective that has to be inferred from a similar, like-kinded group of actors.[210] Within the discourse of foreseeability, however, surprisingly little, if any, attention has been placed on this substantial and influential fact. In court decisions, it can be assumed that the courts imminently implement these considerations without specifically elaborating on the required standards, however, the distinction is also entirely missing from the academic debate. Nevertheless, whether the foreseeability of an individual person or a state is in question is highly decisive for the scope and the requirements posed on the foreseeable outcome. It directly affects the threshold of foreseeability, as well. Influenced is this necessary distinction, furthermore, by different normative principles that underly and transpire the legal doctrines which the overall assessment is ultimately based on. Especially the application of principles of international environmental law can lead to a distinction between the requirements applied in regard to states and contrasting the standards that individuals are

[209] See in this regard Sect. 2.1.1.

[210] See in this regard Sect. 5.3.2.

confronted with. In consideration of the necessity of distinguishing between different actors and in light of the overall climate change setting, it is particularly a three-part distinction that renders appropriate, which also strongly reflects on the scope of foreseeability. The three different groups consist out of states, large private entities—such as large multinational corporations—and smaller private actors, which also include individuals.[211] Such classification and categorization do not counteract the objectivity of the foreseeability consideration; after all, the objectivity continues to exist within the individual groups and is consistent with the differentiated consideration of reasonableness.

5.3.2.3.1.1 States

In light of the general foreseeability of climate change for states, it is the ratification of the FCCC in 1992 that is predominantly used as a timely benchmark.[212] The preamble of the FCCC hereby indicates that at this point in time the general foreseeability of human influence on climate change is not only scientifically given but also predominant in the political discourse. The preamble states in this regard:

> Acknowledging that change in the Earth's climate and adverse effects are a common concern of humankind, concerned that human activities have been substantially increasing the atmospheric concentration of greenhouse gases, that these increases enhance the natural greenhouse effect, and that this will result on average in an additional warming of the Earth's surface and atmosphere and may adversely affect natural ecosystems and humankind.[213]

Based on the ratification of the FCCC by 198 states as of 2022 (initially 165), which runs concurrent with an active acknowledgement of the anthropogenic climate change and its general adverse effects on the natural ecosystem but also on humankind, it is this point in time, viz the year 1992, that can be considered as the latest commencement of foreseeability. Further reference is usually made to the publication of the first Assessment Report of the IPCC in 1990, in which the human influence on the Earth's climate was also explicitly discussed and affirmed from a scientific point of view and which was made publicly available especially aiming at decision makers by entailing an explicit 'Summary for Policymakers'.[214] In the respective summary, it is stated that

> (w)e are certain of the following: [...] emissions resulting from human activities are substantially increasing the atmospheric concentrations of the greenhouse gases: carbon dioxide, methane, chlorofluorocarbons (CFCs) and nitrous oxide. These increases will

[211] See in this regard also Sect. 5.2.1.

[212] See e.g. Zeidler (2022), p. 112, United Nations Committee on the Rights of the Child, 8 October 2021 – CRC/C/88/D/107/2019, *Sacchi et al. v. Argentina et al.*, para 9.11.

[213] Preamble FCCC.

[214] IPCC (1992b), p. 52; IPCC (1992a).

> enhance the greenhouse effect, resulting on average in an additional warming of the Earth's surface [...].[215]

Both references are widely used to infer general foreseeability of climate change for states from the 1990s onwards.[216]

However, the threshold of general foreseeability of climate change for states has to be set much earlier. Critically, it is not actual knowledge of the impact of GHG emissions on the climate system and its respective changes that determines the existence of reasonable foreseeability.[217] Even an explicit declaration of intent in the form of a ratification of international environmental agreements, as proclaimed by some authors, cannot be ultimately regarded as the sole yardstick of foreseeability.[218] There are two arguments against using ratifications as a threshold for foreseeability. On the one hand, although such an approach certainly simplifies the determination of a specific threshold, the use of the active will of states would lead to a subjectivisation of foreseeability. However, foreseeability is a highly objective construct. For this reason alone, active will should only be considered as a further indicator of general foreseeability, but not as the exclusive criterion. On the other hand, ratifications are based on active and explicit knowledge. In view of the long political and diplomatic process involved in such ratifications, with negotiations taking place long before the final draft is presented, states' knowledge does not commence at the time of the ratification. Rather, states know, or should have known, about the adverse effects of GHG emissions and anthropogenic climate change long before ratifying the respective climate and environmental agreements. Nevertheless, ratification by a large number of states can be used as an indicator of the existence of reasonable foreseeability. As a strict threshold, though, they are unsuitable.

Thus, the general threshold of reasonable foreseeability for states needs to be set much earlier. Indications for an earlier threshold can be found, in particular, in the consideration of established principles of international environmental law, which are also reflected in climate matters, as well as in the reflection on further environmental and climate efforts of states.[219] Regarding the latter, a detailed and well-founded overview of the development of climate change-related evidence and possible connecting factors was provided by the claimants in their statement of claim in the case *Kivalina v. ExxonMobil Corp.*[220] Indicators include the Report of the National Academies of Sciences (NAS) in 1979, the 11th Annual Report of the Council on Environmental Quality in 1980, and the Brundtland Report of the World

---

[215] IPCC (1992a), p. 63.

[216] See e.g. Brunnée et al. (2011), p. 35 para 3.22; Verheyen (2005), pp. 182–183; Wagner and Arntz (2021), para 53. For 1990 at the latest, see Voigt (2016), p. 12.

[217] In this respect also Mason-Case and Dehm (2021), p. 173.

[218] See e.g. Hänni (2021), p. 18.

[219] See in regard to the principle of prevention later in this section.

[220] US District Court for the Northern District of California, 30 September 2009 – 4:08-cv-01138-SBA, *Native Village of Kivalina v. ExxonMobil Corp.*, statement of claim, paras 134–162.

Commission on Environment and Development from 1987, just to name a few.[221] Especially in the Brundtland Report it was made clear that "*(c)urrent modelling studies and 'experiments' show a rise in globally averaged surface temperatures, [...] of somewhere between 1.5°C and 4.5°C*" which then "*would lead to a sea level rise of 25-140 centimetres. [...]. Experts believe that crop and forest boundaries will move to higher latitudes; the effects of warmer oceans on marine ecosystems or fisheries and food chains are also virtually unknown.*"[222] Although the case *Kivalina v. ExxonMobil Corp* is located in the private law sphere, it, nevertheless, provides valuable insights into the general, scientific, and political state of knowledge surrounding anthropogenic climate change. Other claimants have followed this strategy and listed numerous reports proving the anthropogenic influence on the climate system and the respective state-related consensus.[223]

Even outside the scientific community, warnings about the harmful effects of greenhouse gases and other activities on the climate system have been issued before the year 1990. This led to the inclusion of a recommendation in the final report of the Stockholm World Conference on the Environment in the year 1972. Therein it states:

> *It is recommended* that governments be mindful of activities in which there is an appreciable risk of effects on climate, and to this end: (a) Carefully evaluate the likelihood and magnitude of climatic effects and disseminate their findings to the maximum extent feasible before embarking on such activities; (b) Consult fully other interested States when activities carrying a risk of such effects are being contemplated or implemented.[224]

An even earlier reference can be built upon the principle of prevention.[225] Since the principle requires states to avoid any transboundary environmental harm it also stretches to climatic damages. The states are hereby not only required to avoid transboundary harm but also to regulate private behaviour. Prevention, however, prerequisites the knowledge of transboundary harmful factors which results in an (at least soft law entailed) duty to assess whether certain behaviour could be harmful to the environment and respectively also to the climate or not. Since the 'no harm' rule was established as early as 1938 (1941) and the principle of prevention is a further development of this original rule, it advocates a timely shift in the threshold of general foreseeability.[226] Those considerations are further emphasized by the establishment and constant acknowledgement of the precautionary principle which

[221] National Academies of Sciences, Engineering, and Medicine (1979); The White House (1980); World Commission on Environment and Development (1987), pp. 338, 342–347.

[222] World Commission on Environment and Development (1987), pp. 343–344 paras 21–22.

[223] See e.g. Hague District Court, 26 May 2021 – C/09/571932/HA ZA 19-379, *Milieudefensie et al. v. Royal Dutch Shell plc*, Essen Regional Court, 15 December 2016 – 2 O 285/15, *Luciano Lliuya v. RWE AG*, Higher Regional Court Hamm, pending – 5 U 15/17, *Luciano Lliuya v. RWE AG*.

[224] United Nations Conference on the Human Environment (1972), p. 20, Recommendation 70.

[225] See for more detail about the principle of prevention Sect. 5.2.2.1.

[226] See for the origin of the no-harm rule Arbitrational Tribunal, 16 April 1938, 11 March 1941 – 3 R.I.A.A. 1905, *United States v. Canada (Trail Smelter Case)*.

requires preventive measures even in cases of scientific uncertainty.[227] That principles of international environmental law can be and are being used to relax certain requirements of causal relationships was also shown in the case of *Southern Bluefin Tuna*.[228] In that specific case the International Tribunal of the Law of the Sea ruled that although it was impossible for the Tribunal to assess the consequences of the defendants conduct with overall scientific certainty, the defendant was nevertheless required to take precautionary measures to safeguard the population of the endangered species.[229]

In view of the broad scientific consensus on the anthropogenic cause of climate change since the 1980s at the latest, and in view of the widespread acceptance and implementation of the principle of prevention in international environmental law, it must be emphatically rejected that there was no general foreseeability in the period up to 1990 with regard to states.[230] Rather, a period between 1970 and 1980 should be taken as the threshold of general foreseeability of climate change.[231] However, the threshold can be moved forward by recognising and demonstrating special knowledge.

5.3.2.3.1.2 Private Entities

In contrast to states, setting a temporal threshold of general foreseeability for private entities and individuals is much more complex. This particularly results out of the fact that neither international environmental and climate principles, nor international climate efforts and agreements can be used as an objective indicator for general foreseeability. Decisive in the case of private entities rather is the fundamental

---

[227] See for more detail about the precautionary principle Sect. 5.2.2.2.

[228] International Tribunal for the Law of the Sea, 27 August 1999 – ITLOS Reports 1999, p. 280, *Southern Bluefin Tuna (New Zealand v. Japan; Australia v. Japan), Provisional Measures*. Similar also Nyka (2021), p. 146.

[229] International Tribunal for the Law of the Sea, 27 August 1999 – ITLOS Reports 1999, p. 280, *Southern Bluefin Tuna (New Zealand v. Japan; Australia v. Japan), Provisional Measures*, paras 73–89.

[230] Opposing foreseeability until 1990 and in citing Tol and Verheyen (2004), p. 1118; Wagner and Arntz (2021), p. 417 para 52. Opposing responsibility for historic emissions in general and raising the concern of constituting a perpetual liability, see Chatzinerantzis and Appel (2019), p. 883.

[231] Presenting a similar approach in regard to foreseeability of transboundary harm from hazardous activities, see Inter-American Court of Human Rights, 15 November 2017 – OC-23/17, *A Request for an Advisory Opinion from the Inter-American Court of Human Rights Concerning the Interpretation of Article 1(1), 4(1) and 5(1) of the American Convention on Human Rights*, para 136. The IACtHR hereby referenced the International Law Commission (2001b), p. 153, Art. 3 para 5. Also in favour of applying the precautionary principle to set a threshold to the criterion of foreseeability, Haritz (2011), p. 25. Setting the threshold even earlier namely in the 1960s, see Schirmer (2021), pp. 1104–1105. Arguing that "*models and reports relating to the risks associated with climate change and the types of activity causing these changes were already known in general terms in the 1980s.*" Nyka (2021), p. 145. Also applying an earlier threshold due to the existence of an "*objectively accessible knowledge of risks*" ("*objektiv zugängliches Gefahrenwissen*") Pöttker (2014), p. 132.

accessibility of scientific information about anthropogenic climate change as well as a broad public consensus on that respective topic. In this context, special knowledge becomes of increased relevance, especially in the case of multinational corporations, based on which the foreseeability threshold per se can be preponed considerably in individual cases. Concurrently, the public opinion and public accessibility to information on the effects of climate change play a decisive role, as well.

The standard of a reasonable observer generally does not refer to the full and current state of science, above all not in the private sphere. Rather, the standard put on the fictional observer to elaborate on whether the outcome was foreseeable or not needs to reflect the equitable and common knowledge as well as the public debate of the respective time. Without, however, any positive obligations or duties to take precautionary measures as it is the case with states based on international environmental principles, the overall threshold of general foreseeability of private entities and individuals must be set significantly later than for states. The relevant period, as has been called for by a large number of authors also regarding states, could relate to the first publication of the IPCC Assessment Report as well as the ratification of the FCCC, which would impose the temporal threshold on the year 1990.[232] In contrast to state actors, nonetheless, the foreseeability standard is not to be shifted forward based on prior reports or deliberations, rather it is here that the year 1990 can function as the threshold of general foreseeability of a reasonable, like-kind observer.

This result still falls under the retention of individual, special knowledge.[233] As it was already previously addressed, such specialized accounts are particularly likely considering multinational corporations and so-called 'global-players'. Individuals, however, are subject to the most reduced standard of general foreseeability. With the Paris Agreement being brought into force in 2015 and the publication of the Oslo Principles on Global Climate Change in the same year, foreseeability of climate change per se as well as its more general impacts can no longer be denied by any actor in question. Increasingly indicative to provide and argue for reasonable foreseeability are also climate lawsuits, which as precedents received a lot of media attention and were, therefore, also comprehensively brought to the public attention.[234] With an increasing number of climate lawsuits, this trend will most likely be persistently used to justify and prove the foreseeability of climate change, as well.

---

[232] IPCC (1992a), United Nations Framework Convention on Climate Change 1992.

[233] In opposition see *Schirmer*, who sets an even earlier threshold and argues for foreseeability starting as early as 1960, Schirmer (2021), p. 1105.

[234] See Regional Court of Kassel, pending – n/a, *Barbara Metz et al. v. Wintershall Dea AG*, statement of claim, 76, Regional Court of Munich, pending – n/a, *Deutsche Umwelthilfe (DUH) v. Bayerische Motoren Werke AG (BMW)*, statement of claim (21 September 2021), 63–65.

5.3.2.3.2 Specific Foreseeability of Climate Change Impacts

5.3.2.3.2.1 General Accounts on Specific Foreseeability

Even a greater obstacle than the foreseeability of general anthropogenic climate change poses the assessment of a timely threshold in light of the foreseeability of concrete climate change induced harm. Based on the broad public debate, the accessibility of scientific knowledge to policy-makers and individuals alike, and the increasingly tangible impacts of climate change, it is now almost universally accepted that specific impacts of climate change are reasonably foreseeable.[235] This applies equally to all actors. Although there are inevitably still climate change-related effects that cannot yet be fully proven scientifically, and it must also be expected that some effects will only become visible in the coming years, the high level of awareness of anthropogenic climate change and the corresponding effects, as well as the lowered and reduced degree of the foreseeability standard, nevertheless allows reasonable foreseeability to be affirmed as a matter of principle even for such specific effects.

However, the situation poses itself different in considering historic emissions and has been the subject of considerable debate in climate change lawsuits as well.[236] The attribution of a specific climate change impact due to the discharge of past emissions was, for instance, at issue in the case *Smith v. Fonterra Co-Operative Group Limited.*[237] In the respective lawsuit, the Judge, while affirming the general foreseeability of climate change, opposed foreseeability for the specific damage the claimant imposed.[238] Although this judgment was widely criticized due to a multitude of different reasons it, nevertheless, stands as a precedent for the difficulties that claimants face when trying to proof foreseeability in regard to a specific damage in light of past and historical emissions.[239] This is further conditioned by the knowledge that climate change will have further socio-economic, ecological and even political effects beyond those already experienced and known of.

The same difficulties arose in a most recent decision in the case *Minister for the Environment v. Sharma.*[240] In this case, the Federal Court Judges disagreed as to whether or not the occurrence of damage in the form of personal injury was foreseeable at the time of the climate-damaging behaviour, in this case the approval of a coal mine. While *Chief Judge Allsop* and *Judge Beach* approved of such

---

[235] See in this regard again the Reports by the IPCC, e.g. IPCC (2023).

[236] See in this regard also Pöttker (2014), pp. 132–133.

[237] High Court of New Zealand, 21 October 2021 – [2021] NZCA 552, *Smith v. Fonterra Co-Operative Group Limited.*

[238] Ibid. paras 81–82.

[239] Bonython (2021), p. 432.

[240] Federal Court of Australia, 15 March 2022 – [2022] FCAFC 35, *Minister for the Environment v. Sharma.*

foreseeability, *Judge Wheelahan* dissented in stating that "*[…] I am not persuaded that it is reasonably foreseeable that the approval of the Extension Project will be a cause of personal injury to the respondents, as the concept of causation is understood for the purposes of the common law tort of negligence.*"[241] This case clearly shows the difficulties that courts face in applying a retrospective view when considering whether a specific outcome was foreseeable or not. Although foreseeability is always stated to be an objective inquiry, in trying to elaborate on what could have been foreseeable at the respective time, courts rather resort to applying an objectified guess than a factual sound assessment. The latter, however, fails a priori due to the necessary ex-ante perspective on grounds of feasibility.

The temporal threshold of a specific climate change impact depends largely on the type of damage, the region in which the damage occurs and the state of scientific research at the time of the action or omission in question.[242] Some types of impact have long been considered to be causally linked to climate change and at least partly attributable to human behaviour. These include, for instance, negative impacts on agriculture and forestry, with the IPCC warning as early as 1990 that "*(t)here may be severe effects in some regions, particularly decline in production in regions of high present-day vulnerability that are least able to adjust. These include Brazil, Peru, the Sahel Region of Africa, Southeast Asia, the Asian region of the USSR and China.*"[243] Other impacts which the IPCC predicted early on include water scarcity especially in parts of Africa and the Sahel, concurrent with increased precipitation in undefined parts of the world, sea-level rise accompanied by socioeconomic issues, and the melting of surface ice shields as well as permafrost resulting in higher risks of landslides and erosions.[244]

However, the IPCC also emphasized in its report that further research on climate change impacts is necessary especially on a regional level.[245] Based on these considerations in 1990, a wide range of impacts have just recently been attributed to anthropogenic climate change and thus to the emission of greenhouse gases or other climate-damaging behaviour. Among them are in particular secondary effects on human health as well as an increase in morbidity and in violent conflicts.[246] After all, for the majority of the impacts, foreseeability can be affirmed at least from the year 2015 onwards. From a political, social and legal point of view, 2015 can be seen as a year of watershed in terms of increased efforts to protect the climate. From a legal perspective, 2015 marks the beginning of the third wave of climate litigation.[247] As a result, awareness of climate issues is expanding to areas of law that

241 Ibid. 135 para 419, 270 para 886.

242 Pöttker (2014), p. 132.

243 IPCC (1992a), p. 87 para 10. The IPCC also considered a potential rise in the agricultural productivity in other areas of the world (see as well at 87 para 10).

244 Ibid. 88–89.

245 Ibid. 90 paras 30–31.

246 IPCC (2014a), pp. 69, 71.

247 See in this regard also Sect. 2.2.2.2.

have primarily not been associated with climate-related issues.[248] With the adoption of the Paris Agreement, as well as the United Nations Sustainable Development Goals and the Sendai Framework, climate change has also been brought to the forefront of political attention.[249] In the same year, a pro-climate movement also began to emerge in the social sphere mainly among the younger generations, leading to the formation of activist groups such as 'Friday's for Future', 'Extinction Rebellion' and 'Last Generation'.

Given this overarching climate positive movement, reasonable foreseeability covers almost all climate change impacts as of today. Nevertheless, foreseeability of specific impacts in light of past and historic emissions does not allow for a final and generally valid statement. Foreseeability hereby strongly depends on the specific outcome in question. Assessments of foreseeability will continue to rely heavily on IPCC reports to determine at what point in time specific impacts are known, at least from a scientific perspective. Although the highly scientific findings cannot be expected to provide an exhaustive assessment, especially when the foreseeability of individuals is in question, they can be used as a comprehensive indicator. In this context, the Summary for Policymakers is of crucial importance.[250] Particularly in relation to states and larger private entities, courts are likely to draw on individual and specialized knowledge of the specific impacts of the action in question in their assessment of specific foreseeability.[251] Judgments will, thus, be based on a case-by-case reasoning reliant on the discretion of the respective courts.

5.3.2.3.2.2 State-Related Peculiarities of Specific Foreseeability

The matter presents itself quite differently, however, when it comes to the foreseeability of states. On the basis of the precautionary principle, states, unlike private actors, are not able to fully invoke the lack of foreseeability of specific impacts of climate change as easily as it is possible for private actors.[252] The precautionary principle requires that states take all feasible measures in the interest of risk prevention, and that the effects of potentially environmentally damaging government behaviour be assessed and evaluated prior to the respective conduct. Such a precautionary obligation also includes the consideration of specific, climate-related damage, regardless of the respective level of scientific certainty.[253] In light of the precautionary principle, the foreseeability test that is applied to state actors can be modified as follows: Foreseeable is what a reasonable observer could have foreseen

[248] See in this regard also Sect. 2.2.2.3.

[249] The UNSDGs are entailed in the Agenda 2030.

[250] See e.g. IPCC (2023).

[251] *Schirmer*, e.g. argues in favour of specific foreseeability in the case *Luciano Lliuya v. RWE AG* as early as from 1960 onwards, see Schirmer (2021), p. 1105.

[252] See for more detail about the precautionary principle Sect. 5.2.2.2.

[253] See for the different certainty and confidence levels Sect. 2.1.1.

from an ex-ante perspective or should have foreseen in the context of risk prevention.

Similar to the assessment of the foreseeability of climate change, the ECtHR has developed a forward-looking approach in the course of positive obligations. In taking an duty-based position, the Court placed particular emphasis on what the actor should have foreseen considering the respective obligation. It, thus developed the so called 'ought to have known'-standard which also entails a strong foreseeability component and reflects the rationale of preventive and precautionary measures, as well.[254] In light of the jurisprudence of the ECtHR, the application of the respective standard presupposes the existence of a positive obligation. Nevertheless, it indicates the strong influence of precautionary perceptions on the overall standard of foreseeability.

The precautionary principle as developed in the realm of international law, however, still remains a controversial concept to this day, despite its far-reaching recognition of a customary provision in international law.[255] Its position is nevertheless considerably strengthened by the implementation of the principle in a large number of international treaties, including the FCCC and the Rio Declaration. Thus, in line with the publication of the first IPCC report and taking into account considerations of prevention and precaution, specific climate change impacts can be assumed to be foreseeable for countries from the 1990s onwards.[256] This only includes impacts that could have actually been determined by adhering to the principles of risk prevention. Which precautionary standard is to be applied is still in dispute, even in regard to the overall scope of the principles. Nevertheless, the foreseeability assessment should at least require an analysis and study of climate impacts based on the current state of science.

This implies that the qualification of concrete, climate change-related impacts as foreseeable for states decisively corresponds to the current state and actual ability of climate and attribution science at the time in question. Thus, such normative evaluations based on the precautionary principle lead to the reconciliation of legal foreseeability and natural science. In contrast to the considerations applied in regard to the interaction of the precautionary principle with general foreseeability, however, preponing the threshold of specific foreseeability in the same way does not function with specific foreseeability at issue. A requirement of such preponderance is the existence of scientific knowledge about the effects in the time of the damaging behaviour and omission. And while this can be affirmed for general foreseeability starting from an early time on, specific climate damage was difficult to be proven long after anthropogenic climate change had surfaced in the understanding of the

[254] For further explanations on the 'ought to have known' standard, see Stoyanova (2020).

[255] In favour of the recognition as customary law, see von Arnauld (2019), p. 409 para 895. Also de Sadeleer (2016), p. 21.

[256] IPCC (1992b).

broad public.[257] The precautionary principle is therefore much less concerned with the threshold of specific foreseeability than it is generally perceived to be. These considerations show that scientific knowledge is indeed the basis of any consideration of climate change, even in its normative form.

The fact that judicial bodies also assume a partly earlier foreseeability threshold for states than for individuals with regard to concrete impacts even outside the application of the precautionary principle, however, is also shown by the statements of the Committee on the Rights of the Child in the case *Sacchi et al. v. Argentina et al.* Here the Committee stated that

> (i)n light of existing scientific evidence showing the impact of the cumulative effect of carbon emissions on the enjoyment of human rights, including rights under the Convention, the Committee considers that the potential harm of the State party's acts or omissions regarding the carbon emissions originating in its territory was reasonably foreseeable to the State party.[258]

In doing so, the Committee accepted the argumentation of the plaintiffs "*that the State party has known about the harmful effects of its contributions to climate change for decades and that it signed the United Nations Framework Convention on Climate Change in 1992 as well as the Paris Agreement in 2016.*"[259]

A similar approach was taken by the Human Rights Committee in the case *Billy et al. v. Australia.* In this case, the Committee had to determine, inter alia, whether the right to culture under Art. 27 of the Covenant on Civil and Political Rights had been violated by the State party by failing to provide adaptation measures to protect the applicants from the adverse effects of climate change.[260] Ultimately, the Committee relied heavily on the special knowledge of the defendant in assessing the foreseeability of the adverse impacts. In using the notification by the claimants as a point of departure for their general foreseeability assessment, they stated that "*(t)he Committee considers that the climate impacts mentioned by the authors represent a threat that could have reasonably been foreseen by the State party, as the authors' community members began raising the issue in the 1990s*".[261] Although a reasonable observer might not have foreseen the impact of climate change on the defendants' cultural life, based on the defendant's notification as well as the positive obligations under Art. 25 CCPR, the risk and outcome were ultimately deemed foreseeable for the defendant.

---

[257] See e.g. the first IPCC – Report in which the degree of uncertainty concerning special impacts was still very high the statement with reference to AFOLU that "*(y)et the fact that there are major uncertainties regarding likely effects in specific regions should be a cause for concern. Studies have not yet conclusively determined whether, on average, global agricultural potential will increase or decrease.*" IPCC (1992a), p. 93 (inter alia).

[258] United Nations Committee on the Rights of the Child, 8 October 2021 – CRC/C/88/D/107/2019, *Sacchi et al. v. Argentina et al.*, para 9.11.

[259] Ibid.

[260] Art. 25 CCPR.

[261] United Nations Human Rights Committee, 22 September 2022 – CCPR/C/135/D/3624/2019, *Daniel Billy et al. v. Australia (Torres Strait Islanders Petition)*, para 8.14.

The foreseeability of concrete climate change impacts is, therefore, to be affirmed for states from 1990 onwards. Here, too, the assessment and proof of special knowledge will play an important role in the assessment of reasonable foreseeability. The determination of foreseeability for private entities and individuals, on the other hand, is mainly based on a case-by-case analysis but will most likely be possible starting from the beginning of the twenty-first century.

5.3.3 Conclusion

Although the foreseeability of anthropogenic climate change and climate change-related impacts is still often described as a problem that is difficult to overcome in climate change litigation, the analysis has shown that it is possible to surmount this obstacle in a broad number of cases. The required standard of foreseeability hereby strongly builds upon an ex-ante perspective of a reasonable observer. The respective observer refers to a fictitious character which derives from the general understanding of 'like-kinded' actors. A distinction is thus made between the action or omission of states as well as private entities and individuals. The distinction between the different actors also determines the threshold of foreseeability. In terms of the general foreseeability of anthropogenic climate change, a threshold can be set for private entities from 1990 onwards, irrespective of their individual capabilities, while the foreseeability for states can be set much earlier, at the latest from 1970 onwards, taking into account preventive and precautionary obligations.

More difficult than general foreseeability, ultimately, is the assessment of specific foreseeability. Due to the complexity of the climate system which strongly corresponds to the difficulty in attributing specific climate change impacts, specific foreseeability can hardly be determined unambiguously and comprehensively, especially in the case of private entities. Even at the present time, the foreseeability of specific impacts of climate change is unlikely to be fully determinable. Nonetheless, in light of the increased awareness about the climate crises, the broad media coverage on the respective topic, as well as based on the comprehensive and ever-evolving IPCC Reports including most recent findings of climate and attribution science, most specific impacts will be foreseeable from the twenty-first century onwards at the latest for private entities. A preponderance of the respective temporal threshold can, however, be achieved in most cases by referring to special knowledge which allows for an earlier legal and moral responsibility. Concurrent to the assessment of general foreseeability and in distinguishing between the different actors, the threshold of foreseeability for states is to be shifted forward concerning concrete climate change induced impacts, as well. On the basis of the precautionary principle, the foreseeability threshold for special impacts can be set from the year 1990 onwards.

5.4 Materiality Threshold

5.4.1 Materiality as a General Principle of Normative Causation

The materiality threshold represents one of the most comprehensive constraints on factual causation. In complying with the core function of the second step of the causal test, the assessment of materiality sorts out contributions to the outcome that are not substantial and legally significant, and thus leads to a negation of overall causation in the law. The concept of materiality denies moral and, consequently, legal responsibility for contributions that fall below its threshold, thereby normatively omitting causation despite the existing factual basis.

Despite its restrictive function it is only in very few cases that the materiality threshold explicitly constitutes a separate test of normative causation. Rather, such a threshold is anchored in other dogmatic-normative structures. These include for example the theory of adequacy, which requires the determination of a legally significant risk.[262] Furthermore, the materiality and scope of an action are also listed as explicit core elements of further normative causal doctrines, including for example concepts such as the 'substantial factor test' or the 'material contribution test'.[263] Contrary to the wording, however, materiality is not the exclusive causal determinant in those so-called 'tests'. Rather, other normative evaluations and principles also find their way into the causal theories mentioned, the explicit terminology, nevertheless, implies the significance of materiality for the assessment of normative causation. In some cases, the rejection of causation on the basis of lack of materiality can, furthermore, arise from considerations of good faith.[264]

As materiality does not constitute an own test of normative causation, and the doctrines in which a materiality test is entailed are rather broadly formulated and carry a great width in their interpretative and evaluative realm, the substance and the requirements of materiality remain unclear to a great extent. This especially affects the issue of the right point of reference and concerns the basic condition whether the requirement of materiality aims at the initial behaviour or omission, or the outcome in question. Whereas the issue of the right reference point can arise in multiple occasions, it does not do so in every case at hand. In some instances, especially concerning cause-effect relations that are characterized by a shorter causal chain, the act and the outcome might be of equal materiality. If A is killed by a blow to the head from B, neither the act, i.e. B's blow, nor the result, i.e. A's death, can be denied materiality. In multi-causal cases in which a great extent of contributions come together to produce the respective result, the materiality of the individual act or

[262] See for the theory of adequacy Sect. 5.6.

[263] See for the material contribution test especially the Canadian and British accounts in Sects. 4.5.2.2.1.1, 4.5.2.2.1.2 and for the substantial factor test that finds application in the American legal sphere Sect. 4.5.2.2.1.3.

[264] Kohler (2017), para 215.

omission and the overall outcome might diverge. With respect to other normative principles and concerning the point of blameworthiness, it is the initial act or omission itself that must be substantial in the first place. As already noted in relation to other normative doctrines, moral blameworthiness and responsibility are anchored in the act or omission itself, rather than in the outcome.[265] It is, therefore, this initial behaviour that must be the starting point for the assessment of materiality. In principle, this does not preclude the inclusion of the scope of the relevant output, which can still be used as an appropriate indicator of materiality. However, the focus of blameworthiness, and therefore of materiality, remains on the act or omission itself.

5.4.2 Materiality and Climate Change

In the determination of causation within climate change litigation, materiality is the second fundamental pillar and guiding principle of the normative adaptation of factual causal chains, alongside the principle of foreseeability. It is in this context that especially two fundamental issues arise. The first concerns whether there is a need for a materiality threshold in climate change litigation at all (Sect. 5.4.2.1). If so, the second question then relates to the most controversial issue of where exactly such a threshold should be set. Current climate change litigation decisions hereby can provide an indication on where the threshold should be placed, without however solving this issue in its entirety (Sect. 5.4.2.2). Therefore, there is a need for further elaboration and analysis to succeed in establishing a materiality threshold for legal climatic causation (Sect. 5.4.2.3).

5.4.2.1 The Need for a Causal Threshold

Under the presumption of scientific provability, nearly every human action and omission is contributing to climate change and provides for factual causation to be established. Such causal relata do not only evolve around obvious emission-generating actions such as fuel-based transportation but also relate to more consequential actions such as consumer choices and general living expenses. Each human being bequeaths a negative environmental and climatic footprint. Should thus every human being be held responsible for their negative impact on the Earth's climate, ergo should causation in the law be established limitless? From a climate-positivistic point of view, such a result might be considered favourable. Depending on the approach used, factual causation in the law can render very broad and consider a lot of different factors as causal. The main aim of normative causation, thus, is to counter such reservations and limit factual causation through the application of

[265] This has e.g. been at issue concerning the vantage point of foreseeability, see Sect. 5.3.2.1.1.

normative-based tests, with one of the possible strategies being to set a causal materiality threshold.

Limiting factual causation through the setting of a materiality threshold is also supported by practical considerations. Unlimited factual and normative causation can lead to the admissibility of a multitude of climate change lawsuits resulting in congestion of the courts. The argument that such a 'flood' of lawsuits would simply not occur due to practical reasons has to be strongly opposed.[266] Climate actions are a rapidly evolving category of litigation based on a dynamic litigation process. Consequently the possibility should not be entirely ruled out that climate change lawsuits in the future will also address minor contributors to limit climate change to its actual extent or to set a precedent for the future tackling of minimal contributions. An extension of actions to micro-contributions would also mean an extension of joint and shared liability, which would again result in major practical difficulties. To avoid such an excess of lawsuits and the associated legal uncertainty, it is necessary to set a certain contributory threshold.

The need for a threshold can also be derived from existing environmental principles, which also limit their scope to a certain type and extent of behaviour or outcome. Foremost among these is the precautionary principle, which applies only in cases of serious and irreversible damage.[267] Although it has already been argued that climate damage is both largely irreversible and serious, micro-contributions often fail to meet the latter requirement. Excluding micro-contributions by the means of implementing a materiality threshold is further necessary given that other normative theories of causation do not serve this specific limiting purpose but rather focus on other normative adaptations. That such perceptions on normative causation and materiality are indeed relevant is also shown by the high number of jurisdictions which have integrated a materiality threshold into their normative causation assessments. However, those materiality thresholds are usually built upon indeterminate legal terms such as 'significant' or 'substantial', which require for further interpretation in regard to climate change scenarios.

Even from a moral point of view establishing a threshold can be justified. The simple idea behind having a materiality threshold is that due to the mere existence of each human being greenhouse gases are produced and other potentially climate-damaging behaviour is favoured. Every human life has a negative impact on the atmospheric greenhouse gas density. However, this would normally not pose a problem provided the Earth's natural climate balance would still exist. A healthy climate system would be able to balance naturally produced human greenhouse gases through the inclusion of those gases into greenhouse gas sinks or the degradation of these by emission-negative-organisms. The moral blameworthiness of such behaviour is, therefore, non-existent in regard to this naturally-occurring amount of GHG. Contributions that exceed this natural amount attributable to the mere existence of humans to the extent that the climate system is no longer able to compensate

[266] Zeidler (2022), p. 116.

[267] See in this regard Sect. 5.2.2.

on its own, however, entail moral culpability for the change in the climate system and the its resulting impacts. Such considerations support the argument that not every contribution should be considered legally causal given that the moral and legal blameworthiness for some, especially minor contributions, is missing. Nevertheless, in terms of climate justice, corrective justice could stand in the way of such a threshold, as it excludes contributions from existing corrective mechanisms. In the light of the above argument, overburdening the courts is not in the interests of corrective justice either. In particular, and ultimately convincing, is the argument that without moral blameworthiness, there is no need for a corrective within the framework of normative justice. As it has been previously elaborated on in light of the foreseeability criterion, corrective justice builds upon legal wrongs. Without the moral blameworthiness of natural contributions, the basis of corrective justice also ceases to exist.[268]

5.4.2.2 Status Quo of Materiality in Climate Change Litigation

Climate change litigation is dominated by the drop-in-the-ocean argument.[269] Defendants argue that their contribution to a changing climate is of such a minor scale that it only constitutes a 'drop' in light of the overall contributions to climate change and would thus be negligible. Although such an argument is not specifically of causal nature but refers to liability and responsibility for climate change and the accompanying damages in general, it nevertheless contains a causal component. The main idea behind the drop-in-the-ocean argument evolves around the consideration that minor emission reduction or mitigation efforts would not constitute a change in the Earth's climate or a deceleration of climate change by itself. A similar rationale is applied to minor greenhouse gas emissions. Transferred to causal considerations, this implies that causation in the law only is relevant and, therefore, is to be established for major contributions that perceive as being more than only a 'drop' in regard to worldwide emissions. Such argumentation was firstly put forward by the defendants in the case *Massachusetts v. EPA*, in which case the Environmental Protection Agency argued that "*its decision not to regulate greenhouse gas emissions from new motor vehicles contributes so insignificantly to petitioners' injuries that the agency cannot be haled into federal court to answer them.*"[270] The Court, however, rejected this argument on the basis that greenhouse gas emissions from motor vehicles are in no way tentative, and even minor contributions should be verifiable by federal courts. Still, not all courts agreed on such argumentation in regard to the handling of minor contributions. *Judge Wakeling* stated in his

268 See in regard to the foreseeability requirement Sect. 5.3.1.

269 See e.g. *Peel,* who calls the therein entailed problem 'the death by a thousand cuts'—problem, Peel (2011), p. 17. See also Sect. 3.3.2.2.

270 Supreme Court of the United States, 2 April 2007 – 05-1120, *Massachusetts v. EPA*, 20–21, Syllabus 4.

concurring opinion in the case *In the Matter of the Greenhouse Gas Pollution Pricing Act* that

> (t)he failure of Alberta Saskatchewan, Ontario or any other province or territory to implement greenhouse gas emission reduction measures that satisfy the federal cabinet will have no impact whatsoever on the climates or environments of other parts of Canada, or any part of the world. What happens in China, the United States, the European Union, India and the Russian Federations seals the fate of the planet.[271]

By pointing to higher contributions from other states, he indirectly implied that the contributions of these Canadian provinces, and even more so the emission reduction measures they are implementing, are of little importance and negligible. More and more courts however refrain from such a strict view and oppose the argument that contributions might be 'too small' and, therefore, would not constitute a liable contribution. The Federal Constitutional Court of Germany, for example, argued in their centennial decision in the case *Neubauer et al. v. Germany*:

> [...] (T)he obligation to take national climate action cannot be invalidated by arguing that such action would be incapable of stopping climate change. It is true that Germany would not be capable of preventing climate change on its own. Its isolated activity is clearly not the only causal factor determining the progression of climate change and the effectiveness of climate action. [...] In view of the global reduction requirements, Germany's 2% share of worldwide CO2 emissions [...] is only a small factor but if Germany's climate action measures are embedded within global efforts, they are capable of playing a part in the overall drive to bring climate change to a halt ([...]).[272]

Concurrently the District Court in the case *Urgenda Foundation v. The State of the Netherlands* stated that

> [...] it follows that a sufficient causal link can be assumed to exist between the Dutch greenhouse gas emissions, global climate change and the effects (now and in the future) on the Dutch living climate. The fact that the current Dutch greenhouse gas emissions are limited on a global scale does not alter the fact that these emissions contribute to climate change. The court has taken into consideration in this respect as well that the Dutch greenhouse emissions have contributed to climate change and by their nature will also continue to contribute to climate change.[273]

Further, the Supreme Court of the Netherlands argued in the same proceeding that

> [...] the defence that a state does not have to take responsibility because other countries do not comply with their partial responsibility, cannot be accepted. Nor can the assertion that a country's own share in global greenhouse gas emissions is very small and that reducing emissions from one's own territory makes little difference on a global scale, be accepted as a defence.[274]

[271] Court of Appeal of Alberta, 24 February 2020 – 2020 ABCA 74, *In the Matter of the Greenhouse Gas Pollution Pricing Act*, 852.

[272] Germany Federal Constitutional Court, 24 March 2021 – 1 BvR 2656/18 – 1 BvR 78/20 – 1 BvR 96/20 – 1 BvR 288/20, *Neubauer et al. v. Germany*, para 202 – English translation by the Court.

[273] The Hague District Court, 24 June 2015 – C/09/456689/HA ZA 13-1396, *Urgenda Foundation v. The State of the Netherlands*, para 4.90.

[274] Supreme Court of the Netherlands, 20 December 2019 – 19/00135, *Urgenda Foundation v. The State of The Netherlands*, para 5.7.7 – English translation by the Court.

Looking at the temporal sequence of the cases and the current pro-climate direction of the courts, a trend towards the recognition of even minimal contributions as causal can be cautiously discerned. Although the drop-in-the-ocean argument will likely continue to be advanced by litigants, the argument at least no longer appears to be fully accepted by courts. This, however, does not contradict the above consideration on the need for a causal threshold. Rather, it suggests that the threshold may need to be lower than the contributions accepted by the courts. The fact that also minor contributions become legally relevant is also advocated by the Oslo Principles on Global Climate Change. The Principles hereby constitute that "*(n)o Country or enterprise is relieved of its obligations under these Principles even if its contributions to total GHG emissions are small.*"[275] In the commentary on the Oslo Principles, the authors specifically address the impact that even minor contributions can have on the global climate and in regard to climate change damages.[276]

Some climate change litigation decisions provide indications on the setting of a possible causal threshold. At least this is true for climate damaging behaviour due to the emission of greenhouse gases. In *Neubauer et al. v. Germany* the Court still considered a share of about 2% of the worldwide CO_2 emissions as sufficient for moving forward in the proceeding.[277] In *Urgenda Foundation v. The State of The Netherlands* the Supreme Court accepted responsibility for The Netherlands' share of global greenhouse gas emissions of around 0.69% by 2020.[278] The Court of Appeal in the same case took another approach which however led to the same result in not referring to the emissions in comparison to global GHG emissions but solely to per capita CO_2 emissions (which amounted to approximately 8.4 t CO_2 in 2019).[279] According to the Court, those are considerably higher in the Netherlands than in other industrialized countries and especially countries of the European Union.[280] Not surprisingly, the Court of Appeals in *Juliana v. United States* also found the contribution of the United States with over 25% of the worldwide emissions between 1850–2012 and 15% of the global emission by the year 2019 significant enough to establish normative causation.[281] In the case *Anvil Hill Project Watch Association Inc v. Minister for the Environment and Water Resources*, one of the more earlier climate change litigation judgements, the Federal Court of Australia had to decide inter alia, whether the decision of the delegate of the Minister for the Environment and Water Resources was correct who found that the emissions

[275] 5 II A para 11 Oslo Principles on Global Climate Change, Expert Group on Global Climate Obligations (2015).

[276] See e.g. Expert Group on Global Climate Obligations (2015).

[277] Germany Federal Constitutional Court, 24 March 2021 – 1 BvR 2656/18 – 1 BvR 78/20 – 1 BvR 96/20 – 1 BvR 288/20, *Neubauer et al. v. Germany*, para 202 – English translation by the Court.

[278] Ritchie et al. (2020).

[279] World Bank (2023).

[280] The Hague Court of Appeal, 9 October 2018 – 200.178.245/01, *Urgenda Foundation v. The State of the Netherlands*, para 25.

[281] United States Court of Appeals for the Ninth Circuit, 17 January 2020 – 6:15-cv-01517-AA, *Juliana v. United States*, summary of the opinion of the Court at 20.

stemming from the project would not constitute a significant impact on the surrounding environment. The mine was responsible for 0.04% of overall greenhouse gas emissions worldwide. Yet, in fine-graining the share of emissions from a worldwide perspective to a mere countrywide point of view, the share of the mines emissions arose to a total contribution of 2% of Australia's greenhouse gas emissions.[282] Still, *Judge Stone* found no legal error in the evaluation of possible impacts by greenhouse gas emissions and the negation of the significance by the delegate of the Minister. Prior to this decision however, was the judgement in the case *Gray v. Minister for Planning*, which concerned the same project as the Anvil Hill case. Here, *Judge Pain* ruled that the greenhouse gas emissions of the project are providing a sufficient proximate link to climate change and climate change impacts, and hence have to be considered in the Environmental Impact Assessment.[283] The divergence of the two decisions on the same project shows the difficulty of the legal evaluation of the materiality of contributions and the broad debate that still persists in that regard.

Similar to the reasoning in the Anvil Hill case, courts in other cases have been reluctant to accept causation for minimal contributions. The prime example is the reasoning in the case *Luciano Lliuya v. RWE AG*. In it, the District Court of Essen stated that

> (i)rrespective of the fact that equivalent causation is negated in the context of cumulative damages, the contribution of individual greenhouse gas emitters to climate change is so small that any single emitter, even a major one such as the defendant, does not substantially increase the effects of climate change.[284]

This statement ultimately led the Court to reject normative causation based on the missing relevance of the contribution of the defendant which constitutes an inherent factor in the theory of adequacy. The contribution of the RWE AG itself hereby accounts for 0.47% of the worldwide greenhouse gas emissions between the years 1751–2010.[285] Nonetheless, the decision is not yet legally binding since the claimant went into Appeal. The Court of Appeal, the Higher Regional Court of Hamm, is likely to differ from the decision of the lower Court due to the high investigative

---

[282] Federal Court of Australia, 20 September 2007 – [2007] FCA 1480 *Anvil Hill Project Watch Association Inc v. Minister for the Environment and Water Resources*, paras 25, 42.

[283] Land and Environment Court of New South Wales, 27 November 2006 – [2006] NSWLEC 720, *Gray v. Minister for Planning*, para 100.

[284] Essen Regional Court, 15 December 2016 – 2 O 285/15, *Luciano Lliuya v. RWE AG*, para 47 – unofficial translation.

[285] Ibid. decision, para 13 as well as statement of claim (23 November 2015), 18 para 8.2 Annex K 24 in its unauthorized translation provided by Germanwatch e.V. The claimant hereby referred to data stemming from Heede (2014).

effort employed by the Court as well as to statements and comments given in its preliminary oral proceedings.[286]

In *Waratah Coal Pty Ltd v. Youth Verdict Ltd & Ors* the question of the 'weight' produced was approached in a completely different manner.[287] The question that arose in the case was whether a specific threshold exists above which a human right is restricted and how such a threshold could be assessed. In affirming the first, Waratah coal suggested that the respective threshold should be considered with the existence of a "*sufficiently strong causal relationship between the act and harm*".[288] In requiring a causal relationship to affirm the excision of a threshold Waratah poses causal factuality as an requirement for the excision of the violation-threshold. The Court later affirmed this approach.[289] In spite of this reasoning, this concept of materiality is highly unconvincing and leads to circular reasoning. The approach concludes from the existence of factual causation to the existence of materiality and thus to normative causation. This, however, is fundamentally at odds with the purpose of normative causation as a criterion of delimitation, and indeed renders it null and void. The materiality threshold would further strongly be dependent on the factual approach used, with some tests of factual causation being broader than, for instance, traditional tests. Due to this uncertainty and the circular reasoning and abolishment of a two-step approach to causation in the law, the Waratah Coal approach must thus be rejected.

While courts more and more oppose minimal contribution arguments, scholars and researchers are still debating whether a materiality threshold can be exceeded by emitting greenhouse gases, at all. Similar to the drop-in-the-ocean argument it is argued that singular contributions are too minor to cause considerable damage to the climate system and would, therefore, in most cases fall under the threshold of materiality.[290] This argumentation however does not convince. Climate change is characterized by the existence of minimal contributions. A denial of materiality as a whole, or with regard to any contributions, consequently does not meet the requirements of climate change and the mitigation of the crisis. Rather, the exclusion of materiality would lead to an exclusion of all liability, which in turn runs counter to the principles of distributive and corrective justice.[291]

---

[286] The Higher Regional Court of Hamm, for example, initiated the evidentiary phase, see Higher Regional Court Hamm, pending – 5 U 15/17, *Luciano Lliuya v. RWE AG*, order to parties to submit evidence (11 December 2017).

[287] Land Court of Queensland, 25 November 2022 – [2022] QLC 21, *Waratah Coal Pty Ltd v. Youth Verdict Ltd & Ors (No 6)*, paras 159, 685, 706.

[288] Ibid. para 1311.

[289] Ibid. para 1352.

[290] Such argumentation was especially expressed in light of the case *Luciano Lliuya v. RWE AG* (Essen Regional Court, 15 December 2016 – 2 O 285/15, *Luciano Lliuya v. RWE AG.*). See further e.g. Chatzinerantzis and Appel (2019), p. 882. Also *Frenz* in Frenz (2022), para 1434.

[291] Arguing in favour of a proportional perception of materiality Schirmer (2021), p. 1103. In drawing on climate change as a 'multiscalar' problem Peel (2011), p. 17. With reference to Osofsky (2009), p. 587.

Similarly, the courts' frequent reference to the principle of common but differentiated responsibilities is used to demonstrate the responsibility of states, even though their contributions may be perceived as minuscule.[292] In relying on the first part of the principle, which is based on 'common responsibility' and requires that, in the face of climate change, mitigation and adaptation to the new challenge be addressed through a collective effort, materiality must not function as an 'easy way out'. The principle therefore requires that the threshold should not be set too high to allow a state to escape its responsibility.[293] However, as with all principles of international environmental law, these requirements apply primarily only to states and are therefore not applied to the materiality threshold of individuals.

5.4.2.3 Setting a Causation Threshold

The analysis of current climate change litigation and decisions has clearly shown that the courts have not yet found an universal approach to the question of which contributions should be considered significant and which should not. At the global level, greenhouse gas emissions of 0.47% and 0.04% have been deemed too low, while in other jurisdictions and climate change litigation, shares of 2% and even 0.69% have been found to be sufficient. One might elaborate following those results that the materiality threshold is to be set exactly between those two levels, namely between 0.47% and 0.69% of the worldwide emissions. However, the case of the Anvil Project has shown that courts might decide differently on the necessary threshold even when considering the same project.[294] And since the above examples represent only a minimal average of climate change litigation worldwide, and are thus not representative of the totality of climate change litigation, it would be wrong to conclude from these parameters that there is a generally valid limit based on them. Again, the parameters can only serve as an indicator of a possible materiality threshold. Deciding on a materiality threshold even becomes more difficult in regard to contributions that are not emission-based such as forestation or the sealing of surfaces.

The following section, therefore, elaborates on different approaches which could be a point of reference for a materiality threshold in climate scenarios. It further aims at introducing different indicators which can be used by parties to the proceeding and

---

[292] See e.g. Administrative Court of Berlin, 31 October 2019 – VG 10 K 412.18, *Family Farmers and Greenpeace Germany v. Germany*, 21–22, Committee on the Rights of the Child, 8 October 2021 – CRC/C/88/D/107/2019, *Decision adopted by the Committee on the Rights of the Child under the Optional Protocol to the Convention on the Rights of the Child on a communications procedure in respect of Communication No.107/2019*, para 9.10. See in this regard Sect. 5.2.2.4.

[293] See for the determination of the specific threshold of materiality Sect. 5.4.2.1.

[294] Federal Court of Australia, 20 September 2007 – [2007] FCA 1480 *Anvil Hill Project Watch Association Inc v. Minister for the Environment and Water Resources*, Land and Environment Court of New South Wales, 27 November 2006 – [2006] NSWLEC 720, *Gray v. Minister for Planning*.

the respective courts to show the existence of materiality in a comprehensive manner. It shall further function as a means to provide legal clarity.

5.4.2.3.1 Emission-Based Causal Threshold

5.4.2.3.1.1 Budget-Based per Capita Threshold

A possible point of reference for the establishment of a materiality threshold within normative causation would be an accessorial account to the residual CO_2 budget of the Earth. The idea of a per capita cap is that each person is entitled to a specific CO_2 budget that must not be exceeded in total in order to limit global warming and changes to the climate system. The excision of that specific per capita budget would than carry moral and thus legal blameworthiness due to the enhancement of climate change. Moral blameworthiness in turn would justify the affirmation of legal and concurrently overall causation in the law. If, however, the individual remains within the per capita budget, meaning the person would fall below the materiality threshold, culpability is omitted and responsibility exempt. In imposing a specific budget on individuals a per capita threshold strongly emphasizes and complies with a distributive understanding of climate justice and thus with the normative perception of equality.[295] In attaining the same budget for everyone, it thus does not meet the requirements set by equity considerations.[296]

For its practical application, however, it is necessary to refer to a specific temperature threshold in order to calculate a CO_2 budget. The Paris Agreement, with its target of 1.5 °C (alternatively 2 °C), offers a possible reference. According to the IPCC Special Report, the world's remaining carbon budget to keep global warming below 1.5 °C amounts to 420 Gt/Co_2 calculated as of 2018.[297] According to the Mercator Research Institute on Global Commons and Climate Change, this implies a residual budget of about 400 Gt/CO_2 in 2020.[298] Converted to an average world population of about 8.8 billion inhabitants and calculated over the next 30 years, this translates to an average CO_2 budget per capita of 1.5 t CO_2 per year until 2050. With an average consumption of about 7.716 t CO_2 per capita in Germany in 2020, the majority of greenhouse gas emissions in Germany would thus be classified as significant.[299] Of course, the per capita budget could also be converted to country-wide budgets on the basis of the number of inhabitants. If a population of 83,695,430 (as of 31 March 2022) is taken as a basis for Germany, this results in a CO_2 budget of 125,543,145 t CO_2 per year. If CO_2 equivalents are

[295] See in this regard Sect. 5.2.3.1.

[296] See in this regard Sect. 5.1.

[297] The budget is evaluated on the base of the global mean surface air temperature with 66% probability, although the budget might change significantly due to the influence of other factors, IPCC (2018), p. 12.

[298] Mercatur Research Institute on Global Commons and Climate Change (2023).

[299] Crippa (2021), p. 114.

considered, Germany exceeded this by a factor of about six in 2021.[300] It should be noted, however, that the figures presented here for Germany's CO_2 share are not representative under the Paris Agreement and are not concurrent and linked to the reduction quotas set out in the respective treaty. This calculation only serves as a simplified illustration of possible starting points for a materiality threshold. In assuming a linear CO_2 reduction path, it illustrates the substantiality of country-wide emissions.

Major difficulties within this approach, however, arise in cases in which the legal question does not tackle current but historic emissions on which a budget calculated on the current provisions is not applicable. A further obstacle concerns emissions that do not stem from individuals but have been produced by either private entities or are attributable to countries per se. Both issues are to receive a further explanation in the forthgoing.

Concerning the former, the Earths CO_2-budget or overall CO_{2eq}-budget can be easily calculated grounded on the latest scientific findings of today. Based on an average calculation of the world's population over the next 30 years, estimating the Earth's total budget in terms of per capita budgets does not pose a major hurdle. Yet, what is not included in such a calculation are the emissions corporations and other bigger private entities contribute to the overall budget. Although private entities are without doubt one of the major producers of CO_2 emissions and other greenhouse gases, they fall short in a budget-based per capita approach.[301] This is caused in particular by the fact that a large number of considerable emitters cannot be attributed to any country specifically on the basis of emissions due to their global and multinational activities. A reference to the company's registered office or the main place of action, as is the case in particular with regard to the question of jurisdiction, would lead to a considerable distortion of the emission quotas. Such a distortion is based, in particular, on the discrepancy between the company's registered office and high-emission production sites. However, a purely production- and thus emission-based allocation is also precluded due to the considerable potential for distortion that this would entail, as well. With regard to states, the problem of setting individual budgets arises once again. The estimation has shown that the application of the per capita budget would result in a considerable overshoot of the budget limit for numerous countries, for example, also for Germany. Although this is not an argument against the application of a per capita approach and would simply establish materiality per se, it does not pose a common way of elaborating on reduction targets, neither in climate science nor in law or politics. Even in the Paris Agreement, such population-based considerations have not found their way into specific reduction targets; rather, the reduction quotas are based on the classification as an industrialized, or developing, country respectively. A materiality threshold of

[300] Germany as a whole emitted 761,591,000 t CO_{2eq} in 2021 (without LULUCF), see Umweltbundesamt (2024a).

[301] See for an analysis of the contribution of multinational corporations Heede (2014).

emissions based on the number of inhabitants would thus run counter to international agreements, which poses a reason for it to be avoided.[302]

The second set of obstacles, revolves around the treatment of historical emissions. The per capita budget referred to here only targets the remaining CO_2 emissions in order to stay within the 1.5 °C target. However, the situation is different when it comes to the allocation of emissions from the past. Applying the same CO_2 budget of 1.5 t CO_2 would be misguided for several reasons. First, the allocation of the residual budget for a 1.5 °C target from an earlier date could be a completely different one. This is especially the case since the last 20 years can be considered as particularly emission intensive. A per capita CO_2 budget in the twentieth century would, therefore, be comparatively higher, assuming the same temperature-based target, than the per capita budget calculated from the year 2020 onwards. Second, the goal of keeping global warming below 1.5 °C also does not form a legitimate benchmark for historical emissions. For one thing, countries did not agree on such a temperature target until 2015, and for another, an earlier budget setting would likely have allowed for a smaller increase in atmospheric temperature, which would have contributed to a more constrained budget under a 1 °C target, for example. Hence, the CO_2 per capita budget would potentially be lower than the budget currently determined. Historical emissions are thus difficult to cast in the per capita budget approach.

There is a clear divergence between the suitability of the approach as a materiality threshold for today's and for past emissions, as well as with respect to individual emitters per se. While the suitability of the budget-based per capita threshold cannot be denied for individuals in today's terms, it proves difficult for private entities but especially for multinational companies and states in general. The same applies to the evaluation of the approach in relation to past emissions. Thus, the approach itself cannot claim universality. However, with respect to individuals, as well as with respect to states, the emission-based causation threshold can provide an indication of whether the materiality threshold is exceeded or not.[303]

5.4.2.3.1.2 NDC-Based Causal Threshold

Art. 4 (2) of the Paris Agreement obliges the parties to the agreement to "*prepare, communicate and maintain successive nationally determined contributions that it intends to achieve*".[304] Those 'Nationally Determined Contributions' (NDCs) should target a limitation of the atmospheric surface temperature increase to 1.5 °C, respectively 2 °C. Within these NDCs, states commit to concrete emission reduction targets which could in turn function as a starting point for the establishment of a materiality threshold. The emphasis for states moral blameworthiness and

[302] See for a possible reference to the Paris Agreement as an indication of materiality Sect. 5.4.2.3.1.3.2.

[303] See for an indication-based approach Sect. 5.4.2.3.1.3.

[304] Art. 4 (2) Paris Agreement.

responsibility for enhanced climate change would, therefore, lie in the excision of the own set targets. Although such an approach seems favourable due to the possibility of taking recourse to specific objectives, it ultimately cannot convince based on a multitude of reasons.

The first objection to an NDC-based threshold relates to the actual targets set by the states. Although the Paris Agreement specifically mentions the aim of keeping the rise in surface temperatures under 1.5 °C or 2 °C respectively, states have failed to initiate necessary emission reduction measures compatible with this goal.[305] The full extent of the misconduct is frighteningly revealed in the current report for the third session of the Conference of the Parties in 2021 in which it became apparent that under the current NDC's the objective of the Paris Agreement would be widely missed.[306] The overall $GtCO_{2eq}$ (without land use, land-use change and forestry (LULUCF)) based on the current NDCs will ultimately even be higher in 2025 (by about 4.3%) and in 2030 (by about 4.7%) than in 2019.[307] With states failing to obtain the 1.5 °C threshold through their emission reduction ambition it is questionable whether the threshold-exceeding NDCs are posing a reliable point of reference for causal considerations. Since the responsibility of states and the legitimacy for establishing normative causation is being founded on the excision of a morally acceptable threshold, the current NDCs, due to them exceeding the 1.5 °C threshold, as well as from a subject of moral blameworthiness, are not able to build a reliable reference for the materiality of a contribution.

Another objection correlates with an argument already previously addressed. The current NDCs are striking for their breadth. However, in order to do justice to the function of normative causation in its role as a limiting factor of factual causation, the causal threshold must be set low enough to allow normative causation to fulfil its function fully. The thresholds set by the current NDCs would, therefore, be too weak.

Last but not least, an NDC based threshold also does not convince due to the discretion of the states in setting their own emission reduction thresholds. For example, linking NDCs to a causal threshold could encourage countries to set targets that are not as ambitious as they would be without the causal link. Building on NDCs would thus be counterproductive and resemble a tool to avoid liability by setting NDCs that are too high. A concurrent issue poses the handling of emissions by states that refrain from submitting NDCs at all. Due to those reasons, NDCs are not fit as a reference point for an overall materiality threshold in light of normative causation.

5.4.2.3.1.3 Indicator-Based Threshold

Establishing an universal approach to a materiality threshold in climatic scenarios has proven to be very difficult. Neither mere scientific derivations, nor international

[305] Art. 2 (1) lit. a) Paris Agreement.

[306] United Nations Secretariat to the FCCC (2021), pp. 5–6, paras 10–13.

[307] Ibid. 5 para 10.

treaties are able to give a comprehensive reference point for the final setting of the materiality threshold. With different principles and standards applying to different actors, which is for example the case with reference to international environmental principles, the threshold is furthermore strongly dependent on the party in question. This again hinders the establishment of an universal standard of materiality. As a result, one needs to refrain from trying to set a specific and fixed verge of causal establishment and be content with a more settle way to decide on the existence of normative causation. Such, for example, can be achieved through the prescription of previously determined indicators by which in the synopsis can be decided on the existence of the materiality of the causal chain. Whether the materiality threshold is exceeded in the end, and causation is to be established is ultimately not a stringent, fixed determination but more so at the discretion of the courts. The following indicators, however, are meant to facilitate the decision-finding process and are built on the moral blameworthiness and responsibility of the actor in question.

5.4.2.3.1.3.1 Scientific Provability

The first prerequisite of the setting of a materiality threshold is the scientific provability of the factual causal dependence between the action or omission and the outcome. This requirement does not constitute a major obstacle for courts in their legal assessment. The facilitation of the fulfilment of this requirement stems from the fact that usually the same has already been assessed at the stage of factual causation. One might, therefore, consider this indicator negligible. It, however, is crucial in cases in which factual causation is simply approved due to a reversal of the burden of proof or due to a legal based presumption of causation. In such instances it is necessary to assess whether it is actually possible to connect the contribution of the respective actor with the specific outcome or climate change in general. In cases in which the contribution is so minor, that attribution science and other fields of science are not able, or only with a high uncertainty quota, to establish causation, materiality is also to be negated. Scientific provability can thus not only be regarded as a strong indicator but also as a prerequisite for the application of all the other indicators and the materiality assessment in general.

5.4.2.3.1.3.2 Ratio to National and International Climate Change Mitigation Targets

Another essential factor in determining materiality is the adherence to national and international emission reduction targets.[308] A large number of countries have set emission reduction targets in an autonomous manner. These targets, which are

[308] Peel (2011), p. 17.

usually sector-specific, set the standard for emission reductions up to climate neutrality and are largely subject to review by the courts.[309] On the basis of this discretionary determination of emission reduction targets by the states, it is not only justified but even necessary to include them in the determination of the materiality threshold. Thus, exceeding specifically set targets is a strong indicator of the materiality of the contribution in question. This is especially the case since moral blameworthiness and legal responsibility automatically go hand in hand with the legal enshrinement and non-compliance of the same. However, the discretionary nature of states in setting emission reduction and climate change targets in general calls for greater caution and scrutiny. Thus, national climate targets may only provide an indication of the materiality of a contribution but not of the insignificance of the contribution or even a lack of materiality. This becomes particularly relevant for climate contributions of states themselves, as well as for larger private entities, falling under the emission reduction obligations imposed by the legislature. The latter can also be influenced by emission targets set by overarching regulatory systems, such as the EU ETS or similar emission trading schemes.[310] Yet, national and international climate protection targets are less relevant for individuals, since climate targets usually (but not exclusively) disregard individuals from strict obligations in light of the target-setting processes.

National emission reduction targets are largely determined by internationally set targets. In this context, the Paris Agreement in particular has a crucial and fundamental role to play in providing an overall goal against which national targets can be measured. Without setting country-specific emission reduction targets, the agreement stipulates the limitation of climate change to a temperature increase of 1.5 °C (but no more than 2 °C).[311] Contributions by states that run counter to this target are automatically considered to be significant. However, as with the national targets, meeting the Paris climate goals does not imply that the contribution is insignificant and, therefore, not substantial. This is especially the case given that the Paris Agreement as well as other international climate protection frameworks such as the FCCC neither provide for a country, nor a sector specific reduction goal but merely entail overall temperature and protection targets.[312] A global temperature target, consequently, only provides a rough indication of the materiality of a contribution, which is further limited to state actors and is generally not transferable to private entities and individuals.

The NDCs adopted and submitted by the states themselves naturally also form an integral part of this process. Nonetheless and in accordance with the criticism already

---

[309] This has, for example, been one of the main topics in the case Germany Federal Constitutional Court, 24 March 2021 – 1 BvR 2656/18 – 1 BvR 78/20 – 1 BvR 96/20 – 1 BvR 288/20, *Neubauer et al. v. Germany*. The German Climate Act presupposes mitigation targets for the following sectors: energy sector, industry, transport, buildings, agriculture, and waste management and others, see § 4 Anlage 1 German Climate Act.

[310] See in more detail especially Sect. 6.2.1.1.2.

[311] Art. 2 (1) lit. a) Paris Agreement.

[312] The FCCC does not even explicitly mention a specific temperature threshold.

mentioned above, these alone cannot be an indicator for the materiality of climate change enhancing behaviour.[313] Therefore, while exceeding and not complying with the NDCs undoubtedly speaks for the affirmation of materiality, adhering to those climate targets does not yet provide an indicator for the exclusion of materiality.

As a result, national and international climate protection targets ultimately lag behind other indicators in their significance. Given the wide discretion of individual countries in setting national climate protection targets and NDCs, the targets mainly serve as a one-sided indicator of materiality but do not fulfil their function of identifying insignificant contributions.

5.4.2.3.1.3.3 Scaling Contributions

The basis of the next indictor is formed by the fact that the assumption of materiality is largely determined by the relation and the setting in which the contribution is placed. The determining factor relates in particular to the specific comparison of the contribution in question at a national as well as on an international level. If contributions, especially those of multinational corporations, are placed in a global comparison, the resulting proportionate share of climate change and its consequences appears to be merely small. However, through a downscaling process to the national level, the contributions that initially appeared insignificant in a global comparison might increasingly exceed the materiality threshold on a national level. A significant example for not only the scaling procedure but also its effect is provided by the already previously mentioned cases surrounding the Anvil Hill project, namely the case *Anvil Hill Project Watch Association Inc v. Minister for the Environment and Water Resources* and *Gray v. Minister for Planning.*[314] Whereas in the first judgment, materiality was negated based on the global contribution of the project to climate change which amounted to about 0.04% of the worldwide emissions, the judges in the second case affirmed materiality in light of a downscaled emission quota.[315] In reference to the national contributions of Australia, the greenhouse gas emissions of the project ultimately amounted to about 2%, which led the judge to affirm the substantiality of the contribution. This does not go contrary to climate change as a global phenomenon. Despite the global nature of the problem, a successful mitigation of its consequences and a further increase in temperature can only be prevented if individual states as well take on their share of mitigating climate change and reducing their contributions to the crisis.

---

[313] See in this regard Sect. 5.4.2.3.1.2.

[314] Land and Environment Court of New South Wales, 27 November 2006 – [2006] NSWLEC 720, *Gray v. Minister for Planning*, Federal Court of Australia, 20 September 2007 – [2007] FCA 1480 *Anvil Hill Project Watch Association Inc v. Minister for the Environment and Water Resources.*

[315] Federal Court of Australia, 20 September 2007 – [2007] FCA 1480 *Anvil Hill Project Watch Association Inc v. Minister for the Environment and Water Resources* paras 25, 42, Land and Environment Court of New South Wales, 27 November 2006 – [2006] NSWLEC 720, *Gray v. Minister for Planning*, para 98.

This does not exclude global efforts but it shows that downscaling is not only feasible but also necessary in determining the materiality of the contribution. For a most comprehensive assessment of the materiality of one's contribution, both, a downscaled, as well as a global and thus upscaled perspective must be taken into consideration. This becomes of special importance not only in regard to states but also in light of multi- and transnational corporations, which cannot be assigned to a specific country with ease.[316] In those cases the indicative quota might even rest in its global contribution rather than its national one. This is especially the case, when corporations are located in countries with an overall high greenhouse gas emission quota. An upscaling approach however is only effective in regard to the biggest overall emitters. The materiality of the contribution of smaller corporations and states, nevertheless, is better assessed on a lower, down-scaled level, always taking into account, their global share.

5.4.2.3.1.3.4 Providing for Comparative Groupings

The fourth and thus one of the most comprehensive indicators is closely connected to the downscaling of the global share of contributions and relates to the determination of the respective comparative group. Depending on the comparison group, the proportional shares differ considerably. This indicator especially aims at analysing contributions of private entities, and can ultimately also be transferred to states and state actors, as well as to individuals. In regard to private entities the starting point for every comparative grouping, apart from the previously mentioned national—international divide, is based in a domestic, sector-specific comparison. Based on the international agreements as well as common structures in national law, particularly the following emission-intensive sectors can be taken into consideration: energy systems, industry, transport, buildings and urban systems, as well as AFOLU.[317] The share of sector specific emissions thus forms a strong indicator of materiality, when, in comparison with other actors from the same sector, the contribution is disproportionally high. Nevertheless, such indicators can never stand alone but must be evaluated in the context of general observations and other, also cross-sectoral comparison groups. The national contribution of a smaller energy company may seem minor compared to the rest of the companies operating in the energy sector. However, if this sector itself accounts for the majority of greenhouse gas emissions in a national comparison (e.g. in Germany with 37% in 2021), the evaluation of the significance and materiality of the contribution changes massively.[318] Conversely, it may be that a company operating in the trade, commerce and services sector generates by far the largest share of greenhouse gas emissions in a sectoral comparison (the trade, commerce and services sector is responsible for 6%

[316] See in more detail especially Sect. 6.2.1.1.2.

[317] A similar differentiation is also applied by the IPCC, see IPCC (2022b). This is also done by the German Climate Act.

[318] Umweltbundesamt (2024b).

of greenhouse gas emissions in Germany in 2020).[319] In comparison with other companies in another sector, such as the energy sector, and in comparison with other countries, the contribution appears to be marginal. This example shows the importance of choosing the right peer group when assessing materiality. It is crucial for the classification of the contribution and thus also for the assessment of normative causation.

In light of the above comparative framework, it is also imperative to consider a variety of different ways in which each party contributes. The contribution to the climate change-induced outcome is likely to be not only the emission of greenhouse gases per se but also a variety of different types of factual contributions. Even in the case of greenhouse gas emissions, it is important to collect and compare different types of emissions on the basis of comparable data. In addition to traditional terrestrial emissions, consumption-based or so-called scope 3 emissions should also be taken into account to ultimately comprehensively address the materiality of one's contribution.[320] Assessing, quantifying and comparing all three different sources of emissions also reduces the potential for handsight-bias and provides a fact-based, objective indication of materiality.

It is, therefore, essential for a well-founded and comprehensive analysis of the materiality of contributions to set them into different comparative groupings. Besides the global and national contribution rate, it is imperative to determine the sector-specific contribution rate as well. In addition, especially outside of economic considerations, the relations to other comparable units must also be taken into account (notably if the contribution of individuals or of states themselves is in question). Further comparative groupings can be the distinction between industrialized and developing countries, geographic alignments like the Global North and Global South divide, population-specific relations or GDP-related comparisons. Besides the application of different comparative groups, it is essential, however, to break down and fine-grain the respective contributions to the smallest comparative criteria possible. Only from a synopsis of all results in different scaled groupings can a comprehensive and factually-based conclusion be drawn on the materiality of a contribution or its insignificance.

5.4.2.3.1.3.5 Per Capita Budget

Another indicator may well be the comparison of the contribution with a per capita budget. This is not excluded by the fact that such a purely individual-based threshold has already been ruled out as the sole criterion for determining materiality in

[319] Ibid.

[320] This was brought forward e.g. by the plaintiffs in the case United States Court of Appeals for the Ninth Circuit, 17 January 2020 – 6:15-cv-01517-AA, *Juliana v. United States*. Against and in favour of one dominant methodology, albeit in a slightly different setting, see Burger et al. (2020), p. 232.

previous considerations.[321] Rather, exceeding a specific per capita budget (e.g. the budget of 1.5 t CO_2) can be a further indication of the materiality of a specific contribution. Another indicative usage of the per capita budget is also achieved by comparing the per capita budget of different states as it was, for instance, done by the Court of Appeal in the *Urgenda* case.[322] As mentioned above, a high per capita budget, such as the Netherlands' approximately 8.4 t CO_2 in 2019, indicates a comparatively high contribution and moral responsibility not only of the individual, but even more so of the state. Especially when the state itself is bound to mitigate climate change based on positive obligations.[323] In turn to high per capita budgets, lower budgets can also form an indication of the insignificance of one's contribution. Whereas, however, it forms a strong indicator for individuals, it has to be approached cautiously when applied on a state-basis as other factors might highly influence the share of the contribution of the state as well. It is also important to bear in mind that a reference to an annual budget works against a dynamic reduction of emissions, particularly in the context of a country specific application. For this reason, the per capita budget must always be considered in conjunction with other indicators.

5.4.2.3.1.3.6 Time-Sensibility of Indicators

Given the long time span of climate-damaging and, thus, climate-changing behaviour, the indicators and the assessment in general also need to be placed in a temporal context. Today's contributions may be assessed differently in terms of materiality than the same contributions decades earlier. Due to the rapid pace of climate change, the proximity of the world's temperature to elementary tipping points, and the large number of current emitters, today's contributions are likely to be classified as significant considerably sooner than contributions of the same magnitude that occurred much earlier in time. Although today's contributions to climate change damages and climate change per se are, in fact, scientifically equal, from a normative-moral point of view, they are much more significant than the contributions made at the beginning of the industrialized era. In the context of the remaining minimal CO_{2eq} budget, today's contributions are subject to a higher moral culpability than contributions that were made decades ago. They, therefore, carry more blameworthiness, which justifies and obliges the application of stricter materiality standards.

A sense of time also requires that emissions be considered in the context of the circumstances at the respective time. While the same contribution today may represent only a fraction of global contributions and thus appear small in percentage terms, the same numerical contribution decades earlier may be significantly higher in

---

[321] See in this regard Sect. 5.4.2.3.1.1.

[322] The Hague Court of Appeal, 9 October 2018 – 200.178.245/01, *Urgenda Foundation v. The State of the Netherlands*.

[323] World Bank (2023), The Hague Court of Appeal, 9 October 2018 – 200.178.245/01, *Urgenda Foundation v. The State of the Netherlands*, para 25.

relative terms simply because there were fewer emitters and thus lower overall contribution rates. However, the earlier contribution would not be classified as larger and thus more significant than the current contribution. Despite this difference in relative percentages, the contribution itself is the same. An assessment of materiality must hence not only take several factors into account but also be sensitive to time.

5.4.2.3.1.3.7 Conclusion

The determination of a clear materiality threshold has proven to be quite difficult and ultimately not feasible. Instead, a large number of different indicators must be used to determine the materiality threshold, which, when taken together, ultimately determines the existence or absence of materiality. The basis for the application of the indicators is the scientific provability of the contribution. In addition, the relation of the contribution to national and international climate protection goals, as well as the per capita budget, provide indications for the conclusion of materiality. A further key indicator is the proportionality within various sector-specific groups. Here, the different groupings are of essential importance. Within the assessment, it is, therefore, essential to both refine and expand the groupings for a comprehensive view. Ultimately and in the absence of legal provisions, the qualification as material is left to the discretion of the courts. Finding that a contribution is material in light of the dangers of overall climate change and the low emission budget that is left to comply with a 1.5 °C target is, however, much easier than concluding on the insignificance of one's contribution, especially in current times. Moreover, law and science provide significantly more indicators for the assessment of contributions by states and larger private entities than is the case for private persons and individuals. Based on the lower emission levels and the fewer indicators that can be turned to, determining materiality in respect to individuals is even more difficult than it is the case with other contributions. Needless to say, the above introduced indicators do not represent an exhaustive list. Rather, it is up to the courts themselves to establish further indicators in order to develop a comprehensive, factual based and stringent case law for determining the materiality of a contribution and thus also to contribute to general legal certainty.

5.4.2.3.2 Threshold for Other Climate Damaging Behaviour

Even more demanding, however, than the setting of a materiality threshold for an emission based conduct is the assessment of materiality in regard to other non-emitting climate damaging behaviour. In the end it is certainly not feasible to present a solution for every possible action and inaction. Nevertheless, some conduct is easier to determine and evaluate than others. On the forefront of overall climate damaging behaviour that does not directly relate to the active emission of greenhouse gases is deforestation. Deforestation of big parts of forests not only results in the secondary release of vast amounts of CO_2 e.g. through the frequently used means of fire clearance and the used wood as material for heating but also leads to a destruction of the forest as carbon sink. Nowadays, the damage caused by the destruction of carbon sinks to the climate system can be easily calculated scientifically and translated into their GHG-resemblance and equivalent. As a result, the indicators introduced above can also be applied here by means of a simple conversion of the relevant behaviour into its CO_2 or GHG equivalent. This also applies to other human changes of land usage such as the transformance of land into agricultural ground and the exploitation of minerals and oils.

Transferring human behaviour to their greenhouse gas equivalent most certainly poses the easiest way in reflecting whether the action falls under the materiality threshold or not. However, some actions are difficult to translate into greenhouse gas emissions overall and need a comprehensive amount of scientific research. This is the case, for example, for accelerated urbanization. Although urbanization is a major driver of climate change it is difficult to transfer those impacts to an unambiguous GHG equivalent, all the more so to a responsible party.[324] In such cases, it must be acknowledged that it is not or only restrictively feasible to work with the above factors. Rather, it is solely at the discretion of the respective courts to decide whether the materiality threshold has actually been overstepped. With regard to individuals, this will most likely often have to be negated. With regard to private entities or states, conversely, a different assessment is quite conceivable. As increasing urbanisation and sealing of land also depends in particular on urban planning, which is largely within the remit of municipalities or the state, materiality seems more likely to be acceptable. Nevertheless, as soon as it is not possible to transfer the action or omission in question to their respective greenhouse gas equivalent, the assessment of materiality is at the discretion of the court. However, in light of increasing scientific methodologies to not only quantify climate change but also its respective impacts and causes, it is most likely, that climate and attribution science will be able to quantify emission-independent behaviour as well in the near future.

5.4.3 Conclusion

The foregoing discussion has shown that a materiality threshold is essential to limit factual considerations. It has further emphasized how difficult it can be to set a precise threshold. Court decisions and judgments in climate change litigation have provided a rough indication of what kind of contributions courts consider significant enough and where a possible threshold for the materiality of a contribution to climate change and climate change damages might lie. Setting an exact threshold however has proven to be a really difficult task and barely achievable in relying neither at a per capita CO_2 or CO_{2eq} budget, nor on a NDCs-based threshold. The only way to facilitate and standardize causal threshold considerations to some extent is by means of using a specific set of indicators. The here developed indicators are meant to

[324] See for the scientific background Sect. 2.1, IPCC (2023).

provide courts and judges with some guidance in assessing the materiality of a contribution. They are in no means exhaustive but give room for a broad margin of appreciation and further development and enhancement by courts.

5.5 Intervening and Superseding Causes

5.5.1 Intervening Causes as Normative Delimitation

The concept of intervening causes refers to situations in which a primary causal chain that hypothetically would have led to a particular outcome, was interrupted by another causal chain that ultimately led to the outcome. Intervening causes are, therefore, often colloquially referred to as 'breakers' of the causal chain.[325] It is further a construct that both arises in the light of the factual determination of causation and its normative realm. Within the first step of the causal analysis, 'interventions' coincide with the concepts of alternative and, in particular, pre-emptive causes, as it questions the existence of mono-causal conceptions and poses a challenge to the correct depiction of the actual causal relata in the law.[326] Within the normative and, thus, the legal determination of causation, it is necessary to determine whether the initial chain-setter should be held causally responsible, even though some event has intervened in the original causal chain. Under some premises, the establishment of normative causation between the initial condition and the outcome can be perceived as contradictory to overall fairness criteria and the very substance of justice in the law. However, such an assessment is only possible in cases where the factual existence of a causal chain has been affirmed prior to the normative evaluation and determination of the intervening event.

How courts and jurisdictions treat and analyse intervening causation varies widely and is truly case specific.[327] Some jurisdictions, particularly in the common law sphere, apply the concept of intervening causation in the context of determining the proximate cause.[328] Others use the intervening cause doctrine as a separate, individual assessment of normative causation or combine the concept with

[325] Intervening causes are also called '*novus actus interveniens*', especially in the common law jurisdictions of England and Ireland. See Infantino and Zervogianni (2017), pp. 607–609. Further descriptions refer to '*causes étrangeres*' and partly also '*superseding causes*' ibid. 621.

[326] On the question of alternative causation, see in particular Sect. 4.2.2.2. Some authors argue that the problem of 'intervening causes' does not arise in the factual assessment of causation, because in the actual and scientific determination of causation there is no such thing as 'interventions', but simply the existence or non-existence of causation. See Moore (2009), pp. 232–233. Similar in referring to 'superseding causes', Hart and Honoré (1985), p. 4.

[327] Whether the intervening cause is actually relevant depends on a large array of different normative principles, see Infantino and Zervogianni (2017), p. 622.

[328] See in this regard Sect. 5.6.

considerations of foreseeability.[329] Despite the different ways and areas of application, the main and core elements within each implementation coincide. Drawing on *Hart* and *Honorés* substantial and arguably one of the earliest assessments of intervening causes (in a normative sense), *Moore* has defined four main elements that are imperative for the existence of intervening causes, which he refers to as the causal, temporal, independence and 'absence-of-culpability' conditions.[330] These four conditions require that the intervening act, in order to be qualified as a cause in the factual sense of the outcome (causal condition), occurs after the initial act and before the outcome has materialized (temporal condition), is independent of the act of the first chain-setter (independence condition), and is ultimately not foreseeable by the respective and primary chain-setter ('absence-of-culpability' condition).

Another qualification that can occasionally be found in legal practice concerns the distinction between intervening causes in general and superseding causes.[331] This differentiation hereby ties in with the fourth element as it was introduced by *Moore* and qualifies superseding causes as cases where the interfering cause was not foreseeable by the original causer. Such distinction, however, presupposes that intervening causes can also be qualified as such, even if the primary initiator foresaw the interfering act. Whether the distinction between these two constructs is recognised, or whether intervening causes are generally presumed to entail the lack of foreseeability, depends largely on the jurisdiction in question and the view of the relevant courts. For the purposes of this work, this specific distinction will be left aside, as only unforeseeable intervening causes come into play and are determined for the normative assessment. This precondition derives from the fact that it is only in cases in which the outcome was unforeseeable for the initiator of the causal chain that the moral blameworthiness of the behaviour is ultimately dispensed with.

5.5.2 Reconciling Climate Change and Intervening Causes

Natural climate variability and the many contributions of others, whether by emitting greenhouse gases or by other climate-impacting actions or omissions, characterise climate change litigation. How these many contributions can be reconciled with the establishment of causation beyond the factual, and to what extent they can be qualified as intervening causes at all, is discussed in the following. This is done by using the common method of distinguishing between natural causes (Sect. 5.5.2.1) and causes of human behaviour (Sect. 5.5.2.2).[332]

---

[329] E.g. in Bulgaria, Italy, France and the Czech Republic, see Infantino and Zervogianni (2017), pp. 608–609.

[330] Hart and Honoré (1985), pp. 68–80; Moore (2009), pp. 234–253.

[331] Some authors equate the terms 'intervening' and 'superseding' cause, see e.g. Hart and Honoré (1985), p. 71.

[332] This distinction was also enhanced by Moore (2009), pp. 233–234.

5.5.2.1 Natural Events

The first group of intervening causes relates to natural events. These can be defined in a negative manner as events that are independent of human influence. In climate change litigation, natural events as intervening causes have often been referred to under the premise of 'force majeure', but they have also found their way into legal jurisprudence as 'acts of God' or 'viz majeure'. The cornerstone of natural events as intervening causes is the scientific uncertainty and unprovability of the origin and the causes of specific events and occurrences.

The concept that some causes of an outcome cannot be explained by, or attributed to, human behaviour has long been present in the legal realm.[333] In climate change litigation, the argument has especially arisen in regard to two distinct lines of defence. The first relates to the negation of climate change as a man-made and, thus, an anthropogenic phenomenon. Under the premise that the climate of the world has always been in a state of flux, and that the temperature increases that are witnessed today have also been present in the distant past, the concept of intervening causes was used to describe those respective changes as force majeure. However, this argument is no longer tenable in the light of current climate science as it is flawed simply based on the point of reference in regard to the compared periods of time in which the temperature changes took place.[334] Apart from the fact that climate science strongly objects this concept in climate change litigation, the argument of force majeure also holds no significance in the normative adaptation of factual causal chains in general. Given that the respective argument serves as a defence to negate causes in general, it aims at arguing against the existence of the factual perception of causation rather than against its normative dimension.

In a second, more moderate line of defence, natural events can serve as intervening acts in their normative perception.[335] This applies in particular to cases in which the anthropogenic origin of climate change is not generally questioned, but where force majeure only relates to specific natural events for which there is a high degree of scientific uncertainty. A normative adaptation is particularly likely to be considered when a factual causal chain that has already been set in motion is interrupted by an extreme weather event such as a flood or storm, which ultimately leads to the outcome in question. Consequently, some authors impose the criterion of extraordinariness on the category of natural events, although this also introduces fundamental legal uncertainty into the normative assessment of the scope and substance of what should and can be considered as extraordinary.[336] The rationale for including a

[333] See for a history on 'force majeure' Dellinger (2017), pp. 455–461.

[334] See for the scientific framework of climate change Sect. 2.1.1.

[335] Outside the realm of climate change litigation has force majeure been acknowledged as an intervening act e.g. in International Centre for Settlement of Investment Disputes, 28 March 2011 – ARB/06/18, *Joseph Charles Lemire v. Ukraine*, Award para 163.

[336] *Moore* hereby refers concurrent to *Hart* and *Honoré* to 'abnormality'. See Moore (2009), pp. 245–247; Hart and Honoré (1985), p. 62.

criterion of extraordinariness lies in the need to distinguish 'normal' natural events from those that were completely unexpected and unpredictable. However, instead of using such a vague criterion as extraordinary, it seems more preferable to use the scientific determinability of an event as a distinguishing criterion. This provides a clearly identifiable, delimitable basis for its qualification. The assumption that an event or act is 'natural' is, therefore, fundamentally based either on the existence of a high degree of scientific uncertainty about the origin of the respective event, or on the existence of a scientific consensus about the actual natural, non-man-made cause.

Irrespective of whether one qualifies natural causes on the basis of their exceptional nature or on the basis of their scientific determinability, the question remains as to whether intervening causes related to climate change can be classified as 'natural' per se. As already argued and discussed in detail in the chapter on the scientific framework of climate change, the changes in climate that are being experienced today can be attributed with a high degree of certainty to human behaviour.[337] The cause of the vast majority of events associated with climate change is, hence, at least partly of anthropogenic origin. As a result, the boundary between natural events and human actions is considerably blurred in the context of climate change litigation.[338] Some authors, thus, refer to a third category that builds on human natural contributions.[339] Even though such a category can certainly be applied within climate science, given the close connection and interaction of the human sphere with the climate system, the basic distinction between natural, human and human-natural does not seem to provide any significant added value. This is especially the case as the category of natural events as intervening causes becomes increasingly irrelevant as science progresses. The only 'proper' natural events that are still conceivable relate to events that are entirely beyond human control and influence, such as meteorites or other phenomena outside the Earth's solar system. Given the high level of scientific consensus on climate change, however, the fundamental causes of climate change are to be classified as anthropogenic.

The category of natural events, therefore, plays only a minor role in climate change litigation, even apart from the concept of force majeure. Even if a situation-specific perspective is applied to the 'exceptional nature' of the natural event, this does not exempt the category of natural events from the accusation of human influence within the climatic framework. Outside the field of climate science, as well, it is doubtful whether natural events in this sense still exist, and whether a distinction between human and natural events still offers any added value.[340] This is likely to be the case only in exceptional circumstances for events outside the Earth's climate system. However, given that storms, tidal waves, precipitation and droughts

---

[337] See in this regard Sect. 2.1.1.3.

[338] *Dellinger* defers this from the close connection and interlacement of the climate system with human behaviour and influences, Dellinger (2017), pp. 461–470. Ultimately, even stating that "*force majeur defies logic and common sense*", ibid. 505.

[339] Infantino and Zervogianni (2017), p. 627.

[340] Negating the relevance of this distinction in practice ibid. 623.

are strongly linked to and interdependent with the Earth's climate system, they cannot be classified as purely natural events.

5.5.2.2 Human Actions

Given the ineptness of natural events as intervening causes in climate change litigation, human action takes on an even greater significance. One of the core elements of interfering human action hereby rests on the requirement of voluntariness.[341] An intervening event can only exempt the initial chain-setter from normative causation if the event in question occurred without coercion, accident or mere reflex. Some even argue that the requirement of voluntariness includes a condition of intent, since the intervening cause must be accompanied by the intervener's foresight, negligence, or at least ability to comprehend and understand the consequences of his conduct.[342]

The voluntariness, however, also raises fundamental problems in light of the qualification of the intervening cause as act or omission. Some authors include the precondition of an act in the requirement of voluntariness.[343] As positive acts cannot be qualified negatively, omissions could not be considered as intervening human actions. This argument is seriously flawed. If the argument is predicated on voluntariness, then it does not stand to reason why omissions should be denied voluntariness. If one decides not to safe a drowning person, although an obligation and the capacity to do so existed, the decision not to do so is of voluntary nature. Omissions can, thus, have the same intentional frame as positive doings. However, if one starts from the assumption of the existence of an act, i.e. an act performed voluntarily, this assumption must already be questioned. On the premise that omissions can be causes, one cannot deny intervening omissions the same qualification.[344] In the light of considerations of stringency and comprehensiveness, omissions can, thus, also qualify as voluntary and as intervening human behaviour.

This finding is also supported by recent decisions on climate change. The fact that omissions can act as intervening causes was emphasised by *Chief Justice Allsop* in the case *Minister for the Environment v. Sharma* in which he stated that

> (i)t can be accepted that the Minister had, almost exclusive, control over any risk created by the approval of the extension of the mine. But bearing in mind the nature of the harm as worldwide global climate catastrophe the control of the Minister of the harm is simply not present. The relevant concept of control is control over the harm, not control over the tiny increase in the risk.

[341] Moore (2009), pp. 241–245.

[342] See again ibid. 242–243.

[343] Ibid. 242–244.

[344] See for a discussion on the qualification of omissions as causes Sect. 4.1.2.

> The extent to which risk may be mitigated by countless others around the world and in particular by international agreement makes the concept of the Minister having relevant control non-existent, or extremely faint at best.
>
> This makes the relationship between the Children and the Minister indirect and mediated by the intervening conduct of countless others around the world (…).
>
> That intermediation of others includes those who decide to buy and use the coal and their national governments who permit it within their obligations under international agreement to be responsible for Scope 3 emissions.[345]

While the qualification of omissions as potential intervening causes is commendable, the shifting of legal responsibility on the basis of intervening omissions to the extent urged by the Federal Court is highly problematic. *Chief Justice Allsop* refers in his judgement especially to two kinds of potentially intervening causes. The first coincides with the general debate on the attribution of scope 3 emissions, which has been addressed on several other occasions in this book, and will be addressed shortly in relation to intervening causes.[346] The other type of potential intervening cause, however, relates to omissions, as national governments are alleged to have failed to restrict the use and purchase of coal and would, therefore, be responsible for scope 3 emissions in light of their international obligations.[347]

Although omissions can be intervening causes, *Chief Justice Allsop's* argument is seriously flawed. This is true not only in relation to the failure to regulate, but also in relation to the objection of the purchase and use of coal by others. The shortcoming of the argument lies in the assumption that both events would initiate causal chains of their own, given that this is a general prerequisite for the affirmation of intervening causes. However, the permission to expand the mine as the initiating cause is not interrupted by either event, but rather both events are part of the entire causal chain. Given that the authorisation is a precondition for the mere possibility for others to buy the coal produced in the mine in question, and that the lack of regulations enables the use of such coal, it is reasonable to show that all these events are part of the same causal chain. The Court's reasoning, thus, contradicts the 'independence' requirement. Intervening causes must be independent of the initial causal chain in order to be qualified as such, which is not pertinent in the case *Minister for the Environment v. Sharma*. Even if one were to argue that the lack of a coal ban by national governments would initiate a new causal chain, this would not lead to the negation of normative causation, as the lack of restrictions and, thus, the use of the coal produced was highly foreseeable for the alleged party ('absence-of-culpability'

---

[345] Federal Court of Australia, 15 March 2022 – [2022] FCAFC 35, *Minister for the Environment v. Sharma* paras 334–337.

[346] See for a discussion on scope 3 emissions especially Sect. 3.3.3.

[347] Permitting or not restricting the use of coal presents a difficult case of the distinction between active doing and omission. However, since Chief Justice Allsop refers to international treaties and thus uses international law, international principles must also be used in the determination and quantification. Since, according to the Lotus Principle, everything is in principle permissible unless it is contradicted by a prohibition norm, the charge lies in the failure to impose a restriction, i.e. in the failure to take measures, and not in actively permitting the act.

condition). Therefore, the defendant cannot be relieved of its legal responsibility by negating the normative causation of its own conduct, which renders *Chief Justice Allsop's* assessment erroneous in this respect.

In addition to the problem of scope 3 emissions as it was in question in the case *Minister for the Environment v. Sharma*, courts have often been confronted with the qualification and attribution of such emissions throughout different jurisdictions.[348] More recently, as mentioned above, courts have increasingly attributed scope 3 emissions to the original chain-setter, which often coincides with multinational energy, automobile and mining corporations.[349] This development is also covered by the previous argumentation in the context of the case *Minister for the Environment v. Sharma* and also by the rejection of qualifying scope 3 emissions as intervening causes. On the one hand, such emissions are at least currently foreseeable, and on the other hand, scope 3 emissions do not constitute a new, independent chain of causation, but are merely further steps within the already existing chain of causation initiated and set in motion by the production of coal, oil or other emitting products.

Even outside of the issue of scope 3 emissions, some authors have indicated that GHG emissions from other emitters can generally function as intervening causes.[350] In difference to scope 3 emissions, those emissions per se comply with the independence condition, as they initiate their own, self-reliant causal chains. Nevertheless, qualifying emissions as intervening causes is accompanied by other obstacles concerning other constituting core elements. Consequently, it is questionable whether the scope of the emissions suffices for the setting of an own causal chain per se. This depends largely on the amount of emissions contributed and can hardly be answered uniformly. On a theoretical basis, and relying on factual causal doctrines that allow for multi-causal conceptions, it is not out of the question that a cluster or set of emissions would give rise to a causal condition of its own. Ultimately, qualifying the set of emissions as sufficient enough constitutes a factual assessment, rather than a question that can and should be answered from a normative perspective.

However, even if the set of emissions would suffice to initiate an own causal chain that would bring about the outcome, one would, nevertheless, have to deal with the question whether the cause can also exclude the normative causation of the setter of the initial causal chain. A precondition for the qualification of the respective bundle of emissions as an intervening cause is the lack of foreseeability and intent.[351] Those requirements stand in question particularly in cases in which

---

[348] See again Federal Court of Australia, 15 March 2022 – [2022] FCAFC 35, *Minister for the Environment v. Sharma* 336.

[349] This was e.g. done by the Court in Hague District Court, 26 May 2021 – C/09/571932/HA ZA 19-379, *Milieudefensie et al. v. Royal Dutch Shell plc.*

[350] Durrant (2007), p. 420.

[351] For a view on the foreseeability of climate change, see Sect. 5.3. By emphasising the importance of intervening causes and foreseeability, and by showing that the existence of reasonable foreseeability does not break the chain of causation, see Swisher (2007), pp. 16–17. Also Lanovoy (2022), p. 70.

the original, initiating action itself consisted of the emission of greenhouse gases. The foreseeability that greenhouse gases will continue to be emitted even after the original emitter has ceased to do so can hardly be denied. Another element that complicates the elimination of causation is the criterion of voluntariness. If under a strict interpretation of the principle intent, foresight or at least negligence on the part of the intervening party is required, this may lead to the qualification as an intervening cause being invalidated, at least for early greenhouse gas emissions. Moreover, such an assumption would also contradict the pure rationality of the determination of normative causation and corrective justice, as by continuing to emit, each emitter could escape its legal and causal responsibility through subsequent emissions. It is, therefore, not straightforward to argue that emissions occurring after the initiation of the primary causal chain would, firstly, qualify as an intervening, factual cause and, secondly, relieve the primary causer of his normative causation and responsibility.

Given the interconnectedness of the climate system and its inherent complexity, it is very difficult to argue that a climate-damaging causal chain was intervened by another climate-damaging act or omission, which then constitutes an entirely new and independent causal chain. In order to justify such a constellation, one would also have to draw on numerous other normative principles. Possible intervening causes, however, could still consist of completely non-climatic intervening causes or events that are independent of the emission of greenhouse gases. Nevertheless, due to the nature of the climate system, climatic causes do not hold up well as a normative argument to negate normative causation in climate change litigation.

5.6 Theory of Adequacy

Unlike the previous principles of foreseeability and materiality, the theory of adequacy is an independent test of normative causation and is applied in most civil law jurisdictions.[352] First developed by *Johannes von Kries* in 1888 as a limiting factor in criminal law, it was later transferred to the field of private law in which it still presents the most common theory of normative causation today.[353] Despite its popularity in the private law of civil law countries and despite its breadth,

[352] The theory of adequacy is, for example, used in Germany, Austria, France and Italy. See for a detailed analysis of the use of the theory of adequacy in European tort law Infantino and Zervogianni (2017), inter alia 604, table 7.2 at 609. The theory of adequacy is also apparent in Spier (2005). Sometimes the theory of adequacy can also be found in decisions issued by courts of common law countries. See, for example, concerning a climate change case United States District Court for the Northern District of California, pending – 3:17-cv-06011, *City of Oakland v. BP p.l.c.*, 5. Stating that the theory of adequacy is in coherence with "*the normative causation test in international law*" Verheyen (2005), p. 302.

[353] von Kries (1888). For further elaborations on the development of the theory of adequacy, see Waldkirch (2018), pp. 301–302.

which in itself includes the evaluation of different notions of normativity, the theory of adequacy is generally not used as the sole criterion of delimitation but can often be found in complementarity with the theory of the protective scope of the norm.[354] It furthermore is not applicable universally but is rejected, for example, for the use in cases of strict liability.[355]

Due to the constant evolution of the law, the theory of adequacy does not lend itself to a single formulation and scope. There are, however, three primary concepts which are usually included in the general theory of adequacy and which are applied both individually and cumulatively. According to the most common definition of the theory of adequacy, a condition is deemed to be adequate if the condition in general and not only under particularly peculiar, improbable and, according to the regular course of events, disregardable circumstances was suitable to bring about an outcome.[356] Other definitions build in their determination of adequacy on the increase in the probability of an outcome occurring or merely focus on the principle of foreseeability.[357] In general, the individual perceptions of adequacy hardly differ, and are often used in the synopsis.[358] The principle of foreseeability and the exclusion of peculiar results are hereby often applied cumulatively. As a result, there is little difference between the various conceptions of the principle.

With regard to the notion of foreseeability that is entailed in the theory of adequacy, a similar understanding can be adopted as the perception already discussed previously.[359] Here, too, are the issues of the right observer and the adequate vantage point up for discourse. In coherence with the assessment of foreseeability, it is commonly acknowledged that the theory of adequacy also builds upon an ex-ante perspective of normative causation based on the view of an objective, reasonable and like-kinded observer.[360]

The fact that adequacy also has a limiting function beyond the notion of foreseeability within climate change litigation is shown by the Court's reasoning in the case *Luciano Lliuya v. RWE AG*.[361] In this case, the Regional Court of Essen negated the existence of adequacy by stating that

> [...] the defendant is not a tortfeasor, since it did not adequately cause the impairment. The theory restricts the conditio-sine-qua-non formula in order to prevent entirely improbable

---

[354] In favour for the application of both theories e.g. Ebert (2020), para 36.

[355] See e.g. Pöttker (2014), p. 232; Brand (2022), para 242; Kohler (2017), p. 162.

[356] Federal Court Germany, 23 October 1951 – I ZR 31/51. See for further elaborations Oetker (2019), para 110; Flume (2022), para 284; Brand (2022), p. 239.

[357] See e.g. Schirmer (2021), p. 1103; Koch et al. (2011), p. 405 para 15.76; Freund (2020), p. 348. Regarding foreseeability-based adequacy e.g. Schirmer (2021), p. 1104. Some jurisdictions however do not question the foreseeability of an outcome at all (e.g. France), see Infantino and Zervogianni (2017), p. 604.

[358] Schirmer (2023), p. 116.

[359] See in this regard Sect. 5.3.

[360] See e.g. Verheyen (2005), p. 302; Oetker (2019), para 111; Flume (2022), para 285; Brand (2022), p. 239. In opposition Ebert (2020), para 32; Schirmer (2023), p. 116.

[361] Essen Regional Court, 15 December 2016 – 2 O 285/15, *Luciano Lliuya v. RWE AG*.

> causal processes from triggering liability. Accordingly, the event must have increased the possibility of an outcome of the type that occurred [...].[362]

In its decision, the Court, therefore, rather relied on the aspect of an increase in risk than on the question of mere foreseeability. However, in opposition to the decision issued by the Regional Court of Essen and in contrast to the question of how to deal with the foreseeability criterion, the requirement of an increase in probability under the risk-increase formula does not pose a major obstacle to normative causation either. Particularly, in the context of general causation, it is undisputed that greenhouse gas emissions, deforestation, and other anthropogenic actions lead to an increase in the risk of climate change and its respective impacts. Since this is not a matter of the probability of the actual occurrence but merely of the increase in the risk of occurrence of a specific outcome, this requirement no longer poses a hurdle even in the context of specific causation. If a materiality criterion is further required in addition to an increase in risk, the assessment of adequacy is likely to be more complex but again does not pose an insurmountable hurdle, as it was shown in the previous section.[363] Rather, in line with the previous explanations, materiality should be determined on the basis of an accumulation of different indicators, with the selection of the relevant peer group playing an elementary role in the consideration and ultimately in the determination of materiality. It is in this area in particular that the incorporation of scientific evidence provides comprehensive and robust results.

Moreover, climate change litigation has shown that the notion of an unlikely and peculiar outcome cannot be used as an argument to deny normative causation. This defence has been proven to be scientifically, politically and legally untenable in the face of the climate crisis and has been particularly evident in cases involving scope 3 emissions.[364] Scope 3 emissions are emissions that are not directly produced or controlled by the action and party in question but are the result of the usage of the product by consumers or further indirect behaviour throughout the supply and value chain. Key areas where scope 3 emissions are of major importance are the mining, fossil fuel and automotive sectors. The treatment of scope 3 emissions was also one of the basic legal questions in the case *Milieudefensie v. Royal Dutch Shell*.[365] The defendants argued that, because of the uncontrollability and remoteness of these emissions, the effects caused by them were not foreseeable and, therefore, attributable to Royal Dutch Shell. However, the court rejected this argument when it ordered the company to reduce its scope 1, 2 and 3 emissions by around 45% by 2030. It specifically included emissions from the use of the company's products, namely the burning of refined oil, and emphasised that fossil fuel companies in particular have a

[362] Ibid. para 47 unofficial translation by author.

[363] See, Schirmer (2023), p. 116. Concerning the materiality criterion see Sect. 5.4.

[364] See in this regard Sects. 2.1.1, 3.3.1, 3.3.3.

[365] Hague District Court, 26 May 2021 – C/09/571932/HA ZA 19-379, *Milieudefensie et al. v. Royal Dutch Shell plc.*

duty of care and responsibility for their scope 3 emissions.[366] In light of this groundbreaking decision, it will be difficult for defendants to argue that scope 3 emissions are failing the test of adequate causation due to their untypical, improbable nature and peculiarity. Even outside the scope of scope 3 emissions, the exclusion criterion of peculiar and highly improbable circumstances in relation to climate change-related factors will only lead to the exclusion of causation in the rarest of cases.[367]

Although several other lawsuits concerning adequacy in the statements of claim are already pending before courts, there is still a lack of empirical values as to how courts will actually deal with this in their decisions.[368] In view of the fundamental criticism of the theory of adequacy that it renders too broad and is not suitable as a normative criterion despite its restrictive purpose, the theory will most likely be a low hurdle for plaintiffs to overcome.[369] The only decisive factor will be how the courts deal with the question of foreseeability.

5.7 Theory of Proximate Cause

5.7.1 The General Perception of Proximate Cause

The equivalence to the mostly in civil law countries applied theory of adequacy forms the theory of proximate cause, which predominates in common law jurisdictions.[370] Originally stemming and also most apparent in the United States, it constitutes a highly indefinite test of normative causation, combining a variety of different normative criteria. Under the most common definition of the proximate cause doctrine, an action must be sufficiently related to an outcome in regard to both time and place to be considered proximate. Proximity in those terms is also occasionally addressed under the principle of a direct causal link or remoteness, although the notion of 'remoteness' is commonly perceived as being even broader and more

---

[366] Ibid. inter alia para 4.4.29.

[367] See in this regard also Sect. 5.5 on intervening causes.

[368] See e.g. Regional Court of Munich, pending – n/a, *Deutsche Umwelthilfe (DUH) v. Bayerische Motoren Werke AG (BMW)*, statement of claim (21 September 2021), pp. 61–67.

[369] In stating that "*(t)his is all the more so given that the minimum probability is required in respect of the loss itself, not in respect of the specific, possibly atypical causal chain of events.*" Koch et al. (2011), para 15.77.

[370] Although the theory of a proximate or direct cause is commonly known to be a common law phenomenon, some civil law countries also apply such tests, among them e.g. France, the Netherlands and Italy. For an overview in the European realm see Infantino and Zervogianni (2017), p. 609 table 7.2 Second-stage Causation: A Map of Theories.

indefinite than proximity.[371] Proximity thus is strongly influenced by other normative concepts such as foreseeability (temporal proximity), substantiality and proportionality.[372] In being one of the broadest accounts of normative causation, the proximate inquiry also takes into account, whether the respective party profited from its conduct or omission and whether it engaged in other harmful and unethical activities.[373] The American Law Institute focuses in its definition of proximate cause (scope of liability), furthermore on a specific risk standard which can be further adapted in cases in which it would still render too broad.[374] Outside of the US legal system, the criterion of proximity can also be found occasionally in international law cases as well as in some European jurisdictions.[375]

What concepts are ultimately applied under the guise of the theory of proximate cause varies from jurisdiction to jurisdiction and is largely at the discretion of the courts.[376] This adds to the difficulty of interpreting and evaluating the theory in the light of the principles of justice and fairness, although normative theories are generally subject to a high degree of interpretation and discretion. Nevertheless, the breadth and vagueness of the theory render its application problematic. This is also shown by the observations of the American Law Institute. In its preface to the section on proximate cause, the American Law Institute prefaces additional remarks to the chapter on the scope of liability (proximate cause).[377] The Institute herein indicates its hopes for a replacement of the terminology in the Restatement Fourth of Torts as it describes the term 'proximate cause' as being an "*especially poor one*".[378]

---

[371] See ibid. 607. Although the 'remoteness' of an effect can function as a test of normative causation and is used in a few jurisdictions, this test has not found its way into this analysis of legal causal theories. The reason for the exclusion of the 'remoteness' test lies in its ultimate breath. Given the results of more restrictive theories of normative causation, and leaving aside the debate about its general usage and functionality in the law, remoteness as a criterion is also highly and generally unsuitable as a limiting factor in climate change litigation.

[372] Affirming inter alia the relevance of "*size of the emissions contribution*", Burger et al. (2020), p. 229. Foreseeability as requirement of a proximate cause was for example at issue in its formation as substantial factor test in Privy Council, 18 January 1961 – [1961] UKPC 2, [1961] AC 388; [1961] 1 All ER 404, *Overseas Tankship (UK) Ltd v Morts Dock and Engineering Co Ltd (Wagon Mound (No. 1))*.

[373] See in regard to fossil fuel producers Burger et al. (2020), p. 233.

[374] See in more detail under the term 'scope of liability'. "*An actor's liability is limited to those harms that result from the risks that made the actor's conduct tortious.*" American Law Institute (2010), § 29, 493. It hereby comes close to the normative principle of the protective scope of the rule see Sect. 5.8.

[375] See for its application in international law Voigt (2008), p. 17. Some similarities can also be found in the international legal framework, especially in Art. 31 (2) DARS which excludes causes that are too distant and not direct (see International Law Commission (2001a), pp. 92–93, para 10). For its application in European law, see Koziol (2007), pp. 63–64; Infantino and Zervogianni (2017), p. 607 table 7.2 Second-Stage Causation: A Map of the Theories.

[376] See for handling of foreseeability Sect. 5.3, for the question regarding the materiality and substantiality Sect. 5.4.

[377] American Law Institute (2010), p. 492.

[378] Ibid. § 29, 492.

It ultimately acknowledges its broad usage in practice which is why they nevertheless included the specific term into the Restatement Third.[379]

5.7.2 *Climate-Relevant Particularities of the Theory of Proximate Cause*

5.7.2.1 The Spatial and Personal Proximity of the Damage

As previously discussed, the theory of proximate cause entails a convolute of different normative criteria, which are applied and weighted differently depending on the respective jurisdictions and even the individual court. Given that notions of the theory have already been discussed prior, especially the issue of materiality, foreseeability, and intervening causes, the main emphasis of this sections rests upon a more general account of the theory of proximate cause which builds on spatial and personal proximity.[380] The emphasis on the spatial and personal spheres of proximity does not mean that these two notions are the only determinants of the theory of proximate cause in climate change litigation. Rather, these two criteria are concepts in which the theory of proximate cause differs from other theories of normative causation, and thus have not yet been addressed in the light of the normative adaptation of the factual causal relation. With regard to the spatial sphere in particular it has already been shown that at least the factual causal chain is per se free of a location-bound account.[381] Yet, this is not the case for its normative dimension and thus for the assessment of normative causation. Here, it is quite conceivable that a local component is involved in the evaluation of normative criteria that can further even lead to an overall denial of causation in the law.

Spatial proximity is particularly relevant for emission-based claims. Given that greenhouse gases are distributed uniformly in the atmosphere, the emission of greenhouse gases may well cause climate change-induced damages in distant locations, which calls into question the local proximity of the reproached action or omission. Even more difficult is the attribution of scope 3 emissions. Due to globalization and the high rate of globally distributed goods, these can be generated far away from the original manufacturer. However, the problem of attributing scope 3 emissions does not only arise in relation to the local sphere, but also in relation to temporal, personal and ultimately general proximity.

In the case *City of New York v. BP p.l.c.* the defendants used the criterion of causal proximity as an argument to reject the plaintiffs' claim for climate change-induced damages. In arguing that scope 3 emissions resulting from the combustion of fossil

[379] Ibid.

[380] See in regard to the materiality Sect. 5.4, for the foreseeability Sect. 5.3, and for the issue of intervening causes Sect. 5.5.

[381] See especially in regard to question of concretizing counterfactual causation Sect. 4.2.3.4.3.2.

fuels represent a cause that is neither spatial or temporal proximate, nor direct or immediate to the action of the defendants, they stated that "*(s)uch allegations, which depend on the use of lawful products by untold numbers of third parties – including Plaintiff itself – over several centuries, are far more remote and attenuated than allegations already rejected by New York courts.*"[382] In another Memorandum of Law, one of the plaintiffs further compared the case to cases based on the usage of tobacco or guns which are not only arguably similar to climate cases due to the so-called issue of indirect causation but the causal proximity in this explicit case was even 'further afield'.[383] In their judgements however, neither the United States District Court of the Southern District of New York nor the United States Court of Appeals for the Second Circuit addressed the issue of proximate causation. Rather, both courts dismissed the plaintiff's claim on the basis of inapplicability of state law and the political-question doctrine.[384] In a few other US climate change cases, plaintiffs, defendants and courts have addressed the issue of proximate causation, but without fully addressing or defining it.[385] However, as regards the lack of proximity with respect to scope 3 emissions, the case is similar to the previously cited case of *Milieudefensie et al. v. Royal Dutch Shell.* In this respective case the Court explicitly rejected the defendants' objections of lacking proximity in light of scope 3 emissions and ultimately, although indirectly, affirmed their proximity to the reproached behaviour of the defendant.[386]

---

[382] United States District Court for the Southern District of New York, 26 July 2018 – 1:18-cv-00182, *City of New York v. BP p.l.c.*, Memorandum of Law issued by BP. p.l.c., Chevron Corporations, ConocoPhilipps, Exxon Mobil Corporation (30 March 2018), 27, 29.

[383] Ibid. Memorandum of Law issued by ConocoPhilipps (30 March 2018), 4–10.

[384] See ibid., United States Court of Appeals for the Second Circuit, 24 May 2021 – 18-2188, *City of New York v. BP p.l.c.*

[385] In New York Supreme Court, 22 October 2014 – 103095/2012, *Wohl v. City of New York*, the Court decided that the city had shown that precipitation was the proximate cause of the damage occurred to the plaintiff and, therefore, rejected the claim of the plaintiff. In District of Columbia Circuit Court of Appeals, 17 April 2009 – 07-1247, *Center for Biological Diversity v. United States Department of the Interior.* The plaintiff also failed in proofing that the conduct of the defendant was the proximate cause of climate change. In New York Federal Court, 15 March 2019 – 2:12-cv-03989, *Cangemi v. Town of East Hampton.* The defendant argued against the existence of proximate causation (see ibid. Motion by the Town of East Hampton (30 July 2018), 14–22). Although the New York Federal Court in the end rejected causation, the judge did not explicitly refer to the existence, or non-existence of proximity. Although rather indirectly, proximity was also addressed in Supreme Court of the United States, 2 April 2007 – 05-1120, *Massachusetts v. EPA*, 21. The Supreme Court rejected the defendants argument that the regulation of GHG emissions from automobiles would only constitute a tentative step. In its dissenting opinion however Chief Judge Roberts. argued against the acceptance of causation since the "*connection is far too speculative*" (see ibid. Dissenting Opinion by Chief Judge Roberts, 11).

[386] Hague District Court, 26 May 2021 – C/09/571932/HA ZA 19-379, *Milieudefensie et al. v. Royal Dutch Shell plc.* See also for adequate causation Sect. 5.6.

Proximity has further been an issue in the Australian case *Smith v. Fonterra*.[387] In this case, the claimant Mr Smith argued for the existence of proximity due to the personal relationship between him as part of the indigenous group of coastal Māori and the defendant.[388] The Court, in the first instance, nonetheless, did not accept such argumentation and rejected not only the personal and physical proximity but also the overall proximity of the damage claimed and the action of the defendant.[389] *Judge Wylie*, furthermore, expressed his concerns regarding the existence of proximity due to the disproportionality of the claim and the issue of indeterminate liability.[390] The Court of Appeal accepted the considerations by the primary judge but added to the requirement of temporal and physical proximity the requirements of relational and causal proximity as well, which it ultimately did not found to be present.[391] However, in another Australian case, *Gray v. Minister for Planning and Ors*, the Court accepted the existence of proximate causation.[392] Without elaborating on the issue of proximity further, *Judge Pain* accepted that "*there is a sufficiently proximate link between the mining of a very substantial reserve of thermal coal in NSW [...] and the emission of GHG, which contribute to climate change/global warming [...].*"[393]

As the above cases have shown, the treatment and reasoning within the discussion of proximity, especially with regard to the local and personal sphere, varies considerably. How proximity is ultimately understood is entirely at the discretion of the courts and judges. That this creates a high and considerable degree of legal uncertainty for the parties to the dispute is therefore beyond question. Whether the theory of proximity in its comprehensive form, and especially in the local and personal sphere, actually constitutes a hurdle will be discussed in the following section.

5.7.2.2 Aligning Climate Change and the Theory of Proximate Cause

As already shown previously, the theory of proximate cause does not consist of specific and delimitable normative criteria, but is understood and applied differently throughout different jurisdictions and courts. Yet, certain basic denominators can be identified across the different usages, with the criterion of temporal proximity on the forefront of general proximity considerations. The notion of temporal proximity hereby also, but not exclusively, includes the foreseeability of the outcome, which is

[387] High Court of New Zealand, 21 October 2021 – [2021] NZCA 552, *Smith v. Fonterra Co-Operative Group Limited*, judgement (6 March 2020) paras 89–93.

[388] Ibid. judgement (6 March 2020) para 90.

[389] Ibid. judgement (6 March 2020) para 92.

[390] Ibid. judgement (6 March 2020) para 93.

[391] Ibid. judgement (21 October 2021) paras 101–103.

[392] Land and Environment Court of New South Wales, 27 November 2006 – [2006] NSWLEC 720, *Gray v. Minister for Planning*, paras 98, 100.

[393] Ibid. 100.

highly decisive for climate claims. In parallel with the theory of adequacy, the previous elaborations on the required standard and the degree of foreseeability can also be applied considering the proximate cause doctrine.[394] Temporal proximity can, however, also be understood as mere temporal vicinity, with the outcome being required to follow the reproached action or omission closely in time. Under such strict perception of temporal proximity, nearly none climate change claim could be considered as normatively causal, given that due to the considerable inertia of the climate system, effects are usually emerging at a much later point in time.

Depending on the understanding of the theory of proximate cause, other notions of proximity can concurrently evolve into a great issue in climate change litigation. Among those is especially the personal proximity as it was required in the case *Smith v. Fonterra*.[395] Conditioned on the narrowness of the interpretation of the standard, the requirement could be negated concurrently with the argumentation provided by the Court in the respective case. Given that climate damaging behaviour does not immediately and directly affect the party in question and does not aim at a delimitable group of people or even individuals, one might argue that personal proximity in those cases is not given. This argument is closely related to the difficulty of spatial proximity, as climate damage is not tied to a specific location, but can occur at a great distance from the place where it was actually caused.

Although these arguments might be persuasive under a strict understanding of the doctrine of proximity, given the extensive case law and its often contested broad and fluctuating understanding, applying a too narrow interpretation of proximity would most likely be contrary to the general view. It would further contradict the general perception of climate justice in its all-encompassing dimension and the integral conceptualisation of fairness. In particular, the associated notions of responsibility and moral blameworthiness require the affirmation of causation in the law despite a possible spatial and personal remoteness. The weight of the blameworthiness produced by someone's action or omission is independent of the place of its realisation. Whether the outcome occurs at the place of the cause or far away from it does not affect the blame that is placed and inherent in the causing action or omission itself. Moral and legal blame thus frequently refer to the respective action or omission rather than to the effect of such behaviour.

Based on this foregoing understanding, temporal proximity must be approached on a more differentiated account. Given that the temporal sphere and, moreover, the foreseeability of the effect are strongly based on the discernment at the time of the reprehensible act or omission, the temporal sphere in its form as a requirement of foreseeability is able to function as a limiting factor, even under the above mentioned perception of moral blame.[396] By contrast, the responsibility of the party in question and the moral blame that is carried by the action or omission itself do not cease to

[394] See in this regard Sect. 5.7.

[395] High Court of New Zealand, 21 October 2021 – [2021] NZCA 552, *Smith v. Fonterra Co-Operative Group Limited*, judgement (6 March 2020), paras 89–93.

[396] See in this regard again Sect. 5.3.

exist if the outcome occurs only after a long period of time.[397] Temporal proximity as it is understood detached from the foreseeability of the outcome, thus, also stands in opposition to fundamental considerations of responsibility, moral blameworthiness and the overall perception of fairness.

The high demands that are occasionally placed on the personal proximity as it was shown in the case *Smith v. Fonterra* also contradict normative principles of causation, especially in the context of climate lawsuits.[398] In contrast to temporal and spatial proximity, however, the contradiction does not primarily lie in the criterion of fairness and in moral blameworthiness and responsibility, but rather in the conditions of climate justice. High standards of personal proximity would in principle rule out the existence of normative causation for the vast majority of climate lawsuits. Despite the existence of a factual causal relationship which, if it exists, confirms the unambiguous presence of an effect on the person concerned, normative causation would have to be denied, especially in the case of emissions-related climate lawsuits. However, this is fundamentally at odds with the principles of corrective justice. Even if the principle of corrective justice is not based on the identification and imputation of all potential causes of climate change, at least the enforceability of a considerable share must be ensured. In the vast majority of cases this would have to be negated by a strict understanding of personal proximity and the exclusion of normative causation. The normative notions of fairness and climate justice invalidate at least the restriction imposed by the requirements of spatial and personal proximity. Nevertheless, other implementations of the theory of proximate cause could still be applied from a normative point of view and limit factual causal chains in law. Among those is especially the temporal proximity in its implementation as mere test of foreseeability, as well as the materiality and the proportionality of the cause-effect relation.

Apart from the normative restrictions that are being placed on the theory of proximate cause by the conceptions of fairness and climate justice, also from a more practical-oriented perspective does the respective theory not contradict the finding of climatic causal relations. At least not in its more general form. Climate change as a global phenomenon factually affects all people of the world in one way or another. Climate and weather extremes, such as heat waves, floods and storms are occurring more frequently each year. From a scientifically point of view and presupposed the causal relation of the respective effect with climate change can be constructed in a factual sense, every person can be considered personal proximate to the causes of climate change. It must therefore be queried whether personal proximity is at all suitable as a delimiting criterion of legal causality.

Finally, the rejection of the proximity of scope 3 emissions in particular no longer seems tenable following the Court's decision in the case of *Milieudefensie*

[397] See for the problem of historic emissions Sect. 5.3.2.3, as well as Sect. 3.3.2.3.

[398] See again High Court of New Zealand, 21 October 2021 – [2021] NZCA 552, *Smith v. Fonterra Co-Operative Group Limited.*

et al. v. Royal Dutch Shell.[399] In addition to the existence of factual and scientifically proven causation, there is now a growing social consensus that responsibility for the consequences of climate change cannot and must not be limited to the immediate and narrowly defined temporal and local effects, but must go beyond this sphere in respect of a fundamental mitigation of climate change and its consequences.[400] Similar social, societal and political objectives can also be observed outside the climate debate. This applies, for example, to the debate on the responsibility of corporations to comply with human rights obligations within their supply chain, which has consequently led to the adoption of specific national legislation.[401]

Both normative and practical elaborations show that the theory of proximity in its broadest sense, and at least with respect to spatial, personal and temporal proximity, comprehensively leads to the affirmation of normative causation in climate change litigation. This view is also increasingly supported by the most recent decisions on climate change. In particular, where reference is made to scientific findings that comprehensively link the action in question to the damage caused by climate change, proximity can hardly be denied. Based on this rather broad understanding and the concurrent un-determinability of the doctrine, it is overall in question, whether the theory of proximate cause under its conception as personal, spatial and temporal proximity, even provides for an effective limiting factor in climate change litigation.[402] Ultimately, and concurrent to the theory of adequacy, proximity does not pose a major hurdle to climate lawsuits and to the establishment of normative causation.

[399]Hague District Court, 26 May 2021 – C/09/571932/HA ZA 19-379, *Milieudefensie et al. v. Royal Dutch Shell plc.*

[400]The subject of scope 3 emissions has already been addressed in previous sections, among those especially Sects. 5.3, 5.4, 5.7.

[401]See e.g. the French Duty of Vigilance Act and the recently enacted German Supply Chain Act. For further details see Nedelcu and Schäferling (2022).

[402]See in this regard also Verheyen (2005), p. 300. Also in referring to the case *Massachusetts v. EPA* (Supreme Court of the United States, 2 April 2007 – 05-1120, *Massachusetts v. EPA.*), Liebesman et al. (2009), p. 11178. In stating that "*(a)ll anthropogenic greenhouse gas emissions are in principle equally 'proximate' to the resulting chain of causation leading to climate change damages.*" Voigt (2016), p. 487.

5.8 Protective Scope of the Norm

The scope of the norm as a limiting factor of factual causation has mainly been known to civil law jurisdictions in which the theory finds its application predominantly in criminal as well as in private law.[403] The theory mainly evolves around the rationale of the rule in question stating that normative causation can only be established in cases in which the rule is intended to protect against the very damage the conduct has factually caused (material dimension). It is further required that the damage is intrinsically related to the hazardous situation and the manner and the evolutionary history of the outcome concurrently falls into the realm of the protective scope of the norm.[404] However, not only on the material level does the protective scope of the norm lead to an adaptation of the legally relevant causal connection; the theory also befalls the personal realm in limiting the causal connection only to the specific group of persons that is protected under the respective provision. The theory thus also carries a personal dimension.[405] Whether it can further stretch to the spatial and temporal sphere is doubtful, but not completely ruled out. The spatial and temporal sphere nevertheless have not carried any fundamental relevance in the general assessment and application of the theory to date, especially given that the temporal sphere is largely covered by separate considerations of foreseeability.

The basis of the analysis of the protective purpose is formed by a conduct- and result-oriented apprehension of the norm. The actual object and purpose of the standard in question must hereby be determined within the framework of a teleological interpretation.[406] Assessing the objective and the protective scope of the provision can further require a balancing of the conflicting interests of the parties to a dispute in light of its overall purpose and can also be influenced by underlying normative accounts of justice and fairness. In contrast to the theory of adequacy, which is usually rejected in cases of strict liability and applied in a more general, abstract manner detached from the specific provision itself, the theory of the protective scope of the rule is a largely norm-specific construct and strongly depends on the norm invoked in each case.

It is, hence, hardly possible to make generally valid statements on the function and impact of the theory in climate change litigation, although the theory can be of great influence in the establishment of normative causation in the respective

---

[403] In German scholarship the theory is known as '*Lehre vom Schutzzweck der Norm*'. The protective scope of the rule is applied in the tort law of e.g. Germany, Netherlands, Spain, Austria and Sweden, see Infantino and Zervogianni (2017), p. 605, Table 7.2 at 609; Koziol (2007), pp. 62–63. The theory of the scope of the rule has also found its way into European Law. See regarding its application to Art 340 AEUV Weitenberg (2014), pp. 136–137. See for European Tort Law Art. 3:201 lit. e) PETL.

[404] Federal Court of Germany, 9 December 2020 – VIII ZR 371/18, paras 26–29.

[405] Ibid. para 28.

[406] See Brand (2022), para 249.

lawsuits. The significance of the theory for climate litigation pertains particularly to two norm-specific areas of application, which shall be discussed in the following. On the one hand, the theory gains relevance in its application to cases in which plaintiffs invoke provisions that are not specifically rooted in environmental or climate law. On the other hand, the theory may find increased use in relation to statutes that, due to their date of adoption, predate the general scientific recognition of anthropogenic climate change and in which the provisions thus did not take climate change into account in their initial drafting.[407]

Most climate change lawsuits build on provisions that are not, per se, norms of environmental or climate law. Rather, plaintiffs make use of provisions enshrined in administrative and constitutional law, and frequently fall back on general norms of liability based in the private legal sphere. This phenomenon is caused by a general lack of climate legislation in almost all jurisdictions, with most climate laws also containing few specific and thus enforceable provisions.[408] As a result, plaintiffs often resort to more general rules of delict and liability. The protective scope of the norm further carries significant relevance for areas of law that have just recently been brought onto the climate change radar, such as the corporate and financial sector.[409] The norms of the latter, in particular, are for the most part not concerned with climate or environmental regulations, but are highly specific to their respective ambit. Whether the scope of protection of the norm might be extended to climate change matters, and whether the particular context is at all relevant for the assessment of these delimitation criteria, may become a major issue in the emerging climate change litigation.

The second area in which the theory of the protective scope of the norm might find increased application in climate change litigation relates to the historical and evolutionary history of the enforced provision.[410] Given that a large number of norms, especially in the private sphere and with particular emphasis on tort and liability provisions, were drafted before a social but also scientific consensus on the dangers or even the mere existence of climate change could be established, climate change was frequently not taken into account in the initial considerations and the scope of the relevant provisions. The fact that the history and the drafting process per se can become decisive in the interpretation of norms is shown by the practice of states in which a historical take is considered a legitimate means for the

---

[407] In denying the applicability of § 1 of the German Environmental Liability Act in relation to aggregate damages ('*Summationsschäden*'), Chatzinerantzis and Herz (2010), p. 597. Opposing *Chatzinerantzis*, see Pöttker (2014), pp. 234–235.

[408] This is also evident in the international legal sphere where, despite the existence of climate standards, enforceability, the possibility of asserting individual claims and the reference to liability constructs is low.

[409] See on the trends in climate change litigation Sect. 2.2.2.3.

[410] This is not to be confused with the temporal sphere of the norm within its protective scope.

interpretation of provisions.[411] Although it often does not constitute the only method of interpretation and therefore does not carry the same weight as other means of interpretation, the historical context does enter into consideration.

Despite the broad consensus on its general interpretative function, it is questionable whether an historical argument, namely the denial of the norm's protective purpose on the basis of the historical legislative intention, can still hold today. In opposing at least a strict application and interpretation, some authors fall back on the methodology of an evolutive and contemporary interpretation of norms, which is recognized at least in German legal methodology.[412] Accordingly, even older norms must be read and interpreted in light of current and contemporary obstacles. Such an approach expands the protective purpose of norms enormously, especially with regard to general norms of liability.[413] An interpretation building on a contemporary account not only bridges the objection of the temporal and historical sphere, but can also play a decisive role in areas of law which do not contain an initial climatic indication. In view of the current challenges, a contemporary interpretation of norms can, thus, also argue for an extension of the protective scope of provisions to climate issues. A progressive interpretation of the protective scope finds furthermore support in general considerations of justice, which imply that the exclusion of entire areas of law from their enforceability in the context of climate lawsuits solely on the basis of evolutive arguments and their overall thematic delimitation is not compatible with the normative aspirations and foundations of general and climate-policy considerations of justice.

Interpreting the provisions in light of contemporary events and with respect to social, political and cultural affairs, is, however, not a construct that is specific to the German legal realm but is also broadly applied in the context of regional and international human rights frameworks in light of a dynamic and evolutive interpretation of human rights.[414] Under the premise that for a universal and all-encompassing standard of protection, human rights have to be adapted and adjusted to new realities, courts increasingly widen the scope of protection of the respective rights. In climate and environmental law, this is also known as 'greening' of human rights.[415] Whether such an interpretation can moreover be applied to other jurisdictions and areas of law respectively depends to a large extent on the

[411] The historical context constitutes one of the four classical 'canones' introduced by *von Savigny* and is still used in some jurisdictions for the interpretation of legal provisions, including in Germany (see von Savigny (2020), pp. 213–214). The historical context and in particular the 'travaux preparatoires' can also be referred to as supplementary means for the interpretation of treaty provisions in international law, see Art. 32 VCLT. The historical context has also been explicitly invoked in light of the assessment of the protective scope of provisions see e.g. Federal Court of Germany, 9 December 2020 – VIII ZR 371/18, para 28.

[412] See e.g. *Pöttker* in referring to Larenz and Canaris (1995); Pöttker (2014), pp. 234–235.

[413] See for the affirmation of climate liability under § 823 German Basic Law, Koch et al. (2011), para 15.77.

[414] In regard to the ECtHR, see Dzehtsiarou (2011) and Ulfstein (2015).

[415] See for the 'greening' of human rights of the ECHR e.g. Pirjatanniemi (2016).

methodological standards employed and recognized in this context. For the purpose of a progressive climate protection, and in light to provide for and comply with overall considerations of justice, the interpretation methods based on a contemporary assessment of legal norms are imperative.

In addition to the possibility of a progressive interpretation of the protective scope, application-oriented aspects also indicate that the theory may well be relevant to climate lawsuits, but does, in principle, not stand in the way of an affirmation of normative causation in climate change litigation. This argument builds on the fact that the protective purpose of statutes largely relates to the specific outcome in question rather than to the circumstance and the reason for its occurrence, and holds especially true for tort law provisions.[416] Whether someone's property is destroyed due to a climate change-induced storm, or directly by another person is not of relevance when the purpose of the norm invoked aims at protecting property in general. The same applies for other legally protected factors. However, this argument finds limitation in the inclusion of further factors into the assessment of the protective scope of the respective provision. As already mentioned prior, part of such assessment is not only the material dimension of the provision, but occasionally also its evolutionary and historic context, which makes the theory of the protective scope of the norm also sensible to time.[417] Nevertheless, it has also been shown that this argument can be rebutted, at least in part, by reference to and engagement with a contemporary understanding and interpretation of the norms in question. How much weight is ultimately given to the other factors is therefore a matter for the discretion of the courts and depends very much on the standard in question. In principle, however, the main point of reference for the theory is the material dimension of the norm and whether the scope of protection of the norm covers the harm caused.

In addition to standards that are inherently independent of climate change in terms of its drafting history and overall substance, the theory of the protective scope of the provision can also be applied to standards and principles that are specifically climate-related. Even climate-specific norms can unfurl the need to determine their objective and purpose for the evaluation under causal accounts.[418] However, the likelihood of negating causation on the basis of the protective scope theory in the case of climate-relevant normative acts, especially on an international level, seems low. Due to the global, multi-layered nature of climate change, limiting causation based on a person-related scope of the norm, or a limitation based on a substantive level and other factors, such as its geographical allocation, is commonly not envisaged, at least not in international environmental and climate agreements such as the FCCC and the Paris Agreement.[419] The fact that a denial of normative causation on the grounds of the respective plaintiff is hardly tenable in the climate context is also shown by the

[416] See in this regard also Spier (2005), p. 63.

[417] Federal Court of Germany, 9 December 2020 – VIII ZR 371/18, para 28.

[418] See for an assessment of the scope of the FCCC rules in regard to state responsibility Verheyen (2005), p. 302.

[419] As it was addressed by *Verheyen* and also ultimately negated (see ibid.).

large number of admissible parties to climate lawsuits, including, in particular, the recent wave of lawsuits raised in the name of future generations. Such argumentation finds further support in considerations of social and climate justice. The only applicable criterion for limiting climate-related statutes, therefore, is the objective of the legal protection pursued by the claim. Given that the main objective of climate provisions rests predominantly in the protection of this very substance renders the normative theory of causation void at least for its application in regard to climate change provisions.

Despite the importance of the protective purpose theory as a normative limiting criterion in a large number of jurisdictions, the theory has so far hardly been implemented in any climate change decision. One of the reasons for its reduced usage might rest in the fact that, to date, only a small number of climate change claims have actually been brought and even more so been decided in jurisdictions which apply the theory of the protective scope of the norm. The cases that have been decided by courts in the respective jurisdictions have often been dismissed for a lack of factual causation, admissibility or further reasons.[420] Another criteria might simply consist in the usage of and reference to climate law provision on a national as well as on an international level, which, as addressed above, are of universal scope and greatly comply with the legal setting and scope of the respective climate lawsuit. The results of the analysis might also indicate that courts are already immanently widening the scope of the protective frame in light of an progressive and contemporary interpretation of the provisions. This could be the case in particular for human, constitutional and fundamental rights, as well as for most liability-based and administrative rules.[421] The only area of law in which the scope of the provision, prospectively, might be of interest in the legal determination of causation and consequently might find appliance, are those areas of law that, given their mere substance, are commonly rather afar from climate change matters such as the financial and corporate law sector.[422]

Conclusively, the protective scope of the norm is a criterion of normative delimitation that is truly case- and even more so norm-specific. Despite its individual nature and the broad discretion of the courts, the theory of the protective scope of the norm does not pose a major obstacle to climate change litigation in general. Naturally, there may be cases in which the damage or the alleged infringement is of such an indirect and exceptional nature that it is no longer covered by the scope of protection of the rule. However, such efforts are not discernible in current climate change lawsuits. On the basis of a progressive and contemporary interpretation of the norms, the common focus of the objective on the harm and infringement and thus on

---

[420] See for example in the case *Luciano Lliuya v. RWE AG*, in which the Court has refrained from addressing the protective scope of the rule and solely based their judgement on factual causation and the theory of adequacy, see Essen Regional Court, 15 December 2016 – 2 O 285/15, *Luciano Lliuya v. RWE AG*, claim (23 November 2015).

[421] Human rights courts, in particular, have tended to broaden the scope of protection and the objectives of the relevant provisions in order to adapt them to overall climate change scenarios.

[422] Although climate change litigation is increasingly affecting these areas of the law.

the outcome in question, and the common understanding of the need to adapt to new realities, many climate-relevant outcomes can, in principle, be subsumed under the relevant provisions.

5.9 Summary of Findings

The second step in the overall causal inquiry in law functions as means to constrain the far-reaching results of the factual inquiry, not only by making factual causation consistent with societal perceptions of what the causal outcome ultimately 'should' be, but by making them actually usable for and in the law. Normative causation hereby grounds itself on conceptions such fairness, justice, responsibility and blameworthiness.[423] Accordingly, climate claims are strongly influenced by the concept of climate justice, which in turn includes principles such as corrective and distributive justice but also entails procedural and social accounts, which are further influenced by intergenerational equity and retributive justice in a North-South divide.[424] Normative causation, furthermore, is influenced by principles of national and international environmental law such as the principle of prevention or the precautionary principle.[425] Due to the different normative principles that have developed in this context, divergences and differences in the evaluation and assessment of normative causation can certainly occur. In particular, the principle of climate justice and its corrective justice component occasionally collide with notions of fairness, responsibility and moral blameworthiness. The dilemma arises in conjunction with the limiting function of normative causation tests, which, while being the primary objective of normative causation, nevertheless and simultaneously interfere with the goal of the best possible achievement of 'corrective justice'.

Ultimately, all those normative notions transpire in climate lawsuits especially in two distinct and relevant legal principles. The foreseeability of the outcome as well as its materiality.[426] Both concepts are used, depending on the jurisdiction, either in a stand-alone manner or as concepts embedded in general theories of normative causation, such as the theory of adequacy and the doctrine of proximate cause.[427]

Foreseeability mainly arises in coercion with the timely inertia of the outcome in respect to the initiation of the causal chain.[428] The underlying notion persists in the understanding that one can only be held legally responsible and set in motion a legally relevant chain of causation if the person could have assessed the questionable act or omission beforehand, which in turn presupposes that the person could have

[423] See in this regard Sect. 5.2.1.

[424] See in this regard Sect. 5.2.3.

[425] See in this regard Sect. 5.2.2.

[426] See for the foreseeability Sect. 5.3, for materiality Sect. 5.4.

[427] See for the theory of adequacy Sect. 5.6, for the theory of proximate cause Sect. 5.7.

[428] See in this regard Sect. 5.3.

foreseen the consequences of the action. The thesis has shown that foreseeability in climate matters and under consideration of normative principles has to be approached from an ex-ante perspective on the basis of a reasonable and objective observer. The general standard of foreseeability, concurrently, should not be set too high. In assessing foreseeability, however, it is crucial to distinguish between the different actors involved, in particular between states, private entities and individuals, as well as between the foreseeability of general and specific causation. The distinction between the different actors is brought about, in particular, by an advanced preponderance of the perception of foreseeability in the case of state actors, based on principles of international environmental law. In this context, foreseeability can be affirmed for general causal statements as early as the 1970s but at the latest since the 1980s. With regard to specific causation, foreseeability can be affirmed from 1990 at the latest but depends on the specific climate change-induced damage and outcome in question. In contrast to state actors, no such limit can be set for private actors. The determination of the foreseeability of non-state actors is strongly influenced by special knowledge, which must be taken into account in the legal consideration, especially in the case of multinational corporations and so-called 'global players'. Since 1990 at the latest it is not possible to deny the foreseeability of general causation any longer. This is a result of the rapid social and scientific developments since the 1990s. As far as specific causation is concerned, the strong dependence on the type of outcome in question also applies here. By 2015 at the latest, however, it will no longer be possible to deny the awareness and inherent foreseeability of a large part of the damage caused by climate change, even for private actors.

Another factor that has emerged as particularly important in the climate context, is the assessment and evaluation of individual knowledge.[429] Differences in access to knowledge and scientific data, as well as the ability to control and monitor, are among the main reasons why it was considered necessary in this book to draw a distinction in the foreseeability standard between different actors, in particular between states, corporations and individuals.[430] The same applies to the distinction between general and specific causal chains.

Materiality, as the second fundamental notion of normative causation, refers to the fact that every human action or omission, no matter how small, ultimately contributes to changes in the climate system.[431] Nevertheless, not all contributions carry legal blameworthiness, as most actions are so marginal and necessary for everyday life that they lack any moral and ethical responsibility. The book has conclusively shown that it is necessary to establish a materiality threshold to exclude contributions that lack such legal blameworthiness.[432] A materiality threshold becomes particularly important under the premise of a reduced understanding of

---

[429] See in this regard Sect. 5.3.2.1.3.

[430] See in this regard later Sect. 6.2.1.

[431] See in this regard Sect. 5.4.

[432] See in this regard Sect. 5.4.2.1.

factual causation, which increasingly allows smaller contributions to be qualified as factually causal.[433] Despite the need for a specific level of materiality, it has been shown that it is neither feasible, nor aspirational to define a fixed and constant threshold. Rather, each contribution needs to be assessed on a case-by-case basis. In order to simplify this task and to provide a way to determine materiality in a comprehensive and dogmatic way, a set of indicators has been developed.[434] Nevertheless, it remains within the discretion of the court to decide which indicators of materiality to use and how to priorities them. Decisive hereby again is the actor in question.[435] However, in order to ensure legal certainty and a degree of consistency and comparability, it is advised that courts not only clarify the relevant indicators in advance, but also adhere to them in comparable situations. The NDCs under the Paris Agreement, national and international emission reduction targets, per capita emissions and the sectoral comparability of the respective emissions are among those decisive points of reference. The latter, in particular, offers a great deal of scope for a comprehensive assessment under the implementation of different comparative groups in a time-sensitive manner.[436]

Both concepts, foreseeability and materiality, are incorporated within the overarching theories of adequacy and proximate cause. And while both theories are to be understood in a broader sense, and especially the proximate cause doctrine contains further normative implications, foreseeability and materiality are the decisive determinants within the application of both theories in climate change litigation. Other approaches, such as the concept of the norm's protective purpose or the debate on intervening causes, have only limited relevance for the causal assessment of climate lawsuits.

Ultimately, the most pressing obstacle to establishing normative causation, and, therefore, the most restrictive criteria, is the question of whether or not the outcome was foreseeable. In this respect, it is the problem of historical emissions that really materialises. Claimants are hereby in the need to prove special knowledge from an early time on to provide for a comprehensive fulfillment of their rights. Whether the 'foreseeability hurdle' will ultimately be overcome also depends to a large extent on the willingness of the courts to prepone the threshold of foreseeability in opposition to frequently voiced other believes. Ultimately, it is generally possible to establish normative causation in climate change litigation, especially in light of lawsuits that oppose recent conduct or omission.

433 See in this regard Sect. 5.4.

434 See in this regard Sect. 5.4.2.3.1.3.

435 See also here later in this Sect. 6.2.1.

436 See in this regard Sect. 5.4.2.3.1.3.4.

Climate Change Cases

A Request for an Advisory Opinion from the Inter-American Court of Human Rights Concerning the Interpretation of Article 1(1), 4(1) and 5(1) of the American Convention on Human Rights – Inter-American Court on Human Rights, 15 November 2017 – OC-23/17

Anvil Hill Project Watch Association Inc v. Minister for the Environment and Water Resources – Federal Court of Australia, 20 September 2007 – [2007] FCA 1480

Arayara Association of Education and Culture and others v. FUNAI, Copelmi Mineração Ltda. and FEPAM (Mina Guaíba Project and affected indigenous communities) – 9th Federal Court of Rio Grande do Sul, pending – 5069057-47.2019.4.04.7100

Argentina v. Uruguay (Pulp Mills) – International Court of Justice, 20 April 2010 – I.C.J. Reports 2010 p.14

Association of Swiss Senior Women for Climate Protection v. Federal Department of the Environment Transport, Energy and Communications (DETEC) and Others – Swiss Supreme Court, 20 May 2020 – No. A-2992/2017

Association of Swiss Senior Women for Climate Protection v. Federal Department of the Environment Transport, Energy and Communications (DETEC) and Others ("Verein KlimaSeniorinnen Schweiz v. Bundesrat") – Swiss Federal Supreme Court, 20 May 2020 – 1C_37/2019

Barbara Metz et al. v. Wintershall Dea AG – Regional Court of Kassel, pending – n/a

Cangemi v. Town of East Hampton – New York Federal Court, 15 March 2019 – 2: 12-cv-03989

Center for Biological Diversity v. United States Department of the Interior – District of Columbia Circuit Court of Appeals, 17 April 2009 – 07-1247

Certain Activities Carried Out by Nicaragua in the Border Area (Costa Rica v. Nicaragua) – International Court of Justice, 2 February 2018 – I.C.J. Reports 2018, p. 15

City of New York v. BP p.l.c. – United States District Court for the Southern District of New York, 26 July 2018 – 1:18-cv-00182

City of New York v. BP p.l.c. – United States Court of Appeals for the Second Circuit, 24 May 2021 – 18-2188

City of Oakland v. BP p.l.c. – United States District Court For the Northern District of California, pending – 3:17-cv-06011

Daniel Billy et al. v. Australia (Torres Strait Islanders Petition) – United Nations Human Rights Committee, 22 September 2022 – CCPR/C/135/D/3624/2019

Decision adopted by the Committee on the Rights of the Child under the Optional Protocol to the Convention on the Rights of the Child on a communications procedure in respect of Communication No.107/2019 – Committee on the Rights of the Child, 8 October 2021 – CRC/C/88/D/107/2019

Deutsche Umwelthilfe (DUH) v. Bayerische Motoren Werke AG (BMW) – Regional Court of Munich, pending – n/a

Duarte Agostinho and Others v. Portugal and 32 Other States – European Court of Human Rights, pending – 39371/20

Ecology Action, et al. v. Minister of Environment and Climate Change – Federal Court, 3 June 2020 – 2020 FC 663

Family Farmers and Greenpeace Germany v. Germany – Administrative Court of Berlin, 31 October 2019 – VG 10 K 412.18

Gbemre v. Shell Petroleum Development Company of Nigeria Ltd. and Others – Federal Court of Nigeria, 30 November 2005 – FHC/B/CS/53/05

Gloucester Resources Limited v. Minister for Planning – New South Wales Land and Environment Court, 8 February 2019 – [2019] NSWLEC 7

Gray v. Minister for Planning – Land and Environment Court of New South Wales, 27 November 2006 – [2006] NSWLEC 720

Greenpeace v. United Kingdom – Scottish Court of Sessions, 7 October 2021 – [2021] CSIH 53

Hearing on Climate Change Before the Inter-American Commission on Human Rights – Inter-American Commission on Human Rights, pending – n/a

In the Matter of the Greenhouse Gas Pollution Pricing Act – Court of Appeal of Alberta, 24 February 2020 – 2020 ABCA 74

Juliana v. United States – United States Court of Appeals for the Ninth Circuit, 17 January 2020 – 6:15-cv-01517-AA

KlimaSeniorinnen v. Switzerland – European Court of Human Rights, pending – 53600/20

Klimatická žaloba ČR v. Czech Republic – Prague Municipal Court, 15 June 2022 – 14A 101/2021

Luciano Lliuya v. RWE AG – Essen Regional Court, 15 December 2016 – 2 O 285/15

Luciano Lliuya v. RWE AG – Higher Regional Court Hamm, pending – 5 U 15/17

L. v. WHO – International Labour Organization Administrative Tribunal, 10 February 2020 – 4239

Maria Khan et al. v. Federation of Pakistan et al. – Lahore High Court, pending – No. 8960 of 2019

Massachusetts v. EPA – Supreme Court of the United States, 2 April 2007 – 05-1120

Mbabazi and Others v. The Attorney General and National Environmental Management Authority – High Court at Kampala, pending – No. 283 of 2012

Milieudefensie et al. v. Royal Dutch Shell plc. – Hague District Court, 26 May 2021 – C/09/571932/HA ZA 19-379

Minister for the Environment v. Sharma – Federal Court of Australia, 15 March 2022 – [2022] FCAFC 35

Ministry of Environment and Forestry v. PT Rambang Agro Jaya – District Court of Central Jakarta, 11 January 2021 – 445/Pdt.G/2019/PN.Jkt.Pst

Native Village of Kivalina v. ExxonMobil Corp. – US District Court for the Northern District of California, 30 September 2009 – 4:08-cv-01138-SBA

Neubauer et al. v. Germany – Germany Federal Constitutional Court, 24 March 2021 – 1 BvR 2656/18 – 1 BvR 78/20 – 1 BvR 96/20 – 1 BvR 288/20

Pabai Pabai and Guy Paul Kabai v. Commonwealth of Australia – Federal Court of Australia, pending – VID322/2021
PSB et al. v. Brazil – Brazil Federal Supreme Court, 1 July 2022 – ADPF 708
R (Finch on behalf of the Weald Action Group & Others) v. Surrey County Council (& Others) – United Kingdom Court of Appeal (Civil Division), 17 February 2022 – [2022] EWCA Civ 187
Sacchi et al. v. Argentina et al. – United Nations Committee on the Rights of the Child, 8 October 2021 – CRC/C/88/D/107/2019
Saonu and Morobe Provincial Government v. Minster for Environment and Conservation and Climate Change and Others – Court of Justice at Wagani, 10 September 2021 – OS (JR) 35 of 2021
Save Lamu et al. v. National Environmental Management Authority and Amu Power Co. Ltd. – Kenya's National Environmental Tribunal, 26 September 2019 – Net 196 of 2016
Sharma and others v. Minister for the Environment – Federal Court of Australia, 27 May 2021 – [2021] FCA 560
Smith v. Fonterra Co-Operative Group Limited – High Court of New Zealand, 21 October 2021 – [2021] NZCA 552
Société Arcelor Atlantique et Lorraine v. [EU] Parliament and Council (environment and consumers) – General Court (Third Chamber), 2 March 2010 – T-16/04
Tatar v. Romania – European Court of Human Rights, 27 January 2009 – 67021/01
The Planet v. Bolsonaro – International Criminal Court, pending – n/a
Urgenda Foundation v. The State of the Netherlands – The Hague District Court, 24 June 2015 – C/09/456689/HA ZA 13-1396
Urgenda Foundation v. The State of the Netherlands – The Hague Court of Appeal, 9 October 2018 – 200.178.245/01
Urgenda Foundation v. The State of The Netherlands – Supreme Court of the Netherlands, 20 December 2019 – 19/00135
Waratah Coal Pty Ltd v. Youth Verdict Ltd & Ors (No 6) – Land Court of Queensland, 25 November 2022 – [2022] QLC 21
Wohl v. City of New York – New York Supreme Court, 22 October 2014 – 103095/2012

Cases

Reichsgericht 31 May 1920 – I 211/20
Federal Court Germany, 23 October 1951 – I ZR 31/51
Federal Court Germany 10 July 1958 – 4 StR 180/58
Federal Court of Germany, 17 March 1992 – 5 StR 34/92
Federal Court of Germany, 9 December 2020 – VIII ZR 371/18
Corfu Channel Case (United Kingdom v. People's Republic of Albania) – International Court of Justice, 25 March 1948; 9 April 1949; 15 December 1949 – I. C. J. Reports 1948 p. 15; 1949 p. 4, 244

Germany v. Great Britain and the United States of America (Samoan Claims Case) – His Majesty Oscar II, King of Sweden and Norway as Arbitrator under Convention of 7. November 1899, 14 October 1902 – 9 R.I.A.A. 15

Joseph Charles Lemire v. Ukraine – International Centre for Settlement of Investment Disputes, 28 March 2011 – ARB/06/18

Overseas Tankship (UK) Ltd v Morts Dock and Engineering Co Ltd (Wagon Mound (No. 1)) – Privy Council, 18 January 1961 – [1961] UKPC 2, [1961] AC 388; [1961] 1 All ER 404

Overseas Tankship (UK) Ltd v The Miller Steamship Co (Wagon Mound No. 2) – Privy Council, 25 May 1966 – [1966] UKPC 10, [1967] AC 617; [1967] 2 All ER 709

Responsibilities and obligations of States sponsoring persons and entities with respect to activities in the Area (Request for Advisory Opinion submitted to the Seabed Disputes Chamber) – International Tribunal for the law of the Sea, – ITLOS Reports 2011, p. 10

Southern Bluefin Tuna (New Zealand v. Japan; Australia v. Japan), Provisional Measures – International Tribunal for the Law of the Sea, 27 August 1999 – ITLOS Reports 1999, p. 280

United States v. Canada (Trail Smelter Case) – Arbitrational Tribunal, 16 April 1938, 11 March 1941 – 3 R.I.A.A. 1905

Vairy v. Wyong Shire Council – High Court of Australia, 21 October 2005 – HCA 62

Wyong Shire Council v. Shirt – High Court of Australia, 1 May 1980 – 146 CLR 40

References

American Law Institute (2010) Restatements of the law third, torts: liability for physical and emotional harm. St. Paul

Aristotle (n.d.) Ethica Nicomachea. In: Baywater I (ed) Oxford classical texts (1894). Oxford University Press, Oxford

Atapattu SA, Simonelli AC (2021) Climate justice, sustainable development, and small island states – a case study of the Maldives. In: Atapattu SA, Gonzalez CG, Seck S (eds) The Cambridge handbook of environmental justice and sustainable development. Cambridge University Press, Cambridge, pp 434–450

Atapattu SA, Gonzalez CG, Seck S (2021) Framing the issue. In: Atapattu SA, Gonzalez CG, Seck S (eds) The Cambridge handbook of environmental justice and sustainable development. Cambridge University Press, Cambridge, pp 1–22

Baatz C (2013) Responsibility for the past? Some thought on compensating those vulnerable to climate change in developing countries. Ethics Policy Environ 16(1):94–110

Barry C, Kirby R (2017) Scepticism about beneficiary pays: a critique. J Appl Philos 34(3):285–300

Benson P (1992) The basis of corrective justice and its relation to distributive justice. Iowa Law Rev 77(2):515–624

Berkey B (2017) Benefiting from unjust acts and benefiting from injustice – historical emissions and the beneficiary pays principle. In: Meyer LH, Sanklecha P (eds) Climate justice and historical emissions. Cambridge University Press, Cambridge, pp 123–140

Birnbacher D (2015) Klimagerechtigkeit – Verursacher- oder Leistungsfähigkeitsprinzip? In: Kallhoff A (ed) Klimagerechtigkeit und Klimaethik. De Gruyter, Berlin, pp 67–80
Blickle P (2022) Climate technologies as emergency solutions: the role(s) of international law. Graduate Institute of International and Development Studies, Geneva
Boer B (2021) The preamble. In: Calster GV, Reins L (eds) The Paris Agreement on climate change – a commentary. Edward Elgar, Cheltenham, pp 5–32
Bonython W (2021) Tort law and climate change. Univ Qld Law J 40(3):421–458
Boyle A, Redgwell C (2021) International law and the environment. Oxford University Press, Oxford
Brand O (2022) § 249 BGB. In: Gsell B, Krüger W, Lorenz S, Reymann C (eds) Beck Online Grosskommentar. C. H. Beck, Munich
Brunnée J, Goldberg S, QC Lord R, Rajamani L (2011) Overview of legal issues relevant to climate change. In: Brunnée J, Goldberg S, QC Lord R, Rajamani L (eds) Climate change liability transnational law and practice. Cambridge University Press, Cambridge, pp 23–49
Burger M, Wentz J, Horton R (2020) The law and science of climate change attribution. Colum J Environ Law 45(1):60–240
Burns W, Dana D, Nicholson SJ (2021) Climate geoengineering: science, law and governance. Springer, Cham
Butt D (2017) Historical emissions – does ignorance matter? In: Meyer LH, Sanklecha P (eds) Climate justice and historical emissions. Cambridge University Press, Cambridge, pp 61–79
Calliess C (2022) Art. 191 AEUV. In: Calliess C, Ruffert M (eds) EUV/AEUV: das Verfassungsrecht der Europäischen Union mit Europäischer Grundrechtecharta: Kommentar, 6th edn. C. H. Beck, Munich, pp 1854–1876
Campfens E (2018) Artefact or heritage? – Colonial collections in western museums from the perspective of international (human rights) law. Available via Völkerrechtsblog. https://voelkerrechtsblog.org/artefact-or-heritage/. Accessed 24 Oct 2024
Caney S (2010) Climate change and the duties of the advantaged. Crit Rev Int Soc Polit Philos Sci 13(1):203–228
Caney S (2018) Climate change. In: Olsaretti S (ed) The Oxford handbook of distributive justice. Oxford University Press, Oxford, pp 664–688
Caney S (2020) Climate justice. Available via Stanford Encyclopedia of Philosophy. https://plato.stanford.edu/entries/justice-climate/. Accessed 24 Oct 2024
Carazo MP (2017) Contextual provisions (preamble and Article 1). In: Klein D, Carazo MR, Doelle M, Bulmer J, Higham A (eds) The Paris Agreement on climate change – analysis and commentary. Oxford University Press, Oxford, pp 107–122
Chatzinerantzis A, Appel M (2019) Haftung für den Klimawandel. Neue Jur Wochenschau 13:881–886
Chatzinerantzis A, Herz B (2010) Climate change litigation – Der Klimawandel im Spiegel des Haftungsrechts. Neue Jur Onlinez 10(11):594–654
Crippa M, Guizzardi D, Solazzo E, Muntean M, Schaaf E, Monforti-Ferrario F, Banja M, Olivier JGJ, Grassi G, Rossi S, Vignati E (2021) GHG emissions of all world countries – 2021 Report, EUR 30831 EN. Publications Office of the European Union, Luxembourg
Cullet P (2010) Common but differentiated responsibilities. In: Fitzmaurice M, Ong DM, Merkouris P (eds) Research handbook on international environmental law. Edward Elgar, Cheltenham, pp 161–181
Czarnecki R (2008) Verteilungsgerechtigkeit im Umweltvölkerrecht – Dogmatik und Umsetzung. Duncker & Humblot, Berlin
de Sadeleer N (2021) The principles of prevention and precaution in international law: two sides of the same coin? In: Fitzmaurice M, Brus M, Merkouris P, Rydberg A (eds) Research handbook on international environmental law. Edward Elgar, Cheltenham, p 152
Dellinger M (2017) Rethinking force majeure in public international law. Pace Law Rev 37(2):445–506

Du H (2018) An international legal framework for geoengineering: managing the risks of an emerging technology. Routledge, London
Durrant N (2007) Tortious liability for greenhouse gas emissions – climate change, causation and public policy considerations. Qld Univ Tec Law Justice J 7(2):403–424
Duvic-Paoli L-A, Vinuales JE (2015) Principle 2: prevention. In: Vinuales JE (ed) The Rio Declaration on environment and development. Oxford University Press, Oxford, pp 107–138
Dzehtsiarou K (2011) European consensus and the evolutive interpretation of the European Convention on Human Rights. German Law J 12(10):1730–1745
Ebbers M, Müller A (2023) New ways to deal with old crimes? Available via Völkerrechtsblog. https://voelkerrechtsblog.org/new-ways-to-deal-with-old-crimes/. Accessed 24 Oct 2024
Ebbesson J (2009a) Piercing the state veil in pursuit of environmental justice. In: Ebbesson J, Okowa P (eds) Environmental law and justice in context. Cambridge University Press, Cambridge, pp 270–294
Ebbesson J (2009b) Introduction: dimensions of justice in environmental law. In: Ebbesson J, Okowa P (eds) Environmental law and justice in context. Cambridge University Press, Cambridge, pp 1–36
Ebert I (2020) Vorb. § 249. In: Westermann HP, Grunewald B, Maier-Reimer G (eds) Erman BGB Kommentar – Band I, 16th edn. Dr. Otto Schmidt, Cologne, pp 908–937
Ehemann E-MI (2020) Umweltgerechtigkeit – Ein Leitkonzept sozio-ökologisch gerechter Entscheidungsfindung. Mohr Siebeck, Tübingen
Expert Group on Global Climate Obligations (2015) Oslo principles on global climate change. The Hague
Farber DA (2017) How legal systems deal with issues of responsibility for past harmful behavior. In: Meyer LH, Sanklecha P (eds) Climate justice and historical emissions. Cambridge University Press, Cambridge, pp 80–106
Flume J (2022) § 249 BGB. In: Hau W, Poseck R (eds) Beck'scher Online-Kommentar BGB, 63rd edn. C. H. Beck, Munich
Frei MA (2010) Der rechtlich relevante Kausalzusammenhang im Strafrecht im Vergleich mit dem Zivilrecht. Schulthess, Zürich
Frenz W (2022) Grundzüge des Klimaschutzrechts. Springer, Berlin
Freund G (2020) Vorb. § 13. In: Erb V, Schäfer J (eds) Münchner Kommentar zum Strafgesetzbuch – Band 1, 4th edn. C. H. Beck, Munich, pp 438–605
Garner BA (ed) (2009) Black's law dictionary. West Publishing, Saint Paul
Germelmann CF (2021) Klimagerechtigkeit – Anmerkungen aus juristischer Sicht. Forschmag Leibniz Univ Hann 02(1):68–69
Giacomini G (2022) Indigenous peoples and climate justice: a critical analysis of international human rights law and governance. Springer, Cham
Godard O (2017) Global climate justice – proposals, arguments and justification. Elgar, Cheltenham
Gosepath S (2021) Equality. Available via Stanford Encyclopedia of Philosophy. https://plato.stanford.edu/entries/equality/. Accessed 24 Oct 2024
Gosseries A (2004) Historical emissions and free-riding. Ethical Perspect 11:36–60
Goudkamp J, Plunkett J (2019) The foreseeability element of the duty of care. Law Q Rev 135:521–526
Greenhouse Effect Working Group (Shell Internationale Petroleum Maatschappij B.V.) (1988) The greenhouse effect. The Hague
Halpern J (2017) Moral responsibility, blameworthiness, and intention: in search of formal definitions. Available via Cornell University. https://www.cornell.edu/video/joe-halpern-moral-responsibility-blameworthiness-intention-formal-definitions. Accessed 24 Oct 2024
Hänni J (2021) The prospects of climate litigation before the European Court of Human Rights: prerequisites and possible challenges. Hum Rights Law J 40(1–12):5–23
Haritz M (2011) Liability with and liability from the precautionary principle in climate change cases. In: Faure M, Peeters M (eds) Climate change liability. Edward Elgar, Cheltenham, pp 15–35

Hart HLA, Honoré T (1985) Causation in the law. Oxford University Press, New York
Heede R (2014) Carbon majors: accounting for carbon and methane emissions 1854-2010 methods & results report. Lambert Academic Publishing, London
Heselhaus (2017) Art. 191 AEUV. In: Pechstein M, Nowak C, Häde U (eds) Frankfurter Kommentar EUV/GRC/AEUV – Band III, 1st edn. Mohr Siebeck, Tübingen, pp 1316–1368
Heyward C (2021) Is the beneficiary pays principle essential in climate justice? Norsk folosofisk tidsskrift 56(2–3):125–136
Honkonen T (2016) CBDR and climate change. In: Farber DA, Peeters M (eds) Climate change law. Edward Elgar, Cheltenham, pp 142–151
Huang J (2017) Climate justice: climate justice and the Paris Agreement. Calif West Int Law J 9:23–59
Hunter D, Salzman J (2007) Negligence in the air: the duty of care in climate change litigation. Univ Pa Law Rev 155(2):1741–1794
Huseby R (2015) Should the beneficiaries pay? Polit Philos Econ 14(2):209–225
Infantino M, Zervogianni E (eds) (2017) Causation in European tort law. Cambridge University Press, Cambridge
International Law Commission (2001a) Draft articles on responsibility of states for internationally wrongful acts, with commentaries, A/CN.4/SER.A/2001/Add.1 (Part 2). Yearb ILC, 2(2): 30–143.
International Law Commission (2001b) Draft articles on prevention of transboundary harm from hazardous activities, with commentaries, A/CN.4/SER.A/2001/Add.1 (Part 2). Yearb ILC, 2(2): 144–170
IPCC (1992a) First assessment report overview and policymaker summaries and 1992 IPCC supplement. Canada
IPCC (1992b) Climate change: The 1990 and 1992 IPCC assessments. Canada
IPCC (2014a) Climate Change 2014: synthesis report – Contribution of Working Groups I, II and III to the Fifth Assessment Report of the Intergovernmental Panel on Climate Change. Geneva
IPCC (2014b) Climate Change 2014: mitigation of climate change – Contribution of Working Group III to the Fifth Assessment Report of the Intergovernmental Panel on Climate Change. Cambridge
IPCC (2018) Global warming of 1.5°C – An IPCC Special Report on the impacts of global warming of 1.5°C above pre-industrial levels and related global greenhouse gas emission pathways, in the context of strengthening the global response to the threat of climate change, sustainable development, and efforts to eradicate poverty. Cambridge
IPCC (2022a) Climate Change 2022: impacts, adaptation and vulnerability – Contribution of Working Group II to the Sixth Assessment Report of the Intergovernmental Panel on Climate Change. Cambridge
IPCC (2022b) Climate Change 2022: mitigation of climate change – Contribution of Working Group III to the Sixth Assessment Report of the Intergovernmental Panel on Climate Change. Geneva
IPCC (2023) Climate Change 2023: synthesis report – Contribution of Working Groups I, II and III to the Sixth Assessment Report of the Intergovernmental Panel on Climate Change – summary for policymakers. Geneva
Jegede AO, Adejonwo O (eds) (2022) Climate change justice and human rights – an African perspective. Pretoria University Law Press, Pretoria
Kahl W (2018) Art. 191 AEUV. In: Streinz R (ed) EUV/AEUV, 3rd edn. C. H. Beck, Munich, pp 1788–1821
Karnein A (2017) Asking beneficiaries to pay for past pollution. In: Meyer LH, Sanklecha P (eds) Climate justice and historical emissions. Cambridge University Press, Cambridge, pp 107–122
Kirby R (2016) The beneficiary pays principle and climate change. Dissertation, The Australian National University
Kleinschmidt J (2009) Kausalität. In: Basedow J, Hopt KJ, Zimmermann R (eds) Handwörterbuch des Europäischen Privatrechts – Band II Kau – Z. Mohr Siebeck, Tübingen, pp 969–973

Kloepfer M (2006) Umweltgerechtigkeit – Environmental Justice in der deutschen Rechtsordnung. Duncker & Humblot, Berlin
Kloepfer M, Neugärtner RD (2021) Liability for climate damages, sustainability and environmental justice. In: Kahl W, Weller M-P (eds) Climate change litigation. C. H. Beck, Munich, pp 23–45
Koch H-J, Lührs M, Verheyen R (2011) National laws: Germany. In: Brunnée J, Goldberg S, QC Lord R, Rajamani L (eds) Climate change liability transnational law and practice. Cambridge University Press, Cambridge, pp 376–416
Kohler J (2017) Einleitung zum Umwelthaftungsrecht. In: Kohler J (ed) J. von Staudigners Kommentar zum Bürgerlichen Gesetzbuch mit Einführungsgesetzen und Nebengesetzen – Buch 2. Sellier & Co, de Gruyter, Berlin, pp 1–363
Koziol H (2007) Natural and legal causation. In: Tichý L (ed) Causation in law. E. Rozkotova, Prag, pp 53–67
Kühl K (2017) Strafrecht Allgemeiner Teil. Vahlen, Munich
Lanovoy V (2022) Causation in the law of state responsibility. Br Yearb Int Law 90:1–84
Larenz K, Canaris C-W (1995) Methodenlehre der Rechtswissenschaft. Springer, Berlin
Law J (2022) Oxford dictionary of law. Oxford University Press, Oxford
Liebesman L, Lake E, Landreth P (2009) The Endangered Species Act and climate change. Environ Law Rep News Anal 39(12):11173–11180
Marti U (2011) Das Vorsorgeprinzip im Umweltrecht: am Beispiel der internationalen, europäischen und schweizerischen Rechtsordnung. Schulthess, Zurich
Mason-Case S, Dehm J (2021) Redressing historical responsibility for the unjust precarities of climate change in the present. In: Mayer B, Zahar A (eds) Debating climate law. Cambridge University Press, Cambridge, pp 170–189
McKinnon C (2009) Climate change and corrective justice. Jahrb Recht Ethik 17:259–275
Mercatur Research Institute on Global Commons and Climate Change (2023) So schnell tickt die CO_2-Uhr. Available via Mercatur Research Institute on Global Commons and Climate Change. https://www.mcc-berlin.net/forschung/co2-budget.html. Accessed 24 Oct 2024
Meyer LH, Roser D (2010) Climate justice and historical emissions. Crit Rev Int Soc Polit Philos Sci 13(1):229–253
Mickelson K (2009) Competing narratives of justice in north-south environmental relations: the case of ozone layer depletion. In: Ebbesson J, Okowa P (eds) Environmental law and justice in context. Cambridge University Press, Cambridge, pp 297–315
Miller D (2021) Justice. Available via Stanford Encyclopedia of Philosophy. https://plato.stanford.edu/entries/justice/. Accessed 24 Oct 2024
Monien J (2014) Prinzipien als Wegbereiter eines globalen Umweltrechts? – Das Nachhaltigkeits-, Vorsorge- und Verursachungsprinzip im Mehrebenensystem. Nomos, Baden-Baden
Moore MS (2009) Causation and responsibility: an essay in law, morals, and metaphysics. Oxford University Press, New York
Mossoux Y (2010) Causation in the polluter pays principle. Eur Environ Law Rev 19(6):279–294
Msafiri AG (2013) Ethics for climate justice and sustainability through value-based approaches: a new Tanzanian model and paradigm shift. In: Ruppel OC, Roschmann C, Ruppel-Schlichting K (eds) Climate change: international law and global governance, Policy, diplomacy and governance in a changing environment, vol II. Nomos, Baden-Baden, pp 661–682
National Academies of Sciences, Engineering, and Medicine (1979) Carbon dioxide and climate: a scientific assessment. Washington, DC
Nedelcu P, Schäferling S (2022) The act on corporate due diligence obligations in supply chains – an examination of the German approach to business and human rights. German Yearb Int Law 64(1):443–457
Neumayer E (2000) In defence of historical accountability for greenhouse gas emissions. Ecol Econ 33(2):185–192
Nitsch S (2021) Liability for climate change damages under the German Environmental Liability Act. In: Kahl W, Weller M-P (eds) Climate change litigation: a handbook. C. H. Beck, Munich, pp 430–447

Nyka M (2021) State responsibility for climate change damage. Rev Eur Comp Law XLV(2): 131–152
Oetker H (2019) § 249 BGB. In: Krüger W (ed) Münchener Kommentar BGB – Band 2, 8th edn. C. H. Beck, Munich, pp 340–529
Okowa P (2010) Responsibility for environmental damage. In: Fitzmaurice M, Ong DM, Merkouris P (eds) Research handbook on international environmental law. Edward Elgar, Cheltenham, pp 303–319
Orakhelashvili A (2022) Causation in international law. Edward Elgar, Cheltenham
Organisation for Economic Co-operation and Development (1975) Report on the polluter pays principle. Paris
Osofsky H (2009) Is climate change 'international'? Litigation's diagonal regulatory role. Virginia J Int Law 49(3):585–650
Page EA (2012) Give it up for climate change: a defence of the beneficiary pays principle. Int Theory 4(2):300–330
Peel J (2011) Issues in climate change litigation thematic focus: climate change governance: policy and litigation in a multi-level system. Carbon Clim Law Rev 5(1):15–24
Peel J, Sands P, Fabra A, MacKenzie R (2018) Principles of international environmental law. Cambridge University Press, Cambridge
Pirjatanniemi E (2016) Greening human rights law – a focus on the European Convention on Human Rights. In: Bos G, Düwell M (eds) Human rights and sustainability. Routledge, London, pp 11–24
Plakokefalos I (2015) Causation in the law of state responsibility and the problem of overdetermination: in search of clarity. Eur J Int Law 26(2):471–492
Posner EA, Weisbach D (2010) Climate change justice – a provocative contribution to the climate justice debate. Princeton University Press, Princeton
Pöttker E (2014) Klimahaftungsrecht. Mohr Siebeck, Tübingen
Rehbinder E (2021) Climate damages and the 'polluter pays' principle. In: Kahl W, Weller M-P (eds) Climate change litigation. C. H. Beck, Munich, pp 46–62
Rengier R (2021) Strafrecht Allgemeiner Teil. C. H. Beck, Munich
Ritchie H, Roser M, Rosado P (2020) Netherlands: CO_2 country profile. Available via Our World in Data. https://ourworldindata.org/co2/country/netherlands. Accessed 24 Oct 2024
de Sadeleer N (2016) The precautionary principle and climate change. In: Farber DA, Peeters M (eds) Climate change law. Edward Elgar, Cheltenham, pp 20–31
Satzger H, von Maltitz N (2021) Das Klimastrafrecht – ein Rechtsbegriff der Zukunft. Zeitschrift für die gesamte Strafrechtswissenschaft 133(1):1–34
Schirmer J-E (2021) Klimahaftung und Kausalität – und es geht doch! Juristenz 76(22):1099–1106
Schirmer J-E (2023) Haftung für künftige Klimaschäden. Neue Jur Woschenschrift 3:113–118
Schulze R (2021) Vorb. zu §§ 249-253. In: Dörner H, Ebert I, Fries M, Friesen S, Himmen A, Hoeren T, Kemper R, Saenger I, Scheuch A, Schreiber C, Schulte-Nölke H, Schulze R, Staudinger A, Wiese V (eds) Bürgerliches Gesetzbuch Handkommentar, 11th edn. Nomos, Baden-Baden, pp 339–350
Schwartz P (2015) Principle 16: the polluter-pays principle. In: Vinuales JE (ed) The Rio Declaration on environment and development. Oxford University Press, Oxford, pp 429–450
Schwartz P (2018) The polluter-pays principle. In: Krämer L, Orlando E (eds) Principles of environmental law, Cheltenham, pp 260–271
Scott J (2004) The precautionary principle before the European courts. In: Macrory R, Havercroft I (eds) Principles of European environmental law. Europa Law Publishing, Groningen, pp 49–72
Scott H (2019) The history of foreseeability. Curr Leg Probl 72(1):287–314
Seibert M-J (2021) Klimaschutz und Generationengerechtigkeit – Der Jahrhundert-Beschluss des Bundesverfassungssgerichts. Dtsch Verwaltbl 136(17):1141–1146
Shelton D (2009) Describing the elephant: international justice and environmental law. In: Ebbesson J, Okowa P (eds) Environmental law and justice in context. Cambridge University Press, Cambridge, pp 55–75

Shue H (2014) Climate justice: vulnerability and protection. Oxford University Press, Oxford
Spentzou D (2021) Climate change litigation as a means to address intergenerational equity and climate change. Queen Mary Law J 2021(2):153–283
Spier J (2005) 3:201. In: European group on tort law (ed) Principles of European tort law – text and commentary. Springer, Vienna, pp 59–63
Stephens JC (2022a) Feminist, antiracist values for climate justice – moving beyond climate isolationism. In: Engle J, Agyeman J, Chung-Tiam-Fook T (eds) Sacred civics – building seven generation cities. Routledge, pp 177–189
Stephens JC (2022b) Beyond climate isolationism: a necessary shift for climate justice. Curr Clim Chang Rep 8(4):83–90
Stoyanova V (2018) Causation between state omission and harm within the framework of positive obligations under the European Convention on Human Rights. Hum Rights Law Rev 18(2): 309–346
Stoyanova V (2020) Fault, knowledge and risk within the framework of positive obligations under the European Convention on Human Rights. Leiden J Int Law 33(3):601–620
Stuart-Smith RF, Roe GH, Li S, Allen MR (2021) Increased outburst flood hazard from Lake Palcacocha due to human-induced glacier retreat. Nat Geosci 14(2):85–90
Sunstein CR, Posner EA (2007) Climate change justice. John M. Olin Program in law and economics working paper 354, pp 1–38
Swisher PN (2007) Causation requirements in tort and insurance law practice: demystifying some legal causation riddles. Tort Trial Insur Pract Law J 43(1):1–34
tagesschau (2021) Deutschland erkennt Völkermord an. Available via tagesschau. https://www.tagesschau.de/ausland/afrika/deutschland-kolonialverbrechen-namibia-101.html. Accessed 24 Oct 2024
Talbert M (2024) Moral responsibility. Available via Stanford Encyclopedia of Philosophy. https://plato.stanford.edu/entries/moral-responsibility/. Accessed 24 Oct 2024
Theurer K (2023) Germany has to grant reparations for colonial crimes. Available via Völkerrechtsblog. https://voelkerrechtsblog.org/germany-has-to-grant-reparations-for-colonial-crimes/. Accessed 24 Oct 2024
Thornton F (2021) Of harm, culprits and rectification: obtaining corrective justice for climate change displacement. Trans Environ Law 10(1):13–33
Tol RSJ, Verheyen R (2004) State responsibility and compensation for climate change damages – a legal and economic assessment. Energy Policy 32(9):1109–1130
Torpman O (2021) Isolationism and the equal per capita view. Environ Polit 30(3):357–375
Trindade AAC (2015) Principle 15: precaution. In: Vinuales JE (ed) The Rio Declaration on environment and development. Oxford University Press, Oxford, pp 404–428
Ulfstein G (2015) Interpretation of the ECHR in the light of other international instruments. PluriCourts research paper 15, pp 1–6
Umweltbundesamt (2024a) Emissionen ausgewählter Treibhausgase in Deutschland nach Kategorien in: Treibhausgas-Emissionen in Deutschland. Available via Umweltbundesamt. https://www.umweltbundesamt.de/sites/default/files/medien/384/bilder/dateien/8_tab_thg-emi-kat_2024-04-02.pdf. Accessed 24 Oct 2024
Umweltbundesamt (2024b) Energiebedingte Emissionen von Klimagasen und Luftschadstoffen. Available via Umweltbundesamt. https://www.umweltbundesamt.de/daten/energie/energiebedingte-emissionen#entwicklung-der-energiebedingten-treibhausgas-emissionen. Accessed 12 June 2023
United Nations Conference on the Human Environment (1972) Report of the conference Stockholm, 5–16 June 1972, A/CONF.48/14/Rev.1
United Nations Secretariat to the FCCC (2021) Revised synthesis report on the nationally determined contributions under the Paris Agreement for the conference of the parties serving as the meeting of the parties to the Paris Agreement of 25 October 2021, FCCC/PA/CMA/2021/8/Rev.1. Glasgow

van der Wilt H (2015) Nullum crimen and international criminal law: the relevance of the foreseeability test. Nord J Int Law 84:515–531
Verheyen R (2005) Climate change damage and international law – prevention duties and state responsibility. Brill, Leiden
Voigt C (2008) State responsibility for climate change damages. Nord J Int Law 77(1–2):1–22
Voigt C (2016) Climate change and damages. In: Carlarne C, Gray K, Tarasofsky R (eds) The Oxford handbook of international climate change law. Oxford University Press, Oxford, pp 464–494
von Arnauld A (2019) Völkerrecht. C. F. Müller, Heidelberg
von Bar C (2000) The common European law of torts – 2 damage and damages, liability for and without personal misconduct, causality and defences. Oxford University Press, Oxford
von Kries J (1888) Über den Begriff der objektiven Möglichkeit und einige Anwendungen desselben. Vierteljahresschr Wiss Philos Soziol 12:179–240
von Savigny FC (2020) System des heutigen Römischen Rechts. De Gruyter, Berlin
Wagner G, Arntz A (2021) Liability for climate damages under the German law of torts. In: Kahl W, Weller M-P (eds) Climate change litigation. C. H. Beck, Munich, pp 407–429
Waldkirch C (2018) Zufall und Zurechnung im Haftungsrecht. Mohr Siebeck, Tübingen
Weitenberg M (2014) Der Begriff der Kausalität in der haftungsrechlichen Rechtsprechung der Unionsgerichte. Nomos, Baden-Baden
White House (1980) 11th annual report of the Council on Environmental Quality. Washington
Wiener JB (2018) Precautionary principle. In: Krämer L, Orlando E (eds) Principles of environmental law. Edward Elgar, Cheltenham, pp 174–185
World Bank (2023) CO_2 emissions (metric tons per capita) – Netherlands. Available via The World Bank. https://data.worldbank.org/indicator/EN.ATM.CO2E.PC?end=2019&locations=NL&start=1990&view=chart. Accessed 24 Oct 2024
Wurmnest W (2003) Grundzüge eines europäischen Haftungsrechts – Eine rechtsvergleichende Untersuchung des Gemeinschaftsrechts. Mohr Siebeck, Tübingen
Zahar A (2021) Historical responsibility for climate change is political propaganda. In: Mayer B, Zahar A (eds) Debating climate law. Cambridge University Press, Cambridge, pp 190–205
Zeidler S (2022) Klimahaftungsklagen – Die internationale Haftung für die Folgen des Klimawandels. Duncker & Humblot, Berlin
Zellentin A (2015) Compensation for historical emissions and excusable ignorance. J Appl Philos 32(3):258–274

Chapter 6
Distinguishing Different Cases of Applied Climatic Causation

The ultimate aim of this book was to find a comprehensive account to approach climatic causation, both factually and normatively. On the basis of the previously conducted analysis, different approaches to and conceptions of climatic causation have been analysed, further developed and tested in the context of causal issues posed by climate change litigation.[1] Decisive for the determination of factual approaches and moreover the usability and utility of the respective doctrines had been their metaphysical soundness, applicability and practicability in climate matters, as well as their depiction of actual causation.[2] On the basis of these determinants, it has become clear that there is no superior doctrine of factual causation, but that all theories, depending on their origin, their metaphysical background, and their mode of application, possess certain advantages over others. The 'correct' doctrine for determining factual causation in practice, therefore, depends not only on the determination of the theories on the basis of the factors already mentioned, but also on additional external considerations of general legal practice. This implies that depending on the specific case, different doctrines might be advisable for different legal settings. This applies to both, the factual, as well as the normative causal inquiry. Within the factual determination, the choice of the applicable causation doctrine fundamentally depends on the jurisdiction and legal system in which the case is being brought (Sect. 6.1).

Even more divergent, however, is the normative determination of causation. While jurisdiction-wide differences persist in the mere choice of theories that are applied to evaluate normative causation, in general and apart from the climate issue, dissimilarities and alterations even exist within the individual theories depending on the legal scenario. This circumstance transpires especially to the assessment of foreseeability and materiality (Sect. 6.2). On the basis of this evaluative account, differences emerge in particular with regard to the actor concerned (Sect. 6.2.1), the

[1] See for a comprehensive account on the analysis Sect. 3.4.

[2] See for the evaluative criteria of factual causation Sect. 4.1.3.

M. Krakau, *Causation in National and International Climate Change Litigation*,
https://doi.org/10.1007/978-3-031-74693-2_6

area of law in which the climate lawsuit is being brought, and the subject of action (Sect. 6.2.2).

6.1 Factual Causation

The varying demands that each factual doctrine of causation places on its application and the theoretical and metaphysical substruction imply that different accounts are suitable for different jurisdictions. In the following, an application of the previously obtained results is provided, which ultimately leads to the formation and distinction of different case groups. Concurrent with the general approach taken within this thesis, accounts are divided into the civil law (Sect. 6.1.1), common law (Sect. 6.1.2) and the regional and international legal sphere (Sect. 6.1.3).

6.1.1 Civil Law Jurisdictions

Civil law jurisdictions commonly apply counterfactual tests in their form as conditio-sine-qua-non doctrine.[3] They are also characterized by a strong legislative structure which places great emphasis on codified law and grants only limited influence to legal precedents. Because of their strong statutory ligation, civil law countries are likely to require a legislative embedding in light of renewed legal structures and concepts, which also applies to altered perceptions of causation and causal doctrines. A new approach to causation, and its legislative foundation, thus, goes hand in hand with a substantial political and even social discourse, which considerably prolongs the legislative process and ultimately also the establishment of a new and comprehensive causal concept. In light of these considerations, adapting yet existing doctrines shows to be preferable in contrast to a complete abolition of traditional understandings of causation.

One avenue that is likely to be pursued in this regard, is the adaptation of the counterfactual approach by concretizing the outcome in terms of time and scope (the strategy of factual concretization).[4] The strategy of factual concretization, hereby allows for a similar test and application as it is traditionally perceived by the courts and further coincides with the mono-causal conception of counterfactual theories. Although multi-causal concepts are generally preferred as they are better adapted to the needs and demands of climate lawsuits, it is the enhanced feasibility and applicability that convinces and argues in favour of the factual concretization

[3] See in this regard Sect. 4.2.

[4] See in this regard Sect. 4.2.3.

strategy.[5] The application of the strategy of factual concretization, furthermore, does not require any intermediate and legislative steps what in turn would be required under the application of other approaches. Since this is not a fundamental metaphysical divergence, it also guarantees a straightforward application by the courts. In civil law countries, the strategy of factual concretization therefore constitutes the preferred way of dealing with factual causation, given its ease of application and the need for a timely solution. Nevertheless, the debate on a broader and therefore multicausal approach should not be completely confined within civil law countries.

6.1.2 Common Law Jurisdictions

In contrast to the civil law sphere, countries of the common law realm rely heavily on precedents and judicial legislation which fundamentally transpires to the specific selection of the factual doctrine chosen to assess climatic causation. Given the enhanced law-making role of the courts in common law jurisdictions, judges commonly enjoy greater discretionary power in their choice of the standard that is to be applied and are not as dependent on its legislative embedding as it is the case in civil law countries. This finds depiction in numerous alternative concepts to the frequently applied but-for test that have already been developed and reaffirmed by the jurisprudence.[6] Common law jurisdictions are, therefore, much better equipped and much more responsive to the new challenges that climate change poses to the causal inquiry, which in turn makes them more open to different, more nuanced conceptions of causation.[7] Although counterfactual tests are perceived as the traditional tests of establishing factual causation, courts are not restricted to a monocausal concept and are able to apply and use multi-causal conceptions instead.

As it has been explained on multiple occasions throughout this work, multi-causal concepts not only facilitate the handling of causation in climate change litigation, they are also generally closer to actual causation and, thus, the ultimate purpose of factual causation in the law.[8] Where feasible, such approaches should therefore be preferred. Alongside the more metaphysically anchored regularity-based and probabilistic theories of factual causation, it is in particular the contribution-based approach that has been present in the discussion about the establishment of factual causation in the law.[9] The latter especially constitutes a progressive account as it comprises a case law grown approach that was developed outside the philosophical,

---

[5]The doctrine does not lose its factuality by applying normative and evaluative criteria in arguing for its applicability. Factuality refers to its ultimate application and not to the choice and decision of why the particular approach should ultimately be adopted.

[6]See in this regard Sect. 4.2.

[7]See for the challenges posed by climate change to the causation debate Sect. 3.3.

[8]See for the preference of multi-causal conceptions especially Sects. 4.3, 4.4, and 4.5.

[9]See in this regard Sect. 4.5.2.

theoretical and metaphysical sphere. Its advantages in light of its facilitated application and the hereby developed dynamic lead to the contribution-based concept being the most compelling account to approach the factual side of climatic causation in common law countries. In favour of its application especially speaks the usage of similar accounts in Canada and the United Kingdom, which depicts and ultimately proves the feasibility to apply a reduced standard of factual causation in common law jurisdictions.[10] Although further research into the metaphysical grounding is necessary as it would greatly enhance the acceptance and legitimacy of a contribution-based approach, its closeness to actual causation by its multi-causal substruction and the existence of other metaphysically grounded approaches that make use of similar understandings (such as regularity based theories) speak in favour of a contribution-based approach.

Theories of regularity, as similar and simultaneously multi-causal conceptions of causation, derive their strength from their dogmatic coherence and metaphysical grounding.[11] By using concepts such as necessary and sufficient conditions, those theories coincide with the terminological usage of traditional, counterfactual understandings of causation. Although their metaphysical substantiation outweighs a mere contribution-based approach by far, theories of regularity have just occasionally found their way into the practical sphere, not to mention in judicial decisions.[12] A simple reason might rest in their theoretical complexity and, thus, difficult application in the law. Those theories have to a large extent not left the philosophical realm which makes them either unknown to the jurisprudence or simply too difficult to apply. Even if the novelty of an approach cannot decide on the preference of one account over the other, the contribution-based approach seems to be more conducive to the application and the general needs of the law and legal practice per se. A contribution-based approach can furthermore avoid the conflict between the two fundamentally different philosophical and theoretical conceptions and embodiments of counterfactual and regularity-based theories.

Similar benefits can be found within a probabilistic account of factual causation.[13] Although a probabilistic approach carries fundamental advantages, such as its comparability with causal inquiries in climate and attribution science and its advanced reflection of actual causation, it also constitutes the approach that is most afar from current perceptions of factual causation. It furthermore poses great difficulties in aligning legal and scientific epistemology, which makes the theory seem not yet fit for simple usage, at least for the time being. Nevertheless, a probabilistic approach should not be completely discounted with. As part of the necessary research, it might be conceivable to draw on lessons and methods from the

[10] See for the usage of the contribution-based approach in Canada and the United Kingdom Sect. 4. 5.2.2.1.

[11] See in this regard Sect. 4.3.

[12] A climate case in which theories of regularity have been briefly discussed was the case Federal Court of Australia, 15 March 2022 – [2022] FCAFC 35, *Minister for the Environment v. Sharma*.

[13] See in this regard Sect. 4.4.

field of evidential science, which is already increasingly operating within the framework of probabilities.

Ultimately it is the contribution-based approach that constitutes the most promising account of factual climatic causation for common law jurisdictions. Naturally, the assessment and the results might vary even within the sphere of common law countries, nevertheless, it is a multi-causal conception that should be on the forefront of climatic causation in climate change litigation.

6.1.3 Regional and International Jurisdictions

Given the fundamental differences between the various regional and international jurisdictions, approaching factual causation on a general account is difficult to assert. What regional and international jurisdictions, however, all have in common, is that, based on the involvement and congregation of different countries and therefore different legal systems, they have a fundamental interest not only in reconciling conflicting interests, but also in avoiding the privileging of traditions and legal elements that are common to some jurisdictions but not to all. Regional and international legal structures are thus characterised by their dogmatic vagueness and disparity. In the absence of a strong legislative base, international jurisprudence is very much characterised by case law and the usage of precedents and, at least in this respect, resemble common law jurisdictions. The fundamental importance of the jurisprudence makes them susceptible to multi-causal concepts of causation. Given that theories of regularity and probability necessitate a comprehensive discourse on the metaphysical understanding of cause-effect relations and thus comprise a specific theoretical approach, it is, again, and even more than in common law jurisdictions, the contribution-based approach that paves the way for a comprehensive understanding of factual causation in the law of regional and international jurisdictions.[14] Although some international courts have occasionally applied other tests, such as counterfactual theories, contribution-based approaches have proven to provide for a consistent and dynamic understanding that suits the needs and demands of regional and international jurisdictions best.[15]

[14] Also proposing such an approach Verheyen (2005), pp. 254–256, as well as Voigt (2008), p. 16.

[15] See for the common understanding of regional and international courts Sects. 3.2.2 and 3.2.3.

6.2 Normative Causation

In contrast to factual causation, normative causation is approached much more diversely throughout different jurisdictions.[16] Differences hereby not only refer to the specific choice of the applied standard but also involves the scope and the content of the theories per se, as well as the emphasis which is placed on the different principles within the ultimately chosen theory. Principles and concepts used to adapt the factual causal results are hereby influenced not only by social, cultural and political norms, but also greatly diverge in accordance to the specific legal setting and the prerequisites posed by it. This in turn not only leads to the fact that the evaluation of normative accounts and normative causation respectively varies even within the same jurisdiction, but also that the approach to the normative assessment is greatly dependent on the respective actor (Sect. 6.2.1), as well as the area of law and the subject matter in question (Sect. 6.2.2).

As it stands, not all normative conceptions are equally influenced by different case scenarios and legal settings. While the respective party to a proceeding has an effect rather exclusively on the theories of foreseeability and materiality (and immanently also the theories that incorporate these two concepts), basically all normative conceptions are influenced by the respective area of law in which the lawsuit is being brought. Commonly unaffected, however, stays the handling and normative assessment of intervening causes, as it has been argued that they generally do not alter the factual causal chain normatively in the case of climate-related interventions.[17]

6.2.1 *Actor-Specific Differentiation*

The fundamental and most significant deviation in the normative assessment of factual causation resides within an actor-specific account. This is the case not only because specific normative principles entail different evaluations for different actors, but also because some normative principles, especially international environmental principles, do not bind all, but only apply and carry obligations for a specific group of actors. Other principles such as overall justice and fairness considerations, are in their application per se independent of the actor in question, but contain differences at the underlying value-based level. On the forefront of the normative assessment and thus also its deviations is the principle of climate justice, which constitutes, similar to its influence in the previous assessment of normative climatic causation, also in its differing character, one of the most decisive criteria in light of climate change litigation.

[16] See on normative causation Chap. 5.

[17] See concerning intervening causes Sect. 5.5.

The distinction based on the actor hereby ties on the specific party of the reproached action or omission in question. As introduced earlier in this work, three different groups of actors are being distinguished: states (Sect. 6.2.1.1), multi- and transnational corporations (Sect. 6.2.1.2), and individuals (Sect. 6.2.1.3).[18] Within the framework of foreseeability, the actor-specific distinction operates at two different junctures. On the one hand, it affects the demands placed on the requirement of a 'reasonable observer'.[19] On the other hand, it alters the inclusion and importance of individual knowledge. Within materiality, normative criteria influence the differentiated application and weighting of indicators.

6.2.1.1 States

States form one of the major and arguably one of the most important groups within current climate change litigation.[20] They are gradually finding themselves as defendants in lawsuits brought by NGOs or individuals challenging the absence or inadequacy of emission reduction targets, climate mitigation goals or protection measures.[21] States, furthermore, appear as parties in inter-state disputes. Within normative climatic causation, the assessment is strongly influenced by the principle of climate justice and international environmental principles, with the precautionary principle and the CBDR being on the forefront of these considerations.

6.2.1.1.1 Foreseeability

States represent the group of actors in which foreseeability is not only assessed most broadly, but also in which the threshold of foreseeability is shifted forward the furthest.[22] The very nature of overarching institutions such as the United Nations or the IPCC, as well as international environmental principles entailed in multinational treaties and convention, provide for a fundamental and universal point of reference on the account of climatic foreseeability. This circumstance constitutes the major difference in regard to other actors, especially considering individuals, and facilitates the assessment of foreseeability considerably. It is thus not only feasible but even

---

[18] See in this regard Sect. 5.3.2.3.

[19] See for the standard of foreseeability Sect. 5.3.2.1.

[20] Most of the precedent cases to date involve states as the defendant party. See e.g. United Nations Human Rights Committee, 22 September 2022 – CCPR/C/135/D/3624/2019, *Daniel Billy et al. v. Australia (Torres Strait Islanders Petition)*, Supreme Court of Ireland, 31 July 2020 – 205/19, *Friends of the Irish Environment v. The Government of Ireland*, Supreme Court of the Netherlands, 20 December 2019 – 19/00135, *Urgenda Foundation v. The State of The Netherlands*, Germany Federal Constitutional Court, 24 March 2021 – 1 BvR 2656/18 – 1 BvR 78/20 – 1 BvR 96/20 – 1 BvR 288/20, *Neubauer et al. v. Germany*.

[21] See in this regard Sect. 2.2.2.

[22] This was already elaborated on in Sect. 5.3.2.3.1.1.

more so demanded to assess the foreseeability of states in an universal matter. The individual knowledge of the actor hereby plays, in comparison to other actor-specific groups, only a minor role.[23]

As already elaborated on in a previous chapter, anthropogenic climate change and its general impacts can be considered foreseeable for states as early as the 1970s.[24] Indicators are not only the drafting process of the FCCC and the first IPCC report, but also earlier consultations and declarations, such as the inclusion of Recommendation 70 in the final report of the Stockholm Conference in 1972.[25] With representatives from 113 states, as well as numerous specialised agencies, international NGOs and intergovernmental organisations attending the conference, its final report and even more so the therein entailed recommendations strive for universality as a strong indicator of foreseeability.[26] Arguing that Recommendation 70 in particular is based on consultations, drafts and preparations that need to be known to the participating and drafting parties in advance of the conference in order to allow for discussion and subsequent inclusion in the report, one could even argue for an earlier threshold. In the absence of generally accessible documents or reports, a pre-1970 threshold can be established and proven individually, but the general foreseeability for states finally takes effect at a universal level from the 1970s onwards. The most important indication, however, and the one that conclusively supports such an early threshold of general foreseeability of states, is the rationale of international environmental principles, with the principle of prevention, and even more so the precautionary principle, at the forefront of the assessment.[27] Under the premise that precautionary measures must be taken even in cases in which there is a lack of scientific evidence, general foreseeability does not depend on full scientific certainty (since this also simply does not exist in natural science) or even on the publication of the first IPCC report, but rather on whether there was sufficient scientific evidence and indications to describe the anthropogenic influence on the climate system and to warn conclusively of the adverse (general) impacts of climate change. This was the case from the 1970s onwards at the latest.

In contrast to the threshold of general foreseeability, the threshold of specific foreseeability is bound to a later point in time. Although the Stockholm Conference indicates a general awareness of anthropogenic climate change and its adverse impacts, the abstractness of the wording indicates a reference only to the most general impacts and does not extend to the specific and more sensitive effects of climate change that are known today.[28] The first IPCC report, in which the IPCC

---

[23] See in this regard Sects. 5.3.2.3.1 and 5.3.2.3.2.

[24] See in this regard Sect. 5.3.2.3.

[25] United Nations Conference on the Human Environment (1972) and Recommendation 70, IPCC (1992a).

[26] United Nations Conference on the Human Environment (1972), p. 43.

[27] See for the principles of international environmental principles Sect. 5.2.2.

[28] The report only *"recommended that governments be mindful of activities in which there is an appreciable risk of effects on climate, and to this end: (a) Carefully evaluate the likelihood and*

already warned and predicted likely impacts not only on the climate and ecosystem in general, but also on a wide range of different areas of life, including energy, human settlements, transport and industry, human health, agriculture and forestry, and water resources, is therefore more indicative of the threshold of specific foreseeability.[29] Specific impacts can thus be regarded as foreseeable from the year 1990 onwards.

Specific foreseeability is concurrent to its general counterpart, strongly influenced by the precautionary principle. This applies in particular to impacts that were either unknown in 1990 or are still unknown today. With regard to the former, the assessment coincides with its application in relation to general foreseeability. However, the principle is also of paramount importance in the latter case, i.e. with regard to impacts that are also unknown today. While climate science has advanced considerably over the decades, and most of the specific impacts are already known today, it is nevertheless likely that anthropogenic climate change will have impacts in the future that are not yet present or fully understood today. However, since it is known that such specific impacts are likely to occur and will affect areas of life that have not been on the climate change radar, the precautionary principle dictates that these specific impacts should also be considered as foreseeable—even if unknown today. Forwarding the specific threshold based on the precautionary approach beyond the year 1990, however, fails, as the principle necessitates at least some degree of foresight and predicament of possible effects. This threshold set by the principle can only be considered reached from the year 1990 onwards. Form this point in time onwards, however does the precautionary principle thus has a fundamental impact on the assessment of the foreseeability threshold for states.

6.2.1.1.2 Materiality

The analysis of climate change decisions that has previously been conducted in this work has shown that states as the defendant party in climate change litigation often serve the narrative of minor contributions and allege their insignificance for climate change and its adverse effects.[30] Also known as the drop in-the-ocean argument, courts have frequently disputed such argument of defence and demonstrated a common obligation under occasional reference to the principle of common but differentiated responsibilities.[31] In providing some substance to this commonly held view and to further ground and undergird this position, the indicators developed in this work can provide a useful tool.[32] Implications for the materiality of the

magnitude of climatic effects [...]" United Nations Conference on the Human Environment (1972), Recommendation 70.

[29] IPCC (1992b), pp. 24–28.

[30] See in this regard Sect. 5.4.

[31] See in this regard Sect. 3.4.3.3.4.

[32] See in this regard Sect. 5.4.2.3.1.3.

contributions of states can especially be given by referring to the ratio to national and international climate change mitigation targets, as well as through the formation of comparative groups and by referencing per capita budgets. Although scaling the respective contribution imminently also affects the formation of different peer groups, this process as its own category does not carry as much weight as it is the case with other actors.

The first and arguably the most universally applicable indicator, consists in the scientific substantiation of the factual causal chain between the action or omission and the outcome in question.[33] This indicator only comes into play in jurisdictions or areas of law which provide for a causal exception in form of a presumption of factuality, or legislatively enshrined 'bridging' of the factual step to causation in the law. This indicator, thus only provides a safeguarding function to ensure factuality even within exceptional cases. With regard to states this indicator commonly does not pose a too much of a hurdle.

The second indication is given by the ratio to national and international climate change mitigation targets, which, however, provides only for a weak indication in light of great discretion that states commonly enjoy in their setting of their respective mitigation targets.[34] Even within an international commitment as it is given by the Paris Agreement and the respective NDCs, complying with their own targets can only give some guidance but is not able to form the sole basis of the assessment. It further provides for a very one-sided indication, as it can speak in favour of the exceedance of a threshold, but, due to the great discretion of states, only grants weak implications for the immateriality of the respective contribution. States that are not able to comply with their own set climate change mitigation targets, indicate a strong case for the affirmation of the materiality of their contribution. At the same time, exceeding or failing to meet nationally set climate change mitigation targets implies materiality. Ultimately, however, the ratio to national and international climate change mitigation targets does not form a stand-alone indicator but has to be read in synopsis with other, indicative factors to provide for a solid and comprehensive assessment of materiality.

One of these further indicators is offered by the formation of different peer groups.[35] Although the flexibility and comparability afforded by these groupings is considerably limited, as is the case with other actor-specific groupings, the comparison of the contribution in question with other contributions can nevertheless provide another strong indication in favour of or against the assumption of materiality. In addition to a general comparison of the contributions of all states worldwide, groupings may be based on regional and thus geographical comparisons, economic factors such as gross domestic product, or on affiliations to a particular confederation of states such as the European Union, the African Union, or other comparable entities. The more such comparisons are made, the more informed the assessment

---

[33] See in this regard Sect. 5.4.2.3.1.3.1.

[34] See in this regard also Sect. 5.4.2.3.1.3.2.

[35] See in this regard Sect. 5.4.2.3.1.3.4.

of materiality becomes. This ultimately also stretches to a comparison with other non-state actors and the addition of scientific data sets and corresponding emissions budgets and thresholds.

Closely connected to the formation of comparative groupings is ultimately also the per capita budget. Relevant in this regard, however, is not the exceeding of a specific per capita budget set by the remaining CO_{2eq}-emission allowance for the compliance with a specific temperature threshold, but more so its comparative function.[36] The per capita budget hereby forms an indicator that is most important for the actor-specific group of states as it integrates the party in question into the global dimension of climate change contributions.[37] However, concurrent to the indication set out by climate change mitigation targets, the per capita budget can only function in synopsis with other parameters as it also carries a certain risk of distortion. With 35.6 t of CO_2 per capita in 2021, Qatar has by far the highest CO_2 emissions ratio, closely followed by Bahrain with 26.7 t, Kuwait with 25.0 t, Trinidad and Tobago with 23.7 t and Brunei with 23.5 t per capita.[38] And although those numbers strongly indicate a certain level of materiality, in their annual share Qatar only accounts for 0.26%, Bahrain for 0.11%, Kuwait for 0.29%, Trinidad and Tobago for 0.10% and Brunei for 0.03% of the global annual CO_2 emissions in 2021.[39] Other countries such as China with 30.90% and the United States with 13.49% of the global annual CO_2 emission surpassed those prior countries by far.[40] This comparison is not intended to suggest that materiality should be dismissed on the basis of the lower annual share of those respective countries, but rather that per capita budgets need to be read into a wider field of other indicators and weighted and assessed from different perspectives.

In principle, however, it can be assumed in most cases within this actor-specific group that the contributions of the industrialized countries, at least, can be classified as substantial. In global terms, the amount of emissions that can be attributed to states by virtue of their economic activities alone means that they are among the world's largest emitters. Under the impression of the results of the previously conducted analysis of climate change decisions and with reference to the different indicators, it can thus be concluded that materiality can generally be affirmed for most of the industrialized countries of the world. Although, the evaluation of the respective contributions is at the discretion of the courts and conducted on a case-by-case basis, the thesis has shown that the objection of a lack of materiality frequently crumbles under the addition of scientific data and on the basis of different points of reference.

---

[36] See for the reasons why the remain CO_{2eq} budget does not form a reliable indicator Sect. 5.4.2.3.1.1.

[37] This indicator can also be used in relation to individuals.

[38] Ritchie et al. (2024a). Emissions by land-use have been excluded from the dataset.

[39] Ritchie et al. (2024b).

[40] Ibid.

6.2.1.2 Multinational Corporations

Multi- and transnational corporations increasingly push to the forefront of climate change litigation.[41] In view of successful precedents, such as the case *Milieudefensie v. Shell*, multinational corporations are more and more targeted by claimants.[42] Within normative causation, however, providing an universal and even more so commonly set account on the approach used to assess the foreseeability and materiality within this actor-specific group is considerably more difficult than it is with reference to states. This especially arises from the fact, that decisive principles such as general environmental principles of international law do not initially apply to private actors.[43] Similar principles, however, can be given effect through their specific implementation in national or regional legislation, although these provisions often exclusively refer to public actors rather than private entities.[44] Precautionary measures for corporations on an international level are furthermore recommended by the OECD Guidelines for Multinational Enterprises on Responsible Business Conduct, without, however, having a binding effect[45] In addition to the lack of binding precautionary principles, the universality and uniformity that the statal-sphere inherits based on the international legal realm and even more so the international organizational structure, is strongly lacking in regard to multinational corporations, as well. The normative assessment of causation is, thus, marked by individual evaluations, leading to the prominent role of indicators and peer groups in light of the assessment of materiality of the respective contribution.

6.2.1.2.1 Foreseeability

The lack of the regulatory effect of international environmental principles greatly affects the specific thresholds that are to be set for both, general, as well as specific foreseeability. It furthermore strongly enhances the dependence of this actor-specific group on the assessment and evaluation of individual knowledge.

Based on the findings presented in the first IPCC report and the ratification of the FCCC, the year 1990 marked a significant turning point in terms of general

---

[41] See for the most prominent ones Hague District Court, 26 May 2021 – C/09/571932/HA ZA 19-379, *Milieudefensie et al. v. Royal Dutch Shell plc*, Higher Regional Court Hamm, pending – 5 U 15/17, *Luciano Lliuya v. RWE AG*.

[42] See in this regard Sect. 2.2.2.

[43] Some debate is already taking place on the extent to which transnational and multinational companies should comply with international law, and human rights in particular. However, this requires explicit legislator regulation, such as that adopted in the context of the supply chain debate. See for a German account Nedelcu and Schäferling (2022). On the general role of private entities in international public law see Tietje (2014).

[44] Such e.g. is the case in Art. 191 TFEU.

[45] See Organisation for Economic Co-operation and Development (2023), pp. 35–39.

foreseeability.[46] However, due to the lack of influence of environmental principles and the stronger focus on public access to information, this does not represent the threshold of specific causation, but based on the previously developed standard, only the general threshold of foreseeability. The determination of a threshold for specific foreseeability, on the other hand, is much more difficult to assess on an universal level and depends strongly on individual evidence presented to prove the specific knowledge of the corporations concerned. However, given the growing public awareness of the adverse effects of climate change, which ultimately led to numerous developments in international law and culminated in the Paris Agreement in 2015, this year can be seen as the latest threshold for specific foreseeability in the corporate sector.[47]

Both of those thresholds, 1990 and 2015, however, are only of diminished importance in assessing the foreseeability of corporations in general. In light of the increasing efforts to hold corporations accountable for historic emissions and past climate harm, both thresholds could be seen as generally too weak, given that a large amount of emissions took place knowingly before the first threshold was even reached. This calls for an increased use of the discretionary power by the courts which corresponds to a greater reliance on the individual knowledge of the corporations concerned.[48]

How individual and special knowledge can shift the threshold of foreseeability and the threshold of reproachability forward in time is also shown by the case of *Luciano Lliuya v. RWE AG*.[49] In 2000, the government of the Federal Republic of Germany signed a climate protection agreement with representatives of the German industry.[50] The agreement set a target of reducing CO_2 emissions by 25% by 2005 (based on 1990 emissions) and a further 21% reduction in greenhouse gas emissions by 2008/2012. As the former president of the Association of German Electricity Companies (VDEW), signed the agreement, and the RWE AG being part of the VDEW, the report and more importantly its content and the therein entailed obligations can be attributed to the respective corporation, as well.[51] The agreement demonstrates the industry's awareness of the harmful effects of greenhouse gas emissions on the climate system in general and emphasises the companies' contribution to it. In relying on yet another statement by the VDEW which was included in RWE AG's own climate report, the plaintiffs date the individual knowledge of the

[46] See in this regard Sect. 5.3.2.3.1.2.

[47] See in this regard Sect. 5.3.2.3.2.1.

[48] In a second step, the question of whose knowledge is relevant becomes crucial. Given the intricacy of this matter, this has to be left aside. Nonetheless, of paramount importance is at least the knowledge that is held by the board of directors and managing directors of the companies that are involved.

[49] Essen Regional Court, 15 December 2016 – 2 O 285/15, *Luciano Lliuya v. RWE AG*, claim (23 November 2015).

[50] Vereinbarung zwischen der Regierung der Bundesrepublik Deutschland und der deutschen Wirtschaft zur Klimavorsorge (2000).

[51] Ibid.

defendant back to the year 1995.[52] On the basis of the individual knowledge and taking into account the general foreseeability discussed above, foreseeability might thus be assumed at least from 1995 onwards. Whether this threshold can be moved even further depends heavily on whether the claimant is able to provide further evidence of prior knowledge, and whether the Court will accept that evidence as part of the proceedings.

Another fitting example of how the threshold could be shifted forward on the basis of individual knowledge was provided by the plaintiffs in the case *Kivalina v. ExxonMobil Corp.*[53] In this case the plaintiffs provided the Court with an extended history of climate science and its findings starting from the discovery of the effects of CO_2 on the temperature by *Arrhenius* in 1896.[54] The plaintiffs ultimately did not take a clear stance on to when the specific climate change and foreseeability threshold should ultimately be set. They, nevertheless, provided the Court with enough information to showcase that climate change in general and its effects have been foreseeable for a long time.[55]

In summary, it can be said that from 1990 onwards a presumption of general foreseeability applies for multi- and transnational corporations. A presumption of specific foreseeability, then takes effect from the year 2015 onwards. In the light of the above, individual and specific knowledge plays an important role, much more so than in the case of other actors.

6.2.1.2.2 Materiality

In line with the assessment of foreseeability, the actor-specific differentiation also leads to different assessments of materiality. This applies both to the choice of indicators and to their weighting within the discretion of the courts. While the per capita budget and, to a certain extent, the ratio to national and international climate protection targets can and should be used to assess state action or omission, these two indicators are only of limited relevance with regard to corporations. However, the latter may have some relevance even within the corporate dimension in situations where the corporation has acted within a delimitable market, as is the case with the EU ETS or the KETS. Within such emission trading schemes and markets, emission allowances and reductions are clearly and legally defined. These targets can

---

[52] Essen Regional Court, 15 December 2016 – 2 O 285/15, *Luciano Lliuya v. RWE AG*, claim 19 (23 November 2015). Due to the lack of accessibility, this information could not further be verified.

[53] This case and the evidence risen by the plaintiffs was already addressed in Sect. 5.3.2.3 although in a different context. See US District Court for the Northern District of California, 30 September 2009 – 4:08-cv-01138-SBA, *Native Village of Kivalina v. ExxonMobil Corp.*, statement of claim, paras 134–162.

[54] See for a brief overview of climate change history Sect. 2.1.1.

[55] US District Court for the Northern District of California, 30 September 2009 – 4:08-cv-01138-SBA, *Native Village of Kivalina v. ExxonMobil Corp.*, statement of claim, paras 134–162.

therefore be held to be indicative for corporations. Nevertheless, and despite the use of these targets as indicators of materiality, the assessment focuses more on other, stronger indicators, such as the scaling of contributions and comparisons within different peer groups.

The assessment of materiality in the multinational corporative sector generally harbours an increased risk and potential of distortion as well as hindsight bias. Given the transnational activities of large corporations it is often not unambiguously determinable to which entity the emissions should ultimately be attributed to. Another factors rests within the handling of scope 3 emissions. It is thus of uttermost importance that courts and the respective parties transparently disclose which kind of attributive component they refer to. The previously conducted analysis of climate change cases, however, has widely shown that courts tend to attribute scope 3 emissions increasingly to the initial producer rather than to the end consumer of the product.[56]

Multinational corporations are generally among the major emitters on a global scale. Studies, e.g. as it was conducted by *Heede* have shown that it is possible to calculate the specific amount of emissions and its contribution in a comprehensive and scientifically accurate manner.[57] The first indicator, the scientific provability of one's contribution, therefore, generally can be perceived as being fulfilled.[58]

As briefly mentioned above, the ratio to national and international mitigation targets acts primarily as an indicator of materiality in relation to states, but can also be consulted in cases where the contribution is part of a delimited legal framework, such as the EU ETS or other similar emission trading schemes. Coincidingly, reference can be taken in cases in which the national or regional legislator has set strict mitigation targets, preferable in a sector-specific manner. Under the inclusion of scope 3 emissions, the failing of mitigation targets can generally function as an indication of materiality, the compliance with or even the over-performance of such goals concurrently as indication of immateriality. In contrast to the indication given by this group in relation to states, the results achieved within this respective assessment carry greater evaluative value, given that the targets are generally not set by the same actor, meaning corporations, but by states themselves. Nevertheless, the ratio to mitigation targets still should not be applied as the sole indication of materiality, but should always be approached under the concurrence with other factors.

Such indicators are for example provided by the third and fourth group, which ultimately can also be considered the most important and decisive ones in relation to multinational and transnational corporations. The scaling process as the third indicator hereby is strongly connected to the fourth, which consists in the formation of comparative groups. Both indicators provide means to combat the distortion of results by using different comparatives and concurrently mitigates the risk of

[56] See in this regard Sect. 3.4.3.3.4.

[57] See e.g. Heede (2014).

[58] See in this regard Sect. 6.2.1.1.1. On a more general note see Chap. 4.

hindsight bias. Especially in regard to the scaling process special attention has to be paid on the way in which the indicator is applied and hence the attribution of emissions and further contributions is conducted. A distortion can easily be achieved by relying on different attributive references, as it is for example the case with the divergence in terrestrial or consumption-based emissions.[59] It is thus imperative to either set a standard beforehand, or, and arguably most preferable, depict the results of both attributive methods to achieve the most comprehensive overview of the impacts of corporative contributions.

Even more important than the specific scaling of the emissions is the formation of different comparative groupings. The most comprehensive one hereby rests in a sector-specific comparison based on the six prominent and commonly used emission-intensive sectors: energy systems, industry, transport, buildings and urban systems, as well as AFOLU.[60] The more indicators are used and the more comparatives are collected, the better courts can assess and evaluate the individual materiality of the action or omission in question.

To provide a further application-oriented perspective on the usage and utility of indicators for assessing the materiality of corporate actions or omissions, the case of *Luciano Lliuya v. RWE AG* can again be referred to as an example.[61] In the present case, it is scientifically proven that the RWE AG is responsible for 0.47% of the global greenhouse gas emissions between 1751 and 2010.[62] The first indicator of materiality, which consists of the scientific verifiability of the contribution and the factual causal chain, is thus provided and accordingly evidenced by both, *Heede's* study and *Stuart-Smith et al.*'s analysis.[63]

RWE, as a German multinational corporation is part of the EU ETS and thus underlies special delimiting structures in their emission of CO_2. The annual reduction in the number of free CO_2 emission allowances is therefore intended to have a steering effect on emission reductions. This factor can be used as an indicator of materiality, i.e. the extent to which the company had to purchase additional allowances, or as an indicator of immateriality, i.e. the extent to which the company had the opportunity to sell the remnants.[64] RWE AG received free allowances in the amount of 1.1 million t CO_2 in 2020.[65] However, according to the company's own figures, actual CO_2 emissions in 2020 amounted to 68.9 million t, which left 66.2 million t CO_2 uncovered by the certificates attributed to RWE by the EU

---

[59] See in this regard Sect. 5.4.2.3.1.3.4.

[60] See e.g. IPCC (2022). This is also done by the German Climate Act.

[61] Essen Regional Court, 15 December 2016 – 2 O 285/15, *Luciano Lliuya v. RWE AG*, Higher Regional Court Hamm, pending – 5 U 15/17, *Luciano Lliuya v. RWE AG*.

[62] Heede (2014), pp. 22, 27, 29.

[63] Ibid., Stuart-Smith et al. (2021), p. 85.

[64] This immediately raises the question of the extent to which a company can be held legally responsible for emissions if those emissions are still below the permitted limit, in this case the allocated allowances. Even if this is a legitimate question, it is not a problem of causality, but rather a general fact or justification outside normative causality.

[65] Pawlik (2024c).

ETS.[66] Such a large difference between the freely allocated allowances and the actual amount of CO_2 produced provides a strong indication of the materiality of the company's contribution.

Additionally and even of greater weight is the assessment of RWE AG's emissions in light of other comparable groups and the scaling of the corporations global emissions to a national and sectoral level. Especially the latter shows the extent of RWE AG's contribution in the current case. Although 0.47% of overall, global greenhouse gas emissions between 1751 and 2010 might initially not seem substantial, they result in a proportion of 14.06% of overall German GHG emissions between the years 1990 and 2014.[67] In the same time span, the global ratio of RWE's contribution resulted in 0.45% of the global emissions. This result is reinforced when the contribution is broken down even further. Looking at 2013 alone, RWE AG's emissions accounted for around 21.95% of Germany's total greenhouse gas emission. Five years later in 2018 and with respect to CO_2 emissions specifically, the RWE AG still contributed 16.6% to the overall CO_2 emissions of Germany.[68] If the CO_2 emissions of RWE AG are taken as a basis and offset against the total CO_2 equivalent emissions of the energy sector in Germany, RWE AG is still responsible for 40.5% of the sectoral emissions in 2018, although the sectoral emissions also include CO_2 equivalents, which ultimately leads to an even higher share of sectoral emissions for the specific contributor.[69] With the energy industry being the biggest sector-specific emitter in Germany, the sector accounted for around 217.9 million t CO_{2eq} in 2020 which makes up for around 29.8% of the overall German greenhouse gas equivalents in the same year.[70] The comparison thus shows that the RWE AG is one of the largest emitters not only in terms of its sectoral share but also on a national level, which gives a strong indication towards the materiality of its contribution. As one of the greatest emitters in Germany, it is no longer tenable to argue that the overall share of emissions is too small to be legally relevant and carry any legal blameworthiness. In the context of climate justice in general, it is the contribution of such multinational corporations that needs to be considered and ultimately declared material in litigation on climate change and its impacts.

6.2.1.3 Individuals

The assessment of normative causation in light of individuals is, in comparison to states and even with regard to multinational corporations, prone by a strong shift of the underlying normative principles. The focus no longer rests on the standards of

---

[66] RWE AG (2020), p. 14.

[67] Essen Regional Court, 15 December 2016 – 2 O 285/15, *Luciano Lliuya v. RWE AG*, statement of claim, 19 (23 November 2015), Heede (2014).

[68] Pawlik (2024a, b).

[69] Umweltbundesamt (2023).

[70] Ibid.

international environmental law, which are generally not binding on individuals, but rather on the principles of climate justice, fairness and equity.[71] These principles are given great weight and, concurrently, are also reflected in the results of the application of other normative doctrines.

Nevertheless, individuals constitute the smallest number of relevant actors within climate change litigation in general and its causal assessment in specific. This mainly originates from the fact that the actions or omissions of individuals in climate-relevant positions are often attributed to higher-level state or corporative actors and not to their private sphere.[72] Given that for this scope of application the actor-specific group of individuals refers exclusively to their private sphere, the group of cases is still relatively limited at this point in time. With individuals commonly also belonging to the smallest emitters, this actor-specific group largely falls under the climate change radar.

6.2.1.3.1 Foreseeability

Within the foreseeability of climate change and its respective impacts, the assessment generally coincides with the foreseeability threshold applied to other private entities. Unlike in the case of corporations, the threshold, however, is strongly dependent on the public sphere and the accessibility of information, rather than on the specific knowledge of the individual. Nevertheless, specific knowledge may come into play for individuals, especially in cases where the individual occupies an important position or is a figure of public interest and therefore had special access to information that had been withheld or not largely shared with the common public. However, such cases are only of minor importance, as they are to be regarded as truly exceptional and are furthermore very difficult to prove. Actions and omission of individuals in this regard are also often attributed to the superior organisation rather than to their private sphere. With the growing public awareness of the climate crisis and the accompanying media attention and coverage, the year 1990 functions as the general threshold of foreseeability for individuals which concurs with the threshold for corporations.[73] With the growing media attention and also enhanced by a growing group of climate change cases pushing to the forefront of public attention, 2015 furthermore forms the benchmark of specific foreseeability for individuals.[74]

Based on considerations of climate justice, individuals constitute the actor-specific group that is to be approached most restrictively when it comes to setting

[71] Exceptions are nevertheless possible under the premise of national legislation.

[72] Occasionally, the attribution may well lead to difficulties. This is particularly the case when individuals have a great deal of regulatory influence. See e.g. in the case International Criminal Court, pending – n/a, *The Planet v. Bolsonaro*. However, the question of attribution must be considered separately from the question of causation.

[73] See in this regard Sect. 5.3.2.3.1.2.

[74] See in this regard Sect. 5.3.2.3.2.1.

a foreseeability threshold. Since the universal standard for assessing foreseeability is the reasonable rather than the optimal observer, it is quite conceivable that there are still some types of specific climate impacts that cannot be perceived as foreseeable by individuals without their acquisition of individual knowledge.[75] Moreover, without the help of temporarily shifting legal principles such as the precautionary principle, individuals cannot be expected to foresee all future impacts of climate change. This would also be contradictory to general principles of justice and fairness. In the midst of the flood of information provided by the media, including a large number of scientifically incorrect facts, individuals cannot be expected to display the same knowledge and ultimately foresight as it is the case with actors that can fall back on large resources and are thus able to not only obtain but also to dissect information more comprehensively. In cases of doubt, the threshold, therefore, needs to be set higher and thus more actor-friendly.

6.2.1.3.2 Materiality

Assessing materiality in regard to individuals greatly diverges from states and corporations. The difference hereby arises under the influence of overall justice considerations. Given that every human being necessarily is of a GHG-positive nature, and ultimately is dependent on emitting, normativity and the therein entailed notions demand that the materiality of one's contribution does not extend to emissions that are per se necessary for its general being and daily life. Materiality is therefore to be denied for indispensable and vital contributions to climate change. This leads to the test of materiality for individuals being reduced in a most restrictive way to a mere test of gross exceedance. Only in exceptional cases can materiality be affirmed for individuals. In such instances, indicators can again prove to be a valuable basis for the determination of materiality.

Under the prerequisite of having a scientific provable action or omission, it is especially the establishment of different comparative groupings that is decisive for the evaluation of materiality in regard to individuals. Coinciding with the second indicator, the comparison of the alleged action or omission with a country's average per capita budget is one of the many possible comparative indicators that should be taken into account by courts in their assessment of materiality. Other comparative indicators are, in a downscaled approach, the average emissions within specific social groups, the contribution in comparison with the GDP, the consumption-based emissions and, in an upscaled approach, the comparison with other countries, groups of countries or even the global average of the per capita budget.

Based on the average per capita budget of Germany, the assessment of an indicator-based materiality could exemplarily lead to the following elaborations:

The average per capita consumption amounted to 7.716 t CO_2 per capita in Germany in 2020.[76] Under an upscaling approach, the individual contribution can

[75] See in this regard Sect. 5.3.2.1.2.

[76] Crippa (2021), p. 114.

thus be compared with the average EU-wide budget, which constituted 5.5 t CO_2 per capita in 2020.[77] On an even broader account, the average worldwide per capita amount of CO_2 emission resulted in 4.5 t CO_2 emissions per capita.[78] The average German per capita budget thus resides over the budgets within its comparable setting. Whether this indication suffices for the affirmation of materiality lies at the discretion of the courts. Under the influence of considerations of climate justice, this book makes a strong case against the materiality of contributions by individuals that still reside within the emissions bound to everyday life.

6.2.2 *Area of Law and the Subject of Action*

Besides an actor-specific differentiation it is especially the area of law and the subject of action that apply a different rationale and thus put different demands and requirements on the assessment and the evaluation of normative causation. Depending on the area of law and the subject of action, different values are given more or less weight, which may well change the account of normativity applied in the respective case. Decisive hereby is especially the nature and the underlying purpose of the legal thought which transpires ultimately to the mere ratio of the legal action. Differentiations within the assessment of normative causation in climate change litigation are restricted to areas in which courts are granted a certain discretion. It, thus, is not able to alter the general standard of the right observer concerning the notion of foreseeability, or even the influence of intervening causes in general.[79] Notions of normative causation that are, however, influenced by the area of law and the subject of action especially reside within the evaluation of indicators in the assessment of materiality and the weight that is given to specific normative principles within general theories of normative causation such as the theory of adequacy and the theory of proximate cause.[80] Highly influenced and strongly connected with the area of law and the subject of action is furthermore the protective scope of the norm. This normative principle is hereby strongly dependent on both of the differing characteristics which makes it a comprehensive point of reference for the inclusion and difference within normative causation.[81]

The differentiation within the area of law and the subject of action strongly grounds itself on the normative principles that underly the legal assessment of normative causation in the first place.[82] Cases in which the claimant seeks redress for wrongful conduct or omissions and which are thus strongly grounded in liability

[77] DC: World Resources Institute (2022).

[78] Ritchie et al. (2024a).

[79] See in this regard Sects. 5.3.2.1 and 5.5.

[80] See in this regard Sects. 5.6 and 5.7.

[81] See in this regard Sect. 5.8.

[82] See in this regard Sects. 5.1 and 5.2.

provisions and often lay within the sphere of tort or criminal law, for example, carry a strong corrective component. This corrective dimension which is entailed in the mere nature and purpose of the action and the areas of law, enlightens the weight and the relevance that is put on corrective accounts of normative causation, which are entailed in principles such as the corrective justice component of climate justice or the environmental polluter pays principle. In light of their increased influence, the room of discretion incumbent on courts might be filled in different ways. The strengthened emphasis on the corrective dimension thus might lead towards a stronger perception of materiality, with courts already accepting smaller contributions as material as it would be the case in other areas of law.

The counterpart to the enhanced focus on the corrective component is formed by lawsuits located in areas of law in which the subject of action focuses more on obligation and rights-based claims, which is the case for example in regard to human and fundamental rights. It is here that the distributive component of climate justice comes increasingly into play and shifts the evaluation within the courts discretion. Affected hereby is again the assessment of materiality as it fundamentally carries a strong evaluative component that needs to be filled out by the discretion of the courts. Based on the enhanced distributive aspect of such areas of law and subjects of action, it is especially the principle of common but differentiated responsibilities that finds entrance into the evaluation of obligation- and rights-orientated lawsuits.

Not as affected as the assessment of materiality is the evaluation of foreseeability given that the standard of the observer in light of its reasonableness has been set universally and independent of the area of law or the subject of action.[83] This is also the case within areas of law in which its rationale and nature rests upon a corrective dimension. Room for differentiation, however, lies within the implementation of special knowledge as this factor, again, rests within the discretion of the court.[84] Here, courts might impose different standards on the soundness and the proof in general, depending on the area of law in which the lawsuit is being brought.

6.3 Summary of Findings

The foregoing elaborations have shown that climatic causation can and necessarily needs to be approached differently depending not only on the jurisdiction in which the lawsuit is being brought, but also on the specific area of law, subject of action and the actor involved. Concurrent with the general assessment of causation in climate change litigation, and with reference to the bifurcated understanding of causation, the concept that is most variable in this regard is the determination of normative causation. Given that normative causation is most susceptible to different approaches and heavily influenced by normative principles, which in turn are

[83] See for the assessment of the standard of the observer Sect. 5.3.2.1.1.

[84] See in this regard inter alia Sect. 5.3.2.1.3.

interpreted and applied differently depending on the cultural, social and political background of the respective jurisdiction, normative causation also alters in light of the influence of external legal factors. Variations may therefore lead to the application of different normative theories and doctrines per se, to different weightings of the importance of different normative accounts within a single doctrine, and ultimately to divergent outcomes within a single normative principle. The latter refers in particular to the scope of discretion involved in the assessment of the respective principles. With regard to the foreseeability of the outcome, this refers in particular to the standard of reasonableness, which varies greatly depending on the specific actor, and the inclusion of individual knowledge. With regard to the assessment of materiality, normativity essentially leads to a differentiation in the application and weighting of different indicators. In addition to actor-specific differentiation, divergences at the level of normative causation also include the area of law. As the rationale of different areas and subject matters diverge considerably, so do the normative principles that influence and ultimately underpin the determination of normative climatic causation, which in turn leads to divergent outcomes, again within the scope of discretion that courts generally obtain in their assessment of causation.

Factual causation, on the other hand, is not as variable and thus different as the normative determination of causation in the law, and differs only in terms of the jurisdiction in which the lawsuit is brought. Given the different legal traditions and the different role of the courts in relation to their law-making function, common law jurisdictions are considered to be better suited to applying a multi-causal conception of causation, leading to the contribution-based approach as the most promising account of climatic causation in these jurisdictions. Civil law jurisdictions, on the other hand, again because of their legal tradition, are more tied to traditional causation accounts, which makes them more inclined to approach climatic causation in a merely adapted way, rather than resorting to an entirely new conception of causation. Even if newer conceptions are ultimately preferable on a general and universal level, based on the arguments presented above, it is the strategy of factual concretization within counterfactual causation that provides a facilitating approach to causation within climate change litigation in these jurisdictions.

Climate Change Cases

Daniel Billy et al. v. Australia (Torres Strait Islanders Petition) – United Nations Human Rights Committee, 22 September 2022 – CCPR/C/135/D/3624/2019

Friends of the Irish Environment v. The Government of Ireland – Supreme Court of Ireland, 31 July 2020 – 205/19

Luciano Lliuya v. RWE AG – Essen Regional Court, 15 December 2016 – 2 O 285/15

Luciano Lliuya v. RWE AG – Higher Regional Court Hamm, pending – 5 U 15/17

Milieudefensie et al. v. Royal Dutch Shell plc. – Hague District Court, 26 May 2021 – C/09/571932/HA ZA 19-379
Minister for the Environment v. Sharma – Federal Court of Australia, 15 March 2022 – [2022] FCAFC 35
Native Village of Kivalina v. ExxonMobil Corp. – US District Court for the Northern District of California, 30 September 2009 – 4:08-cv-01138-SBA
Neubauer et al. v. Germany – Germany Federal Constitutional Court, 24 March 2021 – 1 BvR 2656/18 – 1 BvR 78/20 – 1 BvR 96/20 – 1 BvR 288/20
The Planet v. Bolsonaro – International Criminal Court, pending – n/a
Urgenda Foundation v. The State of The Netherlands – Supreme Court of the Netherlands, 20 December 2019 – 19/00135

References

DC: World Resources Institute (2022) Climate watch historical country greenhouse gas emissions data. Available via Climate Watch Data. https://www.climatewatchdata.org/ghg-emissions. Accessed 24 Oct 2024
Crippa M, Guizzardi D, Solazzo E, Muntean M, Schaaf E, Monforti-Ferrario F, Banja M, Olivier J G J, Grassi G, Rossi S, Vignati E (2021) GHG emissions of all world countries – 2021 report, EUR 30831 EN, Publications Office of the European Union, Luxembourg
Heede R (2014) Carbon majors: accounting for carbon and methane emissions 1854-2010 methods & results report. Lambert Academic Publishing, London
IPCC (1992a) Climate change: the 1990 and 1992 IPCC assessments. Canada
IPCC (1992b) First assessment report overview and policymaker summaries and 1992 IPCC supplement. Canada
IPCC (2022) Climate change 2022: mitigation of climate change – Contribution of Working Group III to the Sixth Assessment Report of the Intergovernmental Panel on Climate Change. Geneva
Nedelcu P, Schäferling S (2022) The act on corporate due diligence obligations in supply chains – an examination of the German approach to business and human rights. German Yearb Int Law 64(1):443–457
Organisation for Economic Co-operation and Development (2023) Guidelines for multinational enterprises on responsible business conduct. Geneva
Pawlik V (2024a) Höhe der CO_2-Emissionen in Deutschland in den Jahren 1990 bis 2022 (in Millionen Tonnen). Available via Statista. https://de.statista.com/statistik/daten/studie/2275/umfrage/hoehe-der-co2-emissionen-in-deutschland-seit-1990/?msclkid=034dbe5283191eb5b20cdad1df6699bf. Accessed 24 Oct 2024
Pawlik V (2024b) Kohlenstoffdioxid-Emissionen ausgewählter Dax-Konzerne im Jahr 2018 (in Millionen Tonnen). Available via Statista. https://de.statista.com/statistik/daten/studie/1090030/umfrage/co2-emissionen-ausgewaehlter-dax-konzerne/. Accessed 24 Oct 2024
Pawlik V (2024c) Menge der kostenlos zugeteilten CO_2-Zertifikate der RWE AG in den Jahren 2010 bis 2020 (in Millionen Tonnen CO_2). Available via Statista. https://de.statista.com/statistik/daten/studie/254083/umfrage/kostenlos-zugeteilte-co2-zertifikate-der-rwe-ag/. Accessed 24 Oct 2024
Ritchie H, Rosado P, Roser M (2024a) Per capita CO_2 emissions. Available via Our World in Data. https://ourworldindata.org/grapher/co-emissions-per-capita?tab=table. Accessed 24 Oct 2024
Ritchie H, Rosado P, Roser M (2024b) Share of global CO_2 emissions. Available via Our World in Data. https://ourworldindata.org/grapher/annual-share-of-co2-emissions. Accessed 24 Oct 2024
RWE AG (2020) Nichtfinanzieller Bericht 2020

Stuart-Smith RF, Roe GH, Li S, Allen MR (2021) Increased Outburst Flood Hazard from Lake Palcacocha due to Human-Induced Glacier Retreat. Nat Geosci 14(2):85–90

Tietje C (2014) Die juristische Person des Privatrechts im Völker- und Wirtschaftsrecht. In: Delbrück JUH, Odendahl K, Matz-Lück N, von Arnould A (eds) Aus Kiel in the Welt: Kiel's contribution to international law – essays in honour of the 100th anniversary of the Walther Schücking Institute for International Law. Duncker & Humblot, Berlin, pp 671–691

Umweltbundesamt (2023) Indicator: greenhouse gas emissions. Available via Umweltbundesamt. https://www.umweltbundesamt.de/en/data/environmental-indicators/indicator-greenhouse-gas-emissions#at-a-glance. Accessed 24 Oct 2024

United Nations Conference on the Human Environment (1972) Report of the conference Stockholm, 5-16 June 1972, A/CONF.48/14/Rev.1

Vereinbarung zwischen der Regierung der Bundesrepublik Deutschland und der deutschen Wirtschaft zur Klimavorsorge (2000) 9 November 2000

Verheyen R (2005) Climate change damage and international law – prevention duties and state responsibility. Brill, Leiden

Voigt C (2008) State responsibility for climate change damages. Nord J Int Law 77(1-2):1–22

List of Instruments

Regional and International Instruments

2000 Millennium Declaration	United Nations Millennium Declaration of 18 September 2000, A/RES/55/2
ACHR	American Convention on Human Rights of 22 November 1969, entered into force 18 July 1978, 1144 UNTS 123
Agenda 2030	Transforming our World: The 2030 Agenda for Sustainable Development of 25 September 2015, A/RES/70/1
Arab CHR	Arab Charter on Human Rights of 22 May 2004, entered into force 15 March 2008
Banjul Charter	African Charter on Human and Peoples' Rights of 27 June 1981, entered into force 21 October 1986, OAU Doc. CAB/LEG/67/3 rev. 5, 21 I.L.M. 58 (1982)
Brundtland Report	Report of the World Commission on Environment and Development: Our Common Future of 4 August 1987, Annex to document A/42/427
Cancun Agreements	Outcome of the work of the Ad Hoc Working Group on Long-term Cooperative Action under the Convention, 1/CP.16, as part of the Report of the Conference of the Parties on its sixteenth session, held in Cancun from 29 November to 10 December 2010 of 15 March 2011, FCCC/CP/2010/7/Add. 1

M. Krakau, *Causation in National and International Climate Change Litigation*,
https://doi.org/10.1007/978-3-031-74693-2

CFR	Charter of Fundamental Rights of the European Union of 2 October 2000, entered into force 1 December 2009, 2000/C-364/01
Directive 2004/35	Directive of the European Parliament and of the Council on environmental liability with regard to the prevention and remedying of environmental damage of 21 April 2004, 2004/35/CE, OJ L 143, 30 April 2004, pp. 56–75
Draft Articles on the Prevention of Transboundary Harm	Draft Articles on Prevention of Transboundary Harm from Hazardous Activities of 11 May 2001, Annex to Resolution 62/68 of 6 December 2007
DARS	Draft Articles on Responsibility of States for Internationally Wrongful Acts of 12 July 2001, Annex to Resolution 56/83 of 12 December 2001, corrected by document A/56/49 (Vo. I)/Corr.4
ECHR	Convention for the Protection of Human Rights and Fundamental Freedoms of 4 November 1950, entered into force 3 September 1953, CETS No. 5
FCCC	United Nations Framework Convention on Climate Change of 9 May 1992, entered into force 21 March 1994, 1771 UNTS 107
Guiding Principles on Business and Human Rights	United Nations Guiding Principles on Business and Human Rights, Annex to the Report of the Special Representative of the Secretary-General on the Issue of Human Rights and Transnational Corporations and other Business Enterprises, A/HRC/17/31, endorsed by the Human Rights Council in Resolution 17/4 (16 June 2011)
ICCPR	International Covenant on Civil and Political Rights of 16 December 1966, entered into force 23 March 1976, 999 UNTS 171
ICJ Statute	Statute of the International Court of Justice of 26 June 1945, entered into force 24 October 1945, 33 UNTS 993
ICTR Statute	Statute of the International Tribunal for Rwanda, Annex to Resolution S/RES/955 (8 November 1994)
ICTY Statute	Statute of the International Tribunal for the former Yugoslavia, Annex to Resolution S/RES/827 (25 May 1993)

Kyoto Protocol	Kyoto Protocol to the United Nations Framework Convention on Climate Change of 11 December 1997, entered into force 16 February 2005, 2303 UNTS 148
London Protocol	Protocol to the Convention on the Prevention of Marine Pollution by Dumping of Wastes and Other Matter 1972 of 17 November 1996 entered into force 24 March 2006
Paris Agreement	Agreement of 12 December 2015, Annex to Decision 1/CP.12, Doc. FCCC/CP/2015/10/ Add.1 (29 January 2016) entered into force 4 November 2016, ILM 55 (2016) 743
Resolution 7/23	Resolution on Human Rights and Climate Change of 28 March 2008, Human Rights Council, A/HRC/RES/7/23
Resolution 71/644	Report of the open-ended intergovernmental expert working group on indicators and terminology relating to disaster risk reduction of 1 December 2016, A/71/644
Resolution 77/276	Request for an Advisory Opinion of the International Court of Justice on the Obligations of States in respect of Climate Change of 29 March 2023, A/RES/77/276
Rio Declaration	Declaration of the UN Conference on Environment and Development 3-14 June 1992, A/CONF.151/26 (Vol.1) (12 August 1992), ILM 31 (1992) 876
Rome Statute	Rome Statute of the International Criminal Court of 17 July 1998, entered into force 1 July 2002, 2187 UNTS 90
Sendai Framework	Sendai Framework for Disaster Risk Reduction 2015 2030, Annex II to Resolution A/RES/69/ 283 (23 June 2015)
Stockholm Declaration	Declaration of the United Nations Conference on the Human Environment 5–16 June 1972, A/RES/27/2994 (15 December 1972)
TFEU	Treaty on the Functioning of the European Union of 25 March 1957, entered into force 1 January 1958, in its consolidated version C 326/49
UNCLOS	United Nations Convention on the Law of the Sea of 10 December 1982, entered into force 16 November 1994, 1833 UNTS 397

UNSDG	United Nations Sustainable Development Goals, Transforming our world: the 2030 Agenda for Sustainable Development of 25 September 2015, A/RES/70/1
VCLT	Vienna Convention on the Law of Treaties 23 May 1969, entered into force 27 January 1980, 1155 UNTS 331

Domestic Instruments

Bolivia

Ley de Derechos de la Madre Tierra	Ley de Derechos de la Madre Tierra of 21 December 2010, Law 071
Ley Marco de la Madre Tierra y Desarrollo Integral para Vivir Bien	Ley Marco de la Madre Tierra y Desarrollo Integral para Vivir Bien of 15 October 2012, Law 300

Bulgaria

Obligations and Contracts Act	Obligations and Contracts Act of 2, 3, January 1950, entered into force 1 January 1951, No. 275/22.11.1950

Canada

Charter	Charter of Rights and Freedoms (*Charte canadienne des droits et libertés*), entered into force 17 April 1982

Denmark

Liability for Damages Act	Liability for Damages Act of 4 September 2002, entered into force 20 September 2005, No. 885

France

Law on the duty of vigilance	Law on the duty of vigilance (*Loi de vigilance*), entered into force 27 March 2017, No. 2017-399

Germany

Civil Code	Civil Code of Germany (*Bürgerliches Gesetzbuch*) of 18 August 1896, entered into force 1 January 1900, RGBl. 1896 p. 195
Climate Act	Climate Protection Act (*Bundesklimaschutzgesetz*) of 12 December 2019, entered into force 18 December 2019, BGBl. 2019 p. 2513
Constitution	Basic Law for the Federal Republic of Germany (*Grundgesetz für die Bundesrepublik Deutschland*) of 23 May 1949, entered into force 24 May 1949, BGBl. 1949 p. 1
Environmental Liability Act	Environmental Liability Act (*Umwelthaftungsgesetz*) of 10 December 1990, BGBl. I S. 2634
Nature Conservation Act	Nature Conservation Act (*Bundesnaturschutzgesetz -BNatSchG*) of 29 July 2009, BGBl. I S. 2542
Penal Code	Penal Code (*Strafgesetzbuch*) of 15 May 1871, entered into force 1 January 1972, RGbl. 1972 p. 127
Supply Chain Act	Supply Chain Act (*Gesetz über unternehmerische Sorgfaltspflichten in Lieferketten (Lieferkettensorgfaltspflichtgesetz LkSG)*) of 16 July 2021, entered into force 1 January 2023, BGBl. Nr. 46 pp. 2959–2969

New Zealand

RMA	Resource Management Act of 1991, royal assent 22 July 1991, entered into force 1 October 1991, 1991 No 69
Te Awa Tupua Act	Te Awa Tupua (Whanganui River Claims Settlement) Act, royal assent 20 March 2017, 2017 No 7

Nigeria

Constitution	Constitution of the Federal Republic of Nigeria of 5 May 1999, No. 24

Portugal

Constitution	Constitution of Portugal (*Constituição da República Portuguesa*) of 2 April 1976, entered into force 25 April 1976

United Kingdom

Compensation Act	Compensation Act of the United Kingdom, entered into force 26 July 2006, 2006 c 29

United States

Constitution	Constitution of the United States of 17 September 1787, entered into force 4 March 1789

Appendices

Annex I: German Summary

Die Herstellung eines stringenten Kausalzusammenhangs zwischen einer Handlung oder einem Unterlassen und einem spezifischen Ereignis beschäftigt die Rechtswissenschaft seit jeher. An der Schnittstelle von Philosophie, Naturwissenschaft und dem Recht, sehen sich sowohl Wissenschaftler als auch Praktiker im Lichte neuer globaler Herausforderungen ein ums andere Mal mit der Frage nach der richtigen Kausalitätsdeterminierung konfrontiert. Eine solche neue Herausforderung ist mit Rücksicht auf ein zunehmendes Bewusstsein für das Klima, dessen Wandel und die damit steigende Anzahl an sogenannten Klimaklagen auch in rechtlicher Sicht der Kausalitätsbegründung erwachsen.[1] Dabei stellen sich innerhalb der Klimathematik nicht nur die traditionellen Dilemmata bzgl. der rechtswissenschaftlichen Begründung von Kausalität, vielmehr begründet die Komplexität des Klimasystems, die lange temporale Ursachenverkettung und die dem zugrunde liegenden normativen und moralischen Determinanten neue Herausforderungen für die Kausalität im Recht.[2] Demzufolge führte die erhebliche Schwierigkeit der Kausalitätsherstellung bereits innerhalb zahlreicher Gerichtsentscheidungen zu der Verneinung klimatischer Kausalität.[3] Entscheidend waren hierbei gleichlaufend Argumente wie der Einfluss natürlicher Klimaschwankungen als eingreifende, intervenierende und überholende Ursachen, die bereits erwähnte Komplexität naturwissenschaftlicher Prozesse und die große

---

[1] Eine ausführliche Darstellung des Inhalts und der Geschichte der Metaphysik findet sich unter *van* Inwagen et al. (2023). Siehe darüber hinaus Kapitel 3.1.1. und Kapitel 4.

[2] Der IPCC stellt einen Anstieg der Treibhausgasemissionen in der Atmosphäre seit dem Jahr 1750 fest. IPCC (2021), 4, A.1.1.

[3] US District Court for the Northern District of California, 30 September 2009 – 4:08-cv-01138-SBA, *Native Village of Kivalina v. ExxonMobil Corp.*, 20, paras 17–19. Ähnlich auch Essen Regional Court, 15 December 2016 – 2 O 285/15, *Luciano Lliuya v. RWE AG*, paras 41–47.

M. Krakau, *Causation in National and International Climate Change Litigation*,
https://doi.org/10.1007/978-3-031-74693-2

Anzahl konkurrierender Beiträge zum Klimawandel.[4] Darüber hinaus scheiterte weitgehend die Anwendung traditioneller Kausalitätstheorien, was wiederum dazu führte, dass diese zum Teil als grundlegend nicht geeignet für die Anwendung innerhalb klimatischer Sachverhalte tituliert wurden.[5] Dabei wiegt der Vorwurf der Kritik jedoch nicht in der grundsätzlichen Verneinung der Kausalität, sondern vielmehr in der umfassenden Funktionsunfähigkeit traditioneller Kausalitätsdoktrinen im Rahmen von Klimaklagen und mit Bezug auf die klimatische Kausalität.[6] Insbesondere die Diskrepanz zwischen natürlicher Kausalität und faktischer Kausalität im Recht fällt hierbei ins Gewicht. Der Kern der Problematik liegt daher in der Dissoziation zwischen naturwissenschaftlicher und insbesondere klimawissenschaftlichen Erkenntnissen und Erkenntnisfindung, sozio-moralischem Rechtsempfinden und der Umsetzung beider Konstrukte in das Recht.

Ziel dieser Arbeit ist es einen Lösungsansatz für die Divergenz zwischen tatsächlichem Kausalitätsbestehen und dessen Transkription ins Recht zu finden. Dabei geht es nicht darum, eine detaillierte Analyse eines bestimmten nationalen Kausalitätsansatzes vorzunehmen, vielmehr liegt der Schwerpunkt in der Erarbeitung eines allgemeinen Ansatzes welcher sich je nach Jurisdiktion und nationaler Besonderheiten auf die spezifischen Begebenheiten anpassen lässt. Dies ist insbesondere deshalb möglich und gar geboten, da sich die grundlegenden Probleme welche der Klimawandel und die Klimathematik für die Kausalitätsherstellung bereit hält aufgrund dessen globalen Charakters nicht innerhalb verschiedener Rechtssysteme unterscheiden.[7]

Auch die unterschiedliche Methodiken und Herangehensweisen wie Gerichte in verschiedenen Jurisdiktionen Kausalzusammenhänge feststellen und begründen steht einem aus einer globalen Perspektive entwickelten Ansatz nicht entgegen. In dem Vergleich und der Übertragung von Ansätzen liegt dagegen eine fundierte Chance der Weiterentwicklung des Rechts. Unterstützt wird ein solcher Ansatz durch die wachsende und durchaus sichtbare Bereitschaft der Gerichte, in Klimafragen auf Ergebnisse und Methoden anderer Rechtsordnungen zurückzugreifen. Monozentrische Ansätze hindern hierbei erheblich, zumal der

---

[4] Siehe u.a. die Argumente der Regierung in *Neubauer et al. v. Germany*, Germany Federal Constitutional Court, 24 March 2021 – 1 BvR 2656/18 – 1 BvR 78/20 – 1 BvR 96/20 – 1 BvR 288/20, *Neubauer et al. v. Germany*, para 89.

[5] Die kontrafaktische Verursachung wird im Allgemeinen als der ‚übliche' Ansatz des Rechts zur Verursachung angesehen. Weitere Erläuterungen zur kontrafaktischen Verursachung finden Sie in Kapitel 2. B. Mit der Ansicht, dass Standardansätze wie der 'but-for'-Test in klimabezogenen Schadensersatzfällen nicht funktionieren, Duffy (2009). Steingart (2021), Nitsch (2021), 446.

[6] Als klimatische Kausalität wird in dieser Arbeit jede Kausalkette verstanden, welche innerhalb eines oder mehrerer Glieder einen Bezug zu dem Klima, dem Klimawandel, oder Klimaschäden aufweist. Dass es sich bei dem Verfahren um eine Klimaklage per se handelt, lässt dabei noch nicht auf das Bestehen klimatischer Kausalität schließen, da Klimaklagen z.T. gänzlich frei von Klimareferenzen in ihrer Kausalkette sein können. Siehe hierzu Kapitel 3.3.2.1.

[7] Siehe hierzu insbesondere Aust (2011), 214. Zitierend Hart and Honoré (1985), 9, Becker (2006), 288, Rigaux (2005), 82–92.

Klimawandel aufgrund seines universellen Charakters globale Anstrengungen erfordert. Selbstverständlich müssen dennoch die grundlegenden Unterschiede gewisser Rechtssysteme mit in die Erwägung mit aufgenommen werden um die Anwendbarkeit der Kausalitätsansätze zu garantieren.[8] Dies gilt insbesondere für die Anpassung traditioneller Tests an die gängigen moralischen und stark kulturell geprägten normativen Konzeptionen von Fairness, Gerechtigkeit, Vorwerfbarkeit und Verantwortung. Dennoch kann diese Arbeit zeigen, dass trotz der Unterschiede innerhalb normativer Doktrinen und Schwerpunkte, sich auch innerhalb dessen bzgl. der Klimathematik gemeinsame Kernelemente herausarbeiten lassen.[9] Prägend für eine gemeinsame Kausalitätsdeterminierung ist zudem die faktische Komponente der Kausalität im Recht, welche sich durch eine weitläufige Kohärenz zwischen verschiedenen Rechtssystemen auszeichnet.

Für die Herangehensweise an die vorliegend aufgeworfene Problematik bedient sich die Arbeit eines starken interdisziplinären Ansatzes, wobei Erkenntnisse der Naturwissenschaft, Philosophie und hierbei insbesondere der Metaphysik und formalen Logik herangezogen werden. Die Tragfähigkeit eines solchen interdisziplinären Ansatzes wird sowohl rechtstheoretisch als auch dogmatisch geprüft und schließlich mit praktischen Erwägungen abgewogen. Grundlegend stützt sich diese Arbeit dabei innerhalb den praktischen Erörterung auf eine zuvor durchgeführte substantielle, sowie empirische Analyse einer großen Anzahl an Klimaklagen. Die gesamte Arbeit ist hierfür in fünf Kapitel gegliedert.

Kapitel 2: Vorbereitende Überlegungen

Kapitel 2 bildet das Fundament der Arbeit indem hierin zunächst die klima-, und naturwissenschaftlichen Grundlagen skizziert werden.[10] Ein Schwerpunkt liegt dabei auf der Erläuterung des anthropogenen Einflusses auf das Klimasystems der Erde, sowie der wissenschaftlich nachgewiesenen Folgen einer Veränderung dessen. Der zweite Teil des Kapitels legt daran anschließend den Fokus bereits auf die juristische Dimension und beleuchtet das Phänomen der Klimaklagen. Ein zentraler Baustein bildet dabei die Definierung der Prozesskategorie ‚Klimaklagen', welche sich innerhalb dieser Arbeit danach wie folgt beschreiben lassen:

"All cases before national, regional and international judicial, quasi-judicial or administrative bodies in which a party directly raises an issue of law or fact or is demonstrably motivated by the substance of the climate, climate change or climate science."[11]

---

[8] Siehe hierzu insbesondere die in Kapitel 6 vorgenommenen Unterscheidungen.

[9] Siehe hierzu insbesondere bzgl. der Vorhersehbarkeit und Wesentlichkeit in Kapitel 5.3, 5.4.

[10] Siehe Kapitel 2.1.

[11] Dt. wohl *„alle Fälle vor nationalen, regionalen und internationalen gerichtlichen, gerichtsähnlichen oder administrativen Instanzen, in denen eine Partei direkt eine Rechts- oder*

Auf Basis dieser Definition gewährt das Kapitel daraufhin Einblicke in die grundlegenden Parameter von Klimaklagen und zeigt dabei aktuelle Entwicklungen auf.[12] Dabei zeigt sich, dass sich die Entwicklung von Klimaklagen grundsätzlich in drei große Klagewellen einteilen lässt, die sich sowohl hinsichtlich der beteiligten Parteien als auch hinsichtlich der Klagegegenstände und Rechtsbereiche unterscheiden. Darüber hinaus wird offensichtlich, dass mit steigendem öffentlichem Interesse und Bewusstsein für die negativen Folgen des Klimawandels auch die Anzahl der Gerichtsverfahren deutlich zunimmt.

Kapitel 3: Kausalität innerhalb von Gerichtsverfahren zum Klimawandel

Kapitel 3 begründet daran anschließend die Beschäftigung mit der Kausalitätsthematik indem zunächst die Grundsätze der Kausalität im Recht abgesteckt werden. Von elementarer Bedeutung ist hierfür zunächst die Erläuterung der generellen Funktion der Kausalität im Recht, welche sich insbesondere, aber nicht ausschließlich, durch die Brückenfunktion zum tatsächlichen Sein und der dadurch zu schaffenden Rechtssicherheit erschließen lässt.[13] Eine weitere fundamentale Weichenstellung erfolgt daraufhin durch die Argumentation für ein zweistufiges Kausalitätsverständis, bestehend aus einer faktischen und einer normativen Komponente.[14] Dabei bildet die faktische Kausalitätskomponente den Grundpfeiler der Kausalität im Recht, während die in einem zweiten Schritt normative Kausalität als rechtliches Korrektivinstrument die Ergebnisse in Kohärenz zu gesellschaftlichen und sozialen Normen stellt. Die Wesentlichkeit dieser Erkenntnis wird daraufhin auch durch die Analyse nationaler und internationaler Kausalitätsansätze bestätigt, welche bzgl. der Zweischrittigkeit übereinstimmen, die grundlegende Konzeption der letztendlichen Kausalitätsdoktrin jedoch insbesondere hinsichtlich regionaler und internationaler Gerichte stark abweicht.[15] Ähnliche Verständnisse ergeben sich im Rahmen der faktischen Kausalität jedoch innerhalb nationaler Rechtsordnungen, in welchen kontrafaktische Kausalitätstheorien im Rahmen des but-for Tests und der conditio-sine-qua-non Formel vorherrschen.

Aufgrund des engen Verbundes zwischen naturwissenschaftlichen und rechtlichen Komponenten innerhalb der Klimaklagen ist es zudem geboten einen Augenmerk auf die natur- und klimawissenschaftliche Kausalitätsdeterminierung zu

---

Tatsachenfrage aufwirft oder nachweislich durch das Klima, den Klimawandel oder die Klimawissenschaft motiviert ist" Vgl. Kapitel 2.2.1.

[12] Siehe Kapitel 2.2.2.

[13] Siehe Kapitel 3.1.1.

[14] Siehe Kapitel 3.1.2.

[15] Siehe Kapitel 3.2.

legen. Von grundlegender Bedeutung ist dabei die Attributionswissenschaft (‚attribution science'), die sich speziell mit der wissenschaftlichen Zurechnung menschlichen Handelns zum Klimawandel und klimawandelbedingten Schäden befasst. In diesem Rahmen erfolgt die Einführung eines deterministischen Modells einer Kausalkette, auf welches im Laufe der Arbeit an zahlreichen Stellen Bezug genommen wird.[16] Unter Verwendung des deterministischen Kausalitätsmodells erfolgt zu dann eine detaillierte Darstellung der spezifischen klimawandelinherenten Probleme im Rahmen der Kausalitätsdeterminierung im Recht.[17] Dabei zeigen sich insbesondere zwei spezifische jedoch stark miteinander zusammenhängende Problembereiche. Zum einen betrifft dies die kumulative Wirkung einzelner Beiträge und Emissionen. Dies wird oftmals unter der Terminologie des drop-in-the-ocean Arguments aufgeführt. Der zweite Problemkreis umspannt die zeitliche Sphäre sowohl des Klimawandels per se, als auch der Verweildauer der Emissionen. Hierunter fällt zum einen die, insbesondere normative Frage nach dem Umgang mit historischen Emissionen, sowie die faktisch begründete Herausforderung langer Kausalketten und dem verzögerten Eintreten von Schäden aufgrund der Trägheit des Klimasystems.[18] Dabei zeigt sich erneut die Divergenz zwischen naturwissenschaftlicher Erkenntnisfindung und rechtswissenschaftlicher Epistemologie.

Als weiteren Baustein schließt das Kapitel mit den Ergebnissen der vorgelagerten Analyse von Klimaentscheidungen in welcher durch die spezifische Analyse von 668 Klimaklagen in empirischer aber auch substantieller Art und Weise der Umgang von Gerichten mit klimatischer Kausalität erforscht wurde.[19] In materieller Hinsicht war hierzu insbesondere die spezifische Verwendung von Kausalitätsdoktrinen auf klimatische Kausalität und deren Ergebnis von großem Interesse. Die Analyse liefert schlussendlich das Fundament für die darauf aufbauende Behandlung und schließlich auch Bewertung spezifischer Ansätze.

Kapitel 4: Faktische Kausalität

Kapitel 4 liefert innerhalb des zweistufigen Kausalitätsverständnisses nunmehr Erörterungen innerhalb des ersten, und somit des faktischen Kausalitätsdeterminanten. Dabei erfolgt zunächst eine allgemeine Grundausrichtung, in welcher insbesondere der Frage nach der Qualifikation und dem Wesen von Unterlassungen und dem Vorkommen allgemeiner faktischer Kausalitätserörterungen im Recht nachgegangen wird.[20] Dass Unterlassungen

[16] Siehe Kapitel 3.3.1.1.
[17] Siehe Kapitel 3.3.2.
[18] Siehe Kapitel 3.3.3.
[19] Siehe Kapitel 3.4.
[20] Siehe Kapitel 4.1.

innerhalb der faktischen Kausalität Ursachen darstellen können und somit neben aktivem Tun Kausalitätsketten begründen, wird in der vorliegenden Arbeit unter Verweis auf eine eindeutige Rechtspraxis bejaht.

Darauf aufbauend schließt sich einer der zentralen Gesichtspunkte der Kausalitätsthematik an, welcher sich in einer detaillierten Auseinandersetzung und Erörterung verschiedener faktischer Kausalitätskonzepte im Recht erstreckt. Diese erwachsen sowohl dem metaphysischen und somit dem theoretischen Diskurs, als auch der Rechtspraxis und finden zum Teil Übertragung aus anderen Disziplinen, wie der Mathematik und der Naturwissenschaften.[21]

Ausgangspunkt der Erörterung unterschiedlicher Kausalitätsdoktrinen ist eine Auseinandersetzung mit dem vorherrschenden Dogma sowohl in ‚civil law‘ Ländern als auch in ‚common law‘ Ländern, welches in einer monokausalen Konzeption kontrafaktischer Effekt-Ursachen Beziehung besteht. Umsetzung findet diese Doktrin durch den weit verbreiteten but-for Test und die conditio-sine-qua-non Formel.[22] Die Anwendung kontrafaktischer Theorien auf die Klimathematik lässt die erheblichen Herausforderungen innerhalb der Kausalitätsdeterminierung aufscheinen, wobei sich zeigt, dass die Kontrafaktizität selbst letztlich als eine der Hauptursachen für die Divergenz zwischen naturwissenschaftlicher und juristischer Kausalität fungiert. Vor diesem Hintergrund ist daher neben einer gänzlichen Abweichung von kontrafaktischen und monokausalen Theorien, auch an eine Anpassung im Wege einer faktischen Konkretisierung zu denken. Die Arbeit zeigt hierbei dass durch eine solche Methodik und unter umsichtiger Anpassung, die faktische Kausalität auf rechtlicher Ebene der natürlichen und tatsächlichen Kausalität angenähert werden kann, ohne jedoch die monokausale Konzeption und die Verwendung notwendiger und hinreichender Bedingungen aufzugeben.[23]

Dennoch offenbaren die Ausführungen, dass im Zuge der Klimathematik monokausale Konzeptionen grundlegend gegen die Ratio und den Gedanken des tatsächlichen Bestehens zahlreicher unterschiedlicher Beiträge arbeiten. Vielmehr sind es multikausale Ansätze die im Rahmen dessen die natürliche Kausalität dem Recht näher bringen, ohne jedoch in rechtlicher Dimension die Anwendbarkeit und den Nutzen der Kausalitätsdeterminierung einzubüßen. Grundlegend sind hierfür die metaphysisch erwachsenen Ansätze Regularien basierter sowie probabilistischer Kausalität.[24] Beide Ansätze überzeugen durch ihre Nähe zur tatsächlichen Kausalität und deren guter Vereinbarkeit mit wissenschaftlicher Ergebnisfindung. Insbesondere ein probabilistischer Ansatz zeigt dabei eine umfangreiche Nähe und Kompatibilität mit klimawissenschaftlicher Ergebnisfindung, wobei jedoch auch hier die Divergenz zwischen naturwissenschaftlicher Methodiken und rechtswissenschaftlichen Bedürfnissen offenbart wird.

---

[21] Dies ist insbesondere im Rahmen eines wahrscheinlichkeitsbasierten Kausalansatzes (‚*probabilistic theories of causation*‘) der Fall, siehe hierzu Kapitel 4.4.

[22] Siehe Kapitel 4.2.

[23] Siehe Kapitel 4.2.3.

[24] Siehe Kapitel 4.3, 4.4.

Den metaphysisch gewachsenen Theorien schließt sich nunmehr die Erörterung rechtsprechungsgewachsener Kausalitätsansätze an, welche sich insbesondere in der ‚market share liability doctrine' und einem beitragsbasierten Ansatz erstrecken. Trotz der bereits in der Literatur erfolgten Übertragung der ‚market share liability doctrine' zeigt sich im Zuge der Erörterung, dass sich ein solcher Ansatz aufgrund dessen Begrenzung nicht für die Kausalitätsdeterminierung innerhalb der Klimathematik im Recht eignet.[25] Vielversprechender ist dagegen ein beitragsorientierter Ansatz.[26] Unter Heranziehung nationaler Modelle abgemilderter und reduzierter Kausalitätsanforderungen und unter Berücksichtigung bereits erfolgter Klimaentscheidungen ist es demzufolge möglich einen rein beitragsbasierten Ansatz auch für die Klimathematik zu entwickeln. Unter dem Versuch verstärkter Legitimierung erfolgt im Rahmen dessen auch eine Rückkoppelung des Ansatzes an metaphysische Grundsätze.

Im Ergebnis zeigen die Erörterungen im Rahmen der faktischen Kausalität, dass es grundsätzlich nicht den einen determinierenden Kausalitätsansatz gibt welcher sich uneingeschränkt für jegliche klimatischen Themen eignet. Jedoch wird deutlich, dass insbesondere monokausale Konzeptionen im Rahmen von Klimaklagen einer erhöhten Diskrepanz zwischen tatsächlicher und rechtlicher Kausalität ausgesetzt sind.

Kapitel 5: Normative Kausalität

Kapitel 5 begründet demzufolge als eingrenzender Faktor faktischer Kausalität den zweiten Teil der Kausalitätsdeterminierung im Recht. Normativer Kausalität liegen dabei eine Vielzahl an unterschiedlichen Prinzipen zugrunde. Dazu gehören insbesondere die Prinzipien der Gerechtigkeit, der Fairness und der moralischen Verantwortung.[27] Jedoch prägen aufgrund der Klimathematik auch klimaspezifische Prinzipien die Abwägung. Maßgeblich ist hierbei das Prinzip der Klimagerechtigkeit in seiner korrektiven, distributiven, sozialen und prozeduralen Dimension, sowie allgemeine Prinzipien des Umweltvölkerrechts, welche sich insbesondere auf das Verursacher – und Vorsorgeprinzip erstrecken.[28] Wie erläutert zeigt sich innerhalb der normativen Kausalität, dass trotz unterschiedlicher Konzeptionen und Wahrnehmung normativer Prinzipien, innerhalb der Klimathematik jurisdiktionsübergreifend insbesondere zwei Prinzipien von erhöhter Relevanz sind; die Vorhersehbarkeit des Effekts, sowie die Wesentlichkeit des Beitrags.[29] Beide Konzeptionen werden je nach Jurisdiktion entweder als eigenständige

25 Siehe Kapitel 4.5.1.

26 Siehe Kapitel 4.5.2.

27 Siehe Kapitel 5.2.1.

28 Siehe Kapitel 5.2.2, 5.2.3.

29 Siehe Kapitel 5.3, 5.4.

Konzepte oder als Teil allgemeiner normativer Kausalitätstheorien wie der Adäquanztheorie oder der Lehre von dem unmittelbaren Kausalzusammenhang (‚proximate cause') verwendet.[30]

Die Problematik der Vorhersehbarkeit innerhalb der klimarechtlichen Dimension ergibt sich im Wesentlichen aus der Schwierigkeit des temporalen Verzugs.[31] Auf Basis moralischer Konzeptionen von Verantwortung und Gerechtigkeit begrenzt das Prinzip die Kausalität auf alle Ursachen, welche für den handelnden, oder unterlassenden Akteur vorhersehbar waren. Ohne eine solche Vorhersehbarkeit entfällt der Vorwurf der Verwerflichkeit. Maßgeblich ist hierbei die ex-ante Perspektive eines vernünftigen und objektiven Beobachters. Die Erörterungen zeigen darüber hinaus auf, dass die Heranziehung individuellen Wissens von erheblicher Bedeutung werden kann.

Die Frage der Wesentlichkeit erwächst der Tatsache, dass jede menschliche Handlung oder Unterlassung, und sei sie noch so klein, letztlich in faktischer und naturwissenschaftlicher Hinsicht zu Veränderungen im Klimasystem beiträgt.[32] Dennoch beinhalten nicht alle Beiträge eine normativ-rechtliche Verwerflichkeit. Dies fehlt insbesondere im Rahmen marginaler und alltäglicher Handlungen, welche sich dadurch und unter Heranziehung von Gerechtigkeitsprinzipen, der moralischen Verantwortung entziehen. Unter der Prämisse reduzierter faktischer Kausalitätsanforderungen, welche es erlauben, auch kleinere Beiträge als faktisch kausal zu qualifizieren, kommt der Erheblichkeitsschwelle eine besondere Bedeutung und uneingeschränkte Notwendigkeit zu.[33] Dabei zeigen jedoch die Ausführungen, dass die Schaffung einer fixen Schwelle der Erheblichkeit nicht nur nicht möglich ist, sondern im weitesten Sinne auch nicht geboten. Vielmehr muss eine Determinierung auf Basis verschiedener Indikatoren erfolgen, welche je nach Akteur unterschiedlich herangezogen und gewichtet werden können.[34] Als Indikatoren dienen dabei die NDCs des Pariser Abkommens, nationale und internationale Emissionsminderungsziele, pro Kopf Emissionen und die sektorale Vergleichbarkeit der jeweiligen Beiträge. Schlussendlich kommt durch die Methodik den Gerichten ein erhöhter Umfang an Ermessen bei der Auswahl der Indikatoren und deren Gewichtung zu.

Wie bereits erläutert, fungieren Vorhersehbarkeit und Wesentlichkeit nicht nur als eigenständige Prinzipien normativer Kausalität, sondern sind auch in andere, umfassendere normative Theorien eingebettet, in erster Linie in die Adäquanztheorie und die ‚proximate cause' Doktrin. Jedoch zeigt sich, dass beide Prinzipien auch über die beiden fundamentalen Prinzipen hinaus, weitere normative Komponenten beinhalten. Innerhalb der ‚proximate cause' Doktrin erfährt in diesem Sinne im

[30] Siehe Kapitel 5.6, 5.7.

[31] Siehe Kapitel 5.3.

[32] Siehe Kapitel 5.4.

[33] Siehe Kapitel 5.4.2.1.

[34] Siehe Kapitel 5.4.2.3.1.1.

Rahmen klimatischer Kausalität insbesondere die Voraussetzung räumlicher und persönlicher Nähe einem erhöhten Diskurs.[35]

Weitere normative Theorien betreffen den Schutzzweck der herangezogenen Normen und den Umgang mit sogenannten ‚intervening causes'. Beide Konstrukte stellen dabei eigenständige normative Determinanten dar. Dabei zeigt sich, dass insbesondere die Schutzzwecktheorie erhebliche Auswirkungen auf die normative Kausalitätsbestimmung haben kann.[36] Dies betrifft insbesondere Rechtsgebiete, Gesetze und Normen, die in ihrer ursprünglichen Entstehungsgeschichte weder auf Umwelt- noch auf Klimaschutzbelange ausgerichtet waren. Die Ausführungen zeigen dahingegen, dass intervenierende und somit Ersatz- und Überholungsursachen im Gegensatz dazu keiner besonderen Relevanz zukommt.[37]

Letztlich sind es die beiden Prinzipien der Vorhersehbarkeit und der Wesentlichkeit, die in der Klimadebatte im weiteren und in Bezug auf die Kausalitätsbegründung im engeren Sinne von zentraler Bedeutung sind.

Kapitel 6: Anwendungsbezogene Fallgruppenbildung

Kapitel 6 dient der anwendungsorientierten Erprobung der in dieser Arbeit erörterten und entwickelten Konzeptionen, indem durch eine fallgruppenorientierte Betrachtung Unterschiede in der Anwendung faktischer und normativer Kausalität im Rahmen von Klimaklagen aufgezeigt werden.

Eine Differenzierung erfolgt dabei innerhalb der faktischen Kausalität insbesondere nach verschiedenen Rechtsordnungen.[38] Im Zuge dessen kann gezeigt werden, dass sich die vorzugswürdigen dogmatischen Ansätze zwischen ‚civil law', ‚common law' und regionalen und internationalen Jurisdiktionen aufgrund der bestehenden Rechtstraditionen unterscheiden. Während in ‚civil law' Ländern kontrafaktische Tests grundsätzlich weiterhin als vorzugswürdig angesehen werden, allerdings in ihrer Modifikation durch die Strategie der faktischen Konkretisierung, sind ‚common law' Länder sowie regionale und internationale Jurisdiktionen durchaus in der Lage, einen multikausalen Ansatz im Rahmen einer beitragsbasierten Kausalität umzusetzen.

Im Gegensatz zur faktischen Kausalität divergiert die Anwendung normativer Prinzipien weitaus stärker.[39] Aufgrund der starken kulturellen, sozialen und gesellschaftlichen Prägung der Berücksichtigung normativer Prinzipien und deren divergierender Gewichtung, ist die normative Kausalität mit einer hohen Abwägungsprärogative verbunden. Dies betrifft insbesondere den handelnden

[35] Siehe Kapitel 5.7.

[36] Siehe Kapitel 5.8.

[37] Siehe Kapitel 5.5.

[38] Siehe Kapitel 6.1.1.

[39] Siehe Kapitel 6.2.

Akteur und das Rechtsgebiet, in dem die Klage erhoben wird. Ersteres nimmt einen starken Einfluss auf die Schwelle der Vorhersehbarkeit und die Anwendbarkeit und Gewichtung der entsprechenden Indikatoren im Rahmen der Wesentlichkeit. In Anlehnung an die vorangegangene Methodik wird dabei eine spezifische Unterscheidung zwischen Staaten, multi- und transnationalen Unternehmen und Individuen vorgenommen. Innerhalb der rechtsgebietsbezogenen Unterscheidung lassen sich im Gegensatz zu den Akteuren keine derart präzisen Aussagen treffen. Es wird jedoch gezeigt, dass in verschiedenen Rechtsgebieten unterschiedliche Prinzipien zum Tragen kommen und dass selbst innerhalb der entsprechenden Prinzipien eine unterschiedliche normative Gewichtung zu unterschiedlichen Ergebnissen innerhalb der Klimakausalitätsbestimmung führen kann.

Annex II: Table of Climate Cases with References to Causation[40]

[40]Decision were considered until 31 December 2021.

Year	Title	Jurisdiction, Court	Responses	Area of Law	Direction of Action	Allocation of Causal Reference	Causal Group[2]
2006	Wildlife Preservation Society of Queensland Proserpine/Whitsundry Branch Inc. v. Minister for the Environment & Heritage and Others	Australia, Federal Court of Australia	Mitigation	Administrative law	pro	Judgment delivered on 15 June 2006 ([2006] FCA 736): paras 56 – 58, 72	1, 4
2006	Gray v. Minister for Planning	Australia, Land and Environmental Court of New South Wales	Mitigation	Administrative law	pro	Judgment delivered on 6, 7, 27 November 2006 ([2006] NSWLEC 720): paras 83-100 (inter alia)	2, 3, 4
2007	Re Xstrata Coal Queensland Pty. Ltd. & Ors	Australia, Land and Resources Tribunal Queensland	Mitigation	Administrative law	pro	Decision delivered on 15 February 2007 ([2007] QLRT 33): para 21 (inter alia)	4
2009	Public Prosecutor's Office v. H Carlos Schneider S/A Comércio e Industria & Others	Brazil, Superior Court of Justice	Adaptation	Environmental, administrative, constitutional law	pro	Ruling delivered on 2 December 2009 (Special Appeal Nº 650.728 - SC (2003/0221786-0)): pages 11-12	3
2010	Société Arcelor Atlantique et Lorraine & Others v. Parliament & Council (Environment & consumers)	European Union, General Court (Third Chamber)	Mitigation	European law	anti	Judgment delivered on 2 March 2010 ([2010] Case T-16/04): paras 132-139	3, 4
2010	Maniototo Environmental Society Inc. v. Central Otago District Council	New Zealand, Environmental Court, High Court	Mitigation	Administrative law	anti	Decision of the Environmental Court delivered on 28 October 2009 ([2009] NZEnvC 293): para 221 Judgment on Appeal of the High Court of New Zealand delivered on 16 August 2010 (CIV 2009 412 000980): para 157	1

Year	Title	Jurisdiction, Court	Responses	Area of Law	Direction of Action	Allocation of Causal Reference	Causal Group[2]
2012	Xstrata Coal Queensland Pty. Ltd. & Others v. Friends of the Earth – Brisbane & Others	Australia, Land Court of Queensland	Mitigation	Administrative law	pro	Order delivered on 27 March 2012 ([2012] QLC 13): paras 533-559 (inter alia)	1, 4
2013	Cherry Tree Wind Farm Pty Ltd v. Mitchell Shire Council	Australia, Victorian Civil and Administrative Tribunal	Mitigation	Administrative law	pro	Order delivered on 4 April 2013 ([2013] VCAT 521): paras 119-128	4
2014	Yayasan Wahana Lingkungan Hidup Indonesia v. Governor of Bali and others	Indonesia, Supreme Court	Loss And Damage	Administrative law	pro	Decision delivered on 22 May 2014 (151 K/TUN/2014): page 90	4
2014	CF Partners (UK) LLP v. Barclays Bank PLC	United Kingdom, High Court of Justice Chancery Division	Mitigation	Contract law	neutral	Judgement delivered on 24 September 2014 ([2014] EWHC 3049): paras 1027-1046	4
2016	Coast and Country Association of Queensland Inc. v. Smith	Australia, Supreme Court of Queensland	Mitigation	Administrative law	pro	Order delivered on 27 September 2016 ([2016] QCA 242): paras 30, 45 (inter alia)	1, 4
2016	Decision C-035/16 of February 8, 2016	Colombia, Constitutional Court	Mitigation	Constitutional law	pro	Decision delivered on 08 February 2016 (C-035/16): para 16	4
2016	Ministry of Environment and Forestry v. PT Bumi Mekar Hijau	Indonesia, Palembang Court of Appeal	Mitigation	Tort law	pro	Judgment delivered on 12 February 2016 (51/ PDT/2016/PT.PLG): pages 160-162, 188-189 (inter alia)	4
2016	Luciano Lliuya v. RWE AG	Germany, District Court of Essen	Adaptation	Tort law	pro	Judgment delivered on 15 December 2016 (2 O 285/15): paras 41-47	4
2017	Australian Conservation Foundation Incorporated v. Minister for the Environment and Energy	Australia, Federal Court of Australia	Mitigation	Administrative law	pro	Judgment of the Federal Court delivered on 29 August 2016 ([2016] FCA 1042): paras 157-163 Judgment on Appeal (on the merits) delivered on 25 August 2017 ([2017] FCAFC 134): paras 40-42	1
2017	Minister of Environment v. PT Kalista Alam	Indonesia, Supreme Court	Mitigation	Tort law	pro	Judgment delivered on 18 April 2017 (1 PK/Pdt/2017): paras 5.16, 5.19	4

Year	Title	Jurisdiction, Court	Responses	Area of Law	Direction of Action	Allocation of Causal Reference	Causal Group[2]
2017	A Request for an Advisory Opinion from the Inter-American Court of Human Rights Concerning the Interpretation of Article 1(1), 4(1) and 5(1) of the American Convention on Human Rights	Inter-American Court on Human Rights	Mitigation	Fundamental law, human rights	pro	Advisory Opinion delivered on 15 November 2017 (OC – 23/17): paras 101, 104	1
2017	Segovia et al. v. Climate Change Commission	Philippines, Supreme Court	Mitigation	Constitutional law	pro	Decision delivered on 7 March 2017 (G.R. No. 211010): page 6	4
2018	Ministry of Environment and Forestry v. PT Palmina Utama	Indonesia, Banjarmasin Court of Appeal	Loss And Damage	Tort law	pro	Judgment delivered on 21 February 2018 (48/PDT/2018/PT BJM): pages 47-48	4
2015/ 2018	Certain Activities Carried Out by Nicaragua in the Border Area (Costa Rica v. Nicaragua)	International Court of Justice	Mitigation	International law	pro	Judgment concerning the merits delivered on 16 December 2015 (I.C.J. Reports 2015 p.665): paras 119, 226 Judgment concerning the compensation delivered on 2 February 2018 (I.C.J. Reports 2018, p. 15): paras 72-87, 99, 105, 112, 118, 121, 123, 129, 144 (inter alia)	4
2019	Gloucester Resources Limited v. Minister for Planning	Australia, Land and Environment Court New South Wales	Mitigation	Administrative law	anti	Decision delivered on 8 February 2019 ([2019] NSWLEC 7): paras 514-525	4
2019	Family Farmers and Greenpeace Germany v. Germany	Germany, Administrative Court of Berlin	Mitigation	Constitutional law, EU law	pro	Judgement delivered on 31 October 2019 (VG 10 K 412.18): page 22	3
2019	Urgenda Foundation v. State of the Netherlands	The Netherlands, The Hague District Court District Court, The Hague Court of Appeal, Supreme Court	Mitigation	constitutional law, Human Rights	pro	Decision of the The Hague District Court delivered on 24 June 2015 (C/09/456689/HA ZA 13-1396 (English translation)): paras 4.79, 4.90	3, 4

Year	Title	Jurisdiction, Court	Responses	Area of Law	Direction of Action	Allocation of Causal Reference	Causal Group[2]
						Decision of the The Hague Court of Appeal delivered on 9 October 2018 (200.178.245/01): paras 62-70 Judgement of the Supreme Court delivered on 20 December 2019 (19/00135): paras 5.7.1-5.8	
2020	Specific Instance filed to the Australian National Contact Point under the OECD Guidelines for Multinational Enterprises by FoE Australia and Others v ANZ Bank Group Limited	Australia, Australian National Contact Point for the OECD Guidelines	Mitigation	Finance law, corporate law	pro	Initial assessment published 24 November 2020: paras 41-43.4	4
2020	In the Matter of the Greenhouse Gas Pollution Pricing Act, SC 2018, c. 12	Canada, Alberta Court of Appeal	Mitigation	Constitutional law	anti	Opinion delivered on 24 February 2020 (1903.0157-AC): paras 763-772, 850-852	4
2020	Lho'imggin et al. v. Her Majesty the Queen	Canada, Federal Court	Mitigation	Constitutional law, human rights	pro	Order delivered on 16 November 2020 (2020 FC 1059): paras: 96-100 (inter alia)	2, 3
2020	Mathur et al. v. Her Majesty the Queen in Right of Ontario	Canada, Superior Court of Justice of Ontario	Mitigation	Fundamental law, human rights	pro	Decision delivered on 12 November 2020 (2020 ONSC 6918): paras 167-171	2
2020	Eskosol S.p.A. in liquidazione v. Italian Republic	International Centre for Settlement of Investment Disputes	Mitigation	Administrative law	pro	Award delivered on 4 September 2020 (ARB/15/50): paras 379-380	4
2020	Greenpeace Nordic Ass'n v. Ministry of Petroleum and Energy (People v Arctic Oil)	Norway, Supreme Court	Mitigation	Fundamental law, human rights	pro	Judgment of the Supreme Court delivered on 22 December 2020 (HR-2020-2472-P): paras 167-171	4
2020	La Rose v. Her Majesty the Queen	Canada, Federal Court	Mitigation	Fundamental law, human rights	pro	Order delivered on 27 October 2020 (2020 FC 1008): paras 74-75 (inter alia)	4
2021	Mullaley Gas and Pipeline Accord Inc v. Santos NSW (Eastern) Pty Ltd	Australia, Land and Environment Court New South Wales	Mitigation	Administrative law	pro	Judgement delivered on 18 October 2021 ([2021] NSWLEC 110): paras 140-153 (inter alia)	4

Year	Title	Jurisdiction, Court	Responses	Area of Law	Direction of Action	Allocation of Causal Reference	Causal Group[2]
2021	Federal Environmental Agency (IBAMA) v. Siderúrgica São Luiz Ltd. and Martins	Brazil, 15th Civil Federal Court	Mitigation	Environmental law / tort law	pro	Decision delivered on 3 February 2021 (1010603-35.2019.4.01.3800): page 5	4
2021	Notre Affaire à Tous and Others v. France	France, Administrative Court of Paris	Adaptation, Mitigation, Loss And Damage	Administrative law	pro	Decision delivered on 3 February 2021 (N° 1901967, 1904968, 1904972, 1904976/4-1): paras 32-33	4
2021	Neubauer et al. v. Germany	Germany, Federal Constitutional Court	Mitigation	Constitutional law, fundamental law	pro	Order delivered on 24 March 2021 (1 BvR 2656/18, 1 BvR 78/20, 1 BvR 96/20, 1 BvR 288/20): paras 201-202	4
2021	Ministry of Environment and Forestry v. PT Rambang Agro Jaya	Indonesia, Central Jakarta District Court	Loss And Damage	Tort law	pro	Decision delivered on 11 January 2021 (No. 445/Pdt.G/2019/PN.Jkt.Pst): pages 208-210 (inter alia)	2, 3, 4
2021	Eco Oro Minerals Corp. v. Republic of Colombia	International Centre for Settlement of Investment Disputes	Loss And Damage	Administrative law	anti	Decision delivered on 9 September 2021 (ARB/16/41): paras 847-849	4
2021	Sacchi et al. v. Argentina et al.	United Nations Committee on the Rights of the Child	Mitigation	Fundamental law, human rights	pro	Decision decided on 22 September 2021, delivered on 8 October 2021 (CRC/C/88/D/107/2019): paras 9.5, 9.7, 9.10-9.12 (inter alia)	1, 4
2021	Idheas Litigio Estratégico v. Centro Nacional de Control de Energía (CENACE) and Secretaría de Energía (SENER)	Mexico, Second District Court in Administrative Matters	Mitigation	Administrative law, human rights	pro	Judgment delivered on 19 April 2021 (586/2020): pages 72-73	4
2021	Smith v. Fonterra Co-Operative Group Limited	New Zealand, Court of Appeal	Mitigation	Tort law	pro	Judgement delivered on 21 October 2021 ([2021] NZCA 552): paras 88-90, 103-113 (inter alia)	2, 4
2022	Ewan McGaughey et al v. Universities Superannuation Scheme Limited	United Kingdom, High Court of Justice, Business and Property Courts of England and Wales, Companies Court	Mitigation	Finance law, corporate law	pro	Judgement delivered 24 May 2022 ([2022] EWHC 1233): paras 173-176 (inter alia)	4

Year	Title	Jurisdiction, Court	Responses	Area of Law	Direction of Action	Allocation of Causal Reference	Causal Group[2]
2022	Sharma and others v. Minister for the Environment	Australia, Federal Court	Mitigation	Administrative law	pro	Judgment delivered on 15 March 2022 ([2022] FCAFC 35): paras 326, 438-439, 882, 887 (inter alia)	2
2022	Waratah Coal Pty Ltd v Youth Verdict Ltd & Ors (No 6)	Australia, Land Court of Queensland	Mitigation	Administrative law, human rights	pro	Decision delivered on 25 November 2022 ([2022] QLC 21): paras 1300, 1314-1316, 1325, 1352, 1362 (inter alia)	2, 4
2022	Challenging criteria and technical requirements to perform fracking in Colombia	Colombia, Council of State	Mitigation	Administrative law, human rights	pro	Decision delivered on 7 July 2022 11001-0326-000-2016-00140-00 (57819)): paras 45-46, 62	1
2022	Klimatická žaloba ČR v. Czech Republic[3]	Czechia, Municipal Court Prague	Adaptation, Mitigation, Loss And Damage	Fundamental law, human rights	pro	Judgement delivered on 15 June 2022 (No. 14A 101/2021): paras 324-327	1, 4
2022	Pavlov and others v. Russia	European Court of Human Rights	Mitigation, Loss And Damage	Human rights	pro	Judgement delivered on 11 October 2022 (No. 31612/09): para 68 (inter alia)	4
2022	Smith v. Attorney-General	New Zealand, High Court	Mitigation	Constitutional law, fundamental law	pro	Judgement delivered on 15 July 2022 ([2022] NZHC 1693): paras 182-183 (inter alia)	2
2022	In re Greenpeace Southeast Asia and Others	Philippines	Mitigation	Fundamental law, human rights	pro	Judgement delivered on 6 May 2022 (CHR-NI-2016-0001): page 147	2
2022	R (Finch on behalf of the Weald Action Group & Others) v. Surrey County Council (& Others)	United Kingdom, Court of Appeal (Civil Division)	Mitigation	Administrative law	pro	Judgement delivered on 17 February 2022 ([2022] EWCA Civ 187): paras 39, 60-63, 85 (inter alia)	2, 4

Annex III: Data Included in Figure 3.2[41]

Jurisdiction	Overall Climate Change Cases[a]	Cases Containing Causal Considerations[b]	Ratio in %
Australia	127	12	9.4
Brazil	31	2	6.5
Canada	34	4	11.8
Colombia	6	2	33.3
Czechia	**4**	**1**	**25**
European Union	**61**	**1**	**1.6**
France	**24**	**1**	**4.2**
Germany	40	3	7.5
Indonesia	12	5	41.7
International	49	6	12.2
Mexico	**18**	**1**	**5.6**
Netherlands	**13**	**1**	**7.7**
New Zealand	26	3	11.5
Norway	**3**	**1**	**33.3**
Philippines	3	2	66.7
United Kingdom	88	3	3.4

[a] Cases have been taken into account until 31 December 2022
[b] Jurisdictions with only one case of causal consideration have not been included in the figure

[41] See for Figure 3.2 Section 3.4.

The manufacturer's authorised representative in the EU is Springer Nature Customer Service Centre GmbH, Europaplatz 3, 69115 Heidelberg, Germany. If you have any concerns regarding our products, please contact ProductSafety@springernature.com

Printed and bound by CPI Group (UK) Ltd, Croydon, CR0 4YY
30/09/2026
02225558-0017